A TO ZAX

A Comprehensive Dictionary for Genealogists & Historians

Third Edition

Barbara Jean Evans

HEARTHSIDE PRESS
Devoted to Genealogy & Local History

DEDICATED
To my husband Rupert
Without whom this book
would not have been possible

ISBN 0-945231-02-4

Printing history:
First Edition published 1978 by Unigraphic
Second Edition published 1990 by the author
Third Edition published 1995 by

HEARTHSIDE PRESS
5735A Telegraph Road
Alexandria, VA 22303
(703) 960-0086

Printed on acid-free paper.

Library of Congress Cataloging-in-Publication Data

Evans, Barbara Jean.
A to zax : a comprehensive dictionary for genealogists & historians / Barbara Jean Evans. -- 3rd ed.
p. cm.
ISBN 0-945231-02-4 (pbk. : alk. paper)
1. Genealogy--Dictionaries. I. Title.
CS6.E9 1995
929'.1'03--dc20 95-38771
CIP

Introduction

Every specialized field of endeavor has its own peculiar vocabulary. Every region of the world, the same. Americans have taken words from the vocabularies of the world, altered, amended, corrupted, redefined, and some may say, completely distorted the author's original meaning or the creator's intended definition.

Word definitions tend to be governed by time as well. Thus, meanings or words in use a century ago have changed, and the correct interpretation of a writing depends upon knowing its definition at the time it was penned or printed.

Archaic words and definitions are the bane of existence of many persons engaged in research. No group is more often perplexed by them than genealogists and local historians. The author has not written her "magnum opus;" rather, she has prepared an aid for those who seek definitions of words which she and others have encountered in their family history pursuits. The omissions are numerous and some of the definitions are wrong. So many will write, and I hope they will. For this is a subject which needs continuous updating, though the author had not planned this to be her full time, all consuming, retirement project.

Congratulations, Jean. This will be a welcomed addition to any personal or public library.

I commend you for your undertaking and bravery. Undertaking, because of the number of years devoted to this project. Bravery, because of the many responses from those who will criticize it for its omissions of their pet words, and those whose word definitions will differ.

James Dent Walker, F.N.G.S.
Washington, DC

Foreword To The Third Edition

More than forty years ago I began collecting words which I did not understand or which I was not certain I understood fully. Many of these words came from my own research, correspondence and discussions about local history and genealogy. They were supplemented by words about which there were questions during my years of teaching genealogy for Parkland College, in my work in the Archives Room of the Urbana (Illinois) Free Library, and most recently during my volunteer days at the Champaign branch of the Family History Center of the Church of Jesus Christ of Latter-Day Saints. Finally, the users of the first edition, which was published seventeen years ago, have made many excellent suggestions for expansion and revision.

It is far easier to accumulate lists of words than to get agreement on their definitions. Definitions differ from time to time, from place to place, and from one writer to another. In searching other books for help, I found many circular definitions or definitions which were as difficult to understand as the word being defined. The goal of this book has been to use language that a lay person can understand. When this has been achieved, much credit is due to the persons listed below.

As in the first edition, the major portion of the book is devoted to terms used in history and genealogy and to their definitions. Many archaic and Norman words are included, not only for those fortunate enough to have the opportunity to read old manuscripts, but because these words have continued to affect those parts of our language and customs which are based upon England and her people.

Foreign language words which are in current use have been eliminated from the second and third editions as there are now many good dictionaries available. Latin phrases have been retained and expanded, but the more common, familiar definitions of English words have been deleted in the interests of conserving space. If that had not been done, this book could have become considerably larger than an unabridged dictionary. Even so, the second edition was almost three times as long as the first, and the third is still longer.

The appendix on nicknames was collected at the request of Harold Felty and the appendix which translates Dutch to English given names comes from my own research. The computer has sorted names from English to Dutch for use by those who have Dutch ancestry and would like to look up a record using Dutch given names.

My deep appreciation goes again to many people: to the late James D. Walker for his help and encouragement; to Stuart Mamer, Esq. for the time he spent in explaining some difficult law terms to me; to Marilyn (Cheney) Stern for her help with medical terms, and to Nancy McNabb for typing all these definitions into a computer and editing them. The responsibility for errors, of course, is mine.

Barbara Jean Evans
101 West Windsor Road
Urbana, IL 61801-6697
July 1, 1995

A 1) adultery (sometimes AD was used). In Massachusetts until 1785 those found guilty of adultery were required to wear a badge of the capital letter A cut from red cloth and sewed to their uppermost clothing; 2) a brand marked on animals belonging to the settlers of East Hampton, Long Island; 3) abstract; 4) acre or acres.

a: 1) age; 2) about; 3) acre or acres; 4) administration; 5) against.

a: prefixed to any word means without.

a., as.: acre, acres.

aac: an oak, oaken.

aad: old.

aaged: aged.

aald: old.

aale: ale.

AAS: American Antiquarian Society.

aat: a fine meal made from oats which was used during cooking as a thickening agent.

ab: when used as a prefix ab means away from a point in time e.g. ab nepos would indicate a further relationship than grandchild, perhaps a great-grandchild.

ab.: 1) about; 2) abbey (which see).

a & b: assault and battery.

aba, abba: a coarse, felted cloth woven of goat or camel hair (but sometimes of silk) which, when sewed into a loose, sleeveless garment, was worn by Arabs.

ab actis: notary public.

abactor: a person who drives a great number of something away. A person who stole an entire herd of cattle instead of one or two would be an abactor.

abade: variation of abode.

abandon: to leave, desert, or give up with the intention of never trying to return or resume interest in property.

abase: to lower, bring down.

abast: bastard.

abastardize: to render illegitimate.

abataylment: a battlement.

abate: 1) to terminate, end, cease; 2) to decrease, remove or destroy e.g. to abate a legacy is to decrease the amount of the legacy because the funds from which the legacy is to be paid are insufficient to cover the entire amount. A nuisance may be abated by removing the object which creates the nuisance 3) to lower as a flag or banner.

abatement: the process of lessening, deducting or taking away in some manner from something.

abates and returns: not guilty, probably settled out of court.

abatis: a fortification made from trees. The branches faced toward the enemy and usually were sharpened to aid in repelling the enemy.

abaty: to abate.

abaut: about.

abavus: a forefather, specifically a great-great-grandfather.

abb: a poor quality sheep's wool.

abba: an abbey.

abbace: an old form of abbess (which see).

abbastre: a cross-bow man (which see).

abbess: 1) a supervisor of a nunnery or convent; 2) a female abbot.

abbey: 1) part of an English church name, e.g. Westminster Abbey; 2) a convent; 3) a monastery.

abbey: when used as a prefix refers to an abbey, e.g. abbeylands would be the ground which belongs to an abbey.

abbod: an abbot.

abbodisse: an abbess.

abbot: a church officer who is chief administrator of a monastery.

abbr: abbreviation.

abbreviate: an abstract.

abbrevyate: decreased.

ABC book: 1) a catechism, hornbook or primer used for teaching children the first rudiments of reading; 2) the alphabet in general.

ABC table: a gambling table, the description and use of which we do not know. The 1798 North Carolina statutes made the use of this table illegal.

abcess of liver: usually a fatal disease in which amebic dysentery has produced many abscesses on the liver.

abdominal typhus: typhus fever characterized by bluish spots on the abdomen which appear on the fourth or fifth day after onset of the disease.

abecedary: 1) a primer, a beginning of

anything; 2) an alphabet book. The abece portion comes from ABC, the beginning of the alphabet.

abed: in bed as in sick in bed.

aberemord: a law term which means murder fully proved, as distinguished from manslaughter and justifiable homicide.

abering: proper and peaceful transportation of a loyal subject.

abesse: absent.

abet: to help or stir another person to commit a crime.

abeyance: 1) the state of being in suspension; 2) expectation; 3) when an estate has no heir or person who is entitled to it, it is said to be in abeyance.

abeyd: abide.

abhor: to protect against or reject solemnly.

abidden: endured.

abigail: a female servant.

abill: to make able.

ab initio: from the beginning.

ab intestate: intestate.

ab intestato: one who died without having made a will.

abit: 1) an obit; 2) a service for the dead; 3) abide.

abitacle: a habitation, a dwelling.

abite: 1) habit; 2) a bite.

abition: dying.

abjuration: a statement renouncing all allegiance to a country, to some one, etc.

abjure: to disavow, or swear never to return without permission.

ablepsy: blindness, either a mental or a physical condition.

able seaman: one well acquainted with and able to perform the expected duties of a sailor.

able whackets: a card game.

able-bodied: 1) refers to an absence of visible defects which would keep a man from performing the duties of service in the militia, armed forces, or an occupation; 2) a skilled seaman.

ablusion: a chemical term which means the cleansing of medicines from any impurities.

ablution: 1) in a religious ceremony to cleanse with water represents a washing away of one's sins; 2) the liquid used in the religious ceremony.

ab nepos: great-great-grandson.

ab neptis: great-great-granddaughter.

abode: 1) where a person lives; 2) delay; 3) waited for.

abofe: abode, dwelling.

abolitionist: 1) a person who was extremely opposed to slavery; 2) a person who favors the repeal of any law considered harmful to others.

aborigines: first inhabitants.

abortivus: prematurely born.

abot: an abbot - which see.

aboun: above.

Abp.: Archbishop.

abracadabra: this word, written in a peculiar manner, was formerly worn about the neck as a cure for the ague.

abraham: the color brown.

Abraham men: a group of men in England who pretended to be down and out seamen and begged on the docks. A seaman who pretends to be ill is said to "sham Abraham."

abraid: 1) to upset the stomach with a degree of nausea; 2) a disagreeable taste in food.

abram: a very poor man.

abreeu: (Norman) April.

abrege: to shorten, abridge.

abric: sulphur.

abroceurs: (Norman) brokers.

abrogate: to repeal, annul, abolish.

abruptio: 1) tear away; 2) divorce.

absence: when a person does not return to his home. When a person is gone from his residence for seven years he may be presumed dead.

absentee landlord: the person who owns land, house, etc., but does not live there.

absey-book: a hornbook.

absinthe: an old medicinal liquid which is never used now.

absolution: to set free, discharge.

absque: without.

abstract: a) the summary of census results sent to Washington, D.C. by the official who recorded the census; 2) an abridgement of a document or book which gives the main points and deletes repetitive language; 3) a separation.

abstract books: these books list land entries by the name of the purchaser in chronological order. They were usually housed in a District Land Office, Bureau of Land Management, etc.

abstracted medical record: see abstract.

abstract index: this is a list of owners of land in chronological order filed by land description. It exists, either whole or partially, in some Ohio courthouses.

abstract of title: a lengthy document, constructed by an abstract company, which sets down the history of a given piece of land. Any conveyances, transfers of title, etc. are included along with facts which might interfere with a clear title to the property.

abstract of will: a summary of a will usually giving only genealogically pertinent information.

abstractor: a person who summarizes transactions affecting one particular piece of property.

abt: about.

abthane: a steward.

abuf: above.

abut, abutt: 1) to adjoin or border; 2) abbreviation for abutter.

abuttal: a boundary between.

abutter: 1) one whose land adjoins, or borders, the land of another at a place where no road or other land is between the pieces of land; 2) an adjacent proprietor.

a.c.: 1) attested copy; 2) anni currentis, current year.

A.C.: Ante Christum - before Christ.

Acadia:old French name of the Canadian province Nova Scotia.

Acadian: an inhabitant of Acadia. Many were driven out in the middle 18th century by the British and therefore they settled in Louisiana. Often abbreviated Cajan, Cajin, Cajun.

acaid: vinegar.

acambre: 1) to encumber; 2) to trouble.

acate: food baked at home, rather than in a bakery.

acater: 1) a caterer; 2) a purveyor of goods.

acatery: a room or place allotted for keeping all provisions which were purchased for the King's use.

acates: 1) victuals; 2) provisions which are purchased.

acazdir: tin.

acc.: 1) account; 2) accompanied; 3) according; 4) accepted; 5) accomplished.

accahints: accounts.

Accelerated Indexing System: computer-generated indexes to various United States censuses.

acceptance: 1) an agreement to the terms named; 2) to take something which has been offered by another person with the intention of keeping and, if called for, paying for it.

accepted: this term is used in Quaker records when any matter brought before the monthly meeting was received and entered into the church records.

accepted mason: see Freemason.

accident: a symptom of illness.

accipitrary: a falconer.

accola: 1) a person who lives near a well-known place such as a stream; 2) an ancient name for a tenant farmer.

accoladed: having been knighted.

accommodation: 1) land given by a colonial town to a family wishing to settle in that town. A legal document sometimes speaks of "to ______ my Accommodations of Land;" 2) a means of travel - coach, buggy, stage coach, etc.; 3) a person who did part-time housework for wages only when needed.

accommodation paper: a document (draft, note, etc.) which has been endorsed and given to another with no charge. The purpose is to allow the second party to raise money or obtain credit. Sometimes called an accommo-dation bill.

accomplice: a partner, associate or companion. This word was not formerly applied exclusively in a bad sense.

accomplished: used in Quaker records when a marriage was reported back to the monthly meeting as done.

accompt: account, reckoning.

accomptant: an accountant.

accot: account.

account: 1) a record of business transactions, as an account book; 2) the report of an executor or administrator of an estate; 3) the story of an event.

account of sale: a list of items purchased

at an auction sale which included what item was sold, how much the item sold for and many times the purchaser's name. These lists are to be found in final estate papers.

accouterments: see accoutrement.

accoutrement: the equipment of a soldier with the exception of his underwear, uniform and guns.

accretions: a growing together of parts which are supposed to be separate.

accrue: to accumulate, e.g. money.

accrument: increase, addition.

acct.: account.

accused: the person against whom a charge has been brought in court, a defendant.

acenseur: (Norman) farmer.

acerote: brown bread.

acertez: (Norman) certified.

achahi: alum water. A chemical term.

achar: pickles.

achatur, actour: (Norman) buyer.

ache: 1) parsley; 2) an ash tree; 3) age.

acheat: see escheat.

achelor: thin stone used to face walls.

aches: convulsions - sometimes called 'pricking aches.'

achete: see escheat.

achetyn: to escheat.

achor: a scalp disease commonly called "the scald."

acicularius: needle maker.

acketon: see acton.

acknowd, acknowled, acknown: acknowledged.

acknowledge: a formal statement made under oath in which a person says that this signature is mine, and therefore the document is valid.

acme: 1) mature age; 2) the crisis of an illness.

acolyte: 1) a young man or lady who helps a clergyman in a worship service, e.g. lights candles, carries standards, etc.; 2) anyone who assists, follows, etc.

acombre: 1) to encounter; 2) to trouble.

aconite: a medicinal potion made from the buttercup family of flowers. Care had to be used, as this flower also had poisonous properties.

acordant, acordend: agreeing.

acorsy: to bury.

acort: (Norman) agreement, accord, consent.

acoulper: (Norman) to accuse.

acoupe: to blame.

acoupement: an accusation.

acquired lands: federal land which was purchased or received as a gift. Such land fell outside public land laws.

acquit: 1) to release from suspicion, accusation or obligation; 2) to behave one's self.

acquittal: the formal finding 'Not Guilty' in a civilian court, or before a military court-martial.

acquittance: a document which says a person is freed from his obligation to pay money to, or to perform a duty for, another. It differs from a release because it is not necessary to have it sealed as well as signed.

acrased: crazed.

acrazed: ill, feeble, weak, impaired.

acre: 1) a measure of land area containing ten square (gunter) chains or 160 square rods or 43,560 square feet. A square measuring 208.71 feet on each side contains almost one acre. Originally it was the amount of land which one man and a yoke of oxen could plow in one day. There are 640 acres in a section, or one square mile; 2) a field. The word at first signified not a determined quantity of land, but any open ground, especially an open area and that sense of it seems preserved in place-names, e.g. Castle-acre, West-acre, etc.; 3) a sort of a duel fought in an open field.

acre-dale: lands in a common field, in which different proprietors hold portions of greater or lesser quantities.

acre foot: the quantity of water which would be required to cover one acre of ground to a depth of one foot. An acre inch would be one-twelfth of this amount.

acre inch: see acre foot.

acre-man: husbandman.

acre right: in New England this was a person's portion of common lands either to own or use. The value was a set amount in each town but the size varied from town to town.

acre-shot: a kind of local land tax or

charge.

acreme: ten acres of land, a law term.

acrotch: to take up, to seize.

acta: official records.

acte: 1) seashore; 2) elder tree.

actg.: acting.

actio in personam, in rem: a court case begun against a person rather than against all persons who might be concerned

action of replevin: see replevin.

action: a lawsuit.

actioner: one who makes the interior mechanism of an instrument.

acto: a court proceeding, a lawsuit.

acton: a leather jacket sometimes worn under a coat of mail, a kind of tunic.

actor: 1) a manager; 2) an agent; 3) a plaintiff.

actoures: 1) governors; 2) keepers.

actuary: a clerk, a person who keeps an account of proceedings.

acture: action.

acuarius: needle maker.

acure: a chemical term, applied to a drug when its power is increased by the addition of some other drug.

acyce: assize.

Ad.: Archdeacon.

AD: adulterer, adultery.

A.D.: Anno Domini (which see).

a.d.: ante diem (which see).

ad: at, before, in, to, towards.

adam: a jocular term for a sergeant or bailiff.

adamantine: 1) a hard wax candle; 2) an extremist member of one of two factions would be called an Adamantine Hard. Named for a type of semi-precious stone.

Adamite: 1) a human; 2) one of Adam's descendants; 3) a nudist is sometimes referred to in this manner.

adam's ale: water.

adam's apple: a kind of citron fruit.

adatis: a fine muslin made in India.

adaz: an axe.

ADC: aide-de-camp (which see).

ad collingendum: refers to a trustee who is appointed to keep an estate in order until an administrator is appointed.

ad curiam: at court.

add.: addatur (which see).

ad damnum: 1) a statement of a person who brings a case into court; 2) monetary loss or damages asked in a lawsuit.

addatur: let there be added.

adderwart: also known as snakeweed, so called because it was believed that its application to a snakebite would cure the bite.

addice: an adze or axe.

addition: a title given to a man over and above his first or Christian and surname, showing his rank, occupation, etc., or alluding to some exploit or achievement. A law term frequently occurring in Shakespeare.

additus: additional.

addle: 1) to earn; 2) to grow; 3) to thrive; 4) a swelling with matter in it: 5) a laborer; 6) wages;7) unsound; 8) unwell.

addle-headed: stupid, thoughtless.

addle-pate: a foolish person.

addlings: earnings from labor.

add. mss.: additional manuscripts.

addoubed: armed, accoutered.

ade: to cut a deep gutter across plowed land.

adec: sour milk.

adeem: revoke a legacy.

adelborst: found in Dutch records, this is a gentleman soldier; rather than a common soldier.

adele: added, annexed.

ademption: taken away, removed (as removing a bequest from a will.

adepcion: an acquirement.

adeps: lard or other animal fat.

ades: an axe.

ad exhaeredationem: an old phrase used in some writs which literally means "to the disinheriting."

adfilliate: an obsolete form of affiliate.

adge: an addice.

ad hoc: 1) for this case only; 2) special e.g. a committee appointed for one purpose and when the purpose has been completed the committee is disbanded.

ad hoc locum: at this place.

adhort: to give advice to another.

ad interim: in the meantime. When an official is temporarily absent from his job another person may be appointed officer ad interim to perform the duties of the absent officer until his return.

a dieu commandez: (Norman) gone to God, departed this life.

adire: (Norman) 1) that is to say; 2) to abandon, forsake.

adj.: adjutant; adjoining; adjourned.

adjacent proprietor: see abutter.

adjournment: to stop until another time or indefinitely.

adjoynauntes: those who are contiguous.

adjoynt: 1) a person joined with another; 2) a companion or attendant.

adjt: adjournment; adjutant.

adjudication: 1) a decision made without an explanation of the degree of guilt, e.g. bankruptcy; 2) (Scottish) an attachment to an heritable estate, security for money, performance, etc.; 3) (Roman) a formula used to determine shares in a property dispute.

adjunction: this term is used to indicate that an article which belongs to another has been permanently attached to an article which belongs to another person by soldering, sewing, painting, etc., for example planting a tree on another's property.

adjure: 1) (Norman) abandoned; 2) to speak to another as if he were under a oath - adjure him to speak the truth.

Adjutant General: 1) a chief administrative officer in the army; 2) a member of the Adjutant General's Corps who has charge of a unit; 3) a high officer in a state or territorial National Guard.

Adjutant General's Report: a publication by the federal government which relates to military matters, e.g. lists of soldiers from a particular state who participated in a war. This report also listed facts relating to the soldier such as rank, place of enlistment and discharge, death, etc.

adjutor: a male assistant.

adjutories: arm bones.

adjutrix: a female assistant.

adle: 1) unsound, unwell; 2) to earn; 3) to addle.

ad litem: for the lawsuit.

ad locum: this place.

adm.: administration.

admeasure: 1) to determine the capacity of a ship for official registration; 2) to divide into portions.

admeasurement: a reapportionment of a previously determined amount.

admeasurement of dower: correction of the amount of a dower by an heir upon becoming of age. The amount had been determined when the heir was a minor and it was likely that his mother had received more than she was really entitled to as a widow, in order to support the child. Now the circumstances have changed and so must the amount of money which she received from her husband's estate.

admerallys: commanders.

admin., adminisn.: administration.

adminicle: evidence which is given either as an explanation or a corroboration.

administration: the process, rather than the record of the management, distribution and other matters concerning the settlement of an estate. The term applies to both testate and intestate estates.

administration bond: money or the guarantee of money is posted by the person who has been chosen by the court to administer an estate. This act is done to ensure that he does his job satisfactorily according to law.

administration c.t.a.: administration cum testamento annexo (see cum testamento annexo).

administration cum testamento: administration of a deceased person's estate which was granted when the deceased left a will but did not name an executor, when the named executor refused to perform the duty of executor, or the person named as executor is unable to perform the obligation.

administration cum testamento annexo: see cum testamento annexo.

administration d.b.n.: administration de bonis non (which see).

administration de bonis non: an additional administration of the estate of a deceased person granted when all the goods had not been distributed by a former administrator or executor because he also has died.

administration of estates: the duties of an administrator or executor of an estate include: (a) the collection of all debts due the deceased; (b) the payment of all debts of the deceased and (c) the distribution of the remainder of the estate.

administration pendite lite: an administration only to take care of an estate until a pending suit against the will is ended.

administrator: 1) a manager; 2) a male person appointed by the probate court to collect the assets, pay the bills and settle the estate of one who died without leaving a valid will.

administrator deed: the deed issued by the administrator of an estate when the deceased person's land or property has been sold on behalf of the estate.

administratrix: a female who administers an estate.

administrs.: administrators.

Admiral: the highest Naval rank which an officer can obtain.

Admiralty court: originally an English court designed to handle matters concerning ships and seamen. After the Revolutionary War these courts were dissolved and maritime matters began to be handled in Federal District courts or state common law courts.

admissible: evidence accurate enough to be acceptable as evidence in a civilian court or a military court-martial.

admission: 1) to allow a citizen of another country to enter a country; 2) to be accepted into an organization; 3) to confess an error, crime, etc.; 4) a concession.

admitted freeman: see indentured servant.

admn.: administration.

admr.: administrator.

admrs.: administrators.

adms.: administrators, usually of an estate, or administration.

admstr.: administers.

admx.: administratrix.

adn.: administration.

adnors: administrators.

adnul: to annul.

adobe: 1) a sun-dried brick made of approximately one-third clay and two-thirds fine sand; 2) buildings constructed of such bricks.

adoption: 1) acceptance of a contract which one could repudiate, e.g. a contract made by a minor child; 2) the act of taking a child born to other parents and making him one's own child, for all legal and moral purposes.

adoption records: documents created by the process of legally making a child who is not yours by birth, your child. These usually list the original name of the child, if known, and the names of the natural parents. As a rule these records are not open for public use.

adoptive parent: one who accepts the responsibility of a child which is not his own and who by law makes the child his.

adorat: a chemical weight of 4 pounds.

adoubers de viels draps: (Norman) patchers or menders of apparel.

ad perpetuam memorium: a perpetual record. Often found on grave markers.

ad quod damnum: a writ which asks what loss, what injury.

a.d.s.: autograph document signed.

ad satisfaciendum: to satisfy.

adsum: here I am. Found on grave markers.

adult: a person who has reached a certain age. In civil law this age is twelve for a female and fourteen for a male. In common law this age is twenty-one for both sexes and in some states it is, by statute, eighteen.

adulterine: 1) born of or involving adultery; 2) not genuine.

adultery: sexual relations by a married person with one who is not his or her spouse.

adust: an early medical term which meant burned, parched, dehydrated due to fever.

adv.: adversus= against.

ad valorem: according to the value.

ad valorem tax: 1) property taxed by percentage according to the value of an item; 2) a tax on real property figured on the basis of the assessed value of the land.

advancement: a gift given by a parent in expectation of an inheritance.

adventayle: the open and moveable portion of a helmet which covered the mouth and but allowed the wearer to breathe.

Advent Sunday: the Sunday closest to 30 November or the Feast of St. Andrew.

adventure: 1) an investment in a business; 2) a venture.

adventurer: 1) a speculator; 2) a person who obtains wealth, power, etc. by questionable means.

ad verbatum: literally.

adversar: an adversary.

adversary proceeding: a case involving opposing parties. The person bringing the suit has given a legal warning and ample time to contest the suit to the other.

adverse possession: a way to obtain a title to real property by possession for a specified length of time. Adverse possession is dependant upon actual possession, not merely paying the taxes due.

adversus: against.

advertacyonne: information.

advertisement: admonition. This is the original meaning of the word in preliminary notices.

advite: adult.

advocacies: lawsuits.

advocas: 1) lawyers; 2) advocates.

advocassie: (Norman) office of advocate.

advocate: 1) the champion of a cause - civil and/or ecclesiastical law; 2) an attorney who advises his client and pleads the client's case in open court.

advocation: the process which allows a case to go before a superior court without a final judgment in the lower court.

advocatrice: a female advocate.

advoue, advoes: (Norman) advocates or persons skilled in the law.

advowson: the right to nominate a person for a church office, e.g. a priest, a curate.

advowtry: adultery.

adward: 1) award; 2) judgment; 3) sentence.

adyet: the innermost part of a temple.

adyld: earned.

adyte: 1) to indite; 2) to write.

adze: a tool, which dates back to the Stone Age, variations of which were used by a 1) hoop binder; 2) cooper; 3) carpenter; 4) bridge builder; 5) log cabin builder; 6) woodworker.

ae: 1) one; 2) one of several; 3) each; 4) aged.

aegteviede: (Norman) married couple.

aele: (Norman) grandmother.

aer: an earl.

aererer: to plow.

aestive: summer.

aet: 1) of age or aged. Sometimes in cemetery records or on tombstones this means aged so many years, months, days; 2) an obsolete word for food.

aetas: 1) age; 2) period of time.

aetat: aged about (preceding a number and years).

aetatis: of age.

aetatis suae: this term followed by a number is a method of describing a person's age, e.g. "aetatis suae 23" means that the person has passed his 22nd birthday but not yet reached his 23rd birthday. This is sometimes found on a grave marker.

aetatula: of a youthful age.

af.: affidavit.

A.F.& A.M.: Ancient Free and Accepted Order of Masons.

afds.: aforesaid.

afeld: 1) felled; 2) destroyed.

afence: offence.

afend: to offend.

afenge: received.

affable: used frequently in old accounts of a wedding "the affable Miss." to mean a lady who was easy to talk to, courteous to equals or inferiors, complaisant, etc.

affair: an engagement not large enough to be called a battle.

affeer: to set a fair price.

affiance: an engagement, a promise to marry.

affiant: a person who make an affidavit and in this sense can be called the deponent. However, deponent should be reserved as the term used for the person who makes an deposition.

affidavit: an oath made before any person who is authorized to administer the oath. In early records this document sometimes was incorrectly called a deposition.

affinage: the refining of metals.
affine: a relative.
affinity: the relationship which exists after marriage between the couple and relatives of each.
affirmation: a statement by a witness who has ethical scruples against taking an oath.
afforn: before.
affray: a public fight between two or more people which is considered to be disturbing the peace.
afft.: affidavit.
affuage: the right to cut wood in a forest for the purpose of maintaining a family fire.
affusion: the act of baptism by pouring of water instead of by immersion.
aforesaid: already been mentioned.
aforesd.: aforesaid.
afoula: (Norman) 1) damaged; 2) wasted.
afsd.: aforesaid.
aft.: after; afternoon.
after-acquired property: property acquired after the date on which a will was written. Usually a will stated each child and what the child was to receive. However, when property is acquired after the will has been written and the will states definitely who will receive what, a problem is created. Usually in that case a person is considered to have died without a will (intestate) as far as that property is concerned. The problem would not have arisen if the testator had included the clause "all the rest and residue" of the property.
after born: born after the father has died or after his will was written.
after coming: following, next.
after grass: the second growing of grass after hay has been cut or in the stubble after harvest.
after kindred: remote relatives.
after the fact: an event which occurs after a court action has started.
A.G.: Adjutant General.
agah: ague.
again say: opposition, objection, to take something without any contention.
again-buyer: to redeem something as from a pawn shop or to pay a ransom for the return of something.
agarified: having ague.
A.G.D.: Adjutant General's Department.
age of consent: the age when a person can marry without a parent's permission. This age varies from state to state and from one period of time to another.
age of contractibility: the age below which marriages may not be made with or without parents' permission, unless the female is pregnant. This age varies in different states.
age of discretion: the age when a person was considered mature enough to make his choice of a guardian or the person to whom he would be apprenticed.
age of majority: the age when a person can make a contract without parental permission. This varies from state to state.
age of reason: the age when a child is considered capable of acting in a responsible manner, sometimes as early as seven.
agenhine: a guest at a house, who after a stay of three nights was considered one of the family.
agent: 1) a person who acts with permission for another whether the permission is implied or express; 2) the person who oversees freight and passenger tickets. He is not a member of the crew of the train, bus, etc. but operates from an office.
ager: an old spelling of ague.
aggregate: to combine or collect into one number, place, etc.
aggrevauns: 1) a grievance; 2) an injury.
aght: 1) possessions, property; 2) the eighth; 3) eight.
aghtand: the eighth.
aghtene: eight.
agiler: a spy.
aginator: 1) a storekeeper; 2) a trader.
agister: a forester who protected a lord's hunting by catching poachers.
agistment: 1) feeding of cattle in a common pasture for a stipulated price; 2) an embankment, earth heaped up, e.g. a dam, a dike; 3) an agreement to provide food or pasture for an animal for an agreed fee.
agler: a needle case.
aglutition: an inability to swallow.

agluttyd: choked.
agnail: a hangnail either on a finger or a toe.
agnate: a person whose relationship to another can be traced through the males in a family.
agnati: relatives on the father's side.
agnation: relatives on a father's side.
agnition: an acknowledgement.
A.G.O.: Adjutant General's Office.
agonist: a champion prize fighter.
Agosto: August.
agreage: to allege.
agreement: a contract between two or more parties specifying items which will or will not be done.
agricola: farmer.
agriot: a tart cherry.
agrippa: apparently the name of an herb.
agrt: agreement.
agst.: against.
agt.: 1) agent; 2) against.
ague and fever: malaria.
ague cake: an enlarged liver or spleen caused by having the ague.
ague tree: sassafras.
ague: 1) malaria type of fever; 2) chills and fever accompanied by sweating; 3) swelling and inflammation from taking cold.
agynus: not married.
A. & H. A. Co.: Ancient and Honorable Artillery Company.
aheritez: (Norman) heir, inheritor.
a.h.l.: ad hoc locum (which see).
ahte: eight.
aid: 1) money paid by a vassal to a feudal lord for a special reason; 2) the revenue obtained from the above tax, which was limited in the Magna Charta.
aid and abet: aid does not suggest guilt. Abet means knowledge as well as encouragement in committing a crime.
aide: Aide-De-Camp.
Aide-De-Camp: 1) a staff officer who delivers a superior officer's orders; 2) aids in the administration of a military unit; 3) aids at social affairs where a hostess is not present. Such an appointment was sometimes called "an aideship."
aidle: 1) to addle; 2) to earn.
aie: an egg.
aiel: 1) ancestor; 2) grandfather.
aiels: forefathers.
aighendale: a measure of seven quarts.
aighs: an axe.
aighteden: the eighth.
aigree: 1) sour; 2) acid.
aik: an oak.
aiker: an acre.
aiker daills: land which was divided into plots of varying acreage for rental.
ailess: (Norman) grandmother.
aim crier: one who helps only by orally giving encouragement.
ainneesche: (Norman) 1) eldership; 2) birthright.
ainznez: (Norman) eldest.
airen: eggs.
airline: also known as "as the crow flies," it was the shortest, straight way between two points. The term preceeds airplanes.
airn: l)iron 2) to earn.
air swellings: bloating of the abdomen due to gas in the stomach or intestines. Also called Tympanites.
airtights: jars for canning fruits and vegetables.
A.I.S.: Accelerated Indexing Systems (which see).
ais: see alias.
aisilyke: vinegar.
aisne fille: (Norman) eldest daughter.
aisne filz: (Norman) eldest son.
aisnecia: primogeniture.
aistre: 1) a house or a part of a house; 2) a fireplace or a part of a fireplace.
aisyll: vinegar.
ait: also spelled eyot. This British term for a small island. Usually refers to a small island in a river.
aitch: 1) an ache or pain; 2) a paroxysm in an intermitting disorder.
aithe: swearing.
aither: 1) either; 2) plowing.
aits: oats.
aixes: an ague.
a.k.a.: also known as.
ake: 1) an oak; 2) early spelling of ache.
aker: 1) an acre, 2) a field; 3) a measure of length.
aker-land: cultivated land.
aker-man: a husbandman.
akler: a custard-like dessert.
aksis: the ague.

A.L.: American Legion.
a.l.: autographed letter.
A.L.A.: American Library Association.
Alabama claims: after the Civil War the United States made claims upon Great Britain for the losses suffered due to the construction of Confederate ships, especially the "Alabama," one of several privateers built in British ports.
alabre: a type of fur.
alack: sometimes also alackaday. An archaic word similar in meaning to alas, expressing concern, grief, dismay, etc.
ala devie a trespass: (Norman) departed this life.
al-hal-day: all-hallows day, November first.
alair: (Norman) allege.
Alamo, the: a fort in Bexar County, Texas where a small number of Texans resisted an attacking body of ten times more Mexican on the 6th of March 1836. All the Texans were killed and "Remember the Alamo" became the battle-cry for Texans in their war for independence from Mexico.
alamode: 1) a thin, glossy, black silk used in Colonial days for hoods and at a later time to make hat bands; 2) fashionable.
alamode pot: a cooking vessel used primarily to cook a pot roast.
alanew: new ale.
alapeen: see alepine.
alaran: a kind of precious stone.
Alarm Act: this law was passed in 1820 and it required a review of all pensions. Those who were deemed not eligible to continue receiving a pension were removed from the pension rolls.
alarm: l) notice of an attack by the firing of guns, beat of drum, etc.; 2) a sudden fear of being attacked.
alay: to mix - generally applied to wines and liquors.
albastere: a cross bow man. Sometimes the cross bow itself.
albatross: a lightweight woolen cloth.
albe: 1) albeit, although; 2) a long, white linen garment worn by Roman Catholic priests.
albeit: an archaic word which means although. Another form is found in medieval English "al-be-it" which means although it be.
Albemarle settlements: land granted by Charles II to Carolina proprietors who hoped to sell part of the land, but keep large estates for themselves and duplicate the English class system of feudal loyalty.
albification: a chemical term for making white.
album: rent which is paid in silver (white) money.
albumen photographs: these were usually mounted on a thick paper to support the thin picture. It was developed with a substance of silver in egg whites which cracked and yellowed with age.
albyn: white.
alcalde: from the Spanish alcaide/ alcade. In areas where the Spanish influence was strong, it denoted governmental officers such as a Mayor, Judge or Justice of the Peace.
alcaly: a kind of salt.
alcamyne/alchemy: a mixed metal.
ald: old.
alder (adnus species): the bark of this plant was made into an ointment which was then used to cure boils, carbuncles, etc.
alderelde: very old age.
alderes: ancestors.
alderman: 1) an elected city officer who represents the people to the city council; 2) a representative of an Anglo-Saxon king who ruled a district, shire, etc.; 3) the person who headed a guild; 4) the person who ranks just below the mayor; 5) the head of a ward in London who was elected for his professional lifetime; 6) men of rank; 7) an old term for a justice of the peace; 8) a man of rank.
alderwoman: the wife of an alderman.
aldurfather: an ancestor.
ale: 1) a party or festival where ale was served; 2) a supply of ale kept for public consumption.
aleberry: a beverage made by boiling ale with spice, sugar and bits of bread which appears to have been given to invalids. Sometimes called alemeat.
aleccioun: an election.
aleconner: an officer whose job was to inspect and sample ale. Also called an

ale taster.

ale draper: a seventeenth century occupation; an inn keeper or alehouse keeper.

alegar: a cheap substitute for vinegar which was made by fermenting ale or beer.

ale-in-corner: new ale.

ale knight: a frequenter of alehouses.

Alemayne: Germany.

alembic: a still.

alemeat: see aleberry.

alepine: fabric made of a combination of wool and silk or mohair and cotton.

alert: vigilant, watching, guarding against surprise or danger of a real or threatened attack.

ale shot: the act of keeping an alehouse in a forest by an officer of the forest.

ale silver: a rent or fee paid annually to the Lord Mayor of London by all those who sold ale within the city.

ale stake: a post set in front of an alehouse which was used as a sign.

alestalder: a stallion.

alestond: an alehouse.

ale stool: the stand upon which casks of ale or beer were set while they were in a cellar.

ale taster: see aleconner.

aleven: eleven.

alewife: 1) a small fish belonging to the herring family which was, in New England, used first by the Indians and then by the Colonists as fertilizer and "planted" along with the seeds. By 1640 the settlers were again using the traditional method of using manure for fertilizer; 2) also used as feed along with corn for hogs; 3) a female keeper of a tavern.

alexcion: an election.

alfarez: a flag or banner.

'alf penny: an English coin made of bronze which was worth half of a penny or two farthings.

algia: used as a suffix means pain.

Algonkin Indians: another spelling of Algonquin.

Algonquins: an American Indian tribe who lived east of the Mississippi River. They entered into fur trading with the French around the St. Lawrence river in the 17th century.

alguazil: an officer in areas under Spanish rule who apprehended criminals and saw that they were punished.

aliant: an alien.

alias: 1) a word inserted between two surnames. For example, a person known by his step-father's name who also wished to be known by his father's name would use "alias" between the two surnames; 2) a name used previously; 3) a name other than your own which you use. It comes from the Latin "alias dictus" (which see); 4) a writ issued after a first writ did not accomplish what was intended.

alias capias: a writ issued in another name; at some other time there was a writ for the arrest of _____ _____.

alias dictus: "otherwise called" when a person is known by two names and is called by both of his names.

alias execution: a second writ issued after a previous writ did not accomplish its intended purpose.

alias subpoena: a second subpoena issued after a previous subpoena did not accomplish its intended purpose.

alias summons: a second summons issued after a previous summons did not accomplish its intended purpose.

alias writ: a second writ issued after a first writ.

alibi: a provable statement which says that a person was not present when a crime was committed.

alibi natua: born in another place.

alienacan: (Norman) kindred.

alien, aliene: 1) a person born outside of the country in which he resides, and who consequently has no legal rights, e.g. to vote: 2) to alienate.

alienate: to transfer property; 2) to cause two people or two countries to part.

alienation: voluntary transfer by sale, gift, will, etc. of property.

alien declaration: documents which support an alien's intention to become a citizen.

alienee: 1) one to whom property is transferred; 2) (Norman) the buyer.

alien enemy: a person whose loyalty lies with a hostile government

alien registration: a method, used especially in wartime, to keep track of non-citizens by requiring them to register and carry a registration card.
alienus: 1) that which belongs to another; 2) a stranger, a foreigner; 3) unsuitable.
aliicide: murder.
aliquot parts: division into equal portions.
alius: an assumed name.
allaboration: toiling very hard.
allaceaulx: (Norman) collateral.
all and singular: 1) all without any exceptions; 2) a phrase used to indicate the whole and each of separate parts which make up the whole.
alleg.: allegiance.
allegation: what a person will try to prove during a lawsuit.
allegiance: loyalty to government, person, cause, group, etc.
allen: unenclosed land that was tilled and left to grow weeds and used as pasture to feed sheep.
allendardy: prevention of a rental agreement for life becoming a perpetual lease.
allepine: see alepine.
aller: an alder tree.
allerbatch: 1) an old sore; 2) a type of a boil.
allers: an acute type of boil or carbuncle.
alleve: 1) eleven; 2) lessen, ease.
alleventhe: the eleventh.
alley: a narrow street or passageway through the middle of a block for convenient access to the rear of houses or business buildings.
alleyde: alleged.
Alleys of the House: church aisles.
All Fools' Day: a facetious name for April Fools' Day - April 1.
allhallown: summer or late summer.
All Hallows' Day: 1 November.
all hands: the total crew, both enlisted men and officers, of an entire ship.
allieny: 1) an alley; 2) a passage in a building.
alligation: an arithmetic process for determining the amounts to be mixed or divided, e.g. liquids in a recipe or shares of money.
allodial title: absolute ownership, free, owned without obligation.
allograph: a signature made for a person who is for some reason unable to sign his own name.
allot: 1) distribute in an orderly manner; 2) to apportion to one or a group of people.
allottery: an allotment.
all overish: neither sick nor well.
allowed: licensed.
allron: a fabric made in France.
All Saints' Day: November 1st.
All Souls' Day: November 2nd.
all's well: a call passed once each hour between sentinels which signifies that each is present and that all is well at his station.
ally: a nation which has promised to fight, or is fighting, on the side of another nation against a common enemy.
almanac: a softbound book published annually both in this country and in England. It contained many articles such as medical remedies for ailments, a schedule of the best times to plant certain crops, and a weather forecast for each day during the year, etc.
Almany, Almayne: Germany.
almarie: cupboard, pantry.
almariol: a closet or cupboard in which ecclesiastical garments are kept.
almesse: alms.
almoner: a person who at the request and expense of a wealthy person, or a church, gave aid to the poor.
alms: gifts of clothing, food, money, etc. to people in need.
almsdish: 1) a collection plate in a church for an offering to be used for the poor of the parish; 2) a receptacle carried by beggars.
almsfee: a payment to the Pope. Sometimes called Peter's pence.
almsfolk: those supported by the public.
alms giver: one who makes gifts to the poor, either personally, or through an almoner.
almshouse: a house where the poor people in a city, county, etc. live and are cared for.
almsman: a person who lives on charity.
alnager: an Englishman whose job was quality control of cloth.
alner: a purse or bag to hold money.

alomba: tin.
a-loryng: a parapet wall.
alpurth: a half-penny's worth.
alriche: a dog.
als.: alias.
a.l.s.: autograph letter signed.
als. wt.: alias writ.
alsene: an awl.
altm.: see at liberty to marry.
alum: a chemical used in early medicines.
alumnus: a foster child. The female form is alumna.
alure: a kind of gutter or channel behind the battlements, which served to carry off the rain water. Sometimes the word was used for an alley or passage from one part of a building to another.
alutation: tanning of leather.
alve: half.
alwes: 1) hallows; 2) saints.
alye: 1) to mix; 2) kindred.
A.M.: Ante Meridian, before noon.
amalgamation: the act or result of mixing two or more together, e.g. metals, corporations, etc.
amalgaming: to mix quicksilver with any metal.
amanuensis: a secretary.
ambassage: an embassy.
ambrotype photograph: a direct image photo which did not have a negative. It had a dark backing which gave it a positive image and sometimes a glass plate was used for support rather than paper or metal.
ambry: 1) a cupboard; 2) a pantry.
ambulatory: 1) an aisle which goes around the end of the chancel or where the choir members sit; 2) a covered walk; 3) capable of walking.
ambuscado: an ambush.
ambush: 1) an attack from a hidden place, either as a military tactic, or as a method used by out-laws to commit a crime; 2) a place where a person or persons may hide before surprising the enemy by a sudden attack.
ame: (Norman) friend.
A.M.E.: African Methodist Episcopal Church.
amen corner: the corner directly to the right of the pulpit, which in some Protestant churches was occupied by persons who would during the services agree with the preacher's sermon by saying "Amen" frequently.
amend: 1) correct; 2) alter; 3) restore; 4) reform; 5) cure.
amendment: 1) an addition; 2) compost laid on land.
a mensa et thoro: "from bed and board." A legal separation after which the couple are forbidden to remarry.
amentia: see insanity.
amerawdes: hemorrhoids.
amerce: 1) to fine an amount of money not set by law but by the court; 2) to punish.
amercements: 1) fines; 2) penalties.
amercts.: amercements.
American Party: see Know-Nothing Party.
American rifle: see long rifle.
American State Papers: first published in book form but now available on microfilm, these papers relate to nearly 80,000 diverse claims on private land. Included are informative notes by states and miscellaneous claims such as Indian Nation Claims, Refugees from Canada, and militia lands but <u>not</u> the patents granted to veterans of wars.
amethodist: a person who does not follow a prescribed method.
Am F.: (Norman) Amen.
amicable: friendly.
amice: a garment worn by Roman Catholic priests.
amicus: a friend.
amicus curiae: a friend of the court. A person who is allowed to speak in court about a matter with which he is familiar. He does not know any of the parties involved.
amicus humani: found on grave markers - a humanitarian.
amita: aunt (father's sister) - sometimes found on grave markers.
ammat: a luncheon.
ammis: the canonical vestment, lined with fur, that served to cover the head and shoulders. Grey fur was generally used.
amnesty: to pardon an offense.
amper: 1) an inflamed swelling; 2) a fault in linen or woolen cloth; 3) decaying of teeth, cheese, etc.

ampulle: a small vessel.
Amrell: Admiral.
amserey: a consistory court.
Amsterdam dium: a Dutch measure of 1.013 inches.
Amsterdam morgen: a Dutch square measure of 2.069 acres.
Amsterdamons: a Dutch weight equalling 1.085 ounces, based upon the avoirdupois weight of 1 ounce contains 16 drams.
Amsterdam pond: a Dutch weight equalling 1 pound 1.34 ounces, based upon the avoirdupois weight of 1 ounce contains 16 drams.
Amsterdam roede: a Dutch measure of 12.071 feet or 13 voeten.
amt.: amount.
Amy Dardin: a widow of Mecklenburg County, Virginia who for nineteen years (1796-1815) applied to Congress at intervals for compensation for a horse seized by the government during the Revolutionary War. Apparently this became a classic case of procrastination.
an.: anno.
Anabaptist: a sect in Germany during the sixteenth century.
anack: oat bread.
anapes: cloth.
anaplerosis: to repair a deficiency, such as a cut healed with new flesh.
anasarca: see dropsy.
anc.: ancestry, ancestor, ancient.
ancelle: (Norman) maid servant.
ancessoure: ancestor.
ancestor: a person from whom one is descended.
ancestor in common: the person from whom you and one or more of your relatives are descended. You all have this common ancestor or ancestor in common.
ancestress: a female ancestor.
anchor: 1) a Dutch liquid measure; 2) a cask used by smugglers to carry their brandy on horseback; 3) a hermit; 4) a heavy iron implement which has a cable attached to one end and a pair of extended hooks at the other end. One or more of the implements are used to hold a vessel steady in a desired area.
anchoridge: a church porch.
anchorsmith: a person who forges an anchor out of iron.
anchyrche: a church.
ancient: 1) a standard bearer; 2) an ensign bearer; 3) an officer now called an Ensign. The work was also used for the flag or ensign of a regiment or of a ship.
ancient documents: wills, deeds, etc. which are presumed to be real and are more than thirty years old.
ancient lights: windows which have let in daylight or air for many years. A person who owns land next to such a window may not build anything which cuts off light and air from these windows. In Japan, for example, a person may not build a barn which cuts off light from ground which is used for growing plants.
ancillary: an assistant, an auxiliary.
ancillary administration: an estate settlement which is held in a state other than the one where the decedent lived. Therefore, it is a secondary administration.
ancille: a maid servant.
ancome: a small ulcerous swelling, formed unexpectedly, or a bump that is hard and hot.
ancomy: a flat iron bar.
ancres: a female hermit.
ande: (Norman) mother-in-law.
andersmas: a mass or festival honoring St. Andrew.
Andersonville Prison: a Confederate prison situated in southwest Georgia which had the reputation of being the worst prison for captured Northern soldiers. Probably this prison and the prison for captured Confederate soldiers at Elmira, New York were the two worst operated during the Civil War.
andesith: previously.
andessorue: ancestors.
andirons: a support to keep logs off the fireplace floor. Used in pairs they allow air circulation underneath the fire. The vertical frontispiece could be quite decorative. Also called dogs or fire-dogs.
An.Do., An. Dom.: Anno Domini.
anelace: a kind of knife or dagger which

was usually worn at the waist.

anemia: an inadequate supply of red blood cells in blood. This may be caused by any number of irregularities: loss of blood, infections, poisons in the blood, lead, inadequate iron, etc.

anens: chains, fetters.

angel: 1) a gold coin; 2) an angular opening in a building.

angel bill of credit: an angel was worth ten shillings sterling in old England and in 1717 the Massachusetts Colony issued a bill of public credit worth ten shillings. In some documents this is shortened to "angel."

angel bread: a purgative cake made of cistern water, ginger, flour and oatmeal.

angelot: 1) cheese brought to England from Normandy; 2) a gold coin - half an angel. It was current when Paris was in possession of the English.

angel's food: apparently another term for heavy ale.

Angevin: a member of the Plantagenet (which see) related families from which fourteen of England's kings descended.

angild: a fine.

angina pectoris: a pain in the chest which may travel the left arm to the abdomen. This is not a disease, but a symptom of heart disease.

Angl.: Anglican, Anglicized.

angle: 1) a corner; 2) an astrological term.

angle-berry: a sore or kind of hangnail under the claw or hoof of an animal.

angle-bowing: a fence built by crossing timber at angles, first one direction then the opposite.

angler: one who begs in the daytime, observing what he can steal at night.

Anglican: 1) of England, the country or the nation; 2) the Church of England; 3) a member of the Church of England.

Anglicize: to cause words, churches, etc. to become English in nature, pronunciation, etc.

anglo: a prefix which means English.

Anglosajone: a derogatory term for Anglo-Saxon in Spanish areas.

angry: painful, inflamed, smarting.

angus: a kind of beef cattle.

anile: imbecile from old age.

animal economy: an old term used in the eighteenth century for bowel movements.

anker: a Dutch liquid measure, especially for wine, equalling 10.128 gallons.

anlepi: alone, single - therefore applies to unmarried person.

anlifen: 1) livelihood; 2) substance.

annals: 1) historical events recorded in chronological order; 2) events of one years listed in chronological order; 3) Roman Catholic masses said with regularity for one year.

annary: a yearly description.

anni currentis: current year.

anno: year.

Anno Dom, Anno Doe, Anno De: Anno Domini.

Anno Domini: "in the year of our Lord." Time dating approximately from the birth of Christ, according to the Christian era. Found on grave markers.

Anno Regni: in the year of the reign.

annot.: annotated.

annual rent: interest received or paid from money which was lent to another.

annual return: a report made for an estate by the administrator or executor on an annual basis, to the probate court.

annuary: annual.

annul: 1) to void; 2) to declare lawfully without a divorce that a marriage no longer exists.

annus bissextus: leap year.

annus luctus: the year of mourning. A widow's year of mourning for her deceased husband.

anodyne: a medicine which will dull pain.

anon.: anonymous.

anonymous: 1) no name; 2) signature on a letter by one who wishes to remain unknown.

anoyle: to anoint. The last sacrament of the Roman Catholic church.

anspessade: an infantry petty officer. Sometimes spelled lanspessade.

answer: a written statement made in court in which the defendant outlines his defence.

ante: before, earlier - either in time or place.

ante bellum: before the war. Usually used when speaking of the Civil War in the United States.

antecessor: an advanced guard, one who runs ahead.

Ante Christum: see A.C.

antedate: to pre-date a document, e.g. a check to pay a forthcoming bill.

ante diem: before the day. Used in dating documents.

antehoc: formerly, before now.

antem: 1) a church; 2) an anthem.

Ante Meridian: before noon.

antenuptial contract: see marriage settlement.

anthelmintic: a substance which is capable of eliminating worms in people.

anthrax: a carbuncle.

anti: prefixed to any word means against.

antients: ancestors.

antifebrile: a remedy for a fever.

antimetic: a medicine to stop vomiting.

Anti-Masonic party: a political party composed of those opposed to the secrecy of the fraternal society known as the Masons. Their candidate failed to receive enough electoral votes in the election of 1832.

antiperiodic: that which prevents periodic recurrent diseases, e.g. ague, intermittent fevers, malaria, etc.

antiphlogistic: a remedy for inflammation.

antiphoner: a psalm book containing the usual church music.

antiq: antiquarian.

antiquarian: 1) the study of customs, history, etc. of a former time; 2) a dealer of rare and second-hand books.

anti-rent: a political party in New York about 1840 which opposed paying rent to a patron.

antiscorbutic: remedy for scurvy such as vitamin C.

antisialagogue: remedy to decrease a flow of saliva.

antispasmodic: remedy for muscle spasms or cramps; quinine (which see).

antisyphilitic: a remedy or preventative for syphilis made out of mercury.

anus: an old woman.

anvel: 1) a priest's yearly salary; 2) an annuity.

anvil: 1) the large iron block which is used by a blacksmith or an armorer as a base on which to hammer hot iron into a desired shape; 2) the handle or hilt of a sword; 3) a narrow flat at the end of a lance.

anynge: union.

a-one: an individual.

A.O.P: American Order of Pioneers.

ap: (Welsh) "son of." Several generations of a lineage may be found on a tombstone: "John ap Robert ap John of ...."

Apache Indians: a tribe who resided in the New Mexico, Arizona area. Their name meant "enemy." Geronimo was one of their most famous leaders.

aparejo: a large saddle designed to carry heavy loads.

apd: see attending places of diversion.

ape ward: a keeper of apes.

aperient: a gentle laxative or purgative.

aperner: one who wears an apron.

apery: an ape house.

aphtha: see thrush.

aphtha chronica: chronic thrush. See thrush.

apis: a kind of an apple tree.

apmt.: appointment.

apock: a small red pimple.

apocryphal: 1) counterfeit; 2) of questionable authenticity; 3) non-conforming.

apodytery: a vestry.

apoplexy: 1) a stroke; 2) a hemorrhage or thrombosis of a blood vessel located in the brain.

apostle spoons: it was anciently the custom for sponsors at a christening to offer gift spoons as presents to the child, which were called apostle spoons, because very frequently the figures of the twelve apostles were chased or carved on the tops of the handles. Wealthy sponsors gave four, while the poorer ones gave one which exhibited the figure of some saint in honor of whom the child received its name.

apothecary: 1) a medical officer's chief assistant, familiarly called "pills;" 2) an old name for a drug store and the pharmacist.

apothecary chest: a chest with many small drawers used to hold various chemicals and medicines used by a pharmacist.

app.: 1) apprentice: 2) sometimes used as an abbreviation for approximately.

Appalachee Indians: once a powerful

tribe in Florida, a portion moved in 1700 to Alabama. It is now non-existent as a tribe.

apparitor: a subordinate court official in ancient Rome.

appd: 1) appointed; 2) appeared.

appeal: 1) the process which allows a case to go from a lower to a higher court to be reheard, or the request for this action; 2) to call a person as a witness or as an authority.

appeal bond: security given by the person who is appealing to a higher court which binds the appellant to pay damages and costs if the suit fails to obtain support of a higher court. This bond is designed to discourage frivolous appeals.

appeal of false judgment: an archaic French court procedure used by persons who were dissatisfied with the outcome of a case in the lords' court. They could charge the papers with giving a spiteful judgment and offer to fight a duel as a final appeal.

appear., appearce.: appearance.

appearance docket: an index to all cases coming into court. From this book one may be able to locate more specific records in various courts.

appellant: one who appeals a judicial decision in another court; plaintiff.

appellate court: a court which hears, reviews and judges appeals from a lower level court. It can correct judgmental errors or can send it back for further hearing.

appellate jurisdiction: the power of reviewing and deciding a legal matter which has earlier been decided by a lower court.

appellee: a person who has been accused of committing a crime and must prove that he is without guilt; defendant.

apple peeler: a device that peeled, and sometimes sliced and cored apples in one operation. As many as a bushel apples could be peeled in an hour.

application: placing a written formal request or petition before a person asking for land, work, etc.

appoind, appotd: appointed.

appointed: used in Quaker records this means a member has been chosen clerk or to be on a committee, etc.

appr.: 1) appearance; 2) appellor; 3) appraisement.

appraisal: an evaluation of property, real or personal, by one or two people qualified to set a fair value on the property.

appraisement: property valuation.

appraiser: a person named to make a fair evaluation of personal property or of real estate.

apprentice: a person, usually a minor, bound to a master of a trade for a specific period of time. The apprentice contributed his labor and sometimes paid a sum of money for the privilege of becoming an apprentice. The master provided instruction and either provided clothing and lodging or a wage. The courts always included that children must be taught reading, writing and arithmetic. Any complaint, from the child, the parents or the apprentice's master would be investigated. The most common complaints concerned runaway boys or pregnant girls. Some parents hid illegitimate children in this system to keep them from becoming wards of the county.

apprentice-at-law: 1) a counselor; 2) the next in rank under a sergeant.

apprilled: partially soured milk or beer.

apprinze: capture.

approver: 1) a person who is an accomplice in a felony and who confesses that he is guilty and then gives evidence against his companions in the crime; 2) a person who turns state's evidence; 3) an obsolete word for a person who proves, tests, or tries, something out; 4) a person who commends another.

approx.: approximately.

apprs.: appraisers.

appt.: 1) appointed; 2) appointment (military).

appt. comm.: found in Quaker records, this is an abbreviation for appointed to a committee.

appted.: appointed.

appurtenance: in land records this word in the singular or plural form refers to a right-of-way, a barn, house, fences, etc.

- anything which is attached to or pertains in some way to the land described.

appx.: appendix.

apres: wool cloth from Flanders.

apron man: a waiter or any worker who wore an apron.

aps: an aspen tree.

apud: 1) near; 2) by; 3) with; 4) at.

apyum: parsley.

aqua vitae: spirituous liquors.

aqua-acuta: a preparation for cleaning armor.

aquaria: water carrier.

aqua vitae: a general term for any kind of alcoholic liquid.

A.R.: Anno Regni (which see).

Arabian: a type of horse prized for its speed and intelligence.

arak: see arrack.

Arapaho Indians: a tribe linked with the Cheyennes. They lived between the South Fork of the Platte River and the Arkansas River headwaters.

arbiter: witness, attestator.

arch.: archives.

archaic: 1) old or ancient; 2) words which were used frequently in old days but now are seldom used.

archbishop: the highest ranking church officer who presides over a church governmental unit.

archdeacon: a church officer who ranks just below a bishop and assists him with church affairs or duties.

archdiacre: archdeacon.

archiater: physician.

archidiaconus: archdeacon.

archidiascalus: headmaster.

archiepiscopus: archbishop.

archipelago: a body of water containing many islands. The term originally referred to the Aegean Sea. It also refers to the islands themselves.

architectus: architect, builder.

archives: a place where records of businesses, churches, families, etc. are deposited for safe keeping. Each organization could either maintain its own archives or use a central depository.

archivist: the person in charge of preserving old materials.

arcularius: carpenter.

arewen, arewes: arrows.

argentan: German silver.

argentine: silver.

argolet: a light horseman.

argonaut: after gold was discovered in California in 1848 those who went to hunt the gold were called "argonauts" after the name of the mythical ship in which Jason sought the Golden Fleece.

argosies: very large ships.

argosy: a merchant ship.

argot, argent: silver.

Arickarees: see Rickarees Indians.

arierevan: a general summons from the King to all his vassals to appear carrying arms.

ark: 1) a large, awkward, but serviceable boat used most frequently on the Ohio River. Both ends were pointed and could serve as a ram to brush aside smaller floating logs and other trouble-makers. It has a "house" built on one end, a fenced in area for animals on the other, and was steered by a large oar which required the strength of two men to use it. As the ark could not go back upstream, when it arrived at its destination it was dismantled and sold for lumber; 2) an enormous freight wagon which had broad wheels with tires, and was pulled by four to ten horses. Also called a market wagon or a Pennsylvania wagon.

Arkansas Indians: a tribe allied with the Dakotas who lived on the Ohio River.

arles: money paid to bind a bargain.

arm: 1) a weapon of attack or defense; 2) to equip men with weapons.

armaments: navy cannon. Also see artillery.

armed guard officer: this naval officer commands a gun-crew aboard a merchant ship during wartime.

armentarius: herdsman.

armiger: gentleman, squire, esquire, shield bearer, knight.

armigorous: the right to use a coat of arms.

Arminian: one who followed the religious beliefs of a Dutch Protestant named Arminius (1560-1609).

armistice: a temporary halting of hostile action by mutual agreement of the parties concerned.

arm of service: a general term used to denote one of the major parts of an army.

armoire: a large, free standing clothes cupboard used to hang clothes in a day when closets were not common.

armorer, armourer: 1) on a fighting ship this man keeps the guns in a serviceable condition. He is also the ship's blacksmith; 2) a maker and repairer of armor.

armory: 1) a drill hall and storage place for arms; 2) a part of heraldry devoted to coats of armor; 3) articles of defense; 4) armor.

armsmaker: a seventeenth century term for the person who made weapons which used gunpowder.

armures (milles): (Norman) a thousand armed men.

armyll: 1) a bracelet; 2) a necklace.

army rank: 1861 = general, lieutenant general, major general, brigadier general, colonel, lieutenant colonel, major, captain, first lieutenant, second lieutenant, cadet, sergeant major, quartermaster sergeant of a regiment, ordinance and hospital steward, first sergeant, sergeant, corporal, private.

Today = general of the army, general, lieutenant general, major general, brigadier general, colonel, lieutenant colonel, major, captain, first lieutenant, second lieutenant, chief warrant officer, warrant officer junior grade, master sergeant, sergeant first class, technical sergeant, staff sergeant, sergeant, corporal, private first class, private.

army structure: entire army commanded by a general, smaller divisions of the entire army commanded by subordinate generals, division or department commanded by a secondary general, regiment commanded by a colonel, battalion commanded by a major, company commanded by a captain, squad commanded by a lieutenant or a sergeant.

Army, U.S.: created in 1789. Those who served in the army were eligible for pensions.

arnaldie: a disease the details of which are unknown.

arnary cheese: an ordinary cheese made of skim milk.

aromatarious: 1) druggist; 2) perfume maker.

aromatic: spicy and fragrant drugs which prevent fainting.

arpent (or arpen): a land measure of French origin which equals 100 square rods or perches. In this measure a rod is 18 feet long. In 1835 in Missouri it equaled .85 acre.

arpentator: a surveyor of land, from "arpent," a measure of land area.

arraign: to call a person to court in order that he may answer a charge brought against him.

arrack: one of several liquors distilled from fermented molasses, rice, etc. in the East or Middle East. It is sometimes spelled arak.

arras: a fabric woven with figures or scenes; a tapestry.

array: the group of people who are assembled in court and from which a jury will be selected.

arrer: (Norman) to plow ground (verb).

arriere-ban: 1) vassals who were obliged to give military service, especially to the French kings; 2) the act of summoning all vassals and freemen for military duty.

arrv.: arrived.

arsenal: a Federal Government establishment for storage or manufacture of arms and military equipment.

art.: artillery.

art and mystery: the principles upon which a person can develop a skill or craft.

arteen: eighteen.

arth-staff: a poker used by a blacksmith.

arti.: artificer.

articlaire: (Norman) artillery.

article: 1) an obsolete word for a critical point in time; 2) a subject of interest, business, etc.

Articles of Confederation (and Perpetual Union): In 1775 for the purpose of making a union of the thirteen American states a set of agreements were proposed by Delegates of the Colonies. The Continental Congress adopted them in

1777, they were ratified in 1781 and were in effect until 1789 when they were replaced by the Constitution.

articules: any multiples of ten.

artif.: artificer.

artificer: 1) a person who makes shells, fuses and grenades; 2) a person who follows a trade (carpenter, blacksmith, mason, etc.) as a military employee; 3) a mechanic.

artificial person: 1) a corporation is called an artificial person, in contrast to a natural person (an individual); 2) a creation of something which has the rights and duties of a real person; 3) once in a while a bankrupt deceased person's estate.

artillery: large guns (e.g. canon) which, along with their specialized equipment are taken into the battlefield to defend or attack fortifications. A soldier in the artillery must posses a knowledge of surveying, geometry, fortifications, etc. as well as skills in firing guns. This term does not apply to naval cannon which are referred to as armament.

artisan: 1) one trained in a trade; 2) obsolete term for an artist.

artist (coach): an artist considered himself above a painter, as the artist would decorate the panels of a coach with appropriate pictures.

arty.: abbreviation for artillery.

arval: 1) the meal served after a funeral. Sometimes the decedent would have made provisions in his will for this meal for the mourners; 2) a funeral.

asafetida: a medicine which was used to control spasms. Sometimes spelled asfetidia.

Ascension Day: the first Thursday forty days after Easter, previously known as Assumptio Domini, Christi.

ascerte: (Norman) certified.

asch cake: bread baked under ashes.

ascites: an abnormally large amount of fluid in the abdominal cavity.

aseth: satisfaction for an injury.

asfetidia: see asafetida.

asgd.: assigned.

Ash Wednesday: the first day of Lent.

askings: the publication of marriage by banns.

asman: driver of asses.

asr.: assessor.

assach: an old custom among the Welsh whereby a person accused of a crime was enabled to clear himself by the oath of three hundred men.

assault: 1) to threaten a person with bodily harm. However, if a blow to the person is delivered, then it is battery; 2) an intense attack upon a fortified area. This attack is usually unsupported and those who are the attackers are sometimes called "the forlorn hope."

assaver 3 mois: (Norman) three months later.

assay: 1) trial; 2) experience; 3) to test ore for a precious metal.

assayer: 1) a person who tests ore for precious metals; 2) a taster of food and wine in barons' houses and other places to guard against poisoning.

assd.: assigned.

assene: asses.

assenel: arsenic.

asseore: an usher.

asser: (Norman) steel.

asserte: (Norman) surety.

assessment: 1) a listing of persons and their property to be taxed; 2) the valuation of the property to determine the amount of the tax to be paid.

assessment rolls: lists of persons eligible to pay taxes on real or personal property.

assessor: an appointed or elected person who places a value on property, usually for tax purposes.

asset: 1) valuable items which could be used by a person to pay debts; 2) things of value which go into an estate.

assheard: a keeper of donkeys.

assignation: 1) the process of giving or allocating something; 2) an appointment for a meeting between two or more people.

assignation house (house of assignation): a house of prostitution that caters to the wealthy.

assignee: 1) a person to whom an assignment is made, usually used in speaking of personal property. In old days an assignee was acting in his own right as opposed to a deputy acting for another;

2) any one who legally possessed a bounty warrant or donation certificate by purchase or gift; 3) a person who had a warrant, but was not the person to whom it had been issued.

assignment: a transfer in writing of the title or interest in any kind of property from one party to another.

assignment of dower: designation by legal description whereby a widow's portion of her deceased husband's estate is given to her.

assigns: a transfer of title from one to another. See heirs and assigns.

assistant marshall: the census taker on the local level during the years 1790-1870.

assize(s): 1) a superior court trial, either civil or criminal, in England which is held periodically; 2) an inquiry by a jury; 3) a judgment; 4) a regulatory statute governing weights and measures.

assize of utrum: a clergyman's suit to recover land which a previous minister had allowed to be improperly removed from the church's control.

assn.: association.

asso.: 1) associate; 2) associated.

assoc.: association.

associators: 1) members of an association; 2) a companion; 3) a colleague; 4) an abettor; 5) a comrade.

asst.: assistant.

assumpit: a type of law suit, usually a breach of contract suit.

asylum: 1) a place for the confinement of lunatics; 2) a place for the care of orphans; 3) a place of refugee in wartime; 4) formerly a place where criminals and/or debtors could find shelter and from they could not be taken without sacrilege.

at large: free, not attached to one particular organization or place.

at lge.: at large.

atavite: ancestral.

atchism: a coin made of copper with a silver wash.

Atherton gag: each year from 1838 to 1844 a resolution in Congress provided that all bills or petitions dealing with slavery should, without debate, be tabled. This resolution was introduced by C. G. Atherton (1804-1853) U. S. Representative and Senator of New Hampshire.

athwart: 1) from side to side or crosswise; 2) to go broadside of the wind; 3) awry; 4) contrary to.

atlas: 1) a book of maps or charts named for their frequent use of an engraving of the mythical character who carried the world on his back; 2) a satin fabric made of silk.

at liberty to marry: used in Quaker records, this means that a couple has announced that they wish to marry. An appointed committee has investigated the couple and reported back to meeting that they may proceed to get married.

atque: and.

atrick: 1) an usher of a hall; 2) a master porter.

atrophy: a wasting away of muscles.

att: in Quaker records this indicates a member attended or is attending.

attabanies: a silk fabric.

attach: to assign a person to a specific duty, or a specific unit on a temporary basis.

attachment: 1) apprehending or taking into custody a person or property involved in a court action, for example, a bond, a writ, a witness, a juror; 2) the order to carry out the above.

attainder: 1) see corruption of blood; 2) loss of all civil rights when one is sentenced to death for a crime such as treason or a felony.

atteach: attachment.

attend: 1) to wait upon, a servant; 2) to minister to a person who is ill.

attending places of diversion: used in Quaker meetings, this term indicates that a member has been to a horse race, a theater, has been gambling, etc. Therefore if, after being counseled, they cannot forgo these pleasures they are disowned at monthly meeting.

atter: poison.

attest: 1) to witness; 2) testimony; 3) to certify that a document is genuine.

attested copy: a reproduction of a document about which an official states that the document is correct and verifies this statement by adding his signature. A certified copy will have a seal attached

to it.
attice: 1) a carpenter's tool; 2) an adze.
attorney: a person who acts for another, a deputy.
attorney-at-law: 1) a legally appointed person who transacts business for another; 2) a lawyer.
attorney-in-fact: a person appointed to act for another in one situation that is not of a legal nature.
attornment: to accept someone as a new landlord.
attt.: attachment.
atty: attorney.
au.: chemical symbol for gold.
aubine: (Norman) an alien, foreigner.
aucte: property.
auction: 1) a public sale conducted by a person (the auctioneer) who asks for the highest price he can get for a wide variety of articles. This method was frequently used to turn estate property into cash which could be divided among heirs; 2) an alternate method of conducting an auction sale was more common in Dutch New York City. The seller offered the item at a higher price than he expected to get and gradually lowered the price until one of the purchasers called out "min." The Dutch called this method "mining."
auctioneer: the person who directs a sale of goods in public, for which he usually earns a commission. See auction.
aud.: auditor.
auditor: a person who inspects accounts, e.g. banks, stores, county records, etc. to make certain they are accurate.
audremantz: (Norman) alderman.
auger: 1) a tool used by a carpenter to make holes in wood; 2) a large tool used to make holes in the ground, e.g. for fence posts.
aught-possessions: property.
aughtene: the eighth.
auhten: eight.
auld thrift: wealth accumulated by the frugality of a long line of ancestors.
auln: a french measure which equals five feet, seven inches.
aulnager: a government official who inspected cloth to maintain its quality.
auma: a pancake.
aumbry: 1) a cupboard; 2) a pantry.
aunceteres: ancestors.
auncian: aged.
auncil: an uncertain kind of land the sale of which was prohibited by law.
aunt: 1) the sister of a persons's parent; 2) courtesy title for an older female friend of a person's parents; 3) a woman of bad character.
aunz/auntz: (Norman) years.
aurifaber: goldsmith.
aurifex: a goldsmith.
auriga: driver.
aurigifex: wagon maker.
aust: (Norman) autumn.
autem: a church.
authentic: proven.
authenticated copy: a reproduction of an original document certified by an official as being accurate. It is legally admissible in court.
A.U.S.: Arm of the United States.
autors: ancestors.
autours: (Norman) 1) the author; 2) the maker.
av: ad valorem according to value.
avage: a rent or fee which was paid to the Lord of the Manor for the liberty of feeding hogs in the manor woods.
availl: 1) value; 2) profit; 3) advantage.
ave: (Norman) cattle.
avenant: (Norman) value, price.
aver: 1) a work-horse; 2) (Norman) cattle; 3) (Norman) money, goods, effects.
averages: a day's work by a subject which was exacted by a feudal superior.
avercake: an oat cake.
averill: (Norman) April.
averish: stubble and grass left in a cornfield after the crop has been harvested.
averland: land plowed by farm tenants for the use of a monastery or for the owner of the soil.
averment: proof.
averpenny: money contributed to the King's averages.
avers, avier: (Norman) money, effects, goods.
aversilver: a rent or tax upon the cattle, or avers, from the tenant farmers.
avery: the place where the provisions for the King's horses were kept.

avet: weight.
avia: grandmother.
a vinculo matrimonii: from the bond of marriage, a final divorce.
avives: a disease found in horses.
avoery: a right of patronage which the founder of a religious order possessed.
avoid: 1) to avoid; 2) to leave; 3) to quit.
avoir: property.
avoir-de-peise: articles of merchandise which were sold by their weight.
avoirdupois weight: a system of weight measurement based upon one pound composed of sixteen ounces, with one ounce containing sixteen drams.
avor: see ave.
avoury: an old law term nearly equivalent to justification.
avoutrer: an adulterer.
avowe, advowee: (Norman) a patron, a follower.
avowtrie: (Norman) adultery.
avunculus: an uncle, a mother's brother.
avunculus magnus: a great uncle, a grandmother's brother.
avus: grandfather. This word is sometimes found on old tombstones.
avy: 1) vow, oath; 2) a navy.
award: 1) to make a judicial decision; 2) to determine judicially an appropriate amount of money as compensation for damage to a person or his property.
awash: a ship which rides very low in the water so that the water repeatedly comes over the sides is said to be awash.
awd: old.
aweld: to govern, rule.
awghtend: the eighth.
awl: a hand tool used to punch holes in leather, wood, etc.
awnber: an almoner (which see).
awner: a possessor, owner.
A.W.O.L.: absent without official leave.
axe: a tool used by 1) a broom-maker; 2) a wheel-wright; 3) a carpenter; 4) a woodworker.
axes: the ague, generally applied to fits or paroxysms.
axle-tooth: a grinder.
ayele: (Norman) grandmother.
ayer: (Norman) heir.
ayere, ayre: an heir.
ayle: (Norman) grandfather.
aylede: possessed.
ayreable: tillable.
ayren: eggs.
ayrshire: a breed of dairy cattle.
ayschis: ashes.
ayselle: vinegar.
ayttene: eighteen.
azzletooth: a grinder.

B: abbreviation for many terms. 1) bondsman; 2) a convicted burglar in Colonial times was branded on the cheek with a B; 3) blasphemy, also in Colonial times was the reason for a B cut from red cloth to be sewed to the arm of a convicted person's clothing; 4) by banns; 5) Baptist; 6) on maps and charts, Bay or Bayou; 7) book.

b.: born; birth.

ba.: bachelor.

baad: a woman of bad character.

baarge: a fat person.

babbler: a gossip, carrier of tales, idle talker.

baberlupped: thick lipped.

baby: a dressmaker's doll used to display her samples.

baby farmer: a person who nurses babies, other than her own, for a fee.

bace chambyr: a room on the lower floor.

bach, batch: abbreviation for bachelor (an unmarried man), or to keep house without a woman's help.

bacon: a clown.

back country: a sparsely populated, partially explored portion of a larger area.

back forty: an area of forty acres which is located some distance from the farm house. This led to referring to any place within a mile or so as "the back forty."

back friend: a secret enemy.

backhander: a blacksmith's helper.

backing knife: a tool used by a cooper.

backlog: 1) a huge wooden log placed at the back of the fireplace used to reflect and conserve heat. It would last for days and many fires without going out. From this came the use of backlog to mean a reserve of money, objects, etc.

backrag: a German wine.

backstep: a backward step approximately fifteen inches long.

backster: a baker.

backstock: a log of wood.

backstress: a female baker of bread.

backwoods: 1) the area situated back outside a town or settled area; 2) also uncharted forest land west of the established eastern states.

bactile: a candlestick.

badger: an itinerant middleman, between a producer of goods and a consumer, who works for a profit. Also called a cadger, hawker, huckster.

Badland, Badlands: an area in Nebraska and South Dakota where erosion has cut deep ravines. The term does not necessarily mean that the land is not fertile - just that it is difficult land to cross. It can provide excellent range for cattle, providing good winter protection.

baggonet: early name for a bayonet.

bagman: 1) a travelling salesman; 2) one who collects illegal payoffs or bribes.

bail: 1) the handle of a pail or pot, sometimes made adjustable; 2) a surety; 3) to dip water out of boat using any container which is handy.

bailbond: the obligations for which a surety is personally responsible.

bailer: the person whose job it is to attach handles to pails.

bailes: (Norman) bailiwick.

bailiff, bailif, bailie: 1) sheriff's deputy; 2) a mayor, or chief officer of a hundred who was nominated by the British King; 3) keeper of a royal castle; 4) same as a Scottish bailie or German landvogt; 5) one who manages and has custody of the property of another; 6) a rent collector for a Lord; 7) a farm manager; 8) an officer of the court who keeps order and announces the arrival of the judge.

bailiwick: 1) an area over which a bailiff has control; 2) the area with which a person is familiar, e.g. his neighborhood.

baillie: 1) custody; 2) government; 3) a custodian of river fisheries; 4) the person who cares for cows on a farm.

bailours: (Norman) sureties.

baily: 1) a bailiff; 2) a steward; 3) a sheriff's office.

bairman: a pauper.

baise: bastard.

bait: 1) a portable work bench which is carried to work; 2) to lower a bargain; 3) food; 4) pasture; 5) an excess of anything; 6) to feed and water an animal; 7) to stop for food or drink while traveling.

baiting sieve: a basket used as a measure

for horse feed.

baize: 1) first introduced in England about 1561 this was a coarse woolen fabric with a long nap used for outer garments. Sometimes if had a fine and light texture and then it was used for clothing; 2) sometimes the name given to an imitation wool felt.

bajardour: 1) a carter; 2) a bearer of any weight or burden.

baked meat: a meat pie.

bake kettle: a Dutch oven.

bakestre: a female baker.

bakpaner: a kind of basket, probably a pannier carried on the back.

bal: a mine.

balastre: a cross-bow.

baldrick: 1) a belt, girdle or sash; 2) sometimes a sword belt.

bale: a compacted bulk of material bound into a shape suitable for shipping or for storage. Cotton usually weighed about 500 pounds, hay about 100 pounds.

baler: a machine which compresses hay or cotton into packages for shipping or storage.

balhier, balhif: (Norman) a bailiff.

baling wire: twine or rope was used as a means of securing a bale of hay before the invention of a thin, strong wire for this purpose. Many a farmer has used baling wire to repair farm machinery or even chair legs.

balister: a man using a cross-bow.

balks: a hay loft.

ball: a bullet.

balla.: balance.

Ballard rifle: patented in America by C.H. Ballard in 1851 this was a breech-loading, single shot rifle. It was perhaps the most popular of the sporting rifles in the days of black powder.

ballast: the stone, gravel, water, etc. which is used to make the ship ride at her proper level in the water when there is little or no cargo. This helps to eliminated the possibility of the ship rolling over. Ballast may be permanent weights of lead or iron.

ballistrarius: gun maker.

balloon brigade: used during the Civil War this group of men ascended by hot air balloon to observe enemy action. Both the Union and the Confederacy had balloon brigades.

ballot: 1) in Colonial days a ballot was a little ball fed through a trough into a closed section of a box. A white ball meant "yes" and a black ball "no." Hence, the expression to be black-balled. Sometimes black and white beans were used instead of balls; 2) the total number of votes in a state, territorial, etc. election.

ball pein hammer: a tool used by a blacksmith.

balle: a sheep.

ballyoe: a bailiff.

balm: a medicinal ointment which soothes an abrasion on the skin.

balm of Gilead (hypericum): a plant whose bark when boiled with sweetgum bark and lard formed a salve used to heal burns.

balsam: a resinous substance which posses healing properties.

balstaff: a large pole or staff.

Baltimore clipper: a long, sharp schooner which was designed to sail faster than any other in the world was made in Baltimore, Maryland - thus said to be of the "Baltimore stamp." Hundreds of this famous ship were built.

balyschepe: the office of bailiff.

bamboozle: 1) to conceal one's true intentions from another in order to gain an advantage; 2) deceive or decoy an enemy by hoisting flags other than the proper ones.

ban (the): used by the Church of England and in other strict churches in this country. Those who were guilty of acts prohibited by the Church were thus "banned" or excommunicated. True believers could not talk to or deal with those who were banned.

band: 1) a bond; 2) a covenant; 3) an engagement; 4) imprisonment; 5) a twenty yard square space of ground; 6) (German) volume.

banded mail: a kind of armor.

banderol: a banner.

banders: 1) associators; 2) conspirators; 3) men bound to each other by mutual ties.

band mill: this kind of a mill had gears

which would allow it to operate more rapidly than a small home mill.

bandoliers: little wooden cases covered with leather, each of them containing the charge of powder for a musket and fastened to a broad band of leather, which the person who was to use them put around his neck. The band itself was also frequently termed a bandoleer.

bandileers, bandoleers, bandoliers: a pair of cases used to carry ammunition in addition to that in a normal cartridge belt.

B and S: Bargain and Sale.

bandsters: those who, in reaping during harvest, bind the sheaves.

bandylan: a bad woman.

baned: age-stricken.

banes: banns of matrimony.

banerer: the bearer of a banner.

bang beggar: a policeman.

bangboard: an extra plank placed high on the far side of a wagon used to haul corn. As the ears of corn where thrown by those harvesting the corn, the ears would bounce against the plank and drop into the wagon.

bang-up road: see corduroy road.

banjo: a later name for bangil, banjor, banger, etc. It is felt that the name and the musical instrument are both African and most likely came to America as a result of slavery.

bank: 1) a bench; 2) paper money; 3) an obsolete word for joint stock; 4) a dealer in money; 5) money to lend to poor people.

banker: 1) a cloth, carpet or covering of tapestry for a bench, seat, etc.; 2) a person employed in making embankments.

banksman: one who superintended the business of a coal pit.

banner: a body of armed men, varying in number from twenty to eighty.

bannerere: an annual custom of walking the bounds of a parish for the purpose of maintaining the local jurisdiction and privileges.

banneret: an old English title sometimes awarded during a battle but unused since the early 1600s, when the rank of baronet was created.

bannering: an annual custom of walking the bounds of a parish for the purpose of maintaining the local jurisdiction and privileges.

bannert: a knight who was knighted in the field. The ceremony involved cutting off the point of his standard, thus making it a banner.

bannier: (Norman) a public crier.

bannock: a New England dish made of cornmeal mush and milk. It was baked on a board and it formed a kind of corn bread.

banns (of marriage): from "Bannen," Saxon for "to proclaim by the sound of a trumpet." Publication of an intended marriages, usually announced at a church service a few weeks in advance of the marriage date.

bannoors, baneours: (Norman) banner bearers.

bannut: a walnut tree.

banqueter: a banker.

banyan: a cotton fabric.

banyan day: a term used for days on which no meat was served to sailors.

banyer: a standard bearer.

bap., bapt.: baptized.

baptism: 1) an initiation into a church which is performed by a recognized leader of the church. The ceremony is performed by immersion in water or by sprinkling of water on the person. Some churches do not baptize infants and Quakers do not practice baptism; 2) a "ceremony" of hazing passengers or members of a crew who are crossing the equator for their first time.

baptismal records: written facts kept by a church official about the baptism of an individual. These usually contain names of parents, date baptized, witnesses, church official performing the ceremony and sometimes other information.

Baptist: a Protestant religious group who believes that baptism by immersion is to be given only to believers above the age of twelve. See also Hard Shell Baptist.

baptistry: the portion of a church designated as the place for baptism, either by sprinkling or immersion.

baptyste: baptism.

bar: 1) baron; 2) boar; 3) a part of a

device to lock a door. The wood is held across part of a door and its frame to prevent it being opened; 4) the gate of a fort; 5) the railing in a courtroom behind which are the judge and witnesses.

baratus: a beard.

barb: a type of horse related to the Arabian horse family.

Barbados liquor: rum.

barbandier: (Norman) a brewer.

barber: to shave or trim the beard. Sometimes there was practiced a double trade of barber and physician. It has been said that the spiral lines still seen on the barber's pole represent the fillets bound around the arm when a person is bled.

barber's stuff: a fabric, the fiber contents are unknown.

barber-surgeon: this man not only cut hair, but performed surgery and dentistry.

barbican: 1) a kind of watch-tower; 2) a parapet or strong, high wall with a gate to a castle or fortified town.

barble: the Bible.

barborery: a barber's shop.

barcary: a sheep walk or pen.

bare trustee: a person whose duties as a trustee are finished. Now he can convey the property to the beneficiary of the trust.

barfray: a tower.

barge: a boat thirty to seventy feet long, seven to twelve feet wide, propelled by men using poles with iron tips. If the boat went with the current, the speed was four or five miles per hour and about two miles per hour when it went upstream.

barge day: Ascension Day.

bargee, bargeman: the captain of or a workman on a barge.

bargood: yeast.

barire: a crowbar.

bark: 1) a sailing sip with three or more masts; 2) a tub used by a tanner of hides; 3) to kill a squirrel; 4) to skin an animal.

barkary: a tannery.

bark cloth: a woolen fabric with a crinkled finish.

barker: 1) a person who tanned hides with bark; 2) a tanner; 3) a whetstone; 4) a person who gives his sales pitch at carnivals, etc.

barkfat: a tanner's vat.

barkman: a boatman.

barlep: a basket to keep barley in.

barley corn: 1) a grain of barley; 2) a measure - the length of a grain of barley is about one-third of an inch; 3) a basket-weave cloth which has a geometric all-over design; 4) a grain from which a liquor is made.

barley corns: a checked fabric.

Barlow knife: a jack knife with one blade, named for its manufacturer.

barmaster: a chief officer among miners who, along with other duties, weighs the ore which has been mined.

barme cloth: an apron.

barmskin, barmyskyn: a leather apron.

barnacle: a marine shellfish which attaches itself to the bottom of a ship.

barnahed: childhood.

barngun: an eruption on the skin.

barn keeper: the man who had charge of keeping a barn clean, filled with hay, etc.

barn mouse: a bat.

barometer: an instrument which measures atmospheric pressure.

baron: 1) a member of the nobility in England. His wife is called a baroness; 2) in Japan, a member of the lowest group of nobility; 3) a person who has gained great influence in industrial work or the business world; 4) a piece of meat such as sirloin which has not been severed from the backbone; 5) a title given for military or some other great service to the king.

baronage: all of the peerage of Great Britain, including dukes, earls, etc.

baroness: wife of a baron (which see).

baron et feme: husband and wife.

Baronet: a title passed from father to son in the United Kingdom.

barracks: living quarters for military personnel.

barratine: a fabric, the fiber content is unknown.

barratry: 1) a fraud upon the owner of a ship committed by the crew or ship's master; 2) the act of stirring up a quarrel or a lawsuit; 3) buying or selling a church appointment or a state appointment. The person who commits a barratry is called a barrator, sometimes spelled barretor or barretry; 4) to cause a disturbance.

barre: a multicolored striped fabric.

barrel (used as a measure): corn - one barrel equals five bushels (in early Virginia); one barrel of corn on the cob equals 196 pounds; one barrel of flour equals 196 pounds; one barrel of pork equals 200 pounds; one barrel for liquors equals 31 1/2 gallons.

barrel fever: a violent sickness occasioned by intemperance.

barrel head: the top or lid of a barrel upon which an artist could paint elaborate "labels" describing the contents of the barrel.

barrel weights: one whole barrel equals 196 pounds; one-half barrel equals 98 pounds; one-fourth barrel equals 48 pounds; one small sack equals 24 pounds.

barriham: a horse's collar.

barrister: an English lawyer who does court work. Only about ten percent of English lawyers are barristers, the remainder are solicitors. Solicitors deal directly with clients; only barristers plead cases in court.

barronet: a silk fabric, perhaps a kind of Barratine.

barrow: 1) a wheelbarrow with one wheel used to haul small loads; 2) a castrated male pig, also called a boar.

bar sinister: illegitimate birth.

barson: a horse's collar.

Bart.: Baronet.

barter system: a direct exchange between two people of goods, not money. For example, garden produce for a shirt. Used on the frontier when goods and services were far more available than money.

barth: a shelter for cattle.

Barton: the manor house - sometimes the term was used for the manor, its outbuildings and yards.

bar vel: a short leather apron.

bas cur: an out yard.

baseborn: 1) a child of an unmarried woman; 2) sometimes used to mean a child of parents who have low social status.

basel: an English coin abolished in 1158 by Henry II.

baseler: a person who cares for neat cattle.

base line: a line used in the survey of the public domain upon which all the rest of the survey is based.

base-son: a bastard.

base tenant: an old English term for a person who performed a lowly service for his landlord as the lord commanded, as opposed to a free-holder.

bashy: 1) fat; 2) swollen.

basilisk: a kind of cannon.

bason: 1) the process of making felt; 2) a term used by the Church of England—a basin.

basoning furnace: a source of heat used in the manufacture of hats.

bastard: 1) an illegitimate child. Born out of wedlock or of a marriage of which the church did not approve. Many times the child used his mother's surname and frequently was prohibited from inheriting property; 2) a gelding.

bastardy bond: a promise to pay a certain sum of money given by the father of an illegitimate child to ensure that no public monies would have to be spent on the child. Sometimes the mother would post this bond, but this was very infrequent.

basteler: a person who bastes meat.

bastille: a fortified castle tower; 2) a little fortress.

batails: provisions.

batea: a Spanish term for a shallow bowl or pan about eighteen inches in diameter, made of wood and used in panning or washing gold ore.

bateau: a flat-bottomed, wide boat fashioned of planks which could carry a family and their possessions. It was helped downstream by long oars called sweeps. Going upstream it was propelled by polling. The steering was done by a sweep at the back end of the craft.

batiste: a high quality, very fine woven lightweight fabric, usually made of cotton.

batln: battalion.

baton: a weapon, such as a policeman's

billy club.
bat-swain: a sailor.
batt.: battalion.
battalion: in Europe a battalion numbered 800 to 1,000 men, in the United States a battalion consists of from two to twelve companies. The name comes from a body of men arranged for battle.
battard: a small, very early cannon.
battery: 1) an obsolete term for a revolver; 2) two or more pieces of artillery (large guns on wheels) on the field of battle: 2) the last and smallest of a series of approximately five kettles used to make sugar before it is poured as a thick syrup into a cooling kettle; 4) the military organization responsible for a number of ordinance pieces; 5) the act of touching another person, however mildly without his approval.
batiste: a high quality, light weight cotton cloth.
baton: 1) a staff used to indicate an officer or official; 2) a stick used as a weapon.
battle: an army.
battle donation: see donation land.
battlement: a notched or indented parapet originally used only on fortifications, but later used on ecclesiastical and other edifices.
battleship: the largest and heaviest of all the fighting ships in the navy. Sometimes it is called a battle-wagon.
Battle of Tippecanoe: this battle was fought in 1811 in Indiana and Illinois. Many men served in both the Revolutionary War and the Battle of Tippecanoe; therefore, they were entitled to a pension and/or bounty land.
battlewagon: see battleship.
bat-ward: a boat-keeper.
battry: tea kettle.
batty.: battery (military).
baubee: a copper coin.
bauciant, baucent: a spy, a informer.
baudekin: a woven cloth. The woof was a silken thread and the warp was made of gold. Later this term included any brocade or heavy silk cloth.
baudroyeur: a currier.
bayberry: the fruit of this tree contains a wax used to make candles.
baydekin: a silk fabric woven with gold and silk threads. Sometimes it was embroidered and later became known as a brocade.
bawaty: a linsey-woolsey material.
bawd: 1) a prostitute; 2) the woman (madam) who runs a brothel.
bawdy house: a house of prostitution.
bawman: 1) a bowman; 2) an archer.
bawn: an enclosed fort. This term now means a yard where cows are milked.
baxter: a baker.
bay: 1) a chestnut color; 2) the fore part of a ship between decks; 3) a horse with a warm, brown color.
bayle: a bucket.
bayman: 1) a resident of Massachusetts Bay colony; 2) one who lives on or near a bay; 3) a Yankee fishing ship was called a "Bayman."
bayn: a murderer.
bayonet: a dagger, usually of triangular cross-section, which is fastened to the end of a musket or rifle in a manner which does not interfere with the firing of the gun.
bayou: a French word used in the south to describe a marshy, sluggish body of water emptying into a larger stream.
bays: a spelling of baize (which see).
B.B.: Bail Bond.
bbl.: an abbreviation for barrel.
bbls.: an abbreviations for barrels.
B.C.: 1) Before Christ; 2) Bail Court; 3) British Columbia.
bd.: 1) see band; 2) buried; 3) bound.
b.d.: birth date.
bds.: beds or boards. A term found in old city directories after a person's name and before the address where he lived.
bead: the upper, sometimes bead-like, portion of a sight on the front of a rifle, which is to be aligned with the target and the rear, notched sight, thus the expression "draw a bead on."
bead house: 1) a dwelling place for poor religious persons which was located near a church and also where the founder of the church was buried. The inhabitants were required to pray for the soul of the church founder. The name bead came from the process of praying and counting the prayers on "telling beads;" 2) a hospital.

beadle: 1) a herald; 2) a town crier of proclamations; 3) the person who delivered an official order.
bead roll: a list of persons who are to be prayed for in church.
beadsmen: those who pray for the welfare of others.
beadle: a minor official of an English parish.
beakiron: an iron tool used by a blacksmith. Also see bick iron.
beakment: one-fourth of a perch measure.
beam drill: a tool used by a blacksmith.
beaming knife: apparently a tanner's tool.
beam maker: a person who made beams for sailing vessels.
beamster: a person who tans hides using a board which supports the hide during the softening process. This board is called a beam.
bear, bere, bar: barley.
bearded: the prickly portion of wheat, oats, etc. which was believed discouraged birds from picking out the grain.
bearers: those who carry a corpse to his grave.
beargrass: 1) a southwestern grass with coarse blades; 2) a variety of the yucca plant.
bearherd: a keeper of bears.
bearing cloth: the fine cloth or blanket with which a child is carried to church to be baptized.
bearing tree: used in land surveying, a tree blazed and marked in someway to indicate a corner in establishing boundary lines.
bearn: 1) born; 2) child; 3) wood.
bearskin: a fabric used for overcoats. This material was made of wool with a shaggy nap.
bearward: a keeper of bears.
bearyng: a funeral.
beas: cows, cattle.
beating iron: a tool used by a basket maker.
beaupere: a priest or friar.
beaver: 1) that part of a helmet which is movable in order to allow a person to drink. Sometimes it is used to shade his eyes; 2) this word sometimes refers to the helmet itself; 3) an imitation beaver fur made of heavy wool; 4) a cotton, napped cloth used for work clothes; 5) the fur of a beaver used as money in early New Netherlands (New York City).
beaver cloth: 1) beaver fur; 2) a felt like cloth; 3) the lower portion of the face guard on a helmet.
beaver pelts: used as money in early New York. Each skin was worth $3.20 to $4.00.
bebered: buried.
becalmed: to be on a sailing ship when there is no wind blowing, the sails hang loosely around the mast and the ship goes nowhere.
becarius: shepherd, sheepfold.
bechic: a cough medicine.
becker: a wooden dish.
bed: a feather bed. A bedstead is what we today call a bed.
bed and bedstead: this term is found in inventories and refers to a cover made of feathers which is used on what we now call a bed.
bed and board: see divorce a mensa et thoro.
bedbere: a pillowcase.
bedder: 1) one who spreads straw for cattle bedding; 2) an upholsterer.
beddle: a husband or wife.
bed house: a hospital.
bedpan: 1) a bed warmer; 2) a pan similar to what we call a bedpan today.
bed rug: a thick, closely woven wool, shaggy outer cover for a bed which today probably could be called a bedspread.
bed sister: a phrase used to describe the relationship between a man's wife and his mistress.
bedstead: the frame of a bed.
bedstone: see millstones.
bed warmer: a covered metal pan which held hot coals. It was placed between the sheets to warm them.
bedwen: a birch tree.
bed wrench: a tool used to tighten the ropes of a rope bed. The rope was strung back and forth across the bed frame serving the purpose of today's bed springs.
bedyer: an officer.

bee but: a beehive.

Beecher's Bible: the Reverend Henry Ward Beecher was instrumental in raising funds to purchase Sharp's rifles to be sent to anti-slavery emigrants who were settling the west, especially Kansas. This led to the popular reference to Sharp's rifles as "Beecher's Bibles."

beedy: chicken.

beefboat: a slang term for a navy supply ship.

beefeaters: the yeoman of the guard.

beegum: a beehive.

beek: rivulet.

been: property, wealth.

beende: bondage.

beerness: a beer cellar.

beestaile: cattle.

beetle: a tool used by 1) a chair bodger; 2) a basket maker; 3) a gate hurdle maker.

bef.: before.

before the mast: this term distinguished the ship's crew from its officers. The crew slept before the mast; the officers' quarters were in the stern of a ship.

before the wind: a sailing vessel which has the wind aft (behind) is said to be before the wind.

beholden: see debt bound.

behoof: a legal term meaning use, benefit or profit which is used in conveyances, e.g. "to his use and behoof."

being: 1) since; 2) seeing that.

beldame: a grandmother. Formerly a term of respect. The original translation from French was "fair lady."

beldyng: building.

belfry: 1) a room for a bell in a tower, especially one attached to a church; 2) a temporary shed for a cart or wagon in the fields, or by the roadside. It had an upright post at each of the four corners and the top was covered with straw. etc.

Belgian horse: a large work horse.

belgrades: a silk fabric used in Colonial days.

belgrandfather: a great-great-grandfather.

bell: in a sailor's language, bells indicate time. The striking of the clapper against the bell at the half hour points of a watch, e.g. a four-hour watch is marked by eight bells.

belladonna: 1) a medicine to calm the digestive system; 2) another name for the plant known as deadly nightshade.

bellhanger: an installer of doorbells.

bellman: a watchman. A part of his duties was to bless the sleepers in the houses that he passed. See also town crier.

bellringer: the person whose job it was to ring the church or town bell to announce a time to attend church, a death, etc.

bellows: a device which draws in air and forces it out through a tube. It is used to blow air to help wood or coal burn more rapidly.

bellus: another spelling of bellows.

bellwether: 1) a castrated male sheep or goat; 2) a leader who is proficient in his field.

belly cheat: an apron.

belly clapper: a dinner bell.

belongings: accessories.

belsire: 1) a grandfather; 2) an ancestor.

belt: 1) In clearing forest land large trees were belted, or girdled; that is, a ring was cut through the bark all the way around the trunk. This killed them by cutting off the flow of sap to the leaves; 2) belt is also used to name tools carried in the belt, for example - a belt knife, belt pistol, etc.

belter: a prostitute.

bench: a widow's bench, a share of the husband's estate which a woman enjoys besides her jointure.

bench (land): usually a narrow level tract of land situated between, bordering upon or separating mountains, lakes, rivers, etc.

bench knife: a tool used by a clogger.

bench mark: in surveying this is one of several marks along a line which indicates a series of levels at different heights. The mark was usually cut into a material that would withstand weather (a rock, a wall, etc.).

bench warrant: a court issued order for the arrest of a person or to force a witness who has ignored a subpoena into court. The use of "bench" distinguishes this warrant from a warrant issued by a justice of the peace, commissioner, etc.

bending table: a tool used by a chair

maker.

bendoarine: a striped fabric, fiber content unknown.

benefice: 1) a tenant's land held by giving service to a feudal lord; 2) an endowed office which enables a church to pay its vicar, rector, etc.; 3) a kindness, service, etc.

beneficial interest: to obtain a profit or some kind of advantage from an estate or a contract but not to own or control it.

beneficiary: one who is named to receive or is receiving profit, advantage or benefiting from property of an estate or contract.

benefit of clergy: 1) this phrase originally meant that a member of the clergy was exempt from common law court jurisdiction. In this country it was recognized by Virginia and the Carolinas, but it is now obsolete in both England where it originated and in this country. Now it is usually used in a negative sense. (He died without benefit of clergy) to indicate an action taken without the ministrations of a clergyman; 2) a law which obviously came from church sources stated that if a man condemned to the death penalty could read (or memorize) a verse from the Bible he would be spared from death. However, at times the crime would be so terrible (breaking into a tobacco warehouse in a state where tobacco was used as money) the culprit would be "without benefit of clergy."

bene quiescat: may he rest well.

bene vixit: he lived a good life.

bengal: 1) a cotton muslin cloth, usually woven with stripes; 2) a general term used for various fabrics exported from Bengal during the seventeenth century. Later many of these fabrics were manufactured elsewhere.

bengaline: striped fabric made of cotton or a combination of silk and wool.

benjoltram: brown bread soaked in milk which was the usual breakfast for a farm worker.

bent: 1) an area covered with bent grass, e.g. a plain, commons, field, moor; 2) chimney; 3) bent-grass.

benters: debentures.

bequeath: when used in a will denotes personal property rather than real property.

bequest: a gift of personal property as stated in a will. Sometimes used incorrectly as synonymous with devise.

berche: made of iron.

bercil: (Norman) a sheepfold.

bere: 1) pillowcase; 2) beard; 3) produce; 4) berry.

bergier: 1) peasant; 2) woodman.

berherie: (Norman) a barkary or tannery.

beriberi: a disease which had the symptoms of dropsy which made a person's legs get numb. It was found in many parts of India.

berie: a grove or shady place.

beriel: 1) tomb; 2) grave; 3) burial.

berlin: 1) a type of carriage; 2) a wool yarn popular for knitting gloves; 3) a Victorian handwork—cross stitch design and worked on canvas.

berners: men who fed the hounds.

berrier: a thrasher.

besant: a gold coin.

besom maker: a person who produces a broom used for sweeping leaves. Usually the broom was made of birch.

bespoke work: products manufactured to the order of a customer. Usually made from the customer's materials, e.g. leather for shoes. If there was not enough such work, the craftsman would make goods to be sold over the counter, using scraps or purchased materials.

bet.: between.

betel: a hammer.

Bethlehemite, Bethlemite: an obsolete order of English monks.

betimes: an earlier time than usual.

betrothal: that portion of the marriage service in which the couple join hands and pledge their troth to each other.

bett axe: a pick axe.

Bettering House: a historical term for a charitable organization in Philadelphia, Pennsylvania fundamentally for sick and poor people. It not only uses an Alms House, but a workhouse and a place for detaining wayward or unpredictable persons.

betterments: 1) usually used in the plural

form meaning the clearing of ground; 2) improving in some way a piece of real property.

betty: a male house-worker. See also cot #8.

beuse: (Norman) a widow.

bevel: a tool used by 1) a wheelwright; 2) a stone mason; 3) a carpenter.

bewgle: a bull.

bewpere: companion.

bglr: bugler.

bgt.: bought.

BIA: Bureau of Indian Affairs.

bias: a preconceived idea or opinion.

Bible clerkship: a ancient scholarship in an English university, so called because the student who was promoted to that office was requested to read the Bible at mealtimes.

bibliography: 1) a list of books, periodicals or articles consulted in the preparation of a book or article; 2) a list of supplemental reading about a subject.

bibliopegus: bookbinder.

Bible records: recorded birth, marriage and death dates of various family members. These were usually written in special pages in a Bible at the time of the event. These are considered proof that the event happened if they antedate the copyright date of the Bible and are in different handwriting.

B.I.C.: born in the covenant. A Mormon term which means children born to a couple who previously have been sealed. Children born after the sealing ceremony are automatically sealed to the parents.

bick iron, beak iron: sometimes called cooper's stake, a tool used by a cooper.

bid-stand: a highwayman.

biennium: two years.

bier: 1) the device upon which a casket is placed before burial; 2) the framework of a litter or stretcher; 3) a burial place; 4) a variation of beer.

bierne: 1) a man; 2) a noble.

biers, bers: (Norman) barons.

bigger: builder.

bigirdle: 1) purse; 2) girdle.

bil.: brother-in-law.

bil: codfish.

bilander: a merchant ship with two masts used in the Netherlands along a coast or canal.

bilbo: this piece of iron was used as a hobble on a prisoner in Colonial days.

bile: a digestive secretion from the liver which is stored in the gall bladder.

bilge: the bottom portion of a ship's hull where waste water and seepage collects. This water is called bilge water and if a navy man is discharged he is said to be "bilged." Bilged also refers to a ship having been damaged severely below the water line.

bilious: an undue amount of bile.

bilious fever: an undue amount of bile in the system accompanied by a fever.

bill: 1) a written statement or charge presented in court; 2) a weapon which has a hooked, sharp blade with a beak at the back. Also called a billhook (which see).

billa vera: a true bill (which see).

billet: 1) a brief document; 2) a label; 3) a short note on paper; 4) a pass to go into a public place such as an exhibition hall; 5) a military order to provide room and board for a soldier who possesses this order; 6) wood cut to a prescribed length to fit into a stove or fireplace; 7) to be put on a list; 8) to assign quarters to military personnel; 9) to give lodging; 10) a metal bar such as steel, silver, gold, etc.; 11) a figurehead on a ship; 12) a kind of fish.

billet head: a curved wooden carving used on the prow of a ship instead of a figurehead.

billets: quarters for troops in civilian or non-military buildings.

bill hook: a sharp, heavy, steel tool which had a wooden handle. It was designed for cutting hedge and brush, but also served as an effective weapon. It was used by 1) a basket maker; 2) a gate hurdle maker; 3) a broom maker; 4) and a laborer.

billman: a man who cut faggots.

bill of equity: a formal, written complaint.

bill of exceptions: a listing of decisions, rulings or instructions.

bill of information: a form of a petition used by a government.

bill of exchange: an order to pay a sum of money by a third party. Also called a draft or, if a bank is to pay on demand, a check.

bill of lading: a receipt for goods from the agent or owner of a carrier. It agrees to provide safe carriage and delivery of the same to the consignee at the destination. Three bills are usually signed: one each for the shipper, the agent and one to be forward to the consignee.

Bill of Rights: the first ten amendments to the Constitution of the United States.

bill of sale: a written statement giving the transfer of title for personal property from the seller to the buyer. It is proof of a sale of personal property such as slaves, furniture, etc. Many times a bill of sale is found in the deed books of a county.

bind-corn: buckwheat.

bind days: the time during harvest when tenants were obliged to reap the Lord of the Manor's corn.

binder: 1) a person who binds books; 2) a document which holds two parties to an agreement; 3) a piece of farm machinery that cuts and ties grain into bundles using binder twine.

Binding day: the second Tuesday after Easter, called also Binding Tuesday.

binnacle list: a sick man list in the navy.

bio.: biography.

biog.: biography, biographical.

bird: 1) a lady; 2) buried; 3) bread.

bird boy: the young lad whose job was to scare birds from cornfields.

birder: bird catcher.

bird's eye: a Colonial fabric marked with varied colors which produced a pattern resembling a bird's eye.

birede: buried.

biretta: a cap of prescribed shape worn by a Roman Catholic clergyman. The color of the tassel on the top of the biretta indicates the wearer's rank in the church priesthood.

birgen: a grave.

birlieman, birlyman, byrlawman: an English or Scottish officer appointed by a court to write byrlaws or attend to small matters.

birny: a coat of mail.

birthdom: birthright.

birye: city or town.

bis: 1) twice; 2) in two ways.

biselet: a carpenter's tool.

bish: a bishop.

Bishop: 1) a church official; 2) a minister who as a church official supervises a church district; 3) a hot drink made of port wine flavored with orange and cloves.

Bishopric: 1) a diocese headed by a bishop; 2) in other churches, the office of the head administrator of a district; 3) a bishop's office.

bissextile: the 29th of February, which occurs every fourth year—leap year.

bi-tartrate of potash: cream of tarter.

bitch: a vagrant's female companion.

bit house: a tavern or saloon where drinks, etc. were sold for a bit (twelve and one-half cents) apiece.

bits: a Spanish dollar was sometimes called "a piece of eight" for its value was eight reals (a standard coin before 1793, when a government mint was established). Change was made by slicing the coin into eight pieces with a chisel. Thus in slang: 2 bits equals 25 cents, 4 bits equals 50 cents, 6 bits equals 75 cents. In the mid-1800s a dime came to be called a "short bit" and fifteen cents was called a "long bit."

bitters: a liquor made of a bitter plant used as a stimulant for a person's appetite or to digest their food better.

bivouac: 1) from the German bei "near" and wache "watch." Troops bivouac when circumstances demand that they camp outdoors for the night; 2) the term also apples to a night-guard for the entire army.

bks.: 1) barracks; 2) books.

blacebergan: blackberry.

black acre: a term used to differentiate one piece of land from another. Different colors were used with the word acre, e.g. tan acre=ripe wheat, green acre=immature wheat. Later black acre came to mean litigation about land. See also white acre.

Black Angus: a breed of beef cattle bred in Scotland. They are hornless, black and have short legs.

black-coat: a clergyman.

Black Cross Day: St. Mark's Day, April

25th.

black death: a plague which caused hemorrhages under the skin which gave the skin a dark, patchy appearance.

black gang: navy slang for the men who work in the engine room of a ship. It originated when ships used coal for fuel.

Black Hawk War: this war, in the year 1832, was fought in Indiana and Illinois by Sauk and Fox Indians, led by Black Hawk. Militia and regular troops fought in this war and veterans' records may be found in the National Archives.

black-jack: 1) a person who looks like a pirate of old; 2) the flag of a pirate ship; 3) a scrubby tree which belongs to the oak family.

black lead: graphite.

blackman: fictitious men who were enumerated during a period when an army was being raised or when making demands where a majority would win.

Black Man: Satan.

Black Maria: a wagon used to transport prisoners to jail.

black measles: a severe form of measles in which the breaking out is dark in color.

Black Monday: Easter Monday.

black plague: cholera.

blackpot: an obsolete word for a beer mug.

black powder: an explosive mixture of charcoal, saltpeter (potassium nitrate) and sulphur, used in guns before the invention of smokeless powder, and in blasting, prior to the invention of dynamite.

black pudding: a dark dessert made of eggs, molasses, baking soda and flour which was popular at the end of the sixteenth century.

black rent: rent to be paid, not in money, but in grain, produce, etc.

blacks: mourning.

black salter: a person who made black salt, a potash.

blacksmith: a man who made and fastened metal shoes on horses to protect their hooves from sharp stones, etc. He also made and repaired farm and home equipment such as plow shares, cooking pots, etc., especially if the objects were made of metal.

blackstrap molasses: a cheap molasses made as a by-product in Southern sugar houses.

Black Sunday: Passion Sunday.

black tin: tin ore ready for smelting.

black-water fever: malaria which has the added condition of dark-blue or black urine.

blameplum: white lead.

blanch duty: an annual rent paid to the Lord of the Manor.

blanket box: a chest similar to a cedar chest.

blede: blood.

bleeding: an old method of trying to cure almost any disease. George Washington died from an excess of letting of blood or bleeding when all he had was a throat infection and was otherwise a healthy man.

blemmere: a plumber.

blenks: ashes.

blessed: a Mormon baby is blessed in a ceremony similar to a christening. It is usually conducted at about the age of one month.

bleystare: a bleacher of cloth, etc.

blinky milk: partially sour milk.

blizzard: 1) a fine blowing snow combined with intense cold. For example, the winter of 1830-31 in the midwest was the "year of the deep snow." It snowed almost constantly for three days, accumulating to a depth of four feet with twenty to thirty foot drifts; 2) an obsolete term for one shot or several shots at a living target; 3) a rapid outbreak of events, e.g. robberies, sales, etc.

BLM: Bureau of Land Management.

B.L.N.: Bounty Land Number.

bloach: a tumor.

blockade: a temporary man-made or natural barrier to stop traffic on a railroad, river, or ocean. The one who tries to get through or elude the man-made barrier is referred to as a blockade runner.

blocker: a broad-axe.

blockhouse: 1) a group of deep iron kettles standing in two parallel rows used in boiling salt water to make salt;

2) also the stand used at slave auctions; 3) an isolated building which may be used for shelter and for protection against enemy fire. It is defended by firing guns through small holes in the walls.

bloman: a trumpeter.

blood letting: see bleeding.

blood relative: people related by having a common ancestor.

blood stone: a green stone (jasper or quartz) which is spotted or streaked with red and was presumed to have the power to stop bleeding.

bloody flux: bloody diarrhea.

Bloody Thursday: the Thursday of the first week of Lent.

bloom: a mass of iron which has gone through a furnace for the second time.

bloomer: a costume consisting of a short skirt with full pants gathered tightly at the ankles. Worn by females about 1851. A later version was gathered just below the knees and was worn with stockings. It was named after Mrs. Amelia Bloomer who championed the costume.

bloomery: a forge which produced wrought iron (the name came from the finished product which was a rectangular slab of wrought iron called a bloom).

bloughty: swelled, puffed.

blown: swelled, inflated.

bluecoat, bluebird: 1) a soldier who was fighting on the side of the Union during the Civil War. Derived from the color of his uniform; 2) a policeman; 3) any blue coat or uniform.

blue disease: see cyanosis.

bluegrass: one of a variety of grasses, found growing naturally in limestone areas of Kentucky, principally around Lexington. It is highly valued as pasture or for making hay.

blue jacket: a seaman in the United States Navy.

bluejohn: a thin, very light blue milk with little or no cream, or milk with water added to it.

blue laws: very strict Colonial laws which prohibit certain activities (especially laws regulating conduct on the Sabbath) and which set forth the punishment for disobedience.

bluelights: this name was used in speaking of New England Federalists who were against the War of 1812. It was derived from the blue lights put out to signal the British of the United States' movements.

bluestocking: a woman who pretends to be intellectual or have literary tastes. A female writer was so called for 18th century literary clubs. Some of their members dressed informally, including blue, worsted stockings.

bluffer: a landlord of an inn.

blunderbuss: a short muzzle-loading musket which made a lout noise and did great damage at short range.

blust: erysipelas inflammation.

BLW: Bounty Land Warrant.

B.L.Wt.: Bounty Land Warrant.

B.M.: 1) Bench Mark; 2) British Museum; 3) Brigade Major.

B'man: Bondsman.

Bn.: Battalion.

bnd.: bound.

bndsmn.: bondsman.

B.O.: an abbreviation found in Colonial records which is presumed to mean British or Burr Oak.

boar: 1) a male hog; 2) a clown.

board cloth: a tablecloth.

boarder: 1) a person who lived with a family and paid rent for his own room. He also ate one or two meals each day with the family or with other boarders; 2) made of board; 3) an animal which is not worth its keep.

boaster: a tool used by a stone mason.

boat: 1) a small vessel carried or stored on a ship. In the Navy a ship is never called a boat. 2) any small vessel used on water.

boatswain: this word is pronounced "bo'sun," and denotes a warrant officer who is concerned with the operation of the ship, rather than its repair.

bobbin: 1) a part of a spinning wheel on which the finished thread is collected; 2) a small fagot.

bobsled: 1) a board with two pairs of runners used for coasting on snow down a hill; 2) a wagon-like sled mounted on two pairs of bobs (runners) and used for hauling heavy objects such as cord wood.

boche: 1) a swelling; 2) a boil.
bocher: (Norman) a butcher.
bochouse: a library.
bodark: variation of bodock - Osage orange tree.
boddle: a small iron instrument which woodmen used for peeling oaks and other trees.
bodicemaker: one who made a quilted garment with stays of whale-bone, similar to a corset worn by women.
bodily heirs: natural-born children, grandchildren, etc. The term was used interchangeably in wills with "heirs lawfully begotten" and "heirs of his (or her) body." It was required that this term be used when property was transferred from one to another. In early America property was given only to a person for his lifetime, but if it were given to him and his "bodily heirs" then he could transfer that property to others.
bodkin: 1) a tool used by a basket maker; 2) a dagger; 3) a type of rich cloth; 4) a long, ornamental hairpin.
bodock: an Osage orange tree.
body horse: the second horse of a team of four.
bodymaker: see bodicemaker.
boffying: swelling, puffing.
boggie meadow: a meadow that is quite wet, marshy or swampy.
boggysche: swelling.
bogus: unsweetened beer or rum.
Bohemia: a province in western Czechoslovakia. Gypsies were believed to have made their home there.
boie: an executioner.
boine: swelling.
bokeler: maker of buckles.
bold hives: see hives.
boldyche: a bowl.
bole: 1) a bull; 2) a bowl; 3) a measure equalling two bushels.
bole holes: the openings in a barn for light and air.
boles: places on hills where the miners smelted or ran their ore, before the invention of mills and furnaces.
boll: 1) a man who managed power looms; 2) a measure used for dry items which varied according to the material being measured. A boll of grain was equal to six bushels.
bollen: to swell.
boller: a drunkard.
bolster: a fat, solid, rolled pillow used for support.
bolt: 1) to desert or refuse to support a political platform, or candidate, sometimes by simply not voting; 2) to split a tree into pieces suitable to begin stave making for barrels.
bolting cloth: silk fabric with a fine weave.
bolting cloth weaver: the person who wove a fine cloth which was used to sift flour during the milling process.
bolus: 1) a large pill; 2) a mass of food which is ready to swallow.
boman: a kidnapper.
Bomb.: Bombardment.
bombaise, bombasine, bombazeen: variation of bombazine.
bombazine: a fabric with a twill weave, made of silk and wool which was usually dyed black and used for ladies' mourning garments.
bombicino: a poor quality of satin.
bombs: 1) hand grenades; 2) artillery shells which are filled with powder. The time from firing until explosion was adjusted by cutting the length of the fuse.
bombardier: 1) a gunner; 2) an artilleryman; 3) a person who uses any weapon which throws out an explosive device.
bon: good.
bona: property.
bona fide: an act done or made in good faith without any intent to defraud or deceive anyone.
bona notabilia: enough possessions to require an estate to be probated.
bond: an instrument, under seal, by which a person binds himself, his heirs, executors or administrators to pay a certain sum of money to another if certain acts are done or not done in a required manner. The date of a bond can give an approximate date of death, which is helpful if it is unknown.
bondager: a cottager or servant in husbandry who had a house for a year under rent. He was entitled to the produce of a certain quantity of seed

potatoes. For these advantages he was bond to work or to find a substitute when called upon to do so. The substitute worked at a fixed rate of wages which was lower than common.

bondeman: husbandman.

bondmaid: 1) a female who has been bound into service with no wages paid; 2) a female slave.

bondman: 1) a male slave; 2) a man who had been bound into service without wages being paid; 3) a tenant who was not free, a villein.

"bond" servant: an indentured servant.

bondsman: a person, sometimes referred to as a surety, who pledges a sum of money as bond for another.

bondwoman: a female slave.

bone: 1) petition, request; 2) command; 3) seize, arrest.

bone ache: ague.

bone-cleaner: a servant.

bone hostel: lodging.

boneset: a willow-like plant, usually found in swamps. The leaves were used frequently in pioneer days as a medicine or as tea. Its name came from the Indian custom of making a poultice from it which was used on the skin above the broken bone after it was set.

bonesetter: 1) a doctor; 2) a rough trotting horse.

bone-shave: the sciatic nerve.

bonhomme: a priest.

boniface: an inn keeper or restaurant owner.

bonnet: 1) a hat with a broad front brim to shield a woman's face from the sun. It was tied with ribbons underneath her chin; 2) the feathered head band worn by some American Indians.

bonny clabber: or bonny clapper. Milk which is thick and curdled and clings to the lid or dasher of a churn.

bontine, bonting: a thin cloth suitable for flags or banners.

bonus: good.

bony: swelling from bruises or pressure.

booby hut, booby hutch: a covered carriage mounted on runners which was pulled by one or two horses.

book accounts: lists of money owed by others to a man who kept the records informally in personal account books, rather than with notes or bonds. Sometimes monies given a child appear in a ledger of this type—a parent was keeping track of what a child had already been given against the child's inheritance.

bookholder: a prompter for actors on the stage.

bookman: 1) clerk; 2) secretary.

boom: any long spar or pole used to extend the bottom portion of a sail, moor a boat, or handle cargo, etc.

boot: the luggage storage portion of a stagecoach.

boot camp: the base where new recruits are trained for the Navy, Marines or Coast Guard.

boot strap: a strap attached to a boot, usually in the back, which was used to help pull on a boot. Hence the phrase, "pulled himself up by his bootstraps," which means that a person made his way in the world to a higher level.

boot stretching plier: a tool used by a boot maker.

b.o.p.t.: both of this parish.

bordarius: tenant.

bordeller: the keeper of a brothel.

bordello: a brothel (which see).

border: the edge of something, e.g. a country, town, pond, farm, skirt, etc.

borderer: a person who lived near the border of an established colony or state.

border state: one of the states situated adjacent to the line between those states which joined the South and those who did not during the Civil War. The northern side states were called border free states and those on the southern side were referred to as border slave states.

borer: a salesman or drummer.

bore-staff: a tool used in weaving to tighten warp threads.

borough: a term used most frequently in the northeastern portion of the United States to indicate a form of self-government similar to that of incorporated towns or villages in other states.

borrier: an auger.

borse: a six month old calf.

borsholder: 1) a constable of high rank; 2)

a tithing man; 3) the chief person who collected tithes from ten persons.

borstax: a pick-axe.

borwage: a surety.

boschloper: a trapper or hunter.

bosel: (Norman) a bushel.

bossloper: a trapper or hunter.

botch: 1) an inflamed tumor; 2) spoiled because poor work or a mistake has been made; 3) to mend in a poor manner; 4) disorderly; 5) mismanage.

boteler: a butler.

botescarl: a petty officer on a merchant ship.

bote et espernonne: (Norman) booted and spurred.

bothan: a tumor.

bothe: 1) a storehouse; 2) a shop where goods were sold.

bottle: 1) a building; 2) a bundle, usually made of hay or straw.

bottoming tool: a narrow, concave shovel used by drainers.

bottomry: a contract in which a ship is security for payment of a loan at the end of a successful voyage.

bouchier: (Norman) a butcher.

boufquelier: (Norman) a woodman.

bought bread: baker's bread.

boughten: a manufactured item sold in a retail store as opposed to a similar item made at home.

boulting mill: this mill either separately or as a part of a grist mill sifted (bolted) grain, for example: flour had the bran (broken skins) of the grain separated, thus refining the flour even further for cooking purposes. The bolting process could be done at home, and was often a cottage industry.

bouman: a person who lives and works on a cattle farm.

boumet: embalmed.

bound: 1) used in speaking of a young person who was indentured or "bound-out" as a servant; 2) obligated.

boundary rider: a person who checked fences for breaks, etc. as he rode around the perimeter of a frontier station.

bound boy: a young man serving an apprenticeship.

bounde: husband.

bounden: see debt-bound.

bounder: a boundary.

bounds: used in land measurement, this term refers to natural objects (such as "two trees") and artificial objects (e.g. a mound of rocks or names of persons whose land adjoins that which is being surveyed).

boune: (Norman) a boundary.

bounty: 1) the premium for a specified amount of land given to men who enlisted in the armed forces for specific period of time during the early wars in this country. The practice no longer existed at the time of the Civil War; 2) money paid men to serve in the army and some militia; 3) governments, such as the British, paid bounties to colonists to produce tar, resin, turpentine, etc.

bounty equalization: a bounty paid to those who remained in the armed forces. It was equal to the bounty paid to a new recruit.

bounty hunter: a person who would hunt escaped criminals for money given by a governing body as a reward for the capture of an escapee.

bounty land (Federal): shortly after the beginning of the Revolutionary War the Continental Congress promised land to those who would serve in the Continental Army. The acreage of land so promised was on a sliding scale based on rank. For example, an enlisted man was to receive 100 acres, while a major general was to have 1,000 acres.

bounty land (State): in some states the promise of issuing land for service in the Revolutionary War was far more liberal than that of the federal government which led many veterans to trade bounty land warrants for state warrants.

bounty land warrant (Federal): a title to a specified amount of land which was issued by the United States War Department upon presentation of evidence that the applicant had served in the Continental Line during the American Revolution. The exact site of the land was not specified, and any licensed surveyor was authorized to survey the land for a warrant holder. It was issued for the full amount of land allotted to the original grantee. This term and donation certificate were used interchangeably when referring to land granted for military service.

bourdour: 1) pensioner; 2) circlet around a helmet.

bourette: cloth made of a thick and a thin yarn of cotton, linen, or silk.

bourmaidne: a chambermaid.

bourn: 1) a limit or boundary; 2) a brook or rivulet; 3) yeast.

bout: in plowing land this is the distance from one side of a field to the other, and back again.

bout-hammer: the heavy two-handled hammer used by blacksmiths.

bouticari: (Norman) an apothecary.

bovate: an old unit of land measure used in England. It was one-eighth of a carucate.

bow: 1) a shaped and bent piece of wood forming, with several similar bows, an arch to support the canvas roof of a covered wagon; 2) a tool used by a brick maker; 3) the front portion of a ship.

bowcer: the bursar.

bowchyer: a butcher.

bower maiden: 1) a lady-in-waiting; 2) a chambermaid.

bowery: 1) an early Dutch settlement farm in New York state; 2) a section or street of New York City frequented by rough or rowdy men around 1835-45, and marked for its sordid and cheap beer halls and theaters.

bowestrenger: a person who strings bows.

bowety: a linsey-woolsey material.

bowie knife: a large knife having a strong, single-edged blade nine to fifteen inches in length and tapered to a very sharp point which was made by blacksmiths from old files, rasps, etc. Though it was designed to be carried in a sheath, it had no particular pattern or design. The first such knife supposedly made by one of the Bowie brothers by whose name it became known.

bowing: a farm where cattle were raised.

bowl alley: a covered space where the game of bowls could be played instead of using the bowling green.

bow pliers: a tool used by a blacksmith.

bowre: a chamber.

bow saw: a tool used by 1) a trug basket maker; 2) a wheel maker; 3) a chair maker; 4) a carpenter.

bowsy: bloated by drinking too much liquid.

bowl turner: a maker of wooden farm and home utensils.

bowyer: a person who made bows and arrows: 2) a small ship.

box: a hollow or "box" cut into the side of a tree trunk with an axe to obtain sugar sap from a maple or turpentine from a pine. A less destructive method is the more modern one of tapping into the tree and collecting the sap in a cup or pail.

boxing day: the day after Christmas, when tradespeople are visited by persons in the employment of their customers to give Christmas boxes, or small presents of money.

boxing engine: a tool used by a wheelwright.

box supper: an old-time party where the girls would fix food for two people from their best recipes. They would then put the food in a box which they would decorate quite elaborately. Then as a money-raising project the boxes would be auctioned to the highest bidder among the gentlemen, who would gain not only the excellent food, but the company of the lady who had prepared the box. Another name for the party would be "box social" and many times the dinner would include music and dancing.

bp.: baptized; birthplace.

bpl: birthplace.

B.P.O.E.: Benevolent and Protective Order of Elks.

bpt.: baptized.

Br.: 1) British; 2) Branch.

br., bro.: brother.

brab: a spike nail.

brace and bit: a tool used by 1) a rake maker; 2) a barrel maker; 3) a wheel maker; 4) a chair maker; 5) a carpenter.

braconer: (Norman) a hunter.

braconier: a man who held the hounds.

brads: 1) small nails; 2) money.

bragot: 1) a kind of beverage which was drunk in Wales; 2) a meadow.

braidery: embroidery.

brain fever: meningitis, encephalitis.

brake: 1) a small plot or group of bushes growing by themselves; 2) an enclosure for cattle; 3) an old instrument of torture; 4) a large barrow; 5) a tool used in dressing hemp or flax; 6) a baker's trough for kneading dough; 7) a bodiless cart used for breaking in horses to harness; 8) a flaw or break; 9) a mortar; 10) a wooden frame to hold horses' hooves while they were shod; 11) to vomit; 12) a bridle.

brakes: a tool used by 1) a basket maker; 2) a rake maker.

braler: a bundle of straw.

bramage: a kind of cloth - carpets were made of this material.

bramble jelly: blackberry jelly.

brand: 1) a mark placed upon a cow or horse by a hot branding iron to denote ownership. This mark was registered with a public official in a nearby town; 2) a piece of wood that is not sufficiently charred to be charcoal.

branding marks: the law required that cattle be marked at twelve months of age and swine at six months. When any animal was killed in the woods, the hunter was obliged to show, within two days, a magistrate or two freeholders the head and ears of each hog and the hide and ears of each cow.

brandreth: a fence set around a well to prevent anyone from falling in.

brandy wine: brandy.

brash: wood which is so brittle as to be difficult to bend enough to use in the weaving of baskets.

brasiator: brewer.

brasier: a spelling of brazier (which see).

brass: 1) copper coins; 2) a general term for money.

brassfounder: the person who cast articles from brass.

braudesters, brouderers: (Norman) embroiderers.

brawls: blue and white cotton cloth made in India.

brawtherer: an embroiderer.

brayard: (Norman) a crier.

brazier (brasier): one who used brass to make various articles, such as a pan which holds live coals for cooking.

bread baskets: 1) baskets in which bread was carried; 2) baskets in which bread dough is placed for the rising process.

bread colonies: the section of land between New England and Virginia which was particularly suitable for growing wheat.

bread riots: during the panic of 1837, when the price of flour rose to $12.00 per barrel, the poor in New York City helped themselves to flour stored in warehouses until the state militia suppressed the raiders.

breakbone fever: see dengue.

breaker: 1) a type of plow used in plowing or breaking land and which is referred to as a clipper plow or prairie breaker: 2) a person who plows the land; 3) a person whose job is breaking hemp.

breast bib: a tool used by a chair maker.

breck: a piece of unenclosed arable land.

bredaws: a silk fabric used during the eighteenth century.

bredchese: cream cheese.

bredere, bredurne: brethren.

breeches: trousers.

breeches maker: one who made men's trousers.

breech-loader: a gun which is loaded at the end opposite the muzzle (which see).

breech-loading carbine: a short breech-loader, especially a Sharps 50-70 caliber gun used by the Union cavalry during the Civil War.

breechman: sailors.

brennage: a payment made by a tenant, sometimes in bran, to the lord for use as feed for hunting dogs.

bressine: (Norman) a mill to grind malt.

Brethren: 1) a religious denomination of German-American origin, also called Dunkers or Dunkards and German Baptists; 2) a general term used as part of a denominational name, or in speaking of the full group of church members "The Brethren."

Brevet: a higher honorary rank given to an officer for meritorious service instead of a medal which was non-existent for many years. This commission did not include a pay raise nor the right of command, except by special assignment.

An officer so honored could serve at a higher rank with Brevet as a prefix. Therefore, when promotion time came, he would have a slight advantage over a fellow officer of equal rank who did not hold a higher Brevet rank.

brevet: 1) a little brief or letter; 2) to search diligently into anything.

brewer: a maker of beer or ale.

brewis: an early American food made by stewing bread crusts in milk until it became a mush. It was used as a gravy or as porridge.

brewster: 1) a female brewer; 2) a term used to describe a hat with a nap which was glossy in appearance; 3) a chair named for William Brewster, a leader of the Pilgrim church, who is said to have possessed one of these many-spindled chairs; 4) a group of Mormons who split off from the church in Illinois and settled in Socorro, New Mexico. They followed James C. Brewster a dissident Mormon and this group became known as "Brewsterites."

bribour: 1) a robber; 2) a beggar.

brick-dust: bricks were pounded to a fine powder which was the equivalent of today's scrub powder.

brick keel: a brick kiln.

brick mason: see mason.

brick mould: a tool used by a brick mason.

bridges: a kind of thread.

bridris: breeders.

brief: 1) money or goods collected by a minister or other approved citizen for a person or family in need of aid; 2) an abstract of title; 3) a summary of legal arguments; 4) an official letter; 5) a letter which requests money, help, etc.; 6) a letter authorizing a church to take a collection for a specific cause.

briefs of title: abstracts printed in Philadelphia in pamphlet form for builders.

brieve: a document which authorizes a trial by jury.

Brig.: Brigade.

brig.: brigantine.

brig: a navy jail for short-term offenders.

brigade: troops of cavalry, infantry, artillery, or a mixture, which included two or more regiments under one command. A Brigadier General usually commanded the brigade.

brigant: a robber or plunderer.

brigantine: a two-masted, square rigged sea-going sailing vessel.

Brig. Gen.: Brigadier General.

Brigadier: a Brigade commander.

Brigadier General: see Army rank and brigade.

Brighamite: The Church of Jesus Christ of Latter-day Saints (Mormon) was divided into two principal groups after Joseph Smith's murder in Illinois. One followed the convictions of Brigham Young and went to Utah. The other was loyal to the son of Joseph Smith and returned to Missouri. Members of one group refer to members of the other as Brighamites or Josephites, respectively.

Bright's disease: nephritis, qv.

brightsmith: see whitesmith.

brilliantine: a tightly woven cloth made from angora and cotton.

Brill's disease: typhus, qv.

brimstone: sulfur.

brindle: this term is usually used when referring to an animal with dark spots on a gray or tan background.

britain crown: a gold coin.

bro.: brother.

broad axe: a tool used by 1) a rake maker; 2) a cooper; 3) a carpenter.

broadcloth: 1) a plain weave lustrous wool cloth; 2) any fabric woven on a wide loom; 3) square sails.

brocour: a seller or broker.

broadhorn boat: a flatboat which had two huge oars, one on each side which made the boat look somewhat like the Western long-horn cows. A third oar for steering purposes was at the rear of the boat.

broadside: 1) a type of newspaper which was placed in a prominent place for all to read. Sometimes a series of these papers would continue personal quarrels, sad happenings of the day, etc. Broadsides often emphasized crime and were frequently decorated with coffins or other equally cheerful decorations; 2) the side of a vessel which is above water; 3) the simultaneous firing of all guns on one side of a warship; 4) an extra edition of a newspaper which reported one terrible event.

broadweaver: one who made a fine, plain woven cloth that was used to make clothing for men.

broggours, broggage: (Norman) brokers, brokage.

broiderer: one who does embroidery.

bro-il, bro-i-l: brother-in-law.

broken beer: remnants of beer.

broken money: any single or odd money.

bronchia: a branch of the windpipe.

bronchocele: enlargement of the thyroid gland, an enlarged neck or cystic goiter.

brond iron: sword.

bronstrop: prostitute.

Bronze John: another name for yellow fever.

broo: brother.

brook: 1) boil or abscess; 2) to keep food on the stomach or digest.

broomfield: 1) to inherit one person's property; 2) to get possession of the whole of anything.

broom horse: a tool used by a broom maker.

broom squire: see besom maker.

brothel: 1) a house where prostitutes live and practice their profession either as an individual business or on a commission basis for the proprietor. The house usually has an older woman (the madam) who runs the establishment and makes appointments for her "girls;" 2) a worthless person.

brother: 1) brother-in-law; 2) son of one's mother or father; 3) male member of one's ethic group, lodge, or other close-knit group; 4) a half brother; 5) a stepbrother.

brother and sister: 1) kinsmen or members of a common family, e.g. a church; 2) having both parents in common.

brotherhed: brotherly affection.

brother-in-law: 1) a half-brother; 2) brother of a person's spouse; 3) in old documents this term sometimes was used to mean a step-brother.

brother-law: a brother-in-law.

brow denster: an embroiderer.

brown holland: see holland.

brownstone: 1) a sandstone, reddish brown in color, used for building; 2) a building made of brownstone; 3) when only the front wall of a house was made of this stone, it was called a brownstone front house; 4) a term also used to denote well-to-do people, used usually on the east coast.

brown swiss: a type of dairy cattle.

browse: 1) cattle feed which consists primarily of twigs and shoots.

Brumaire: the name of the second month of a calendar used during the French Revolution. It ran from 22 October to 20 November.

brumble gelder: a farmer.

brunswick: a name of an obsolete fabric.

brussels carpet: a looped wool carpet made in Brussels.

bruzz: a tool used by a wheelwright.

B/S, B.S.: bill of sale - abbreviation found sometimes in a court index.

Bt.: Baronet.

B.T.: Bishop's Transcripts.

Btry., Bty.: Battery (army unit).

bu.: buried, burial.

buccaneer: piratical rovers of different European nations who frequented the coasts of Central and South America.

buck: a deerskin used as a gauge of value by Indians when selling or purchasing goods or services.

buckaroo: a cowboy.

buckboard: a wagon which had a single seat on the front of a resilient platform which connected the two axles. In the beginning the seat was only a plank, but the later models had a back to the seat.

bucke: a book.

bucket shop: a brokerage house which had the reputation of operating in an unethical or very aggressive manner. Originally it referred to a cheap place to obtain liquor, when drinks were mixed or sold in buckets.

buck rake: a device rather like a comb used for scooping up hay.

buckram, buckrum: an early fabric of fine linen or cotton. Later it was made stiff with gum or paste. This appeared in a 1475 estate inventory.

bucksaw: a wood cutting, sharp, notched metal bar usually set in an H-shaped frame with one end of the frame extended to form a handle.

buckshot: a lead shot smaller than a bullet, but large enough to kill deer, etc. It had a diameter of .24 to .36 inches.

buckskin: a backwoodsman, especially a Virginian, probably because the suits they wore were made of deerskin.

buckwasher: a laundress.

buckwheat: a grain which has triangular shaped seeds used as feed for animals. Milled into a flour, it is consumed by humans in pancakes, cereal, etc.

buffalo chips: see bull chips.

buffalo lick: see lick.

buffalo soldier: a black soldier so-called by Indians who thought kinky hair resembled a buffalo's coat.

buffalo trace: a "road" made by buffaloes (wide enough in places for two wagons to go abreast) heading straight for a lick (salt). Explorers travelled these roads in the expansion to the west.

buffer: a tool used by a farrier.

buffin: a coarse wool fabric used for the dresses of middle classed ladies during the reign of Elizabeth I.

buggy: a two or more usually a four wheel passenger vehicle with a collapsible top which was pulled by one horse. It was quite popular because it was inexpensive and lightweight.

bugler: a soldier whose duty is to sound calls (general commands) upon a bugle. The bugle is similar to a cornet, but it has no keys.

bule: 1) a boil or swelling; 2) the handle of a pan.

bulkhead: any vertical partition which divides the inside of a vessel into compartments.

bull chips: a fuel which was the dried manure of oxen or buffalo. It was used by frontiersmen to make a very hot, but short lived, fire for cooking.

bullock: a young or castrated bull.

bullpen: 1) a fence made of heavy logs to enclose bulls or cows; 2) a jail or enclosure which served as a temporary prison.

bull-rake: a tool used by a farmer to pile hay.

bullseg: a gelded bull.

bull's noon: midnight.

bull stag: a castrated bull.

bull-wacker: a driver of horses who used a long whip called a bull-wacker.

bumbershoot: an umbrella.

bumboats: small boats which were used to take provisions from shore to anchored ships where the goods were sold. These boats were in common use in Cuban and Philippine harbors during the late 19th and early 20th centuries.

bummers: a nickname given to those who helped General Sherman's troops to obtain local supplies on their "march to the sea" during the Civil War.

bundle: a low woman.

bundling: a way for an unmarried couple to occupy the same bed. They did not get undressed and many times would have a rolled up blanket between them. It was a way for parents to deal with courtship when people did not want to burn expensive candles.

bung: 1) a pickpocket; 2) a stopper.

bung hole: the opening in the bottom of a cask. The stopper is called a bung.

bung maker: a maker of bungs. See bung hole.

bunker: 1) a coal bin in a steam-drive vessel; 2) a protection built of dirt for a gun or men.

bunkum: a congressman from Buncombe County, North Carolina was giving a long-winded, irrelevant speech and, when rebuked, he said that he was not speaking for anyone but Buncombe. Thus, this word has come to mean talk which has little, if anything, to do with the subject under discussion.

bunter: 1) a rag woman; 2) a word of contempt for a vulgar woman.

bunting: a cheap, thin cotton cloth more suitable for decorating buildings than for making garments.

bur.: 1) buried; 2) burial.

burden: 1) a nautical measure of cargo; 2) used to indicate the weight or capacity of a ship; 3) a heavy or oppressive load; 4) the main idea.

burdett: a cotton fabric.

Bureau of Land Management: a Federal government office which had charge of buying, selling and developing Federal land. Its name was formerly the General

Land Office.

Bureau of Pensions: a government office which has charge of issuing pensions, keeping the pension information current, etc.

burgess: 1) a freeman in a borough; 2) in pre-Revolutionary War days a representative in the Virginia or Maryland legislatures. Today, this person would be called a delegate; 3) a man whose citizenship in a British borough gave him the right to vote for two Members of Parliament; 4) a member of the group of men who governed a town; 5) in Britain this was a representative of a town, borough or university to the Parliament; 6) see also House of Burgesses.

burgh: a town.

burgher: an inhabitant of a town.

burgomaster: a mayor or head magistrate in Europe.

burgundy: a red wine.

burial records: pertinent facts about a person who is buried in a cemetery. These facts are kept in books by the sexton or other responsible person. They will note the name of the deceased, age, cause of death, the number of the lot where the person is buried and sometimes other information.

burlap: a coarse, rough cloth made of hemp which is used for feed sacks, etc.

burler: 1) a person who removes defects from cloth; 2) a person who mends minor imperfections in rugs.

burmaydene: a chambermaid.

burness: men of New Sweden (a section along the Delaware River) so known because they had refused to obey a Swedish law which did not allow land to be cleared by burning.

burn-heat: to clear a piece of land by cutting growth and brush off, then setting fire to the weeds and finally spreading the ashes over the ground. Sometimes called denshire.

burnisher: 1) a person who polished articles: 2) a tool used to rub an item smooth.

burnwin: a blacksmith.

bursar: a treasurer.

burse: 1) a purse; 2) a square case in which a church's communion cloth is kept when not in use.

burying a wife: a feast given by an apprentice at the expiration of his contract.

bush: 1) uncleared wilderness consisting of large and small trees, bushes, grasses, etc. Used with other words, e.g. (a) bush arbor - a shelter for shade which was made of boughs, shrubs, etc.; (b) bush meeting - a religious group holding a meeting or service in a grove of trees or a forest; 2) the sign of a tavern which in former times was generally an ivy bush.

busheler: a person who mends garments for a tailor. Also called a bushelman.

bushfighters: a battle fought by ducking behind trees, rocks, etc. and using underbrush for cover from the enemy.

bushment: ambush.

bushpick hammer: a tool used by a mill peck.

bushwackers: men who claimed to be non-fighters when they were outnumbered. However, if the opportunity arose, they did not hesitate to ambush soldiers. If they were caught, the punishment was severe. 2) see also bushwacking.

bushwacking: when a simple boat was going upstream, instead of being poled or rowed it was sometimes towed by a long cable pulled by men walking along the banks of the river. The men were called bushwackers.

busker: an entertainer who danced, sang, or recited on streets or in public places.

buss: a fishing vessel which had square sails.

butlands: waste ground

butler: 1) the keeper of the wine casks; 2) the supplier of wine to royalty; 3) the head servant in a large household who supervised lesser employees; 2) a housekeeper.

butt: 1) a large cask; 2) a measure which varied but usually was considered equal to two hogsheads.

butternut: 1) the edible nut from a butternut or white walnut tree; 2) the bark of a butternut tree was used as dye for cloth and the name designated a kind of cloth: butternut flannel, "butternut grey" homespun, butternut woolsey, etc.; 3) some Confederate soldiers were designated as butternuts, especially those from Mississippi and Texas. Named for the color of the home-dyed clothes which they wore, they supported the Democratic party during the Civil War. The term "butternuts" was used as a term of contempt to describe Peace Democrats in the North. The Peace Democrats wore this color as a badge of honor, for they supported common people.

buttery: a room (sometimes called a pantry) located near the kitchen or dining room where food and drink were kept.

buttillary: a buttery.

butt knife: a tool used by 1) a tanner; 2) a currier.

buttrice: a farrier's tool used to pare the hoofs in shoeing a horse. This term was sometimes spelled butteris or buttress.

Bvt.: Brevet.

"by experience:" one way in which the Baptist church accepts members. It usually means that the new member has been convinced that he can accept the beliefs of the church and be baptized.

"by letter:" one of the ways members are received from one Baptist church to another Baptist church. A written statement confirms that the transferring member left in good standing.

byre: a cowbarn.

"by relation:" another way that members are received from one church to another. It apparently means that the person is a member of a recognized denomination. Now this phrase has been replaced by a statement of faith.

byrewoman: an English woman who takes care of cows.

byrlaw: a law or local custom established by landowners in the area which settles boundary disputes, dates when plowing should start or be finished, use of commons, etc.

byrlawman: see birlieman.

C

1) cape, on maps and charts; 2) circa; 3) cousin; 4) chancery; 5) century; 6) Roman numeral for one hundred.

c.: 1) copyright; 2) when preceding a date it stands for circa or about; 3) copy; 4) the Roman numeral for one hundred; 5) a hundred weight; 6) codicil; 7) cousin.

2c 3r: second cousin, three times removed. (c and r used with numbers in this manner is a short method of describing the degree of relationship of cousins).

C.A.: 1) Court of Appeals; 2) Chief of Artillery.

ca.: circa.

cabbage plane: a kraut cutter.

cabbis: a coarse, cheap fabric which had a tight weave. Sometimes it was called serge.

cabby: a garden hoe.

cabin: 1) the area on a ship designated for the captain's living and working accommodations; 2) a covered area for boat passengers; 3) a small, crude house.

cabin boy: a young lad who works on a ship to attend to the needs of the passengers and officers in the cabin.

cabinet card: a larger card than a carte de visite card, it measured about six by four inches and was in use from the late 1860s to about 1900. The edge would be decorative and the photographer's name and city were across one corner.

cabinet maker: a craftsman skilled in the art of making furniture of wood.

cabin raising: a gathering of neighbors to build the framework of a log cabin or a barn. When the task was completed, there would be a party with food and music.

cable length: in the Navy this is 600 feet or 100 fathoms.

cabriolet: a light carriage which had two wheels and was pulled by one horse.

cachalot: see sperm whale.

cache: an often hidden supplies of food, ammunition, etc.

cachere: a hunter.

cachet: 1) an official seal; 2) a feature which distinguishes from others; 3) prestige; 4) a hollow capsule which is designed to hold a foul-tasting medicine; 5) condensed to a small size.

cachexia: the look of death due to a total wasting away of the body, especially when cancer has spread throughout the body.

cacopathy: a bowel movement.

cacosphyxy: an obsolete term for an irregular pulse.

cad: a very small pig.

cadastral maps: the proper name for county atlases. These maps usually have a scale of twenty-five miles to an inch and give the names of landowners in the county together with the acreage they own. They also show the boundaries of properties, political subdivisions, and location of main buildings. They probably originated in Babylonia about 2300 B.C. and are the oldest known maps. In the late 1800s these maps were drawn and used for the purpose of taxation.

cadastral survey: measurements to locate the boundaries of a parcel of land for the purpose of determining ownership.

cadastre: a base for taxation. Registers of property which state the name of the owner, how many or how much, value, etc. in a given area.

caddice: 1) a person who works at odd jobs, performs the service of running errands, etc.; 2) a sturdy device which has wheels and is designed to carry heavy objects.

caddis: 1) a ribbon or tape made from wool; 2) a woolen cloth.

caddow: a woolen coverlet which had a rough texture.

cade: 1) a barrel of 500-600 herrings; 2) any quantity of beef under a quarter; 3) a favorite foal, lamb, child, etc.

cadet: 1) a young man who is being trained as an officer in a military service; 2) a younger, junior family member.

cadette: 1) a sister; 2) a younger daughter.

cadger: a packman or itinerant huckster. See also badger.

cadre: the officers and enlisted men who are assigned to form the core of an entirely new unit.

caducous: 1) gifts from a testator which for some reason the donee failed to take; 2) deciduous; 3) epileptic.

caedes: kill, slaughter.

caelebs, coelebs: bachelor.

caffa: 1) made in India, this heavy silk cloth was somewhat like damask in appearance; 2) a painted cotton fabric which was produced in India.

cag: 1) an obsolete word for a small cask; 2) a small fishing boat.

Cahokia: a fort erected near St. Louis in the Illinois territory.

cairn: a pile of stones used as a mark in surveying, to mark a grave, a landmark, or to lead to something.

caisson: a two-wheeled cart in which ammunition for artillery guns is carried.

Cajan, Cajin, Cajun: see Acadian.

calamanco: a woolen fabric which was glossy on the surface. On the under side there are checks made by the weaving process. This material was quite popular during the eighteenth century.

calash: 1) a light carriage which had room for four passengers and a separate seat for the driver. It also had a top which folded back in fine weather; 2) in the late eighteenth century as women's hair styles became higher, hoods of cloaks became larger. A calash was an awkward affair made of hoops which folded back as did the top of the vehicle from which its name came.

calasses: almshouses.

calcar: an astrologer.

calciator: shoemaker.

calcocos: brass.

calder: tin.

calefactory: a sitting room in a monastery which is heated in cold weather.

calendar: 1) a schedule of cases to appear in court; 2) the account book of a moneylender; 3) a method of visibly showing divisions of a year into months, weeks, and days. Many times this will include ecclesiastical dates; 4) any kind of a list.

calendared: when records have been arranged in chronological order.

calenderer: see calender man.

calender man: the person who put fabric, rubber, or paper through a rolling or embossing machine called a calender.

Sometimes called a calenderer.

calends: in the old Roman calendar this was the first day in a month, the day from which the preceding month's days were counted backward until the ides were reached.

calenture: a high fever.

calibogus: a beverage made of rum and spruce beer.

calico: 1) originally this was a general term for all the cotton cloth imported from Callicut (now Calcutta) India and from the Far East. Now calico seems to refer to an inexpensive cotton cloth which is printed only on one side, usually with a small flowered or figured pattern; 2) also used to describe a several colored animal with a spotted or patchy marked coat.

calicuts: an early name for calico.

caligo: failing eyesight.

calipers: a tool used for measuring diameters by a blacksmith, farrier, turner, or machinist.

calligrapher: 1) a person who could write elegantly and was employed to write the names in diplomas, etc.; 2) a professional copyist who copied deeds, wills, etc. into the permanent courthouse records.

calligraphy: the art of writing clearly and beautifully. Sometimes used as a general term for handwriting.

calliope: a musical instrument associated with a circus or parade. It has a key board much like a piano and the sound is shrill and ringing, since it is really a series of steam whistles of various sizes.

calmative: a medicine which acts as a sedative, has a calming effect.

calmendar: see calico.

calo: 1) the servant of a soldier; 2) one who does menial tasks around a military camp; 3) also spelled kalo, which refers to religious ceremonies.

calomel: a laxative.

calotype: an early photographic process in which the picture is printed on paper. See talfotype.

calumny: slander or fake and malicious charges against another person.

cambe, cambage: (Norman) a brewery.

cambist: 1) a person who deals in foreign exchange; 2) a book which lists money, weights, measures, etc. of various countries and which also gives the equivalents.

cambletteen: a variation of camlet (which see).

camber: (Norman) brewer.

cambric: a soft, finely woven cotton fabric.

cambric tea: a children's drink made of weak tea to which sugar and milk were added, making a thin, white, weak substitute for real tea.

cameist: a maker of cameos.

camerarius: 1) valet; 2) groom.

camerist: 1) a lady's maid; 2) a female in charge of bedrooms.

camlet: 1) a beautiful and expensive fabric made of silk and Angora wool imported from the Far East. Later the fiber content was silk and wool and became heavy and sturdy enough to make tents and blankets; 2) the name of a piece of clothing made from camlet.

camlet maker: the person who made fabric of silk and wool, called camlet, which was an imitation of a fabric made of camel hair or angora wool. He could also make a plain weave lustrous wool usually dyed a bright red.

campaign: a series of military operations which are connected and are designed to form a battle plan in a distinct part of a war.

campaigner: a veteran member of the armed forces.

campanator: bell ringer.

Campbellites: a popular name for a religious denomination known as Disciples of Christ, so named for one of its founders, Alexander Campbell.

Camp Douglas prison: a prison in Chicago, Illinois, used during the Civil War for captured Confederate soldiers, which had miserable conditions for the prisoners.

campestres: (Norman) pastures.

camp fever: a transmittable fever, usually typhoid, which occurred in an army post where many men were kept together in close quarters.

camp follower: 1) a female prostitute who associated with the soldiers; 2) any one who follows the army from post to post without being in the army.

camphor: a medicinal vegetable oil with a pungent smell that was used externally.

camp-meeting: a revival, usually of Methodists, commonly held in a tent or open field. Families often brought food and bedding, and stayed for two or three days. See also revival.

campn.: campaign.

can, cann: a Colonial term for a tankard or mug, with or without a lid.

canacin: the plague.

canal: a watercourse dug deep enough to allow boats which carried goods, merchandise and passengers to move from one point to another. Indiana developed an extensive canal system which caused the state and many individuals to go bankrupt.

canal boat: a flat-bottomed boat designed for use on a canal system. It could be propelled either by oars or by horses who walked along the banks and who were tied to the boat.

canal lands: an extensive canal system was planned for Ohio, Indiana, and Illinois. When the canal system became outdated much of that land became park and recreation land.

canary: 1) a kind of sweet wine used especially in the earlier part of the 17th century; 2) a kept mistress.

candle: 1) to help a wicked person with his crimes; 2) to sell by a candle meant to accept bids at an auction sale as long as a small candle burned. When the flame died, the bidding was finished; 3) to candle eggs meant to hold an egg in front of a light to see if there was an embryo in the egg.

Candlemas Day: 1) a religious holiday—Feast of the Purification—which falls on the second of February; 2) a day in Scotland which occurs quarterly, when school taxes are due.

candle rent: rent collected from a house which was deteriorating from a lack of repairs.

candleshears: snuffers to extinguish the flame of a candle.

candlewood sets: pitch pine pieces put in cracks of the fireplace hearth. When lighted, they smoked badly, but gave a bright light.

candy butcher: a peddler on a train or at a railroad station who sold small goods to passengers.

candyman: 1) a traveling candy salesman; 2) process-server in northern England.

canine madness: hydrophobia (rabies).

canker: an ulcerous sore.

cannel bone: collar bone.

cannel coal: a choice coal mined in Scotland which burns slowly with a bright flame. It is used also to make coal oil and gas.

cannon: a gun mounted on either a movable or fixed base. Generally a name applied to large guns.

cannoneer or cannonier: the man who cared for and fired a gun or cannon as a member of a gun crew.

cannon stove, cannonball stove: a wood burning, vertical, cylindrical stove which resembled a cannon. It was used to heat large public rooms around the middle of the eighteenth century.

canoa: a sloop-rigged fishing boat.

canoe: developed and used by the American Indians, a canoe was made of a large tree hollowed out. It was very suitable for a light cargo and the settlers quickly adopted this type of boat for their shipping.

canon: 1) a rule; 1) a law; 3) a church law; 4) a portion of a deceased man's goods exacted by the priest; 5) a quit-rent.

canonizle escrite: (Norman) canon law.

canon law: legal rules for dealing with matters over which the Church has jurisdiction. This law was observed by most of our states in establishing relationships, e.g. who could not marry based on the degree of descent from a common ancestor.

canons of descent: rules by which property is given from a deceased person to his heir.

cant: 1) language used in the underworld; 2) an auction; 3) a corner of a field; 4) a crowd.

cantaloon: a tightly woven wool made in western England during the eighteenth century.

Cantate: the fourth Sunday after Easter.

cant dog: see cant hook.

canteen: a tin, capped bottle carried by military personnel. It was usually kept filled with water.

canter: 1) a nickname for a Puritan; 2) a Spanish fishing boat.

cant hook: a hooked took used to grasp and turn logs. Also called a cant dog.

canting caller: an auctioneer.

canton: a portion of a flag, shield, or country, especially a corner.

cantonment: buildings which are temporary and are used to house soldiers, or for other military purposes.

canvas: hemp cloth used for sails or ships. The phrase "under canvas" means the ship is being moved by the wind filling her sails.

cap-a-pie: covered from head to foot by clothing; e.g. armor or rainwear.

cape bonnet: a bonnet which instead of ending under the chin and at the nape of the neck continued to elbow length forming a cape.

capellanus: chaplain.

cape merchant: 1) an obsolete term which was used for the cargo carried on early voyages; 2) the head parts keeper in a factory.

caper: 1) a privateer of the seventeenth century; 2) an obsolete word for a captor or seizor; 3) bread, butter and a slice of cheese.

capias: "that you take." A general term for several kinds of writs.

capias ad computandum: to force an accounting.

capias ad respondendum: to answer, a written order to the sheriff to keep the defendant safe in order that he may appear in court.

capias ad satisfaciendum: that you take to satisfy a written order to arrest and detain, until he can pay his debt, a person who has been ordered by the court to pay a sum of money.

capitation: 1) a tax imposed on each person 2) the total of a poll tax; 3) a fee paid for each member of a group to the parent organization.

capitol of county: the county seat of government.

capitus: see caput.

Capt.: Captain.

Captain: 1) see army rank; 2) an honorary title given to those in command of a vessel. This could be the owner, the pilot, etc.

Captain Lieutenant: this rank, used during the Revolutionary War, indicated the first lieutenant who had the great seniority in a battalion.

Captain's district: a sub-division of a county. Usually used to denote the area allotted to one person. Usually found on tax lists and censuses that are not related in any way to military service.

captal: (Norman) 1) a captain; 2) a chief.

caption: the title or first lines of a document, article, etc.

caput, capitis: head, chief.

carabins: light cavalry from Spain who were so named from their guns, carbines, or muskets.

carage: 1) measure; 2) quality.

caravel: a small light ship.

carbine: a medium-sized gun usually used by those in the cavalry.

carbonarius: 1) collier; 2) coal miner.

carcelage: prison fees.

carcinoma: cancer.

card: 1) a tool used to smooth the nap of cloth; 2) a tool with teeth used to comb wool fibers; 3) to mix together; 4) a plan; 5) a stiff paper with holes punched in it which is used to control the patterns in Jacquard weaving.

carde: a fabric whose fiber content is unknown but which was used to make curtains, linings, etc.

card abstracts: these cards contain without exception all information from the original documents concerning an individual's military service.

carder: a person who smoothed wool for the spinning process.

cardiacle: a disease which affected the heart.

cardicue: one-fourth of the coin known as a French crown.

carding: the second of two steps in loosening and straightening fibers for a spinning wheel. See teasing.

card maker: the person who made the card with compass directions on it (compass rose) attached to a mariner's compass and rotated with the needle.

cardours: (Norman) a quiver.

carecarius: 1) carter; 2) plowman.

care cloth: a fine silken fabric shaped like a canopy which was held over the heads of a bridal couple as they knelt during the wedding ceremony.

caresme: an obsolete word for troublesome.

cark: 1) a weight; 2) a pain; 3) to burden.

carl: 1) a bondsman; 2) a rude country clown.

carnifex: 1) hangman, executioner; 2) a scoundrel.

caroche: a luxurious town carriage.

Carolus: the Latin form of Charles or Karl. When a coin was minted under a monarch named Charles or Karl, Carolus preceded the name of the coin.

carpe diem: this phrase is found in cemeteries. It means enjoy the present day.

carpentarius: 1) carpenter; 2) cartwright.

carpenter: a person who made wooden objects, houses, etc.

carpet: a thick, usually made of wood, fabric which was used as a table or bed cover.

carpet bagger: 1) a person who was reputed to carry all of his possessions in one carpet bag and who went south to gain profit from the social and political aftermath of the Civil War; 2) a term used in speaking of a stranger, foreigner, etc. in a contemptuous manner.

carpet knights: knights dubbed at court by the King as opposed to those so honored on a military field for distinguished service.

ca. resp.: capias ad respondendum (which see).

carnitate: to build stone houses.

carriage: 1) cost of transportation; 2) a heavy support on wheels for moving cannon; 3) administration; 4) the act of transporting.

carrier: 1) a laborer who carries mortar to a brick layer; 2) one who takes messages from one person or group to another.

carrousel: a merry-go-round, originally hand powered, then steam powered and now powered by a gasoline or diesel engine or by an electric motor.

carrucage: 1) a tax on land; 2) a tax on a plow.

carrucate: as much land as a man could till with a plow and team of eight oxen during one year.

carryall: 1) a light vehicle pulled by one horse. The term was later applied to a larger, heavier carriage; 2) a bag or large purse used for carrying an assortment of miscellaneous articles.

carrying coals to Newcastle: this phrase means that someone was carrying coal to Newcastle, England in a coal mining area. Thus, to take a product or provide a service in an area where there were several like products or services would be carrying coals to Newcastle.

carsey: see kersey.

carta: a deed, a chart, or a map.

carte blanche: authority to do as one pleases in a given set of circumstances.

carte de visite: used from the 1860s to the 1920s, this photo on a card was most popular during the 1880s. Many times the picture was a portrait which could be sent through the mail. This mounting often had on it the photographer's name and town where he had his studio.

cartel: any agreement between opponents, especially an understanding about the exchange of prisoners between two enemy forces.

carter: 1) a person who drove a cart which carried freight; 2) a charioteer.

cartography: the art of drawing maps.

cartulary: a book or register which has duplicate copies of the title deeds in an estate. Also spelled chartulary.

cartwheels: silver dollars.

cartwright: a person who made carts, wagons, etc.

caruage: plow.

carucate: an old unit of land measure used in England. It varied from 96 to 160 acres. This measurement was based upon how much land could be plowed with one plow and eight oxen in a season.

carve: 1) to plow land; 2) as much land as could be tilled in one year with one

plow.
carver: (Norman) plowman.
carver's chops: a tool used by a wood carver.
ca.sa.: capias ad satisfactum (which see).
casa execution: an action which orders the sheriff to imprison a debtor because the debtor does not have sufficient property, real or personal, to pay his debts.
cascos: one-half black, a child of two mulatto persons.
cas de frument: (Norman) a load of wheat.
case: 1) a general term used to indicate some kind of an argument brought into court to be settled; 2) (Norman) a house.
case law: common law determinations based upon earlier written court decisions.
casement cloth: light-weight curtain material.
cashd: cashiered.
cash entry files: a group of records, created by cash land sales in some states, which are housed in the National Archives. They contain lists of land purchase applicants, receipts, and evidence which allowed a man to purchase land from the government.
cashier: 1) dismiss from a job or group; 2) in the military sense, to disband a unit; 3) to issue a dishonorable discharge;
4) to make something void.
cashiered: dismissed from military service in disgrace, usually as the result of a court martial.
cashmaire: a dealer in fish.
casked tobacco: at one time tobacco was packed and shipped in a cask or hogshead.
casket girls: poor girls who were brought from charitable institutions in France to Louisiana during the eighteenth century. The name came from the fact that the clothes they had with them were packed in cassettes (small chests).
caskmaker: a person who makes casks.
cassinette: a type of light-weight cloth woven with a cotton warp thread and a filler, or woof thread) of silk and wool or fine wool alone.
cassock: a long garment worn by ministers.
castelano: cloth.
castelet: a turret.
castelle: a large cistern.
caster, castor, casterstand: a set, usually of glass containers set in a metal or wooden revolving frame. The containers were filled with salt, pepper, mustard, vinegar, or other condiments.
castlewards: a tax to support a garrison which was paid by persons who lived within a specified distance of a castle.
castor: beaver fur, or an imitation of beaver fur, which was usually made into hats.
cata baptist: a person who is against baptism.
catalepsy: a physical condition in which the muscles are rigid. At times the afflicted person does not know where he is.
cataplasm: a mustard plaster used to draw poison from the portion of the body on which it was placed.
catal: (Norman) movables of any kind.
catarrh: inflammation of <u>any</u> mucous membrane, e.g. catarrh of the throat. Earlier it was thought that this liquid ran down from the brain.
catarrh epidemic: influenza.
catarrhal croup: see catarrh.
catarrhal fever: see catarrh.
Catawba Indians: members of the Sioux nation, these Indians lived along the Catawba River in the Carolinas. As a rule, they were friendly toward settlers.
catch land: border land whose title was disputable. It was taken by the first claimant who could catch it.
catchpole, catchpoll: a sheriff's assistant, particularly one who arrests people for non-payment of debts (from chacepol, a tax gatherer).
catch rogue: constable; bailiff.
catch water: a reservoir of water in a newly designated common.
catechism: an instructional oral summary in question and answer form regarding the basic principles of a religion.
catechumen: a person who was in the process of receiving pre-baptismal instruction in the doctrines of the early church.

cater: caterer.
cater-cousin: a friend who is very close.
catery: the place in a large house or palace where provisions were kept or distributed.
catgut: a strong thread made by twisting dried animal intestines.
cathartic: an active laxative.
cat mallisons: cupboards near chimneys where dried beef and other provisions were kept.
cat o'nine tails: a flogging whip with nine knotted cords.
catshead hammer: a tool used by a farrier.
catted chimney: chimneys made of wood with a mud plaster on the inner portion. This mud hardened with the heat of many fires and lasted for quite some time. However, when a chunk of mud would drop out, the chimney became a fire hazard.
cattle: years ago this term referred to all types of four-footed domesticated animals.
cauceage: (Norman) toll paid toward repairing causeways.
cauciour: surveyor.
caudibec: a French hat worn in England about 1700.
cauer: (Norman) a knight.
caul: swelling.
caulker: a person whose job is to caulk the seams of a ship.
caupo: an innkeeper.
causa: a reason or cause. Used as a part of a phrase in Latin.
causa mortis: by reason of death.
causary: an obsolete word which meant a medical discharge from military service.
cause: a case brought before a court.
cause of action: the reason for bringing a lawsuit into court.
cause number: case number in court records.
causidic: a lawyer.
caution: a pledge; security.
cautioner: a Scottish law term which means a surety or sponsor.
cav.: cavalry.
cavalier: a gentleman accomplished at using arms.
cavalry: the portion of the army that served on horseback.
caveat: 1) a written document filed by an interested party which stops the process of obtaining a grant until the opposition can be heard, e.g. stopping the court from probating a will; 2) previously, a notice filed at the Patent Office by an inventor who was trying to forestall the granting of a patent to another inventor for an invention claimed by both. So long as the caveat was in force, a patent could not be issued without approval of the one who filed the caveat; 3) a warning against a certain action or practice.
caveat emptor: "let the buyer beware," let the purchaser see that the title is good or that he receives the quality for which he is paying.
Cave-in-Rock: a notorious hang-out for criminals in the first half of the 19th century. Located in southern Illinois, and known by a succession of names: Wilson's Tavern, Cave Inn, Rock Cave Inn, Cave Inn Rock, Cave-in-Rock. Now a State park.
cayon: (Norman) a grandfather.
Cayuga: Indians who belonged to the Iroquois nation and who sided with the British during the Revolutionary War.
C.B.: chain bearer.
C.C.: 1) Clerk of Court; 2) chain carrier; 3) County Court; 4) County Commissioner; 5) Company Commander.
C.C.C.: Clerk of the County Court.
C.C.P.: Court of Common Pleas.
C.D.A.: Colonial Dames of America.
C.E.: 1) Church Elder; 2) Caveat Emptor; 3) Christian Era; 4) Chief of Engineers.
cedar basket: country men felt that water tasted better when a wooden bucket was used instead of a metal one, though the dipper for drinking from the bucket was usually made of metal. An uncouth person would put the dipper back in the pail after drinking from it, whereas a well-bred person would lay the dipper alongside the pail or hang it on a nail provided for that purpose.
cedula: a Spanish governmental order or permit. This term sometimes was used for some South American government-

issued securities.

cedules: (Norman) seats or pews.

ceel: (Norman) a saddle.

ceinz (de): (Norman) of this court, here.

celerity (celerity coach or wagon): a vehicle adjusted for use on muddy roads or through mountainous areas to provide a faster way of travel on rough sections of road.

cellar: until the 19th century, any place for storage, above or below ground.

cellarman: a person whose job was bringing supplies upstairs from a basement.

celle: a religious house.

cem.: cemetery.

cementers: (Norman) 1) bricklayers; 2) masons.

cemetery: a piece of land set aside for the burial of deceased persons. There are several types: family burial grounds on the farm where the deceased lived; commercial cemetery enterprises; churchyards, which were next to the church; and military. Some churches buried their members in chronological order, with a space reserved for the spouse.

cemetery company: ground is purchased by a group of people for a cemetery. The grave sites may be purchased by anyone for a fee. Some funeral homes own such a cemetery.

cen.: census.

cenfables (en chofes): (Norman) in things to be taxed.

cense: (Norman) rent.

censeo: 1) a valuation; 2) an estimate; 3) to express an opinion.

censour: (Norman) a farmer.

census: an official counting of people within the boundaries of a country. The Bible says that the Lord told Moses to take a count of the children of Israel before he took them out of Egypt. The Romans took a census every five years and at the time of Christ's birth all men had to go to their town of birth "to be taxed." In the United States, a census has been taken every ten years by the Federal government since 1790.

census abstract: a statistical compilation of material contained in a census which is useful to determine how many people of a certain vocation are in a given area, how many own or rent their house or farm, etc. This does not contain names, only figures.

census bureau: see census office.

census day: the day, established by law, when the ten year counting of people was to begin and it was also the day when the special statistics were to be taken as follows: first to fourth censuses on the first Monday in August, fifth to twelfth censuses on June first, the thirteenth census on April 15th, the fourteenth census on January first and the fifteenth to eighteenth censuses on April first.

census marshall: see marshall.

census office: this office was set up on a temporary basis for each ten year census before the permanent Census Bureau was organized in 1902.

census schedule: a completed questionnaire.

census year: the year which preceded the census day. Events which took place during this year were to be recorded (e.g. deaths, births, marriages). This term was used first when the act for the seventh census was passed. It refers to the year immediately preceding the census day. Some states took a census also every ten years in the fifth year after the Federal census, e.g. 1835, 1845, 1855, etc. In these early censuses they contained no more information than the Federal census and in later years, less information.

cent.: century.

centiesme partie: (Norman) hundredth part.

central: an old term used in calling ("Hello, Central") or in referring to a telephone operator.

centry-garth: a cemetery or burial place of a monastery.

centurion: a Roman peace keeper.

cenz: (Norman) hundred.

ceper (al): (Norman) to the jailer.

cephalic: pertaining to the head.

cepi: "I have taken." This term is frequently found in sheriffs' returns, e.g. cepi corpus—I have taken the body.

cere cloth: cloth saturated with a gummy or waxy substance which was used to wrap a dead body, thus waterproofing and preserving it for a short time.

cert.: 1) certificate; 2) certified.

certes: (Norman) verily, truly.

certificate: 1) a statement of title to land, or concerning possession of land; 2) a written declaration stating the truth of a fact; 3) this term was used interchangeably with "warrant;" 4) in Quaker records this term indicates that a person has written permission to transfer his membership to another monthly meeting.

certificate of removal: a Quaker title for a written introduction of a church member in good standing to another Quaker church.

certified copy: a copy of a document, signed and sworn to by the officer in whose office the original document is housed.

certiorari (writ of): an order from a higher court to a lesser court asking for a record of a particular case.

cert-money: an annual fee paid by tenants for the use of land which belonged to the manorial lord.

ces freres: (Norman) his brothers.

cess: a tax on land.

cessaunt: (Norman) sixty.

cesse: stop; give possession.

cessure (un): (Norman) 1) a receiver; 2) a bailiff.

cession: a thing yielded or surrendered.

c.f.: confero, compare.

C.H.: 1) Court House; 2) Custom House.

Ch.: 1) Chief; 2) Chaplain.

ch.: child; children; church.

chaches, char, charet, charette: (Norman) a cart.

chafer house: an ale house.

chaff: 1) fodder; 2) something of no value.

chaffer: 1) a business; 2) one who bargains over prices.

chaffering: buying and selling.

chaffers: an obsolete word for merchandise.

chaffery: 1) the art of selling and buying goods; 2) furnace (industrial, not heating).

chain: a lineal measure of land. One chain equals 100 links or 66 feet. Sometimes called a "gunter's chain" to distinguish it from an engineer's chain, which is 50 or 100 feet long.

chain carrier: a surveyor's assistant, sometimes called a chain bearer; sometimes called a "chain bearer."

chain, engineer's: 100 feet in length, consisting of one foot long links.

chainman: 1) the person who assists a surveyor by measuring, etc. Also called a lineman, a rodman, or a tapeman; 2) the person who searches land records to construct an abstract of title; 3) a sawmill worker.

chain measures (surveyor's): one link equals 7.92 inches, one chain equals 100 links or 66 feet, one furlong equals ten chains, one mile equals eighty chains.

chain of title: the succession of ownership changes for a particular piece of land. This chain will begin with the government or original owner and end with the current owner.

chain of transfer: after a bounty warrant had changed hands a number of times, proof of ownership was required before the warrant could be used. The holder needed all the sale and transfer evidence from the original holder to himself.

chain, square: 66 feet. 10 square chains = 1 acre. 1 square chain = 16 square poles.

chair: see sedan chair.

chairbearers: persons who carried others in chairs supported on poles.

chair bodger: a wandering craftsman engaged in making the turned parts of chairs, especially the legs and stretchers of Windsor chairs.

chaise: 1) a two-wheeled, light, open carriage pulled by one horse; 2) a fourteenth century French gold coin; 3) a copy of the French gold coin minted in England.

chalk: 1) a term for 25 cents, used in multiples, for example: $1.75 would be seven chalks. This term was used in the late 1700s and early 1800s; 2) a mark on a person's hat used as an indication that the person could travel free of charge.

chalk box: used to mark a straight line. This was a small box containing a marking substance, charcoal, chalk or a mixture of lime and pokeberry juice and a coiled piece of string. The string would be pulled out of the box, stretched tight the length of, and along where, the mark was to be. The string would be given a sharp flip and a clear visible line would remain. The worker then rewound the string in the box to absorb the marking substance, making it ready for use again.

chalkstone: a secretion which resembles chalk and is found in the small joints of a person who has gout.

challis, challie, chally: a finely woven silk and wool fabric, easily draped, which was first introduced in Norwich, England about 1632.

chalunge: (Norman) claim.

chamber: 1) a bedroom; 2) an apartment over a stable; 3) a palace reception room; 4) a judge's office.

chamberer: 1) a chambermaid; 2) a wanton person; 3) a concubine.

chamberlain: 1) a valet; 2) a man who visits ladies' chambers.

chambermaid: a person who makes the bed and cleans a bedroom in an inn or large house.

chambermaster: a shoemaker whose workroom is in his own home.

chambray: a two-colored plain weave cloth; one color is used for a warp thread and another for the woof.

chamois: 1) a soft, very pliable leather used to polish, etc. Originally, this leather came from an antelope called a chamois; 2) a fake chamois leather made of cotton.

chamoising: the art of curing animal skin by pulling it in all directions and applying oil, producing a very tough, flexible and soft skin.

champartie: 1) a share of land; 2) partnership in power.

chance bairn: a bastard.

chancel: the area around the altar in a church and the railing around this area.

chancellor: 1) legal counselor to a church Bishop; 2) the judge who presides over a chancery court.

chancery: a legal term very seldom used now. The first courts were simply called law courts and as this system needed refinement, chancery courts were added. There are no juries used in chancery courts as they deal with matters such as divorce and foreclosures. These were not considered important enough to require jury trial.

chancery court: 1) an equity court; 2) in England, an ecclesiastical probate court. See also chancery; 3) an equity court presided over by a deputy governor and council.

chancery records: books containing various types of records, for example: partitions, petitions, civil cases, etc. Each geographic area had its own rules for the types of records to be included.

chandler: a person who made or sold candles, tallow and, at times, soap.

chandry: a place where candles were kept.

change house: a small inn or tavern.

changerwife: an itinerant female huckster.

change of venue: to choose another place for a court trial, usually because it is felt that the defendant cannot get a fair trial in the original location. However, it can mean only a change from one court to another court in the same county.

changerwife: an itinerant female huckster.

change(s) society: used in Colonial documents to indicate a change in church membership.

channel opener: a tool used by a boot maker.

chantry: 1) an attached chapel used for small church services; 2) in the Catholic church this term refers to a Mass for the souls of persons named by those who pay for this Mass to be said.

Chap.: Chaplain.

chaparral: a thicket made of brush.

chapchurch: a parish clerk.

chapel: a printing house.

chapelle: a chaplain.

chapel room: a closet-like, very small room used for prayer or contemplation.

chaplain: a clergyman who serves in the armed forces as a non-combatant, commissioned officer, and is responsible for the spiritual well-being of personnel. In early times chaplains entered the service as privates and were not commissioned officers nor even paid.

chapman: 1) a merchant; 2) a buyer; 3) a peddler in England; 4) a salesman sometimes known as a "yankee peddler."

chappellet: a small chapel.

charbokull: a carbuncle.

chare: 1) a chore; 2) occasional work.

charet: a carriage, cart, wagon, etc.

charetter: (Norman) a wagoner or carter.

Chare Thursday: Maundy Thursday.

chargehouse: an obsolete word for a boarding school.

charger: a cavalry horse.

charger (loader): a small horn-shaped container used to hold the amount of powder for one charge to be used in a muzzle-loading gun.

charges: (Norman) charters.

chariot: a four-wheeled carriage used by wealthy colonists.

charioteer: the driver of a two-wheeled passenger cart used in Colonial days.

charmed milk: sour milk.

charmer: magician.

charnel house: a mausoleum, a building in which the dead are buried.

charter: 1) a deed; 2) a grant issued by the government of a state or country.

charter chest: in Europe, this was a box for family papers.

charterer: a freeholder.

charter party: a corruption of the Latin, *charter partita*, or divided contract. An agreement between businessmen and ship owners regarding merchandise. Each group received one section of the contract.

charter rolls: a list of priveleges granted to individuals, or to a group of people.

chartulary: 1) a book which lists charters, title deeds, etc.; 2) an archivist.

charwoman: a female who cleans offices on a contract basis, or one who does domestic cleaning by the day.

chased: jewelry ornamented with engraving or a raised design is said to be chased.

chasour: hunter.

chastelain: lord of a castle.

chastity belt: a locked belt worn by a woman, designed to prevent her from indulging in sexual intercourse. Sometimes a suspicious husband would put one on his wife before he left on a long trip.

chatelaine: 1) one who cared for a large house in the country, especially a feudal French castle; 2) a fancy pin with a hook from which a purse, watch, keys or small tools are suspended. The housekeeper of a large establishment wore this as she went about her supervisory tasks.

chattel: 1) moveable personal property; 2) at one time, before the Civil War, a slave was considered personal property and, therefore, was a chattel.

chattel mortgage: a bill of sale on moveable property, for example: cattle, furniture, etc., with a condition that it shall be void on the happening of a certain event; usually the payment of money.

chauffer: a small, portable, box-shaped stove in which one could carry a fire to stay warm, start another fire, etc.

chauffeur: when cars first came on the market not everyone could drive them. The person who could and did drive them had oftentimes attended school, not only to learn how to drive cars but also to repair them. This raised his standing among fellow workers.

chauncelrie (en la): (Norman) in chancery.

chaundler: candlestick.

chautauqua: a meeting, both instructional and religious, named for Chautauqua, New York where the first of these meetings was held. The name was used for like meetings held in other states.

check (chequer): 1) in farming, a method of plowing at right angles, thereby marking places for planting seeds at the intersections of the rows; 2) the rectangle formed by the plowing of land, or the points at which the rows meet at right angles; 3) see bill of exchange.

checks: refers to a fabric either printed or woven with a checked pattern.

cheesemonger: a seller of various kinds of cheese.

cheese press: a tool used to separate curds from whey in the cheese making process.

cheesery: the factory where cheese is made.

cheivsauns, chevissance: (Norman) an agreement between debtor and creditor, in relation to the loss of money.

chello: a fabric imported from India during the 1700s.

chepier: (Norman) a jailer.

cheping: market; sale.

Cheraws: these Indians lived in the Carolinas and were probably members of the Sioux family.

cherche: church.

Cherokee Indians: originally found in the southeastern United States, these Native Americans were forced out of Georgia to what is now Oklahoma, where they became on of the Five Civilized Tribes.

cherriderry: a cloth, resembling streaked calico, used for work clothes.

cherry bounce: a Colonial drink made from rum or whiskey and flavored with cherries. It was made quite frequently at home.

chersit, chersid: Christened.

chesford: cheese vat.

chest: coffin.

chest complaint: an infection in, or an inflamation of the respiratory system, a cold, pnuemonia, etc.

chest on chest: a piece of furniture with deep drawers on the bottom and shallow drawers on the top.

chester: a person who embalms, or places corpses in coffins.

chetel, chetil, chetyl: an obsolete word for a kettle.

chevance: (Norman) goods, money, riches, bargains.

chevener: usually a young girl who embroidered designs on knitted stockings.

cheventeins: (Norman) chieftains, captains.

cheviot: 1) a breed of sheep originating in England; 2) a nineteenth century woolen fabric with a twill-weave used to make suits and coats, etc.

Cheyenne Indians: members of the Algonquin tribe, these were the most hostile of the Indians who lived in the plains area. Today surviving Cheyenne Indians live in Montana and Oklahoma.

cheyney: a woolen fabric which has a pattern produced by various colors of warp thread.

Chickasaw Indians: a warlike tribe who lived in Alabama and part of Mississippi until they were removed to the west in 1837.

chief: 1) a familiar name for the senior engineer on a ship; 2) the usual way of addressing a chief petty officer; 3) the leader of an Indian tribe.

chief mate (chief officer): this term denotes the officer next lower in rank to the master of a merchant ship.

chief-of-staff: a senior staff officer of a division or higher organization who is the main advisor to a commanding officer.

chief petty officer: an enlisted man who holds a rank below the warrant officers and above all the other petty officers.

chienquante: (Norman) fifty.

chiez d'ostiez: (Norman) the head of a family.

chiffonier: 1) a rag picker; 2) a tall, narrow chest of drawers.

chilbladder: chilblain.

chilblains: redness, swelling and blisters on fingers, toes, etc. due to being cold.

child bed fever: see puerperal fever.

child of tender years: a person under fourteen years of age.

childwit: a fine paid to the Saxon lord when his bondwoman was unlawfully pregnant. The reputed father of the child paid the fine to the lord.

chillumchee: a tin-lined copper or brass basin for hand washing.

chillum house: a separate building used in southern slavery days where baby sitting for the children of slaves was provided while their parents worked in the cotton fields.

chime mawl, chime maul: a tool used by a cooper.

chiminage: a fee paid in order that a person could travel safely through a forest.

chimney cloth: a valance used as a decoration hung from the mantel over a fireplace. When the fireplace did not draw well this cloth was used to shut off the top of the opening, thus keeping the smoke from filling the room. In wealthy homes the cloths were trimmed with lace or fringe.

chimney dogs: andirons.

chimney money: in England and Wales this money was a tax imposed upon each fireplace hearth or a similar tax.

chimney sweep: a small boy who cleaned out chimneys once each month. If you failed to keep your chimney swept and a fire resulted, you were obliged to pay a fine for neglect.

chimney viewer: householders were required to have their chimneys inspected periodically (fire danger was great) and if there was not a tree close enough for the viewer to climb and do his inspecting, the householder had to provide a ladder. The person whose job it was to conduct this inspection was called the chimney viewer.

China silk: made in China, this plain weave, fine silk was used for women's clothing, especially as a lining.

chinchel: small hammer.

chinchilla cloth: a wool fabric which had a long nap. It was given the appearance of fur by gathering the fibers into little tufts. This fabric was popular at the turn of the seventeenth century and was usually made into coats.

chin cough: whooping cough.

chink: to fill crevices in the walls of a house or cabin made of logs, using sticks, mud, clay, etc. in order to make the building more nearly weatherproof.

Chinook: a jargon developed by the Hudson Bay Company employees in order to converse with Indians. It consisted of about one hundred words, some French and some Indian.

Chinook Indians: tribes who lived in Oregon and Washington.

chintz: a cotton fabric usually painted with an all-over design.

chip ax: broad axe.

chiragra: gout in the hand.

chirographer: a person who practices the art of beautiful handwriting.

chirotherarus: glover.

chirurgeon: a surgeon.

chisel: a tool used by 1) a chair bodger; 2) a saddler; 3) a carpenter; 4) a turner.

chit: 1) a note or written message; 2) a signed note promising to pay a small sum for food or service.

chiv: a tool used by a cooper.

chiveret: one of several fabrics made of a mix of wool with silk.

chivisaunce: (Norman) an unlawful bargain.

chldn: children.

chlorosis: anemia in young girls.

chm: 1) see condemned in Quaker records; 2) abbreviation for chairman.

chn.: children.

ch/o: child of.

Choctaw: a southeastern Indian tribe which moved to the Indian Territory (now Oklahoma) where they became one of the Five Civilized Tribes.

choak-damp: foul air in a colliery.

Choice: a place chosen for establishing a home or number of homes, which bears the name of the owner or developer. For example, "Taylor's Choice," "Parker's Choice," etc.

cholagogue: a medicine to promote the flow of bile.

cholecystitis: inflammation of the gall bladder.

cholera: an extremely infectious disease of the digestive system which many times brought death. Symptoms included severe diarrhea which caused a loss of fluids (dehydration) and a painful muscle cramping.

cholera infantum: an acute childhood disease, symptoms of which include vomiting, very high fever, diarrhea. The disease has a tendency to occur in the summer months. See also cholera.

cholera morbus: a disease usually caused by contaminated food which is not as life-threatening as cholera.

cholera nostras: another name for cholera morbus.

choore: thirty bushels of flour or meal.

chop church: an obsolete word used to indicate a dealer in church favors or one who exchanges one favor for another.

chop house: an early restaurant where steaks, chops, etc. were sold.

chopper: see zax.

chopping cotton: the back-breaking task

of using a hoe to thin cotton plants to one foot apart, repeated every few days for three weeks followed by breaking up the ground between the rows with a small plow.

chore: a narrow passage between two houses.

chorea: muscular twitching beginning with the head.

chorister: a person who conducts the singing of a choir or the congregation of a church.

chowder: fish seller.

chr.: christened.

chris.: christened.

christen: 1) to baptize with water and receive into a Christian church; 2) to give a child a name at baptism; 3) to name a new ship as it leaves the shipyard for the first time.

Christian name: first, or given, name.

Christian servant: a white, indentured servant.

Christ-tide: Christmas.

chronic: an ailment of long standing (as opposed to acute).

chronological: arranged in order by the date of event.

chun: bad woman.

churching: church service.

church litten: a church yard or burial ground.

churchman: an officiating minister.

church masters: church wardens.

church mouse: a mouse which is presumed to be a resident of a church. As mice are quiet we have the saying "quiet as a mouse." As the mice own no property and are not fed as well as they would be in a household, we say "poor as a church mouse."

church records: records written in the principal language of the individual church. These are varied in content and can include confirmations, baptisms, membership lists, excommunications, births, marriages, deaths, orphans, disciplinary actions, minutes of governing bodies, etc. Sometimes a minister went beyond the call of duty and added his own notes to the records. Sometimes not even births and deaths were noted.

church scot: contribution to the church.

church stile: pulpit.

church town: a village near the church.

church warden: a church officer.

churn: a container to hold cream which was agitated by a paddle to make butter.

churner: a person who makes butter.

churn milk: buttermilk.

C.I.C.: Clerk of the Inferior Court.

cigar finder: a person who retrieved cigar butts and sold them to be used again in "new" cigars.

cimbick: miser.

cincater: a person who has entered his fiftieth year.

cincaunt: (Norman) fifty.

cink: (Norman) five.

cipher, cypher: 1) the zero mark on a thermometer; in speaking of the temperature one would say "eight below cypher." 2) to write out, with considerable effort, the solution to a mathematical problem.

ciphering, cypering: arithmetic.

cippus: 1) stocks or pillory; 2) a short column without a base but which has an inscription. A landmark or marker in a cemetery.

cir.: sometimes used as an abbreviation for circa.

circ.: see c.

circa: 1) round; 2) about. Usually used in speaking of a time period.

circiter: about (speaking of time).

circle: a tool used by a surveyor to measure compass directions and angles.

circuit court: before 1911, this was a Federal court presided over by any two of the following: a justice of the Supreme Court, the judge of the district court or a special circuit judge. See also superior court.

circuit court of appeals: an appellate Federal court, started in 1891, directly below the Supreme court in authority.

circuit preacher: a minister who had a pastorate in each of several churches and performed church duties at various churches on a prescribed route.

circuit rider: see circuit preacher.

circular meeting: a Quaker gathering requested by a monthly meeting and authorized by the quarterly meeting.

They were held at various places and at different times.

circum: around (speaking of time).

circumforancus: tinker.

circumferentor: a surveyor's compass.

circumstantial evidence: a "fact" which is assumed from known facts. It is not admissible in a court of law, but can be considered as a clue in historical research.

cistern: 1) an underground container for rain water collected from draining the eaves of a house by pipes to the cistern; 2) a word used for the container to hold the molasses in the sugar making process; 3) a bowl to hold water for washing.

citation: 1) an order issued by a court requiring a person to appear on a specific day; 2) a reference to the decision made in a previous court case; 3) a commendation by a military unit to one of its members for a special deed; 4) a listing of a specific author, title, publisher and copyright date in another book, article or a quotation from the original publication.

cite: 1) notification to a prospective defendant of the charges against him which will require him to appear in court; 2) a reference of a title, author, etc. of a book or article which has been used as a source for a statement.

citified: a colloquial term used by country folk to describe a person who had adopted some of the manners of city dwellers.

city directory: published annually as an aid to business establishments, these books list alphabetically the inhabitants of a town. Also listed are residents' addresses; street and house number. Early directories listed occupations of the inhabitants. Boarders were listed with a special abbreviation to distinguish them from family members. The directories are valuable sources for several facets of history and family history.

civ.: civil.

civic: citizen.

civil: 1) pertaining to citizens and their rights; 2) obsolete meanings are orderly, well-governed, refined, educated; 3) the commons area of a village; 4) a municipality; 5) non-military.

civil action: a lawsuit to protect the right of an individual or correct a wrong.

civil cases: lawsuits heard in a court designed to make decisions in small, not serious, cases.

civil condition: marital status.

civil court records: documents recording the legal business of individuals, e.g. probate records and suits.

civil law: the law descended from the Roman law, as opposed to law descended from English common law (which see).

civil township: a division of a county made by government for legal purposes.

Civil War: 1) the major war in the history of the U.S. Every age group from 14 years to 70 years was involved. It was fought from 1861 to 1865 and most of the battle grounds were in the South. It was a conflict between the Northern states of the U.S. and the seceding Southern states, extending from a variety of disputes of political, economical and social issues. A great destruction of property and records ensued. From 1861 to July 1, 1863 the draft for military personnel was controlled by each state. Therefore, records will be found among state records. After July 1, 1863 to 1866 the draft was controlled by the federal government and these records are located in the National Archives; 2) in England this name referred to the differences between Parliament and King Charles I during the seventeenth century.

C.J.: County Judge.

ck.: cook.

clabber: in the butter-making process this is cream which has soured or "turned," after the "blinky" stage, but not quite to the separation of liquid and solid stage.

clacker: a rattle to frighten away birds from a cornfield.

claim: 1) acreage in public lands for which a prospective settler has made application. Sometimes used to refer to a certain settler's home, for example: Johnson's Claim; 2) in mining, claim means the land staked out by a prospector searching for gold, silver, etc.

clamp: a tool used by a saddler.

clan: 1) people descended from a common ancestor; 2) used especially to mean a Scottish family.

clap: gonorrhea.

clapboard: long, thin pieces of wood which vary in thickness from one edge to another and are used to face or cover the outside of a house. Sometimes used in describing a roof or a shutter.

clapse: a device made of wood designed to hold a cow's head while she is being milked. Hobbles are used on her hind legs to keep her from putting her foot in the milk bucket. The end of her tail is caught in the hobbles to prevent her from switching her tail.

clarence: a four-wheeled, four-seated, enclosed carriage which had a glass front behind the driver's seat.

clatch: a brood of chickens.

clatterfert: a tale-teller.

claustrarius: locksmith.

claw hammer: a tool used by a carpenter, joiner, or farrier.

claw tool: a tool used by a stone mason.

cleaning off iron: a tool used by a chair maker.

clearance papers: documents issued by all ports where cargo was loaded or unloaded, and required to be kept on board the vessel.

clear title: ownership of land without liens or any other impediment to a fair, good sale.

cleaver: a tool used by 1) a basket maker; 2) a butcher.

cleaving breaks: a tool used by a hoop bender.

cleaving knife: a tool used by a basket maker.

cleft: 1) black slate; 2) timber fit for coopers' wares: spokes, etc.

cler., clr.: clerk.

cler: (Norman) clerk.

clerex, clerkus: (Norman) clerks, clergy.

clergeresse: (Norman) a learned woman.

clergyman: a church authority, usually the minister.

clerical survey records: in some areas Lutheran pastors kept detailed records of facts about his congregation, e.g. how well each person knew and understood Lutheran doctrine, how often each person attended communion, etc. When he made his annual visit to each family he also noted children born, deaths in the family, etc.

clericus: clergyman.

clerk: (pronounced as "clark" in England and certain areas of the United States) 1) the person in charge of a civil office; 2) a layman who holds a minor office in a religious group; 3) an ancient term for a clergyman; 4) a person who copies records; 5) a salesperson; 6) one who keeps accounts and answers letters; 7) the person who handled freight on a boat or ship, as well as passengers on board; 8) in the Quaker church, the clerk presides at a meeting for business or discipline and then formulates conclusions and decisions. After reading these conclusions they are approved by the meeting and he then writes them down as minutes in the record book; 9) a now obsolete term for a pupil.

clerk of the court: this person entered each order that the court made, read petitions, recorded animal identification (marks, brands, etc.), filed pleas, declarations, etc. When an action was appealed the clerk forwarded all papers to the higher court.

clerk of the crown: see clerk of the peace.

clerk of the market: this person's duties were to attend each market day to check weights, keep the premises clean, to enforce rules of the sale, open the market on market day by proclaiming aloud, "You may buy and sell," etc.

clerk of the peace: clerk of the peace and clerk of the crown were early offices whose duties were essentially the same as a clerk of the court in civil cases. Later, they were combined into one office: clerk of the court.

clevis: a U-shaped fastening device with a pin closing the open end of the U, used to allow the quick connecting or disconnecting of two articles. The tongue of a wagon with a hole drilled through it can be secured to the clevis by threading the pin through the holes.

clicker: the operator of a machine which cut shapes from leather, paper, cloth, etc.

clicker's awl: a tool used by a bootmaker.

climacteric: "change of life;" stopping of the reproductive period in a woman's life; menopause. It most often occurs between the ages of forty-four and forty-eight.

clime: (Norman) kindred.

clipper: a large, fast, sailing vessel built first at Baltimore. They had more sail area for their size than had previous ships.

clipperman: a sailor on a clipper ship.

clipping coins: Colonists would sometimes file a very small part of the edge from gold and silver coins. This was called "clipping" and resulted in merchants weighing the coins in order to determine their value.

clk.: clerk.

clob: some rough material used for building cottages.

clobber: a black filler used to hide cracks in leather boots or shoes.

clock-jack: a spring-wound clock works designed to turn a spit with roasting meat on it.

clod-hopper: 1) a farmer's laborer; 2) also, the shoes he wears when walking over rough ground.

clod-mall: a wooden hammer used for breaking clods of soil.

clog: 1) any mass of solid material; 2) the act of breaking lumps of land with a harrow; 3) a log for a fireplace; 4) a heavy wooden piece which was attached to the leg of a man or animal to prevent an escape.

clogger: 1) a person who makes the wooden soled shoes called clogs; 2) a tool used by a clogger; 3) a tool used by a boot maker.

clogger's tacking hammer: a tool used by a boot maker.

cloister: 1) a covered walk in a religious building; 2) a courtyard in a religious area, especially one that has covered walkways; 3) a quiet place; 4) secluded; 5) a monastery or convent.

cloom: clay or cement.

close: 1) a tract of land; 2) obscure lane; 3) farm yard; 4) enclosure of any kind; 5) public walk; 6) an entry or hall; 7) to put a jewel into place in its setting; 8) to finish; 9) to join together or agree.

close rolls: transcriptions of actions which have been closed or sealed.

close season: a Quaker term used to describe an event during which spiritual unity prevails.

close stool: see commode.

closh: Dutchman.

clothespeg: a clothespin used to hang wet clothes to dry on a line.

clothier: 1) a person who treats cloth by washing and pressing after weaving to take the oil out of wool, etc. His place of work is called a fulling mill; 2) the person who sells various types of cloth.

clothier general: the officer in the Continental and United States army who furnished the clothing for the non-commissioned officers and soldiers, now called a quartermaster general.

cloth rash: see rash.

cloth worker: a person engaged in the manufacture of cloth.

clotter: clothier.

clough: a ravine or valley which has steep sides and usually a stream running through it. See coomb.

clown: sometimes used to refer to a person who lived in the country; a rustic.

clr.: clerk.

clurs: (Norman) clerks.

cluster: people, animals, or like objects gathered together.

Clydesdale: a huge work horse, originating in Scotland.

clyster/glyster: an enema.

C.N.: a type of land sale in early Illinois, the land was sold to finance the Illinois and Michigan Canal.

cn.: census.

C.O.: 1) Colonial Office; 2) Commanding Officer; 3) Chief of Ordnance.

Co.: 1) County; 2) Company.

coach: an enclosed four-wheeled carriage. Inside the seats face each other with the driver's seat outside.

coachee: a pleasure carriage which resembled a surrey. It was lighter and longer than a coach, had a top, and seated four passengers.

coach lace: in the 18th century the interior of a coach was decorated with hand woven bands of lace. These were made of bright colors in addition to the more commonly used black, and had geometric, flower, or scroll designs. The introduction of the power loom ended this old craft, which had been imported from England. Earlier a coat of arms or an insignia suitable to the use of the coach was used as the design.

coachmaker: a maker of coaches.

co-administrator: a person who shares the responsibility of an administration with one or more other people.

coajer: a shoemaker.

coal: in 1810 charcoal was referred to as coal. Bituminous coal was called pitcoal. "To coal" was to make charcoal or to load coal pit coal on a steam ship.

coal heaver: a person who shoveled coal.

coal heuch: a coal pit.

coal oil lamp: a lamp designed in the mid-nineteenth century which burned coal oil (kerosene). It was replaced by electric lamps.

coaly: 1) a lamplighter; 2) a shoveler of coal.

coast guard rank: the same ranks as those used by the navy except that fleet admiral and admiral are not ranks in the coast guard.

Coast Guard, United States: the military traditions of this organization resemble those of the navy. In peace-time they enforce maritime safety and laws and operate under the Secretary of the Navy. Congress created the Coast Guard in 1790 as the Revenue Marine. Later it was called the Revenue Cutter Service.

coasting trade: trade carried on between towns which are located on the same coast.

coatee: originally a military coat that was tight fitting and short, and sometimes had as many as forty-four buttons.

cobbler: 1) a pie-like fruit dessert with a thick crust baked in a rectangular pan two to three inches deep; 2) a drink made of wine, sugar, fruit juice and crushed ice; 3) a maker of shoes.

Cobbler's Monday: any Monday.

coble, cobble, couble: 1) a ferry boat; 2) a flat-bottomed fresh water fishing boat.

cochen: the kitchen.

Cochranite: a participant in a religious movement in Maine begun in 1816 by Jacob Cochran. It apparently did not last very long and was confined to New England.

cock: a small heap of hay or dung.

cocket: 1) an official record issued by the customs office which certified that the duty on goods was paid; 2) a slightly inferior bread; 3) a joint used in buildings; 4) a seal of the King's custom-house.

cockey: a common sewer.

cockquean: 1) a beggar; 2) a cheat.

cock's comb: a tool used by a stone mason.

cocus: cook.

cod.: codicil.

cod: 1) a contemptuous word for a fool; 2) a kind of fish; 3) penis.

code: laws in effect on a certain date in a certain place, town, county, etc. These are usually compiled into a book for easy reference.

codicil: an addition to a will by which the will is altered, explained or added to, but is not wholly revoked. There is no limit to the number of codicils that can be added, as long as it is done properly. A will with the latest date always supercedes previous wills.

codman: a dealer in codfish.

coel: single, unmarried.

coelebs: bachelor.

coemeterium: cemetery.

coer: (Norman) commoner.

co-executor: a person named with one or more persons to distribute an estate as specified in a will.

coferer: a chest maker.

coffeehouse: an early restaurant.

coffer: 1) a box to hold valuables; 2) a treasury; 3) an ornamental sunken panel in a ceiling, etc.; 4) to deposit in a chest (coffer).

coffle: animals and/or humans fastened together in a chain.

cogmen: dealers in coarse cloth.

cognate: relationship on the mother's side.

cognati: blood relatives, especially when

the relationships are on the mother's side.

cognatus: persons who are related by blood, especially those from the mother's side.

cognomen: surname.

cohabitation: the act of living together as man and wife under the same roof.

cohabitation record: a record usually found in a county office which states the legal marital status of emancipated slaves. These records were made at the end of the Civil War.

co-heir: a joint heir. One who shares an inheritance with others.

co-heiress: a female who shares in an inheritance equally with another female.

coher: 1) reaper; 2) sell by auction.

coif: 1) a cap which fitted close to the head and was tied under the chin. It was worn by both men and women; 2) a head dress worn by a head churchman; 3) a white cap worn at one time by lawyers; 4) a leather cap worn under a helmet; 5) a cap worn by surgeons; 6) to arrange hair; 7) an obsolete form of cove (which see).

coillours: (Norman) collectors.

coistrel: 1) a person who cared for a knight's horses; 2) a groom; 3) a squire.

cojoints: owners of property, as husband and wife.

cojoint will: see joint will.

coke: charcoal made by heating coal without enough oxygen to allow it to burn.

Col.: Colonel.

cold catarrh: runny nose and/or redness around the eyes.

cold child: ague fit.

cold chisel: a tool used by a blacksmith.

cold plague: severe malaria.

cold set: a tool used by a blacksmith.

cold water: used in referring to one who did not drink. For example: the term of office of President Hayes was a cold water regime, for he allowed no spirits to be served in the White House.

colic, infantile: a condition where a baby appears to have pain in the abdominal area which usually disappears during the first six months of life.

collapse: a recession of the blood from the surface (fainting).

collarage: a tax imposed on the collars of horses who hauled wine to merchants.

collar maker: the craftsman who made only horse collars, a part of the craft of a saddler.

collar stuffing iron: a tool used by a saddler.

collar stuffing mallet: a tool used by a saddler.

collateral: 1) something of value to be used as security for a loan or other obligation; 2) belonging to the same ancestor, but not in the direct line, for example: aunts, uncles.

collateral heir: a person who receives property from a relative other than a direct relative (father, mother, etc.). For example, a brother who inherits from a brother would be a collateral heir as would a niece who inherits from an uncle. A son who inherits from his father is a direct heir. Direct heirs are preferred to collateral heirs (cousins, brothers, aunts, uncles, etc.) in lines of inheritance. A collateral heir would inherit only if no direct heirs could be found.

collateral record: a document which mentions a fact which was not the reason for which the record was made. For example, a deed which mentions a daughter for whom there is no birth certificate substantiates the birth of the daughter.

collector of customs: the officer who supervises the customs service at a port.

collector of rates: a town tax collector of which there were two types. One was responsible for the taxes levied upon each male citizen and upon land. The other was the collector of church taxes which were used primarily for the support of the minister. He was elected by the church and was not technically a town official. Both collectors were responsible for collecting special taxes levied for the repair and maintenance of meeting houses and public buildings. They also kept account books which were audited by the town or parish treasurer.

collier: 1) a man who makes wood into charcoal; 2) a coal miner; 3) a vessel for carrying coal.

colliery: a coal mine.

collodion plates: these negatives of pictures were produced on glass plates hand-coated with an emulsion. Usually these are recognized by a plain corner where the photographer held the glass while applying the emulsion.

collogue: 1) to band together, generally for an unlawful purpose; 2) to cheat; 3) to converse secretly.

collybist: 1) a money changer; 2) a lender of money; 3) a miser.

colonel: see army rank.

Colonial Court: the Proprietors and Nobility divided 2/5 of each county's land into four precincts. Then each of these precincts was divided into six colonies. Later the precinct courts became county courts; their duties stayed the same and only the name changed.

Colonial Dames of America: this society was founded in 1890 for descendants of those who arrived in the United States before 1750 and who performed some significant role in developing the nation.

colonus: settler, farmer, peasant.

colony: 1) a group of people who live apart from others; 2) a group of people from another land who live under the government of their home country.

color: when color is noted in a census or another listing, it does not necessarily refer to a person who is black. It could indicate a Chinese, an American Indian, an Italian, etc.

colorator: dyer.

color of title: an apparent land title which is not correct and therefore not valid.

colors: the silken banners or flags of each infantry regiment carried in battle, campaigns or on ceremonial occasions.

colporteur: a man who traveled around the country as a representative of the American Tract Society which published religious romances, Bibles, and other religious literature bearing titles like "The Lost Soul," "The Swearer's Prayer," etc. This high pressure salesman concentrated on isolated rural areas, thus adding to the limited amount of literature, other than the Bible found in a pioneer home.

colter: a plow share.

columbarium: a space approximately one foot square where ashes of deceased person may be buried.

Comanche Indians: this warlike tribe of Indians roamed from Texas to Wyoming to Mexico. After settling in Oklahoma, they became cattle raisers.

comb: 1) valley; 2) sharp ridge; 3) brewing vat; 4) mallet.

comber: a person who straightened wool for the spinning process.

combine: a harvesting process by a piece of machinery called a combine, which heads, threshes, then cleans grain, especially wheat.

combined force: armed forces (members of all military units of a nation) of two or more allied nations banding together against a common enemy.

com day: an abbreviation for company day (which see).

"come and get it" clause: a most common clause in a will that encourages a reluctant wife, sons, or daughters to join the head of the family during his lifetime, e.g. "provided son John comes into the province and makes use of it," "on condition that he shall come and reside on my plantations within seven years," "entire estate to brother Daniel's eldest son, but if he does not come then the entire estate is left to any of his children that shall first come."

comfit: a candy-covered nut or piece of fruit.

comforter: 1) a heavy, puffy, tied quilt; 2) a long wool knitted scarf to wind around a person's neck; 3) when capitalized, this mean the Holy Spirit; 4) in England this term means a pacifier.

com'tatus: county.

comm.: committee.

Comm.: Commissioner.

commandant: the commanding officer of a ship, fort, regiment, navy yard or station, etc.

commander: a tool used by a basket maker.

commander-in-chief: the President of the United States is the commander-in-chief of the army and navy, but an independent fleet or squadron may be commanded by a commander-in-chief when he is appointed as such by the Navy Department.

commandery: 1) a lodge, usually secret; 2) an area which is commanded by a military officer.

commissary: 1) a person representing the government who had certain duties to perform. For example: the Commissary of Indian Affairs; 2) a store where the items stocked were for use by people engaged in a particular kind of work such as mining, the armed forces, railroading, etc. The store usually was at the site of the business and was some distance from the nearest town.

commission: 1) an appointment of rank to officers in the armed forces; 2) authority to fill a government office.

commissioner: in Scotland a person who is elected to manage the business affairs of an unincorporated town.

commissioner of roads: persons appointed or elected to oversee the construction or maintenance of public roads.

commissioner of sinking fund: the person in charge of this special fund (which see).

commissioners: an elected county office of three men which usually met once a month. They had the duty of conducting the business of the county. Also men appointed to carry out a specific duty were called commissioners.

commissioners' books: sometimes called day books. These are the records of business conducted by a county kept by the commissioners. In these books can be found who were called to petit or grand jury duty, who worked on which road, where the roads went, who were granted licenses to sell, run taverns, etc. Many times these unindexed books will be the only reference to an ancestor's existence in a county.

commissioners' deed books: in Kentucky these books contain the deeds written by court appointed commissioners. These deeds were the result of land disputes which were settled by courts.

commissions of oyer and terminer: in Pennsylvania this court went to any county which asked for it, to hear cases formerly heard by the provincial court.

committee of correspondence: a group of persons appointed by towns or by the American Colony Assembly about 1772. These groups consulted with each other and were prepared to take immediate action against the British if deemed necessary.

committees: groups of citizens in frontier areas who banded together to perform the tasks of local government, e.g. law enforcement, vigilance for community emergencies, etc. Usually they were disbanded when their duties were finished and were replaced by governmental agencies.

commode: 1) a large piece of furniture which had drawers and shelves suitable for use in a bedroom or living room; 2) a chair which holds a chamberpot and sometimes called a close stool or night stool; 3) a high head ornament made of silk-covered wire that was fashionable in the seventeenth and eighteenth centuries.

commodore: the commander of a squadron of ships.

common ancestor: see ancestor in common.

commoner: 1) a person not of the nobility; 2) a person who has an interest in land held in common; 3) a student who paid for his own room and board; 4) a member of the English House of Commons; 5) a common lawyer.

common house: that part of a monastery in which a fire was kept constantly in winter for the monks to warm themselves.

common law: based upon English law, it is the most prevalent and useful type of law in the United States. It was built up over centuries by customs, judicial decisions and by Parliament without statutes. It is many times called "ordinary law."

common-law marriage: a mutual agreement between a man and a woman to live together as man and wife without a marriage ceremony, either civil or church.

common pleas: see court of common pleas.

commons: 1) an area held in common by a community which all may use, but none destroy. In New England a "commons" was a public park; 2) an obsolete term for pasture ground; 3) provisions; 4) English citizens, as opposed to the royal family and members of the nobility.
common school: a district school consisting of primary and secondary grades which is supported by public funds.
Commonwealth: a republic, nation or state governed by the people. The first constitutions of Kentucky, Pennsylvania, Massachusetts, and Virginia specified this form of government. Actually, all the United States govern themselves, but only the four listed above are so constituted.
commother: a godmother.
commotion: a concussion.
comms.: commission.
community property: land, goods, etc. owned together by both husband and wife as a type of partnership. In states who laws are based upon Spanish customs all land, goods, etc. obtained by either husband or wife during the time of their marriage is community property.
comnant: an obsolete spelling of covenant (which see).
comotion: concussion.
comoun: a town, township.
Comp.: Company.
compaigne: (Norman) wife.
company: two or more platoons under the command of a captain. It is also called at times a battery or troop and is part of a regiment or battalion.
company day: this term, found on lists of militia men, apparently referred to those who failed to appear on muster day for inspection.
company servant: a minister in the Jehovah's Witness Church who cares for the local congregation, which is called a company.
compas: a countess.
compasser: a tool used by 1) a stone mason; 2) a carpenter; 3) a blacksmith.
compatre: godparent.
compear: a Scottish law which obliges a person to appear in court or send his attorney to represent him.
comperte: narrative.
competent person: one capable of managing his own affairs.
compier: (Norman) a godfather.
compiled military service record: an envelope (jacket) which contains on cards, abstracts of an individual's service records and, at times, original documents which pertain to the service rendered. These records are in alphabetical order and are kept in the National Archives.
compl: complained of (which see).
complainant: the person who brings a legal action into court (plaintiff). Specifically, the person who files the action in an equity pleading.
complained of: found in Quaker records, this phrase indicates that someone stated that another member of the Quaker Church did something against the rules.
complaint: 1) a plaintiff's statement of facts as he sees them; 2) a formal charge against one or more people.
complimentary days: an extra day added to various months of the Revolutionary calendar, used during the French Republic after the revolution.
composition: an agreement between a debtor and his creditors to accept less money than the whole amount of the claim. This was to be distributed pro rata in discharge and satisfaction of the whole claim.
composition money: a sum of money, set by law, which was required to buy a warrant for land from the government.
compos mentis: of sound mind: a person in such a state of mind as to be qualified legally to sign a will, deed, etc.
comprizing bill: a summation of charges.
comprobate: proved.
compter: an English debtors' prison.
Comstock Lode: in 1859 in Nevada a miner held the rights to a huge silver deposit. Henry Comstock, or "Old Pancake" as he was known, sold these rights for virtually nothing. The silver petered out after 1880 leaving wealthy owners and bankers in San Francisco but not benefiting Virginia City, the settlement at the mine site.

comsy: commissary.

comyn: an obsolete spelling of common.

con: 1) against; 2) conduct; 3) see condemned.

concealers: an old term which referred to persons who hunted out land kept by people without titles, from the crown.

concern: 1) an estate; 2) a business.

concianator: preacher.

concord: 1) an agreement between people, nations, things; 2) a treaty.

concord coach: a vehicle manufactured in Concord, New Hampshire around 1820-30, braced with strong leather straps called thorough braces which acted more or less as springs. It held nine passengers, had a luggage rack on the top, a high driver's seat and was more commonly known as a stagecoach.

condemn: to proclaim the seizure of property for public use, under the right of eminent domain.

condemned: in Quaker records this word means that a member has made an acknowledgement that she/he did wrong. After due consideration, the monthly meeting will inform the person of the result of deliberation by those attending the monthly meeting.

conditio: 1) a variation of condicio. To settle, make an agreement, etc.; 2) to preserve fruit; 3) a seasoning.

conditional line: a boundary based upon an unofficial line.

conductor: 1) the person who had charge of the mail, gold, etc. on a stagecoach; 2) a person who aided in the escape of slaves during the Civil War on the Underground Railway.

condutcz: (Norman) lodgers.

conestable: an obsolete spelling of constable.

conestoga bonnet: this woman's cloth bonnet had a crown which resembled the lines of a conestoga wagon roof.

conestoga wagon, scoop wagon: a large, heavy, brightly painted covered wagon named for the Conestoga Valley in Pennsylvania where it was first built. It had broad wheels, and a roof consisting of a frame of wood which was covered with canvas. The ends curved upward at both the front and back ends to prevent loads from spilling out when it was pulled up and down hills.

Conf.: Confederate.

confectionery store: a shop where candy, ice cream and other sweets were sold.

confederacy: 1) a union between two or more people or groups of people to support a common cause; 2) a group of people who commit an illegal act; 3) states which banded together. Although the United States was originally a confederacy, the term is used more in speaking of the southern states during the Civil War.

Confederate States: the group of Southern states that seceded from the United States at the start of the Civil War.

confederation, articles of confederation: during the Revolutionary War, this was the agreement under which the American States united. It was replaced by the Constitution.

confessed judgment: this term is used when a debtor agrees to decision against him by a creditor.

confined: engaged as a laborer for one year to one master.

confinement: 1) in jail awaiting trial; 2) childbirth.

confiner: 1) a neighbor; 2) an inhabitant.

confirmation: a church rite, which after a series of lessons, allows a person to become a member of a particular denomination.

confiscation bill, the: this Bill, or Act, provided for the emancipation of slaves and the appropriation of property of those persons advocation the cause of the South during the Civil War.

confrontations: (Norman) borders.

congeable: done in a lawful manner.

congestive chills: the characteristic chills of malaria.

congestive fever: another name for malaria.

congius: an ancient Roman liquid measure of about eight-tenths of a gallon or 3.2 liters.

Congo: a type of tea.

Congregationalism: a principle of a religious organization in which each local church has complete independence in its affairs.

Congress lands: acreage sold in Ohio according to laws which were enacted by the Federal legislative branch. This land was surveyed into the township system of land division and was sold through the land offices established for this purpose.

Congs.: Congress.

coniunx: 1) spouse; 2) wife; 3) sometimes a husband.

conjectural passengers: persons on board a ship about whom few facts are actually known. Therefore, the notations about these passengers are only presumed to be correct.

conjoined: united or joined together.

conjoints: persons who have been legally married to each other.

conjoint will: a name used sometimes to mean a joint will. These wills were at one time used frequently by the Dutch in New York as the couple's children were protected better from the orphan masters.

conjunx: wife.

conjur doctor: see root doctor.

conjus: wife.

connected draft: a document which lists several tracts lying together and which enclose a limited area.

Connecticut Reserve–1786: Also called "New Connecticut," these three million plus acres in the northeast corner of Ohio were given to Connecticut as the result of a compromise in a land dispute between New York, Massachusetts, Virginia, and Connecticut.

conner: a log canoe found in the tidewater area of Virginia and on the east coast of Maryland.

consanguinity: relatives or blood relationship.

conscription: compulsory enrollment in military service in accordance with national laws which require citizens to serve in some branch of the armed forces. See draft.

consensual: formed by a mutual consent.

consent: to give approval, e.g. to allow underage children to marry.

conservator: a person appointed by the court to see that the income from, or sale of the holdings of another was used for the support of the owner. The appointment was made after the owner was adjudged incapable of managing his own affairs.

conservators pacis: a keeper of the peace.

conservatory: 1) a greenhouse; 2) a school of fine arts; 3) a safe place where objects were preserved.

consideration: the price or the motive which is mentioned in a contract to buy and sell property.

consesus: consent, agreement.

consistory: 1) a meeting place of a council or a court; 2) the meeting of a council or a court; 3) a council of deans.

consistory court: an English ecclesiastical probate court.

consobrina: female cousin.

consobrinus: male cousin.

consociation: a convention composed of the ministers and one layman from each church, sometimes called a council of churchmen.

consolidation fund: public income in England.

consort: "Jane, consort of William." Consort means companion, therefore this phrase means that William was living when Jane died. If William had died before Jane, the tombstone would have read: "Jane, relict (or widow) of William."

constable: an English term for a policeman which was used in the early United States. In addition to his regular police duties he was obliged to collect any taxes levied by the General Assembly. All these duties made the job undesirable. Penalties of heavy fines were imposed upon persons who chose not to accept the post. Colonial records show, however, that many men paid fines rather than serve as constable.

constables' watch: 1) a duty maintained much as policemen are now for protection; 2) the military watch used in case of war or threat of war.

constablewick: the area which a constable served.

constabularius: constable; warden.

constitute: 1) to appoint to an office; 2) to enact a new law.

constituted with prayer: found in the

Baptist church records, this term was used in such a way as to indicate that a church business meeting was opened with a prayer.

Constitution, the: 1) the document setting forth the principles of government for the United States written at Philadelphia, Pennsylvania in 1787; 2) a sailing vessel which achieved its fame during the War of 1812.

Constitutions of Clarendon: a series of sixteen articles written in England which stated the relationship between church and state. They were later enlarged to limit rights of clergymen.

construction: an interpretation of what a particular law means.

construction suits: usually brought into a chancery court, this suit seeks to clarify the technical meaning of legal terms used in a document. In this case a judge will try to determine what the author of the document intended.

consummate: finish; fulfill; complete.

consumption, consumptions: tuberculosis.

contd., contind.: continued.

contee (le): (Norman) the county court.

contest a will: an attempt by a person who has an interest by law in the estate of another. He seeks to say that the testator was 1) mentally incapable of making a will; 2) influenced unduly by someone else; 3) was tricked into signing a will or that the will was not properly executed. Thus, a will can be found in a circuit or chancery court as well as a probate court. The person who brings this suit into a circuit court must have a legal interest in the estate, e.g. he would receive from the estate if the will had not been written.

Continental: 1) a soldier (or his uniform) in the Continental Army; 2) an upholder of the American cause, as opposed to a Loyalist; 3) currency of paper notes issued by the authorization of the Continental Congress.

Continental Army: the army supported by the Continental Congress during the Revolutionary War.

Continental Line: these troops were organized first as state militia, then were placed under the Federal government and referred to as a Continental Line. State militia records are usually found in the state from which the militia served, and the federalized troops or Continental Line records are found in the Federal Archives.

contingent: rights which are dependant upon a future event taking place.

contingent estate: a property right that depends upon a certain event which may or may not occur in order for the right to be effective.

continuance: a postponement of a court case from one day to another, or one court term to another.

continuance docket: a book found in a courthouse which names the cases which have been continued from a previous session of court to a later date.

continuation: dismissed until a later date.

continuation schools: schools which provided classes after work hours for people who had quit school in order to work.

contl.: continental.

contr.: contraction.

contrabrand: a black former slave who found shelter with the United States government during the Civil War. The camps where the blacks were housed were referred to as contraband-camps.

contract: an agreement, verbal or written, between two or more people to do or not do a certain thing.

contract bond: a promise to pay money if another will lose money due to a breach of contract, e.g. if a contractor gave his bond that a building will be finished by a certain date and it is not and the owner will lose rent, then the contractor must pay.

contribution box: a long-handled wooden box (or sometimes a bag) passed along the pews of a church for the purpose of collecting money to pay the minister's salary, etc.

control document: any legal document which governs to what use public lands and resources are put. Also, any documented action which affects the ownership of public land and its resources.

conubium: marriage.

conversion: in old court records this means that one person is charged with stealing personal property from another.

converter: one who reduces rough lumber to small pieces; a sawyer.

convertible: something that can be exchanged for another of equal value.

convey: transfer ownership.

conveyance: a document which transfers real property rather than personal property. A building attached to the land becomes real property.

convince: 1) to change by argument, evidence, etc.; 2) an obsolete word for to find guilty; 3) an old word, meaning vanquish.

convocation: 1) people who have gathered together in answer to a summons; 2) clergymen who have appeared as part of a diocese or church unit; 3) a college assembly for graduation, welcoming new students, etc.

convoy: vehicles, or ships, which move in a group and are escorted for protection during travel time.

convulsions: a violent muscle spasm which many times accompany a high fever.

cooking irons: household cooking utensils consisting of a round fat pot with a lid, a heavy frying pan, and a deeper pan similar to what we call a dutch oven.

coomb: 1) an English measure of four imperial bushels, which is about 4.13 bushels in the United States; 2) a small cup, possibly a measure; 3) a ravine or hollow valley, sometimes called a clough.

coonskin cap: plainsmen or hunters wore these caps which were round in shape, made of the skin or skins of a raccoon, with the animal's tail hanging from the back of the cap.

cooper: a person who made casks, barrels, wash tubs, pails, butter churns, and other wooden vessels. A "dry cooper" made cheap containers which would not hold liquids.

cooper's block: a tool used by a cooper.

cooper's stake: see bick iron.

cop: 1) mound or bank; 2) heap of anything; 3) enclosure with a ditch around it; 4) top, summit; 5) a fence.

coparcenary: joint inheritance. A property right held by two or more heirs of a common ancestor, usually children. Sometimes these children are referred to as parceners.

coparceners: persons who have an inheritance which has come to them jointly and who hold it as an entire estate.

copeman: 1) a buyer; 2) a peddler; 3) a merchant; 4) one who receives goods which have been stolen.

coper: an Englishman who buys and sells horses. Also called a horse coper.

coping: a tool of several shapes used by a brick maker.

copist: used in early English as a variant of copyist.

copperheads: during the Civil War, a group of Southern sympathizers were people from Northern states. They were called copperheads and actually inflicted military chaos during the Civil War upon this country. Records of Southern sympathizers from Southern portions of Northern states may be found military records. Sometimes they were referred to as Peace Democrats.

copperplate: 1) a style of handwriting, very precise, very beautiful and sometimes quite ornate; 2) a fabric very fashionable during the eighteenth and early nineteenth centuries. This material was so closely woven that patterns, landscapes, etc. could be printed on it from engraved copper plates, hence the name.

coppers: 1) a ship's cooking utensils, which are usually made of iron or copper; 2) an English penny.

coppersmith: 1) a person who works with copper; 2) a person who makes utensils from copper.

copyhold: a right to occupy and enjoy land according to the custom of an English manor. The people were listed on a roll of records in the manorial court.

copyholder: a peasant who owned no stock and who was bound to hard work. He was not a freeman.

copyyoke: cop, as part of a word, usually means "top." Therefore, the top of a yoke.

coqueluche: whooping cough.
cor.: cornet.
coracle: a simple, bowl-shaped fishing boat without a keel, which can be carried quite easily by one man.
coram me: 1) "before me." A preposition used in Latin phrases; 2) sometimes used with a signature to a document; 3) at times used by mistake for quorum; 4) obsolete form of currant (dried fruit).
coram nobis: "before us ourselves," e.g. a "writ of error coram nobis" is based on the fact that there was an error in the proceedings of the court. The writ asks for a review of the decision by the same court who issued it.
corarius: currier.
cord: 1) a cord of wood eight feet by four feet by four feet; 2) also a stack of wood.
cord (de la): (Norman) 1) the agreement; 2) consent.
corded: corduroy.
corded bed: see rope bed.
corder: the Colonial town official whose job was to pile saleable wood into standard-sized cords.
cordewaners (de): (Norman) leather, etc.
cordial: 1) a medicine designed to stimulate the heart; 2) a strong, sweet liqueur; 3) an old word used when speaking of the heart; 4) sincere; 5) friendly.
cordiner: (Norman): a shoemaker.
Cordon Bleus: children of a relationship between a black woman and a Frenchman. These children were usually wealthy enough to have been educated in France, but were not accepted by either black or white society.
cordone: an honorary award given to a successful combatant.
corduroy road, bang-up road, ribbed road: a rough road built across swampy or muddy areas by laying branchless tree trunks side by side across the road. The trunks were often close together, but in some areas they would be several inches apart. Small bridges were also made of these trees with the bark still on.
cordwain: leather. The first leather was made from goat skins; later, of horse or cow hides.
cordwainer: shoemaker, now only a guild name.
cordwinder: a folk term for cordwainer or shoemaker.
coresur: a courier.
corf: 1) a large basket; 2) coal; 3) fish.
coriarius: tanner.
cormorant: a servant.
corn: 1) any small grain: barley, wheat, etc. See also maize; 2) a grain of salt, e.g. corned beef salted; 3) oats.
cornage: a tenure which obliges the landholder to give notice of an invasion by blowing a horn. The rent was determined by the number of horned animals a man owned. One out of each ten was reserved for the landlord.
corn chandler: a person who sells corn and related products in his store.
corn cracker mill: a mill which did no more than crush the grain and left the work separating the flour from the meal (bolting) to be done with a hand sieve.
corn crib: see crib.
corneser: (Norman) a maker of horns.
cornet: 1) from the Italian cornetta (small flag). In the Colonial army it was the lowest of commissioned officers in the cavalry. The duty of a cornet was to carry the flag. The rank no longer exists; 2) a commissioned British cavalry officer who served as a standard bearer.
cornhusking: in the fall of the year at harvest time neighbors would gather together to husk (remove the fibrous layer from) corn. It was a social gathering as well, with fiddles playing lively music for a dance at the end of the husking.
cornhusk rope: the husks of ears of corn, braided together to form a rope.
cornlaiters: newly married peasants who beg corn with which to sow their first crop.
corody: a sum of money or an allowance of food and clothing allowed by an abbot to the king for the maintenance of any one of his servants. It could be purchased on a plan similar to an annuity.
coronel: a colonel.
coroner: the duties of this person consist of investigating deaths of all persons not

under the care of a physician, or who appear to have died under peculiar circumstances.

coroner's jury: citizens who officially inquire into a death thought to be not of natural causes. The coroner presides over the inquiry.

corpl.: corporal.

corporal: see army rank.

corporeal property: property which can be seen, for example, a house, as opposed to incorporeal, which cannot be seen, for example, life interest in a house.

corporeal hereditaments: tangible property which is inheritable.

corps: 1) a body of troops under one commander; 2) troops which are a part or division of the army; e.g. corps of engineers.

corpse viewer: a coroner.

corpus, corporis: a body.

Corpus Christi: a festival occurring on the Thursday after Trinity Sunday which honors the Eucharist.

correction house: a type of jail for minor criminals, especially young ones.

corregidor: 1) a chief magistrate of a Spanish town; 2) in Spanish America this is a minor administrative district or the chief officer of this district.

correours: (Norman) curriers.

corretier: a horse dealer.

corridale: a breed of sheep which originated in New Zealand.

corruption: an old term for an infection.

corruption of blood: when a criminal is sentenced to die, his property rights are forfeited and he cannot inherit property, nor can he bring a suit against anyone. The declaration of forfeiture was called attainder or corruption of blood.

corse: a corpse.

corse present: 1) (Norman) a mortuary; 2) a gift due a clergyman from an estate at the owner's death.

corsere: 1) a horseman; 2) a war-horse; 3) sometimes a horse dealer.

corsetiere: a person who makes, fits, sells, and repairs foundation garments for women.

corspresant: a mortuary .

corve: about one-eighth of a ton of coal.

corvisor: shoemaker.

coryar: a currier.

cos.: 1) counties; 2) companies.

cosces: (Norman) husbandman.

cosher: to live with relatives, without charge for rent, food, etc.

cosier: cobbler.

cosin: 1) a cobbler; 2) kinsman.

cosinage: kindred.

cost: 1) loss; 2) risk; 3) a dead body.

coste (en), coste de coste: (Norman) collateral.

coster: see costermonger.

co-state: a state affiliated or connected with other states in the Federal Union.

costermonger: a person who sells fruit and vegetables from a cart on the street.

costiveness: constipation.

costyfhed: see costiveness.

cot: 1) a small house; 2) a pen for cattle; 3) a shelter for sheep; 4) felted wool; 5) an Irish dug-out boat; 6) a lightweight portable bed; 7) a child's crib; 8) a male house-worker, sometimes called a betty; 9) to live with another in the same house.

cot-betty: see cot 8).

cote hole: usually an animal shelter.

coteller: the second person who helps to count votes in the House of Commons.

cotellers: (Norman) cutlers.

cotenancy: joint ownership of land of which there are four kinds: community property, tenancy by the entirety; joint tenancy; tenancy in common.

coterie: a group, sometimes exclusive, who work together closely.

coteret: a fagot.

cotiers: (Norman) cottagers.

cotquean: a housewife.

cotrelle: a cottager.

cotsetta: a cottager (which see).

cotswold: a breed of sheep which originated in England.

cottage industry: 1) production of goods by people in their homes rather than in a factory; 2) a small business conducted from a person's home.

cottager: 1) a farm laborer; 2) a person who owns or rents a small house at a resort; 3) a person who lived in a small house in a rural area and paid rent, usually by work instead of money.

cotter: in early England this person farmed a very small amount of land and worked part-time for the lord, sometimes as a servant.
Also called a cottager.
cotterils: money.
cottonade: a fabric, which frequently looks like wool but is cotton or a mix of fibers, that is heavy and coarse and is suitable for work clothes.
cotton domestic: see domestic.
cotton factor: see factor.
cotton flatboats: these were light, high-sided boats which carried bales of cotton down the rivers to the seaports. Upon arrival, after unloading, they would be dismantled and sold for lumber.
cotton lord: a person who was prominent in the field of raising, buying, or selling cotton. This term usually was used to indicate a man who made a lot of money dealing in cotton.
cotton spinner: 1) a person who spun cotton into thread; 2) a cotton mill owner.
cou., cous., csn.: cousin.
coulee: a small creek, the bed of which may be dry in the summer, but flooded during the spring of the year or other wet seasons.
coulter: the sharp, knife-like portion of a simple plow which cut the soil ahead of the share, which in turn made the deep row and threw the soil on to a wooden moldboard which turned the dirt over and pushed it to one side.
councillor: 1) a member of a Colonial town council; 2) a member of the council of a city, district, etc.; 3) not an alderman.
counselor: a lawyer.
count: 1) a member of the European noble family. His rank is equal to that of an Earl in England; 2) in old days this was the sum of some money or of goods; 3) a way of measuring yarn involving how many hanks, balls, etc. there are in a pound; 4) in a woven piece of cloth this is the number of threads per inch, both vertical and horizontal; 5) the point in a case tried before a court "he is guilty on three counts."
counter jumper: a salesperson in a store.
counterpane: this was a woven cotton bedcover or bedspread. The word is a corruption of "counterpoint" which refers to the patterns of squares which were used in these spreads.
counter stick: a tool used by a boot maker.
Countess: 1) the wife or widow of a nobleman on the continent who holds the rank of Count; 2) a woman who is entitled to hold a rank equal to that of an Earl or a Count; 3) see also Earl.
counting house: a bank.
countre rouler: (Norman) controller.
country: sometimes used to mean a county.
country pay: a barter method which was used in rural areas to purchase goods at a store, pay the preacher's salary, etc. with products grown or made at home instead of using cash which was a rare thing for a person to possess.
country side: a tract or district.
country squire: 1) a wealthy man who lives on a large farm; 2) a person whose income comes from agriculture; 3) see also squire.
country store: a large building which housed the post office, displayed curios, contained a supply of herbal medicines and drugs, groceries, liquor (primarily whiskey), cloth by the yard and sewing supplies, hardware, household supplies and, of course, neighborhood gossip.
county: 1) a count; 2) a nobleman; 3) a division of a state.
county agent: a person appointed by a state to aid, advise, and promote agriculture within a county.
county atlases: see cadastral maps.
county clerk: an official who performs the duties of a clerk of a county court, or secretary of the county board.
county commissioner: an officer of the county who is elected to oversee the affairs of a county, especially the roads. Not all states have this officer.
county court: this court was a step higher than a precinct court. The sheriff served as judge until 1694 when the office of provost marshall was introduced.
county directories: similar to city directories, these books listed rural residents

of a county. Some named family members and their ages, acres owned or rented, etc.

county history: a book comprised of a fairly detailed account of the county from its beginning to the date of writing. Many times there would be a biographical section which included many of the leading citizens of the county. These books were many times subscribed to in advance, primarily by those whose biographies were included. Sometimes there would be a general history of the state written by one person. The county history section was written by a local citizen and at least the facts of citizens' lives were given by themselves. These books have many truths in them, but are not considered a primary source.

county home: a poorhouse supported by a county. Sometimes called a county house.

county line: a boundary of a county. Sometimes a road will run along the county line which divides two counties and thus will earn the name of "county-line road."

county palatine: the territory governed by a person who enjoys royal privileges. See also palatine.

county recorder: see recorder.

county seat: a town, usually close to the middle of a county, where the courthouse is located.

coup: (Norman) damage.

coupe: 1) poultry coop; 2) basket; 3) vat; 4) cup; 5) ice cream topped with fruit, liqueur, etc. which is served in a stemmed dish of the same name; 6) a closed, four-wheeled carriage which carried two passengers. The driver had an outside seat.

couranteer: an obsolete word for a journalist.

coureur: (French) a runner. (Coureur de bois referred to men who hunted, traded with Indians, lived in the wilderness for long periods of time, etc.).

courier: a person who carries a message from one person to another.

courser man: groom.

courses: compass directions.

courses and distances: in the metes and bounds method of surveying, the compass directions are the courses and lengths are the distances used to describe the land.

court: 1) principal house in a village; 2) the yard to a house, also called a courtain.

court baron: an English manorial court which dealt with the manor tenants and their real property.

court calendar: see docket.

Court Christian: a church court.

court docket: see docket.

courtelage: 1) a garden; 2) a courtyard.

courtesey: see curtesy.

courthouse: a large public building where the business of the county is conducted. This building also houses the records created over the years from the beginning of the county.

court journal: see court minutes.

court keeper: a master at the game of racket or ball.

courtledge: see curtilage.

court leet: an English court similar to our petit court which was later replaced by the quarter sessions.

courtlet: a small court.

courtlodge: a manor house.

courtman: courtier.

court martial: officers (army, navy, etc.) appointed to conduct the trial of persons alleged to have committed a crime under military or naval laws.

court minute books: see court minutes.

court minutes: in some states a variety of records will be found in these books which contain the daily record of matters which came before the court. For example, licenses of various types, guardianships, some items usually found in a probate court, depositions for federal pensions.

Court of Assistants: In Colonial Connecticut this court replaced the Particular Court. It dealt with civil and criminal cases and probate actions. Later this court became the quarter or county court.

Court of Assize, Oyer and Terminer: this court met two times a year as an extension of the general court, thus bringing it closer to the people it served.

Court of Chancery: see chancery court.

Court of Chivalry: an old English court.

Court of Common Pleas: a court which heard cases between common folk, in contrast to a court which heard cases which involved the government. Sometimes cases were heard by a different court for no particular reason other than a judge was present and his docket was not full. All cases except those brought by the king were held in this court.

Court of Errors: This was the highest court in the state of New York from 1784 to 1846, when it was abolished. It heard cases appealed from the state supreme court, chancery court, etc. Its records are held by the New York State Archives and Records Administration.

Court of Exchequer: an old civil court, which merged with another court, where cases which could affect the King's income were tried.

Court of Guard: place where the guard gathers together.

Court of Hustings: 1) a court held in some Virginia cities; 2) a court held before the lord mayor and other high-ranking officials.

Court of King's or Queen's Bench: this was the highest court in England which handled common law cases. It later became a division of the High Court of Justice.

Court of Last Resort: the highest court in England; a court which puts an end to further appeals.

Court of Lodgings: principal quadrangle in a palace or large house.

Court of Ordinary: a probate court.

Court of Orphans: an English court which handled cases of orphans whose parents died in London and were free of the city.

Court of Piepowder: the lowest court of justice in England held at a fair to hear minor cases occurring during the fair.

Court of Probate: see probate court.

Court of Probate (New York): this court was established in 1797 and abolished in 1823. It was a state court created by law and is located in Albany, New York. The records are kept in the office of the clerk of the court of appeals.

Court of Quarter Sessions: suits brought by the king were heard in this court.

Court of Sessions: Scotland's highest civil court.

Court of the Admiral: see Admiralty Court.

Court of the Ordinary: in some states this is the court which handles probate business.

court records: a little-used, but most useful source of records about a county's citizens. These are the records of court proceedings.

court roll: a manorial record which consisted of entries such as rent, holdings, deaths, tenant successions, etc.

court roller: the writer or keeper of the rolls of a court of law.

Courts of Pleas and Quarter Sessions: these county courts existed in some states from Colonial times until the middle 1800s. They met quarterly with the Pleas portion considering minor civil actions and the Quarter Sessions considering criminal matters which were not punishable by loss of life. These courts also oversaw public roads, licensing, etc. as handled by county commissioners in some states.

court week: at one time judges traveled a circuit much like that of a preacher. When court was in session a general relaxation of routine occurred and an almost party-like mood existed.

cous.: cousin.

cousin: 1) child of a sibling; 2) sometimes used to indicate a relationship by marriage rather than blood; 3) in early New England it can mean a niece or nephew; 4) sometimes used to refer to a close friend; 5) used to refer to someone who is kin, but the exact relationship is unknown.

cousin german: first cousin.

cousinhood: an association of cousins or kinfolk. A group of cousins is called a cousinry.

cousin red: the relationship of cousins.

cove: 1) the meadow or low land next to an inlet, sometimes quite swampy; 2) the inlet itself; 3) a strip of grassland penetrating the edge of a forest; 4) a small inner or bedroom; 5) a bay, inlet or creek along a coast where boats can seek shelter; 6) a sheltered spot in woods or hills; 7) a peddler; 8) an arch.

covenant: 1) a valid agreement or pact; 2) conditional promises of God to man; 3) a reason for a court action to recover monetary damages.

covenantor: the person who fulfills the promise contained in a covenant.

coventure: a cooperative venture which is ended when the project is finished.

covered bridge: a bridge with a roof and sides to protect the flooring from the weather. Many were toll bridges which was a fair practice considering the amount of money involved in the building of the bridge and toll gate.

coverlid: a woven bedspread, sometimes called a coverlet.

covernour: governor.

covert: married.

coverture: legal status of a woman while she is married.

cowble: see coble.

cowboy: 1) at the time of the Revolutionary War groups of men functioned between the American and British lines plundering and killing. These shameless men earned the derogatory title of cowboys or skinners; 2) an employee of a ranch who, riding horseback, drove cattle into a corral or along a trail.

cow calf: female calf.

cow catcher: a sturdy, sloped frame on the front of a locomotive which was designed to push aside cows or other large objects from the railroad tracks.

cow clap: cow dung.

cow clatting: spreading manure on the fields.

cow common: in the Colonial days a piece of public land would be set aside to allow cows, sheep, etc. to graze. A share in a cow common would be sufficient to keep one cow, or eight sheep. One horse required two cows' commons as did sixteen sheep.

cowdy: a small cow.

cow ground: pasture.

cowherd: a cow keeper.

cow jockey: a dealer in animals.

cowkeeper: 1) a person hired to watch and move, as necessary, the town herd, composed of cows which belonged to the area farmers; 2) a person who owns or works in a dairy. One who tends cows.

cowl: a monk's hooded garment or a scarf draped to look like a hood.

cowltes: quilts.

cowpenning, cowpenned: after land was cleared of trees, bushes, etc. it was common to enrich the ground with manure by using moveable fences to pen in cows.

cowpoke: see cow puncher.

cow puncher: a man whose job was to poke cattle with poles to make them move into cattle cars and also keep them from lying down so more could be loaded into the railroad car.

cowshard: cow dung.

Coxey's Army: a United States political reformer led a group of out-of-work men from Ohio to Washington, D.C. This group of men was called Coxey's Army for their leader, Jacob Coxey. They wanted Congress to pass legislation creating jobs and thus relieve poverty.

coxswain: pronounced kahk'sun. An enlisted man in charge of a small boat carried by a larger ship

coyre, coure: (Norman) copper, brass.

coz: a familiar term for cousin.

C.P.: 1) abbreviation for a Catholic Priest. It is found in county books of marriages after the name of the man who performed the marriage ceremony; 2) also an abbreviation for court of common pleas; 3) abbreviation for Circuit Preacher.

cpl.: corporal.

cr.: abbreviation for creek.

cracker: 1) a lawless frontiersman and boaster, which later came to mean a "poor white" in some southern states; 2) the driver who cracked the whip to move the horses pulling wagons of freight.

cracklings: the browned residue that results when fat meat (usually pork) is heated to extract lard.

craftiman: an artificer.

craftsman: one skilled in making all or a portion of a product. These craftsmen fall into three groups: 1) those who work in their own ship and sell the product at the shop; 2) those who work near the source of their supply of raw material and are forced to move on as the supply is exhausted; 3) those who work on the site of the person who hires them and are referred to as travelers.

cramer: a tinker.

cramp colic: 1) appendicitis; 2) typhlitis.

cramp iron: quick-acting iron clamps used to hold material in place while work was performed or while glue set, etc.

crash: linen fabric used to make towels.

cratch: see crib.

crateman: itinerant vendors of earthenware.

creacures, creansours: (Norman) those who were creditors.

creamer: one who has a stall in a market or fair.

creauncer: a creditor. Another spelling for creacures, creansours.

creaunser: a tutor.

crebulle: cripple.

credit entry final certificate: the document given to a purchaser of land from the federal government upon completion of their payments.

credit land sales: acreage in the public domain sold by the United States in a credit plan. Many times the records of these sales will show the county and state where the purchaser lived when he made his first payment. Thus a migration pattern is proved.

creed: 1) a statement of religious faith; 2) a summary of the beliefs of a church.

creek: 1) originally a tributary to a larger body of water, it can be described as a stream smaller than a river, but larger than a brook; 2) servant.

Creek Indians: a large, powerful tribe who lived in Georgia and Alabama until they moved west of the Mississippi River. During the Colonial period this tribe allied themselves with the British and fought against the United States in the War of 1812. They settled in the Indian Territory (Oklahoma) where they became one of the Five Civilized Tribes.

creel: 1) wicker basket; 2) butcher's stool.

creep hedge: vagrant.

Creole: 1) a person of mixed parentage; 2) in Louisiana one descended from the French or Spanish settlers; 3) a black born in the United States as opposed to an African born black; 4) in Alaska, a person born of native Indian and Russian parents.

cresset: 1) a tool used by a cooper; 2) an early light or beacon made from a resin-soaked rope, oil suspended from above, or attached to a pole

cretonne: a heavy cotton fabric which had a bright, colorful pattern and was used as a drapery or upholstery fabric.

crew: the group of men necessary for efficient operation of a ship, vehicle or wagon.

crew's lists: a roster of crew members which will give names, ages, etc. and at times a description of their physical appearances. Reasons for any change such as death, illness, transfer to another ship, etc. are added.

crib: a well ventilated (by slats or holes) barnyard structure used to store corn. Sometimes called a cratch.

cricker: 1) a collier's horse; 2) a man who carries heavy loads on a horse.

crier, cryer: 1) the instructions and orders of a court; 2) the person hired to make public announcements in a strident voice, a town crier; 3) see also auctioneer.

crieynges: prayers.

criminal courts: sessions before a judge where public offenders are tried and the case decided.

crimp tool: a tool used by a blacksmith who made decorative wrought iron.

cristendom: baptism.

cristing: baptism.

crk: creek.

crocheteur: a porter.

croft: 1) enclosed pasture or field; 2) small parcel of land farmed by a tenant; 3) small farm in Scotland worked by a peasant; 4) a crypt or vault; 5) to spread cloth on grass to be bleached by the sun.

crooked axe: tool used by a spoon carver.

crooked knife: a tool used by a spoon carver.

crone: an old ewe (female sheep).

cropper: 1) a machine that cuts cloth; 2) a

person who raises a crop of anything; a farmer. When a person plows, plants, reaps, etc. for another and is paid by sharing in that crop, he is called a sharecropper.

crop sick: a stomach ache as a result of overeating and drinking.

cross bow: a medieval bow to shoot arrows, stones, etc.

crossing sweepers: children who worked in groups to clear streets of horse manure.

cross saw, cross-cut saw, thwart saw: 1) a saw designed to cut across the grain of the wood, it became the saw most commonly used to fell trees; 2) a tool used by a chair bodger; 3) a tool used by a carpenter.

crote: a clod of earth.

crouche: 1) a piece of money; 2) to sign with the cross.

crouchmas: Christmas.

croup: a congestive condition in which spasms cause breathing to be very difficult and almost suffocating.

crowbarrow: wheelbarrow.

crowcoal: inferior coal.

crown: 1) a coin made of silver and minted in the United Kingdom; 2) a unit of money in the Scandinavian countries.

(the) Crown: the name of the Sovereign, the English King or Queen. This is used instead of using the title and name, e.g. the Crown granted land to ...

crowner: a coroner.

crownet: a coronet.

croze: a tool used by a cooper.

crspd.: correspond; correspondence.

cruciar: a crucifier.

cruive, cruve: a fish trap placed in a river.

cruller: one of a variety of sweet cakes made from a rich egg batter in different shapes, which then were fried in deep fat.

crundles: swellings caused by scurvy.

crupel: a cripple.

crusado: a Portuguese coin, minted originally from gold and later from silver.

cryer: see town crier.

crypt: a vault under the floor of a church where bodies of important persons are buried.

c.s.: copy signed.

C.S.A.: Confederate States of America.

C.S.C.: Clerk of Superior Court.

csn.: cousin.

ct.: citation; court.

c.t.a.: cum testamento annexo (which see).

cucking stove: a form of punishment used in early days. It was a chair, into which the offender was securely strapped. Then fellow citizens could pelt him with objects, call him names, or duck him into water.

cuckold: a man whose wife is unfaithful to him. The name comes from a cuckoo's custom of laying eggs in another bird's nest.

cudgel: a tool used by a wattle hurdle maker.

cuers: (Norman) leather, skins.

cui bono: for what good?.

cuinse: to carve a wild bird called a plover.

cuirbouly: tanned leather.

cuis susceptores: godparents.

culiours: (Norman) collectors.

cull: to separate the poorest or smallest from the best of a product. The less desirable items removed are called culls. The person who sorts items to select the best or to reject the worst is called a culler.

culler of hoops and staves: see sizer of pipe staves.

cullers of fish: a Colonial office. The holder of this office selected or gathered fish.

cultellarius: cutler.

culter, cultor: farmer or farm laborer.

cum: with or when.

Cumberland Gap: a passage through the Appalachian Mountains to the Cumberland River.

cum onere: subject to an impediment of which the purchaser is aware. For example, a lien.

cum testamento annexo: an administration of an estate where there was a will but no executor was named, and the will was attached.

cuntrere: a country.

cunty: countess.

cupalo: smelting house.

cupping: 1) a method of drawing blood; 2) a drinking binge; 3) a tavern.
cupre (de): (Norman) of copper.
cuprifaber: coppersmith.
curate: 1) a clergyman who has been hired to assist a vicar or a rector; 2) any clergyman who cares for a parish congregation.
curation: a guardianship.
curator: 1) guardian; 2) a person who has been named to act as an administrator of an intestate estate until the court appoints an administrator.
curator ad hoc: a special guardian for one specific purpose.
curb: see wheel hoop.
cure: 1) to restore health; 2) to preserve meat by smoking it, salting it, etc.; 3) a religious charge of all the people in a particular district; 4) an office or district of a curate; 5) a parish priest in France.
cure-all: a remedy or healing compound which had the reputation of curing all diseases.
curer: a person whose job is to cure fish.
curfew: an evening bell rung to tell people to put out their fires. It was a method of fire control.
curia regis rolls: the schedule of proceedings of the English King's court.
curretter: 1) a canvasser; 2) a broker.
currency, preferred: in Colonial days corn in New England or hemp in Virginia and beaver in New Netherlands (New York) were more valuable than many types of coinage.
curreye: wagon train.
curricle: a two-wheeled lightweight carriage drawn by a team of horses, side-by-side.
currier: the craftsman whose work begins where a tanner's stops and who makes the tanned animal skins highly polished and more supple.
currier's knife: a tool used by 1) a tanner; 2) a currier.
currifex: cartwright.
cursen: to christen.
cursenmas: Christmas.
cursetor: vagabond or vagrant.
cursitor baron: a junior court officer who attended to matters of revenue. In the middle 1850s this office was abolished.
cursor: messenger.
curtesy, courtesey: interest which a husband has in the property of his deceased wife. A husband's counterpart of a wife's dower. The dower applies to one-third whereas the curtesy applies to all land owned by a wife which the husband takes if the wife has not disposed of it otherwise. This differs from state to state.
curtilage: the ground and outbuildings which surround a house.
curtle-ax: a cutlass.
curz: (Norman) courts.
cus.: course.
cushies: armor for a man's thighs.
cushion lord: a lord made by favor, not for good service.
cushion man: chairman.
cushion thumper: a Methodist preacher.
custode: an obsolete word which has recently come into use again. It means a person who has custody of anything; a custodian.
customal: collection of customs.
customer: 1) an obsolete word for a customs official who collects duty on goods; 2) a companion; 3) an obsolete word for a prostitute; 4) a person who has ownership by long possession or use.
customs: the fee paid by merchants for goods imported from other lands. Sometimes called duty.
customshouse: a government office in a port city where duty is collected.
cut: 1) a measure of linen yarn equalling three hundred yards; 2) canal; 3) skein of yarn; 4) door latch.
cut meat: hay, fodder.
cutpurse: a thief; pickpocket. In early days this person actually cut a purse from the belt where it hung.
cut up well: to die rich.
cutlass: a short, heavy naval sword.
cutler: one who makes and sharpens knives, scissors, and other cutting tools.
cut money: similar to bits, except that a silver dollar was used. This was quite common practice in the western states.
cutter: 1) a light sleigh with iron runners, usually pulled by one horse; 2) an apparatus used to slow a wagon going

down a hill; 3) beef from an animal of a poor grade; 4) in the navy this refers to a boat pulled by ten oarsmen or a single-masted, sharp-built ship. However, in the coast guard this term refers to a ship of more than sixty-five feet in length; 5) robber; 6) ruffian; 7) engraver.

cutting box: a mitre box.

cutting nipper: a tool used by a boot maker.

cut throat: highway robber.

cuz: contraction of cousin.

cv.: caveat.

C.W.: 1) Church Warden; 2) Civil War.

cwith: a will or testament.

cwt: abbreviation for hundred weight.

cyanosis: a bluish tinge to the skin due to a lack of oxygen.

cyanotype: a photographic process which produces a drawing such as those which architects use; a blueprint.

cymytere: (Norman) a churchyard.

cynanche: a severe sore throat.

cy pres: "as nearly as possible." When a gift or trust is impossible to administer as the testator desired, this statute will allow the administrator to act as closely as possible in agreement with the testator's wishes.

cystitis: an inflammation of the bladder.

D: 1) the letter D in Colonial New England stood for Drunkard and, as was the custom, the convicted person was made to wear the letter stitched to his clothing. Many times he could no longer hold a public office, and could be whipped or made to serve in a work gang; 2) Dominus (The Lord); 3) deputy; 4) Roman numeral for five hundred.

d.: 1) decessit (died); 2) dies (day); 3) died; 4) dominus; 5) symbol for pence, an English coin; 6) used to indicate the size of nails; 7) demi, one-half.

da.: daughter.

D.A.B.: Dictionary of American Biography.

D.A.C.: Daughters of the American Colonists.

dafter: a daughter.

dagger: 1) a two-edged, sharp-pointed weapon which looks like, but is shorter than, a sword and is used in close contact fighting; 2) the name given to any board which lies in a diagonal position in a sailing vessel.

daguerreotype: an early method of printing pictures on metal developed by a French inventor whose name was Daguerre.

Dahlgren: an improved cannon invented in 1856 by Lt. J. A. Dahlgren. It had a smooth bore and was somewhat bottle shaped.

daie: to die.

dairer: a dairy man.

dairy house: 1) the building used for milking cows; 2) the house where a person engaged in dairy farming lives.

dairyman: a person who rented cows from a farmer.

daker: 1) to work for wages after the usual day's work is over (now called moonlighting); 2) a dispute.

Dakota Indians: a collection of tribes sometimes called Sioux, who wandered between the Missouri and Mississippi Rivers until they moved west.

dalder: (in England) a foreign coin.

dalk: a pin or buckle.

dama, damaga: damages.

damage-chere: a fee in use during the seventeenth century. It was collected by the English courts at the time when damages were paid.

damage-feasant: damage done to property which belonged to another, e.g. an animal grazing without permission.

dame: 1) a married woman; 2) the name given to a lady of rank; 3) the head of a nunnery; 4) a housewife; 5) the principal of a private elementary school; 6) the person in charge of boarding the student body of an all-male school.

damnum: damages; injury.

damsel: 1) an unmarried young lady. Originally used to indicate a young lady of noble birth; 2) a bed warmer; 3) a maid-in-waiting.

Dan: sir or master.

dance: a journey.

d and coh: daughter and coheir.

dander: ire, temper, anger, e.g. "got my dander up."

d and h: daughter and heiress.

dandiprat: a small sixteenth century English coin worth about three half pence.

dandy: 1) a man so elaborately dressed in the very latest fashions that he disgusted the more serious hard-working men of the late 1700s; 2) breakbone fever or dengue (which see).

dandy brush: a small stiff brush used to curry horses.

dandy cart: a cart with springs which was used by tradesmen.

dandy horse: a forerunner of a bicycle which consisted of two wheels connected by a bar on which the rider sat while he pushed against the ground with first one foot and then the other.

Danegeld: an additional tax in England on land. This tax was believed to have been collected as a tribute to the Danes, who invaded England, and this tax was never removed. Also called Danelage and Danelagh.

dangue: see dengue.

Danz: (Norman) five hundred years.

dap nor: baptism.

D.A.R.: Daughters of the American Revolution.

darg: work done in a day; a task.

darg days: day work done to pay rent due to a feudal lord.

darg man: a man who worked by the day.

darnacle: see dornick.

darnex: see dornick.

darning egg: a small gourd that was slipped into the worn stocking. It made a smooth surface to aid in mending or darning the sock. Egg shaped wooden, china, or even rock pieces were also used.

darps, drops: (Norman) clothing, covering.

darrees: (Norman) money, goods, chattels, effects, merchandise.

dasser: (Norman) to assess.

dater: an old spelling of daughter.

dative: a court appointment.

daturine, datura: daturine, a drug used in the past to treat seizure and mental disorders.

dau.: daughter.

dau, daou: (Norman) two.

daub: see chink.

daughter-in-base: a daughter born out of wedlock.

daughter-in-law: 1) a son's spouse; 2) sometimes a stepdaughter is referred to in this manner

daughter-law: a daughter-in-law.

Daughters of the Confederacy, United: this organization is open to descendants of those who aided, in some way, the Southern cause.

dau-i-l: daughter-in-law.

daus.: daughters.

Davis' quadrant: a navigational instrument.

Davy (Davey) Jones' locker: a naval slang term for the bottom of the ocean.

daybed: a couch by day and a bed by night.

day book: 1) a log book or ship's log; 2) a ledger or daily record of business transactions; 3) a diary.

day fever: a fever which lasts but one day or one that appears during daylight hours. Also called sweating sickness.

day house: a dairy.

day laborer: an unskilled worker who was hired for a day at a time.

dayman: a man hired by the day.

day math: the area of a meadow which could be mowed by one man in one day.

day name: the name given a black child

born to parents who observe African customs. The name indicates the sex and the day of the week on which the child was born. Beginning with Sunday, a male child could be named Quashee, Cudjo or Cudjoe, Cubbena, Quaco, Quao, Cuffee or Cuffy, and Quamin or Quame. A female would be named Quasheba, Juba, Beneba, Cuba or Cubba, Abba, Pheba or Phibbi, and Mimba.

day tale: in the daytime.

day tale man: 1) a dayman; 2) a chance laborer; 3) one not regularly employed.

day tale pace: slow.

day work: 1) work done by the day; 2) the amount of land that one man could plow, mow, etc. in one day.

D.B.: 1) deed book; 2) Domesday or Doomsday Book.

d.b.a.: doing business as, e.g. "John Brown doing business as Brown Co."

d.b.n.: de bonis non.

d.b.n.c.t.a.: de bonis non cum testo annexo.

D.C.C.: Descendants of Colonial Clergy.

D.C.G.: Descendants of Colonial Governors.

dd: deed

d'd.: deceased.

de: 1) day; 2) to die; 3) dead; 4) God; 5) of.

Dea.: Deacon.

deacon: a church official, responsible in various churches for different duties. In pioneer days a deacon was one who would conduct the church service in the minister's absence.

deacon seat: 1) the seat, usually directly in front of the pulpit, which was reserved for the deacon; 2) in a log cabin this was a long bench in front of the fire.

dead earnest: earnest money.

dead horse: "to pull a dead horse" means to work for wages already paid.

dead house: a place for the reception of drowned persons.

dead man: old works in a mine.

dead pay: pay given to or in the name of a soldier who was no longer in the army because he was dead, discharged from the army or because an officer appropriated the pay.

deaf: 1) decayed; 2) tasteless.

deal: 1) timber measure; 2) a Dutch wine; 3) a fractional part of a whole; 4) a pine board; 5) to separate one thing from another; 6) to divide into shares; 7) to share with another; 8) to take action in some affair.

deanery court: an English ecclesiastical probate court.

de anno in annum: from year to year.

dear: used to indicate that the price of an item is expensive, almost more than one can afford.

Dearborn: a little, light, four-wheeled carriage or wagon with a roof and side curtains. It probably received its name from general Henry Dearborn (1751-1829) who rode on a battlefield in this type of vehicle.

dearn: 1) door post; 2) stone gate post.

death certificate: issued by a governmental authority when a person dies. Much of the information is obtained from the next-of-kin, such as names of father and mother (and her maiden name), age, place of birth, etc. If unknown, nothing is recorded other than what the attending physician knows to be factual.

death rattle: a characteristic sound in the throat often just prior to death.

deathsman: a hangman or executioner.

deathsnear: a rapid and fatal disease common to children which is now obsolete.

deauscens: (Norman) two hundred.

deaux: (Norman) two.

de avo: from the grandfather.

debar: 1) to prevent an action; 2) to exclude from a place or from a condition in a contract.

debatement: contention.

de bene esse: something done out of normal sequence. For example, evidence given before a trial for fear it would be lost due to age, infirmity, or the impending death of the person giving the evidence.

deberbiz (peaux): (Norman) sheep skins.

debility: 1) weakness; 2) failure to survive. A term used to describe a death due to either old age or an infant death; 3) sometimes used to describe a loss of weight or appetite; 4) an undianosed case of cancer or tuberculosis; 5) sometimes used as a cause of death when the reason was unknown.

de bonis non: an administration in which the original administrator of an estate died without having finished his duties and another person was appointed to administer the estate.

de bonis non cum testamento annexo: an administration granted when an administrator died without having finished his duties, and the will was attached.

de bono et malo: of good and evil.

debt: a court action to collect money owed because an agreement or contract was not fulfilled.

debtbook: a day book, account book, etc. in which only debts were written.

debtbound: an obligation, must pay because of a duty to do so.

dec.: deceased.

Decalogue: the Ten Commandments.

decan: one in charge of a group of ten.

dec'd.: deceased.

decedent: used in speaking of a person who is dead.

deceder: (Norman) to die.

deceit: similar to fraud.

decennial census: authorized by the Constitution of the United States, this is the counting of people taken every ten years. It began in 1790.

decesd.: deceased.

decessit: deceased, died.

decessit sine parole: died without children. Sometimes shortened to s.p.

decessit sine parole mascula: see d.s.p.m.

decessit sine parole supersite: see d.s.p.o.

decessit vita matris: died in his mother's lifetime.

decessit vite patria: died in his father's lifetime.

decet: descendant.

decido: to fall dead; die.

deck: 1) the roof of a stage coach or railroad car; 2) a horizontal compartment in a freight car or truck to transport small animals such as hogs or sheep; 3) to pile logs on a skidway, using a horse pulling a decking chain.

deckhand: a worker on a boat or ship under the supervision of a first mate.

Deckhard rifle: named for the maker in Lancaster, Pennsylvania, it was about three and a half feet long, weighed seven pounds and used bullets of the size "seventy to a pound of lead." It was quite precise and a bullet from it could travel a long distance.

decla.: declaration.

declae.: declared.

de clamo: of a claim.

declaration of intent: an announcement that a couple is about to marry. This may be written or oral and the practice still exists in many states today.

declaration of intention: a sworn statement made by an alien in which he announces that he plans to become a citizen.

declaration of trust: a written admission by an individual that title to property which he holds is held by him as trustee of another.

decoct: 1) to reduce by boiling away; 2) to waste or squander; 3) to cook something in water; 4) to devise.

decoction: the result of a boiling down process or steeping in hot water, an old way of making medicine.

decree: 1) a court order. Also see judgment; 2) a fianl judgment of a court.

decree nisi: see nisi.

decree of distribution: the document which declares how an estate is to be distributed. It should name all heirs or devisees.

decrepitude: the effects of old age.

decsd.: deceased.

dect.: deceased.

de die in diem: from day to day.

dedimus: a document which permits a civilian to do something in court. For example, acting instead of a judge, whose normal duty would be to perform the act. The full term is dedimus potestatem.

deed: the written legal document that transfers the ownership of property. The most common deed is a deed in fee, which gives a fee simple title to property. The name is usually shortened to deed. Also made for slave sales.

deed, acknowledged or proved: a deed which has been authenticated by its signer before a court, notary, or other public official.

deed in fee simple: a conveyance of the absolute ownership of land.

deed of acquittance: when a patented survey was found to have more acreage when resurveyed than it had the first time, the extra acres were purchasable by the original patent owner if he so desired. Deed of acquittance was the name given to the deed under these special circumstances.

deed of agreement: this document is concerned with the sale of personal property. It can deed land to persons who agree to take care of the grantor for the remainder of his life. At the death of the grantor the debt is canceled.

deed of bargain and sale: a deed of property from one person to another.

deed of conveyance: see conveyance.

deed of decree: a deed of this type shows that a petition asking to sell the property has been brought into court. A widow's dower should be filed and then the decision of selling belongs to the court.

deed of division: the document which states how property which has been held as a unit by two or more heirs is divided.

deed of gift: property given to another, usually a relative. Sometimes the phrase "love and affection" is used rather than a sum of money.

deed of mortgage: a deed which promises property as security for a debt of money.

deed of partition: a document signed by all the persons who hold real property jointly, e.g. an estate with several heirs is sold to another party, and all the heirs must sign it.

deed of release: this document is made when a debt has been paid and the property which has been held by the person who made the loan no longer needs this pledge of security.

deed of trust: a type of mortgage. The title to property is given to one or more persons to secure the payment of a debt.

deed poll: a document signed by one person representing several persons. Sometimes grantee names were added at a later date.

de ejectionne firmae: see ejectment.

deemster: a judge whose court was on the Isle of Man.

de facto: based upon fact.

default: if a person had been called into court for three consecutive sessions and failed to appear, the court could make a binding decision without him.

defeasible: an action which is voided, especially an event such as laying claim to an estate by an underage person.

defeasance: making void by having fulfilled the conditions stated in a deed. Another deed may then be made stating the action which has been completed.

defendant: a person who has been brought into court charged with a crime, or sued by another person.

deferred debt: during the American Revolution money was borrowed from supporters of the American cause. The responsibility for part of this domestic debt was assumed by the federal government and the 6% interest payments were not due until 1801.

deforceant: a defendant.

defrisher, defrischer: (Norman) to work by tilling the ground.

deft.: defendant (which see).

defues: (Norman) widows.

defunct: dead, deceased.

defunct county: a county which no longer exists, yet knowledge of this county is essential for the use of local records. Sometimes they are quite difficult to locate.

degener: an obsolete form of degenerate.

degrade: when wind was the main way of propelling a ship, and an adverse wind or bad weather would cause a journey to pause, the ship's log would say that they had made a "degrade" (a word of French origin).

degree of relationship: this is not the same as relationship. A legal term which does not specify an exact relationship, e.g. brother or cousin. The word degree merely indicates that there is a varying distance between blood relatives.

degrees of descent: see descent.

deguerpys: (Norman) abandoned.
Dei gratia: by the grace of God.
de jure: legalized, legitimate.
dekyne: deacon.
del.: delegate.
delaine: an expensive woolen cloth popular in the early 1800s.
delair: (Norman) December.
delare: an almsgiver.
Delaware Indians: a native tribe who lived in the Delaware River Valley of New Jersey, New York, Delaware, and Pennsylvania. They traded peaceably with the Dutch and later sided with the French against the British. They eventually joined with the Cherokee tribe in Oklahoma.
delayed registration: this can be filed many years after the fact by an affidavit stating that the facts are true.
deld.: delivered.
delinquent: a person who is able to pay but is lax in doing so. Sometimes a person would not pay the taxes on poor land; therefore, you will find him in a delinquent tax list.
delirium tremens: usually found in persons who use excessive amount of an alcoholic beverage. Hallucinations, both visual and auditory, are usually present. Commonly referred to as the "D.T.s."
delirium tremors: an older term for delirium tremens.
de lunatico inquirendo: an inquiry by jury as to whether a person is, or is not, of sound mind.
dem: 1) an abbreviation for demi, one-half; 2) an abbreviation for the law term "demise" (which see).
demandant: plaintiff.
deme: 1) a dime; 2) a tenth part; 3) a tithe.
demenge: (Norman) Sunday.
demesne: 1) legal possession of land; 2) the main manor of an English lord; 3) a group of similar activities, knowledges or interests.
demi: one-half.
demi-castor: a hat made of inferior fur.
demierkes: (Norman) Wednesday.
demihag: a long pistol, used much in the sixteenth century.
demi-john: a one to ten gallon jug enclosed in a wicker case with a wicker handle.
demi-lune: a small cannon.
demise: 1) a lease given by a landlord to a renter for a certain number of years or life. It also is given for leases which will terminate when the landlord so chooses; 2) death; 3) to transfer an estate from one to another, either by will or by a lease; 4) to let go or dismiss; 5) to resign the crown as Edward did in order to marry Mrs. Simpson.
democrat wagon: a high, two-seated, lightweight wagon drawn by one horse.
demographic: the study of population growth or decline.
demster: a judge.
demulance: 1) a light horseman; 2) one who carried a lance.
demur: 1) a charge that facts presented in a case are not enough to continue the case. The question is not so much a question of facts as a question of law; 2) to delay; 3) an abode; 4) raise an objection to a plan; 5) doubtful; 6) a way of saying that even if facts are true, they are not sufficient to put the one who is demurring to the trouble of answering or proceeding further.
demurrage: 1) undue detention while loading or unloading of a vessel in port by its owner; 2) a tax imposed on a vessel under the above conditions.
den: 1) a valley or a hollow area in a woods; 2) an obsolete form of Dan; sir or master; 3) to dam up a water way.
denarius: an English coin usually abbreviated to "d."
denaturalization: to deprive a person of his rights, either as a citizen or as a naturalized citizen.
dengue: known also as break-bone fever. A tropical fever, described as early as 1780. The fever was complicated by pains characteristically in the joints and extremities, but is seldom life threatening. We now know that it is caused by a virus transmitted by a type of mosquito. Also called dandy.
denial: the defense in a suit.
denicalis: a funeral.
denier: an old French coin made of copper, worth one-thirteenth of a

farthing.

denier, deniast: (Norman) denied, refused.

denization: the act of issuing citizenship to a foreigner.

denizen: one type of colonial citizenship where a person born outside England or her possessions was eligible for civil rights after naturalization. The person could hold, inherit or sell property, but not hold public office, vote or participate in political matters.

denoicer: (Norman) wages.

denomino: to name, to call.

de novo: begin again. For example, a second trial which is held as if there had never been a decision in a previous trial.

denshering of land: a way of improving soil. A pile of dried weeds, grass, etc. is burned and then plowed into the ground. Some farmers burn off a field and then plow the ashes back into the earth. In modern farming this is not considered a very good way to enrich soil but it is still used in some parts of the world.

denshire: 1) see burn-heat; 2) a shortened form of Devonshire where the practice of denshire began.

dentition: 1) teething in a child; 2) infant convulsions or seizures; 3) an infected tooth; 4) mercury poisoning from a teething medication.

dentor: an indenture.

denubo: to marry, especially beneath her.

deodand: an old English custom whereby personal property which caused the death of a human being was given to the church as atonement for the use of the poor.

Deo valente: God willing.

dep.: 1) depot; 2) deputy.

de parte domus: of part of the house.

departer: a refiner of metals.

de partition facienda: of making a division. The name of an ancient writ which directed the sheriff to make a partition of the lands.

deplume: 1) to pluck feathers from a chicken; 2) to take away honor, wealth, etc.

deponent: a person making an oath that certain facts are true. This statement is put in writing and is called a deposition.

deported alien: a non-citizen who was banished from a country.

depose: 1) to remove from a high office or rank; 2) to make a statement by a witness who is under oath; 3) to put away or place in safekeeping; 4) to take a burden or obligation away.

deposition: written testimony of a witness, answering questions (not it court) to be used during a trial in court.

depositum: treasury, e.g. paid out of the depositum for 1789.

depot: 1) the station building where a train makes a stop; 2) a place of storage and distribution for army supplies.

depot.: deposition.

depreciation lands: men of the Pennsylvania Line were paid in Continental money for their service during the Revolutionary War. This money dereciated in value, while gold and silver did not, which caused great hardships for the citizens. In order to encourage men to continue in the service, certificates of depreciation were issued at a rate determined by a monthly graduated scale. These certificates could be used to pay for confiscated estates of persons convicted of treason, or to pay for parcels of unclaimed lands in an area called the depreciation tract.

depredation: 1) plundering; 2) to drive away cattle by force (Scotland); 3) robbery; 4) waste of anything.

Dept.: 1) Department; 2) Deputy.

deputy: a person authorized to act in the interests of another as a substitute for that person. See also assignee.

derelict: anything abandoned at sea by consent or compulsion, but still afloat.

derrai: (Norman) damage.

derringer, deringer: this small pistol was named for its inventor Henry Derringer of Philadelphia. It used a large diameter single bullet and as it was small, easy to conceal and most useful at close range it was carried by ladies in their muffs or by gamblers inside a sleeve.

desc.: descendant.

descent: when ownership of land or personal property is leased upon one's relationship to a deceased person. Sometimes it is called degrees of descent.

descendants: those living after a person, son, grandson, etc., who are in a direct line.

descent: when ownership of land or personal property is based upon one's relationship to a deceased person. Sometimes called degrees of descent.

descheterie: (Norman) escheator.

descres: (Norman) decrease.

descry: to become aware by intense observation. The word is now almost obsolete.

descs.: descendants.

Deseret: "land of the honey bee," which was the name given by the Mormons to the area where they lived. They were refused statehood under the name Deseret, but in 1850 became a part of the Territory of Utah.

deserie: to disinherit.

deserite: (Norman) disinherited.

deserter: a person who leaves his unit with no intention of returning in order to avoid service or dangerous duty.

deses: (Norman) decease.

deseurer: (Norman) to divide, separate.

desgaynnes: (Norman) untilled.

desinarietz: (Norman) unmarried.

de son tort: of his own twisting. This term is used to denote a person who has not been appointed to act as the executor, but performs the duty anyway.

desportes de payer: (Norman) exempted without paying.

despot: an absolute ruler.

dessuisy: (Norman) seized.

destrere: a war horse.

det.: detachment.

detached duty: duty performed while not with one's permanent assignment.

detail: 1) a soldier or group of soldiers appointed to perform a special duty; 2) or to designate someone to fulfill a certain task.

de tempore in tempus: from time to time.

detinue: action to recover personal property which has unlawfully been kept by the defendant. The "question" is not the unlawful taking but the unlawful keeping.

detinue non detinuit: a form of action brought into court to secure the return of personal property from another person who obtained the property legally, but who has kept it without the right to do so. The question to be decided by the court is who has the right to retain the property.

detur: let there be given. The will of a wealthy man, Edward Hopkins, specified that books were to be distributed impartially to some of the best students at Harvard University. The books were called "Deturs."

Deu, Deus, Deux: (Norman) God.

devastavit: waste of the property of a deceased person by the one responsible for settling the estate. He is liable for this act.

de ventre inspiciendo: of examining the abdomen. A writ sometimes issued by a presumptive heir-at-law which requires the sheriff to summon a jury of matrons and a jury of twelve men to inquire if the widow was pregnant or not. The matrons examined the widow and reported to the male jury who returned the decision to the court of chancery.

devers: (Norman) dead.

devers pere ou mere: (Norman) of the father's or mother's side.

deviation from plainness of dress and address: a charge in the Quaker church of not dressing in a plain manner or not using Quaker terminology in speech. Both subjects can be brought before the church for consideration.

devil: 1) a tool used by a chair maker;) an apprentice in a print shop, more frequently called a printer's devil; 3) a portable furnace used in a foundry, construction work, etc.; 4) an obsolete term for device, invention.

devise: 1) the act of making a gift of real estate by a person through his will to take effect at his death; 2) to direct; 3) to order; 4) to relate.

devisee: a person named in a will to inherit land, or other real property.

devisor: a person who by his will gives his land to another.

devolution: the transfer of a right, title, office, etc. from one person or group to another.

Devonshire colic: so called because cider

which was a popular drink in Devon-shire was made in presses fashioned from lead. This caused a slow lead poisoning in the person who drank the cider. Also called a dry bellyache.

devoterer: an adulterer.

devy, day: (Norman) death, died.

dewbit: first meal in the morning, not as substantial as a regular breakfast.

dewdrink: the first allowance of beer given to those who harvested the crops.

dey: 1) a female dairy worker, although the term is sometimes used for a male worker in a dairy; 2) a friendly title given to old people.

deyes: (Norman) drivers of geese.

deytron: daughters.

deywife: a dairywoman.

dez, deze: (Norman) ten.

dezick: a day's work.

D.F.P.A.: Daughters of Founders and Patriots of America.

dft.: defendant.

d.g.: degree of gift.

D.H.D.: Daughters of Holland Dames.

di: abbreviation for demi, one-half.

diaper: a fifteenth century linen fabric woven in a diamond pattern. The diamonds were filled with lines, dots, etc. Sometimes diaper was a blend of linen and cotton.

diaphoretics: anything which produces perspiration .

diarrhea: looseness and frequency of bowel movements.

diary: 1) an obsolete word for daily; 2) something which lasts for one day.

dibendre: (Norman) Friday.

ditcher: a digger.

dicker: 1) to bargain or haggle, finally reaching a mutual agreement on the price or on the trading of goods or services; 2) ten of any commodity, e.g. ten hides of leather, ten bars of iron, etc.

dico: 1) to indicate, appoint; 2) to tell, speak to.

didymi: twins.

die: 1) day; 2) a tool used by a metal worker. A variation of a dic is used by a woodworker.

died without issue: died without having any children of his/her own.

diem: day.

diemane: (Norman) Sunday.

dies: 1) day of burial; 2) days.

dies natalis: birthday.

diet: a food supply. This term can be found mentioned in a contract, "if he does not get drunk above once in three months, he will be paid a pair of stockings and his diet."

diets: a term found in Revolutionary War records which means meals.

dieux, diaulx: (Norman) two.

Digger Indians: a contemptuous name given by pioneers to some western Indian tribes who chose not to eat meat but dug roots and ate seeds, grasshoppers, etc.

digitalis: a medicine derived from fox-glove, used as a heart stimulant.

dijau, dijou: (Norman) Thursday.

dike-grave: dikerve (Norman). 1) in Holland, this man is responsible for maintaining dikes and sea walls; 2) in England this man maintains drains, ditches, sea banks, etc.

diker: 1) a hedger; 2) a ditcher.

dikerve: an official who oversaw dikes and drains located in marshlands.

dil: daughter-in-law.

diligence: 1) a French stagecoach; 2) an obsolete term for care, caution.

dilling: 1) a baby born to older parents; 2) a country term used to indicate the weakest piglet in the litter.

dimaigne, dimeine, dimeins, dimeignt, dimenche, dimegne: (Norman) Sunday.

dimar: (Norman) Tuesday.

dimecre: (Norman) Wednesday.

dimity: a stout fabric of cotton which was woven with raised stripes or fancy patterns. It was used for bed or window curtains, clothing, etc. Sometimes called Dimothy.

dimming: dawn.

Dimothy: see dimity.

dimpse: twilight.

dinders: an ancient small coin.

dingy, dinghey, dinghy: a small boat carried by a man-of-war and used for light, rough work.

dinner horn: in New England this was a large horn from an ox which, when blown by a man, could be heard over his farm, and which was later made of tin.

dinner on the grounds: the noon meal at a revival meeting where everyone brought food from home and shared with others by putting it on a table with the food of other families. At an all-day auction sale it usually means food prepared and sold by ladies' charitable groups.

dinner pail: the container in which food was placed at home for working men, school children, etc. to carry with them to eat at noon at work or school.

diocese: the religious district over which a Bishop has authority.

diphtheria: an infectious disease which caused a false membrane to form, usually in the throat, and made a person unable to breathe. The disease is seldom seen today, due to vaccines.

dipper: a long handled cup-like container made of iron coated with tin and used to dip water from a bucket. In earlier days it might be made of a gourd. Sometimes referred to as a ladle.

diptych: 1) a hinged, wooden tablet. On one side are the names of living people and on the other are the names of deceased people. Mass is said for both and prayers are offered; 2) a pair of pictures, etc. hinged together.

direct evidence: information obtained at the time an event occurred, which is given about the event at a later time and can lead to a legal conclusion.

direct heir: one who inherits from a relative in a direct line, e.g. son from a father. See also collateral line.

direct index: an index to a court's books of documents which lists the main names contained in the documents.

direct line: descent from an ancestor to one's self from great-grandparent to grandparent, to parent without consideration of other relatives.

direct passenger list: those ships which went directly to destination.

direct tax: a poll tax, property tax, income tax which will not be reimbursed by others.

dirk cane: a dirk is a dagger and a dirk cane is a cane with a dagger concealed in it, which can be quickly released.

dis-: a negative prefix which indicates something is taken away, e.g. disfavor, no longer well regarded, disliked, etc.

dis.: 1) discharge; 2) see disowned.

disabled: 1) to be made unfit for duty by an enemy or by weather; 2) if a vehicle becomes unserviceable.

discharge: 1) the certificate terminating an individual's service in one of the armed forces; 2) a document which gives one person's interest in property to another who already has an interest in the same property. For example, a son might release interest in his deceased father's estate to his mother; 3) a documented release from prison; 4) to satisfy a debt, a duty, etc.; 5) (Scottish law) forbid.

dischd.: discharged.

disclaimer: see renunciation.

discontd.: discontinued.

discovert: (Norman) an unmarried woman.

discretionary trust: power given to a person called a trustee to use his own judgment, within broad guidelines, in the investment of funds, lands, etc. belonging to another person.

disenest: (Norman) nineteen.

diseset: (Norman) seventeen.

disfoith ataunt: (Norman) ten times as much.

dished wheels: these light, wooden wheels used on coaches and buggies had a shape that was similar to that of a saucer, with the hollow side of the saucer facing away from the coach body. This shape added strength without weight.

dishon.: dishonorable.

dish timber: a large knot of wood, especially soft maple, birch, beech and white ash from which a carver could make a nest of bowls.

dismables: (Norman) tithable.

dismarie: (Norman) unmarried.

dismd.: dismissed.

disme: 1) one-tenth, from which the word dime comes; 2) a tithe.

dismiss: 1) send away; 2) dispose of; 3) discontinue a court action.

dismission: usually written in the form of a letter, this stated that the subject of the letter was of good standing in his church and that he was leaving for a good reason, usually a move. The letter itself is usually found with church papers and it will indicate the location of the former church. The fact that a letter of dismission was written will usually be noted in the former church's minutes.

disowned: dismission from membership by the Quaker church after due process, for disobeying the church Discipline. Anyone who was disowned had the right of an appeal to the Quarterly Meeting and the Yearly Meeting.

dispensation: 1) something given out or dispensed; 2) a relaxing of a church law, a pardon.

dispensator: steward.

dispone: 1) to set in order, an obsolete meaning; 2) to expend; 3) to assign something to another; 4) to make a disposition; 5) obsolete form of dispose.

disposal: 1) to sell, give away, use anyway of getting rid of a thing; 2) to assign something to someone else by sale or gift. This word is frequently used in the sense of "sale" only or by disposition in a will.

disposition: 1) a final settlement; 2) a right to dispose of something; 3) regulation; 4) an arrangement such as placing troops, etc.

dissate: (Norman) Saturday.

disseizin: ouster of a tenant from possession of property.

disseizor: 1) an intruder or trespasser; 2) a person who turns a tenant out of possession.

dissent: to not take property given by a will. A wife may dissent if her husband left a very small part of his estate to her and take her share as if her husband died intestate. Beneficiaries other than the wife may decline to take their share, but they may not take something else instead.

dissenter: 1) a person who leaves a church; 2) a person who disagrees with a popular action or school of thought.

dissisme: (Norman) tenth.

dist.: 1) district; 2) distinguished.

distaff: 1) a female; 2) part of a spinning wheel.

distances: boundary line lengths.

distiller: a person who makes alcoholic liquors which are stronger than beer or wine.

distrain: to seize and hold something of value in lieu of rent, damages or satisfaction of a claim.

distress: 1) to take, without due process of law, personal goods from a wrong-doer; 2) to compel payment, e.g. a debt; 3) state of misfortune.

distribute: 1) to apportion; 2) to disperse; 3) to promote sales; 4) to divide into various stages.

distributee: a person who shares in an estate which has been or is probated.

distribution: after all debts and costs have been paid the estate of the deceased and intestate person is divided (distributed) among his or her heirs.

district: a division of a town, city, or state for the purposes of holding elections, establishing schools, representation in state and federal legislatures, etc.

district attorney: the lawyer who is the prosecuting officer for a governmental body in a court.

district court: 1) a United States trial court serving a judicial district; 2) a state court which attends to cases within the limits of the court's jurisdiction. In some states this is an appellate court.

district land office: divisions of the general land office, these offices were located in strategic points throughout the United States. Each office would record purchases of land by settlers and were responsible for recording all transfers of land from the federal government to the settlers.

district land office books: maps bound together which show the exact location of each piece of land sold by the government to persons in that region.

district land office tract books: these contain each land entry by the legal description within the area governed by the district office of the Bureau of Land Management.

disturbing the peace: causing public turmoil or annoyance.

disutime: (Norman) tenth.

disvyt, dysiout: (Norman) eighteenth.

dit: a French way of denoting a nickname or alias, e.g. Peter dit Pete Smith.

ditch back: a fence.

ditcher: the man or machine which digs ditches.

ditching shovel: a shovel designed for use in digging a trench or ditch.

dito: an unusual abbreviation for ditto used in some census records in place of the surname of one family. Not a Dito family.

ditto: the same as above.

ditty bag: a bag made of stout cloth used by seamen for carrying their small possessions. At one time this was made by a lady-love and was a treasured article.

diurnal: 1) daily; 2) during daylight; 3) an obsolete word for a diary; 4) an old word for a daily newspaper.

diurnal women: women who sold the daily papers about the streets.

div.: 1) division; 2) divinity; 3) divorced.

divers: 1) different; 2) an unspecified number but more than one.

diversory: an inn.

divide: a watershed formed by land which slopes in two directions separating two drainage systems.

divided land: a term found in colonial documents which means land allotted to, or divided among, the colonists.

dividend land, divident: 1) land included in a patent or grant; 2) one person's allotted share of such land.

dividende: (Norman) 1) a schedule; 2) a list; 3) an indenture.

dividers: 1) men, usually four in number, appointed by a probate court to divide an intestate estate into portions; 1/3 to the widow and the children received the rest, in equal portions. Any three of the four men could do the work; 2) a tool used by a surveyor, a carpenter, or a machinist.

division: 1) the part of a district to which an assistant census taker was assigned during the census years 1790 through 1840; 2) one section of an army consisting of two or more brigades. If the regimental system is used, a division consists of two companies of battalions or regiments; 3) a court document describing the procedure of distributing real or personal property among heirs of an estate.

division land: an area of land allocated to one or more settlers.

divorce: originally, no matter how much a couple desired to have their marriage dissolved, this action simply was not available. While the court system did not recognize divorce, on occasion the church would grant an annulment.

divorce a mensa et thoro: not a total divorce, but a legal separation from "bed and board."

divorce a vinculo matrimonii: an absolute divorce, with no restrictions.

divorce, migratory: a divorce obtained by moving to a more permissive state than the one in which the couple lived.

divorce of bed and board: (a mensa et thoro) a divorce that prohibited a remarriage, it was used primarily for wife abuse.

divorce, migratory: a divorce obtained by moving to a state where divorce laws were more permissive than those of the state where the couple resided.

dixet: say, said.

dld.: delivered.

D.N.: Dominus Noster Our Lord.

Do., do., ditto: which see.

d/o: daughter of.

doarium, doayre, doans, dowarie: (Norman) dower.

dobbouts des draps: (Norman) sellers of cloth.

dobla: a Spanish coin minted in the 1590s.

doblon: a Spanish coin of gold which was also circulated in South America.

dobra: a Portuguese gold coin, also known as double Johannes and sometimes called a joe.

docent: a teacher.

dock: the place in an English courtroom where the accused stands during his trial.

docker: 1) a stevedore; 2) one who cuts off animals' tails; 3) the name of the device used to cut the animals' tails off.

docket: 1) a calendar of the actions of a court kept by the clerk of the court, sometimes called a court calendar; 2) a woodman's bill; 3) a list of court cases awaiting trial in court.

docket books: these books house the

collection of papers for a case including what the case is about, the papers pertinent to the case, and the final decision of the court. They are sometimes called registers of actions.

dock fever: yellow fever.

dock walloper: a slang expression for a laborer who works at odd jobs around a wharf.

dock yard: 1) an area near water where ships are built, repaired, supplies stored, etc.; 2) a British navy yard.

doct: document.

doctor: an apothecary.

doctoress: a female doctor.

doctor of skill: a physician.

doctor's stuff: medicine.

docu.: document.

document: any "matter" written down upon any material for preservation. This would include writings from the stone age.

doen estat: (Norman) due estate.

doer: 1) agent; 2) manager.

d of g: degree of gift.

d of t: deed of trust (which see).

doftyr: daughter.

dog: 1) a miserable beef cow incapable of producing good meat; 2) prostitute; 3) a bad investment of money.

dogger: 1) a Dutch fishing ship which had two masts and operated in the North Sea; 2) an assistant metal worker at a drawbench (which see).

doggeres: a mechanical clamp.

dog hanging: a wedding feast at which money was collected for the bride.

dog-leech: 1) an old word for a veterinarian who treats dogs. Often used as a term of contempt; 2) an ignorant or quack doctor.

dog-leg: an angled road or path, as a dog's hind leg is crooked at the joint. From this name we get the saying "as crooked as a dog's hind leg," meaning a crooked road or a dishonest person.

doglope: a narrow slip of ground between two houses, the right of owner-ship of which is questionable.

dogs (fire-dogs, andirons): see andirons.

dog trot: an area with only a roof between two cabins set closely together. This space was used by both occupants of the cabins to set in shade, work under cover and the dogs also rested here. Thus the name, which was also used in the area between the living area of a large house and its kitchen.

doioers: (Norman) dowers.

doit: a small Dutch coin.

dol.: dollar, dollars.

dole: 1) a lump of anything; 2) any division of goods or property; 3) money, bread, etc. distributed to the poor; 4) a boundary mark; 5) unplowed ground; 6) a low, flat place.

doleator: cooper.

dolet: (Norman) an ax.

doling: 1) almsgiving; 2) a fishing boat with two nets.

dolor: pain.

Domain, public: see public domain.

domescart: the hangman's cart.

Domesday Book: a record of surveys of land begun in each county of England by five justices in 1081 and completed in 1086. It is contained in two volumes of unequal size and is deposited in the Treasury of England. The book was also called Doomsday Book for it judg-ed without bias all the landowners, as the Last Judgment will.

domesman: a judge.

domestic: 1) a category used by a census enumerator to denote a sister or other female relative who lived with the family and helped with the house work. Sometimes the person would not be related to the head of the house; 2) an unbleached muslin-type cloth which was called domestic or cotton domestic in order to differentiate it from cloth which was imported; 3) a person who was on an intimate basis with a family, as if at home; 4) a person who helped in the management of a home but was not a servant, e.g. maiden aunt; 5) made in this country as opposed to being manufactured in another country.

domicile: more than a residence, this is the place where a person intends to return. The state where a person's domicile was may not be the one where he lived or died. Under these circumstances, you may find an administration in another state.

domicilium: a dwelling.

domina: 1) a wife; 2) the lady who keeps the house; 3) a mistress.

domine, dominie: 1) the title for a minister of the Dutch Reformed Church; 2) the head of a boarding house where Eton students live outside the college grounds.

dominicum: absolute ownership or inheritance.

dominie: a preacher.

dominion: 1) during the Civil War the area covered by the Ku Klux Klan called "The Invisible Empire" was divided first into realms, and realms into dominions rather like congressional districts; 2) a group of states or countries under the control of a central government such as Canada under England, counties in Virginia under state government, etc.

dominus: sir.

dominus Rex: our Lord the King.

dominus vobiscum: the Lord be with you.

Doms Rex: see Dominus Rex.

domus: a house, home.

donatio: a gift, a donation.

donatio inter vivos: a gift among living persons.

donatio mortis causa: a gift in anticipation of approaching death.

donation certificate: see bounty land warrant.

donation land: 1) this was land granted by Texas for service in the Texas Revolution. It had not been promised in advance and fell into two classes. The first was called "battle donations" granting 640 acres to participants in specified battles. If the soldier died in service before he received his donation his heirs received it. The second class was "veteran donation," which see; 2) a few other states used this, or a similar method, to lure settlers to a specific area.

Donation Tract—1792: This land, situated in Washington and Morgan Counties, Ohio, was donated by the Ohio Company. Each settler was given, or "donated," one hundred acres, for which he had to have a gun and ammunition and keep an able-bodied man upon the acreage. At the end of five years the donee received a deed to the land. The purpose of this plan was to create a barrier against the Indians who resented their territory being taken. This land is sometimes referred to as the "Ohio Company's Third Purchase." Later, any settler could live on the land and receive a deed for one hundred acres from Congress.

donative: a gift, donation.

donee: a person who receives a gift or grant.

donne: (Norman) a lady.

donor: a person who gives a gift to another.

doomage: when a town or a person neglected to send a return of taxable property, the general assembly or selectmen would set the tax according to their discretion, from which there was no appeal. This assessment was referred to as doomage.

Doomsday Book: see Domesday Book.

door-keeper: a whore.

Dorhman's Grant: In 1801 land was granted to Arnold Henry Dorhman, a Portuguese merchant, who aided American prisoners in Portugal and provided the United States with supplies. The 23,000 acres given Dorhman were located in southeastern Tuscarawas County and in Harrison County, Ohio.

dornick: 1) a woolen or part woolen fabric used for window drapes, carpets, vestments, etc. as early as 1527; 2) a Scottish linen tablecloth.

dorp: a term for a Dutch village or hamlet found in many Colonial New York documents.

Dorrite: a supporter of Thomas W. Door in Rhode Island who led a rebellion designed to give more people the right to vote.

dorse: 1) a back of a document which has been folded, a book; 2) an obsolete word for dossal, a hanging at the back of an altar or in the sides of a chancel.

dorset horn: sheep bred in England in the 1890s.

dos rationalis: a dowry or gift of a reasonable size.

dosce, dudzime, duides: (Norman) twelve.

dossal: see dorse.

dosser: a basket.

doster: a daughter.

dotalis: that which belongs to or forms a part of a dowry.

dotter gauge: a tool used by a chair maker.

double cousins: two-way relationships between both pairs of parents.

double eagle: an American twenty dollar gold coin authorized by Congress in 1849.

double faced shoe hammer: a tool used by a bootmaker.

double iron: a tool used by a bootmaker.

double Johannes: see dobra.

double ribbed: pregnant.

doubloon: a Spanish gold coin circulated by the American colonies, South America, and the West Indies, so named for it was twice the value of a pistole.

dough-ball: see dough-boy.

dough-boy: 1) a brick made out of mud and dried in the sun; 2) a dumpling, hard in consistency and boiled in salt water. Sometimes called a dough-ball; 3) this term did apply to all soldiers, but later came to apply only to United States Army infantrymen.

dougherty wagon: 1) an ambulance; 2) a forerunner of the station wagon.

doughface: 1) a mask, a funny or hideous false face; 2) a Northerner during the Civil War who supported the South, and did not oppose slavery.

doughtren, doughtern: daughters.

Douglasite: a follower of Stephen A. Douglas, who split the Democratic party approximately ten years before the Civil War, by objecting to Kansas being admitted to the Union as a slave state.

dous, doux, dues: (Norman) two.

dovant: customs house.

dovecot: the hole cut in the side of a barn to allow pigeons to nest. This was before pigeons became pests.

Dover egg beater: an egg beater with loops on independent shafts which revolve toward the middle, thus bringing the eggs up and toward the center of the bowl. It received its name from the town where it was manufactured, Dover, New Hampshire.

dowager: a widow who has a dower from her deceased husband.

dowaire: a dower.

dower: a provision of law which entitles a married woman to receive a portion of her husband's estate for her and her children's support upon his death, if he dies without leaving a will. Usually a life interest in her husband's estate.

dower chest: a wooden chest, sometimes made by the bride's father, which was given to her when she was of an age to marry. In Pennsylvania the decorations can be traced to determine which county the chest was made in, but the final painting was done by a traveling painter as one can tell the work is not that of an amateur.

dower house: a house in England where the widowed mother of the lord of the manor lived.

dower release: usually found at the end of a deed. The clerk questions a wife, separately from her husband, if she is of her own free will agreeing to the sale and gives up all right to that land.

dower right: that portion of an estate which is given to a widow by law from her deceased husband's estate to be used for her lifetime.

dowery, dowry: now called a "portion." Property a bride brings to her husband, to be used by him so long as the marriage lasts. In the case of real estate it cannot be sold unless there is a clause in the marriage contract permitting such a sale.

dowlas: a coarse linen material which was originally made in Britany. It was a quite popular fabric in the sixteenth and seventeenth centuries.

down: small, fine, soft under feathers on fowl. The best quality comes from a goose, however duck feathers are suitable for pillows or down overcovers.

downright shave: a tool used by a cooper.

dowser: a person who attempts to detect the presence of water beneath the ground by using a divining rod.

dowsing rod: a divining rod.

doxies: women of doubtful reputations; prostitutes.

dozen: a course English cloth made of

wool which was woven in twelve-yard lengths.

dozze, doze, dozime, dozine: (Norman) twelve; the twelfth.

dp: see deviation from plainness of dress and address.

dpl.: deathplace.

Dr.: 1) a doctor; 2) a dealer, e.g. dealer in dry goods, etc.

dr.: 1) dram; 2) debtor; 3) when found in Quaker records this term stands for drinking spirituous liquor to excess.

drab: 1) one of several fabrics so named for its muddy, dull color; 2) a prostitute; 3) a dirty woman.

drachm: see dram.

draft: 1) fabric made of silk and worsted fibers which was either plain or had a pattern; 2) selective requirement for service in the United States armed forces was for native or naturalized white American males, age twenty-one and above. After 1863, blacks and American Indians were included. Exceptions were allowed (as opposed to conscription, which allowed no exceptions, except by law); 3) to pull a load, e.g. a draft horse; 4) the number of fish caught in one pull of a fish net; 5) a more modern spelling of draught or draw; 4) a drink; 5) a dose of medicine; 6) beer in a cask is called beer on draft; 7) a wing chair is sometimes called a draft (breeze) chair; 8) a preliminary drawing, writing, etc.; 9) see also bill of exchange.

draft horse: a large, strong horse used to pull heavy loads.

drag.: dragoon.

drag: a tool used by a stone mason.

drag knife: a tool used by a bootmaker.

dragoons: at one time these soldiers were trained in both infantry and cavalry procedures; a mounted infantry.

drain (prairie drain): a small run, brook or branch of a larger stream or river.

drainer: a person who fills and empties wood pulp vats during the paper making process.

dram: 1) a liquid measure which contained about a sixteenth of an ounce; 2) a small drink of spirituous liquor; 3) a pharmacist's weight which equally about an eighth of an ounce.

dramshop: a shop which sells liquor, e.g. an inn, tavern, etc.

draper: 1) a dealer in cloth, linen, etc.; 2) at one time a person who made cloth; 3) a tailor of clothes.

Draper Manuscripts: Lyman C. Draper (1815-1891) acquired several thousand notebooks of papers, including some regional papers of pioneers. He made trips, interviewed, and corresponded with hundreds of people. His collection is housed in the Wisconsin State Historical Library at Madison and deals with Illinois, Kentucky, Pittsburgh, and northwest Virginia and includes personal papers other historians added to the collection after Mr. Draper's death.

drappeaux quarrez: (Norman) banners.

draught: 1) many landowners wanted to have their land surveyed, perhaps to sell piece or only to make certain of their boundaries. These usually have only the necessary notations to identify the land and its boundaries but some will contain locations of streams, roads, woods, fields, buildings, etc. They are also called land draughts or surveyors' draughts; 2) an old way to spell draft (which see); 3) a British game of checkers; 4) to pull a plow; 5) a team of horses used to pull a plow, a cart, a wagon, etc.; 6) the number of fish taken in one net; 7) a measure of how much work a sawyer has done; 8) a dose of liquid medecine; 9) a stream or the current of a river; 10) a plan, chart, map, etc.; 11) the floor-plan of a building; 12) an extract made by distilling the ingredients; 13) a poultice; 14) an outdoor toilet; 14) liquor ready to draw from a cask; 15) to separate a several people or animals from a large group for a special purpose; 16) to draw warp threads through the heddles of a loom.

draught horse: a work horse.

draw: see draft.

drawbench: a workbench where equipment to make (draw) wire, tubes, etc. is manufactured.

drawday: after the Civil War, the government gave food to the poverty-stricken. The day when the food was distributed was called drawday.

drawer: 1) a bartender; 2) a waiter.

drawers: undergarments worn on the lower part of the body.

draw knife: a tool used by 1) a chair bodger; 2) a basket maker; 3) a rake maker; 4) a gate hurtle maker; 5) a cooper; 6) a wheelwright; 7) a carpenter.

draw latch: a thief; literally a house-breaker.

draw shave: a tool used by a rake maker.

dray: 1) a vehicle (sled, wagon, etc.) used for hauling freight in return for drayage (the cost or fee); 2) the occupation of driving the horse who pulled a dray.

drayage: see dray.

dray horse: a huge horse, such as a Belgian or Percheron, capable of pulling a heavily laden wagon.

drayman: a hauler of freight.

dregister: a druggist.

dreng: 1) a servant; 2) a young apprentice.

dresden: a coarse fabric woven from wool yarn.

dresser: 1) a finisher of commercial goods; 2) one who cares for a wardrobe of an actor and assists the actor with costume changes; 3) one who assists a doctor in dressing wounds; 4) a name for a variety of tools used to prepare goods for market; 5) see walker.

dressing: see millstones.

drgs.: dragoons.

dribble: servant.

drifts: tools used by a blacksmith.

drill: 1) a small stream sometimes called a rill; 2) to sow seed in a shallow trench. The machine used for this purpose is called a drill; 3) a strong cloth woven with a twill-weave which can be used for clothes and in heavier weights it is suitable for drapes, etc; 4) a tool to produce holes in many materials.

drill sergeant: the non-commissioned officer who trains new soldiers in their military duties.

drinkshankere: a cup bearer.

drive: 1) a large forest or place where deer are hunted; 2) to bring cattle together from many places or to conduct them from one area to another; 3) a quantity of logs which are floated down a river or a stream.

driver: 1) an authorized official who would collect and impound stray animals; 2) previous to the Civil War on a plantation where there was no overseer, a dependable and skillful slave was in charge of a number of his fellow slaves. Sometimes also called a sub-foreman; 3) a tool used by a cooper.

driving pike: a steel tool with a sharp point, a hook, and a strong wooden handle. It is used in driving logs downstream to pry the logs out and break up logs jammed together.

drofman: a herdsman.

drogman: an interpreter.

droit: a right.

drombeslade: a drummer.

dromon: warship.

dropped: found in Quaker records this term indicates that if a person did not attend the monthly meetings for quite some time their membership would be cancelled and their name dropped from the rolls.

dropsy: a symptom. It is retention of water in tissues and cavities which can be caused by a heart disease, kidney disease, cirrhosis of the liver, etc.

dropsy of the brain: see hydrocephalus.

dross: inferior grain which was given to chickens instead of sold.

drover: 1) one who is responsible for a group of slaves; 2) one who goes with (drives) a sizeable number of cattle which are being shipped on foot or by railroad to the market.

drowner: a person who regulates the irrigation of a farm.

drpd: see dropped.

drugger: a druggist.

drugget: a fabric of wool and either silk or linen which was used for clothing.

drugster: a druggist.

drum major: the person whose duty is to supervise the drummers of an infantry regiment and to direct the band during a parade.

drummer: 1) usually a young lad, generally a soldier's son, who played a drum. In early days one part of a drummer's duty was to flog men who had been sentenced to punishment; 2) a person who is seeking commercial business by taking orders; a salesman. He "drums up" business.

druthers: this word is used to indicate a person would like to have a choice: "if I had my druthers."

dry bellyache: symptoms resulting from lead poisoning.

dry dripes: see dry bellyache.

dry farming: the method of farming in areas which are not irrigated. Begun in California during the 1850s, drought-resistant crops are planted to take advantage of the periods when rain can be counted on to fall.

dry goods: clothing.

dry salt: preservation of meat by a process of drying it and then adding salt.

drysalter: 1) a British merchant who sells dyes and chemicals; 2) a druggist; 3) a dealer in chemicals; 4) a dealer in dyes; 5) a person who dyes fabrics.

dry trustee: see bare trustee.

D.S.: document signed.

d.s.: died single.

d.s.p.: decessit sine parole. Died without issue.

d.s.p.m.: decessit sine parole mascula. Died without male issue.

d.s.p.s.: decessit sine parole supersite. Died without surviving issue.

DT: deed of trust (which see).

dt: in Quaker records stands for daughter or daughters.

dto.: ditto.

"DT's:" see delirium tremens.

duary: a widow's dowry.

duatoon: a silver coin used and minted in the Netherlands during the seventeenth and eighteenth centuries.

ducape: a plain weave, stout silk fabric which had a soft texture and, at times, was woven with a stripe. This material was first introduced in England by the French refugees in 1685.

ducat: a coin of varying worth which was minted in several European countries of either silver or gold.

duces tecum: "you will bring with you." Used in a variety of legal orders, it requires a person who has been ordered into court to bring whatever is asked for in the writ with him into court.

Duchess: 1) a wife or widow of a Duke; 2) a woman who by inheritance has the right to this title.

ducking stool: used more commonly in Southern states, this was a device which worked on the principle of a lever. It was a form of punishment for wrong-doers. It had wheels in order that it could be pulled through the streets of a town for all to see, then to a pond where the convicted person would be ducked several times.

duco: to draw, as in draw along from place to place.

due bill: a written certificate acknowledging a debt and stating the date on which it was due to be paid.

duffel: a cloth which usually was made of wool but sometimes of silk. It was coarse with a thick nap and was first made at Duffel, Germany (near Antwerp). It was sometimes called "shag" or "trading cloth." Some inventories show that blankets and overcoats were made of this material.

duffer: a peddler, especially one who sold women's shoes.

dug-out: a hollowed or dug out tree trunk forming a canoe-like boat.

dugout (house): made by digging out a squared hole in the side of a hill. What roof was needed consisted of logs put together with sod. The front of this most primitive "house" was made of upright logs with a door for the single opening, which when open afforded the only light. The door itself was a piece of canvas or animal hide, the floor was dirt and there was usually a fireplace opposite the door. The roof dripped dirt in dry weather and mud in the rainy season, but the cavelike room was reasonably warm in winter and certainly many families never knew a better home.

dugway: a cleared roadway. Better than a path, but not as well constructed as a road.

duim: a western German linear measure of 1.03 inches. The Dutch measure was 1.013 inches.

duke: 1) a captain; 2) a leader.

Duke: a male member of a royal family who ranks immediately below a Prince.

Duke's laws: laws of an autocratic nature adopted in 1664 for the colony of New York after the Duke of York appointed Nicolls as Governor.

dum, dumb: a term comparable to, and used in place of, damn.

dumb-betty: a name for 1) a washing machine; 2) the dumbwaiter invented by Thomas Jefferson.

dumb chill, dumb shakes: symptoms of a fever, a chill combined with shaking.

dumb stove: a German stove made of sheet iron, resembling a military drum. It had stove pipes vented through, thus warming the second floor rooms of a house.

dummy: a tool used by a stone mason.

dung: solid waste of an animal.

dung drag: apparently a device for spreading manure.

dungaree: a stout, coarse cloth called blue denim suitable for use in the manufacture of work clothes.

dung cart: see tumbrel.

dung ground: the area where cattle produced fertilizer. This was a choice spot and, if a public road was run through a cowyard, the farmer would be allowed to remove the manure before the road was built.

Dunkards: see Brethren.

Dunkers (Dunkards, Duncards, Tunker): members of the German-American Baptist denomination. The sect was established first in Germany around 1719. Members began coming to Pennsylvania, from which they spread to Ohio and other sections of the United States.

Dunstable: a lady's straw bonnet first made in Foxboro, Massachusetts.

duplicate deed: an exact copy of a document made so that all parties may have their own copy.

duplicate warrants: this certificate was issued under conditions when the original warrant was said to be lost or destroyed. This act caused confusion, as many were issued for land already patented by other people..

duPont: gunpowder made by a company founded in 1802 named "E.I. duPont de Nemours and Company," which is now a chemical company whose name has been shortened to duPont.

dur.: during.

durable: a lease in which the renter had a permanent interest.

durance: enprisonment. See durant.

durant: sometimes called durance, this wool fabric had a long-wear or everlasting quality and was a variety of tommy cloth (which see).

durante viduitate: during widowhood.

durante vita: during life.

durchfall: dysentery.

Durham boat: a long keel boat, resembling an Indian canoe, named for Robert Durham of Pennsylvania who built many boats which were used on east coast rivers.

duroc: a breed of hog which is brownish-red in color. Sometimes called a Duroc Jersey.

duroy: a coarse wool fabric used mainly for men's garments. It was made in western England and was similar to tommy cloth (which see).

durrsucht: tuberculosis.

durst: a dare.

duscenz: (Norman) two hundred.

dusesme: (Norman) twelfth.

dusse: (Norman) two.

dussipere: nobleman.

dustman: a janitor.

dustyfats: peddlers.

dusty foot: see pie powder.

dusty poll: a nickname for a miller.

Dutch: people from the Netherlands, but in many localities it refers to German or people of German origin.

Dutch auction: an auction sale of property which has been priced at an inflated figure, which is gradually lowered until the item has been sold.

Dutch belted: a breed of dairy cattle black in color which had a white band around the middle. It originated in the Netherlands.

Dutch gold: a mix of copper and zinc which is produced in thin sheets and used as a fake gold leaf. Sometimes called Dutch metal.

Dutch names: see Appendix A.

Dutch oven (old-timey oven, old bread oven): a large, round pot made of iron, which sometimes had three or four legs. It had a heavy, close fitting lid. When the oven and lid were heated properly, filled with batter, and coals heaped over the lid, cornbread could be baked in the open fireplace. The oven was also used for stews, roast, soups, etc.

Dutch West India Company: founded in 1621, this Dutch merchant company was formed to trade with Africa, the West Indies, North and South America, and Australia.

dutton corn: a fruitful, early ripening yellow corn. It had a large cob and small kernels.

duty: 1) a period of time served with one of the branches of the armed forces; 2) see customs.

D.U.V.C.W.: Daughters of Union Veterans of the Civil War.

duxit: 1) husband; 2) leader.

D.V.: Deo Volente. God willing (found in cemeteries).

D.V.M.: 1) Verbi Dei minister, which means Minister of the Word of God; 2) Doctor of Veterinary Medicine.

d.v.m.: decessit vita matris (which see).

d.v.p.: decessit vita patria (which see).

dweesken: twin.

dwelling house: where a person lives with his or her family.

d.w.i.: died without issue (which see).

dwindler: a swindler.

d.y.: died young.

dyehouse: a dairy.

dying declaration: admissable in some courts under certain circumstances, this statement is made by a person who realized that death is close.

dynasties of England: the families which supplied the approximately sixty-six Kings and Queens of England during 1,150 years. They are: Saxons, Normans, Plantagenets, House of Lancaster, House of York, Tudors, Stuarts, Hanoverians, Saxe-Coburgs and Windsors.

dys___: prefixed to any medical term means abnormal or diseased.

dysentery: inflamed digestive tract.

dyspepsia: indigestion.

E

E: east.

ea, eius, ejus: this.

ead.: eadem.

eadem: in the same way.

eage: (Norman) 1) age; 2) life.

eagle: an American ten dollar gold coin authorized by Congress in 1792.

eald: 1) old; 2) age.

ealdren: elderly.

eam: 1) uncle; 2) sometimes any friend or neighbor.

eare: (Norman) to plow.

earer: a person who plows ground.

earike: a tax paid for the privilege of plowing.

earing: plowing or cultivation. Sometimes referred to a day's plowing.

Earl: 1) an English nobleman whose rank is below a marquess and higher than a viscount. His wife or widow holds the title of countess; 2) in feudal days this rank could be held by a prince.

ear mark: a method of identifying cattle by placing a distinctive mark on an ear of the animal. This could be one or more notches in one or more of several places. These marks were usually registered with the town officials and were transferable from father to son.

earmnesse: poverty.

earth: a day's plowing.

easement: a right which a land owner sells or gives to another permitting limited use of his land. For example, a way over the land by a power company, railroad, etc. The land title itself is retained by the land owner.

easy beef: lean cattle.

eatage: 1) grass used for grazing, usually after the hay has been cut; 2) the stubble left in a field after a crop has been harvested. Animals are let in to clean the field; 3} the right to use pastureland.

eaters: servants.

Eaton code: in 1657 this practical interpretation of biblical law was published in London. Each householder in New Haven, Connecticut was required to own a copy.

ecclesia: church.

ecclesiastical: church affairs, principles, organization, not related to civil affairs in any manner.

echelon: 1) a particular arrangement of military units in which each unit is lined up in a parallel fashion. Each unit is to the right or left of the one ahead, so all units form a stair-step pattern. No two are in a direct line. In battle formations there are functional names: rear echelon, forward echelon, support echelon, etc.; 2) level of command.

eclampsia: a blood condition during pregnancy characterized by swelling, fluid retention, etc.

eclectic: the use of many resources in a person's profession.

eclectic physician: one who professes to be liberal in views, independent of party, and who favors progress and reform in medicine.

economy: to manage an efficient household, group, etc. to ensure that it will be, or continue to be, productive.

ecumieur: (Norman) a pirate.

ecux.: a female executor.

e.d.: 1) enumeration district; 2) eodem die.

edema: fluid in tissue and/or cavities in the body.

edema of lungs: congestive heart failure or a form of dropsy.

edge leams: edge tools.

edge shave: a tool used by a saddler.

edge toolmaker: 1) the maker of chisels, knives, or other sharp tools; 2) the maker of weapons used to cut, e.g. swords and daggers.

edging: the waste wood remaining after slab wood from logs was sawed to width to make lumber.

editicius: 1) jurors chosen by the plaintiff in a case; 2) announced.

edom die: when this term appears in court records it means same place, same day.

eelde: age.

eel thing: St. Anthony's fire.

effects: personal and moveable property.

e.g.: exempli gratia. For example.

egg candler: see egg viewer.

eggler: a person who went about the country collecting eggs for sale.

egglise, einglise: (Norman) church.

eggpop: a New England drink similar to an eggnog.

egg viewer: a person who inspected eggs to dispose of spoiled ones. Today he would be called an egg candler.

eghte: possessions, property.

eight-day man: a scornful term for a man who joined the army for a short length of time during the Civil War.

eighty-niners: these were the settlers looking for homesteads in 1889 when a large acreage of land was opened in Oklahoma.

einsnes: (Norman) eldest.

eir, eirs: (Norman) heir, heirs.

eire: a heir.

ejectment: a suit brought into court by a property owner to recover the use of property for either failing to pay rent or for misusing the property.

Elapso tempore: the time having passed.

eld: old age, old people. Sometimes used for age in general.

elder: 1) an ancestor; 2) a former name for a justice of the peace; 3) a church officer whose duties vary according to different denominations; 4) an older person.

elderly man: 1) a chief; 2) a principal.

elderman: a nobleman.

elderne: 1) elders; 2) ancestors.

elderynges: 1) parents; 2) ancestors.

eld father: a grandfather.

eld mother: a grandmother.

El Dorado: the west, especially California, was often called El Dorado during the nineteenth century, meaning it was thought to hold great prosperity for adventurous pioneers. El Dorado was the name given by sixteenth century Spaniards to the gold-rich areas of South America.

elected guardian: a guardian chosen by a child if he or she is over fourteen years of age. This contrasts with the court appointing a guardian.

election: to choose one person from several to perform a specific duty.

eleemosynary: 1) in old records this was a charitable gift; 2) a non-profit organization.

elephantiasis: a form of leprosy transmitted by mosquitoes.

elephant size: an eighteenth century measurement (22" x 32") used for paper for printing and wallpaper. Later on these pieces were pasted together to form lengths of twelve yards.

elmother: a stepmother.

election court: In the seventeenth century, the general assembly of certain New England colonies, when meeting to elect colonial officials, was called an election court.

eleven-penny bit: a coin used in New York and Pennsylvania which was at times called a York Shilling. See also Spanish real.

eligible: a person who is qualified either legally or physically to be chosen to perform a duty.

elin: (Norman) a gentleman.

elixir: a liquid medicine prepared with more than one ingredient.

ell: 1) an old measure of distance used in several countries with a scale which varied. The distance used in England was forty-five inches; 2) an addition to a house, either included in the original plans or added later, which is usually set at right angles to the first structure.

ellipsis, printing: an omission in writing or in a quotation, indicated by a series of dots. "______ ... _____."

Elmira, New York prison: A Union prison in south-central New York state to retain Southern military captives. It was as frightful as the Andersonville, Georgia prison. Some doctors got what medical training they had by riding troop trains back and forth between prisons for the exchange of prisoners.

elopement: this term was used to indicate that a man seduced or stole another man's wife.

elsen: a shoemaker's awl.

elugeo: to mourn for the full time.

Embargo Act: an act giving the President of the United States the right to control ships departing from American harbors. It was passed by Congress in connection with the War of 1812.

embarment: an old term for embargo.

embellisher: a person who added designs to books, etc.

embleer: (Norman) 1) a seedsman; 2) to sow.

emblements: crops or profit from farm land.

embrasures: the opening in a fortification through which cannon or wall arms are fired.

eme: 1) an uncle (mother's brother); 2) an elderly friend.

emery bag: a very little bag filled with powdered emery which was, and is still, used to polish sewing needles in order that they can go through cloth more easily.

emfauntz: (Norman) children.

emigrant: 1) a person who leaves a country to settle in another country. For example, a person who leaves the United States to settle abroad; 2) a person who left the eastern portion of the United States to seek new land in the west or the south.

emigration: to leave a place, e.g. a country, to move to another place for temporary or permanent residence.

eminent domain: land which is owned by a state or the federal government, or is controlled by one of these agencies.

eminent domain, the right of: the right of a state or federal government to pay a reasonable amount of money to a person for his real estate, for the use of the public, without the consent of the owner.

emolument: benefits, advantages or wages which come to an employee.

emorior: to die off.

empanel: see impanel.

emperales: coins called imperials.

emporium: 1) a general store which carries a great variety of goods; 2) a market place.

emposses: to possess.

emptor: a buyer.

empyemia: gas in a body cavity.

enate: a person whose relationship to another can be traced through the female side of a family.

enbofognez: (Norman) engaged in business.

enceinte: pregnant.

encephalitis: inflammation of brain tissue.

encroachment: the process of slowly expanding your property on to another person's property. For example, to plow a little further over on your neighbor's land each year. This procedure is also applied to the rights of another person.

encumber: to retard an action placing a legal obstacle such as calling for a lien to be placed upon an estate, thus slowing a probate process.

end: see endorsed.

endemic: used in discribing a disease which is always found in a particular locality.

endleve: 1) eleven; 2) eleventh.

endorse: see indorse.

endorsed: found in Quaker records, this term indicates that a certificate addressed to another monthly meeting was properly signed and was forwarded to another monthly meeting.

endow: 1) to give a source of income to a person or institution; 2) an obsolete word for to provide a dower.

endowed: a Mormon who has made certain religious vows is said to have been endowed. This usually is done before a young person goes on a missionary term. It must be done prior to marriage in a temple.

endowment: 1) to give a widow her portion of her husband's estate; 2) a gift to an institution.

endware: a small hamlet.

enfeoff: transfer of land from the person selling it to the purchaser.

enfo, enfovie: (Norman) buried.

Eng.: England.

engage: (Norman) 1) mortgaged; 2) betrothed.

engagement child: a Southern phrase used to describe the first born child of a couple who were living together while waiting for the circuit preacher to come to their community and perform their marriage ceremony.

engendrure: (Norman) issue.

engendure: generation.

engineer: 1) a builder of engines; 2) a designer of engines; 3) a professional person, for example one skilled in mining; 4) a supervisor of stationary steam engines; 5) a person who drives a locomotive; 6) the person on a ship or boat whose duties are to care for the engines, boilers, etc.

engr.: engineer.

engross: 1) to copy an entire document or a record with a clear, large handwriting; 2) to finish a deed so it is ready to sign and record.

engrossing and forestalling: these laws are against the process of buying necessary goods and selling these goods at far higher prices. In other words these laws prevent profiteering.

enjoin: 1) a court order which commands or forbids a person to commit an act which he intended to do; 2) join together; 3) a direct order.

enlimn: to illuminate a book.

enlist: to voluntarily enroll in any of the branches of the armed forces.

enlisted man: 1) a non-commissioned officer or private in the Army or Marines; 2) any chief or petty officer or non-rated person in the Navy or Coast Guard.

enlistment paper: this document is a contract to serve in the armed forces and states the conditions of service of an individual. Some personal data is included.

enlistment register: an entry on two pages which repeats the information on an enlistment paper and adds information obtained at the time of discharge from the service.

ennui: lassitude, dullness of spirit, boredom.

enrolling clerk: the person who wrote on parchment the copy of a bill or resolution after passage by Congress and prior to inspection, or action, by the President. Then the bills were filed away as a permanent record of the business of Congress.

Ens.: Ensign.

enseal: 1) to fasten a container; 2) to put one's seal on a document.

ensifex: armorer, bearer of arms.

Ensign: 1) the equivalent of a cornet in the cavalry, an ensign carried the flag in the infantry. Now the lowest rank of commissioned officers in the United States Navy; 2) the national flag.

entail: 1) a common English practice which reserved the entire inheritance to the eldest surviving male heir and it could not be sold or given, even a part of the inheritance, to anyone who was not on a list which specified the line of heirs. Any heir who wished to dispose of the inheritance had to get an act passed by the state before he could make any land deals, sell worn out lands, move his labor force, etc.; 2) to impose a burden; 3) to limit an estate so it cannot be transferred, bequeathed, etc. by any of a prescribed list of heirs; 4) any line of upward order, as in an office; 5) a rule of descent for an estate.

entailed estate: property which can ben inherited only by certain children according to prescribed rules.

entd.: entered.

enter: to make a record according to a prescribed form.

enterclose: 1) a passage between two rooms in a house; 2) a passage leading from the door to the hall.

enteric fever: typhoid fever.

enteritis: inflammation of the digestive tract.

enterocolitis: inflammation of the small intestine and the colon.

enterpriser: a manager of a business who takes upon himself all the risks of conducting a business. Sometimes he was called an undertaker.

entg.: entering.

entirety: a whole, the total.

entitled land: real estate which can not be sold by its owner without permission of the government. Books do exist which list the acts passed by a vote of the Legislature giving permission for certain lands to be sold.

entity: a person, a state, a thing which is real and clearly seen. To view as entire by itself.

entradas: 1) rents; 2) revenue.

entrants: to enter into something, e.g. a college, games, country.

entresse: 1) interest; 2) business.

entry (land): a claim filed, or recorded, at an appropriate public land office by a person who has fulfilled the legal requirements for filing a claim.

enubo: 1) to marry a lower-class man; 2) to marry and leave a childhood home.

enumeration: a count, as of people in a census.

enumeration district: for the purpose of taking a census an area was divided into districts and a person was assigned to conduct a census in that part.

enumerator: a person who takes a census of a given area.

enure: see inure.

enutrio: to bring up a child.

enveillez: (Norman) grown old.

eodem: to the same place, just so far.

eo die: on the same day.

e.o.e.: errors and omissions excepted (which see).

epaulet, epaulette: the shoulder ornament on a dress uniform on which is indicated the commissioned officer's rank.

epilepsy: a chronic nervous disorder with convulsions and sometimes unconsciousness.

episcopus: bishop.

epistaxis: a nose bleed.

epistles: letters of goodwill and encouragement exchanged annually between nearly all of the Yearly Meetings of Friends (Quakers) in the world.

epistoler: the priest at a mass who chants the epistle.

epitaph: verse or sentiment on a tombstone.

epitaphulm: a funeral sermon.

epithelialize: to cover a wound with new skin.

epizootick: an old term for "an ailment going around."

epposant: (Norman) the petitioner.

Equal Rights Party: a portion of the Democratic party which was formed in 1835-37 in New York state and was active from time to time into the 20th century.

eques: cavalry soldier; a knight.

equipage: see accoutrements.

equitable: fair and reasonable.

equitable ownership: fair treatment of each of a group of owners.

equity court: this court had the power to make new rules or to adapt old ones to fit the circumstances of a particular case, whereas the common law court had to adhere strictly to the law. In certain matters the equity court could enforce a moral obligation.

equity of redemption: the rights of a

person who has lent money which as not been repaid on time and in full. These rights include payment of all costs.
erantz, arantz: (Norman) plowing.
erberage: (Norman) provision for cattle.
erberger: (Norman) to lodge or harbor.
erchdekene: (Norman) archdeacon.
erchevesqe: an archbishop.
erding: a dwelling.
ere: to plow.
ereable: arable.
erelle: an earl.
eremite: a hermit.
erendrake: 1) an ambassador; 2) a messenger.
ergo: therefore, hence, accordingly, consequently.
erite (l'): (Norman) the inheritance.
Erland: Ireland.
erminette: a rabbit fur which has been dyed to look like the more expensive fur, ermine.
errare humanum est: to err is human.
erresdeken, ersdekne: an archdeacon.
errors and omissions excepted: a notation found on a financial statement which indicates that the figures are as correct as possible.
erysipelas: an acute disease characterized by a fever, redness and swelling of the skin. Also called St. Anthony's fire. In frontier days a black cat with ears and a tail was rare as the pioneers believed that the blood of a black cat was the only remedy for this disease of the skin.
esche: ash tree.
escheat: the transfer of personal property or land to the state for reason of being abandoned or in the event of the owner dying without legal heirs. Sometimes spelled ascheat, achete.
eschele: 1) troop; 2) company.
escolin: a Dutch six-penny piece.
escoted: 1) paid; 2) supported.
escrow: money, deeds, etc. which are in the care of a third person who releases the item to the new owner when the conditions governing the escrow are fulfilled.
escryeurs: (Norman) writers.
escuquiteur: (Norman) an executioner.
espie: an overlooker.
espouse: spouse or wife.
esprit de corps: an individual's pride in his own unit or branch of service, etc.
Esq., Esqr.: Esquire.
esquire: a title used in this country to mean a person of considerable influence or even wealth.
ess: ashes.
essence peddler: a person who sold patent medicines, cure-alls, flavoring for food, etc. Sometimes he sold other unrelated items.
est: is.
est.: estate.
establie: a guard.
Established Church of Scotland: Presbyterian.
estafet: a footman.
estafette: a courier who rides a horse.
estasion: a shop or stall.
estate: 1) what a person owns or has an interest in, at the time of death; 2) assets of a person who has a guardian; 3) (archaic) state; 4) condition; 5) a wealthy person; 6) administration of government.
estate at will: a lease held at the will of the person who owns and leases property.
estate for life: use of property during the lifetime of the person who was given this life estate.
estate for years: interest in property which will be finished, done, terminated after a specified number of years.
estate from year to year: interest in property which does not have a termination date.
estate papers: a collection of documents created by the settlement of an estate. They can include the original will, inventories, accounts of the administration renunciations, etc. They are usually found in the county probate office where the decedent lived. While they may not provide "new" information, they can add color and an understanding of an ancestor's lifestyle.
estate sale: when an estate is to be divided among the heirs, it is sometimes easier to convert personal property to cash, which can be divided more easily. Sometimes only the items the family does not want are sold. This is usually

an auction sale.

estate tail: property which is limited to a person and does not go to his heirs in general, but to his lawful issue in a direct line. When a person who owns the property dies without any issue the estate is terminated.

estellacioun: astrology.

estole: (Norman) a school.

estovers: essentials taken from another allowed within the law, e.g. wood for repairs to a landlord's house may be taken from the owner's estate.

est quod: there is a reason for.

estray(s) book: the book kept in the courthouse which contained the description of valuable domestic animals and slaves which were missing.

estray notice: 1) a descriptive advertisement placed in a newspaper or on a broadside, to the effect that a slave had escaped or that an animal had disappeared. Usually a reward was offered for the capture of either; 2) Many times it was used to avoid accusations of theft, a landowner would post a written notice when a horse or cow strayed onto his property. This estray notice notified the county clerk of the animal's presence on a farm.

estrays: cattle, slaves, or convicts who appear to have left their domicile by escaping or straying away.

estreat: 1) an extract of an original; 2) to send an extract to an authority who has the power to enforce the recognizance.

estreynerye: (Norman) tin works.

et: and.

et al: 1) et abbi, and elsewhere; 2) et alii, and others.

etc.: et cetera, and so forth.

et cetera: and so on, so forth.

ethyndel: one-half bushel.

et sequentes: and those that follow.

et sic de caeteris: and so of the rest.

ettick fever: the ague.

ettlings: earnings, wages.

et ux, et uxor, et uxoris: and wife.

etyck: a fever.

Eucharist: 1) the Lord's Supper; 2) a consecrated part of Holy Communion, especially the bread; 3) giving thanks.

euchologion: a prayer book.

euiz (nous) desunes: (Norman) we have above mentioned.

evacuate: to leave a combat zone, first if possible, removing casualties from the battlefield.

Evang.: Evangelical.

evangelical: a religious person who seeks to convert others to his or her beliefs.

eveck: a goat.

even cristen: 1) a fellow Christian; 2) a neighbor.

evening gun: a gun fired at tatoo (evening hour) in the navy.

everlasting: also called durant, this popular cloth was used during the sixteenth and seventeenth centuries where durability was needed. Later it was called "lasting" and its strong, twill weave was used frequently to make women's shoes.

evidence: a statement given to an official in an attempt to prove or disprove a situation under investigation.

evito: to avoid.

ewangel: (Norman) evangelists.

eware: a water bearer.

ewe: a female sheep (pronounced "you").

ewer: a pitcher with a handle and spout and/or a base.

ewert (molin): (Norman) a water well.

ex: out of, from.

ex, exs: excess.

examinations: a document used when a person did not have a settlement certificate. He was required to make a sworn statement and answer many questions before an official, who would determine where he belonged.

examining court: in some states, the name of a court which questioned persons charged with a crime. Sometimes the cases before this court are found in the book containing commissioners' minutes.

exanthema: a symptom of an eruptive disease, as small pox, scarlet fever, measles, etc.

ex assensu patri: with the father's consent.

excd., execud., exed.: executed.

Exceldy, Excly: Excellency.

excess acreage: when a parcel of land upon being resurveyed is discovered to contain more land than the original survey stated.

exchange: a saloon in the early 19th century.

exchange warrant: issued in the place of an original military, preemption or treasury warrant.

exchequer: an English treasury in charge of public revenue.

excise man, excise master: a person appointed to collect taxes on liquor. The job was later expanded to include tea, coffee, jewelry, etc. and to make certain that retailers of these goods were properly licensed.

excise tax: an internal tax on the manufacture of liquor, cigarettes, etc.

ex contractu: a lawsuit started by a dispute over a contract.

excrescence: an unnatural out-growth of the skin.

ex curia: out of court.

ex dem: an abbreviation for ex demissione, meaning upon the demise.

ex donatione regis: by gift of the king.

exec., exectr.: executor.

execute: to finish. When a person executes a deed it is finished by his signature and delivery to the other party.

execution: in a court of law, when a debtor who had a judgment against him did not pay his debt, the next step was for the court to satisfy the debt in an orderly manner. The debtor's personal property would be sold and if this were not a sufficient amount to pay the debt, his real estate would be sold. If this failed, the debtor would be imprisoned until he could pay his debt.

executor: a person named in a will to settle the estate of the testator.

executor dative: a court-appointed person who will administer an estate.

executor deed: when a deceased person's land is sold by the administrator or executor of the estate an executor deed is issued. In order to locate this type of deed the name of the executor or administrator should be known.

executor de son tort: a person who unlawfully acts as an executor of an estate.

executress, executrix: a female named in a will to administer the estate.

exempd.: exempted.

exemplification: a copy book which shows how the letters used in writing should be formed.

exemplifications: a true copy. In Pennsylvania after the state government moved from Philadelphia to Harrisburg it was discovered that many of the Philadelphia land records had been transcribed into state record books instead of the county books. The Recorder of Deeds for Philadelphia went to Harrisburg and made "true copies" of all records which related to the city and county of Philadelphia. These records included property sales outside of Philadelphia, naturalizations, manumissions, etc.— anything which a person would like to have recorded. These are in twelve volumes titled *Exemplifications* and can be found in the Philadelphia County Courthouse.

exempt: 1) a man who was not required to fulfill a military obligation; 2) an honorably discharged member of a fire department.

exempt from tax: many court order books state that a person was exempt from paying his taxes. At various times and not all the time, the following people were exempt from paying their taxes: high ranking officers of the state, the Governor and his servants, clergymen, older males who were either infirm physically or mentally, those who were in the military service and those who were settling new lands.

exequy: a funeral.

exers., exors.: executors.

exercises: 1) public meetings for special occasions; 2) school displays of pupils' skills in orations; 3) body motions encouraged by preachers at revival meetings; 4) weekday sermons, so called by the Puritans.

ex facto: from or by the deed.

exheres: disinherited.

exhibit: a document which is produced in court, and duly recorded, to enable the court to reach a decision.

exhibition: 1) stipend; 2) allowance; 3) support, e.g. money to support another; 4) a gift; 5) a scholarship.

exhort: to urgently advise or caution another.
exidemic: an epidemic.
exile: 1) endowed with a small income; 2) poor.
ex officio: officially, by virtue of one's office.
ex parte: 1) of one part; 2) uncontested by any person adversely affected; 3) a one-sided viewpoint; 4) a report prepared by one contestant which has not been countered by the views of opponents.
expatriate: to live no longer in your own country.
expd.: expired.
expdn.: expedition.
expede: 1) to extricate; 2) to complete; 3) to issue (a document) officially; 4) obsolete word for to speedily dispatch.
expert: the highest recognition a person can receive for his skill in the use of small arms.
express rider: the man who worked for a pony express company and who carried mail or messages.
exr.: executor.
ex rel, ex relatione: a state action taken by the attorney general at the instigation of persons who have pertinent information to give about the case.
exs: executors.
exscribo: to copy; to note down.
extant: in existence.
extendour: 1) surveyor; 2) one who extends property.
extent: a violent attack.
ex testamento: in accordance with the treatment of.
extm.: ex testamento.
extr.: executor.
extract: a quotation or part of a written document as opposed to an abstract which sets out certain facts or sections.
extravasated blood: an old term for a ruptured blood vessel.
extreme unction: an old term for what is now called anointing of the sick. A sacrament given by a Roman Catholic priest to a person who is very ill or near death.
extremity: a term applied to the arms and legs, called upper and lower extremities.
exx., exor., ecux.: executrix.
eyegrass: old pasture ground that has gone a long time without animals eating there.
eyot: see ait.
eyrus: years.
eytendelle: 1) half a bushel; 2) one-eighth of a coomb (which see).

F: folio (large book).

f.: 1) father; 2) female; 3) filius; 4) folio; 5) following.

F.A.: Field Artillery.

fa.: father.

faber: smith, literally "maker."

fabricator: 1) artificer; 2) maker; 3) framer.

fabrick lands: lands given toward the maintenance, building or repair of churches or cathedrals.

factor: 1) an agent who buys and sells for another. He is paid a commission for his duties; 2) one appointed by law and charged with the care of an estate.

factorage: the commission paid to an agent (factor) who has been hired to sell goods for another.

factum: a deed, an act.

faculty: 1) the capacity of a mind, including memory, reason, speech; 2) the entire teaching staff of a school; 3) a privilege awarded by state government; 4) license or authorization.

fader: a father.

fagots, faggots: 1) small branches, brush, twigs, etc. bound together into a bundle for a fire, to fill in ditches, or to strengthen fortifications. In the latter sense it is called a fascine; 2) pieces of wrought iron which are bound together before being forged into bars.

fai: faithful.

fa-in-law: father-in-law, the father of one's husband or wife.

fair copy: a final copy of a document which includes all changes and corrections.

Fairfax proprietary: a huge estate of five million plus acres in Virginia was held by Lord Fairfax, who had inherited the land. Virginia took possession of this estate after Lord Fairfax's death in 1781, an action which showed a revolutionary opposition to this survival of the feudal system.

fait accompli: a thing already done.

faithful-brother: a Puritan.

falconer: a person who trained falcons or other varieties of hawks to hunt game.

faldstool: 1) a folding chair used by a church official when away from his own church; 2) a folding stool placed by the altar for use during a coronation ceremony.

falling-down: epilepsy.

falling leaf table: drop-leaf table.

falling-sickness: epilepsy.

fallow: 1) cut trees which are ready to be burned; 2) land which is allowed to stay in an unplanted state for at least one year.

fallow-field: a common field.

falls: the divisions of a large arable field attached to a village.

false measles: Roseola qv.

false pretenses: deceptive statements made in order to defraud.

falwes: 1) fallow ground; 2) newly plowed fields; 3) fields recently made tillable.

fam.: family.

fame: 1) (Norman) wife; 2) surgeon's lancet.

family of love: a sect introduced into England about 1560. They believed in love to all men and passive obedience to established authority.

familier de la chauncery: (Norman) a clerk belonging to the chancery.

familists: name for members of the family-of-love sect.

family Bible: a Bible in which is written the birth, marriage and death dates of a family. Usually the oldest child inherits the Bible and the responsibility of keeping it updated upon the death of the owner.

family burial ground: in early America deceased persons were buried in as high and dry a spot as could be found on a family farm. Many of these still exist.

family group record: a list containing names of a husband and wife plus all of their children with dates and places of births, marriages and deaths.

family plot: in a cemetery, graves are sold in groups of varying numbers. They usually are deeded as in other land transactions, therefore permission to bury is required of the deed holder. As a result, seldom are strangers found in a family plot. There is usually a relationship between the deceased and owner of the plot.

famular, familiar, famulus: (Norman) 1)

one of his household; 2) a familiar, intimate friend; 3) a servant.

fancy: used as a name for a home or acreage with a man's name as a prefix. For example: "Rogers' Fancy, 100 acres surveyed the 22nd of September 1674 for John Rogers."

fancy chair: usually the word fancy applied to a chair means that the frame of a lightweight simple chair was painted and parts of it were decorated with stencilled designs.

fancy man: 1) a pimp; 2) a male lover.

fancy woman, fancy lady: 1) a prostitute; 2) a mistress.

F & A M: Free and Accepted Masons.

fane: 1) a banner; 2) enemies.

fanega: the Spanish bushel.

faner: a winnower.

fanger: 1) a guardian; 2) a capturer.

fanning mill: a machine which separates dust and chaff from grain by means of a current of air.

farandine: this material, which was popular in the seventeenth century, was developed by a man named Ferrand. The content was a combination of silk and wool or hair.

farandman: a traveler. In Scotland a law provided that a stranger could bring a citizen into court for a felony if he did so within a specified amount of time. Most areas did little to protect a stranger from a crime.

fardel: 1) a profit; 2) a bundle or package; 3) one-fourth of anything.

fardel de terre: (Norman) a fourth part of an acre.

fardingale: the fourth part of an acre.

farer: a traveler.

farmed out: 1) when captured Hessians were in a Lancaster, New York prison, they were farmed out or put out to work on a farm as laborers; 2) land which has been used year after year for the same crop without rebuilding by the use of fertilizer, etc. or by rotating the crops.

farmer: 1) a tax collector; 2) the eldest son of the occupier of a farm. 3) anciently, a yeoman or county gentleman; 4) the man who did the work on his own land with the help of his family or a hired man.

farmery: infirmary.

farm let: to lease a farm for a set amount.

farren: half an acre.

farrier: a specialized blacksmith, also sometimes called a shoeing smith, who had great knowledge of horses' hooves and could make the shoes and nails and fit them in place.

farron: litter of pigs.

farron cow: barren cow.

farthing: 1) a measure of land, one-quarter of an acre; 2) a British coin; 3) an ancient English coin minted of gold; 4) a small Roman coin.

farthing ale: a hoop skirt, or the petticoat worn beneath it.

F.A.S.: see Free African Society.

fascinator: a scarf, either crocheted or knitted, triangular or oblong, worn over a lady's head and loosely wound around her throat.

fascine: see fagot.

fashion baby: a doll used by mantua makers which was dressed in the latest fashions and sent to the colonies as an example of their wares.

fashioner: a tailor.

fastening penny: earnest money.

fast estate: realty (real estate) as opposed to personalty (personal property). See also realty.

father-in-law: in Colonial days this term not only meant a spouse's father, but it could mean a step-father.

father-law: father-in-law.

fathom: a naval measurement (especially of depth) which equals six feet.

fatt: sometimes spelled fat or fatte 1) a wine cask, a vat, or a large tub; 2) a barrel used for dry material; 3) a quantity measure which varied with the material to be measured.

faunt: an infant or small child.

Faverer: (Norman) February.

fawdyne: a notary.

fawkenere: a falconer.

fayters: 1) facts; 2) acts.

f.b.: family Bible

F.C.P.: Free Person of Color.

F D: a type of federal land sale in early Illinois.

feal: a fee.

fealty: faithfulness which is owed to

another because of law or custom.

feasors de drapes: (Norman) cloth workers.

feast: an annual day of merry making in country villages. In some places the feast lasted for several days.

Feast of St. Andrew: see Advent Sunday.

feather bed: a very soft bed which has a mattress stuffed with feathers, and which sometimes had a top or over cover also filled with feathers.

feather merchant: slang for a person who is a loafer.

featlet: four pounds of butter.

febrifuge: a medicine to reduce a fever.

febrile: having a fever or high temperature.

Federalist: a member of the Federalist political party which endorsed the adoption of the Federal Constitution. This was shortened to Feds as opposed to Antis.

fee: 1) an estate consisting of property to be given to the owner's heir unless the owner disposes of it before he dies; 2) a charge for professional services; 3) a servant's wages.

fee bill: the itemized list of charges by a lawyer or officer of the court for his services.

feedbag: a bag (woven or of canvas or leather) which slipped onto the head of a horse or ox. It held grain which the animal could eat by pushing the bag against the ground.

feeder: a servant.

fee simple absolute: complete and unlimited interest in land.

fee simple title: property which the owner can do with as he pleases. It can be subject to easements, restrictions, etc.

fee tail: property which goes to the owner's legal heirs, if he dies without selling, or otherwise disposing of it.

feile: (Norman) daughter.

feisours: (Norman) makers.

feitt: 1) a paddock; 2) a field.

fell: 1) an animal hide, sometimes hair-like fleece; 2) high land.

feller: a person who cut down trees.

felling axe: a tool used by a cutter of trees.

fellmonger: a person who removes hair from animal hides preparatory to making leather.

fellmonger's shears: a tool used by 1) a tanner; 2) a currier.

felloe pattern: a tool used by a wheelwright.

felon: 1) a deep abscess of the finger, involving the bone; 2) a wheel rim usually made of seasoned oak; 3) a criminal.

felony: a serious crime. At one time even minor crimes were punishable by the taking away of property, death, imprisonment, etc.

feltmaker: a person who makes cloth which, instead of being woven, is made of fibers matted together.

feman: a fugitive.

feme: wife, woman.

feme-covert: a married woman.

feme sole: 1) an unmarried woman; 2) a married woman who became single again by death or divorce.

feme sole trader: a married woman who can hold, buy, or sell real property in her own name, rather than her husband's. Sometimes referred to as a free trader.

femina: woman.

femme de chambre: a lady's maid.

fen: a low marshland.

fenage: a hay crop.

fence viewer: his duties were to supervise the establishment of boundary lines and the construction of fences and walls in these boundaries. He also was responsible for arbitrating boundary disputes and seeing that the fences were kept in good repair.

fender: a protective fireplace screen designed to keep children from being burned. It may be attached to the grate.

fenerator: a lender of money for interest.

fennies: see tennies.

feod: an obsolete form of feud.

feodary: 1) a vassal in feudal days; 2) an obsolete word for an accomplice.

feofee: grantee.

feoffer: grantor.

feoffment: a public delivery of a deed of an English freehold estate between the grantor and grantee. This ceremony was called a livery of seisin. Also spelled enfeoffment.

fere: a companion or wife.

ferriage: 1) boat or ferry hire; 2) (Norman) payment for using a ferry.

fermacie: a medicine.

ferme: 1) a farm; 2) a rent in lieu of all other payments; 3) duty.

fermeald: a farm.

fermerere: the officer who had the care of the infirmary.

fermistier: (Norman) wage.

ferramentum: any tool but especially one used in agriculture.

ferrarius: relating to iron.

ferrement: (Norman) ironwork.

ferrer: 1) a farrier; 2) a barrel with iron hoops.

ferriage: 1) the fare to cross a river on a ferry; 2) the business of operating a ferry.

ferrotype: a tintype (which see).

ferruere: (Norman) the shoeing of horses.

ferrum: iron.

ferry: 1) a flat floating platform which was propelled across water carrying passengers, animals, cargo, etc. from one shore to the other; 2) the right to operate a ferry.

ferryman: the owner and/or operator of a ferry.

festing penny: earnest money.

fet, fetes: (Norman) 1) was, had been, caused, done, made; 2) the fact, deed, business.

fetz: (Norman) deeds, grants.

feu: a perpetual lease.

feu (argent): (Norman) pure silver.

feudal system: the medieval scheme of land ownership. The king owned the land but granted its use to others, who in turn could grant their interests to third parties. These grants were made in return for past services, or on the promise of service in the future.

feudatory: 1) an estate held by feudal tenure; 2) a feudal vassal.

feust: (Norman) wood.

feust nostre fitz: (Norman) our late son.

feut: (Norman) son.

fever: a blacksmith.

Feverez: (Norman) February.

fewterer: a dog-keeper.

fey, feyets: (Norman) deeds, actions.

feyne: (Norman) 1) a fine; 2) hay.

fez: (Norman) fees.

feze (treis): (Norman) three times.

ff: following.

FF's: First Families. A slang expression for a supposedly elite society.

fft: an abbreviation for fatt.

F.F.V.: First Families of Virginia.

fiables (gentz): (Norman) persons of credit.

fiancer (per): (Norman) by pledging his faith. This was allowed a poor man, or a foreigner, who brought an action, because he could not find pledges to prosecute. This was to prevent malicious prosecution.

fichere: a fisher.

ficicion: physician.

fidei defensor: defender of the faith.

fidejussore: godparent.

fiduciary: a person who invests or holds funds in trust for another.

fie: (Norman) fee, salary.

fie (en): (Norman) in fee.

fief: 1) an English manor or estate; 2) a term rarely used now which indicates something over which a person has rights or can exercise control.

field: a plowed field as distinguished from grass or pasture.

field bed: 1) a bed used for sleeping outside; 2) a small canopy bed which was popular in the middle 1800s.

field day: 1) the day when troops practice field maneuvers, such as marching; 2) the day set aside for thorough cleaning by the navy.

field driver: a local officer whose job was to catch and confine animals roaming on roads or lands. This was necessary as there were few fences and animals could wander far from home.

field notes: notes pertaining to a particular subject or about a particular survey, etc. made by a researcher or surveyor before returning to his office.

field officer: regimented officers who are out in the field with their troops, as opposed to officers with duties which keep them in quarters.

field rates (surveying): a type of diary kept by a surveyor of land. In this diary he recorded details as he established land boundaries. It is a permanent record.

fielle, fillie, filie: (Norman) daughter.

fiere en lay: (Norman) brother-in-law.

fieri facias: "cause to be done." A court order which tells a court officer or sheriff to raise money from the sale of possessions belonging to the person who owes the court money.

fi fa: fieri facias (which see).

fife: a small, shrill flute made of wood. It was used in combination with a snare drum to produce military music.

fife-major: the person in charge of the regimental fifers.

fifer: the person who played a fife.

figulus: potter.

figure flinger: an astrologer.

fil.: father-in-law.

fil day: an abbreviation for field day (which see).

file: 1) a collection of papers arranged by subject; 2) to place documents with a county office to be recorded.

file cutter: a person who makes a tool from hardened steel which is designed to smooth metal, fingernails, etc. by means of small teeth cut into the metal.

fileresses: (Norman) spinners.

filia: daughter.

filia fratris: brother's daughter.

filial portions: a child's inheritance from an estate.

filia sororis: sister's daughter.

filia vitrici: stepsister.

filibuster: 1) a political tactic consisting of a long speech, maybe of several days, designed to prevent passage of a law or force a decision; 2) an unauthorized military expedition to encourage and support a revolution in a foreign country.

filiola: diminutive form of filia, or daughter. A little daughter.

filiolus: a diminutive form of filius, or son. A little son.

filius: son.

filius fratris: brother's son.

filius novercae: stepbrother on mother's side.

filius nullius: a son of nobody; an illegitimate person.

filius populi: a son of the people, a bastard.

filius sororis: sister's son.

filius terrae: a son of the soil.

filius vitrici: stepbrother on father's side.

fill dyke: the month of February.

"filled" jewelry: at the beginning of the 1800s, the New Englanders made jewelry stamped out of pewter, or other base metal, with a gold covering. This was cheap and soon the demand was for more than the supply.

filly: a young female horse or a young lady.

final: a certificate, with interest, issued in 1780 by the Continental Congress to replace the Continental money which was depreciated.

final account: see settlement.

final records: see settlement.

Fincastle County, Virginia: an area which is now the state of Kentucky.

find: fined.

finding out: a point in a sermon where a prolonged discussion upon a verse in the Bible was analized.

fineez: (Norman) ended.

fingerboards: a directional sign erected at a crossroads. They pointed in the direction of towns.

finishing horse: a tool used by a bowl turner.

fip: half of a bit or one-sixteenth of a coin.

fireboard: a board, used to fill the fireplace opening during the summer months. Some were painted with scenes of historical events, designs or in some cases were made of frames enclosing cloth, embroidered or done in needlepoint on canvas.

firedogs: see andirons.

Firelands or Sufferers' Lands—1792: This land replaced property destroyed along the coast of Connecticut by the British with the aid of Benedict Arnold. This land is located in Erie and Hudson Counties, Ohio. Upon petition of these people whose property had been destroyed, Connecticut set aside 500,000 acres at the west end of Connecticut's reserve lands.

fireman: 1) a man stationed at a gun; 2) one who feeds the fire for a steam engine (a stoker); 3) a worker on a boat or ship under the authority of the engineer.

fireroom: a room which contained a fireplace.

firescoop: a shovel-like device with a short handle and a perforated lid in which one carried coals borrowed from a neighbor to start a fire in the stove. Stove coals had to be kept and tended carefully, for matches were hard to get.

fireship: prostitute.

firkin: 1) a wooden tub used for storage, especially butter; 2) an English measure which equalled about a fourth of a barrel; 3) a measure. Eight gallons of a liquid or six and one-half pounds of a solid.

firlot, firlat, firlet: a grain measure.

firman: 1) a permit or license; 2) a passport.

firmarius: farmer, renter.

first mate: a person who is second in command on a non-military ship.

fisechiens: (Norman) physicians.

fisher: a man who catches fish from a lake, ocean, etc. for his living.

fish fag: a fish-woman.

fishmonger: the person who sold fish.

fistula: an abnormal tube-like pouch in the body.

fitpence: five pence.

fits: epilepsy qv.

fitter: one who fits pieces who that they work well together.

Five Civilized Tribes: a term used in the early 19th century to identify the Indian tribes which were considered to be the most advanced in civilized life and customs: the Cherokee, Chickasaw, Choctaw, Creek and Seminole.

five-share-men: men who enlisted for service on a whaling ship, as a group. They received one-fifth of the profits.

fixtures: goods attached to a house which go with it when it is sold. For example, light fixtures or kitchen cupboards.

fk: fork, as in the Salt Fork of the river.

flagging iron: a tool used by a cooper.

flag fallen: out of work.

flagman: 1) a surveyor's assistant; 2) a rear brakeman on a train.

flag officer: a naval officer who holds the rank of rear admiral or higher.

flagon: a container for liquid, usually a large bottle with a handle, spout, etc. for use at a table.

flail: a tool used by a farmer to pound or thrash (separate grain from the stalk) before the invention of a threshing machine.

flakewhite: white lead.

flank: the side of a military formation. The side which is to the right as one faces the enemy is called the right flank.

flankers: gun emplacements for protection against Indians, usually made of planks or timber.

flannel: a soft woolen fabric with a nap on one side which was used for clothing, sheets, etc. When made of cotton it was called flannelet.

flaptable: what we would today call a small drop-leaf table.

flatboat: this term seems to cover many varieties of boats designed to transport families by waterways. It would appear that they sometimes resembled the houseboats of today, but were far larger.

flat box tongs: a tool used by a blacksmith.

Flathead: 1) a lawless man, as opposed to a Regulator. See Salish; 2) a member of the Chinook Indian tribe, so called for their flat-topped heads.

flat milk: skimmed milk.

flatter: a hammer with a four inch square laid on top of a piece of metal. It was hit with another hammer to flatten the metal.

flax: a plant with blue flowers which was cut, soaked or retted, and stripped in fibers. It was woven into linen.

flax dresser: the person who prepared flax for the spinning process.

flax swingle: a large knife made of wood used by a farmer to beat and clean flax. Also called a leasestick.

flax wheel: a small spinning wheel.

fleam: 1) a doctor's instrument for opening a vein when "bleeding" a patient; 2) a river, either natural or man-made.

flecher: (Norman) a bowyer.

fleet milk: skimmed milk.

flem: a farrier's tool.

flesh axe: a butcher's cleaver.

flesher: a person who removes animal

hides from their flesh or the tool he uses.

flesh fork: a large fork used for lifting and turning meat during the cooking process, or for serving.

fleshing knife: a tool used by a tanner.

flesh marks: see brand.

fleshmonger: a butcher.

fletcher: 1) an arrowmaker, more properly the one who put the feathers on the arrow; 2) one who deals in arrows.

flip: a Colonial drink made of beer, sugar and rum. It had a distinctive flavor made by inserting a hot poker in it before serving.

flirt-gill: a woman with few morals.

flitting and removing: moving to another house.

float: a certificate issued by the federal government 1) to Indians when their lands were acquired. These certificates were to be used for land in certain areas farther west, but unethical speculators many times exchanged trifles for the certificates; 2) to settlers who were then entitled to stated acreage in public lands. The location was to be selected by the settler. While these certificates were designed to protect the settler when claims overlapped, corrupt land speculators were again the ones who profited.

floating entry: a land claim with a vague land description, which was done on purpose.

floating shovel: a shovel used for cutting turf.

flock bed: a mattress stuffed with cast-off cotton or wool material which has been cut into small pieces.

floor mandrel: a tool used by a blacksmith.

florentine: 1) a one crust meat pie; 2) when capitalized, a native of Florence, Italy.

florin: 1) a coin first minted in Great Britain of silver and later of an alloy; 2) equal to a guilder in the Netherlands; 3) a gold coin minted during the thirteenth century in Florence; 4) an English gold coin; 5) an early Austrian gold coin.

flotilla: a number of fleet of small vessels.

flouring mill: the mill where wheat was ground into flour by a pair of millstones.

flourish: 1) to embellish with ornamental lines; 2) to prosper; 3) a trumpet fanfare.

F L T: an inscription on the cemetery stone of an IOOF member. It is an abbreviation for Friendship, Love, Truth.

flummery: 1) a porridge or soft jelly made of a grain sometimes used as a dessert, sweet and cold with nuts or fruit; 2) fruit custard; 3) any one of several custard-type dishes; 4) nonsensical; 5) something trashy, not worth keeping, or a compliment without real meaning.

fluttergrub: a field laborer.

flux: 1) the drainage or discharge of a liquid from a body cavity, for example diarrhea; 2) dysentery.

flux of humour: the circulation of blood.

fly: a small amount of land. Also called fly-land.

flying camp: 1) a temporary military encampment; 2) a military group which is temporarily housed, for example, an extra troop during wartime; 3) troops ready to move rapidly from place to place.

fly-land: or fly. A small amount of land.

fly-scarer: this was a device resembling fringe which hung over the table from the ceiling and was operated by a woman's foot operating a treadle, thus keeping it moving and scaring flies away from the food.

f.m.: free mulatto.

f.n.: free negro.

f/o: father of.

foal: a baby horse.

foaled: the word used to indicate that a mare has given birth to a foal.

focage: a medieval English tax levied upon each chimney in a house. Also called fumage.

fodder: dried corn plants used as winter food for cattle. A device to chop the corn stalks was developed in the early 19th century.

foddering ground: a grass enclosure for feeding cattle.

F.O.E.: Fraternal Order of Eagles.

fogger: 1) a laborer who cared for cattle; 2) (archaic) a huckster; 3) a manservant; 4) a cheat.

foites: (Norman) duds, writings.
fol.: 1) folio; 2) following.
folde: farmyard.
fold garth: a farmyard.
folht: baptism.
folio: 1) both sides of a leaf (page) make a folio and sometimes these pages will be numbered as one; 2) a large size of book, made of sheets folded only once.
foll.: follows.
folly: 1) used as a means of identification for newly surveyed land, this word derived from the Latin "folium" (foliage). At first it was usually used for shaded areas, then the use was extended to any tract of land. 2) Another meaning of folly comes from the French "follie" (foolish) and was applied to partially finished or poorly financed large houses.
foolscap: a size of paper which varied in dimensions from about 12" by 15" to 13 1/2" by 17". Its name came from a watermark in the shape of a pointed cap.
"football" coach: this was a wooden coach shaped like a watermelon or football and slung on several through-braces, drawn by four horses, and carried six to nine passengers.
foot-boat: a boat used solely for conveying foot passengers.
footbridge: a rough bridge only large enough to accommodate a man on foot.
footlog: a log, or several lengths of logs, which have been cut in half lengthwise and fastened together to form a narrow bridge. A crude hand rail made of smaller logs was attached to one side.
foot-maiden: a waiting maid.
foot man: 1) a pedestrian. It was common during the first two centuries of our country to go barefoot as much as possible. When a man would reach his destination, he would put on the shoes he had carefully carried with him; 2) a servant who runs errands and performs other duties; 3) a foot soldier.
foot pad: a robber who is on foot.
foot peddler: a person who walked from area to area selling small items that he could carry on his person.
forage: to gather together supplies for both animals and men wherever these supplies can be found.
forbearance: permission to delay payment.
for-burthe: 1) birth-right; 2) the first-born of a family.
forced sale: a sale made without the consent or concurrence of the property owner,but made by a judicial process such as a writ of execution, or an order under a foreclosure decree.
forcible detainer: 1) to keep a building or land by a person who does not legally own it; 2) sometimes a refusal by a person not the legal owner to return property to the one who owns it.
for compliment: for completion; accomplished.
ford: a place at which a body of water may be crossed safely. Infantry depth of safety is three feet, four for cavalry and two and one-half for artillery.
foreclosure: the act of stopping the person who owes money on property from redeeming it, usually because he has not paid what he owed.
fore-elders: ancestors.
fore-family: the ancestors of a family.
foreman: an ancestor.
forepart iron: a tool used by a bootmaker.
foreroom: a parlor where the best furnishings of a house were used and visitors were received.
foresd.: aforesaid.
forestaller: a broker.
forestarius: forester.
forester: an official in charge of a forest.
forester-of-the-fee: a person who had, for some service to the crown, the perpetual right of hunting in a forest upon paying to the crown a certain rent for the privilege.
forge: an implement which contains fire and uses a blast of air to heat metal in order that it may be reshaped. During the Revolutionary War iron ore was heated in a forge until iron could be produced. Workers in the shop were referred to as blacksmiths.
form: in Quaker records this stands for formerly.
formal: done well in order to meet all legal requirements.
formfaderes: fore-fathers.
formulary: 1) a book which lists pharma-

ceutical formulas; 2) a book of forms used in a church service.

fornication: sexual intercourse other than that between a married couple.

fornissors: (Norman) framers.

forolded: worn out with age.

forsary: a slave who worked in the kitchen.

forspeak: an advocate.

fort: 1) a reinforced strong place; 2) the name usually given a permanent army post.

for-taxed: wrongly taxed.

fortelace: a fortress.

Fort Necessity: built by George Washington early in the French and Indian War, Washington was defeated here by the French and forced to go back to Virginia.

Fort Ninety-Six: located in South Carolina, this fort was given its name because it was ninety-six miles to the nearest Indian village. The British held this fort during the Revolutionary War.

Fort Pickering: a fort which was on the site where Memphis, Tennessee is today.

fortnight: a time period of two weeks.

fortress: 1) a very large fort or several forts placed in a group; 2) a city or locality defended by forts.

fortuit: French law; accidentally, by chance.

forty: 1) one-sixteenth of a section of land or forty acres; 2) this word also refers to forty acres, more or less, of land which is quite some distance from a farmhouse. A long distance, e.g. "I parked in the back forty," meaning I parked a long way away.

foss: a pit in which criminals are punished by drowning.

fosse: a ditch, moat, canal which is usually filled with water.

foster: (Norman) a park keeper.

foster child: a child not old enough to care for himself and whose parents are unable to care for him. He lives with an unrelated family for an unspecified period of time.

fosterage: the process of bringing up another person's child.

foster father: one who raises a child as his own but does not adopt him.

fother: a great number or quantity.

foulard: usually made of silk, this lightweight fabric had a twill weave and was mainly used to make clothing accessories. Sometimes the fiber content was cotton.

foullons, fullours, fullons: (Norman) fullers.

founday: a space of six days. A term used by iron workers, being the time in which they make eight tons.

founder: 1) in the navy this means that the ship fills with water and sinks; 2) in animals it means that they eat too much, bloat and sometimes die.

foundry: a work place which produces objects cast of metal.

fourbour: a furbisher.

fourte: fourteen.

four to: quarts.

Fox Indians: a tribe of Algonquin stock who lived on both sides of the Mississippi River.

fowertie: forty.

fowling piece: a light-weight gun designed for shooting birds. It fired birdshot (many small lead pellets) instead of a solid bullet.

F.P.C.: Free Persons of Color.

Fr.: French.

fr.: from.

fractur: a pen and ink art form, also called illuminated handwriting, which was probably introduced in this country by the Moravians and was used in two main forms: religious and secular. Religious included baptismal and marriage certificates, etc., and the secular included "pictures" which were used to decorate the usually barren walls, title pages of books, etc.

fractura: fracture.

frail ladies: ladies of the evening, more commonly called prostitutes.

frake: a man.

framer: a person who built the skeleton of a house to be finished by others. As an occupation the framer is obsolete with his work done now by a carpenter.

framer's block: a tool used by a chair maker.

framer's hammer: a tool used by a chair

maker.

frame saw: a tool used by a stone mason.

frame work knitter: a person who made knitted stockings on a machine which belonged to someone else, who provided raw materials and bought the finished product. The worker had no control over the price of yarn or the finished product.

franchise: 1) a privilege given by a governmental body to a person or a group of people; 2) to set free from restraints.

frank: 1) a pig sty; 2) to fatten an animal; 3) to pay another's fare on public transportation.

frankalmoin: a situation where a church, or other religious group, owns land forever as long as they fulfill the obligation of praying for the souls of the deceased donor and his heirs.

frankferm: a lifetime rental agreement at a fixed rate without being obliged to give extra service to the lord.

Frankland: see State of Franklin.

frank law: no longer used, this phrase means that a freeman has all the rights of a citizen, including the right to serve as a juror or as a witness in court.

franklein, franklyn, franklin: a country gentleman or farmer of considerable worth.

franklin: an English freeholder of the 14th and 15th centuries.

Franklin: see State of Franklin.

frank marriage: the right of a man and wife to hold land given to the wife by a blood relative, either before or after the wedding. This land was tax-free until it passed to the couple's great great grandchildren.

frank pledge: a division of a village into groups, often for the purpose of overseeing the conduct of others in his group. If a member erred he would be charged with a breech of law in court. Each group was called a tithing (which see).

frater: 1) brother; 2) a person who solicited alms under the pretence that the money would be used for a hospital.

frater germanus: a full brother.

frater house: the hall in a monastery.

fream: arable or plowed land that has been worked too much.

Free African Society: A beneficial organization for blacks. This group offered burial insurance and help for the elderly, poor or ill black families. Other similar groups had different names.

Free and Accepted Masons: see Freemason.

free and common socage: see free socage.

freebooter: 1) a pirate; 2) a member of a band of marauders.

freeborn: a person born to parents who were neither slaves nor in bondage.

free church: 1) a church open to all with no charges; 2) a church which is not under state control; 3) a nonconformist church.

freedman: a male released from slavery.

Freedman's Bureau: authorized by Congress, this department of the War Department existed from 1865 to 1872 to help not only blacks but loyal white refugees during the Reconstruction period. It distributed clothes, provided transportation home for these men, established hospitals and schools, and worked to relieve the terrible conditions existing in the postwar South.

Freedman's Savings and Trust Company: after the Civil War when many banks operated by white people were insolvent, they could not accept new accounts. The Freedman's Savings and Trust Company was formed to allow both black and white people to open accounts. Their records furnish many personal details about their depositors.

freedom dues: the sum of money given to an indentured servant along with clothes and a set of the tools of his trade at the close of his term of service.

freed stool: a seat or chair in churches near the altar, to which offenders fled for sanctuary. It was their last and most sacred refuge.

free from restraint: a phrase used in wills to indicate that the testator was not deceived as to the contents of his will. He was also not forced or induced to sign a will.

freehold: real estate which can be used by the holder only during the lifetime of a specified person.

freeholder: in early England, a person who farmed a fairly large number of acres for which he paid rent in money. The freeholder, unlike the serf or the cotter, was not obliged to give the lord extra service.

freehold estate: see freehold.

Freeman: in Colonial days this term referred to any male over twenty-one years old who owned personal property or real estate valued at a prescribed amount. He also was obliged to be a peaceful man, endorsed by a majority of the town's Freemen. Only after this vote at a semi-annual meeting of the selectmen, could the man take the Freeman's Oath. His duties were to elect deputies to the General Assembly of the colony and to elect new Freemen. He was a member of a local church and had the right to vote and pay taxes.

freeman of color: this usually means a black man who had been freed from slavery.

freemason: 1) a stone mason who was above the grade of rough mason, and who was qualified to carve freestone (fine ground limestone and sandstone); 2) a member of the Free and Accepted Masons, a large secret lodge known better as Masons or Masonic Order; 3) a stoneworker of the Middle Ages who was skilled also belonged to a secret lodge for workers. Sometimes, later, this lodge included other honorary members who did not work in building trades. They were called accepted Masons.

freendesse: a female friend.

free socage: land held by a tenant who was required to give his lord the same service as a free man would give. It is also called free and common socage.

free state: the term applied to a state where, before the Civil War, slavery was not allowed.

free tenant: a man who paid rent for land.

free trader: see feme sole trader.

freighter: 1) a sailing ship used to transport goods; 2) a man engaged in hauling goods by wagon across the western plains.

French and Indian War: This war was fought from 1754 to 1763 in Eastern North America. In Europe it was known as the Seven Years War. It was the last of a long series of wars fought by England and France. The chief issue between the two nations became the Colonies in America and India. The peace of 1763 eliminated France from North America; the land between the Appalachians and the Mississippi and Canada was ceded to England; Louisiana was ceded to Spain.

French Canadian: a small diary cow, brown in color, which was raised in Quebec during the middle eighteenth century.

French Grants: two grants, one in 1795 and the other in 1798, gave land in Scioto County, Ohio to French immigrants who had been swindled out of their money by a bogus land company. The land was given by the United States government.

French pox: venereal disease.

fresco: 1) a way of painting on newly plastered walls before the plaster dries; 2) wall painting.

freshet: 1) a fresh water stream which empties into the ocean; 2) a stream which is made to overflow by a heavy rain or melting of a large amount of snow.

friar: a male member of a religious group which did not have community property and no headship. He did not take a vow to remain a friar for his lifetime.

friars' cloth: see monks' cloth.

fricandeau: a dish made of veal and bacon.

friendly estate: an estate which remains in probate for an undetermined period of time. There are four kinds: fee simple absolute, defeasible fee, fee tail, and life estate.

Friendly Society: originally this was the name of a fire insurance company. Later many, as members of other associations, would purchase insurance against illness, death, etc. from a company doing business under this name.

friendly suit: a suit brought to court by a creditor against the executor or administrator of an estate to force persons to take their assets from the estate. Many times this suit is brought by the executor or administrator against himself, in the name of the creditor.

Friends: Society of Friends, see Quakers.

frier, fryer: (Norman) brother.

frieze: 1) ornamentation on a wall or around a door frame; 2) a woolen fabric with a long pile, usually on one side only.

frigate: a warship which operated as an independent unit against enemy threats.

friperer: 1) one who cleans old apparel for sale; 2) a seller of old clothes and rags; 3) a broker.

fripery: an old clothes shop.

friseur: a French hairdresser.

frobicher: a furbisher.

frock: a loose outer garment slipped over the head, with the waist-length neck opening closed by buttons. Sometimes the opening was gathered on a string. The length usually was halfway between the knees and feet with a short length worn indoors.

frock coat: a knee-length, close-fitting man's coat. It had a vent in the back and could be either single or double-breasted.

frodmortell: a free pardon for murder or manslaughter.

froe: a tool used by 1) a hoop bender; 2) a basket maker; 3) a gate hurdle maker.

from bed and board: a wife has left her husband, his bed, and support.

fronstead: a farm yard.

frontier: in the United States this was the area where there were few settlers. It was adjacent to the wilderness or unoccupied area.

fruiterer: a seller of fruit and vegetables.

fruitestere: a female seller of fruit.

Ft.: Fort.

fueler: the servant who laid the fires.

fuelle: (Norman) a daughter.

fugere: a satin weave used for several centuries as a fancy material for petticoats, bedspreads, etc.

fuit: was.

fulker: a pawnbroker or money lender.

full: this term indicates that siblings have the same parents, e.g. a full brother or full sister.

full age: see adult.

full cousin: first cousin.

fulled: baptized.

fuller: 1) a tool used by a blacksmith; 2) see walker; 3) the person who cleans or finishes cloth.

full hand: a person who could do as much work as an adult, able-bodied male.

fulling mill: see clothier.

fulling stocks: a machine used in a mill for fulling cloth.

fullynge: baptizing.

fumade: smoked herring.

fumage: see focage.

fumer: an old word for a manufacturer of perfume.

funambulist: a tightrope walker.

funarius: rope maker.

funeral gifts: in Colonial days gifts (rings, scarves, gloves, etc.) were given to those invited to the funeral as a way of paying tribute to the dead. The custom came from England and was so strongly ingrained that even pauper funerals required a minimum of gifts. Prominent persons' funerals could require the distribution in excess of, for example 2,000 pairs of gloves. The cost of the gifts was deducted from the estate of the deceased, which eventually led to laws prohibiting the custom, which frequently had left a widow and her children virtually paupers.

funeral meats: a meal served after a funeral to relatives and friends who had some distance to travel home.

funeral pie: a raisin pie which was served at funerals, according to a Pennsylvania-Dutch custom.

funeral trolley: in areas where the streets were too muddy for a hearse to be driven, a trolley car built especially for the occasion was used. It carried the coffin, pall bearers and mourners to the cemetery gate on a spur track where the coffin was placed on a flat car by the pall bearers and taken into the cemetery. After the service the trolley car was reversed and the trip was made back into town.

furbisher: a person who cleaned and polished armor.

Furier: (Norman) February.
fur(les): (Norman) the gallows.
furlong: 1) a linear measure of one-eighth of a mile, forty rods or two hundred and twenty yards; 2) the line of direction of plowed lands; 3) a division of an unenclosed corn field.
furlough: an enlisted man's leave of absence with permission .
furnage: the charge to either use the lord's oven or permission to have one's own oven.
furner: a baker.
furnish: a term used during the Revolutionary War to indicate who would provide the necessities of life for women and children whose husbands and fathers were in the army or who had been killed while in service. The donors were reimbursed by the county treasurer.
furniture: this word signified any kind of movable property. A country well stocked with animals, etc. was said to have good furniture.
furnour: a baker.
furor: a very violent unreasonable temper tantrum, not accompanied by fever.
furrow: the deep trench made by a plow as it breaks ground.
furunculus: a small-time thief.
fusileer: in early times, a British member of a regiment.
fust: a wine barrel.
fusterer: a maker of pack-saddles.
fustian: this cloth was at one time made of a cotton and linen mixture, but now the term refers to corduroy or velveteen.
F.W.K.: frame work knitters.
fylesoferus: philosophers.
fyschere: a fisher.
fysyschons: physicians.
fyvire: fever.

G

G: grand, as in grandson, granddaughter, etc.
g., gt.: great.
gabel: 1) a tax or excise; 2) a sheep's ear mark.
gabelle: 1) a tax; 2) a law in early France which created a tax on salt. At the end of the eighteenth century that law was repealed.
gabeller: a tax collector.
gaberdine: 1) a loose garment worn by pilgrims; 2) a woven cloth of cotton or wool.
gableck: a crowbar.
gad: 1) a Colonial term for a mark or cut in the ear of an animal to prove ownership. Many times these marks would be registered with the town officials; 2) a tool used by a stone mason.
gad bit: a nail passer.
gadger: a gauger or exciseman.
gaffer: 1) an old man; 2) a grandfather; 3) a head laborer or workman; 4) in some areas a former, quite common mode of address, equivalent to a friend or neighbor.
gage (en): (Norman) in mortgage.
gage: a measure of slate one yard square, about one ton in weight.
gager: a person concerned with seeing that a merchant did not give a short measure. This job today is concerned with both weights and measures.
gagez, gages: (Norman) 1) sureties; 2) fees; 3) wages.
gaigiers: (Norman) hirelings.
gaignarie, gainery: (Norman) husbandry.
gaille, geaule: (Norman) a jail.
gainage: 1) profit from farming; 2) the art of agriculture.
gainure: (Norman) tillage.
gait: 1) the pace at which mounted men, or groups of men, move; 2) the type of motion with which a horse moves.
gaiter: 1) a shoe which had an ankle high top to it; 2) an overshoe which covered the ankle and sometimes extended further up the leg; 3) an extension of a shoe which reached to the ankle, calf, or knee and was constructed of leather or cloth.
gaitor, gaitor legs: a covering from instep

to ankle, midcalf, or knee which was made of cloth or leather and was held down by a strap under the sole of the foot.

gal.: 1) gallant; 2) gallon.

galding: a vagabond.

galena: lead.

galena pills: bullets.

gall: 1) bile; 2) an abrasion; 3) gallon.

galleon: 1) a good catch or prize; 2) a large merchant ship with sails which could also be rowed.

gallery: 1) an open-sided, covered walkway attached to the outside wall of a house; 2) a ship's platform sometimes used as a gun site.

galley: 1) a sea-going sailing ship rowed by slaves or condemned criminals; 2) the name by which a ship's kitchen is called.

galley year: navy slang for a rumor.

gallier: a person who keeps teams for hire.

galliot: a small boat with sails and oars.

galloon: a trim which had scalloped edges made of silk, wool. Sometimes it had gold or silver threads woven into it.

galloping: when this term precedes a medical term for a disease, it indicates that the disease progressed more rapidly than usual.

galloway: 1) a big pony; 2) a small horse; 3) a breed of Scottish beef cattle.

gallows: a frame constructed from wood which had a rope used to hang criminals or to butcher cattle.

gallow tree: a tree which served in place of a frame gallows, from which to hang a criminal.

galluses: suspenders.

gally team: a team of horses kept for hire.

galowe-tre: the gallows.

gammer: 1) an old wife; 2) a grandmother; 3) an old woman.

gammon: a ham.

gangdays: Rogation Days (which see).

gangrel: a vagrant.

gangrene: the death of tissue which will spread if not removed.

gangsman: a foreman.

gangweek: Rogation Week.

gannok: standard, ensign.

gannoker: 1) a tavern; 2) inn keeper.

gantier: (Norman) a glover.

gaol: jail.

gaoler: a jailer, so pronounced.

G.A.R.: 1) Grand Army of the Republic, an organization of former Union soldiers (the last member died in 1956); 2) garrison.

garant: (Norman) 1) a warrant; 2) a commission.

garauntage: (Norman) warranty.

garbal teind: a tithe; the tenth sheaf or bundle which the parish rector was due.

garbvil: an old word for confusion.

garceons: (Norman) 1) servants; 2) journeymen.

gardeen: guardian.

garder (les): (Norman) the judgment.

gardior: (Norman) guardians.

gardydoo: "beware of the water." A warning to passersby shouted from an upstairs window just before a slop bucket was emptied out of it.

garnementz: (Norman) garments.

garner: 1) a granary; 2) a storeroom of any size.

garnish: the fees paid by a prisoner upon entering jail.

garnishee: to attach a man's wages or his property in order to recover a debt.

garnishment: 1) an order to appear in court; 2) advance notice to a person who holds property belonging to another not to give it to him, but to account to the court for it.

garrant, guarant: (Norman) forty.

garrant: a gelding.

garrantie: (Norman) a justice's warrant.

garret: at one time this term meant a watchtower on a fortified wall. Now it refers to an attic in a house.

garrison: 1) troops stationed in a military post or a fort to maintain its security; 2) the act of assigning men to a military post; 3) a military post.

garrison house: a log house, fortified against invasion. Every village had at least one house of this type which could shelter the town inhabitants from enemies. These houses were better constructed than most, had a single low door, and small slit openings to accommodate the barrel of a gun. The overhang of the second floor provided openings in the floor through which not only could a gun be fired, but boiling water poured upon those unfortunate to get so close. A flaming arrow on the roof could cause a garrison house to burn, but a remarkable number survived. These houses and forts were surrounded by pointed log fences, the forerunners of our "picket fences" of today.

garth: 1) a yard; 2) a churchyard; 3) an orchard; 4) a warren; 5) sometimes a fence or hedge fence; 6) an area of water where watercress is grown, fish are caught, etc.

garthynere: a gardener.

gastro enteritis: inflammation of the stomach and intestines.

garzon a pee: (Norman) a footboy.

gate: farmyard.

gatehouse: 1) a gatekeeper's home near or over a gate where he could supervise the traffic flow through it; 2) a building near a dam where equipment, controls, etc. are located.

gate hurdle maker: a person who makes sections of fence from willows. These sections, which look like gates, are joined end to end to form the fence.

gate penny: a fee paid by tenants for permission to pass through one or more of their lord's gates in order to have easier access to their own lands.

gate post bargain: when payment for a purchase of stock was placed in the gate post before stock which has been sold leaves the field, it is called a gate post bargain.

gate room: 1) a yard; 2) a paddock.

gate-schadylle: the division of a road into two or more ways.

gate-shord: 1) a gateway; 2) a place or gap for a gate.

gateward: 1) a porter; 2) a gate keeper.

gatherer: a money taker at a theatre.

gathering: inflammation, swelling.

Gatling gun: a type of gun invented by R. J. Gatling around 1862. It was light, mounted on a pair of wheels and fired rapidly.

gauger: a person who supervised the packing of liquids, usually distilled liquor. The cask was to be of a standard size and filled as specified by law. If the casks were deficient in any way, the gauger was subject to a rather stiff fine.

gauky: 1) a simpleton; 2) a clown; 3) awkward.

gavel: 1) a hammer used by a mason; 2) an early English term for rent; 3) a presiding officer's hammer.

gavelkind tenure: an English law in some areas whereby lands of an intestate father descended to all sons equally. This custom excluded all female heirs and bastards. It was abolished in 1925.

gayles: gaols, jails.

gaynours: (Norman) the tillers.

gazet: a Venetian coin.

gazette: 1) a newspaper; 2) one who spreads news.

gazetteer: 1) an early news reporter so-called because the newspapers were known as gazettes; 2) a collection of facts about towns, townships and counties contained in a book covering one or more states.

G.B.: Great Britain.

gch., g.ch.: grandchildren.

gct: see granted a certificate.

gdn., grdn.: guardian.

gdp.: grandparent.

gear: any kind of moveable property.

gebur: a copyholder.

gee: the command given to a working horse or ox telling the animal to turn right.

gelatin dry plate negatives: these are coated with an emulsion by machine which spreads the emulsion evenly. They are of standard size and sometimes have a foggy appearance.

geld: 1) a tax paid by landholders to the Anglo-Saxon and Norman kings; 2) a payment; 3) to castrate a horse; 4) to weaken.

geldable: (Norman) liable to be taxed.

gelding: a male animal which has been castrated. Usually used when speaking of a horse.

geltif: guilty.

gemel: 1) a pair; 2) a twin.

gemelli: twins.

geminus: twin.

gemman: a gentleman.

gemelli: twins.

gemmery: a jewel house.
Gen.: General.
geneat: a tenant farmer.
gener: 1) son-in-law; 2) granddaughter's husband; 3) sometimes a brother-in-law.
generation: an average period of time between one group of people and the next, about twenty-five to thirty-three years.
General: see army rank.
general court: this court heard civil and criminal cases, administered estates, appointed guardians, laid out roads, etc. They observed common and statutory law.
General Land Office: the earlier name for the Bureau of Land Management.
generationis: baptisms.
generosus: of noble birth.
genitores: parents.
gen'l.: general.
genner: January.
gent., gentm., gentn.: gentleman.
gentieux hommes: (Norman) gentlemen.
gentifeme: (Norman) gentlewoman.
gentile: used in some religious groups to denote a person not of their faith.
gentle birth: well born, born to parents of some social standing.
gentle craft: 1) shoemaking; 2) fishing as a sport.
gentleman: 1) used in this country to denote a person of influence or wealth. In Colonial days it was used more strictly for a person who was a step beneath a man using Esquire after his name; 2) a valet; a gentleman's gentleman; 3) a representative of a legislative group; 4) a formidable opponent.
gentleman commoner: a young man who was fortunate enough to attend Oxford or Cambridge Universities in England, but who was obliged to pay higher fees than other students paid.
gentleman farmer: a man wealthy enough to be able to farm for pleasure rather than because he must earn a living.
gentleman of fortune: a polite way of referring to a pirate.
gentlemen's agreement: a bargain between two persons not legally, but morally, binding.
gentleman usher: a state officer, attendant upon queens and other persons of high rank. Later a sort of upper-servant, whose duty it was to hand his mistress into the coach and walk before her bareheaded, though in later times she leaned upon his arm.
gentlery man: the gentry.
gentry: 1) an independently wealthy man in New England as opposed to a man who must work for his living; 2) a person who owns a large amount of land and has social political and economic influence in the area where he lives.
gentry cuffin: a gentleman.
gentz de mestire: (Norman) masters of trades.
genus: ancestry.
geographer's line: this line was surveyed as required by the Ordinance of 1785 and ran due west from the point where the Ohio River crossed the Pennsylvania border. The first township system of surveying known as the Seven Ranges began south of this line.
geolier: (Norman) jailer.
geometer: a gauger.
geoter: a person who casts metal.
Ger.: German.
gereve: 1) a guardian; 2) a governor.
german: a brother.
german (germane): this term refers to a close relationship, for example: brothers german would be children of the same parents instead of half-brothers. However, cousins german are what we usually call first cousins.
germana: sister.
German-American: an American, whose ancestors came from Germany.
German Baptists: see Brethren and Dunkers.
German measles: a mild form of measles.
germane: see german.
gernier: a granary.
gerrymander: an unfair division of a state, country, etc. into election districts designed to favor the political party in power.
gersing: pasturage.
gerund grinder: a schoolmaster.
gesine: childbed confinement.
Geskerech: (Norman) August.
gest: 1) a deed; 2) history; 3) tale; 4)

guest; 5) lodging during a journey.
gestour: a tale-teller.
getee: a part of a building which projects beyond the rest.
getoun: a banner about two yards long.
geylere: a jailer.
gf.: grandfather.
gg.: great-grand (great-grandson, great-granddaughter).
ggf.: great-grandfather.
2gg: great-great-grand (great-great-grandson, etc.)
ghenting: a fine handkerchief linen originally made in Ghent, Flanders.
gib: 1) obsolete term for an old woman; 2) a tomcat; 3) a cat.
gib door: a dutch door, probably so-called because one could let the gib (tomcat) in through the bottom half only.
gidere: a standard or banner.
giderne: 1) a standard; 2) a banner.
gift causa mortis: a gift made in anticipation of death, although it can be revoked during the giver's lifetime.
gift deed: see deed of gift.
gig: 1) a two-wheeled, lightweight carriage; 2) a boat which only a ship's captain may use; 3) the process of raising nap on fabric; 4) see also tim-whisky.
gigour: a fiddler.
gihall: (Norman) guildhall.
gild: 1) a tool used in preparing fibers to make cloth; 2) an old spelling of guild; 3) to apply gold or gold leaf to a surface; 4) an old word which means to make as red as blood.
gilder: a person who decorates an object with a layer of gold leaf.
gilds: village greens or commons.
gill: 1) in the United States, about one-fourth of a pint of liquid; 2) to clean fish; 3) a brook, stream, etc.; 4) a combing process used in textile manufacturing.
gillet: a tool used in thatching.
gimlet (auger bit): a steel tool used for boring holes in wood. A gimlet makes small holes, while an auger bit makes large holes.
gimp: 1) a trim made of wool or silk; 2) a glazed, coarse thread used in making lace.
gin: 1) an enclosed place within which colonists inspected their livestock, held them ready to move to another field or sheltered them for the winter; 2) a machine which separated seeds from cotton fibers.
ginner: a cotton gin operator.
ginour: 1) an engineer; 2) a craftsman.
gip gill: a horse.
girder: jester.
girdle: 1) see belt; 2) a round iron plate for baking.
girdler: maker of girdles.
girdle wheel: a spinning wheel small enough to be used while hanging from the waist.
girty wheel: milk porridge.
given letter to: a Quaker term found in church records. After the middle 1870s letters of membership from and to other Protestant churches were issued and honored.
given name: first name, or the first and middle names chosen by parents.
givetall: household items.
gl, gll: an abbreviation for gill.
glade: an open area surrounded by a forest.
gladstone bag: see portmanteau.
glass plates: see collodian plates.
glass tax: an early tax levied by the federal government on house windows. The information collected consists of not only how many windows in a house but how many acres a person owned, size and type of buildings, how many doors, owners and tenants names, etc.
glazener: a glazier.
glazier: a person whose trade was to install glass, oiled paper, parchment, etc. in windows.
glazing irons: tools used by a bootmaker.
gleaning: gathering loose corn in the fields. By common law and custom in England, the poor were allowed to enter and glean upon another's ground after the harvest, without being guilty of trespass.
glebe: land which provides income and is owned by a church, or the house which is given to the minister to use during his pastorate as a portion of his salary.
gleet: the discharge caused by chronic

gonorrhea.
gle-man: a minstrel.
glises: (Norman) churches.
GLO: General Land Office.
globber: a miser. At times it referred to a glutton.
Gloria Patri: Glory be to the Father.
glory hole: usually a small, cramped area on a ship where menial laborers employed on the ship are housed.
glosser: a polisher.
glove money: 1) a tip given to servants. It was supposed that this would be to buy gloves; 2) an out of the ordinary gift to any officer of an English court.
glover: a maker of gloves.
glt: see given letter to.
glut: a wooden wedge.
gm.: grandmother.
G.M.D.: Georgia Military District.
goal: 1) a boundary; 2) a contest.
goal delivery: the process, by hearing cases, of emptying jails of prisoners. Originally, those persons awaiting trial were kept in jail and, by the time they were convicted, they had served time.
goat house: brothel.
go-between: see marriage broker.
godcept: 1) a godfather; 2) an obsolete word for gossip.
godchild: see godparent.
godf.: godfather.
godm.: godmother.
god parent: the sponsor at a baptismal service who holds the child during the ceremony and promises to raise the child in the church if the parents died. Sponsors are usually related to the child.
god pays: a profane expression formerly used by disbanded soldiers, implying that they had no money themselves and must, therefore, borrow or beg. Hence God to pay, a hopeless debt, nothing.
godphere: a godfather.
god's penny: earnest money.
God's sake: a child kept for God's sake, for example, a foster child.
goffer: crimping (curling) iron.
goffram: a clown.
gofle: a small basket.
going: the right of pasturage for a beast in a common area.
goiter: a disease of the thyroid characterized by a swelling in the front of the neck.
gold end man: 1) one who buys broken pieces of gold and silver; 2) an itinerant jeweler.
goldfinch: 1) a piece of gold; 2) a purse; 3) a sovereign (coin).
gold finder: a jocular name for a person who cleaned a privy.
gold house: a treasury.
goldsmith/silversmith: a person who not only worked with gold or silver, but acted as a money changer or a banker before banks were founded in this country. He also melted coins to make ornaments or tableware.
goldsmithrie: a goldsmith's work.
gome: 1) a man; 2) black grease; 3) a godmother.
gone-goose: a deserted ship.
gonmer: an old person.
gonorrhea: a venereal disease characterized by an inflammation of mucous membranes, usually of the reproductive organs.
goochy: Indian rubber.
goodale: a type of beer.
goodale, goodall: a person who brewed goodale.
good brother: a brother-in-law.
goodfather: 1) a father-in-law; 2) a stepfather.
goodger: husband.
gooding: begging.
good lord: a term applied to a patron or benefactor.
goodman: 1) used in Colonial days to denote a male head of a household; 2) a landlord.
good mistress: a patroness.
goodmother: 1) a mother-in-law; 2) a stepmother.
goods and chattels: a term used to de-note personal property (furniture, jewelry, livestock, etc.) as distinguished from real property.
goods cattle: dairy produce.
goodsire: a grandfather.
goodsister: a sister-in-law.
goodson: a son-in-law.
goodwife (goody): used in Colonial days to mean a housewife.
good woman: a wife.

goody: 1) the shortened form of goodwife; 2) good-wife. This term was addressed only to poor women.
goose: a tailor's smoothing iron.
goose feast: Christmas.
goose herd: a person who takes care of geese.
goose herder: at the start of the trade of tailoring, this occupation was looked down upon because sewing was considered woman's work. The itinerant tailor carried his tailor's goose (an iron which had a handle shaped like a goose neck) with him which led to the uncomplimentary name of goose herder. Later a male tailor was considered a respectable man, practicing a respectable trade.
goosehouse: a small temporary prison.
goosier: a gooseherd.
G.O.P.: see Grand Old Party.
gore: 1) an irregular piece of land left over after other surveys have been made. It is often found where a river is used as a boundary or in a hilly area; 2) an unassigned or disputed parcel of land lying between two larger political areas; townships for example.
gorge: 1) the throat; 2) the mouth.
gorger: armor for the throat.
gorn: a small pail with one handle.
gospeller: 1) an evangelist; 2) the priest who chanted the gospel.
gossib: a sponsor at baptism, since corrupted into "gossip."
gossip: 1) a close friend; 2) a godparent or baptismal sponsor.
gossips wheel: a spinning wheel designed to be operated by two persons simultaneously.
gossone: a god-son.
gotfer: an old man.
goud gulden: a Dutch coin.
gouge: a tool used by 1) a chair bodger; 2) a bowl turner; 3) a wood carver; 4) a carpenter.
gourd: the fruit of a vine belonging to the squash family. It served the pioneer family as a dipper for water, cider, whiskey, etc., and as a container for salt.
gout: 1) painful inflammation of the joints of the toes or fingers; 2) the gateway bridge over a water course.
Gov.: Governor.
gover: governor.
govt.: government.
gowarge: a round chisel used in making hollows.
gowt: a vault.
gp.: grandparents
gr.: grant; granted.
Gr.: Greek.
grace cup: a large cup used in a monastery or college. It was passed around the table after grace was said.
graceship: a Duke's title.
grace wife: a midwife.
graciadei: a medicine.
graduate: a physician.
graffer: 1) a notary; 2) (Norman) one who writes.
grafmakere: a sexton.
grain: 1) grain (medical); 2) great; 3) grand; 4) grant.
grainer: a person who removed hair from animal skins and then softened the skins and raised the grain in the leather.
gramer: a granary.
gramfer: a grandfather.
grammer: a grandmother.
granary: the bins in a barn where the wheat and other grains were stored to be used later for animal feed, for grinding into flour, or for seed.
grandam: a grandmother.
grandaevus: very old.
Grand Army of the Republic: the Union army in the Civil War. See GAR.
grandfather clause: a condition, written into the constitution of some states. It deprived persons, especially blacks, of their vote unless their immediate male ancestors had voted before 1867.
grandil: grandmother.
grand jury: a group of twelve to twenty-four persons who hear evidence in a prospective case and who decide if there is sufficient evidence to hold a trial.
Grand Old Party: the Republican political party. Earlier this term referred to the Democratic party, but in that context the words were not capitalized.
grandonkel: (Norman) granduncle.
grandsher, gransher: a great-grandfather.

grandsire: an older man who is serious, wise, settled, firm, etc. The qualities associated with human older age.
graner: a granary.
grange: 1) a farm house and its outbuildings; 2) a barn; 3) a granary; 4) a small hamlet; 5) sometimes a lone farm house; 6) a house in the country; 7) in England, a yeoman or gentleman farmer's country house and buildings.
(the) Grange: Patrons of Husbandry, a social and cultural society formed for and by farmers. Now the Grange's responsibilities extend into the business world, e.g. lobbying for laws favorable to farmers, offering varying types of insurance to farmers, etc.
granger: a person who cared for a farm.
gran'man: an older woman.
grannep: a grandmother.
granny: 1) midwife; 2) nurse; 3) grandmother; 4) old woman.
grant (land): a grant of land which was for military duty, or by a special act of Congress only. Actually, a grant was not a document but the process of obtaining land which created several documents. However, documents called grants are sometimes found.
grant: to sell, convey, or donate.
granted a certificate: in Quaker records this phrase indicates a member who is moving and has asked to be dismissed from their monthly meeting to one near their new home. If they neglect to obtain this certificate before moving, they may apply for one from their new home. And after ascertaining there is no reason to withhold a certificate, the new one will be sent immediately.
grantee: a buyer of property.
grantee index: pages which list the buyers of land in courthouse deed books.
grantor: a seller (or donor) of property.
grantor index: pages in courthouse deed books which list the sellers of land.
Granville District: roughly, the northern half of North Carolina.
grap: an ear of Virginia corn.
grapnel: a three or four pronged hook used to lower a pail containing food down into a dug well to be kept cool during the summer months. Also the hook was used to make certain that nothing had fallen into the well.
grasiers: sheep, or other animals, which were fed grass only.
grass hearth: a feudal service of a day's plowing.
grass widow: an unmarried woman who has had a child.
graunt-fader: grandfather.
grave deed: a document issued by a church or cemetery company transferring ownership of a burial plot.
graver: 1) a sculptor; 2) an engraver.
graviditas: a pregnancy.
gravowrys: engravers.
grayback: 1) a Confederate soldier during the Civil War, also called a gray coat or a gray jacket; 2) paper money issued by the Confederate treasury.
gray coat: see grayback.
gray jacket: see grayback.
grazier: a rancher or a person who raises cattle on pastureland.
grd.: guardian.
grdn.: guardian.
grd/o: granddaughter of.
grdt: in Quaker records this stands for granddaughter.
great: used to show a more distant relationship by generations. Used to compound words, for example, great-grandmother.
Great Charter: see Magna Charta.
greatcoat: an overcoat.
great gudsire: a great-grandfather.
great guns: cannons.
great men: members of parliament and noblemen.
great pox: syphilus.
greave: cracklings.
greenback: 1) a person who, at the end of the Civil War, was a member of a political party which opposed reduction in the amount of paper money which was in circulation at that time; 2) U.S. paper money.
greengrocer: a British seller of fruit and vegetables.
green hand: a person who is new at a job.
greenhorn: a person who is not experienced at whatever he is doing; a newcomer.
greenland: pasture land.

greenman: a savage.

Green Mountain boy: 1) a person from Vermont; 2) a member of a militia formed to protect the interests of settlers who held grants to land in New Hampshire against those persons claiming to have grants from New York state.

green sickness: an old term for anemia.

greenside: grass, turf.

gregorian: a particular kind of wig said to have been invented by a man named Gregory. He was a barber in the Strand area of London during the seventeenth century.

Gregorian calendar (new style): devised by Pope Gregory to correct accumulated errors in the old (Julian) calendar. It was accepted by Great Britain and her colonies in 1751 and the 2nd of September 1752 was chosen as the day which would be followed by the 14th of September, thus making the necessary correction and causing us to take it into consideration when figuring a birth date. For example, whether a person was born before or after that date could make a twelve day difference.

grenadier: a soldier who specialized in throwing grenades, but who today is a member of a regimental group such as the grenadier guards.

greves: leg armor.

grey coat: 1) parson; 2) a tenant who hires someone else to do his work.

greyve: magistrate.

grf.: grandfather.

grid: the system of imaginary lines which go around the earth (east-west longitude and north-south latitude) upon which surveying is based.

Griff, Griffe: 1) a person who is three-fourths black and one-fourth white; 2) a person who is part black and part American Indian; 3) see also Sambo.

grimgribber: 1) a lawyer; 2) the technical language used by a lawyer.

grinder and stuffer: a machine used in making link type sausage.

grindery: 1) a workshop where knives, tools, etc. are sharpened; 2) in Britain this term refers to the materials which a leatherworker uses in his trade.

griot: an African storyteller or oral historian. Each family clan had its own griot.

grippe: an acute virus, the symptoms of which resemble influenza. Sometimes called la grippe.

grisette: a very inexpensive, sleazy fabric.

grist mill: a mill for grinding grain. If it was large, it was housed in a special building, but some mills were small enough to put on a stump and to be turned by hand.

grizet: see grisette.

grm.: grandmother.

groat: an English silver coin.

grocer: originally meant a wholesale merchant who speculated in various things at markets and fairs.

grock: a very small child.

grog: a Colonial drink made of rum with water, sugar, and lemon juice. It was usually served cold but sometimes it was heated.

groggery: a cheap tavern.

grogram: a coarse silken fabric, sometimes mixed with mohair or wool and frequently stiffened with gum.

grome: a man.

gromer: a boy.

grondy: a grandmother.

groom grubber: an officer in the royal (English) household whose duty it was to see that the barrels brought into the cellar were tight and full, and to draw out the lees from casks that were nearly empty.

groom porter: 1) an officer of the royal (English) household whose business it was to see that the king's lodging was furnished with tables, chairs, stools, etc. He also was to provide cards, dice, etc. and to settle disputes arising at games. Earlier he was allowed to keep an open gambling table at Christmas; 2) loaded dice were sometimes called groom porters.

groop: a pen for cattle.

groove: a mine or shaft.

groovers: miners.

grosgrane: see grogram.

gross: a unit which equals 144 or 12 dozen. It was used to count eggs. People who were otherwise illiterate could count to twelve in order to take eggs to market.

gross up: to buy up all the market.

ground rain: a plentiful, but gradual, rainfall which works its way deep into the earth.

ground rent: the price charged for farm land at the time when it is rented to a tenant.

grover: a miner of lead.

grove wood: a small timber for the use of mines to support the roof or sides.

growblor: a digger.

grower: a cultivator.

grownder: founder.

growth halfpenny: in some places a tax. It was paid on every fat animal.

grs: in Quaker records this stands for grandson.

grs/o: grandson of.

grub: food.

gruff: a mine.

g.s.: gravestone.

g.s.w.: a military abbreviation for a gunshot wound.

gt.: great.

Gt.Br.: Great Britain.

guano: 1) fertilizer made from the droppings of seabirds only; 2) a fertilizer which acts or smells similar.

guannys: (Norman) husbandman.

guard: a group of men responsible for the safety of the place they are guarding.

guardian: the person who is appointed by the court to oversee 1) the affairs of a minor. Many times a child of fourteen was considered capable of choosing a guardian but, if the child was under fourteen, a mother alone was many times not considered as a guardian. Many times a guardian would be appointed by the court until the mother remarried and the stepfather would be appointed guardian. A father alone was considered a guardian; 2) the business of a person deemed incapable of handling his own affairs.

guardian ad litem: a person appointed by a court to represent another (who is incapable of managing his affairs) for only one particular court action.

guernsey: 1) a breed of dairy cattle which originally was found in the Isle of Guernsey. They give a very rich milk with a high butterfat content; 2) a knitted sweater originally worn by men who lived in the Channel Islands. The patterns were peculiar to the Isle of Guernsey.

guerr: war.

guffer: a miner.

guggler: a funnel.

guide stoop: a guide post.

guidon: 1) a little flag carried by army troops in battle; 2) the person who carries this flag; 3) a small flag used to distinguish a company of soldiers.

guidresse: a female guide.

guidsire, gudesirr: a grandfather.

guild: (Saxon) "gilden" to pay. A fraternity or company, each member of which was required to pay dues. It regulated prices, quality of work, and determined who could make and sell the goods and services for which it took responsibility.

guilder: 1) a Dutch coin used in areas of the United States populated by the Dutch people; 2) a coin of silver, or sometimes nickel, which was used in the Netherlands. At one time this coin was also minted in gold. Also called a gulden or florin; 3) one of several gold coins minted in Germany.

guindors: (Norman) governors.

guinea: a British coin minted of gold for more than one hundred years.

gulden: a Dutch gold coin minted during the late 1500s and early 1600s.

gull gropers: usurers who lend money to gamblers.

gully washer: a heavy rain.

gundalow: a fairly general term for river sail boats which differed in structure depending upon the cargo to be carried and period of time involved.

gunner's mate: 1) the highest non-commissioned officer in charge of guns; 2) an assistant to the gunner or to the gunnery officer.

gunny: burlap made from jute and used for sacks to hold grain, etc.

gunsmith: a person who makes or repairs guns.

gunter: see acre.

Gunter's chain: see chain.

Gunter's scales: tool used by a surveyor.
gutcher, gowcher, geetcher: 1) a grandfather; 2) a relative; 3) a cousin.
gut scraper: a fiddler.
gutt: (Norman) hay.
gutter blood: a low-bred person.
guttersnipe: 1) a street child; 2) a member of a city's lowest social group.
gutter viewer: a person who inspected guttering along a roof to make certain that no undue amount of moisture would fall on a passerby.
guyour: guide or leader.
guyte: a guide.
gyderesse: a female guide.
gz.: gazeteer.

H

H: 1) husband; 2) heir.
1/h, 2/h: first husband, second husband, etc.
habeas corpus: that you have the body. A legal document requiring jailers to produce a prisoner, rather than keeping him or her in confinement indefinitely.
habendum et tenedum: a clause, sometimes called the habendum clause, found in deeds. To have and to hold by (the grantor's name) his heirs and assigns.
haberdasher: 1) men's wear salesman; 2) a schoolmaster.
haberdyne: dried, salted codfish, a staple foodstuff which was carried on ships such as the Mayflower sailing from England to America.
habere facias possessionem: a writ of ejectment from land to restore the land to the rightful owner. Sometimes abbreviated het fa.
habeus corpus: an order written by a court to a person demanding that he bring into court another person who is detained by the first person. For example, to a jailor, telling him to bring a prisoner into court. The day on which he is to appear is stated as well as the cause or reason.
habitacle: a dwelling or habitation. Sometimes applied to a niche for a statue.
hable: a seaport or haven.
habot: an abbot.
hac, hic: here.
hack: 1) a strong pickaxe or hoe; 2) half door; 3) the place where newly made bricks are set to dry; 4) a hard-working man; 5) a hedge.
hackle: a device used to comb flax or hemp prior to the spinning process.
hackle board: a tool used by a rope maker.
hackney: 1) a hired carriage, also called a jarvey; 2) a hired menial worker; 3) a saddle horse; 4) the person who drove a hackney or jarvey carriage.
hackney man: a person who lets out horses for hire.
hackney saddle: a riding saddle.
hack saw: a tool used by a metal worker.
haemoptysis: see hemoptysis.

hag: 1) a nightmare; 2) an enclosed pasture; 3) a tree stump; 4) to chop or hew wood; 5) a variation of hake (firearm).

hag clog: chopping block.

hagger makers shop: a public house.

haggler: the upper-servant of a farm, this person owned a cart and a large work horse. He used them to haul heavy materials.

ha house: a mansion.

haircloth: a sturdy cloth made of hair used for coal sacks, tents, towels, etc.

hake: 1) a book; 2) a hand gun; 3) a sixteenth century short firearm; 4) a pot hook; 5) a wooden frame which hung from a roof and was used to dry cheese; 6) a frame used to dry bricks; 7) the wooden rack where a cow feeds; 8) to fish for a fish called a hake.

half: when used as a prefix to sister, brother, etc. means having one parent in common with another sibling.

half-baptized: the result of a deathbed baptism; private, without full rites.

half-blood: 1) the relationship between children who have only one parent in common; 2) a person who had one parent of one race and the other parent of another race.

half-breed: a person who has an American Indian for one parent and a white person for the other.

half-crown: a British coin no longer minted which was of silver or an alloy of copper and nickel.

half disme: considered to be the first coin minted in the United States in 1792.

half-faced cabin: a temporary house or shelter on the frontier. It had three sides and a roof.

half-faced camp: a primitive pioneer cabin entirely open on one side with no doors or windows.

half-groat: a mid-sixteenth century English silver coin.

half guinea: an eighteenth century English gold coin.

half marrow: 1) an obsolete word for a spouse; 2) a partner in a mining venture.

half-mask: a mask of black velvet or linen, depending upon the season, with holes to see through and strings to tie it to the head to prevent recognition at a masked ball. With the addition of lace to the bottom edge, a mask was also worn in summer to shield a woman's face from the sun and in winter from the wind.

half-mast: a navy term for a flag flown half-way down a flag pole as a symbol of mourning. The army refers to this as half-staff.

half-moon knife: a tool used by a saddler.

half mourning: the period of time after the first, or full, mourning, when a widow's black dresses are replaced by ones in lighter colors such as gray, lavender, pastels, etc.

half named: privately baptized.

half orphan: one parent is dead.

half penny: an English coin. See also 'alf penny.

half-round bottom glazer: a tool used by a blacksmith.

half-section: three hundred and twenty acres, one-half of a section of land.

half-staff: see half-mast.

hall: a chief house. The manor house in many parishes is called the Hall.

hallage: the fee or toll due to the lord of a fair or market.

hallucinations: delirium.

hamald: a general term for homemade fabrics.

hame: part of a horse's harness.

hamesucken: this crime of attacking a person in his own residence was a serious crime in early England. The term is still used in Scotland.

hamlet: 1) a small group of houses clustered together in a sparsely populated area; 2) a high constable.

hammer: a tool, called "the king of tools," which dates back to Biblical times. A hammer is used for impact, e.g. driving nails, heading rivets, etc.

hammercloth: a special covering for the driver's seat of a carriage.

hammer head chisel: a tool used by a stone mason.

hammil: 1) a village; 2) a hovel.

hamper clot: a plowman.

Hampshire Down: 1) an English sheep noted for fast growth of lambs. They have a dark face and legs; 2) a black hog which has a wide white band around the shoulders and which originated in England.

hanaper office: an office where writs were deposited in a basket called a hanaper.

hand: a person who works at a task and is paid by the day, e.g. helps a farmer.

handbarrow: instead of having a wheel as a wheelbarrow does, this device is carried by two people.

hand cannon: a musket.

hand card: a tool used by a wool worker.

hand comb: a tool used by a wool worker.

handelyt: found in Dutch records this is June, July, and August when beaver skins and other pelts were brought to Beverwyck by Indians for the purpose of exchange for goods.

handful: measure of a hand (four inches).

hand woman: a midwife.

hangboard: a sign positioned by a store door to advertise the merchandise which was sold inside the store.

hangby: a dependent.

hanger on: a dependent.

hanging month: November.

hank: a definite number of yards of yarn tied in a loose coil which must be wound into a ball before use.

Hanover: the Stuart family's rule of England came to an end when Parliament passed an Act which stated that no Catholic (or any one married to a Catholic) could be the sovereign of England. The closest Protestant relative of the Stuarts was Sophia, a daughter of Elizabeth and granddaughter of James I. Consequently, Sophia's son George became the first Hanover King of England. Because the House of Hanover ruled both Great Britain and Germany, Germans who emigrated to England, Ireland, Scotland, Wales, and the British colonies were not required to pledge allegience anew to their king. This eliminated many records which would have been helpful to genealogists.

hantin: (Norman) an uncle.

happy hunting ground: an Indian's Heaven where the souls of their hunters and warriors went after death to enjoy hunting plentiful animals and birds.

harbergage: 1) an inn; 2) lodging.

harbinger: 1) the person who goes ahead of others to secure food and lodging; 2) a herald who warns of another person's approach; 3) anything that forecasts an event.

harchiers: (Norman) archers.

hard by: near by.

hard corn: wheat and rye.

hardmen: men who, by eating a certain herb, became impervious to shot, it is said, except when the bullet was made of silver.

Hard-Shell: a strict, exacting 1) person; 2) church; 3) member of the New York Conservative Democratic political party.

hard-tack: a large cracker to be eaten by troops out in the field or by those on a ship at sea.

hardware: 1) liquor; 2) weapons; 3) tools and related objects.

hardy, hardie: a cutting tool used by a blacksmith on an anvil. The name came from the hardened metal from which it was made.

harman-beck: a constable.

harness maker: the maker of all the harness for a horse except a saddle or a collar, but is classed as a saddler.

harper: 1) a person who played a string instrument for the amusement of others; 2) an English coin minted for circulation in Ireland.

harrateen: a linen fabric used for curtains, bedspreads, etc.

harrow: the early plain harrow consisted of heavy beams fastened together in a rectangular or triangular shape with twenty to forty iron or hardwood teeth or tines driven into the wood beam. This piece of machinery when pulled over plowed ground further broke up the soil for planting. Not all early farmers had a harrow, but would drag a heavy branch over the ground unless they could hire a harrow.

harvest lady: the second reaper in a row. The first and primary reaper's motions regulate those of his followers. He was called harvest lord and the second reaper was called harvest lady or sometimes harvest queen.

hashmark: a slang term for the stripes worn on an enlisted man's sleeve. This service stripe shows the number of enlistments to the man's credit.
hasp: 1) a simple door or casement window fastening; 2) a catch for fastening a garment or a book together; 3) a handle on a trunk or box; 4) to lock in a small place.
hastary: a spearman.
hasteler: the person who roasted meat.
hasty pudding: a New England food. Cornmeal mush served hot with a sweetener of molasses or maple sugar and milk.
hatchel: variant spelling of hackle (which see).
hatcheler: a person who cleans flax or hemp.
hathill: a nobleman or knight.
hat money: a small amount of money paid to a ship's crew by a merchant or the one who receives the ship's cargo.
hatter: 1) a person who makes hats; 2) a seller of hats; 3) one who cleans and repairs hats.
hauberk: a coat of mail.
haunieck: (Norman) a person born in Flanders.
havage: 1) race; 2) family.
haveles: poor, destitute.
haversack: see knapsack.
haw: the command given to a working horse or ox, which means turn left.
hawk: 1) to sell goods by calling out loudly to passersby; 2) to spread rumors or news among others; 3) to clear one's throat noisily.
hawk bill: a tool used by a bootmaker.
hawker: a person who travels from house to house, carrying his goods with him, selling directly to the purchasers, and drawing attention to his wares by calling out or by printed signs. See also badger.
hawkey: the harvest supper.
hawkey load: the lost load.
hawk goods: to sell merchandise.
hawrawde: a herald.
hayboute: 1) brush used to mend fences; 2) this term also means the right to take brush from a common area or from a landlord.
hay house: hayloft.
hayward: 1) the man whose duty it was to catch stray cattle and fine their owners for allowing them to stray; 2) a person who guarded the corn and farm yard in the night time, and gave warning by a horn in case of alarm from robbers. The term was afterwards applied to a person who looked after the cattle, and prevented them from breaking down the fences; 3) the warden of a common was so called in some areas; 4) the official (also called a hog reeve) whose duty it was to see all the hogs had nose rings and yokes. They were to be warded off the highway; 5) at a later time, all newly married men were appointed haywards. It was said that young men were adept at putting rings on young ladies' fingers.
Hdqrs.: Headquarters.
heading chisel: a tool used by a wheelwright.
heading knife: a tool used by a cooper.
head money: a type of poll tax levied upon individuals.
head of the family: a person, male or female, who legally and morally is responsible and has accepted this responsibility for the welfare of a family.
headright: 1) public land given to the head of a household who would settle upon it. Headright grants were made to original colonists and early citizens of Texas whether or not they served in the Texas army; 2) this term also refers to the land that was given under this system.
headsman: 1) an executioner; 2) a leader; 3) a chief; 4) a miner who moved coal from a mine; 5) a commander of a whaling boat.
headswoman: a midwife.
head tax: see head money.
healer: a tiler or slater.
hearsay: 1) gossip; 2) rumor; 3) evidence which the witness did not see or hear himself, but has learned from another person. In most cases such evidence is not admissible in court.
hearth: 1) the complicated fireplace used by a blacksmith; 2) a fireplace floor (or the space in front of it).
hearth money: see hearth tax.
hearth penny: see hearth tax.
hearth tax: two shillings were charged for

every hearth in every house except those of poor people and churches. Also called hearth money or hearth penny.

heath: 1) a heather plant which has a purple blossom; 2) a field covered with low-growing weeds and no trees.

hebberman: a fisherman on the Thames River below London Bridge.

hectare: a metric measure of land equaling approximately one hundred acres. Used in old surveys of California and Texas.

hectical complaint: probably a chronic complaint.

hedare: one who beheads others.

heder: a male sheep.

hedge: to mend hedges.

hedge alehouse: a very small obscure alehouse.

hedgepriest: an uneducated clergyman.

hedger: the person who repairs, plants, and prunes hedge fences.

hedge school: an inexpensive open-air school in Ireland.

hedge tacker: a hedge mender.

heel awl: a tool used by a bootmaker.

heel parer: a tool used by a bootmaker.

heer: an old measure for yarn which used yards or meters.

heeretraet: any public street.

heerewegh: a public road or highway.

heers: a hearse.

heir: 1) a person who inherits property, rank, leadership, etc. at the death of the owner; 2) (Norman) inheritance.

heir apparent: a person who is likely to receive an estate after the death of another person.

heir-at-law: usually the eldest son who would inherit all of an intestate person's real property. This occurred under the primogeniture system; 2) sometimes used to mean "legal heirs," e.g. a person who by law inherits an intestate estate.

heirs and assigns: in common law this term was at one time considered essential in a deed which gave absolute ownership of land. It meant that the person sold to John Johnson's heirs and those to whom John's property would at some time be sold.

heirs lawfully begotten: see bodily heirs.

hairs of the body: see bodily heirs.

heirs to his/her body: this is a term which is necessary in the "establishing" of a fee tail estate. It refers to a natural child, but not an orphan.

hellier: 1) a thatcher; 2) a tiler.

helmsman: the person who guides a ship by the use of the tiller or helm. Sometimes he is called a steersman.

hematemesis: vomiting blood.

hematuria: blood in the urine.

hemoptysis, haemoptysis: spitting up of blood.

hemp: 1) a tall, corn-like plant used to make rope, cloth, rugs, etc.; 2) a rope used for hangings; 3) a narcotic (hashish); 4) a hanging; 5) a gray-olive color sometimes called Quaker gray.

hemp heckler: a flax-dresser.

hemton: made of hemp.

henter: a thief.

hepatitis: inflammation of the liver.

Her.: heraldry.

herald: 1) an officer whose duties included caring for people's genealogies and their right to bear arms. He visited each family in order to examine and question them, and to copy their answers into his book of "visitations." Also see town crier; 2) an old word for a royal or official messenger or sometimes an ambassador; 3) something or someone who goes ahead, a forerunner; 4) an official in charge of tournaments, funerals, parades, etc.; 5) to announce.

heberjours: (Norman) lodgers.

herd: a group of animals, usually rather large, which is kept together or belongs to one person.

herdess: a shepherdess.

herdsman: a person who owns a number of animals or cares for them.

here, heurs: (Norman) heir, heirs.

hereditas: inheritance.

hereditaments: all that property which may be inherited in a prescribed order.

heres esse alicui: to make a person one's heir.

heriot: 1) military equipment, such as a horse, which was returned to a lord when one of his retainers died; 2) a sum of money commonly given to a lord in lieu of a horse.

Heroes of America: a secret group in

North Carolina at the time of and immediately after the Civil War.

hespe: a hank of yarn.

Hessians: troops hired by Great Britain during the American revolution. They were Prussians who were sold by Prussia at forty pounds sterling each, nine pounds of which was to be repaid if the soldier returned alive. However, if they were captured in this country, they could either become indentured to Americans or enter the American army.

hetchel: variant spelling of hackle (which see).

hewe: 1) a husbandman; 2) a workman.

hewer: a coal worker.

hewing: the skill of fashioning beams and logs for a log house. The round log is changed into a flat sided log using an adze or a broad axe.

hewing-dog: an iron device used to hold a small log in place while an adze was used to shape it.

heyman: a nobleman.

heyment: a boundary or fence.

hhd., hhds.: an abbreviation for hogshead, hogsheads (which see).

hiatus: 1) a gap, especially of time; 2) an opening in a fence caused by a missing part.

hic: here.

hic iacet: here lies ...

hickory broom: this broom was fashioned from a young tree several inches in diameter with the root end slivered, the heart cut out, at which time the slivers were spread out. Sometimes a centerpiece would be inserted. The bottom end was then bound and the top cut down to handle length.

hic sepultura: here is buried.

Hicksite Quakers: a conservative branch of the Society of Friends (Quaker) church. They did not believe that women should participate in the church service, nor should any member join a reform movement. The several yearly meetings of this branch were brought together biennially in a group known as the Friends' General Conference.

hide: an English land unit measurement of 120 acres, which was the measurement used in collecting material for the Domesday Book.

hide of land: an old term which denotes land measures varying in size from eighty to one hundred and twenty acres.

hier: (Norman) heir.

hierdesse: a shepherdess.

higgledy-piggledy: 1) in disarray, not orderly; 2) confusion in which lot of ground belonged to which person.

higger: a huckster.

High Church: an Anglican church service is highly ritualistic. Sometimes used in speaking of a formal service as opposed to a small country church's more informal service.

High Court: 1) a superior court; 2) a Supreme Court, the highest court in the state, land, etc.; 3) sometimes a combination of courts to form a higher court.

High Court of Admiralty: see Admiralty Court.

high tea: a late afternoon tea or early light supper which usually consisted of meats, sandwiches, cake, etc. plus tea.

highwayman: a robber, mounted on horseback, who stole from those who were travelling in the countryside.

high yellow: a term used to describe a black person who was light skinned or who the speaker thought was more mannerly than necessary.

hind: an English or Scottish skilled farm laborer. Many times he was given a cottage for himself and his family as part of his pay.

hinehead: kin, with a distant degree of relationship.

Hingland: England.

hip gout: osteomyelitis.

hippodome: a trainer or tamer of horses.

hire: to take a farm.

hired hand: see hand.

hired man: in the early 1800s a redemptioner was referred to in the north as a "hired man" which put him in a higher economic class than he would have enjoyed in the south. This was also true in the middle states where manual labor was considered respectable.

hiredman: attendants.

hireling minister: a paid minister.

hist.: 1) history; 2) historical.

historical index: a summary of all transactions which affect title or use of public lands.

hitching post: a post with a ball or ornate top to which a horseman could tie his horse's reins. The post was for the use of a visitor who would not be staying long enough to stable the horse. Sometimes the visitor would have along a piece of iron to be put on the ground and thus "anchor" the horse.

hither: to come toward this place.

hither, thither: to go from place to place, often aimlessly.

hives: an itching rash which may be caused by allergic reaction.

hiytan jour: (Norman) eighth day.

H.J.S.: Hic Jacet Sepultus here lies buried.

hk, hks: abbreviation for hank, hanks.

H.L.S.: Hic Loco Situs. Laid in this place.

H.M.: His or Her Majesty.

h.m.: see hoc mense.

H.M.S.: Her or His Majesty's Service or Ship.

h/o: husband of.

hoastman: an ancient fraternity at Newcastle, England which dealt with sea-coal.

hobbler: a longshoreman.

hobbles: a device for fastening together two legs of an animal to prevent it from straying far or to keep it from kicking. See clapse.

hobby: a small horse or pony, originally from Ireland.

hobeler: 1) a light horseman; 2) a person who rode on a hobby horse; 3) tenants who were obliged to maintain hobbies (small horses) for use in case their services were needed in defense of their country.

hoblers: sentinels who kept watch at beacons located on the Isle of Wight. They reported directly to the governor.

Hobson's choice: "that or none." This saying is attributed to a livery man named Hobson. He was in business at Cambridge, England and never permitted his customers to choose their horses but required them to take the horses in succession.

hocktide: the second Monday and Tuesday after Easter. At one time money was collected to support a church on these two days; later, this time was used for a festival. The custom lasted until the nineteenth century, when it was abolished.

hoc mense: this month.

hoc tempore: at this time.

hodman: a person who carries supplies to a mason.

hog: an adult pig.

hogget: a sheep or colt after it is a year old.

hogleg: a revolver used in the west by cowboys.

hoglin: a boar.

hogmena: a name given to December.

hogmena night: New Year's Eve.

hog reeve: see hayward.

hogshead: 1) a cask or barrel which contains sixty to one hundred and forty gallons of liquid; 2) used also in an enlarged version to contain tobacco weighing 750 to 1,200 pounds.

hoict: (Norman) eight.

hoirie: (Norman) inheritance.

hoirs: (Norman) heirs.

hoker: a shoplifter.

holland: a fabric made in Holland of linen, which when not bleached was called "brown Holland." It was used for head scarves, handkerchiefs, undergarments, etc.

hollow: the area between two hills.

hollow mouthed tongs: a tool used by a blacksmith.

hollow square jawed tongs: a tool used by a blacksmith.

hollowing adze: a tool used by a chair maker.

hollowing knife: a tool used by a cooper.

holm: 1) flat land; 2) small island; 3) deposit of soil found where two bodies of water meet.

holographic will: a will believed to have been written by a person entirely in his own handwriting.

holstein: a black and white dairy cow which gives a large quantity of milk with a low butterfat content.

Holy Thursday: see Ascension Day.

homa: (Norman) man.

homage: 1) a tribute; 2) a public declaration of service given by a vassal to his lord.

home: to avoid taxes levied upon taverns or inns they were referred to sometimes as a "home."

home dwellers: inhabitants, as opposed to strangers.

home lot: the plot of land upon which a home is built. This distinction is used in Colonial documents to denote land used for homes rather than farms. It also referred to the area surrounding the house, enclosed with a high protective fence. Inside it were rail fences used to separate garden, pigpen, cowyard, barnyard, etc.

homemade soap: a strong all-purpose soap made from fat and lye (which was made from ashes). It was usually yellow in color and "strong enough to take hide off."

homespun: cloth produced from fiber by spinning and weaving entirely at home.

homestead: 1) the place where a family lives; 2) house, barn and other buildings on a developed plot of land; 3) a tract of land obtained from the government by a settler under a homestead law.

Homestead Act of 1862: Congress passed this law, which gave a settler one hundred sixty acres of land after he had cultivated and improved it for five years. After the five year period he was then exempt from cash payments. To qualify, he had to meet age and citizenship requirements.

homestead application: a person was asked to fill out forms proving his residence and fulfilling certain conditions in order to be granted usually one hundred and sixty acres of land.

homestead entry file: see homestead application.

homo: man.

Hon., Honl., Honr.: Honorable.

Hon. dis.: Honorably discharged.

honour: several manors grouped together and owned by one baron or lord.

hons: (Norman) a man.

hont: 1) a huntsman; 2) haunt.

hoof cleaning knife: a tool used by a farrier.

hoof parer: a tool used by a farrier.

hook: a tool used by a 1) tanner; 2) currier.

hookah, hooka: a Near Eastern water pipe which cool tobacco smoke.

hooking knife: a tool used by a 1) chair maker; 2) wood carver.

hoop: see wheel hoop.

hoop bender: a person who made the hoops used to bind together barrels in which dry products were stored.

hoop bender's easel: a tool used by a hoop bender.

hooper: the person who made hoops for casks.

Hoosier: a native-born or a resident of Indiana, which is nicknamed the Hoosier State.

Hoosier cabinet: a tall piece of kitchen furniture which had an enameled work surface and storage space for flour, sugar, etc.

hora: an hour.

horcap: a bastard.

horder: 1) a treasurer; 2) a person who kept another's savings.

hordeyne: appointed.

hornage: a quantity of corn given annually to the lord of the manor for every ox used to plow land within the lord's jurisdiction.

horn-book: 1) an elementary treatise; 2) a piece of wood with pieces of translucent horn attached to both sides. Between the wood and the horn was a piece of paper marked with the alphabet, and perhaps the Lord's prayer. On the reverse side would be a picture. This formed the first schoolbook and was usually suspended from the child's belt.

horned: mitred.

horned cattle: 1) cows, bulls, steers, etc. of the bovine kind; 2) any animal with horns.

hornwork: constructed of stone.

horrors: delirium tremens.

hors de combat: a French term meaning unable to continue combat.

horse and foot: cavalry and infantry.

horse artillery: the part of the artillery which serves in cooperation with cavalry units and has its cannoneers mounted on horses for more rapid movements.

horseblock: an arrangement for mounting a horse or getting into a buggy. It could be a rock with a step chipped into it, wood with a step cut out, or a shelf-like "step" at the end of a porch.

horse coper: see coper.

horse courser: 1) a horse thief; 2) a horse dealer.

Horse Guards: an especially chosen cavalry group who guard a royal palace. The horses are perfectly matched and the men are extremely well trained. It is an honor to be chosen to be a member of the group.

horse knave: a groom.

horse leech: 1) a horse doctor; 2) a farrier.

horseshoe: the piece of iron shaped to fit a horse's foot, the style and weight of which varied with the task to be done: work, pull a carriage, race, walk through a swampy area without sinking, etc.

horseways: see tote-road.

hosier: a tailor who sold men's ready-to-wear garments.

hosp.: hospital.

hospitalers: religious persons who attend the sick in hospitals.

hoste: to swell or ferment.

hostel: an inn; a place to obtain lodging for the night.

hosteler: a hostel keeper.

hostelery, hostel: an inn.

hostelier, hostillers, hostillurs, hosteler: (Norman) an innkeeper.

hostery, hostry: (Norman) an inn.

hostielx tenauntz: (Norman) householders.

hostilements: household furniture. Any kind of utensil or implement.

hostler: 1) an innkeeper; 2) a groom; 3) a cleaner and oiler of steam engines.

hot chisel: a tool used by a blacksmith to cut hot metal.

hot evil: a fever.

hot house: in salt-works, the room between the furnace and the chimney towards which the smoke is conveyed when the salt is set to dry.

hot presser: 1) one who operates the machine which puts a gloss on paper or cloth; 2) one who presses hot wood or metal flat or in a shape.

hot punches: a variety of (punch) tools used by a blacksmith.

hot set: a tool used by a blacksmith.

hot shot: an iron ball which was to be fired from a cannon was heated red hot in a furnace. This was done in the hope that the sails or woodwork on an enemy's ships would be set on fire.

hot toddy: a drink made of brandy, sweetening and hot water, sometimes consumed for the purpose of warming a person suffering from exposure to cold weather.

hougher: the public whipper of criminals, or the executioner of criminals.

hours of the day: in the armed forces time is numbered from midnight to midnight, to twenty-four. Therefore, 2:35 A.M. is 0235, whereas 2:35 P.M. is 1235.

house agent: 1) a real estate agent in England; 2) a person who rents houses or collects rent for others.

household: a group of persons who are not necessarily related, but live together. The census refers to households in this sense.

householder: a person who lived on property which he did not own. When found on a tax list, this indicates a resident on a particular property.

house joiner: this person built house frames of wood.

housekeeper: 1) the person in charge of making a house a home; 22) a hotel employee who supervises those who do the actual cleaning, making of beds, etc.; 3) a person employed on a regular basis, either in supervising other employees or by taking the place of a deceased wife; 4) a householder, either male or female; 5) a person who offers the hospitality of a home to another.

housel: an obsolete word for the Eucharist (which see).

house of assignation: see assignation house.

House of Burgesses: 1) formed by the Virginia Company to satisfy politically unhappy settlers, this representative assembly consisted of the governor, his councilors who were appointed by the company, and two burgesses elected by the settlers from each plantation. It became a model for Colonial govern-ment; 2) the lower chamber of the legislature of some states.

House of Lancaster: see Lancastrians.

House of York: see Yorkists.

housewife: in the military sense this is a small case which contains needles and thread for repairing clothing.

housewife's cloth: see huswives.

housewright: a high grade carpenter who worked on houses.

hout-wood foot: a Dutch measure of 11.15 inches which was used for all short measurements.

howdy wife: a midwife.

Hq. Co.: Headquarters Company.

H.R.I.P.: Hic Requiescit in Pace. Here rests in peace.

H.S.: Holland Society.

hs.: horseshoer.

H.S.A.: Huguenot Society of America.

huckster: a traveling street peddler who was not very popular with the established town merchants. See also badger.

huech: (Norman) eight.

huem, hucm: (Norman) a man.

Huguenot: a person of Protestant faith who lived in France in the sixteenth and seventeenth centuries. Many left France to live in England or Holland because of religious persecution.

hujus (quatre): (Norman) 1) four boundaries; 2) hedges.

hulk: a ship which has been worn out and is unable to move.

hull: the body of a ship without sails, masts, etc.

humanitian: 1) a grammarian; 2) a person skilled in polite literature.

hume: a hymn.

hund.: hundred.

hundred: 1) in Colonial days in some parts of the United States, this term was used to mean one hundred acres. It may have come from the English use of "hundred" to designate a part of a county having its own court. Other authorities feel that the term meant enough land to support one hundred colonists. Many estates were named (e.g. Job's Hundred) presumably from this term; 2) a Danish system was part of a shire and was so called apparently from its having been composed of one hundred families at the time the counties were originally divided, about 897; 3) in England this term meant a subdivision of a division of a county which was used as a basis for the organization of military service of one hundred men. This division was brought into the colonies of Pennsylvania, Virginia, Maryland, and Delaware.

hundred-court: based upon the early Danish court system, this was a court held for all the inhabitants of a hundred instead of a manor.

hunks: 1) a miser; 2) a mean old man.

hunt: a huntsman.

Huntington's chorea: a serious hereditary disorder which does not appear until adulthood. See chorea.

hurdling bill: a tool used by a wattle hurdle maker.

hurer: (Norman) a hat maker.

Huron Indians: a tribe who lived in Canada and the United States and fought against the United States in the War of 1812. They were also called Wyandots.

hus.: husband.

husband: 1) a husbandman or farmer; 2) a thrifty man.

husbandman: a farmer.

husk: see wheel hoop.

husking hoe: another time for a party among neighbors in early rural New England was the harvest-time husking bee when the picked corn had the outer covering removed in order to allow the corn to dry for storage. It is said that the man who found an ear of red corn could choose a girl to kiss.

husking pin: a tool used to husk Indian corn.

Hussar: this term comes from huszar which means twentieth man. Therefore, this means one man out of twenty who was chosen for service in the Hungarian army.

hussy: 1) a trollop or slut; 2) an impudent girl.

hustings: an ancient Anglo-Saxon court of London convened on a weekly basis. Later other English areas were granted hustings courts.

huswives: housewife's cloth made of a medium grade of linen which was used for household items ("family uses").

hutch: a measure of coal.

hydro-: used as a prefix means fluid on the ...

hydrocephalus: abnormal collection of fluid in the head. Also known as dropsy of the brain.

hydrops: dydropsy or dropsy.

hydropericardium: fluid around the heart. Also known as pericardial dropsy.

hydrophobia: 1) an abnormal fear of water; 2) rabies.

hydrothorax: excess fluid in the chest area.

hypertrophy of heart: enlargement of the heart.

hypothecate: a kind of mortgage; anything given as security for a debt without giving a title of ownership.

I

I: in New England this letter was sewed to a person's outer garment as punishment by the court after conviction of the crime of incest.

i: sometimes used interchangeably with the letter j or y in the spelling of English words.

Ia: in early census records the letters Ia. meant Indiana instead of Iowa.

ibid, ibid, ibidem: the same case, place or book; last mentioned place.

ice cutter: a person who cut chunks of ice from frozen lakes, streams, etc.

ice house: during the winter months when bodies of water would be frozen, blocks of ice were cut out and hauled to buildings for storage. There the ice would be buried in sawdust. Sometimes sawdust insulation was placed in the walls.

iceman: the person who deals in ice; buying, selling, delivering, etc.

icterus: jaundice, a bilious disease which first appears in yellowness of the eyes and skin.

idem: same.

idem sonans, rule of: use of a law rule which states that a word, usually a name, in a document which is misspelled but has the sound of the word as intended is valid, e.g. Cathy, Kathy, Kathi.

ides: the fifteenth day of March, May, July and October in the Roman Calendar. The ides of the remaining months fell on the thirteenth day.

id est: that is.

idlemen: gentlemen.

i.e.: see id est.

I.G.: Inspector General.

I.G.I.: International Genealogical Index, an on-going project of the Church of Jesus Christ of Latter-day Saints to list ancestors. It is a good finding aid.

ignoramus: when less than twelve members of a grand jury agreed, the case would be dismissed and the accused was freed.

ignota, ignotus: unknown.

-il: in-law (mil = mother-in-law, fil = father-in-law, bil = brother-in-law, etc.).

ileus: intestinal obstruction, also known as

intestinal colic.
illeg., illegit.: illegitimate.
Illini Indians: several tribes, mostly Algonquins. They lived in what is now Illinois, and gave the state its name.
illuminate: to draw in gold and silver the initial letters and occasional pictures in a manuscript.
illus.: illustrated.
immersion: baptism by lowering a person into a body of water.
immigrant: a person who comes to a country to settle permanently from another country, e.g. a person who comes to the United States from abroad.
immigration: to enter a place from another for the purpose of temporary or permanent residence.
imner: a gardener.
imp.: see imprimis.
impanel: 1) to choose; 2) to record the names of persons available, e.g. those for jury duty. Sometimes spelled empanel.
imparl: to settle a suit peaceably or to gain a delay for a settlement. It occurs when all the interested parties discuss a case with an amicable agreement as a goal.
imparlance: 1) time provided before a law suit begins in order that a friendly settlement might be made; 2) postponement of a lawsuit; 3) a petition asking for the delay of a lawsuit.
impeach: to call a public official before a court to answer a charge of misconduct while in office.
impediment: something which hinders the process of making a contract.
imper: a person who plants seed.
impetigo: an inflammation of the skin, most common in children.
Also known as scrumpox.
impn.: impanelled.
impressed seamen: see impressment.
impresseur: (Norman) a printer.
impressment: forced servitude in public service of a country, e.g. a navy. Able-bodied young men were forced into the British navy by a "press gang."
imprimis: in the first place; used many times in wills.
imprint: date and place of publication, plus the name of the book's publisher.
improved: 1) build home and outbuildings, plant crops; 2) employed.
improvements: 1) buildings; 2) additions to an existing object.
Imps: abbreviation for imprimis (which see).
impts.: improvements.
in: found frequently in old court records, "in" is a flexible preposition or prefix which assumes a variety of meanings. It usually means for or about, e.g. "____ vs. ____ in trespass" may mean "for trespassing" or "about trespassing." In real estate law it can be a title or an abbreviation for <u>in</u>vested with a title. In other cases it indicates an existence and, governed by the context with which it is used, can be about, on, etc. An example is "in debt," when a person owes money to another.
in: in France and Germany this suffix when used on a surname indicates a female.
inalienable: may not sell or purchase.
in articulo mortis: at the point of death.
inc.: incorporated; incomplete.
in case: found frequently in old court records, this term means "if it does happen."
in chancery upon petition: this term, used in some old court records, indicates that a case in the chancery court has received a petition which relates to the case.
inchoate: 1) unorganized; 2) incomplete; 3) just started.
incl.: included.
incle: see inkle.
Incle Manchester: see inkle.
incognitus: unknown.
incola: an inhabitant or dweller in any place.
incommode: 1) delay; 2) disturb; 3) inconvenience.
incompertus: unknown, uncertain.
incompetent: a person who is legally judged unable to handle his own affairs, insane, idiots, etc.
incorporeal: change to incorporeal property. See corporeal property.
incorporeal hereditament: see easement.
in cos: in partnership.

incumbent: the current rector of an English parish church.

I.N.D.: In Nomine Die. In God's name.

inde: hence, from there, from that place.

indebitatus: indebted.

in debt: see in.

in debtitatus assumpsit: a type of law suit, over a debt.

indefeasible: 1) not to be made null and void; 2) not subject to a forfeit.

indented servant: see indentured servant.

indenture: England did not have a system for recording documents, so a lawyer's clerk would make two copies of a document. The original document was cut in half and each party took a half. An indenture was the actual cutting apart or indenting.

indentured servant: a person who was unable to pay his fare to America and had to work out the cost of his trip. He was "sold" by the captain of the ship who had given him passage to another person as a servant to learn or practice a trade for a given number of years.

independent city: a large metropolitan area which has been incorporated and whose charter declares it free of county government. Services which would normally be administered by the county are administered by the city.

independent meetings: Quaker meetings of considerable size and importance which do not report to a higher meeting.

independent planter: a person who owned land and farmed it with no assistance other than that of his family.

Independents: see Separatists.

indexes (indices): in courthouse records names of grantees, grantors, testators, etc. are found for most records roughly alphabetized by surname. Some of these lists will be found at the front or back of the record book and others will have a small accompanying index book.

Indian bannock: used in Colonial New England this form of bread, about one inch thick, was made from cornmeal and water and baked. When rye meal was used it became a brown bread.

Indian file: to march or walk, one following another, which was the common way Indians walked through a wooded area.

Indian pudding: similar to, or perhaps another name for, hasty pudding. However, the difference could be that Indian pudding ingredients are mixed together and baked for a long time, and it is more likely to be used as a dessert.

Indian wars: a major civilian war fought from 1838 to 1891 during which American Indians were pushed to the west coast. The men involved were local residents and the regular army.

indictment: a written notification to the court which states that a grand jury has found reason to bring a criminal matter to trial.

indidem: from that same place.

indigent person: see pauper.

indirect tax: a tax upon materials levied during the manufacturing process. Eventually the purchaser pays this tax by paying a higher price for goods which includes all these taxes.

indiscriminate surveys: see metes and bounds.

indorsed: to sign a name on the back side of a document.

Inds.: Indians.

Ind.S.O.: Indian Wars Survivor's Original Certificate.

indt.: indictment.

Ind. Terr.: Indian Territory.

indulged meeting: a neighborhood meeting of Quakers authorized by a monthly meeting for those who are unable to attend monthly meetings because of bad roads, bad weather, or long distances.

Ind. W. C.: Indian Wars Widow's Certificate.

ineditus: unpublished.

in esse: in being; alive. Sometimes indicates a child not named or a child conceived but not born.

in extremis: in his last moments.

inf.: infant; informed.

Inf.: Infantry.

infair: it was common, two or three days after a wedding, for the parents and friends of the groom to make an "infair" or to renew the festivities.

infamy: shameful notoriety, disgraced.

infans: child.

infans puer: boy.

infans puella: girl.

infant: a person, who although he may be six feet tall, is not of legal age and therefore is still a minor.

Infantile debility: used when a child could not absorb nutrients from food, thus suffering from malnutrition, also known as marasonus, which see.

infantry: foot-soldiers. Men who were equipped with small arms and marched and fought on foot.

inferior court: a low court which handles small cases.

infirmarian: a nurse in a hospital.

infirmary: a place where ill or aged persons are housed and nursed.

info.: information.

influenza: an acute viral disease accompanied with fever and aches. Several years it reached epidemic proportions, for example: 1830, 1833, 1836, 1889 and 1890, 1897, and the largest of all 1918 and 1919 which claimed many lives.

in forma pauperis: an action allowing a poor person the right to sue without being liable for the court costs.

infra: beneath, below.

infusion: liquid medicine.

in futuro: henceforth.

ingener: an inventor or creator.

ingenere: not precisely alike but in kind.

ingenuus: freeman, yeoman, freeborn.

inhabitant: 1) a person who has made his home in an area. Historically transients, indentured servants, slaves, and women did not qualify as inhabitants. In order to participate in town affairs those who qualified were age twenty-one and possessed land or personal property of sufficient value to be taxed. Only then could he attend town meetings and cast his vote in the elections of town officers; 2) sometimes used in Colonial days to denote an area settled by colonists (plural only).

inhumatus, inhumata: unburied.

initiate injury: a wrong done to another.

injunction: the power of a court to require or prevent a person from committing a certain act or deed. Sometimes called a restraining order. See enjoin.

ink horn maker: the person who made inkwells from the horns of animals.

in kind: see ingenere.

inkle: a strong, woven, narrow tape of linen which was used for apron ties, shoestrings, to tie packages, etc.

in-law: this phrase used after brother, sister, mother, etc. denotes a relationship by marriage, e.g. a mother-in-law is your spouse's mother.

in loc. cit.: see in loco citata.

in loco: in place of.

in loco citata: in the place cited.

in loco parentis: "in the place of a parent." A person in loco parentis is one who acts as a parent for a child who is not his own.

inlot: 1) a plot of land lying inside a larger plot; 2) a lot surveyed and platted within a new or established town or village.

in manu: in possession.

inmate: 1) in an early tax list this term means a boarder, roomer or renter of land who is taxable for personal property; 2) a person may also be an inmate in a home for the aged, etc.

in memoriam: in memory of.

inn: a public house where travelers may obtain food and shelter; a tavern.

innholder: inn keeper, not necessarily the owner of the building.

Innig: (Norman) June.

innkeeper: the owner or operator of an inn.

in nomine Domini: in the name of the Lord.

inns of chancery: an English "college" which taught students elementary law, allowing them to be admitted to an inn of court.

inns of court: founded at the beginning of the 1300s and located in London, these institutions were practical schools (but not universities) for the teaching of law. Today, they give lectures and hold exams.

innubus: unmarried, without a husband.

innupta: unmarried.

in pari delicto: "in equal fault" or "equal in guilt."

in perpetuam: forever.

in personam: an individual, a character.

in posse: it is possible. The phrase

"children in posse" sometimes is used in a will rather than "any child my wife may be pregnant with."

in propia persona: in proper person. A person acting for himself as his own attorney.

inqr.: inquiry.

inquest: 1) a judicial inquiry made into the death of a person presumed to have died suddenly under peculiar circumstances; 2) an inquiry not necessarily concerned with death, e.g. an inquest into what damaged would have to be paid when a road was built. This term is found in many old records.

inquiline: a lodger.

inquilinus: 1) a tenant; 2) a lodger.

inquisition: 1) an investigation; 2) an inquiry; 3) an examination.

inquisition jury: twelve men assembled together to determine whether or not a man's real estate was of sufficient value that he could continue to own the land and work to pay off a debt.

in re: see re.

in room of: 1) in the place of. For example: James Black in room of John Smith, constable would mean that James Black was appointed to the position of constable instead of or succeeding John Smith; 2) also used in Quaker records with the same meaning.

insanity (amentia): amentia is intellectual defect of varying degrees (feeblemindedness). Insanity is: a legal term for mental derangement. Note: one who is feebleminded is not insane.

in secula seculorum: forever and ever.

inseller: (Norman) to occupy a stall in a church.

insignia: embroidered or metallic symbols worn on military uniforms which denote the rank, branch of the service, organization, etc. of the person wearing the uniform.

insolvent: unable to pay debts.

insolvent estate: an estate which does not have enough money to pay debts. Many states have a minimum amount for probate and under that amount an estate is not admitted to probate. Sometimes it will be mentioned in the probate records as of less than _____ dollars.

in specie: 1) written in as exact language as is a contract; 2) specific identifiable, "in the same form."

inspector: a county official who evaluated goods which could be used to pay a debt.

inst.: instance; instant.

inst., instant: within the same period of time. A term used to mean the current close date, e.g. on a document written in May: Inst. June.

Inst.: Institute; Institution.

instance court: a district admiralty court convened to try a civil case which involved admiralty matters.

instant: a term used to mean the current close date, e.g. on a document written in May; Inst. June.

instanter: immediately.

instd.: instructed.

in stirpes: same as per stirpes (which see).

instrument: any formal document which is acceptable in court.

insurgent: a rebel.

int.: 1) intentions (marriage); 2) intestate; 3) interred or buried; 4) interest, e.g. money.

intelligencer: a spy.

intendant: a governmental or public business official.

intentions: see banns (of marriage).

inter: between.

inter alia: among other things.

intercourse law: passed in June 1834 this law was designed primarily to protect Indians from dishonest land searchers.

interest in: ownership of a portion of land or commodities, e.g. "my interest in the cotton planting."

interfector: one who kills.

interim: 1) in the meantime; 2) meanwhile.

interlocutory: temporary.

intermarriage: to join two families, castes, tribes, etc. by the marriage of a man and a woman, one from each group.

intermittent fever: a condition where temperature falls to normal range for a period of time before rising again, such as in undulent fever or malaria.

interred: buried.

interment records: burial records. Sometimes quite informative.

in terrorem clause: the statement in a will which says that a person may or may not do a certain thing or he will be disinherited, e.g. marry into a specific family. This is usually considered against "public policy."

interval: the period between paroxysms of periodic diseases, e.g. ague, etc.

intervenor: a person who interferes in some manner in a lawsuit.

inter vivos: among the living.

intest.: intestate.

intestate: when a person dies without a will he dies intestate.

intestinal colic: a condition where pain may be present throughout the abdomen and which is frequently caused by an improper diet.

intestinal stricture: a contraction (tightening) due to pressure on (or changes in) the wall of the intestine.

In the Name of God, Amen: used in wills. This phrase originated in the English church probate courts.

intituled: entitled.

in toto: 1) in the whole; 2) altogether; 3) entirely.

intra quatuor maria: within the four seas.

intrd.: introduced.

intussusception: the condition where part of the intestine has slipped into another part just below it, as though it were a telescope.

inure: to become accustomed to something by prolonged exposure.

inv., invt.: inventory.

in viva, in vivus: at birth. Often used to indicate that the child died at birth.

in vacation: the period of time during which a court is not in session with a judge, but during which the work of the court goes on as usual, e.g. filing of cases or documents.

inventory: a verified itemized list of property. Sometimes an occupation can be determined by the contents of an inventory, e.g. one lot blacksmith's tools, one lot surveyor's tools, etc. This list, by its contents, can tell us how an ancestor lived; what tools he possessed tells us his occupation, what grain and animals tells us what type of farming he engaged in, etc.

inventory of estate: a list of all items in the possession of a person at the time of death. It is used for an equitable division of property among his heirs.

inventory of taxable property: this is a list of items which are eligible to be taxed. It is not to be confused with an inventory of an estate.

in ventra sa mere: in his mother's womb.

in vita testatorius: in the testator's lifetime.

inward maid: housemaid.

I.O.O.F.: Independent Order of Odd Fellows.

Ionic Indians: a tribe who lived in Texas.

Iowa Indians: a tribe who lived in the area that is now Iowa. They were of Dakota descent.

ipsa senestris: grown old by oneself or senilty, old age.

ipso facto: by the deed itself.

iretage: (Norman) heritage, inheritance.

ironclads: ships which have a coating of iron over a wood frame for protection against enemy fire.

Iron Horse: an early nickname for a railroad locomotive.

ironmaster: a person who owned or operated a foundry.

ironmonger: a person who sells hardware.

Ironsides: 1) the frigate "Constitution" was known as "Old Ironsides," a familiar name for this favorite old ship; 2) also a nickname for any well known veteran man-of-war.

Iroquois Indians: a confederacy of tribes, named by the French, of which the Cayugas, Mohawks, Oneidas, Onondagas, and Senecas were members. The Tuscaroras were added after they were driven from North Carolina.

Iroquois League: this group of Seneca, Cayuga, Onondaga, Oneida and Mohawk Indians, who all lived in central New York State, was founded to end wars between tribes and to establish peace through justice. The Oneidas and the Tuscaroras, who later became the "sixth" nation in this group, were allies of the British against the French. They also allied with the British during the

Revolutionary War.
ischewe: issue, progeny.
issud.: issued.
issue: 1) there is no special meaning in land terminology for "issue," but it is found without a form of the verb "to be" in old documents. Thus, a document might read "no patent can issue on this warrant;" 2) child or children usually limited to legitimate children. In wills it may mean children or lineal descendants who are alive at the time of the testator's death; 3) in a court case this is one particular point, claimed by one side and denied by the other; 4) a direct descendant, e.g. a child, grandchild, great-grandchild, etc.
it., item, itm.: also, likewise.
It.: Italian.
Italicino: a poor quality satin.
itch: a common frontier disorder of the skin for which a remedy was an ointment of brimstone (sulphur) and lard.
item: 1) from the Latin word idem which means also or likewise and is used to introduce a new section in a legal document; 2) a Colonial term meaning imitation.
itinerant: a person who traveled from one area to another in pursuit of his vocation, e.g. preacher, peddler, tinner, etc.
itinerant occupations: many, many persons of varying backgrounds with a skill or an object to sell, would take to the road and peddle their product. Some of these occupations in the wealthier areas of early America were: dancing masters, lecturers, mimics, school-teachers, etc. The forerunners of theatres were traveling waxworks shows, fortune tellers, balloon voyages, magic shows, minstrel shows, singing groups, trained animals, medicine shows, all of which were ready to amuse the amusement-hungry country folk.
-itis: inflammation of.
ivory turner: a person who carved objects from elephant's tusks, using a lathe.

J: 1) see i; 2) in Quaker records this is the abbreviation for joined.

J.A.: Judge Advocate.

jack: 1) a coat of mail; 2) half or quarter of a pint; 3) underground slang for a farthing; 4) a kind of water engine turned by hand and used in mines; 5) a poor parson; 6) a figure outside old clocks on public buildings. These figures struck the clock's bell.

jackalent: 1) a foolish fellow, hence jack-o-lantern; 2) one who looks rather seedy.

jack-bed: rails and slats forming the bed frame were laid from each side of the corner of a cabin to a single vertical post, forming a simple, unmovable bed.

jacket: the envelope which contains a person's service records or abstracts of his service records.

jack-in-the-box: a person who is around until help is needed, at which time he disappears.

jack-of-all-trades: a person who can do many things, but is not skilled in any one area.

Jack Raker: see raker.

Jacob's ladder: this ladder had wooden or metal rungs with rope sides and was used especially on ships, but also in fortifications.

jades: worn-out horses.

J.A.G.: Judge Advocate General.

jagger: a person who drove work horses for hire.

jail fever: typhus.

jalap: the root of a Mexican plant which when dried was used as a purgative medicine.

janders: jaundice.

Janevoir, Janner, Jaynuer: (Norman) January.

janti fame: (Norman) a noblewoman, gentlewoman.

jarvey: see hackney.

jarvis: a tool used by a wheelwright.

jas: see joined another society.

jASF: see joined Anti-Slavery Friends.

jaundice: a symptom where the skin and whites of the eyes become yellow. It occurs when liver bile gets into the blood. Although it is incorrect, many people use the term "jaundice" to mean liver disease.

javel: 1) a jail; 2) a worthless person; 3) a number of stalks of corn, flax, etc. which have been laid out to dry in the sun.

jaylarde: a jailor.

jC: found in Quaker records this indicates that a member joined a group of Conservative Friends.

J.C.: June Court.

jeans: a cotton and flax twill cloth.

Jeaundie, Jeady: (Norman) Thursday.

jehu: a coach-driver.

jerico: a slang expression for a retirement area or a place where a person could be concealed. Also used to indicate a far away and difficult to find place.

jerky: meat which was cut in strips and dried in the sun to preserve it. This would sustain life for a man on a journey.

Jersey: 1) usually referred to either or both of East New Jersey and West New Jersey at the time when New Jersey was not one state. Many times Jersey was used in the plural form; 2) short for a light wagon used in the New Jersey area; 3) a dairy cow, originally bred on the island of Jersey, which has a high butterfat content.

Jesse: the tree of Jesse was a representation of the genealogy of Christ in the form of a tree.

jetsam: goods thrown into the sea.

Jew's money: a name given to old Roman coins found in some parts of England.

jH: an abbreviation found in Quaker records which meant that a member joined the Hicksite Friends.

jib: the triangular forward sail on a sailing ship.

jigger pump: this device was used in breweries to force beer into vats.

Jim Crow laws: a name given to the laws which were designed to keep blacks and whites separated in this country. These laws were passed in a reaction to thirty years of freedom for blacks after the Civil War. The name came from a popular song sung in minstrel shows.

jMeth: a Quaker abbreviation indicating that a member joined the Methodist church.

jobber: 1) a person who buys and sells for other people; 2) a dealer in cattle.
joclet: small manor or farm.
joe: a master, superior.
Joe: see dobra.
joel, joer: (Norman) day.
jogelour: a minstrel.
Johannes: a Spanish coin, sometimes called "Joe."
johnny-cake: a common food cooked by pioneers on their journeys. Two staples usually carried on the trips were cornmeal and flour. These were the base for johnny-cakes with molasses, buttermilk and possibly soda added.
Johnny Reb: 1) a soldier who fought on the side of the south during the Civil War; 2) any citizen of a southern state, especially of one which was a member of the Confederate States of America.
johnny wopstraw: a farm laborer.
Joignet, Joign, Joil: (Norman) July.
joined another society: a phrase found in Quaker records indicating that a church member joined another religious group.
joined Anti-Slavery Friends: a Quaker term. Members of the church sometimes joined the Separatists or participated in establishing a Monthly Meeting whose beliefs were contrary to the church rules (Anti-Slavery Friends). This took place in 1843 and the following decade.
joiner: this person made more inexpensive items than did a cabinet maker.
joint and several: the binding of two or more persons, individually or all together. A plaintiff who is successful in his court case could recover damages from any defendant or from all of them.
joint store: this was an arrangement made early in the building process which allowed the general store to build the first floor to house merchandise. The Masonic Lodge (who would share their hall with other organizations) would build the second floor. The cost of the roof would be shared by both parties. The Masonic emblem often would be placed on the ends of the gables, but this arrangement could backfire if the organization was opposed to the high prices downstairs. After the Lodge could build its own building the storekeeper could expand his lines of good upstairs.
joint tenancy: this type of ownership is not limited to husband and wife, but can be entered into by any two people who have the same interest in the property. It has the right of survivorship, but can be ended by a mutual agreement to sell.
jointure: 1) two or more persons holding property together; 2) in early days this was property given to a wife in place of her dower; 3) the act of joining, as in a marriage.
joint will: usually this document is made to dispose of joint property and is made by two or more persons with each person signing it.
joist: a beam placed in a horizontal position as in a floor or ceiling.
jollacks: a clergyman.
jone home: (Norman) young man.
jonglours: (Norman) minstrels.
jordfesting: (Norman) burial).
jorrours, jorres: (Norman) jurors, juries.
Josephite: see Brighamite.
jour: abbreviation for journeyman.
journeyman: a worker who has completed his apprenticeship and is free to leave the establishment of his master and practice his trade independently. He may teach an apprentice under the direction of a master, but so long as he is employed by another, he is not a master but a journeyman (from French, jour, day, indicating that he was paid by the day).
jours (apres la): (Norman) after the decease.
jouster: a retailer of fish.
Jove: Thursday.
Joynter: jointure.
J.P.: abbreviation for Justice of the Peace. It is found in courthouse marriage books after the name of the man who performed the ceremony.
Jr.: 1) Junior; 2) the younger of two persons by the same name who may or may not be related.
Jubilate Deo: rejoice in God.
Jubiliate Sunday: the third Sunday after Easter.
J.U.D.: Juris Utriusque Doctor, Doctor of Laws.
judg., judgmt.: judgment.

Judge Advocate: the officer appointed to conduct a military trial or court-martial.
Judge of the Plains: an early California judge who settled arguments over cattle ownership and had control over the livestock driven through his area. This appointment was made each year.
judgment: a record of the court's decision of a case. The books where these are recorded may also be called order, decree or judgment books.
judgment debt: an obligation to pay which has been confirmed by a decree issued by a court.
judgment note: a document issued when a person does not pay a debt. It says that the creditor may ask for a judgment in court without being obliged to notify the debtor of the same.
Juen: (Norman) June.
Juesday: (Norman) Tuesday.
jugeable (ne foit): (Norman) cannot form any judgment.
jugh: judge.
Jug (le): (Norman) the judge.
Juig, Juignel: (Norman) June.
Juil: July.
Julian (Old Style) calendar: the calendar used in Europe during the Middle Ages which was inaccurate by about three days in every four centuries.
julio: an Italian coin.
jument: (Norman) an ox.
jumentz: (Norman) mares.
jumper: a tool used by a 1) cooper; 2) stone mason; 3) a rough sled; 4) a sailor who leaves his ship not intending to return; 5) a slang term for a driver; 6) a person who jumps or tries to obtain land, a mine, etc. from another person who was there first; 7) a mallet.
junamey: land sown with the same grain that it grew the preceding year.
Jung, Jun: (Norman) June.
Junior/Senior: until the nineteenth century this term did not necessarily mean father and son. It was used to separate persons of the same name living in the same town. If there were more than two of the same name, numbers were then used. Upon the death of one, the remaining would move up the numerical line. It was sometimes used when the person is a nephew or cousin.
Junr.: Junior.
jur.: see jurat.
jurat: it has been sworn.
jure, jurere: (Norman) to swear.
jure uxorix: in right of his wife.
jurges: (Norman) oaths.
jurisconsultus: lawyer, jurist.
jurisdiction: 1) the legal right to hear a case and make a decision; 2) the area of an authority, e.g. state, county, township, city; 3) a judge's right to speak. If a judge does not feel that he has the right to make a decision in a court case, he says that he does not have jurisdiction.
jurs: jurors.
jury: 1) a group of citizens called together to hear evidence produced in court and to reach a fair decision about a lawsuit. In Pennsylvania jury members were called from freeman lists; 2) sometimes used to mean a committee of twelve to "lay out a road" or perform other orders of the county commissioners.
juryn: jurymen.
jury of inquiry: see coroner's jury.
Just: Justice (as in a title).
Justice of the Peace: a person who has the power to perform marriages, levy fines for minor offenses and who has limited power to try certain cases; for example, one person sues another for his week's wages.
justicer: 1) a judge; 2) a justice of the peace.
juvenca: young girl, maiden, or cow.
juvenilis: youthful, juvenile.
juvencus: a young man or bullock.
Juyl: (Norman) July.

Kaintuck: see Kentuck.
kalo: see calo.
Kaskaskia Indians: a tribe that lived in southern Illinois.
kaite: a dresser of wool.
kalender: a guide or director.
kayn: a nobleman.
kaysere: emperor.
K.B.: Kirchenbuch, parish register.
K.C.: see Queen's Council.
kecker: an overseer at a coal mine.
kedger: a fisherman.
keel: the lowest and principal timber in a ship. It goes from front to back and supports the frame of a ship much as a backbone.
keelage: the tax which a merchant ship was obliged to pay when entering a port.
keel alley: a bowling alley.
keelboat: a flat-bottomed, sturdy, large boat approximately forty to seventy-five feet long and seven to nine feet wide which always had a heavy four by four the entire length of the bottom which was designed to withstand collision with under-water obstructions. It usually had a mast, oars, and poles, one of which would be used according to river and weather conditions. There were even many varieties which came to be separated by the name of the river where they were built and used.
keeler: a shallow tub which could hold water for washing, etc.
Keeper of the King's Conscience: the early chancellors were priests and out of their supposed moral control of the king's mind grew the idea of an equity court as opposed to the law courts. The keeper of the king's conscience then became the person who presided over the court of chancery in England.
keeping room: the room usually sat in by the family.
kenman: half a bushel.
kenting: a fine linen fabric made first in Kent, England.
Kentuck, Kaintuck: 1) an old term for Kentucky; 2) an old term for a person from Kentucky.
Kentucky boat: a small flatboat designed for use on the smaller Kentucky rivers along the Ohio River.
Kentucky rifle: a very accurate, long-barreled rifle which was used by the first hunters and citizens in Kentucky. It was also called a long rifle and was likely to have been made in Pennsylvania.
Kentucky vital statistics: see Sutton law.
ker: (Norman) a city.
kerk: church.
kersey: a coarse wool fabric woven in narrow, ribbed lengths used for stockings, petticoats, men's clothing, etc.
kerseymere: a fabric made of fine wool woven in fancy twill weaves.
kersin: to christen.
kerver: (Norman) a carver.
kesson: a Christian.
ketch: a two-masted sailing vessel.
keykeeper: a person who built and maintained (but did not make the survey for) a pound for stray animals, usually on his own property. Sometimes called a pounder.
Kickapoo Indians: a member of the Algonquin tribe, these Indians were forced from Wisconsin south into Indiana and Illinois and finally to Oklahoma.
Kickapoo ranger: a Kansan who strongly supported slavery.
kickine: kitchen.
kidnapped: 1) sentenced by a court and sent abroad to do forced labor, especially from England to the colonies in America; 2) seized illegally and forced to work for another.
kilderkin: eighteen gallons; one-half or sometimes one-quarter of the size of a barrel.
kill-devil: cheap, poor quality rum.
kilometer: five-eighths of a mile.
kimmel: a round wooden tub used in salting and working with meat.
kin: see kith.
kindred: people who are blood relatives.
kine: cows.
king: Friday was sometimes called the king of the week.
King George's War: from 1744 to 1748, New Englanders assembled troops and ships at Boston and captured Louisburg on Cape Breton Island. It was part of the struggle for control of the St.

Lawrence and Mississippi basins. It was a fruitless conflict beginning when France and England declared war against each other in the War of the Austrian Succession. Peace following this was only an interlude.

King Philip's War: Philip, son of Massasoit, the Indian friend of the Pilgrims at New Plymouth, was induced by real and imaginary wrongs to make war on the European settlers in America and exterminate them. He struck his first blow in 1675 and the white settlers sprang to arms. Philip ordered other New England Indian tribes to join him and a blood war was fought in the more remote New England settlements until in 1676 Philip was shot by a faithless Indian. His son, the last survivor of his family, was sold into slavery in Bermuda.

Kings, Queens, and other rulers of England

Saxons (802-1017):
- 802-839 Egbert
- 839-858 Ethelwoulf
- 858-860 Ethelbald
- 860-866 Ethelbert
- 866-871 St. Ethelred
- 871-901 Alfred the Great
- 901-925 Edward the Elder
- 925-940 Athelstan
- 940-946 Edmund I the Deed-doer
- 946-955 Elred
- 955-959 Edwy the Fair
- 959-975 Edgar the Peaceful
- 975-979 Edward the Martyr
- 979-1016 Ethelred II the Unready
- 1016-1017 Edmund II Ironside

Danes (1017-1042)
- 1017-1035 Canute
- 1035-1040 Harold I Harefoot
- 1040-1042 Hardicanute

Saxons (1042-1066)
- 1042-1066 Edward the Confessor
- 1066 Harold II

Normans (1066-1154)
- 1066-1087 William I the Conqueror
- 1087-1100 William II Rufus
- 1100-1135 Henry I Beauclerc
- 1135-1154 Stephen of Blois

Plantagenet Kings (1154-1399)
- 1154-1189 Henry II
- 1189-1199 Richard I Coer de Lion
- 1199-1216 John Lackland
- 1216-1272 Henry III
- 1272-1307 Edward I Longshanks
- 1307-1327 Edward II
- 1327-1377 Edward III
- 1377-1399 Richard II

House of Lancaster (1399-1461)
- 1399-1413 Henry IV Bolingbroke
- 1413-1422 Henry V
- 1422-1461 Henry VI

House of York (1461-1485)
- 1461-1483 Edward IV
- 1483 Edward V
- 1483-1485 Richard III

House of Tudor (1485-1603)
- 1485-1509 Henry VII
- 1509-1547 Henry VIII
- 1547-1553 Edward VI
- 1553 Jane (Lady Jane Grey)
- 1553-1558 Mary I "Bloody Mary"
- 1558-1603 Elizabeth I

House of Stuart (1603-1649)
- 1603-1625 James I
- 1625-1649 Charles I

Commonwealth (1649-1659)
- 1649-53 Council of State
- 1653-1658 Oliver Cromwell
- 1658-1659 Richard Cromwell

Restoration of the House of Stuart
- 1660-1685 Charles II
- 1685-1688 James II
- 1688-1702 William III and Mary II
- 1702-1714 Anne

Kings of Hanover and England (1714-1837)
- 1714-1727 George I
- 1727-1760 George II
- 1760-1820 George III
- 1820-1830 George IV
- 1830-1837 William IV

Hanoverian Queen of England
- 1837-1901 Victoria

House of Saxe-Coburg (1901-1917)
- 1901-1910 Edward VII
- 1910-1917 George V

House of Windsor (1917-)
- 1917-1936 George V
- Jan-Dec 1936 Edward VIII (Duke of Windsor)
- 1936-1952 George VI
- 1952- Elizabeth II

See also Dynasties.

King's attorney: during the period when this country was a British Colony, the prosecuting attorney was appointed by, and served under, whoever was the King of England.

King's evil: scrofula, a swelling in the lymph glands of the neck. There is an old tale that claims the disease is curable by a king or queen's touch.

King's passengers: English convicts who were shipped to America under court orders. The convicts paid no passage money and were sent as servants. Certainly this was preferable to the severe punishment which could then be imposed for a small crime in England.

King's pasture: money.

King William's War: this was fought from 1689 to 1697 and was an intercolonial war. Military enterprises were generally on a small scale, with raids in the enemy frontier and the burning of forts and towns. It was closed with the treaty of Ruswick in 1697 with no real settlement. The troops were all volunteer.

Kiowa Indians: a once powerful tribe who roamed through Colorado, Kansas and northern Texas.

kirk: a church.

kirke: (Norman) a church.

kirk garth: a church yard.

kirk master: church warden.

kirsome: Christian.

kiss-me-quick: 1) a curl which hangs down in front of an ear; 2) a fashionable bonnet from the 1800s which was small and rested far back on a lady's head.

kisting: a funeral.

kith: friends and acquaintances as opposed to kin (relatives).

kit kat, kit cat: a member of an eighteenth century political club which met in London.

K.K.K.: Ku Klux Klan.

Klamath Indians: a tribe who lived in northern Colorado and southern Oregon.

Klan: see Ku Klux Klan (which see).

Kliketats Indians: a tribe who lived in the Washington Territory.

kln: an abbreviation for kilderkin (which see).

kn.: known.

knacker: 1) a person who makes used of carcasses of animals for purposes other than human consumption, e.g. as fertilizer, dog or cat food; 2) a collar and harness maker, chiefly employed by farmers; 3) a collier's horse; 4) a person who buys old buildings or ships for the material in them which can be used in other ways.

knapsack: a bag made usually of canvas which was designed to be carried on a soldier's back and contain his necessary items. Also called a haversack.

knave: 1) a lad; 2) a servant.

knight: a servant, generally a servant in a war; a soldier.

knight bachelor: a man who belonged to the oldest and lowest class of knights in Great Britain.

knight errant: a medieval knight who would wander around searching for an adventure, a wrong to make right, a way of showing off his strength, etc.

knighthode: valor.

knight of the pestle: an pharmacist.

knight service: military duty under the feudal system.

Knights of Columbus: founded in 1882, the members are Roman Catholic men.

Knights of Labor: begun in 1869 by nine Philadelphia tailors, this was a secret organization until it expanded to include all workers except lawyers, bankers, gamblers, and saloon keepers.

Knights of Pythias: a charitable and social organization founded in 1864.

Knights of St. Crispin: an organization established in 1867 by shoemakers, it lasted for ten or eleven years when it dissolved and its members joined the Knights of Labor.

Knights of the Golden Circle: a secret organization formed before the Civil War to support slavery and Southern causes.

Knights Templars: 1) a military and religious fraternity established during the twelfth century; 2) a member of the York rite of Masons.

knitster: a female who knits.

knitting cup: a cup of wine handed around immediately after a marriage ceremony to those who assisted in the ceremony.

knobstick: 1) a cane or walking stick which had a knob instead of a crook; 2) a name given to a person who continued to work instead of joining his fellow workers in a strike; 3) an employer who hires non-union workers.

knock-knobbler: the name of the person who walks about the church during the service to maintain order.

knockledeboinard: hard-working clown.

knot: 1) a naval measure of speed, one nautical mile (608,027 feet) per hour; 2) a nautical mile.

Know-Nothing party: a political party prominent during the early 1850s whose members wanted the government controlled by native-born citizens. They professed ignorance of their party's principles or activities, thus gaining the name of the Know-Nothings. Now the term is used to mean a person who knows nothing of politics.

Knt.: Knight.

K. of C.: Knights of Columbus.

kok: a cook.

kommies: in Dutch records this person is a deputy or clerk.

kommissaries: found in Dutch records, this person is the magistrate or commissioner.

Koran: a sacred book written about 610 by Mohammed, who said that it had been revealed to him by the angel Gabriel in twenty-three years. Its general aim was to unite those who worshipped idols, Jews and Christians in the worship of God and that Mohammed, as an apostle of God, was to be obeyed.

kowke: a cook.

krib: one hundred square feet of cut grass.

kuke: a cook.

Ku Klux Klan: a society whose membership is secret. Founded after the close of the Civil War, it believes in the superiority of whites over blacks.

kuntiput: a clown.

Kusine: (Norman) female cousin.

ky: cows.

kyack: a bag which hangs on both sides of a packsaddle.

L

L: 1) license; 2) Latin; 3) Liber; 4) Law; 5) an English pound (money).

l.: lived, lives.

labor: an old Texas unit of land equal to approximately 177 acres.

laborer: frequently used to describe a man who owned no real estate.

lacewoman: a lady's maid. The term probably came from the fact that a maid was required to pull tight the lacings on her mistress' corset.

laches: negligence, undue delay.

lackland: one who did not own land.

lad: a man servant.

lade saddle: a saddle which allows a horse to carry a load on its back.

ladle: see dipper.

laddle adze: a tool used by a wood carver.

lady: 1) a mistress of servants; 2) a female head of a household or lady of the house; 3) the wife of a lord or a woman who holds the title equivalent to a lord; 4) the Virgin Mary; 5) a name used in speaking to a woman of rank, e.g. My Lady Sarah; 6) a obsolete prefix for a female office holder, e.g. Lady Mayoress; 7) wife or consort; 8) a measure of roofing slate (15" x 8").

Lady Day: 25 March.

lady-in-waiting: a Queen's companion, assistant.

laer: a barn.

lafter: the number of eggs laid by a hen before she sits on her nest to hatch the eggs.

lageman: jury man.

lagniappes: 1) a small gift which a Louisiana tradesman gave to his customers; 2) a payment in return for the use of influence.

la grippe: see grippe.

laid down: a Quaker term used to mean discontinued. It was used especially to indicate that a meeting was adjourned by direction of a higher meeting.

laity, the: non-professional persons.

lake: a kind of fine linen from which shirts were made.

laker: a navigator of a boat on the Great Lakes.

lameter: a cripple.

lamplighter: a person who lighted the

street lamps at dusk and extinguished them the following morning.

Lancastrian: 1) a member of the Plantagenet (which see) families from which fourteen of England's kings descended; 2) a supporter of the Plantagenents.

lance knight: a foot soldier.

lancet: a surgical instrument used for opening infections, etc.

land agent: 1) a company or an individual who, for a fee, obtained grants for public land or negotiated a sale of privately owned land; 2) the government official who managed public land; 3) in England this was the person who managed an estate.

landau: a carriage used in the middle 18th century. It had two seats which faced each other and a two-part collapsible top which could be let down. The carriage was first made in Landau, Germany.

land certificate: a certificate which was negotiable and assured the grantee of a clear title to public land.

land classification: the process of deciding that a piece of public land is particularly suited for a certain purpose.

land day: a specific day on which a certain portion of public land would be sold.

land descriptions: S1/2 NW1/4 S14 T19N R10E. This is a description of land. It is read from back to front, first finding on a map the Range, then Township, then Section. This piece of land would be the south 1/2 part of the northwest 1/4 part of Section number 14 in a specific Township.

land drain fork: a tool used by a brick maker.

land draughts: see draughts.

land end: the piece of turf left at the end of a plowed field.

land entry: a specific piece of land obtained from the government by a warrant, purchase, etc. which was filed with the area land office authorized to sell land.

land entry book: the book usually kept in the county courthouse, which contains the entries for public land, listed by names of the individual owners.

land entry papers: documents concerned with acquiring public land; receipts for cash or installment payments, bounty land warrants, land applications, etc. They are filed in a land office.

landerer: a person who washed clothes.

land grabber: 1) a person who obtained another person's land in a dishonest manner; 2) a person who acquired large tracts of land many times by dishonest methods.

land grant: see grant.

Land Grant Act: an act, sometimes called the Morrill Act, which in 1862 gave public lands to states for the purpose of establishing colleges to teach agriculture and mechanics.

landgrave: an early South Carolina title for a holder of 48,000 acres of land.

landholder: a person responsible for taxes on land which he did not necessarily occupy.

land jumper: see land grabber.

land lien dockets: courthouse books which list all lands, sold and unsold, upon which there was money due the government. Many times these books will note ancestors who did not pay for their land.

land looker: 1) a person who claimed to have appraised the value of land in a given area. This person would also claim that he could furnish water, particular types of land, etc. immediately 2) a person whose job was to hunt for good timberland.

landlord: a person who owns land or other property which he rents to another person for a monthly or annual fee.

landloupers: persons who flee a country for a crime or debt.

landlubber: a slang term which means one who has never been on the sea in a ship.

landmale: a reserved rent or an annual sum of money which was charged for a piece of land by the chief lord of the manor or his successor.

land marker: a post, or some other object, used to mark a survey point on land, e.g. a boundary.

landmate: he who in harvest time reaps the same ground as another.

land measure: in some states the early

method of specifying the boundaries of land was quite vague. This early system of metes and bounds used tree, water courses and other temporary markers to separate a person's land from that of his neighbors. The system of Range, Sec-tion and Township was accepted in the United States in the early nineteenth century. This system used geometrical surveying with lines running north-south and east-west.

land measures: 1) length: one mile equals 5280 feet, eighty chains, 320 rods, or 1760 yards. One rod equals 5.50 years, 16.5 feet or 25 links. 2) area: one square mile equals 640 acres or 102,400 square rods. One acre equals 4840 square yards or 43,500 square feet. One square rod equals 30.25 square yards, or .006 of a square acre.

land mend: to level the ground with a shovel after wheat has been sown.

land office: a center for sale of land previously owned by the government. This office was a part of the Treasury Department, but later was transferred to the Interior Department.

land patent: the document which states the a settler had permanent claim and was the first purchaser of a piece of land.

land records: documents which give facts about transfers of land from one person (or the government) to another person.

land right: the legal obligations which are attached to ownership of land.

land scrip: a certificate for the purchase of land which entitled a person or a land company to a specified amount of land. Much scrip would be purchased by persons who wished to obtain large parcels of land.

landsman: 1) a dweller on land; 2) a novice seaman; 3) a fellow countryman.

"lands, tenements and hereditaments:" a comprehensive description of real estate which is found in old deeds.

land waiter: a customs officer in England whose job was to enforce regulations, collect the duty due on goods, etc.

land warrant: a certificate issued by a land office which entitled the possessor to a certain number of acres of land. The certificate was negotiable.

lane: see lawn.

langrets: loaded dice.

lanius: butcher.

lanspessade: an infantry petty officer. Sometimes used without the l.

lantern staff: a weight tied to a horse's foot which enabled him to be caught more easily.

lapicide: a stone-cutter.

lappior: a dancer.

lapse: this term is used to indicate that a person who was to inherit under a will has died before the testator. Therefore, whatever the deceased person was to inherit is said to lapse and is integrated into the rest of the testator's property.

lapstone: 1) a cobbler's tool; 2) (archaic) the stone on which a shoemaker beats his leather to soften it.

laquear: a ceiling.

laras: round pieces of wood turned on a lathe by a turner.

larboard: a nautical term for the left side. It was replaced by "port" because "larboard" and "starboard" were difficult to distinguish when shouted.

lardering stick: a tool used to pierce holes in poultry while it cooked.

lardery: a pantry; food cupboard.

lardyner: (Norman) the officer in the king's household who presided over the pantry.

lare: a rate or a tax.

lare-father: a schoolmaster.

largess: 1) a bounty; 2) the cry of minstrels at feasts.

larks leers: 1) tillable land not in use; 2) poor or barren land.

lart: a wooden floor.

lartin nails: nails used to fasten down a floor.

laryngismus stridulus: a condition where muscles of the voicebox go into spasms causing shortness of breath and a "crowing" sound. This condition was usually associated with boys under the age of two who had the disease known as rickets (which see). It was considered a grave condition because the throat would swell until one could no longer breathe unless surgery was performed.

last: 1) a measure: eighty bushels of corn; twelve bushels of fish; fourteen barrels of pitch, tar, or ashes; twelve dozen hides or skins; twenty thousand herrings; twelve sacks of wool, etc.; twelve dickers of leather; 2) a court which levied rates for preserving marsh land; 3) a Dutch dry measure.

lastage: 1) an obsolete tax paid for each booth at a fair or market; 2) a ship's ballast; 3) a port tax to load ships; 4) a tax upon a catch of herring; 5) an obsolete word for garbage.

last day: yesterday.

laster: a person who makes a part of a shoe over a wooden form which is known as a last.

last generals: this term was used in some English records when referring to the most recent meeting of a group, general assembly, council, etc.

last hook: a tool used by a bootmaker.

lasting: see everlasting.

lasting pincers: a tool used by a bootmaker.

latchstring: a piece of cord or leather which ran from the inside to the outside of a door. It allowed the latch to be raised from the outside. The string could be kept inside, thus effectively locking the door, or it could be left on the outside to invite guests to come in.

late: 1) recently deceased person; 2) a person who has just moved from another town, e.g. "name of person," late of "name of town."

latent: hidden, concealed, or not visible. For example a latent defect is one so concealed that a reasonably careful inspection does not reveal the defect.

lath: a court in about 1033.

lathe: 1) a division of a county containing three or more hundreds; 2) a barn.

lather: 1) part of a mill; 2) a ladder.

lathing: an invitation.

latimer: an interpreter.

latitude: see grid.

latten: plate tin, a mixed metal which resembles brass.

lattice: an ale house was generally distinguished by a lattice, not a glass window. A glass window was expensive and could be broken.

lauchaids: terraces on the side of a hill, either natural or artificial.

laudanum: a morphine drug which produces sleep and relieves pain when given in small amounts. Larger amounts result in poisoning and even death. Intentional overdoses were a common method of committing suicide.

laundre: a laundress.

Laus Deo: praise to God.

lavandre: a laundress.

law case: a legal matter usually tried before a jury.

lawn: a fine, plain weave linen fabric.

law of entail: this forbids the division of large estates.

lay: 1) (usually followed by man, woman, person or other similar noun) a person who is not trained in a profession, but at times is called upon to do the work of a professional. For example, a person who conducts a church service in the minister's absence; 2) a tax or rate.

lay preacher: a person who is not an ordained minister but in the absence of a minister conducts the church service and gives the sermon.

lay subsidies: taxes in England levied by Parliament to meet costs of government, support the military and the royal family as demanded.

lazaretto: 1) a hospital which specializes in caring for person who have contagious diseases; 2) a building or a ship which has been named a quarantine unit; 3) a small room used for storage in the hull of a ship. Sometimes called a glory hole.

lazer house: a place for persons afflicted with leprosy.

lb.:: pound. The Latin word for pound is libra and the abbreviation for libra is lb.

L.B.C.: Letter Book Copy.

L.C.: Library of Congress.

L.C. or l.c.: legitimate child.

ld.: land.

Ldr.: leader.

L.D.S.: The Church of Jesus Christ of Latter-day Saints.

l.e.: local elder in a church.

lea board: a plank fixed to the bottom of a flat vessel in a way designed to slow down the drift to leeward.

leach: 1) a lake or large pool; 2) a common way.

leachman: a surgeon.
leachroad: a road used for funerals.
leader: the first pair of horses of several who pulled a vehicle, or the first horse in a tandem team.
lead paint: in the early 1800s the use of a lead compound to make paint (lead compound and linseed oil) was discovered. This began the protection of buildings from decay.
lead palsy: a paralysis of muscles due to a large amount of lead in a person's body. See also Devonshire Colic.
lead poisoning: a disease which affected persons who had a prolonged contact with substances containing lead—painters, those who made lead bullets, potters, dyers of cloth, etc. Materials used today do not contain large amounts of lead. See also smelter.
leaf: a page.
leaf hammer: a tool used by a blacksmith for making decorative wrought iron.
leaf tool: see above.
league: 1) an English measure on land of approximately three miles; 2) an ocean measure of distance, usually about three nautical miles; 3) a square league was a Spanish land measurement used in California. It equalled 4439 acres or 1796 hectares. In Texas it equalled 4428.4 acres or 1792.1 hectares.
lean-to: a temporary shelter constructed from whatever kind of material was at hand.
leap: half a bushel.
lease: 1) to rent; 2) a legal contract in writing whereby a person conveys a portion of his interest in property to another, in consideration of a certain rent or other recompense; 3) a pasture.
lease and release: a technical way of avoiding English court fees for transferring land. The possessor of the land would *lease* it for a year to the person who wanted to buy it. The leaseholder would take possession of the land, and then could purchase the remaining rights to the land through a *release*. The entire process had the same effect as a sale of land.
lease for "lives:" in Colonial days the customary time for a lease to be in force was twenty-one years, but at times it was for three "lives." This could be for the lives of any three people: a man, his wife and child, a man and two friends, or any other combination. At the death of the last of the three, the use of the land reverted to the owner. This type of lease usually was not recorded in the local land register.
leasehold: land which has been rented.
leasestick: an earlier name for the flax swingle.
leasing: an armful of hay or corn which has been gleaned.
leather breeches beans: young, tender green beans strung together with a needle and strong thread and hung by one end to dry.
leather clothing: the "cloth" used by a frontiersman for outer garments, which was most practical as it resisted briars better than woven cloth.
leatherdresser: the person who worked with animal hides to preserve them.
leatherhead: a policeman.
leatherneck: a slang term for a Marine.
leatherparer: one who reduces binding leather to the proper thickness for use.
leathersealer: a person who inspected tanned leather to determine if it was of sufficiently good quality to bear a "seal of approval."
leatherworker: a person who made or repaired straps, parts of a gun slings, etc. of animal hides.
leave: 1) to change one's residence; 2) to permit.
leavenor: a luncheon.
leche: 1) a physician; 2) to heal.
lectur: a reader.
ledger: an account book.
ledger stone: a flat stone large enough to cover the top of a grave.
leech: 1) a blood-sucking worm which may be used to treat wounds; 2) part of a sail; 3) an old name for an instrument used to draw blood; 4) an obsolete word which meant to heal or cure; 5) an old word for a physician.
leech house: a hospital.
leet: see court leet.
leetman: 1) a member of a committee or a group commissioned to perform a

certain task; 2) a general term used to indicate a district; 3) a person eligible for nomination to an office.
legacy: a gift of personal property left to a person in a will.
legal age: this varies in different states. It is the age at which one is considered competent to manage his own affairs.
legal description: a method of identifying a certain piece of land. See also metes and bounds and rectangular survey system.
legal residence: a person's permanent address to which he intends to return ultimately.
legal tender: currency authorized by the government for use in business transactions, debts, taxes, etc.
legate: 1) the Pope's assistant; 2) a general, consul or magistrate's assistant; 3) an emissary; 4) a provincial governor who was appointed by the emperor.
legatee: a person who receives property, either real or personal, by a will.
legator: a person who receives property by a will, either real or personal.
legerdemainist: a magician.
legget: a tool used by reed thatchers.
legn.: legion
leiger: a resident ambassador at a foreign court.
leightonward: a gardener.
leland: a cow pasture.
leman: 1) an old word for a lover or sweetheart; 2) an obsolete word for a mistress.
Lent: from the Saxon "lencten" (spring). The forty days' feast observed in the Roman Catholic church from Ash Wednesday to Easter day. In early times Lent began on Sunday, now called the first Sunday in Lent, and the four days beginning with Ash Wednesday were added by Pope Felix III in 487 in order that the fasting days should amount to forty.
lent-evil: the ague.
lentz monet: (Norman) the month of March.
leprosy: a disease of humans and animals which eats away flesh and formed white scales on the skin. At one time people were banished to islands or leper houses to restrict the spread of this disease.
lerare: 1) a learner; 2) a teacher.
lessee: a person who receives a lease.
lessor: a person who grants a lease.
lestal: saleable, good and proper weight.
lesur: pasture.
letter, letters: a written message, request, etc. which is sent to another person and which gives permission or authority to act, e.g. letter of attorney, a power of attorney (which see).
letter of attorney: see power of attorney.
letter of dismission: see dismission.
letter of marque: a ship's paper which authorizes a privately owned ship to take prize vessels at sea to be given to an Admiralty Court for condemnation.
letters of administration: a document from the probate court which allows an administrator of an intestate estate authority to settle the estate.
letters of admission: a letter from one Baptist church to another when one in good standing moves to another community.
letters of guardianship: see letters of tuition.
letters of guardianship: a document from the probate court which allows a guardian to begin his duties of caring for a minor child and his affairs. Sometimes called letters of tuition.
letters of marque: 1) documents pertaining to shipping which name the master of a ship, the owner of the ship, and sometimes the destination of the ship; 2) authorization for a private ship to seize enemy ships (prize ships) and to bring them before an admiralty court for condemnation.
letters of transfer: a letter of introduction from a Church of England congregation for a member in good standing to another church of the denomination.
letters of tuition: a court-issued document which allows a guardian to start his duties, e.g. conservation of an orphan's estate from parents, conservation of an incompetent person's assets, etc. Sometimes called letters of guardianship (which see).
letters patent: see patent.
letters testamentary: a document from the

probate court which allows the executor of an estate authority to settle the estate.

letting of blood: see bleeding.

levellers: persons who advocate an equalization of property ownership.

lever scale: see steelyard.

levetennante: a deputy.

Leviticus: the third book in the Bible which lists laws of the Jewish religion, Levites (the descendants of Levi), along with the prescribed rites and ceremonies.

levours: (Norman) those who levy any tax.

levy: 1) to assess or to collect a tax; 2) to raise troops for service; 3) to wage war.

lewd: ignorant, untaught, useless.

lewis: a tool used by a stone mason.

lewn: a tax or rate for church or parish dues.

lexicon: an alphabetical list of words in one category, e.g. in one language or relating to one profession, along with a definition for each word.

ley, lea: fallow or untilled ground.

leyare: a stonemason.

leze majesty: see treason.

LGAR: Ladies of the Grand Army of the Republic.

L.G.O.: Land Grant Office.

lht.: light.

L.I.: Long Island (New York).

li.: 1) lines; 2) abbreviation for pound.

lib.: 1) see liber; 2) library.

Libby prison: a Confederate prison housed in warehouses to hold captured Union officers during the Civil War. Located in Richmond, Virginia, it got its name from the company which owned the warehouses.

libel: to injure the reputation of another by publishing degrading material.

liber: book.

liber homo: a free man.

liberi: children.

liberoriem: children.

libers: the large, bound books into which deeds, wills, etc. have been copied in chronological order. These are kept in the appropriate office in a courthouse.

liberty-wife: a sailor's mistress.

libr.: an abbreviation for library.

libra: a Roman measure of weight (a pound) which equalled about 327 grams or ¾ pound avoirdupois. See lb.

libro: see liber.

lic.: license.

license: issued by some states, this document gave permission for a land grant applicant to buy a certain tract of land.

lich gate: the gate through which a corpse was carried into church. It had a roof over it which sheltered the bier and the bearers could rest until the funeral began.

lick: named by the first settlers because they noticed buffaloes, elks, and deer went to lick a salt deposit on the surface of the earth. Hunters waited at the licks and killed a few animals as they came for salt. Pioneers also by crude methods of evaporation "made salt" for their homes. Also see salt suck.

lidgitts: gates set up on the edge of a village to prevent cattle from straying on to planted fields.

lie (de la): (Norman) of the lineage.

lief coup: sale of goods at the place of manufacture.

liege man: 1) a vassal; 2) a devoted follower.

lieger: an ambassador.

lien: the right to retain interest in another's property until the debt he owes is paid. There is no transfer of title and it is not a land record, but is usually kept in the recorder's office along with deeds.

lien release: see release of lien.

lientery: a form of diarrhea.

lieton: a church-yard.

lieu: in place of.

Lieutenant: see army rank.

Lieutenant Colonel: see army rank.

Lieutenant General: see army rank.

lievies (de leur): (Norman) of their heirs.

lieux: (Norman) bonds.

life estate: 1) a partial interest in property which ends with the owner's death; 2) an interest in property owned by another, which lasts only as long as the life of the person who holds the life estate. For example, a man wills land to his son with his widow having income from the land which income ends with her death.

life-guard, Washington's: a corps of from sixty to two hundred and fifty men formed in the spring of 1776. These men were of uniform height, not less than five feet, nine inches and not more than five feet, ten inches and were selected from the Continental Army for their moral and personal perfection. Their duty was to protect General Washington, his person, baggage and papers. The last survivor died January 1856.

life rent: income received during a lifetime from property which belongs to another. For example, a father gives in his will a farm to his son but the widow receives the farm income for the rest of her life.

ligatus: husband.

lightage: a fee paid by each ship to support the port's lighthouse.

light artillery: mobile guns of 105 mm (about four inches) or smaller caliber.

light dragoons: a cavalry man armed with light guns, etc. and able to move rapidly.

lighter: a barge which loads or unloads ships which cannot maneuver to dockside.

lighterman: a person employed on a barge or harbor freighter.

lightfoot: a messenger who ran rapidly.

light heeled: loose in character.

light horse: soldiers who are mounted on horses and carry small arms. Sometimes called light cavalry.

light infantry: these soldiers were used after 1656 and carried no camping equipment. Their arms were lighter than regular infantrymen carried. They were used as skirmishers, etc. and were trained to move quickly.

lights: the lungs of a hog, chicken, etc.

light troops: formerly this term applied to all troops who were equipped for detached duty. They were lightly armed and equipped.

lightwood: a piece of wood cut from a pine or fir tree to be used as a torch. It burns well because of the high fat content in the wood.

ligne: 1) lineage; 2) lineal descent.

lignie, lin: (Norman) lineage, race.

limb trimmer: a tailor.

limey: see scurvy.

limner: 1) a person who illustrated (illuminated) early manuscripts; 2) a self-taught travelling artist.

lincey: a variation of linsey (which see).

lincoln: a breed of sheep originating in England which was raised not only for wool, but meat.

lindabrides: a mistress.

line: 1) direct ancestors with the same family name; 2) soldiers who fight, e.g. cavalry, infantry. In Britain this term was used to distinguish regular infantry men from volunteers. During the Revolution troops paid by the Continental Congress were called the Continental Line and those who were paid by a state were the Virginia Line, Pennsylvania Line, etc. This term was used frequently in pension applications.

lineal: in a direct line from an ancestor. This would not include aunts, uncles, etc.

line biline: (Norman) the collateral or by-line.

lineman: see cracker man.

linendraper: a yardgoods dealer.

linener: a dealer in linen cloth.

link: a lineal measurement of land. One link equals 7.92 inches.

linman: a flax seller.

linsey-woolsey: a combination of linen and wool, often homespun. The linen thread used for warp supplied durability and the wool for the weft or filler gave warmth to the fabric. This cloth was common in this country where the Scotch-Irish settled.

lintel: a horizontal portion of framework which spans doorways or similar openings and supports the structure over it.

lipped tongs: a tool used by a black-smith.

lis: a lawsuit.

lis pendens: a pending lawsuit filed in land records.

list: 1) the official description of property for the purpose of taxation; 2) the dirt thrown to one side by a hoe or plow.

lister: 1) the person who wrote down the list of persons and their property to be taxed. Sometimes called a listmaker; 2) a device used to plant corn.

listmaker: see lister.
listre: a person who read some part of the church service.
literator: a critic of literature.
lit house: a place where cloth was dyed.
liten: (Norman) little.
litigant: a person who is involved in a lawsuit.
litigation: a law suit or series of law suits.
lit morant: (Norman) death bed.
litster: a dyer of cloth.
litterman: a groom.
little house: a privy.
little master: a schoolmaster.
liv.: lived, living.
liv. abt.: lived about.
liver complaint: found on old death certificates, this term indicates one if any number of diseases of the liver.
livering: a kind of sausage.
livery: 1) a servant's ornate uniform provided by his employer; 2) a commercial stable engaged in boarding horses; 3) an ancient, formal delivery of a freehold estate; 4) to give food, clothing, etc. to servants; 5) dependence upon another; 6) lodging or quarters provided for another; 7) a kind of wool.
livery of seisin: a ceremonial delivery of land or buildings to a new grantee. The grantor usually handed the grantee a clump of dirt, a door key or some other part of the property which was being transferred.
livery stable: a barn where rental horses and horse-drawn vehicles were kept. Also, overnight accommodation for horses was provided.
living: a farm.
livre: 1) an old French monetary unit; 2) an obsolete form of livery.
loader: see charger.
loadsaddle: a pack saddle for a horse or donkey.
loblolly boy: an assistant to a ship's surgeon.
local: a local preacher was a dissenting clergyman who preached at different places.
loc. cit.: see loco citato.
lock chain: log chain.
lock-keeper: see locksman.
lockram, lockrum: a linen fabric of several qualities used for household items or clothing.
locksman: a jailor. Also called a lock-keeper.
locksmith: the person who makes locks or repairs broken locks.
loco: 1) to place; 2) to give; 3) to let for hire; 4) to invest; 5) to contract for.
loco citato: in the place cited.
loco parentis: in the place of the parent.
locorum: location, place.
locus: location, place.
locus sigilli: see L S.
lodemen: carters, carriers.
lodesman: pilot, guide, carter, carrier.
lodged: a complaint filed with a court but which is waiting for one of several conditions to be fulfilled.
lodged land surveys: a lodged survey is a term created by a local land office (in Virginia) for a document which the person requesting a survey was to return to the registrar's office. The return was not accomplished, sometimes by reason of death, for insufficient funds to pay the attached fees, for assignment to another, etc.
loftes: (Norman) foster child.
log book: the official daily record of all transactions and observations on board a ship.
loker: a carpenter's plane.
lombard: a banker.
lond buggere: a buyer of land.
London Company: see Virginia Companies.
longaevus: old, aged.
long bit: see bits.
long cloth: a fine muslin type of cloth made during the sixteenth century of cotton.
"longest liver:" the last of the (usually three) participants in a "lease for lives" (which see).
Long Hunter: in 1770 men left their Virginia settlements going through the Cumberland Mountains with rifles, dogs, horses, a surplus of powder and lead, traps and tools to fix their guns if necessary. Apparently, the name Long Hunters derived from the long time (six to nine months) these men could be hunting without returning for supplies.

longitude: see grid.

long jointer plane: a tool used by 1) a cooper; 2) a carpenter.

long knife: an Indian name, especially for Virginians on the frontier, but also used for any white settler.

"long paper tails:" these were purchase orders written on any kind of paper which was easily available and carried by a servant or child to the store. This system was a part of the debit and credit system against crops kept by the general store, and sometimes represented the wages of the bearer of the store order.

long rifle: a reliable gun used by frontiersmen as soon as they were old enough to hold it steady. Sometimes called "Kentucky rifle," "American rifle," or "Pennsylvania rifle," after the state where it was first manufactured.

long saw: a tool used by a chair maker.

longshoreman: a man who works on the docks of a seaport, loading and unloading a ship's cargo.

long sickness: tuberculosis.

long-tails: a nickname for a native of Kent County in England.

long tongue: a tale teller.

looker: a shepherd or herdsman.

lorarius: saddler.

lord: 1) a person who exercises authority, power, etc. over others; 2) a land owner; 3) a proprietor of a manor; 4) a titled nobleman; 5) a formal, polite title given to high officials; 6) an informal title for earl, viscount, etc.

loreman: a bit maker.

loresman: a teacher.

lorimer: a person who makes small iron goods, wrought iron, metal mounts for horses' harnesses, etc.

Lost State of Franklin: a state in the United States of America for a short while (1784-1788). It was located in that part of North Carolina that is now Tennessee.

loteby: 1) a bedfellow; 2) concubine.

lothe: to offer for sale.

lot layer: a person officially designated to lay out town lots.

lot of old iron: this term is found frequently in estate inventories. Discarded iron was saved to use for repairs, to be remade into something useful by a blacksmith.

lot teller: a witch.

loukers: weeders.

lounge: this phrase is found in inventories. "Lounge and clothing" indicates a type of a daybed, a davenport with a blanket, pillow, etc.

lount: a small piece of land in a common field.

love apple: a tomato which in the early 19th century was grown only as an ornamental plant, for it was considered poisonous. It was said, "If a hog won't eat them, why should I?"

love day: a day appointed for settling differences by arbitration. Later the term came to mean any peaceful day.

low Sunday: the first Sunday after Easter.

Lower Creek Indians: members of the Creek tribe who lived on the Alabama-Georgia border along the Chattahoochee River.

Loyalists: Americans who were loyal to the King of England who fled to Nova Scotia, Canada or back to England in the 1780s.

l.p.: local preacher.

L S: abbreviation for the Latin term Locus Sigilli (place of the seal). This abbreviation will be found after a signature on a legal document. It does <u>not</u> mean legal signature.

L.S.: Letter Signed.

Lt.: 1) Lieutenant; 2) (lower case) letter.

Lt. Arty.: Light Artillery.

Lt. Battry.: Light Battery.

Lt. Col.: Lieutenant Colonel.

Ltd.: Limited.

lues venera: venereal disease.

lug lain: full measure.

lumbago: rheumatic pains in joints.

lum swooper: a chimney sweep.

lunatic: when used in a census taking, this does not necessarily mean insane, but can refer to a person who is senile or born afflicted.

Lune: Monday, literally on the day of the moon.

lungee: a fabric imported from India. This material was originally made of cotton but later of silk and cotton dyed in rich, deep colors.

lung fever: pneumonia.
lungi: see lungee.
lungs: a fire-blower for a chemist.
lung sickness: tuberculosis.
lutestring: a silk fabric with a glossy side, varying in colors from pale to black.
lyceum: 1) a place provided for instructional lectures; 2) an association formed by persons who had no formal education but desired to learn. The meetings featured lectures in the arts, sciences, timely topics, etc. It was replaced after the Civil War by Chautauquas.
lye: hundred.
lynch law: not a proper law, but the process by which a person was punished by hanging without a legal trial for a crime, either real or said to be real.

M

M 1) Month; 2) Roman numeral for one thousand.
m.: 1) married; 2) male; 3) month; 4) mother.
m/1, m/2, ... : first marriage, second marriage, etc.
M.A.: Military Academy.
Mac: a name prefix which means son.
mace proof: free from arrest.
macel: (Norman) a butcher.
macheronerie: (Norman) masonry.
macstar: 1) a person who cared for chickens; 2) an egg seller.
madam: see brothel and/or bawd.
madel: shaped like a dunce's cap five to six feet tall and two feet in diameter, this tool was used to form bands and hoops.
madstones: a poultice of either natural or man-made material which has been soaked in body-warm sweet milk or water. Superstitious persons believed that when this poultice or stone was applied to a wound made by a mad dog, snake, etc., and when it dried and dropped free from the wound, the poison would be gone.
maere, maire: (Norman) mother.
maeur: (Norman) a mayor.
magazine: a storage place for ammunition which has been built to be as safe and dry as possible, and is lighted by daylight only (to eliminate the possibility of explosion from an overturned lantern).
magistrate: 1) a non-military governmental official; 2) a minor judicial officer who can issue a warrant for arrest.
magna: large, great.
Magna Charta: a document, restoring old liberties, which was signed by King John of England at the insistence of the English barons. It guaranteed civil and political liberties, among which was fair judicial procedures and thirty different statutes were involved in the confirmation. Also called the Great Charter.
magnate: 1) a person who holds rank or has distinguished himself: 2) a person who was of noble rank or held a high office.
maiden: 1) a ship's first trip after construction is referred to as the "maiden

voyage;" 2) a fortress which has never fallen to an enemy.

maiden name: the surname of a female's father.

maiden rents: a noble was paid a fee by every tenant upon the noble's marriage in lieu of the ancient marchet.

maide (si Dieu): (Norman) so help me, God.

mail: rent.

mail coach: a vehicle built to the specifications of the Post Office Department. It was the speediest of the early wagons and carried only three passengers in addition to the mail. It proved to be impractical, however, and it was not long before the stage coach lines also carried the mail.

mail land: a land measure unit which equalled three soums (which see).

mainburnie: (Norman) 1) guardianship; 2) government.

mainour: property which has been stolen and later found either on the person or in the possession of the thief.

mainpernor: 1) a surety; 2) a person who promises money to guarantee that a prisoner will be in court at the appointed time.

mainprize: to become a surety.

mains: a farm or fields near a house and occupied by the owner.

maior: older.

maiores: ancestors.

maisonette: 1) a small house sometimes attached to an apartment building; 2) a two-story apartment with an inside staircase or a duplex.

maisterlyng: a mayor.

maistresse: mistress, in sense of master and mistress.

maistrise: masterly workmanship.

maire (a): (Norman) to marry.

maison-dewe: a hospital.

maisterman: 1) ruler; 2) governor; 3) husband.

maize: corn, which was an Indian crop, not well-liked by the English settler, and considered more difficult to raise than other grains.

Maj.: Major

Majeure: (Norman) Major.

Major: see army rank.

majority: see age of majority.

Maj. Gen.: Major General.

majority: see age of majority.

majr.: major.

mala fide: 1) in bad faith; 2) with intent to deceive.

malaria: a parasitic blood disease produced when a person is bitten by an infected mosquito. As the parasite multiplies, it causes fever and chills.

malarial fever: see malaria.

mallet: a tool used by 1) a stone mason; 2) a saddler; 3) a carpenter.

mallet head chisel: a tool used by a stone mason.

malls: the measles.

malt: see maltster.

malthorse: a slow, heavy horse used by a brewer.

maltster, malster: a person who makes malt. This is the process of softening grain in water and allowing it to sprout. Malt is used in the brewing or distilling of alcoholic beverages.

Man: (Norman) a Norman.

manchester: a general term for cotton fabric made in Manchester, England.

manciple: 1) a steward; 2) an officer who had the duty of purchasing provisions for an Inn of court, a college, etc.

mandamus: an order compelling a person who had signed a contract to do what was called for in the contract.

mandillion: a mantle; great coat (top coat).

mang fodder: feed for cows which was mixed with hay and straw.

Mango: seven-eighths black; a child of a Sambo and a black.

mania: mental disease; insanity.

mania puerperium: insanity following childbirth. The "postpartum blues" is a mental disorder of new mothers which is usually temporary and not serious.

manifest: 1) the official and complete list of cargo carried by a merchant ship. This list contains the name of the ship, nature of the goods shipped, and the shipper and receiver with all identifying marks; 2) to prove beyond a doubt.

mann: (Norman) man, husband.

manner: 1) manure; 2) to be caught in a criminal act.

man-of-war: a general term for a warship. This category is further divided into fighting ships and auxiliary craft.

manor: a large holding of lands usually named for the family or group who owned the acreage: a king, a nobleman, a religious order. There would be a church and the manor hall or house in the center. These two buildings were surrounded by the small homes of those who did the actual farm work.

manorial court: an English feudal court in which the lord of the manor handled probate matters.

manors: manors are as ancient as the Saxon times in England and imply a territorial district with its jurisdiction, rights, etc. They were formerly called baronies and later lordships. Each lord was empowered to hold a court called the court-baron for straightening out misdemeanors and settling disputes among the tenants. In other words, an individual economic unit.

manse: 1) house or mansion; 2) a minister's home; 3) (Norman) a farm; 4) also the amount of land sufficient to support a family.

manslears: murderers.

manta: 1) a cloak-like wrap used in Spain or South America; 2) a type of blanket used on a horse; 3) a mobile shelter used by the assailants of a fort.

mantle: 1) a cloak; 2) the portion of a kerosene or gasoline lamp which glows with a brilliant white light.

mantua: an Italian silk fabric.

mantuamaker: a maker of a mantua, which was a loose robe, open down the front to show the petticoat. This person would likely be called a dressmaker today.

manufactory: the word for which factory is an abbreviation.

manumission: the act of formally freeing a slave. Many times the papers relating to this process are found in deed books.

maple-sugar candy mold: this was a board with many shallow, carved cavities in which maple sugar was shaped.

mar.: married.

marasmus: emaciation (wasting away) of the body.

marauder: one who roams, hunting booty or plunder.

marastre: (Norman) a mother-in-law.

march: 1) a land-mark or boundary; 2) to border on, or be contiguous to; 3) the region bounded.

marchale: a marshall.

marchande (ville): (Norman) market town.

marchant: (Norman) adjoin to, bounded by.

marches: the old boundaries between England and Wales, and England and Scotland.

marchet: an obsolete form of market.

marchpane: by the Old Style calendar New Year's Day fell in March and this led to the small, sweet New Year's cakes being called March Pan, Marchpane or New Year bread. The fancy shapes were made by using wooden molds, which after the Civil War were replaced by metal molds.

march stone: a stone which marks a boundary.

mare: a female horse.

marenne: (Norman) land bordering on the sea.

mariages: (Norman) marriage portion.

Marine Corps: this branch of the armed forces was founded in 1775 and now operates under the Secretary of the Navy. The men are trained to fight on land briefly or to participate in naval battles. Their rank corresponds with that used in the Army. Those who served in the Marines were eligible for pensions.

marisne (loy): (Norman) maritime law.

marita: wife.

maritassent: (Norman) married.

marite: husband.

mariti, maritus: marriage.

maritus: 1) husband; 2) relating to marriage.

mark: 1) see X; 2) a type of brand (which see); 3) an old Scottish coin.

marker: a surveyor's assistant.

market wagon: see ark.

marking iron: a surveyor's tool.

marksman: a man who is skilled in shooting a rifle, but is not yet rated as a sharpshooter or expert.

Marquis: a member of the nobility, above

an earl or count but below a duke.

Marquise: 1) the wife or widow of a Marquis; 2) a female who holds the rank in her own right.

marquisette: a lightweight, gauzy fabric made from cotton.

marriage bond: in Colonial days, this was a sum of money promised, usually by the parents or a close relative of a young couple, to the governor of the state. This was asked to ensure that there was no reason, moral or legal, for the couple not to marry and that they would not become charity cases. Money did not actually change hands, but could be called for if the marriage did not fulfill the requirements.

marriage broker: a person who, for a fee, arranges that a couple meets and then arranges for the marriage. In some countries this go-between is responsible that the lineage of each is suitable, e.g. in Japan a child of a survivor of the Hiroshima bombing may not be suitable for a mate from another area.

marriage certificate: usually a printed and suitably illustrated document which is filled in by the minister who performs a marriage and given by him to the couple. These vary in size from 9" by 12" to 20"" by 24". Sometimes an illustrated booklet with poetry and the certificate bound in the middle was presented to the bride.

marriage contract: entered into by a couple when one or both parties have been previously married. In this document they seek to protect monies inherited from a previous spouse to pass on to his/her children. See marriage settlement.

marriage contrary to discipline: this Quaker term indicates that a man and woman, both of the Quaker faith, were married in a civil ceremony. Sometimes called married out of unity. See marriage out.

marriage license: a document issued by a county giving permission for a couple to be married.

marriage out: a Quaker church term which means a person has married one of another faith. Sometimes called marriage out of unity or marriage by priest.

marriage records: after the marriage ceremony is performed, the official (church or government) files a record of the marriage with the church, and/or county officials.

marriage register: a book which lists marriage licenses issued and, frequently, marriage returns. This book is kept at a clerk's office in the courthouse.

marriage return: notation by a minister which states on which date he married a couple.

marriage settlement: a written contract usually made before and in anticipation of a marriage. In it the estate of either or both of the parties is settled or limited in a certain way, e.g. children of a wife's former marriage would inherit their mother's estate which was hers from her previous husband. Also called marriage contract or ante-nuptial agreement.

married out of unity: see marriage out.

marriglier, merriglier, maruglies, marguelier: (Norman) a church warden or sexton.

marry out of meeting: see marriage out.

marseilles: a heavy cotton cloth suitable for bedspreads. It has raised figures or stripes woven into it.

marsh.: marshall.

marshall: 1) in England, the person who took care of horses for the lord; 2) later, a person who had charge of military affairs; 3) from 1790 to 1870, the title of the supervisor of census taking in a judicial district; 4) a person who performed minor police duties.

mart: 1) an old word for a fair; 2) an obsolete word for a bargain; 3) an English term for beef cattle fattened for slaughter.

martel: a hammer.

martello, martello tower: a round fort made of stone or brick.

Marti: Tuesday.

mash hammer: a tool used by a stone mason.

masle (le): (Norman) the male.

mason: a craftsman who shaped and/or laid brick, stone and similar materials to form structures.

Mason and Dixon line: a line, named for the men who surveyed it, which formed the boundary between Pennsylvania and Maryland. The term later came to mean the entire southern boundary of Pennsylvania dividing the North and the South during the Civil War.

Masonic Lodge: a fraternal organization.

Masonic Order: see Freemason.

Massachusetts Indians: the general name given to the tribes who were living in Massachusetts in the early Colonial days. There were six main tribes: Massachusetts, Nausets, Pennacooks, Nepmucks, Pokanokets and Wampanpoags. These tribes were reduced in size considerably during King Philip's war.

masser: 1) mercer (which see); 2) privy.

mast: food such as acorns, nuts, and berries.

master: 1) an old term for a person who employed others. He sometimes employed journeymen and apprentices; 2) the commanding officer of a merchant ship; 3) a prefix denoting a chief, e.g. master sailmaker, master boat-builder, etc.; 4) husband.

Master and Commander: the title used until 1814 in the British navy. It was simplified to Commander.

master-at-arms: the chief petty officer of a man-of-war, this officer's duties were to act as the chief of police on a ship, confine prisoners, etc.

master-in-chancery: an assistant judge who heard cases and made recommendations to the judge of the chancery court. Land which had been foreclosed would be sold by the master-in-chancery and therefore would appear in the deed and deed book index under "master-in-chancery" instead of under the ex-owner's name. Land disposed of in this manner would be found in the deed books instead of the probate books, even if the foreclosure occurred while the estate was in probate.

master mariner: a captain or shipmaster of a merchant vessel.

masters: (Norman) mistress.

Master of the Rolls: an equity judge.

mast road: a road in New England made by hauling long, straight logs to be used in making masts for sailing vessels. These were comparable to the "rolling roads" of Virginia.

mat.: maternal.

match-coat: a garment made of coarse woolen cloth.

mate: 1) a petty officer in the navy who was an assistant to a warrant officer, e.g. gunner's mate, armorer's mate, etc. He held his position by appointment and was not in a line of promotion; 2) a person who keeps a boat or ship in working order, supervises loading and unloading, landings, etc.; 3) a spouse; 4) a consort; 5) an equal in social standing, courage, strength, etc.; 6) to defeat another.

mater: mother, matron.

maternal: used in speaking of a mother.

materta magna: grandmother's sister (grand aunt).

matertera: mother's sister (aunt).

mathook: a variation of mattock (which see).

matria: mother.

matron: 1) a mature married woman; 2) the woman who is in charge of a school, hospital, or prison.

matross: a private in the army who aided the artillery gunners to load, fire, sponge, etc. the guns.

mattock: a tool used for difficult digging. Rather like a pick-axe.

maug: a brother-in-law.

maul: a large wooden mallet with a handle about two feet or more in length.

maules: the measles.

maunder: beggar.

Maundy Thursday: the Thursday before Good Friday. On this day it was the custom of the kings (or queens) or their representatives to give alms, food, and clothing to as many poor persons as they were years old. Edward III began the custom when he was fifty years old in 1363.

maw bound: constipated.

maupuses: money.

Mayflower Society: a hereditary society comprised of members descended from the families who were transported to this country on the Mayflower, a ship arriving in Plymouth, Massachusetts in 1620.

McClellan saddle: the standard army saddle used by the United States Cavalry units.

m. bn.: marriage banns.

mbr: member.

mbrp: a Quaker abbreviation for membership.

M.C.D.: Municipal Civil District.

mcd: see married contrary to discipline.

Mch.: March.

M.D.: Doctor of Medicine.

md.: married.

mead: a Colonial drink made from wild honey and water.

meader: mower.

mead month: July. So called because it is the season for mowing.

meadow: a field shut up for hay, as opposed to a pasture.

meander lines: a term used in surveying to denote imaginary lines drawn on land which borders waterways in order to determine how much land is involved.

meat earth: cultivated land.

Mecklenburg Declaration of Independence: on 31 May, 1775 prominent citizens of Mecklenburg, North Carolina signed and published a document virtually declaring their independence from the British colonies in America. This was more than a year before the adoption of the Declaration of Independence by Congress.

Mecurio: Wednesday.

med.: medical.

medicine peddler: a person who sold herbs, elixirs, pills, etc. which were purchased in large lots and were labeled with his name. Another peddler might have pills from the same batch, but under his own name, which he prescribed for another illness. His trade later expanded to the Medicine Show, with the flashy, circus-like medicine man.

medicus: physician.

medrinacks: also called medrinix. It was a coarse canvas used by tailors as an interlining.

medulary sarcoma of bladder: tumor (usually malignant) of the bladder.

medulary: in the center of.

meemer: (Norman) an arbitrator or mediator.

meer: a boundary.

meeting for sufferings: a Quaker term. The 1778 annual meeting held in Baltimore was made up of representatives of smaller meetings. Known by various names, it was empowered to act in place of the annual meeting when it was not in session. The power of this committee was considerable and its duties comprehensive. In 1780 it was called the Representative Committee and in 1913 it was changed to the "Executive Committee."

meeting for worship: this Quaker term refers to a meeting at which business is not discussed.

meeting house: 1) a New England church building; 2) a church used for meetings other than those sponsored by the church; 3) a Quaker church building; 4) a place where dissenters worshipped.

meeting seeds: the seed of dill carried to the long church services to be eaten by children. Supposedly the seeds dulled the senses and therefore kept restless children quieter.

meinie: 1) a family; 2) members of a household, e.g. retainers, etc.

melanuria: a condition that causes one's urine to turn dark blue or black.

melanuric: see black-water fever.

mele tide: dinner time.

meliorist: a person who believes that the world can or will become better by human effort.

mell doors: a passage through the middle of a house.

melte: two bushels of coal.

membraneous croup: diphtheria.

membraneous sore throat: diphtheria.

memorial: a petition.

"memorial of:" 1) used in Colonial documents to mean a statement, a memory of an event, a deposition; 2) a petition drawn up by one or more persons and presented to an official or body of officials.

menage: 1) family; 2) a household; 3) housekeeping.

menageoers: (Norman) farmers, husbandmen.

menistres: (Norman) 1) ministers; 2) officers.

men of straw: 1) an old term for persons who gave false evidence in a court; 2) shiftless, no good persons; 3) unimportant parties involved in a transaction. Sometimes called straw men.

mensa et thoro: "from bed and board;" a legal separation of a married husband and wife.

mensager: a messenger.

mensal: the book of accounts of articles purchased for a table.

mensis: month.

ment.: mentioned.

mente captus: mentally incapable; insane.

mentle: a coarse apron.

meollen: mills.

mer: 1) mayor; 2) meritorious.

mercantile marine: a term embracing all persons and ships engaged in transportation of goods.

mercator: merchant, trader.

mercenary soldier: a person who fights for money, not for loyalty to a cause, especially one who fights for a foreign power.

mercer: a fabric dealer, especially costly fabrics. This term was British and came to America with the Colonists.

merchant: 1) a dealer who buys and sells goods, especially one whose business is with foreign countries; 2) a retailer; 3) a parts dealer; 4) in the merchant marine, one who carries on a commercial trade.

merchant man: a ship engaged in transportation of goods on all seas.

merchant tailor: a person who does custom tailoring from his own shop.

merchant venturers: a company of merchants who traded with Russia, Turkey and other distant places.

meridian: see principal meridian.

merino: 1) a breed of sheep which originated in Spain and has very fine wool; 2) a dress fabric, or yarn, which was made from the wool of merino sheep.

Merkedy, Merdie, Mercuredi: (Norman) Wednesday.

merkland: acreage on which a tax of one merk (or mark) was paid.

mershalle: 1) one who attended to horses; 2) a farrier; 3) a blacksmith.

mesa: a flat-topped mountain.

mesne: 1) now, immediately; 2) middle; 3) intermediate, between two times; 4) a lord who has charge of the land of another, usually a superior lord.

mesne conveyance: the transfer of a title to land between the first title-holder and the present one. In some large counties of southern states these are filed in a separate mesne office.

mesnier: (Norman) a public crier.

mess: meals in the armed forces and the place in which meals were served.

message: a messenger.

messe: 1) the mass; 2) a messuage or tenement.

messenger: 1) a constable, mailer, etc. in the Plymouth Colony; 2) a representative or delegate to a church convention from a member church.

messer, messour: (Norman) an officer in a manor who had the overseeing and care of the fields at the time of the harvest, for which he was entitled to certain profits.

messrs.: plural of mister.

messuage: this term, found in early American documents, means a dwelling house with its barns and other adjacent buildings. Messuage is found primarily in wills and deeds.

mestize: a person who has a mixed ancestry. In South America, a person whose ancestry is a native American and European. In the Philippine Islands, a person who is a native-foreign mix.

metal man: a person who takes used type (from a printer's shop), melts it, and recasts it for use.

meterer: a poet.

metes: water courses, distances, etc. given in a land survey. This term is used in land measurement and refers to the direction and distance of a line.

metes and bounds: a combination of terms used to describe a type of survey. Also known as an indiscriminate survey and sometimes called courses and distances. See metes, bounds, and land measures.

metesel: dinnertime.
metreza: a mistress.
mew: 1) mow; 2) a stack of hay.
mews: an English alley, now quite fashionable with remodeled carriage houses.
Mexican War: from 1846 to 1848 there was a struggle between the U.S. and Mexico, caused by a desire to expand westward. The Mexicans accused the American military and Naval forces of trespassing on their territory. A treaty was signed in 1848, resulting in annexation to the U.S. of territory extending from the Oklahoma panhandle to the Pacific Ocean. Every state and territory mustered troops to fight in this war.
meyne: the company or crew.
meyre: a mayor.
M.G.: abbreviation for Minister of the Gospel. It is found in county books of marriages after the name of the person performing the marriage, indicating that he was a clergyman.
M.H.: Meeting House (which see).
M.I.: Monumental Inscription (which see).
Miami Indians: a tribe of Algonquin descent who lived in Indiana and Ohio and fought against the United States as British allies in the War of 1812. Their lands were ceded to the United States under the Treaty of Greenville and they joined other tribes in Oklahoma.
miasma: 1) a poisonous gas emitted from decomposing matter; 2) a foreboding atmosphere.
micco: an Indian tribal leader. This term was used in a Georgia deed.
Michaelmas: Christmas. Sometimes called Mickellies.
Michigan Survey, 1836: when Ohio was admitted to the Union in 1803, it was without a northern boundary. The survey was used to resolve the land dispute between Michigan and Ohio.
middlegood: an old type of linen cloth.
middle night: midnight.
middle states: in early days this term referred to the states lying in the middle between the northeastern and southern states consisting of New York, New Jersey, Pennsylvania, Delaware and, at times, Maryland.
midshipman: a young aspirant to commissioned officer rank in the navy. In England the oldest son of an upper class family usually inherited the family wealth. Younger sons traditionally went into the military or the church at about the age of fourteen. The midshipman could command a group of much older sailors and non-commissioned officers and was always addressed by them as "Sir." His first promotion would be to the rank of Ensign.
midwife: a woman who is trained to help other women in childbirth without the assistance of a doctor.
midwifery: the art of assisting at childbirth.
Midwinter: Christmas.
migrant: a person who moves from one place to another and, perhaps, on again.
migratory divorce: see divorce, migratory.
mil.: 1) military; 2) militia; 3) mother-in-law.
milch: milk.
mile: a lineal measure of land. 5280 feet, 80 chains, 32 rods, or 8 furlongs.
miles: soldier.
miles endways: very long miles.
mile way: 1) the amount of time it takes to walk a mile on foot; 2) twenty minutes.
milice: 1) militia; 2) military service.
military certificate: a document stating that a person's proof of military service had been presented to the proper authorities and, therefore, he was eligible for a specific amount of land as compensation. There was only one claim to this type of land available to each person.
military land: public land which was reserved for Revolutionary or War of 1812 soldiers to receive as part of their compensation for service.
military police: the men in charge of all military law enforcement in areas which are occupied by troops.
military rank (Revolutionary War): **Army**: General (only George Washington), Lieutenant General, Major General, Brigadier General, Colonel, County Lieutenant, Major, Captain,

Captain-Lieutenant, First Lieutenant, Second Lieutenant. **Navy**: Admiral, Vice-Admiral, Rear-Admiral, Commodore, Captain (40 or more gun ship), Captain (20-40) gun ship, Captain (10-20) gun ship, Lieutenant.

military reservation: this land was put aside for military purposes by the President of the United States. It was then from the public domain.

military reserve: public land set aside to give to veterans, upon proof of service to the United States. Ohio was the Virginia Military District for soldiers from Virginia (which see).

military uniforms, first: the uniform approved by George Washington was the simple, and in many cases already owned, homespun shirt made like a hunting shirt with pants of the same material and gaiter legs. The rank of the first officers was marked by the use of ribbons of various colors placed over the shoulder. For example: colonel, red; captain, yellow, subaltern, green. A captain wore the epaulet on his right shoulder, while a lieutenant wore his on his left. It was not until 1779 that an official army uniform appeared with different colors denoting different regiments.

military warrant: a document issued by the land office requesting that land be set aside for a veteran entitled to it for his military service. The land was located in Ohio and Kentucky and eligibility for its ownership was based upon the veteran's military certificate.

militia: at the time of the first Thanksgiving in 1621, New England male citizens formed a group to bear arms and held the first formal "Training Band," or military day. The word "militia" comes from the Latin "miles" which means a soldier. In early days this meant the entire fighting force of the country. The militia was responsible to the governor of a state, or if a county or city militia, to the head of the governing body of the county or city. However, in a later army structure the militia became a reserve organization under individual states. Since 1898 the National Guard is the organized militia in the United States.

militia district: a geographic area containing one hundred or more men, twenty-one years and over, who were eligible for militia duty.

milk broth: gruel made with milk.

milk fever: 1) a fever due to an infected cut; 2) an acute disorder which affects dairy cows after calving.

milk leg: 1) thrombosis in a femoral vein. This occurred frequently after childbirth; 2) listed as a cause of death which resulted from a pulmonary embolism.

milkman: 1) a hired man who earned his living by milking cows for another person; 2) one who led a cow to a central location and sold milk by cupfuls; 3) the person who delivered milk in containers to customers.

milkmeat: 1) food made with milk, e.g. custard; 2) cheese.

milkness: 1) a dairy; 2) any white dishes made with milk.

milk sickness: a disease of which the symptoms are vomiting, constipation, muscular "tremors." This disease is usually caused by eating the meat or milk of cattle who have eaten certain poisonous plants. Sometimes called trembles or slows.

mill: 1) 1/1000 of a dollar or 1/10 of a cent; 2) when referred to in taxation, it would be calculated at one mill per dollar of the valuation of property; 3) usually refers to the building where the machinery for grinding was housed. Many different items were ground into more versatile forms: corn to cornmeal, wheat to flour, apples to cider, etc. The mills were powered by water, horses, wind, or men. The mill was also a place for men to swap stories.

milled dollar: see real.

miller: a person who ran a mill. He was called a millward.

milleray: a gold coin.

milleress: the wife of a miller.

mill fleam: see sluice.

milliner: 1) the person who sells women's hats; 2) the person who makes women's hats.

mill lodge: an old term for a mill pond.

milln, millne, miln: a mill.
millpeck: the person who sharpened millstones.
mill pick: tool used by a millpeck.
mill pond: a reservoir above the mill dam which stored water used to power a water wheel.
mill race: the man-made wooden ditch, wooden pipe, or penstock which brought water from a stream to the mill for power.
mill ring: the ground grain which clung to the millstone after the grinding was finished. This was considered a portion of the miller's pay.
mill run: see sluice.
millstank: an old term for a mill pond.
millstones: the cutting stones in a mill which are always in pairs rubbing one against the other. The top stone was called the runner or upper stone and the immovable bottom stone was called the nether or bedstone. Even when the stones were made of New Hampshire granite, they needed dressing or sharpening at least once a month.
mill stream: see sluice.
mill sweep: see sweep mill.
mill tail: see spillway.
millward: see miller.
mill wash: see spillway.
millway: see sluice.
mill wheel: a water wheel which furnishes the power to run a mill.
millwright: a person who designs and builds mills, windmills, watermills, etc. Usually a skilled mason and carpenter.
milne, milner: the old spellings of mill and miller.
minch: a nun.
minimus: youngest.
mining: see auction.
minion: a type of gun.
minister: 1) an agent for another; 2) the pastor of a church; 3) a servant; 4) the title of a high-ranking government officer, e.g. Minister of the Interior.
Minister of the Gospel: an ordained minister.
ministers: minstrels.
ministers and elders: these Quakers, both male and female, not only preached and served as examples but kept uninformed ("without edification") people from speaking.
ministres: officers of justice.
Minnetarre Indians: a branch of the Crow tribe who formerly lived on the upper Missouri River.
minny: mother.
minor: a person under twenty-one, or eighteen in some states.
minours: (Norman) 1) miners; 2) engineers.
mint master: 1) the person in charge of the place where a country's coins are produced; 2) a person who invents words.
minute book: the written record of a court's actions during its session. Sometimes called order book.
minute men: 1) members of militia during the Revolutionary times who had agreed to be ready to perform their military tasks the minute this was required; 2) members of numerous southern groups who were organized about the time of the Civil War and were ready at once to oppose anyone who was against the interests of the South.
mire, miers, mier: (Norman) mother.
misadventure: an accident, catastrophe.
miscall: to abuse.
miscegenation: marriage or cohabitation between a man and a woman of the black and white races. This was an offense under the statutes of many states.
Miscellaneous Survey, 1817-1833: these were small grants of land given to Indians by treaty and a few to white people who had been captured by Indians and lived with them. The Auditor of Ohio office has a book which lists the plats by name of the Indians and whites who lived and intermarried with the Indians. In Athens County, Ohio land owned by John Paul Jones, who died unmarried, passed to his sister, nieces and nephews, who sold this land which had once been part of the Ohio Company's purchase. In Franklin County, Ohio a Polish patriot who became a general in the U.S. Army was paid five one hundred acre plots in one tract of the U.S. military survey for his

services.

misdemeanor: a crime of less seriousness than a felony.

misericord: 1) a room in a monastery reserved for the use of monks who are allowed to relax monastery rules; 2) a dagger used to kill a wounded enemy; 3) a seat affixed to a church stall which gives support to an occupant while standing.

misnomer: an inappropriate name.

missel: a cow house.

Missouri Compromise line: the southern boundary line of the state of Missouri used to separate the North and South in that area, as far as slavery was concerned.

mister: a title applied only to those who had some social standing, through their family or an office, before they emigrated.

mistery: also mystery. 1) work, business; 2) guild.

mistress: see Mrs.

mite: 1) a small English coin; 2) Amish church members who were corrected for not obeying a church law were "mited;" 3) see also widow's mite and mite box.

mite box: a small container used to collect a Sunday School offering which was to be used for a special purpose.

mittimus: authorization to send a person to prison.

mixed blood: a combination of two or more races by intermarriage; e.g. black and white, white and Indian.

mixer: bartender.

mizzel: (an underworld expression) "he told them to sell and mizzel." In other words sell and leave, decamp, get out.

mizzy: a quagmire.

M.L.: Military Land.

M.L.E.: Military Land Entry.

M.L.W.: Military Land Warrant.

M.M.: Monthly Meeting of Society of Friends (Quakers). Which see.

m.n.: abbreviation for Latin term "more novo," which means "in the new manner" (of determining calendar dates).

M.O.: mustered out.

m/o: mother of.

mo.: 1) month; 2) mother.

mobles: 1) goods; 2) movables.

moblys: (Norman) movables.

moccinego: a small Venetian coin.

mockado: a cloth made during the 16th and 17th centuries which was tufted with pieces of wool. First made in Flanders, later in England by Flemish refugees, this cloth was used primarily as an accent fabric, e.g. sleeves.

mocke: (Norman) 1) a bride; 2) a spouse.

mod.: moderator.

Moderator: this person was elected at the December town meeting to preside over that meeting and the meetings for the following year. He kept order and chaired the meeting. When a person addressed the moderator he took off his hat and put it back on when he was finished. Some churches used a moderator in their church business meetings.

modir: mother.

moerge: (Norman) dies.

mogul: a person who is prominent in a certain field, e.g. advertising.

Mohave Indians: ferocious members of the Iroquois League who lived in the Mohawk Valley of New York.

Mohawk Indians: a tribe who lived in the Mohawk Valley in New York, which was named for them. They were allies of the British during the Revolution, and after the war moved to Canada.

Mohegan Indians: a tribe who lived in a considerable portion of New England and part of New York. Norwich, Connecticut, which was called "Mohegan" by the Indians, is situated near the center of their territory.

moidore: a Portuguese gold coin which was also circulated in Brazil.

moiety: an equal share in something: a half, a third, etc.

moirent: (Norman) die.

moison: 1) harvest; 2) growth.

Mojave Indians: this tribe of Apache descent lived in Arizona and are sometimes known as Mojave Apaches.

moldboard (plow): see coulter.

molder: in the navy, a petty officer trained in foundry operations.

moleday: a day of burial.

moleine: scabs, swellings, or cracks in the

skin.

molener: (Norman) a miller.

moleskin: a stout cotton fabric with a twill-weave suitable for clothing or as a polishing cloth.

molour: a grinding stone.

molours: (Norman) mills.

molter: the charge due the miller for grinding corn.

Monanday: Monday.

money: 1) silver; 2) in early America British money was used: pounds, shillings and pence. There are 20 shillings in a pound and 12 pence or pennies in a shilling. A change was later made to dollars but we cannot equate them with today's dollar. Almost the only way of calculating the value of money would be to consider how much a man earned in a day and use that figure as the base. In early Virginia tobacco was considered legal money, for metal to make coins was scarce. The Dutch of New York used beaver pelts (called beavers) along with wampum for deals involving money.

moneyage: a payment made for the privilege of minting coins.

money maker: 1) a minter of coins; 2) a person who makes counterfeit coins.

money monger: a lender of money.

_____**monger**: when used as the second portion of a word or phrase, this term usually means "seller of."

moniours: coiners.

monition: 1) a legal notice; 2) a court order which obliges a person to appear before the court.

monk: a member of a male religious order who lives with others of the same order and carries on his work and other activities almost entirely within the walls of a monastery.

monk bag: a small bag suspended around the neck in which sailors carried their money.

monkey tool: a tool used by a blacksmith in making decorative wrought iron.

monkhood: 1) a group of monks; 2) men whose profession is being a monk.

monk's cloth: a cotton fabric with a basket weave which was heavy enough to hang well when used to make draperies. Sometimes called friar's cloth.

Monroe Doctrine: foreign policies set by the United States government as spelled out in a message delivered to Congress on December 2, 1823 by President James Monroe. It forbade further colonization in the Western Hemisphere.

montenance: amount, extent.

Monthly Meeting: a business meeting of the Society of Friends (Quakers) which is held once each month. Records of these meetings include births, marriages, deaths, discharges from the church, etc. One set of meetings was held for male and another for female members.

month's mind: a Requiem Mass said in a Roman Catholic church on the thirtieth day following a person's death or his funeral.

monture: 1) a saddle; 2) a riding horse.

monumental inscription: an English tombstone.

moon men: thieves, robbers.

"moons:" a reckoning of time based on the phases of the moon used by American Indians. Approximately 29 1/2 days.

moonshine: liquor which has been distilled without a license to do so.

moot court: a mock court designed to teach law students how to conduct a case, how a court works, etc.

moothall: a town hall in an old English village.

mor: (Norman) mother.

moraine: a small hill deposited by a glacier.

Moravian Lands: during the period of time from 1786 to 1796 three pieces of land, four thousand acres in each piece, were given to the Moravian Brethren of Bethlehem, Pennsylvania for the use of "Christianized" Indians in Ohio who were living in Tuscarawas County, Ohio.

Moravians: followers of John Huss who first called themselves Unitas Fratum (the Unity of Brethren), but later were called Moravians for most were from the central province, Moravia, in what is now Czechoslovakia. The Moravians from Pennsylvania were the first permanent settlers of the North Carolina backwoods, under the leadership of Count Nicolaus Ludwig von Linzerdorf.

morbo loacteo: milk sickness.

morbus: disease.

morbus coxarius: disease of the hip joint.

moreen: a fabric used for ladies' petticoats, curtains, etc. which had a taffeta or moire finish. It was made from cotton or a blend of cotton and wool.

more novo: "in the new manner." This term was used when calculating calendar dates.

more or less: a clause which qualifies a measure, e.g. 30 acres more or less means it could be more or could be less than thirty acres.

morfound: a disease found in animals, especially horses who have not been cooled down properly after exercise.

morg.: morgen; which see.

morgan: a breed of saddle horse.

morganatic marriage: a marriage statement used when a titled person marries a commoner. It says that the lower-ranking person may not have a claim to either the title or entailed property of the other.

morgen: an old Dutch measure of land used in New York state which equaled about two and one-tenth acres. Originally, it was the amount of land which one man or one team of horses could plow or mow in one morning.

morgive: a wedding gift.

moriant (en son lye): (Norman) on his deathbed.

morine: dead.

mormal: 1) cancer; 2) gangrene.

Mormon (LDS): a short, more common name for a member of the Church of Jesus Christ of Latter-day Saints, whose headquarters is in Salt Lake City, Utah. It is not used for a member of the Reorganized Church of Jesus Christ of Latter-day Saints (RLDS). See also Brighamite.

Mormon War: this was fought from 1857 to 1858 and did involve military personnel. Militia groups were assigned to escort Mormons from one state border to another. Therefore, records of militia participants may be found in the National Archives or among state records.

morphew: a leprous eruption on the face.

morphine: a narcotic which is used as a pain reliever and as a sedative. It is a habit-forming drug which is used mainly in terminal illnesses.

Morrill Act: see Land Grant Act.

mors: 1) death; 2) corpse.

mors necessaria: a natural death.

mors omnibus communis: death is common to all.

mort: mortally.

mortality schedule: a list of persons who died during the year from June 30 to June 30 of the census year.

mortar: a short barrelled artillery piece fired at near vertical angles. Many times used in sieges.

mortar and pestle: dried herbs and other plants of medicinal value were placed into a container (mortar). These were pounded and ground together into powder form with a pestle. Early doctors ground their own medicines until pharmacists began maing medicine.

mortar beds: see beds.

mortgage: money borrowed from another, pledging real or personal property. The person who is borrowing the money may continue to operate his farm, business, etc. but the title is not his until he repays the money. If the full amount, plus interest, is not repaid, the mortgage is treated as a true deed. Early mortgages are many times found in county deed books.

mortgage release: when a debt has been repaid the mortgage becomes void and a release of mortgage or mortgage release is given.

mortgage satisfied: a claim against property which has been paid in full.

mortice knife: a tool used by a gate hurdle maker.

mortification: slow death of the flesh, such as gangrene or necrosis.

mortifie: to render quicksilver into a usable form for medicine.

mortis: 1) death; 2) corpse.

mortis causa: cause of death.

mortise: 1) to cut a mortise; 2) a square

or rectangular hole in the side of a piece of wood. It is used as a socket into which fits a tenon, a projection of the same size, cut on the end of another piece of wood. Mortise and tenon joints do not require the use of expensive metal fasteners.

mortmain: 1) the dead hand that reaches beyond the grave. The conditions which a testator makes in a will that affect heirs for years and years; 2) land held by churches or corporations.

mortman: this law, or statute, prohibits acquisition of land by a church without the approval of the legislature, from which the clergy were excluded in Maryland.

mortua, mortuus: died.

mortuary: a gift or payment to the church on the decease of a parishioner. The gift was brought with the corpse when it came to be buried and offered to the church as satisfaction for supposed negligence or omissions the deceased had been guilty of, in not paying his personal tithes.

Moses law: a piratical term for the punishment of thirty-nine lashes ("forty save one") on a bare back.

mossback: a slang expression for a very conservative person.

mosshorn: a steer which is so old that his horns are scaly.

mot.: a motion.

mothering: a custom of going to visit parents on mid-Lent Sunday and giving them a gift of money, trinkets, or fancy food.

mother-in-law: 1) the mother of a person's spouse; 2) a Colonial term for stepmother.

mother law: a mother-in-law.

mother's son: a man.

moti., moto.: a motion.

motion: when made in court a motion is usually written but may be spoken, as opposed to a petition which is always written.

mottows: the rent of a piece of meadow ground in two parcels (or mottows) to be used for the poor.

mou: 1) mowing; 2) see married out of unity.

moudy: a catcher of moles.

moulder, molder: a person who 1) shapes sand into which molten metal is poured in a foundry; 2) shapes the clay to make bricks.

moulding stick: a tool used by a brick maker.

mound: 1) fence; 2) hedge.

mountaineer: a person who is born in the mountains or chooses to live there.

mountain of piety: a company which granted loans at a reasonable interest.

mountance: amount, quantity.

mountebank: 1) a charlatan; 2) a person who sells quack medicine in public places; a type of medicineman or peddler.

mounted infantry: soldiers who fight on foot but are mounted on horses at times as a way of moving quickly.

mourning articles: see funeral gifts.

mousel-seab: distemper in sheep.

mov.: moved.

movable estate: personal property.

movables: personal property which can be carried from one place to another; furniture, animals, etc.

mow-burnt hay: hay which has fermented while in the stack.

mowche: spy, eavesdrop.

Mr.: used sparingly in Colonial days, this title usually indicated a person of some social standing in the community.

Mr. Lincoln's War: the Civil War.

mr. gun.: master gunner.

mr. sgt.: master sergeant.

Mrs.: short for "mistress." In Colonial times, Mrs. did not necessarily mean that a woman was married.

ms., mss.: manuscript, manuscripts.

MT: a type of land sale in early Illinois. Military Tract.

mtd.: mounted.

mtg.: 1) meeting; 2) mortgage.

muck: dung, manure.

muck worm: a miser.

mudboat: a "land raft" on runners, useful in the wet springs for it was more easily pulled by a horse on muddy ground than any other vehicle.

mudde: a Dutch measure consisting of four schepels.

mudlark: 1) an Englishman who searched mud or low tide beaches for coal, iron, etc.; 2) see also street cleaner.

muffled drum: at military funerals the sound of the drum is muffled by passing the spare cord through the snares or cords across the bottom of the drum.

mug books: county history books which included biographical sketches of residents. They were sold by subscription in advance of printing at the end of the 19th and beginning of the 20th centuries.

Mulatto: 1) one-half black, a child of a black and a white; 2) soil which has a brownish color.

mule: 1) a cross between a donkey and a horse; 2) a small engine used to pull railroad cars in a yard, tow canal boats, etc.; 3) a machine used to spin fibers into yarn.

mule skinner: a driver of mules.

muleteer: a driver of a team of mules.

muletrain: 1) a line of mules which are loaded with goods; 2) a line of mule-pulled wagons.

mulharde: a keeper of mules.

mulier: 1) a woman, generally applied to a married woman; 2) a matron; 3) legitimate.

mull: 1) a thin, muslin-like cloth made of cotton, silk, etc. or a combination of several fibers used in bookbinding and in clothing; 2) a dressing with a high melting point which was spread on mull to form a kind of plaster; 3) to heat a sweetened and spiced liquid, such as a wine, by inserting a hot poker into it.

mulley: a cow.

mulne: a mill.

multiplication: the art of making gold and silver.

multon: sheep.

multure: the price paid to a miller for grinding grain. Sometimes the price paid was a percentage of the flour which had been made. See also sucken.

mum: a German beer or strong ale served frequently in Colonial America.

mumper: a beggar.

mumping day: December 21st, when the poor went about the country begging corn, etc.

mundaine: worldly possessions.

muniment room: English manor houses frequently had a room where deeds, inventories, rent rolls, copies of wills, etc. were kept. The term derived from a Latin word meaning to fortify or strengthen, and since deeds, etc. strengthened the validity of ownership they were kept in this room. It was not essential that this room be a giant safe.

muniments: the documents which enable a person to defend the title to an estate or a claim to the rights or privileges.

munture: (Norman) a riding horse.

murderer: former name for a blunderbuss gun.

murenger: a superintendent of the town or city walls.

murours: (Norman) men employed in building walls and fortifications.

murrain: 1) an obsolete word for a plague; 2) any one of several cattle diseases.

musard: 1) a wretch; 2) a vagabond.

musiker: a musician.

musket: a moderate length shoulder weapon with an effective range under fifty yards. "Brown Bess" was the common name for this type of gun.

must: 1) ground apples; 2) new wine; 3) to turn mouldy.

must.: mustered.

muster: to inspect a group of soldiers.

Muster Day: by law, the day when state militia men from 18 to 45 met for military inspection and training. After the Civil War this law was repealed.

muster in: to enlist in a military unit.

muster out: a discharge from military service.

muster roll: the list of all officers and men in a military organization which includes name, rank and other information about the men along with reasons for any absences or other reductions in the strength of the unit.

Mustifee: one-sixteenth black, a child of an Octoroon and a white.

Mustifino: one-thirty-second black, a child of a Mustifee and a white.

muthe: an army.

mutiny: 1) insubordination by two or more persons to lawful military authority; 2) disobedience accompanied by violence.

mutton: the meat of an adult sheep which

is usually tougher as the animal gets older, especially a male.

mutual will: or mutual testament. A disposition of property by two people who make reciprocal bequests or devises. Sometimes this is a binding contract.

muzzle loader: the front end of a gun is called the muzzle. Therefore this name applies to any gun that is loaded at the muzzle.

m.v.: abbreviation for the Latin term "more vetere," in the old way (calendar dates).

myelitis: an inflammation of 1) bone marrow; 2) spinal cord matter.

myleware: an old word which meant a dam strong enough to hold back water or a twig and stake "net" which was used to trap fish.

myneurs: (Norman) minors.

myocarditis: inflammation of the heart muscle.

N

N: 1) in old records indicated Negro; 2) North.

na: naturalized.

N.A.: National Archives.

naam: to take another's possessions by force.

nabob: a very wealthy man.

nacion: (Norman) birth.

nackendole: eight pounds of meal.

nail: 1) eight pounds, generally applied to articles of food; 2) an old cloth measure which equalled 2 1/4" or 1/16 of a yard; 3) to do a carpenter's work.

nailage: a fee charged by a customs house after inspection to renail a container of tobacco.

nailburn: a temporary brook which is irregular in its path and the time that it is present.

nailer: 1) a maker of nails; 2) the person who uses nails; 3) the person who makes lids for wooden boxes; 4) a slang word for a capable (in at least one area) person.

nailery: a peace where nails are manufactured.

nail heading tool: a tool used by a farrier and other blacksmiths.

nail marker: a tool used by a bootmaker.

nailor: a carpenter.

nainsook: a soft cotton fabric suitable for babies' clothing or for underwear.

naked: not what it appears to be, e.g. a naked contract, something is wrong with the contract; incomplete.

nale: ale, alehouse.

nammet: luncheon.

nankeen: a fabric first made in Nanking, China and was a durable unbleached cotton whose fiber came from a tree cotton. There was also an imitation which was a twill that had been dyed the pale yellow of real nankeen. It was later made in England.

Naperer: an old use of a word for a person who was in charge of royal linens.

napery: 1) linen, generally table linen; 2) obsolete word for personal linen; 3) a linen closet; 4) make linen cloths, napkins, petticoats, etc.

napier: the person who took care of table linens.

Napier's bones: a 17th century tool made of rods which was used to speed arithmetical calculations. It was invented by Lord Napier.

narle: a hard swelling on the neck.

Narragansett Indians: a tribe of Algonquins who lived in the area occupied by the present state of Rhode Island.

narrow bed: a grave.

N.A.R.S.: National Archives and Records Service.

narthex: a church's main entrance.

nasci: to be born.

nascor: to be born.

nata: daughter.

natches: the battlements of a church tower.

Natchez Indians: this tribe of farmers and mound builders lived in Mississippi near where Natchez is today. They were unsuccessful in fighting the French.

nation: family.

National Highway: U.S. road 40, running from east to west through the United States, was called the National Highway and sometimes called the National Pike or National Road. It has been replaced by U.S. 70.

National Union Catalogue of Manuscript Collections: a publication by the Library of Congress. It is an index of material by the Library of Congress which is not limited to genealogy. First published in 1962, the first issue covered cataloguing of books by the Library of Congress done from 1959 to 1961. The next publication of NUCMC was a cumulative index for the years 1963-66, 1967-69, and 1970-74. Beginning in 1975 the indexes cover five year periods of cataloguing, bound together in one volume. Although there are one and two year indexes, collection held by libraries and repositories other than the Library of Congress are included. A good finding tool for elusive genealogical material.

Native American: an American Indian or eskimo.

natty-boxes: the contribution paid periodically by workmen in various branches of trade to the trade union to which they belonged.

natty lads: young pickpockets.

natu maximus: firstborn, oldest.

natural: did not mean an illegitimate child, but a person related by blood instead of by adoption or by marriage.

natural affection: warm feelings which naturally exist between close relatives are considered a legal payment in a deed.

natural child: 1) a term used to describe a child born out of wedlock rather than an adopted child; 2) in Louisiana a child born out of wedlock but whose father has admitted that the child in question is lawfully his.

natural father: a father who is not necessarily legally married to the mother of his child.

natural life: in a will usually indicates during widowhood.

naturalization: the process by which a person of foreign birth becomes a citizen.

natus est: was born.

nauta: sailor.

Navajo Indians: a large tribe of the Shoshone family in New Mexico.

nave: the area in a church where the congregation sits.

navegor: an auger (a carpenter's tool).

navies: excavators.

navigator: 1) a person who digs and constructs canals; 2) a person who constructs earthen fortifications.

navy: a canal.

Navy rank (in order): Commissioned officers: fleet admiral (only since 1944), admiral, commodore (a wartime-only rank), captain, commander, lieutenant commander, lieutenant senior grade, lieutenant junior grade, ensign. Warrant officers: chief warrant officer, warrant officer. Non-commissioned officers: chief petty officer, petty officer first class, petty officer second class, petty officer third class. Seaman, apprentice seaman, seaman recruit.

Navy, U.S.: a branch of the armed forces which was created in 1798. Those who served in the navy were eligible for pensions.

naysmith: a maker of nails.

N.B.: note bene. These letters usually indicate a footnote of further explanation and are found in scholarly writing.

N.C.I.C.: National Cartographic Information Center.

N.C.O.: non-commissioned officer.

n.d.: no date.

N.E.: 1) New England; 2) northeast.

near side: left side.

neat: horned oxen.

neat cattle: in Colonial New England to nineteenth century days, neat cattle were what we now call cattle: cows and their calves.

neatery: an obsolete term for a place where beef cattle and other animals used for food were sold.

neatherd: a person who owns or keeps a herd of cattle.

neat house: a barn.

neatress: a female keeper of herds.

necantur: the account book of a slaughter house.

nece: 1) a niece; 2) a cousin.

necessaries: articles of clothing prescribed by the military organization but not issued by the government, therefore paid for by the men.

necessary house: a polite term for an outside toilet.

neck verse: the beginning of the 51st psalm which was read aloud by criminals who claimed the benefit of clergy.

necrology: 1) an account of a deceased person's life; 2) a church's death register.

necrosis, neckrosis: see mortification.

nedeller: a maker of needles.

nee: born. This word is used after a married woman's surname to indicate her maiden name, e.g. Mrs. Marian Johnson, nee Baker.

needle house: a case for small needles.

needments: necessaries.

ne exeat: a written order that forbids the addressee to leave the jurisdiction of the court or the area.

neeveye: descendants.

negro cotton: a name for cheap material such as the material used in jeans or clothing worn for work.

neicence: (Norman) birth.

neighbor: something which completes a pair.

neme: uncle.

neph.: 1) nephew; 2) sometimes in old documents grandchildren, both male and female, were referred to as nephews and occasionally this term was used to mean the daughter of a sibling; 3) any descendant.

nephew: 1) the male child of a person's brother or sister; 2) sometimes in old documents can refer to other relatives: grandson, cousin, etc.; 3) a descendant.

nephritis: inflammation of the kidney.

nephrosis: deterioration of the kidney without inflammation.

nepos: a grandson.

nepos ex filio: a brother's or sister's child.

nepotis: a grandson.

neptis: granddaughter.

nervine: a nerve disorder.

nester: see squatter.

net: to wash clothes.

nether stone: see millstones.

nettle house: a privy.

neuralgia: pain along or in a nerve.

neutral ground: an area controlled by neither side.

neuz: (Norman) nephew.

neve: 1) nephew; 2) spendthrift.

nevon: (Norman) nephew.

nevy, nevo, nefo, nevey, nevoy: nephew.

New Amsterdam: the original name of New York City, which was settled by the Dutch in the seventeenth century.

new bear: a cow who recently had a calf.

New Connecticut: see Western Reserve.

New England: in a French account of the siege of Charleston, South Carolina in 1780, the term "New England" was used to distinguish all of British North America from England, the mother country. Usually, however, it referred to the six states in the northeast part of the United States.

New English: in Colonial days this term referred to New England or the people who lived there.

Newgate: a well-known prison in London.

New Lights: members of numerous revivalistic, usually non-conservative, groups, each led by an eloquent preacher.

"new mother:" a Colonial term for a stepmother.

New Netherland: settled by Dutch families sponsored by the Dutch West India Company, this group established New Amsterdam and Fort Orange near the present town of Albany, New York.

New Orleans boat: a very large flatboat designed for use along the whole length of the Ohio and Mississippi Rivers.

New Style calendar: this term refers to a date written after 1752, when the use of the Gregorian calendar began. See Gregorian.

next day: the day after tomorrow.

next friend: a person, not a guardian, but one who files a suit in behalf of an infant or a person incapable of handling his own affairs. This is usually a relative who assumes the court costs.

Nez Perce Indians: this tribe, who lived in the Pacific Northwest, were friendly with settlers until they were forced to disperse. The name was given them by the French because they wore nose ornaments (nez perce means "pierced nose").

nfi.: no further information.

nfk.: nothing further known.

niccanee: a cotton fabric imported from India.

nicky: a small bundle of wood.

niece: 1) a female child of a person's brother or sister; 2) in old documents, used to indicate a relative in general; 3) an obsolete term for a granddaughter; 4) a polite way to say an illegitimate daughter of a clergyman; 5) rarely, but on occasion, a nephew.

nieghend: the ninth.

nies, niez: (Norman) 1) a grandson; 2) a nephew.

niffle: a spur for a horse.

nigger consumption: a term found in old records which refers to a black person afflicted with tuberculosis.

niggle: small, tight handwriting.

night magistrate: a constable.

night riders: 1) men on horseback who banded together and came after dark to subdue the recently freed blacks after the Civil War; 2) also tobacco growers in Kentucky in the early twentieth century who were violent in their struggles to form an association to protect their interests; 3) another name for Ku Klux Klan members; 4) sometimes called a Silent Brigade.

night stool: see commode.

nihil dicit: a judgment issued against a defendant who has not responded to a complaint of a plaintiff.

nil: nothing.

nil debet: he does not owe what is claimed or alleged.

nilla: a cotton fabric imported from India.

ningimmer, nimgimmer: 1) a surgeon; 2) an apothecary or anyone else who cures a pox or clap.

nipcheese: a ship's purser.

nippers: 1) a tool used by a stone mason; 2) a slang expression for handcuffs; 3) young lads who help sell vegetables and fruit from a cart; 4) small boys.

nipte: 1) a niece; 2) a granddaughter.

nisi: this means "unless" and is usually used in the sense that a decision will be valid unless within a certain time limit steps are taken to show why the decision should be invalid.

nisi prius: no number. 1) a court which hears cases before a judge and jury; 2) a British writ to summon a jury to the court in Westminster on a particular day. If the assize judge came to that county at an earlier time; 3) a court system whereby judges are assigned to various courts.

nm.: name.

n.m.i.: no middle initial.

n.m.n.: no middle name.

nms.: names.

no.: 1) number; 2) an abbreviation for neglected attendance of meeting. Found in Quaker records, the member did not attend church of a period of time.

nobbler: a person who constructed fences of stone by cutting the stone into small shapes.

noble: a gold coin used in early England.

nob thatcher: 1) a person who made wigs; 2) a peruke maker.

nolle prosequi: no further prosecution. A notation made in the records of a court when a plaintiff will go no further with a suit.

nolo contendere: "I will not contest it." This phrase says guilty but it cannot be used as proof of the act of which the person is accused.
nol pros: see nolle prosequi.
nomen: name.
nompere: an arbitrator.
non: not; by no means.
Non-Associators: these men did not believe in fighting (Quakers, Mennonites, etc.), as opposed to Associators who were willing to go to war. If exempted from military service, they were still obliged to contribute a sum of money to the cause.
non assumpsit: he did not promise.
Non-commissioned officers: these men, usually of great ability, are appointed not by Congressional commission, but by commanding officers of regiments or ships.
non compos mentis: 1) not of sound mind; 2) in a state of lunacy.
non compotes: 1) idiots; 2) madmen.
non-conformist: 1) a person who will not observe any established customs, ideas, etc.; 2) a Protestant who lives in England.
non culpabilis: not guilty.
non est inventus: not found. This is added to the court order when the defendant is not found to be within the court's jurisdiction.
non ficet: he did not make it.
nonne: men.
nonresident: a person who does not live in the area mentioned in a document.
non vivus: not alive. Usually indicates that the infant was stillborn.
nooning: the meal harvesters eat at noon.
noonsheen: a luncheon.
no papers: when this is found in a Revolutionary War pension jacket, it means that the papers were burned in either 1801 or 1814.
nord, nordre: (Norman) north, northern.
no record: the original papers referred to were never transcribed in any record book.
nore: (Norman) a daughter-in-law.
nori: (Norman) a foster child.
norice, norices: (Norman) nurse, nurses.
noristry: a nursery.
Normans: the first of the Norman kings of England was William I (The Conqueror). Before William became King only three kings had immediately succeeded their fathers. With William's reign, the principle of primogeniture was adopted.
norred: northward.
norrel ware: a bit maker.
norterer: a notary.
North Britain: Scotland.
Northern Department: Northern Area. This phrase is used on maps, in Revolutionary War records, etc. when a general rather than a specific area is indicated.
Northwest Territory: a great interest in settling land on the frontier was recognized by Congress, who created the area called the Northwest Territory in 1787. It included much of the land occupied today by Ohio, Indiana, Illinois, Michigan and Wisconsin.
norway: a whetstone.
nosebag: see feedbag.
nostalgia: home sickness.
nostra: our, ours.
nostrum: a quack medicine.
notary: 1) clerk; 2) secretary.
notary, notary public: 1) a person who administers oaths, witnesses signatures, etc. and signs his name to the documents involved, attesting to their authenticity; 2) in England it is an ecclesiastical office for the same purpose.
notaries public: said to have been appointed by the early fathers of the Christian Church to collect the acts or memoirs of the lives of the martyrs of the first century.
notary seal: a stamp affixed to a document which attests that the signature on the document was witnessed by the notary and is genuine.
note of hand: see promissory note.
noterer: a notary.
note shaver: a person who sells stocks, bonds, etc. for a fake financial company.
nothus: spurious, illegitimate, a bastard.
nou, nouve, noun: (Norman) nine.
noughty: possessed of nothing.

nounne: (Norman) noon.
nout-gild: cornage rent which was paid in neat or cattle.
nouveau riche: having sudden wealth, as opposed to having "old money."
noverca: stepmother.
novercae: stepsister.
now: present wife or house. Indicates a man is married.
nowells: see noyals.
now house: used in wills to indicate the house in which the deceased lived at the time of death. It was common to allow the surviving spouse to continue to live in the "now house."
nowt: cattle.
now wife: used in wills to indicate the last wife of the deceased. If a will mentioned a wife by name, e.g. "my wife Sarah," and if Sarah had died and had been replaced by wife Ann, then Ann would not be protected. "Now wife" does protect her.
noyals: a canvas fabric made in Noyal, France.
noyles: see noyals.
n.p.: 1) no page; 2) no publisher.
N.P.: Notary Public.
n.p.: no place, no page, no publisher.
n.r.: 1) none recorded or not recorded; 2) an abbreviation used at times for naturalized; 3) near.
N.S.: when used with a date after 1752 this indicates use of the new style or Gregorian calendar.
N.S.D.A.R.: National Society of Daughters of the American Revolution.
nubblings: small coal.
N.U.C.M.C.: National Union Catalogue of Manuscript Collections.
nudum pactum: agreement made without "consideration" (money).
nugging house: brothel.
numb palsy: loss of sensation.
numerals: see Roman numerals.
nunc.: nuncupative; oral rather than written.
nunc pro tunc: now for then. A court order to correct errors or omissions, effective as of the earlier date.
nunch: luncheon.
nuncle: uncle.
nuncupative will: an oral will which is later spoken of in court by those who heard the testator speak; then it is written for the records. In some states it is not a legal will. In a state which does not honor this type of a will, the testator is regarded as having died without a will.
nuncle: uncle.
nuncupative will: oral, rather than written. In a state which does not honor this type of will, the testator is regarded as having died without a will.
nunnery: a slang term for a brothel.
nunrye: a nunnery.
nuntius: messenger.
nun's cloth: this probably was a thin wool fabric used for a nun's veil.
nugging house: brothel.
nupt, nupta, nuptial: relating to marriage or the wedding ceremony.
N.W.: northwest.
N.W. Terr.: Northwest Territory.
N.X.N.: no Christian name.
nybgger: (Norman) settler.
nynon: eyes.

Oath of allegiance: 1) the oath taken by an alien in which he renounced the government of another country and accepted that of the United States; 2) the oath taken by a recruit in the army or by a public official.

oath of fidelity: similar to oath of allegiance (which see).

oavis: eaves of a house.

O.B.: Order Book.

ob.: abbreviation for the Latin word obit, meaning he (or she) died.

obelisk: a four-sided stone shaft which is tapered to a point, e.g. the Washington Monument in Washington, DC.

obiit, obyt: died.

ob. unm.: died unmarried.

obit: 1) died; 2) a requiem mass for the dead; 3) abbreviation for obituary; 4) a memorial service held regularly upon the anniversary of a person's death; 5) a funeral service; 5) (Norman) forgotten.

obiter dicta: last words.

obituary: an account published in a newspaper giving the details of a person's life, date of death, etc.

obligation: (Norman) tenure.

obsetetrix: midwife.

occany: a compound metal which was intended to imitate silver.

occupant: a prostitute.

occupation: (Norman) encroachment, seizure.

occupier: a tradesman.

octavo: a book which is 6" wide and 9" high. It has been printed on paper which is folded to form eight pages printed on both sides.

octoroon: one-eighth black, a child of a quadroon and a white.

odame: brother-in-law.

O.E.D.: Oxford English Dictionary.

oel: (Norman) she.

oept: (Norman) eight.

oeptisme: (Norman) eighth.

oet, oite: (Norman) eight.

of color: non-Caucasian. This term does not necessarily mean black but can refer to any color: Indian, Oriental, etc.

off., offc.: office, officer.

officer: in the military this is a person who has been given a commission by the chief magistrate of a country and the authority to command a military unit.

office survey: sometimes a patent would be issued without a surveyor physically surveying the land. Sometimes called a projection survey.

off side: right side.

O grab me laws: a name for Embargo Acts (which see).

Ohio Company: 1) a group of Virginians who controlled the colonization of land lying south of the Ohio River; 2) a corporation organized to buy and settle land between the Ohio River and Lake Erie.

Ohio Company Purchase: this land lying along the Ohio River contained about a million and a half acres. It was purchased in 1787 from the federal government by the Ohio Company. This company was formed in Massachusetts for the purpose of settling Ohio lands, which sold for a least one dollar per acre. Poor land was allowed a one-third reduction in price.

Ohio Company's Third Purchase: see Donation Tract.

Ohio packet boat: a larger boat than a barge, it was seventy-five to one hundred feet long and fifteen to twenty feet wide. These boats had a regular run between Pittsburgh and Cincinnati and one could make a round trip in a month with a couple of days to do business in Cincinnati while the boat went on to Louisville. It carried both passengers and freight and the power for the upstream trip was man-power until steamboats were invented.

Oictoure: (Norman) October.

oil of barley: strong beer.

oir masle: (Norman) male heir.

oirs (pur ses): (Norman) for his heirs.

okere: to loan money.

(The) Old Bailey: London's central criminal court, a stone building built on the site of the infamous Newgate prison. There are eighteen separate criminal trial courtrooms in The Old Bailey.

old-bread oven: see dutch oven.

Old Colony: the Plymouth Colony territory which was absorbed into Massachusetts.

Old Dominion: The old name for Virginia, named at the time when King Charles II made Virginia into a dominion. The phrase "the colony and dominion of Virginia" is found in old documents.

oldefar: (Norman) great grandfather.

Old Lights: a name given to orthodox Colonial clergymen to distinguish them from New Lights (which see).

old ling: urine.

old milk: skimmed milk.

old settler: a person who was one of the first to live in a given area.

Old Southwest: this name originally referred to the area of Tennessee and Kentucky as we know them today, but was extended to include Alabama, Mississippi and portions of Louisiana and Arkansas.

Old Style Calendar: this term refers to a date written before 1752, when the Julian Calendar was in use. See Julian Calendar.

old-timey oven: see dutch oven.

oliver's scull: a chamber pot.

olographic will: see holographic will.

O.M.: Organized Militia.

oman: a woman.

om, omme: (Norman) 1) man; 2) person.

oncl: (Norman) uncle.

Oneida Indians: one of the Five Nations of the Iroquois Confederacy who lived in New York and for whom Oneida County, New York was named. The Oneidas aided the Americans against the British during the Revolutionary War.

Onondaga Indians: one of the Five Nation (Iroquois) tribes who lived in New York state in the county which was named for them.

onset: a dwelling house and out buildings.

on stand: a payment by the incoming farm tenant to the outgoing tenant to reimburse him for the value of a crop not yet ready for harvest or for crops harvested before the change was made.

onstead: a single farmhouse.

"on sufferance:" in some rural areas this term meant that a family which was very poor were dependent upon kind neighbors for food, clothing, etc.

onus: burden.

o.p.: out of print.

op. cit.: opere citato (Latın), in the work cited.

ope land: land constantly tilled and plowed up every year.

open court: any court which has a clerk.

open field: a system of farming in which the tillable land is made up of unfenced strips owned and/or cultivated by farmers who may be known as "open field men."

opere citato: in the work cited. See also ibid.

opiate: a sedative or narcotic used to induce sleep and relieve pain.

opificer: 1) a workman; 2) a person who makes things.

opine: to state an opinion.

opium: a drug made from the dried juice of poppies.

opodeldoc: a liniment made of camphorated soap.

oppidan: 1) a townsman; 2) a citizen of the town in which a university is located. He is not a member of the faculty.

oppiddani: inhabitants of a town.

"opportunity with:" a Quaker interview with a church member to obtain facts in a case or to issue an admonition.

optimas: parish.

oral will: see nuncupative will.

orator: a male plaintiff in an equity suit.

oratory: 1) a chapel or room set aside for prayer; 2) a society of clergymen who do not belong to a religious order and do not take vows, but live in a religious community; 3) the art of speaking in public with eloquence.

oratrix: a female plaintiff in an equity suit.

ord.: 1) ordinance; 2) order.

ordain: 1) to appoint to an office; 2) to install a graduate of a church seminary as a minister in that denomination.

ordemments: (Norman) ordinances or statutes.

ordenours: (Norman) a church official and/or barons who in 1310 were appointed by the king's commission to reform and settle the state of the king's household and of the kingdom.

order: see judgment.

order book: 1) the book in which are copied a senior officer's successive commands; 2) see also minute book.

orderly: 1) one who bears official messages; 2) a private or a non-commissioned officer in the military who has been assigned the task of working in a post hospital.

order of admission: see admission.

"order the town:" to "order the town" was to distribute the land in a new town to each settler in his "due proportion." This was a power given by a Colonial governing body to select men or town leaders. The allocation was usually similar to that used in the section of England from which the settlers had come.

ordinal: order, as first, second, third, etc.

ordinance: a local law; established public rule.

ordinary: 1) a tavern, inn or in some areas, a saloon; 2) a probate judge in some states of the United States; 3) not unusual, not peculiar; 4) the section of a chancery court which handles common-law matters; 5) a church official of high rank; 6) an ecclesiastical order for a service; 7) an obsolete term used to identify a clergyman appointed to prepare prisoners for their approaching death; 8) an early bicycle which had a large front wheel and a small back wheel.

ordnance: 1) artillery; 2) all types of weapons used by the military; 3) the branch of the army in charge of military weapons, munitions and vehicles used in combat.

ore: 1) seaweed used for manure; 2) a type of fine wool.

orfever: a goldsmith.

orfrays: embroidery.

organic disease: where the structure of the organ is impaired rather than infected.

organized militia: see militia.

original attachment: an action used to force a debtor to appear in court. This was used when the debtor had left, or was about to leave, the court's jurisdiction. The name came from the fact that the debtor's goods were attached by the court, thus assuring that he would promptly appear in court.

original records: those made at the time of an event. See primary record.

original survey: a survey which created the boundaries of a piece of land for the first time.

origo familiaris: the genealogy of a family.

orison: a prayer.

orloger: a man who keeps clocks running properly.

ormuzine: a fabric made of silk

orphan: a minor child who had lost one or both parents by death. Sometimes limited to a child whose father only has died.

orphan asylum: another name for an orphanage.

orphan book: in some areas, records concerning orphans and their affairs are kept in a special book in the courthouse. Other areas keep such records in records of the court which generated them.

Orphan's Court: the Pennsylvania probate court which handles estate accounts and petitions to court regarding estate matters, e.g. petitions for guardians, petitions for auditors, returns of valuations, and renunciations. Children above the age of fourteen choose their own guardian and those under fourteen have a guardian appointed by the court. Sometimes, rough maps of farm land locations will be found. The orphan's court records do not always relate to orphans.

Orphan Trains: these trains ran west from large east coast cities. They took poor children in orphanages, etc. west to families who needed children to help out on a farm, do domestic work, etc. The arrival of an orphan train was announced by a county sheriff. People who wished to take in children to work would pick out the child they preferred; very few were adopted and many families were never reunited.

orpharion: a musical instrument which looked like a lute.

orrie (l'): (Norman) the inheritance.

ortus: birth.

O.S.: Old Style. Used with a date, this means the Old Julian Calendar which was used before 1752.

Osage Indians: a branch of the Dakotas who were divided into bands: Beavers, Big Chiefs, Big Hills, Black Dogs, Clammores, Half-Breeds, Little Osages and White Hairs.

osey: a kind of wine.

osmond: a kind of iron.

osnaburg: a coarse fabric made of linen at Osnabruck, Germany.

o.s.p.: obit sine parole, died without issue.

ossembrike: see osnaburg.

ossification: hardening into bone.

ostayle: inn, lodging.

ostel: (Norman) 1) household, at home; 2) an inn, lodging, entertainment; 3) diet.

osteo sarcoma: cancer of the bone.

ostery: an inn.

osthouse: an inn.

ostiller: an innkeeper.

ostler: a person who cares for horses in a stable.

ostre: (Norman) eastern.

ostregier: a falconer.

"other lumber:" a phrase used at the end of a sentence which meant odds and ends made out of wood. "And other old iron" would be odds and ends made out of metal.

"other old iron:" see "other lumber."

otitis: inflammation of the ear.

Ottawa Indians: a tribe of Algonquins who lived on the shores of Lake Erie before they moved to Kansas and on west.

ottoman: a low, backless, armless, cushioned seat which would sometimes be tufted or have a fringe. It became quite popular in the early 1800s.

ounce: a measure of liquid volume; one-sixteenth of a pint. Also a measure of weight; one-sixteenth of a pound.

ousen: oxen.

Oust: (Norman) August.

oustead: one farmhouse and its outbuildings.

out-crier: an auctioneer.

out-cry: an auction sale.

out-door-work: field work.

outener: a foreigner, a non-resident.

"outgoing:" a Quaker term referring to a sufficient ground to dismiss a church member for an infraction of church rules, e.g. marrying someone other than a Friend. If the offender gave satisfaction this could be cancelled.

outhorne: an outlaw.

out house: most commonly this term refers to a privy or latrine. However, it can be used to describe a building for a household use, such as summer kitchen, wash-house, etc. It does not refer to a barn or buildings of that type.

outing: 1) a feast given to his friends by an apprentice at the end of his apprenticeship. In some parts of England this ceremony was called "burying a wife;" 2) an evacuation.

outlay: expenditure.

outler: an animal which has not been housed.

outlers: outstanding debts.

outlese: the privilege of turning cattle out to feed on a commons area.

outlot, outlying lot: a plot of land lying outside town or village limits used for tillage, grazing or woodland.

outner: a stranger.

outpartners: thieves.

outriders: 1) bailiffs errant employed by the sheriff to summon persons to court; 2) highwaymen.

outrop: a public auction.

outsetter: an emigrant.

ousettler: a person who lives in a remote area.

out shot: a projection of the upper story in an old house.

out take: to deliver.

out winders: bow windows.

oven rubber: a pole used for stirring the fire in a large oven.

overbug: to give more for anything than it is really worth.

over (de): (Norman) to work, to labor.

overganger: one who escapes.

overhouse-men: men who draw out small wire.

overland farm: a parcel of land without a house on it.

overling: ruler, master.

over live: to outlive.

over-roller: an oxen-pulled roller used to flatten out snow drifts to make roads more passable.

overseer: 1) a Colonial official appointed

to do one of any number of supervisory jobs, e.g. a road supervisor; 2) an officer of the Quaker church who had the duties of the business affairs of the meeting, preparing answers to queries, giving advice to members and pre-venting the introduction of unnecessary matters and premature complaints into meetings for business and discipline; 3) the ordnance officer in charge of construction. Sometimes he is called a superintendent; 4) a person in charge of work on a plantation; 5) an overlooker frequently appointed in wills. Sometimes the executor was called an overseer; 6) a man in the pillory.

overseer of the poor: in Colonial days the person appointed to this post purchased the materials to be used in work done by the unemployed. He also dispensed aid to the poor.

overseer of the road: a person appointed to maintain a specified stretch of road. He obtained workers to care for the road from the people who lived along it and used the road most frequently.

owels: (Norman) goods.

owler: a person who enjoys nightlife.

own cousin: first cousin.

owune: an oven.

ox: this animal outnumbered horses at one time. They were less expensive to keep than a horse.

oxey: of mature age.

oxford down: a hornless sheep bred in England.

oxgang: the amount of work which could be done on a farm by one team of plowing oxen.

ox goad: this had no lash as a whip does, but instead it had a pricking point at the tip to urge the animal to obey.

ox muzzle: a light, loosely woven basket used on the animal while it was working, thus keeping it from trying to eat grass, etc., but still allowing it to breathe easily.

ox yoke: the neck "harness" which enabled two oxen to work together. The style differed somewhat between the North and the South. A pair of oxen are referred to as a yoke of oxen.

oye: a grandchild.

oyer: to hear.

Oyer and Terminal Court: a court held when a circuit rider judge appeared in the county. Local justices of the peace staffed the court and held over cases until the judge arrived.

oyer and terminer: an order which told English judges to hear and judge criminals accused of felony, treason, and trespass.

oyez, oyez: (Norman) "hear ye, hear ye." An old beginning of a will.

oynt: (Norman) eight.

oyster peddler: a seller of oysters.

oytiesme: (Norman) eighth.

oz.: ounce, which see.e

oznabrig: see osnaburg.

P: 1) British pound; 2) page; 3) pater (father); 4) parents; 5) poll, polls; 6) pence, an English coin.

p2: pair.

p., pp.: 1) pagination, the number of numbered pages in a book; 2) pages.

P.A.: Power of Attorney.

pace: 1) the distance traveled in one step, commonly two and one-half feet, however, it is considered a rough measurement for one yard; 2) what we call Easter eggs.

pace tua: by your leave.

pack: 1) to carry on one's back; 2) a group of dairy cows; 3) a flock of any animals; 4) a heap or quantity; 5) a measure of coal, about three bushels; 6) a peddler's bundle.

pack cloth: a coarse, stout cloth used to wrap packages for shipping.

packer: 1) a person who supervised the packing of casks for export with solids (fish, pork, etc.) rather than liquids. As with most of these town officers, stiff fines were imposed for defective casks; 2) a person whose business was to transport goods on pack animals, usually mules; 3) persons employed in barrelling or packing up herrings.

packet boat: a ship which carried freight, passengers, and mail on an established route, sometimes buying and selling goods from port to port.

pack-horse man: this man rode the wilderness trails with horse and rifle, leading one or more horses carrying supplies.

packman: an itinerant salesman or peddler.

pack Monday: the first Monday after the tenth of October.

pack paper: paper used in packing a merchant's goods, etc.

pack-rag-day: a day in May when servants packed up their rags or clothes preparatory to going home or to a new job.

pack-road: see tote-road.

pack saddle: a device of wood and leather to support freight carried on horseback.

pack staff: the stick on which a peddler carried his pack.

packway: a narrow road by which goods could be conveyed only on pack horse.

padaway: see padusoy.

Paddington fair: an execution. The most common place for executions in London was in the parish of Paddington.

paddle steamer: a steamship moved through the water by paddle-wheels driven by a steam engine.

paddock cheese: asparagus.

paddy wagon: see Black Maria.

padusoy: a strong silk fabric of a serge weave, first made in Padua and later in England.

page: 1) an "appendage" of nobility; 2) a boy-child or boy-servant; 3) the common and almost only name of a shepherd's servant, whether a boy or man; 4) a carrier of messages in a governmental body.

paine maine: a fine bread.

painted paper: early wallpaper which was colored by hand.

painter: a rope attached to the bow of a ship to fasten the ship to a dock or buoy.

paintice: the shed where blacksmiths shoe horses.

pairing: a wedding feast where gifts were given.

Paiute Indians: peaceful for most of the time except for a few fights with miners, these Indians lived in Nevada, Utah, Arizona, and southeastern California.

palace: 1) a storehouse; 2) the residence of a king.

Palatinate: an area of southwest Germany from which came immigrants. Some people referred to all immigrants as Palatines regardless of their area of origin.

Palatine: 1) a person who enjoys royal privileges; 2) a high officer of a palace; 3) a native-born or resident of the Palatinate; 4) a short cape made of lace or fur. See also Palatinate.

Palatines: see Palatinate.

Palatine's court: in North Carolina this court was composed of original proprietors presided over by the senior proprietor, called the Palatine. The other proprietors controlled other government courts. One headed the treasurer's court, one headed the admiral's court, one headed the chief justice's court, etc.

pale: 1) a small fortress; 2) an enclosure for cattle; 3) a stripe in heraldry; 4) a limit or boundary.

paleography: 1) old writing; 2) the study of old documents to determine their content, origin, age, etc.

palfreis: saddle horses.

palfrey: a riding horse.

palimpsest: parchment from which all writing has been removed preparatory to writing another text.

palingman: a fishmonger.

pallhorse: a horse carrying a pannier.

palliard: a born beggar.

palmer: 1) a person who made a pilgrimage to the Holy Land and, therefore, was entitled to wear two crossed palm fronds; 2) a wandering religious person.

palm iron: a tool used by a saddler.

palpitation: quiver, flutter or throb, usually said of the heart but may also refer to the stomach or uterus.

palsy: loss of sensation, especially the inability to control movement of certain muscles of the face, arms, or hands.

palveise: a shield.

pam., pamph.: pamphlet.

pampilin: a many-colored coat worn by servants.

panacea: a cure for all ailments or an answer to all problems.

panary: a storehouse for bread.

pancake bell: bell-ringing on Shrove Tuesday, a signal to cease work and begin a holiday.

pancake Tuesday: Shrove Tuesday, was a pancake feast day for all of England.

pandel: a shrimp.

pandemic: a disease of epidemic proportions which has spread over a whole country, large area, etc.

pandoulde: a custard.

panhandle: a narrow projection of land belonging to one state which lay between two others, e.g. "panhandle" of West Virginia which lies between Virginia and Maryland.

pannage: a forest pasture for hogs, cattle, etc.

pannier: one of two wicker baskets which was used to carry the load on a pack animal.

pannier man: a servant belonging to an inn of court, whose duty was to announce dinner.

pannifax: cloth worker.

panoply: 1) a full suit of armor; 2) an impressive display of something; 3) a covering design to protect the contents; 4) complete ceremonial attire.

pantalets: long bloomers or drawers with a ruffle at the bottom which showed beneath a woman's or child's dress in the first part of the 19th century.

pantaloons: trousers which fit closely with straps going under the soles of the feet to hold them down.

panter: 1) a net or snare; 2) a baker; 3) now a butler.

panterer: the keeper of the pantry.

pantile-shop: a meeting house.

pantler: a butler.

pantry: see buttery.

papau: see pawpaw.

paper hanging: wallpaper, as opposed to a tapestry hanging.

paper stainer: a person who painted coats of arms and other things pertaining to heraldry, linen cloth and, later, hand-painted wallpaper.

Paper town: one planned and drawn carefully into a county deed book, but which never materialized. If lots were advertised, sold and resold, it could become a money maker and still not have a building in it.

papist: a demeaning term for a Roman Catholic.

par: piece.

Par.: Parish.

par., pars.: parent, parents.

parage: noble lineage, rank, descent.

paragon: 1) a kind of double camlet used for dress and upholstery in the 17th and 18th centuries; 2) a large pearl, perfectly round in shape.

paralysis: loss of function, especially sensation or movement.

paraments: furniture, drapes, ornaments.

parapet: the portion of a fortification wall which protects occupants from outside attacks.

parasangue: a measure of roads, 30-60

furlongs, which was used by the ancient Persians.

parcel: a term used to define land with specific boundaries.

parcener: a person who had an equal share in the inheritance of an ancestor; a joint heir.

parceners: see coparcenary.

parched corn: dried corn, light in weight for travel, inexpensive, but nutritious.

parchment: 1) a kind of lace; 2) animal skin from sheep, goats, etc. which has been prepared for use as paper; 3) stiff paper which resembles animal parchment; 4) a manuscript written on parchment or a parchment-like material.

parchmenter: a parchment maker.

parchmynmaker: a parchment maker.

pardoner: a dealer or seller of pardons and indulgences.

paregoric: a medicine composed of opium, which was used to ease pain.

parens: parent.

parent, parentz: (Norman) kindred.

parent country: the country where an emigrant was born.

parent county: when a new county is formed, the county from which the new one was taken is referred to as the parent county.

parentele: kindred.

pargemin: (Norman) a manuscript or parchment.

pariage (de): (Norman) on the part of the father.

paring knife: a tool used by a 1) bootmaker; 2) a clogger; 3) farrier.

parish: 1) a subdivision of a county in Britain; 2) a unit of both civil and ecclesiastical government. This term is used in the Colonial United States, e.g. Virginia; 3) a cluster of towns assigned to one priest who was to take care of their religious needs. The boundaries were identical to those of the civil townships.

Parish: in the state of Louisiana this is the equivalent of a county. Early Virginia also had the parish system. In England a parish is a county subdivision and a unit of both civil and church government.

parish council: a governmental body of a civil parish.

parishing: a hamlet or small village adjoining and belonging to a parish.

parishioner: 1) a member of a church; 2) an inhabitant of a civil or ecclesiastical parish.

parish register: the register records the church ordinances which were performed: christenings, baptisms, marriages, etc. Early records are less complete than the more recent registers.

parity of hands: comparison of two handwriting samples which prove to be the same.

parker: a park keeper.

paroch: a parish.

parochia: a parish.

parochial: 1) relating to a church-operated school; 2) local; 3)narrow.

parol: unwritten; oral.

parrott's bill: a surgeon's pincers.

parson: a church minister, clergyman, vicar.

parsonage: living quarters of a clergyman and his family. The church bears the expense of running this house as a portion of the minister's salary.

partaker: an assistant.

partel: a part or portion.

Particular Court: this Colonial Connecticut court settled differences between citizens, both civil and criminal cases, and served as a probate court, much as commissioners' courts did in the midwest. It ceased to exist in 1664 and was replaced by the County or Quarter Courts and the Court of Assistants.

particular meeting: this Quaker meeting is the same as a preparative meeting.

partition: a dividing of property which may be found in both probate and land records. If a man dies without a will, his property may be divided among the heirs in this manner. If a very small portion is involved, the court may recommend that the eldest heir buy the property from the younger ones at market prices.

partition deed: see deed of partition.

partition records: see chancery records.

partition suits: lawsuits brought by dissenting heirs to force the division of real estate so that each could have personal possession of his inheritance.

partnership: an agreement between two parties in a venture, usually on a share and share alike basis.

parturition: following childbirth.

party fellow: a co-partner.

parva: little.

parvenu: a person who recently acquired wealth but has not yet developed manners, refinement, etc. to go with the wealth or position.

parvis: a church porch.

parvoisiers (vallez): (Norman) valets who were well-trained in their military duties.

paryard: farmyard.

Pasch: 1) Jewish passover; 2) Easter.

pase day: Easter.

pasquinade: satire.

pass: 1) to toll the bell for the purpose of announcing a death; 2) an opening by which one can travel through an otherwise impassable area.

passage: a ferry.

passamen: a type of lace.

passance: a journey.

passenger: a passage-boat.

passenger boats: boats which provided overnight accommodations such as one would expect at a hotel.

passim: confusedly, indiscriminately.

passing bell: a bell rung to announce a death in the community, rung to remind people to pray for a soul leaving this world.

Passover: the most solemn festival of the Jews held in commemoration of their coming out of Egypt because the night before their departure the destroying angel who put to death the first born of the Egyptians "passed over" the houses of the Hebrews without entering them (the doorposts being marked with the blood of the Paschal lamb killed the evening before).

passport: a document which gives a person permission to travel 1) outside of the United States and to return; 2) into Indian lands to recover stolen goods or collect debts during the early 1800s.

passport applications: although passports were not required until the beginning of the twentieth century, some were issued upon request by the Federal government. Found in the National Archives, the information on these applications will be of interest to genealogists.

pasteler, pasterer, pastler: a maker of pastry.

pasticump: a shoemaker's tool.

pastor: 1) a minister; 2) a sheep herder.

pastoral: 1) a shepherd; 2) rural scenery or country life; 3) duties of a clergyman or pastor; 4) pasture land.

pasture: acreage where livestock may graze.

pat.: 1) patented; 2) paternal.

patache: 1) a small boat which operated between larger ships in a fleet; 2) a small kind of French transportation.

patacoon: a Spanish coin.

patch: a highly glazed cotton fabric with a printed floral design. It was used in window drapes and bed hangings. Some came from England and some was imported from India.

patchbox: a thin, small decorated box used by a woman in the late 18th century to carry her face patches which were fashionable at the time.

patching: mending clothes.

patchwork quilt: pieces of cloth of various sizes and colors sewn together to form a top for a piece of bedding. These would sometimes be of irregular shapes and other times would be put together in a definite pattern.

patent entry books: registers in a county courthouse in which are kept records of the original land patents for the area.

patent (land): the first deed to a piece of land from the government.

patentee: the person who receives land from the government.

pater: father.

paternal: used in speaking of a father.

patriotic service: during the Revolutionary War these persons did not serve on the field of battle, but served as wagoners, furnished ammunition or supplies and therefore were eligible for pensions. Many services to the Continental Army are now a part of the regular army: chaplains, physicians, veterinarians, paymasters, quartermasters, etc.

patrius: uncle (father's brother).

patrol: an established route which an officer (county, military, etc.) must walk or ride, maintaining security, order, etc.

patron: 1) a sea captain; 2) one who supports a cause or a person, usually with money; 3) any superior person.

Patrons of Husbandry: see Grange.

patronymic: a name formed by the use of a prefix or suffix which denotes a child-parent relationship, e.g. Anderson, son of Anders; O'Neil, son of Neil.

patroon: 1) in South Carolina, a black who held the very responsible job of master of the boats. He knew in great detail the rivers and the boat he navigated down these rivers; 2) in New York this was a person who transplanted at least fifty people to become colonists. For this act, he received a very large grant of land and the right to administer it.

patroonship: a Dutch ownership of land in New York and New Jersey managed in a manner similar to that of an English manor.

patruelis: a cousin german.

patruolus: a nephew.

patruus: a father's brother.

pattens: 1) thick soles usually made of wood which fastened with leather straps to a woman's thin-soled shoes to make her fashionable shoes more suitable for walking on unpaved streets; 2) round wooden blocks designed to fasten on a horse's hind feet, to keep it from sinking into mud.

pattern: a device to describe the shape of an object made of wood, metal, etc.

pauling: a covering for a cart or wagon.

paunce: a coat of mail.

pauper: a person unable to provide for himself and his family who is often supported by public funds. An indigent person.

paupusses: paupers.

pavage: a toll or duty payable for the liberty of passing over the soil or territory of another.

pavilioners: men who pitched tents.

paviour, pavior, pavier: 1) the material of which a road was made, e.g. stone, brick, etc.; 2) the tool which tamped paving material into the ground; 3) a building brick which was quite hard and of uniform size.

pavise, pavis: a large shield.

paviser: a soldier armed with a pavise.

pawn: an object which can be used for security.

Pawnee Indians: as a rule, this tribe was friendly to the whites who lived in the Platte River area of Nebraska. After disease and war had dwindled their numbers, they settled in Oklahoma.

pawpaw: a small tree.

paxbread: a small tablet with a picture of the cross upon it to be kissed by the faithful in church.

paymaster: 1) an officer in charge of paying salary to personnel in the United States army; 2) a civilian who paid the personnel and kept accounts for the federal government.

paymr: paymaster.

pc.: precinct.

P.C.C.: The Prerogative Court of Canterbury. From the fourteenth century until 1858, all wills in the north part of England were probated by this court.

pce: piece.

pchd.: purchased.

P.C.Y.: The Prerogative Court of York. The court in which all wills from the fourteenth century until 1858 in southern England were probated.

pd.: paid.

P.E.: Presiding Elder.

Peace Democrats: see butternuts.

peace warrant: an English order for the arrest of a person. It was issued by a justice of the peace.

peager: a person who collects a toll.

peaiges: (Norman) 1) tolls; 2) customs.

pea jacket: a short, loose top coat made of rough cloth, favored by sailors. Sometimes spelled p-jacket.

peale: an oversized wooden spatula used for putting a pan into or out of an oven.

peautre, peantre: (Norman) pewter.

peaux deberbiz: (Norman) sheepskins.

peavy, peavey: a tool used by a 1) logger; 2) saw mill operator; 3) woodsman.

peck: 1) a measure of one-half bushel; 2) meat; 3) victuals; 4) pickaxe; 5) a large quantity.

peculiar: 1) in New England this term

referred to land which did not belong in either a village or a township; 2) the person who built on this land was also called a peculiar; 3) a territory, office or job which is exempted from ordinary supervision, e.g. a piece of land which is not a part of a town, or a parish which is not controlled by a church authority which controls the land around it; 4) not ordinary.

peculiar court: an English ecclesiastical court on a parish level in which the local priest could probate a will.

peculium: private property or possessions.

pecuniary: pertaining to money: payments, penalties, honoraria, difficulties with, etc.

ped: a basket which sometimes had a lid.

pedagogue: a teacher.

pedaile: 1) footmen; 2) foot-soldiers.

pedant: a language teacher.

peddler: see hawker.

peddlery, pedlary: this term refers to a peddler's goods or his trade. It can also refer to a business so small it resembles that of a peddler. See also hawker.

peder: a small farmer.

pedigree: a record of ancestry, usually shown on a chart.

pedigree sheet: an outline form of a person's direct ancestral line giving parents, grandparents, great-grand-parents, etc. These sheets range from four or five generations to fifteen or more.

pedisequent: 1) a footman; 2) a follower.

pedlary: see peddlery.

peeler: 1) a policeman; 2) a yarn spun from a cotton raised along the Yazoo and Mississippi rivers. When the yarn is used to weave cloth, the cloth assumes the name "peeler;" 3) a peg or pin; 4) a person whose job it is to peel vegetables or fruit; 5) a log suitable to make veneer.

peer: 1) an equal; 2) a person who holds a rank of a noble: earl, duke, viscount, etc. in England.

peerage: 1) an English noble rank; 2) a book which lists peers and their genealogies. Many times peerage records are passed over by researchers who feel that there is no chance of their families being mentioned, as they were not members of the nobility. For plain dirt farmers this is likely true. However, many wealthy families suffered financial reverses and merged with more common folk. Many times, members of peerage married into families of well-to-do merchants and the landed gentry. Therefore, some pedigrees can go far back in non-noble lineages.

peeress: a wife or widow of a peer or a woman who has the rank of peer in her own right.

peipe (fon): (Norman) his father.

peire: (Norman) father.

peise: a weight.

pell: a skin, hide.

pelles: a kind of oats.

pell wool: an inferior wool cut off after the sheep is dead.

pelrine: a poor pilgrim.

pelter: (Norman) skinner.

pelt not: a disease that killed sheep. It was caused by poor feeding methods.

peltrie: (Norman) all kinds of fur.

pemphigus: many blisters which appear on normal skin. When they disappear the skin is discolored.

pence: an English coin; actually the plural of penny.

penistone: a coarse wool fabric which was used for clothes and was made in Penistone, England.

penniston: see penistone.

Pennsylvania Dutch: immigrants from southern Germany and Switzerland who lived in Pennsylvania during the seventeenth and eighteenth centuries. Their descendants are the Pennsylvania Dutch which has become the common usage of the more proper term Pennsylvania Deutsche or Pennsylvanian Germans.

Pennsylvania rifle: see long rifle.

Pennsylvania wagon: see ark.

penny wedding: a Scottish wedding at which money is given to help with the cost of the refreshments. Any money left over is given to the bride and groom.

pennyroyal: a plant belonging to the mint family which was supposed to have medicinal value.

Penobscot Indians: a tribe related to the Algonquins who lived near Bangor,

Maine and were allies of the American Colonies in the Revolutionary War.

pension: the set stipend paid by the government for past service to retired military personnel, widows, etc.

penstock: see mill race.

Pentecost: the seventh Sunday after Easter, when the apostles were visited by the Holy Spirit. Also called Whitsunday.

Pentecostal church: one of a group of fundamentalist sects or the building it uses.

penthouse: the shed where a blacksmith shoed horses. See paintice.

pepastic: a digestive medication.

peppercorn: a term which meant a nominal sum of money, e.g. rent of one peppercorn.

pepperers: grocers.

peppernel: a lump or swelling.

Pequot Indians: this tribe belonged to the Algonquin nation, who lived in Connecticut. They fought against the Colonists of New England and the remaining Pequots joined other tribes in the area.

per: by.

perambulator: 1) a surveyor; 2) a person who made a journey on foot; 3) a person who made an inspection trip; 4) see also processioner.

per annum: by the year.

per capita: when property is distributed among grandchildren, it can be done in two ways: per capita and per stirpes. Per capita means "by the head," so grandchildren would inherit equally, with a certain amount of money going to each child. The choice is the testator's. See per stirpes.

perch: a linear measure of five and one-half yards or sixteen and one-half feet. Also called a rod or a pole.

perchemear: a parchment maker.

percheron: a heavy gray or black work horse, originally bred in France.

per curiam: an opinion by the whole court anonymously, as opposed to an opinion in the name of one particular judge.

per diem: by the day.

per diem allowance: a specific sum of money allowed each day for expenses.

perdue: 1) a soldier sent on a hopeless task; 2) any person in a desperate state; 3) an ambush.

peregrinator: a traveler or one who wanders around the countryside.

peregrinus: 1) foreigner; 2) traveler.

performance bond: a promise to pay money if a contract is not fulfilled.

periaqua: boat, canoe.

pericardial dropsy: see hydropericardium.

pericarditis: inflammation of the sac around the heart.

perigord pie: a highly seasoned meat pie.

periodic tenancy: same as periodio tenancy.

periodio tenancy: rental reckoned by time, whether it be month, year, or week. It may be ended by issuing a written notice in advance.

peripatetics: persons who, as they traveled, preached or taught the principles of Aristotle's philosophy.

peripneumonia: inflammation of the lungs, sometimes accompanied by pleurisy.

peripneumonia notha: congestion of the lungs.

perishable: the part of an estate which can decrease in value between the time a will is admitted to probate and the estate is settled, e.g. crops in the field or harvested, cattle raised for market, etc. This term does not include land.

perpetual: continuing without time limitations.

perpetuana: an English fabric similar to everlasting or durance. It was made of wool and woven in a way that made it very durable. A poor quality satin.

perpetuating testimony: written testimony of a witness for use in a trial which has not yet begun. This occurs when testimony is likely to be lost, e.g. the witness is ill, quite old, going abroad, etc.

perrier: a short mortar, used for shooting a stone ball high in the air above an enemy.

perry: a Colonial drink of fermented pear juice.

pers: (Norman) peers.

pers.: personally.

per se: by itself, in itself.
persian wheel: an engine invented to raise a quantity of water that is sufficient to flood the land near the banks of a river which is too low to flood the land without help.
person: 1) a mask; 2) an actor.
personal property: goods other than land which many times are declared in a will, e.g. crops and feeder cattle.
personalty: personal property, but not including land.
persone: a man. Generally a man of dignity, e.g. a parson or a rector of a church.
per stirpes: when property is distributed among grandchildren it can be done in two ways: per capita and per stirpes. Per stirpes means "by the steps." Therefore, grandchildren inherit as a family unit, which divides the parents' share among their children (the testators's grand-children). The choice is the testator's. See per capita.
per testamentum: by will, one of the ancient ways of freeing a slave.
pertussis: whooping cough.
peruke, peruque, perrugue: a wig.
peruker, perukier, perruguier: a wig maker.
per verba futuro: future tense usage of words.
per verba praesenti: present tense usage of words.
pessoners: (Norman) fishermen.
pesteresces: (Norman) bakers (female).
pest house: a hospital for people who are ill with a harmful disease, such as bubonic plague.
pestorer, pesture, pescour: (Norman) a baker.
pestrine: (Norman) a bakehouse.
pet., petn., pettn.: petition.
petd.: petitioned.
pete: pettit.
petechia: a rash of small round hemorrhages on the skin.
Peter's pence: see almsfee.
petechial fever: severe fever accompanied by small skin hemorrhages.
petered out: gradually failed, became exhausted.
peterman: a fisherman.
petit: small, as in a petit court or small claims court.
petition: 1) this document from the people to the governor says "we want this or that." Petitions can be used for some historical purposes in lieu of tax lists or census records which may be missing for a particular area; 2) an application to a higher authority for a decision on some subject must be written, whereas a motion, which is usually written, may be spoken.
petitioner: 1) a person who signs a petition; 2) a person who presents a petition on behalf of others.
petit jury: twelve citizens, gathered together in a court and charged with the task of listening to evidence and making a fair decision in a case which is being tried in that court. Also called a petty jury or traverse jury.
petit larceny: see petty larceny.
petticoat: 1) a fancy undergarment for women, usually attached to a waistband, which showed or did not show beneath the outer garment as fashion dictated; 2) earlier it was the outer skirt part of a dress worn by women or young girls; 3) the skirt part of a riding costume for a woman.
pettifog: 1) to quibble over small trifles; 2) unethical, dishonest conduct in small matters (petty); 3) to conduct a shady law business.
pettigrew: a pedigree.
petty: see petit.
petty jury: see petit jury.
petty larceny: a theft where the amount stolen is less than a certain sum. Also called petit larceny.
petty officer: a naval rank corresponding to non-commissioned officers in the army or marines.
petty treason: an ancient term for 1) a wife killing her husband; 2) a servant killing his master.
peutre: (Norman) pewter.
pew fellow: 1) a companion; 2) one who sits in the same pew at every service.
pew rent: a source of church income. Pews were assigned to church families and the charge for each pew varied, depending upon a family's ability to pay.

pewter: an alloy of tin and lead used to make various utensils and dishes.

pewtner: a pewterer.

peysuns: (Norman) peasants.

ph.: parish.

phaeton: a nineteenth century light, four-wheeled carriage.

pharmacopoeia: 1) a published book containing a list of drugs, their properties, methods of combining, tests for purity, etc.; 2) a pharmacist's supply of drugs.

Philadelphia lawyer: a clever attorney who knows the fine points of law thoroughly and all the loopholes and points of trickery with which he can operate within legal bounds. It is said that this phrase originated because Benjamin Franklin, a native of Philadelphia, was so skillful a businessman in Europe on behalf of his city, state, and country.

philip: a common quality woolen fabric.

Philippine Insurrection: many men served in this war (1899-1901) and in the Spanish-American War.

phlebotomy: blood letting as a medical treatment.

photo cases: in use from the mid 1840s to the 1860s, these hinged cases provided a mounting for tintypes and earlier photographs. The left portion was lined with cloth or paper, the right side held the mounted photograph and the whole was covered with leather. In 1854 a case called a Union case was made of a thermoplastic, such as celluloid.

photograph types, negative: collodion wet and dry plates (1850s-1880s), gelatin dry plates (1880s-1920s).

photograph types, positive: daguerreotypes (1839-1860), ambrotypes (1850s - 1860s), tintypes (1850-1930s), salted paper prints (1839-1860s), albumen prints (1850s-1890s), silver gelatin prints (1880s-present).

phrenitis: delirius, a condition caused by inflammation of the brain.

phrenologist: a person who makes a study of human skulls in an effort to determine the mental faculties of the persons whose skulls are being examined.

phthiriasis: infested with lice.

phthisis: 1) tuberculosis of the lungs, consumption; 2) any disease which causes wasting, e.g. coal miner's black lung.

phthisic: asthma.

phunky: land saturated with rain.

physic, physick, physique: 1) to treat with medicine; 2) to purge or cleanse; 3) an early term for a medical doctor.

picaroon: a piratical ship.

picayune: a small coin worth half a real which was used in Louisiana and some other southern states. It came to mean something quite small or insignificant.

pick: 1) a tool used by a stone mason; 2) a pitchfork; 3) a basket for drawing coal up out of a pit.

pickeer: 1) an obsolete word for a skirmish before the arrival of an army; 2) to scout or survey a situation.

picker: to rob or pillage. Properly, to skirmish before a battle begins.

pick hammer: a tool used by a slater.

picking hammer: a tool used by a slater.

picking knife: a tool used by a basket maker.

pictor: painter.

piece: 1) a cask or vessel of wine; 2) a field or enclosure; 3) a coin; 4) an indeterminate measure of cloth which varied as to length: "a piece of cloth."

pieces of eight: see bits.

Piedmont area of Virginia: this area, east of the Blue Ridge mountains in Virginia, is 250 miles long and about 25 miles wide. Loudoun, Rappahannock Fauquier, Culpeper, Madison, Nelson, Greene, Orange, Albemarle, Amherst, Bedford, Franklin, Henry, and Patrick Counties are included in the Piedmont ("foot of the mountain") area.

piepoudre court: an early English summary court of justice formerly held at fairs and markets. It handled cases which concerned non-residents. Also called a piepowder court.

piepowder/piepoudre: 1) a traveling salesman; 2) also called a dusty foot; 3) an abbreviation for piepoudre court (which see).

pigeon pair: a pair of twins, one boy and one girl. It was believed that pigeons and doves always sat on two eggs which produced a male and female chick.

pie plant: rhubarb.

piggin: a wooden pail-shaped container which has a handle formed by continuing one of the staves above the rim. Occasionally, it is made of glass or silver in approximately the same shape.

pightle: 1) a small meadow; 2) any small, enclosed piece of land.

piglet: a baby pig.

pig poker: one who drives pigs from one place to another.

pigsty: the shelter where hogs or pigs were kept, usually dirtier than a barn. The style of housing hogs varied in different parts of the country from under a horse barn in New England to a pigpen built on stilts in Virginia.

pike: 1) a long pole with a sharp iron point on one end. Several pikes could be used to raise one side of a building which had been assembled flat on the ground; 2) a main highway which was constructed or maintained as a toll road; 3) a hay fork; 4) a hilltop; 5) a large heap of hay; 6) an abbreviation for a turnpike; 7) a tollgate; 8) the price charged at a tollgate; 9) the painted end of anything, e.g. an arrow, spike, etc.

pikeman: an infantry soldier who carries a weapon known as a pike.

pile mow: a wooden hammer used when putting up a fence.

Pilgrim, pilgrim: 1) a first settler of Plymouth Colony, Massachusetts; 2) an early settler of other areas; 3) a tenderfoot in the West; 4) also used in combination with other words to denote a first church, city, etc., or to honor the Pilgrims.

pill: an obsolete word for losing one's hair; to become bald.

pillage: 1) violent robbery; 2) wartime plundering; 3) to take something as booty.

pilled: having no hair, nap, feathers, etc.; bald, shaven, threadbare.

piller: a robber.

pillion: a small cushion strapped to a horse's back just behind the saddle where a wife would sit sideways of the horse for a journey in the days before carriages and roads were in use.

pillory: to pillory was a form of punishment in which the criminal was compelled to stand with his head and hands placed in holes between boards for hours on end. See stocks.

pillowbeers, pillowberes, pillowbers: pillowcases.

pilot: the person experienced in guiding a ship or boat through dangerous and intricate waters. Unless the boat operates less than twelve hours per day, there will be two such people on board. They are licensed for certain sections of a trip so that if a river boat were travelling on a long river, several pilots would be hired.

Pima Indians: a peaceful tribe who lived in Arizona and used irrigation to grow crops on desert land.

pincer tongs: a tool used by a 1) blacksmith; 2) farrier.

pinchbeck: the metal from which cheap jewelry was made. Later the word came to mean cheap jewelry.

pincteur: (Norman) a painter.

pinder: the petty officer of a manor whose duty it was to impound all of the strange cattle straying upon the commons.

pine box: a coffin made of plain pine boards.

piner: a pioneer.

pinetree shilling: a Colonial coin with a pine tree pattern on it which was minted in Boston. It contained less silver than an English shilling. Therefore, the government did not want pinetree shillings to leave the colony. However, the coins were shipped to Europe as bullion to pay for European goods.

pinfold: a pound of stray animals.

pingle: 1) a small, long, narrow enclosure; 2) to work hard with little progress.

Pin Indian: Cherokees who believed in the north's anti-slavery position. They gained their nickname from the custom of wearing on their shirts two crossed pins signifying to other Indians which side they favored.

Pinkerton Agency: a detective agency formed by Allen Pinkerton. An employee of this agency served as Abraham Lincoln's personal security officer during the early part of the Civil War and later became the head of the Union Army's secret service.

pin maker: a maker of pins.

pin money: a wife's allowance from her husband for her own expenses.

pinner: 1) a seventeenth and eighteenth century cap worn by a woman;) a person who works with pins in some manner, e.g. placing or removing pins, etc.; 3) a person who works in a bakery sticking pins in cookies prior to dipping them into icing; 4) the person who fastens two parts of an object together with pins (rivets); 5) the person who cuts and puts the brim of a hat together by pinning the brim to the main body of the hat; 6) a small stone used by a mason to support a larger stone; 7) a British officer who catches stray animals and impounds them.

pintado: a chintz cloth.

piol: a type of lace.

pion.: pioneer.

pioneer: 1) a frontiersman; 2) an early settler; 3) a leader of other people into a new area.

Pioneer Day: a holiday in Utah, on July 24th, to celebrate the founding of Salt Lake City by the Mormons, led by Brigham Young.

pioneers: members of a regiment furnished with pickaxes, saws, spades, etc. who performed the duties now delegated to the corps of engineers.

Pious Fund: money raised and used by the Jesuits for their missionary work among Californian Indians.

pipe: 1) a cask of liquid which was equal to 126 wine gallons; 2) a large cask used to hold wine.

piper: an innkeeper.

Pipe Roll: abbreviation for "The Great Roll of the Pipe of the Exchequer," an English tax roll which also included fines imposed by the civil and criminal courts which were payable to the Crown. These accounts grew so large that they required a special services court whose accounts were called Fine Rolls.

pipe staves: the boards which form the sides of a cask.

piroque: a large canoe approximately forty to fifty feet long and six to eight feet wide which was capable of carrying a whole family with several tons of their goods.

piscator: fisherman.

pistole: a Spanish gold coin.

pistolero: 1) a roving band of armed and mounted bandits who operated in Central America and Mexico; 2) a hired killer.

pistor: baker.

pitancer: a person who gave out provisions.

pit and gallows: a sentence of death by hanging and drowning.

pitch: 1) a fur skin; 2) the amount of hay on a hay fork; 3) a crowbar with a thick point used to make holes in the ground; 4) to pave a road roughly.

pitch fork: a hand tool used to load or unload hay.

pitching pence: money which was used to pay for each bag of corn bought at a fair or market.

pitching tool: a tool used by a stone mason.

pit-coal: see coal.

pithole: a grave.

pitman: the man who works in the bottom of the saw pit.

pityriasis: 1) a variety of diseases of the skin, characterized by shedding scales of skin; 2) a skin disease affecting domestic animals which also is characterized by dry scales.

p-jacket: see pea jacket.

P.J.P.: Probate Judge of the Peace.

pl.: place.

placer: an area where valuable minerals are mined by a washing process.

placing: becoming a servant.

placing out: see apprentice.

placket: 1) a sixteenth century map; 2) a piece of armor; 3) the side opening of a petticoat designed to make it easier to put on and take off.

plague: any contagious disease which is of epidemic proportions and has a high mortality rate.

"plain people:" religious groups from the Palatinate (Mennonites, Dunkards, Moravians, Schwenkfelders, etc.) who were sometimes collectively called the

"plain people."
plainsman: a person who lived in a prairie area.
plaintiff: a person who starts a lawsuit against another.
plain tongs: a tool used by a blacksmith.
plane: a tool used by a 1) wheelwright; 2) carpenter.
plank road: this road, like the corduroy road, was made of wood which would last about five years. This plank road was made of milled lumber which was placed on the right side of the road going into town in order that farmers would have easier going with the heavier loads. Coming out of the town they would drive on dirt alone. As these were more sophisticated roads, they were laid with uneven sides to enable a heavily loaded wagon to get back on the road after slipping off. They were also slightly sloped so rain would drain off the planks.
plant.: plaintiff.
Plantagenet: a member of the family that ruled England from Henry II through Richard II (1154-1485). Henry II's father was Count Geoffrey of Anjou, who was called Plantagenet. The name came from planta genista, a bright yellow broom flower whose emblem was a part of the family arms.
plantation: 1) a large estate or homestead; 2) an Indian village; 3) a large farm in the southern United States; 4) in some states a unit of government between a township and an incorporated town; 5) in Delaware, a legal term for cultivated oyster-beds.
plantation house: the main dwelling on a farm.
planter: 1) a farmer; 2) a person who owns a farm or plantation, usually more than 100 acres.
planting: an old term used instead of platting or surveying an area. Sometimes states are referred to by this term, but it usually refers to a township.
planting by signs: some time ago, and at times yet today, farmers plant seed by the sign of the zodiac and/or the phase of the moon and the type of crop which is being planted. Many farmers believe that in this procedure lies the success or failure of a crop. Also called "planting by the moon."
plasterer: 1) a person who fills in holes, makes rough areas in walls smooth, applies plaster to cover lathe; 2) a maker of plaster casts for decorating; 3) the worker who installs plaster trim.
plastering hair: hair (from animals or human hair from barber shop floor sweepings) used in plaster as a reinforcing agent.
plat.: 1) platoon; 2) plaintiff.
plat: 1) a planned division of land; 2) a map, especially of a newly established town; 3) a small area of ground. See also survey.
plat book: maps (usually of townships) which show who owns the land, how many acres and where the land is. The maps are bound into books, each covering one county.
plate: a coin of silver.
plate (le): (Norman) bullion, uncoined gold or silver.
platf.: an abbreviation for plaintiff (which see).
platoon: in the English service this was a group of men who fired together, but in the United States, it is a subdivision of a company. Usually it has two or more sections or squads and is under the command of a lieutenant.
plaustrary: a wagoner.
P.L.B.: Poor Law Board.
plea: 1) a claim or allegation of fact; 2) the answer of a person accused of an unlawful act; 3) (obsolete) a court case or lawsuit.
pleadings: statements usually written by a plaintiff and a defendant in which they set forth the case and the defense.
plea rolls: a list of cases in different law courts. Sometimes a generation can be established by the study of these lists.
pleasauntes: 1) lawn fabric; 2) gauze.
plebe: 1) the populace; 2) a freshman member of a military school.
plebian: a common person, as opposed to one of high rank or birth.
pleurisy: inflammation of the membrane around the lung.
pleuritis: see pleurisy.

plewed: plowed.
pleytyre: (Norman) poultry.
plier tongs: a tool used by a blacksmith.
plinth return (right hand or left hand): a tool used by a brick maker.
plinths: tools of varied shapes used by a brick maker.
plith, plyth: an obsolete form of plight.
plo: an obsolete form of plough, plow.
ploshett: a swampy meadow.
plot: this usually refers to a small piece of land, e.g. a garden plot.
plt., pltf.: plaintiff.
plu capius: a blanket claim used when apparently there is more than first was thought and it is not known exactly what. It is used quite commonly in order that nothing is missed.
pluffe: a plow.
plumber: one who dealt or worked with lead (plumbum).
plough, plow: used by a farmer to prepare ground for planting. It is pushed by one or more men and pulled by one or more men or animals.
plough jogger: a plowman.
plough land, plow land: 1) tillable land; 2) an archaic term for an English land unit, as much land as one plow will till in a year.
ploughman: 1) a farmer; 2) a laborer on a farm..
ploughwright, plow-wright: a person who makes or mends plows.
plow-alms: a source of income for old English churches, a penny each year for each small farm. At this time a piece of plow land was as much as one man could plow, using a team of eight oxen, in one year. Sometimes this measure included pasture land as well as tilled soil.
plow-bote: wood which a tenant farmer had available and had the right to use in repairing agricultural tools.
plow driver: the person who guided and walked behind a horse pulling a plow.
plow foot: an early farm tool; a plow without wheels, which was somewhat easier to use than a spade.
plow land: see plow alms.
plow tree: the handle of a plow which was pushed by a man or pulled by a horse and guided by a man.
plow wright: the person who manufactured plows.
plt., pltf.: plaintiff.
plumb bob, plumb line: a string with a weight attached to one end. When suspended it forms a vertical line to use as a guide for construction, surveying, etc.
plumb rule: a tool used by a stone mason.
plumbum: lead (as in lead pipes).
plumbum man: a maker of lead pipes; 2) later a plumber.
plumbum worker: a plumber.
plummet: a tool used by a 1) surveyor; 2) mason; 3) carpenter.
plumper: a small ball made of ivory used by men who had had some of their teeth extracted. This system filled out the person's cheeks to improve their appearance.
plunder: 1) to take another person's property by force, usually during a war; 2) to rob, steal; 3) property taken by a plunderer.
pluralism: a person who holds two offices at the same time.
pluries: a third writ used when an original or an alias writ goes unanswered.
Plymouth Company: see Virginia Companies.
plyth: see plith.
P.M.: 1) Post Meridiem, afternoon; 2) Post Mortem, Latin for after death; 3) Police Magistrate; 4) Preparative Meeting (which see).
pneumonia: inflammation of the lungs.
P.O.: Post Office.
poa.: power of attorney.
pocosin, poquosin: wooded swampland.
podagra: gout in the feet or big toe.
podunk: in Colonial days, this word was an Indian place name in the Connecticut and Massachusetts area of New England. Later it came to be used as a name for any small hamlet or in speaking of an imaginary place.
poinding: a Scottish law which allows a creditor to take personal property to settle a deal and be entitled to a bill of sale.
point: a tool used by a 1) stone mason; 2) saddler.
pointing horse: a tool used by a farrier.

pointoure, pointourne: a painter or artist.

poke: a preventive device in the form of a collar with a metal stick protruding from it. It was put around the neck of a cow, horse or hog which had the habit of trying to jump over or root under a fence; 2) a sack or bag; 3) a plant which produces a dye; 4) tobacco or other plants used for smoking; 5) the front part of the brim on a woman's bonnet.

poke bonnet: a hat which had a brim similar to that worn by women in the Salvation Army.

poke cart: a miller's cart filled with sacks or pokes of meal.

poke day: the day on which an allowance of corn is made to laborers. In some locations they received part of their wages in this manner.

pokerwork: a form of handwork consisting of decorative designs, pictures, etc. which are burned into the surface of wood or leather articles.

polail: (Norman) poultry.

Poland China: a black and white hog raised in the United States.

pole: a measure of distance used in surveying. Equal to a rod or sixteen and one-half feet.

pole axe: sometimes called a felling axe. Used for cutting down trees.

poledavis: see poledavy.

poledavy: a sacking or coarse canvas used to make sails.

pole fence: see rail fence.

poleman: a surveyor's assistant.

polenta: a barley porridge.

poler: 1) a barber; 2) a person who uses a pole to move a barge, boat, etc. through water.

police jury: a coroner's jury.

poll: 1) the place where an election of officials is held, a church, school, etc. Sometimes called polls; 2) usually this term meant a person was free to vote in his county, providing he had paid his poll tax and was twenty-one years of age or older. At age fifty he became exempt from the poll tax.

pollage: a head tax.

poll deed, deed poll: a deed made by one person as opposed to an indenture which was torn into two pieces so each of two parties could have half. The deed poll or poll deed usually begins: "Know all men by these presents, that ..."

poll (tax): 1) a list of persons eligible for a tax of an equal amount without regard for the value or amount of property which is owned by the people. Usually, this term meant a person was free to vote in his county providing he had paid his poll tax and was 21 years of age or over. At age 50 he became exempt from a poll tax; 2) in England, any male fifteen and over was obliged to pay this tax. Wealthy men paid more than poor men.

poltaire, polter, polentier: (Norman) a poulterer; the officer in the king's kitchen who had charge of the poultry.

polther: an obsolete form of poultice.

poltroon: a person who was mean and cowardly.

polygamy: to have more than one wife or husband at the same time.

pomander: 1) a box with little holes in the top containing perfume for a lady, or a powdered disinfectant for a doctor. His was usually carried in the top of his cane so that with a tap on the floor the disinfectant would be scattered in the air; 2) sometimes a mixture of scented substances formed into a ball and carried in a box or bag with small holes, as a prevention against being infected by disease; 3) an apple or orange covered with whole cloves stuck into it and hung in a closet as an air freshener.

pompadour: 1) a cloak imported from France, favored by wealthy women in the late 1700s, which was of satin or velvet with a hood and slits for the wearer's arms; 2) a women's hair style which was a high roll supported by a colored roll called a rat, over which the hair was combed.

Poncas Indians: a small group of Indians, who belonged to the Dakota tribe and were driven beyond the Missouri River.

pond: a Dutch measure of weight.

ponche: tobacco used for trading.

ponder: 1) to weight something; 2) an obsolete word which meant to estimate the value of something; 3) to consider.

pond vlaamsch: a Dutch coin.

pony express: a man who carried mail on horseback. He had a special light saddle, was armed with a gun, and changed his horse for a fresh one quite frequently.

poole: a measure of work used when roofing a house with slate. Every poole of work was either 6' broad and 14' on both sides or 168' in length and 1' in breadth.

poor accounts: records which concern distribution of money to the poor.

poorhouse: a home for the elderly poor people which is supported by a county.

poor law: a system of public relief used in England.

poor school: a term used at times when referring to a public school.

poplin: a fabric which was woven with silk warp threads and wool woof threads. It had a corded surface.

porcarius: swineherd.

porcelain pottery: this pottery has a glass-like, translucent appearance, fired at high temperatures. It was likely to be used in wealthier homes.

porgy: a variety of edible fish.

porr: 1) a plumber; 2) a glazier.

porridge: 1) not only made of oats cooked for a long period of time until quite soft, but also of beans, peas, etc. which was a staple food for pioneers; 2) sometimes a meat and vegetable soup which has been thickened with a cereal.

porringer: 1) the dish in which porridge is served. It usually is a shallow cup-like dish from which it is easy for children to eat or be fed; 2) a hat which is shaped like a porringer.

port: the left side of a ship as you face the front.

portage: 1) tonnage; 2) carrying of a small boat, e.g. a canoe, overland between two bodies of water.

portague, portigue: a Portuguese gold coin minted in the sixteenth century.

porter: 1) a combination of two malt beverages, ale and stout; 2) a door keeper; 3) a person who helps carry the coffin at a funeral. The modern term is pallbearer; 4) a person who carries heavy items for others.

porterhouse: 1) a tavern or inn which sold malt liquors; 2) an excellent cut of beef.

porticullis: a coin struck during Elizabeth I's reign.

portmanteau, portmantua: a traveling bag or gladstone bag which was hinged in the middle and opened into two separate compartments.

portmantles: an archaic form of portmanteau (which see).

port sale: an open sale of wares.

P.O.S.A.: Patriotic Order Sons of America.

posse: horse-mounted citizens who aided the sheriff in apprehending fugitives, etc.

possessioners: an uncomplimentary name for those religious committees which were endowed with land.

post: 1) after; 2) a courier; 3) a special messenger.

postage currency: at the beginning of the Civil War there was a shortage of silver coins and postage stamps were used as legal tender. The post office soon ran out of postage stamps, which were not desirable as money for they turned into sticky messes in purses and pockets. Then the Treasury issued currency in small denominations.

postal services: travelers of the roads were also the early method of carrying mail. Not many could read or write, so most were oral messages. However, state papers or letters of importance would be handed to the sheriff who would take them to the sheriff of the next county, etc. until the destination was reached. Post riders then appeared, and while this job was to carry the mail, the rider would wait until he had enough letters (at a certain price per letter) collected to make his expenses. It was a fairly expensive method of communication in Colonial days. Later mail was carried by stage coach.

posterity: descendants not in a direct line.

post hole auger: a drill used to make holes in the ground, e.g. for fence posts.

posthumous: an event occurring after a person's death. For example, a baby born after its father's death.

posthumous child: a child born after the death of its father.

postilion: a man who held the position of

a groom on the Cumberland-National Road. He would have ready, at the foot of a steep hill, a pair of horses which were added to the coach's team. At the top of the hill the extra pair would be back to the bottom of the hill and wait for the arrival of the next coach.

postman and tubman: ancient offices in the English court of the exchequer held by a lawyer with certain privileges.

postmasters: the job of postmaster was often held by a printer who also published a newspaper. Two Boston papers had "post-boy" as a portion of their name and the price of the paper was quoted in cash, rye, corn, etc.

post mill: a type of wind mill which was a little corncrib-like house built on a post at least two feet in diameter. The entire house was turned to face the wind.

post mortem: 1) after death; 2) an investigation to determine the cause of a death.

postoure: a pastor.

post house: a house or an inn where fresh horses were kept and where the post rider could spend the night.

post rider: a person who carried mail on horseback.

post road: 1) a route used to carry mail between two points; it could be a road, a waterway, a railway, etc.; 2) a road with several post offices or stations along it

post runner: a person who carries the mail on foot; a speedy messenger.

post town: 1) in this country it is the town where the main post office for an area is located; 2) in Britain a town with a post offices which serves as a distribution office for smaller towns.

potagre: the gout.

potash: a chemical derived from the ashes of wood.

pot boiler: a housekeeper.

potecary: an apothecary.

potestat: a chief magistrate.

pot house: 1) an obsolete word for the place where pottery is made; 2) a public house or tavern.

potlikker, potlicker: the juice left in a kettle after cooking greens with the jowl of a hog. Relished especially by southerners.

pot metal: an alloy of lead and copper which was used to make pots and pans.

pottage: a thick vegetable soup.

Pottawatomie Indians: a tribe of Algonquin stock who lived in a large part of Michigan. They were against the Colonists in the Revolution and allies of the British during the War of 1812 after which they went to Kansas.

potter: a person who made pottery.

potter's asthma: a lung disease caused by dust which makers of pottery are exposed to daily in their work. Also called potter's bronchitis, potter's consumption, etc.

potter's field: this burial place may be either an entire cemetery or a section of a cemetery. They are usually found near a county seat and are reserved for paupers, suicides, executions, etc.

pottle: 1) four quarts out of a bushel of ground grain used as the fee or "toll" for grinding; 2) a liquid measure of two quarts.

potwalloper: 1) a house owner who had the privilege of voting and owned his fireplace where he could cook in pots. Also called a potwaller; 2) a washer of pots.

poulter: a keeper of poultry.

poultice: a cloth, usually wool, to which was applied a suitable "medicine" and the medicated side then applied to the skin. Used mostly for congestion.

pouncet-box: see pomander.

pound: an English monetary unit which originally was worth the weight of a pound of silver. Sometimes abbreviated to a capital L.

pounder: 1) see key keeper; 2) the person who impounded stray animals, then notified the owner who had to pay a small fine to retrieve his animal.

powdering tub: a large tub for salting or pickling meat.

powder monkey: a person who carried gun powder from storage areas to the guns.

powdering tub: a vessel for salting or pickling meat.

powder(s): medicine at one time came in

powder form and in some countries it still comes as a powder wrapped in a piece of paper. A fever powder is a medicine to reduce fever, a headache powder is a medicine to quiet the headache, etc.

power of attorney: authority which gives another person permission to act on behalf of the giver. Generally, this is to do a specific act—execute a deed, make a contract, etc. It expires with the death of the giver.

power of investigation: the power of a grand jury to call witnesses.

powler: a barber.

pp.: pages.

ppa: per power of attorney.

pr.: 1) proved; 2) probated; 3) per; 4) pair.

practical printer: a person who did the actual work of printing. One who did not have a printer's skill would sometimes publish a newspaper, etc. in another person's print shop and would be referred to as a printer, thus leading to the need for the phrase "practical printer."

praecipe: 1) a writ which forces a defendant to either do something or give a good reason why it should not be done; 2) an order which tells the clerk of the court to issue the above writ.

prairie breaker: a person who accepted free land from the federal government and lived on it while he "developed" or homesteaded it.

prairie drain: see drain.

praline: a candy, which originated in France, made of sugar and nuts which was (and is) quite popular in the south.

prater: to talk too much without saying anything worthwhile.

prayg.: praying.

praying: respectfully asking.

praying Indians: during King Philip's War these friendly Indians, who lived in New England and had been converted to Christianity, acted as scouts and spies for the Colonists.

prc: produced certificate.

prcla.: proclamation.

pre: prefixed to any word means before.

preacher: in frontier days a man needed no formal divinity school training, for any one with a knowledge of Biblical quotations and a "gift of gab" could get by. This was not always true in the more established New England area. Country folk accepted the preacher for, although most were "unlarnt," they were sincere according to their beliefs.

preachment: a sermon.

prebend: 1) a stipend given to a clergyman from the church's income; 2) the part of church-owned land set apart for income for clergymen.

precept of sasine: a document which orders the delivery of property as described in the document.

prechovrez: (Norman) preachers.

precinct: a geographic area, similar to a war, used to designate a local police protection area, an election area, etc.

precinct court: this court judged all civil actions and criminal cases brought before them which were not punishable by death.

precisian: 1) a serious person; 2) a Puritan.

predial lands: farmlands.

predial tithe: a tenth of a farm's income which belongs to a church.

prediator: 1) a real estate dealer; 2) a person who buys land which is mortgaged.

predicator: preacher.

prediction: a sermon.

pre-emption: 1) the right to obtain land when certain conditions set by the federal government have been fulfilled; 2) the right to purchase anything before another person may.

pre-emption application: papers filed by a person who had already settled on public land, but later wished to buy it at the minimum sale price.

prenella: see prunella.

prentis: an apprentice. A barrister was called a prentice or prentice-of-law.

Preparative Meeting: a Quaker business meeting to discuss matters which might properly be discussed during a Monthly Meeting.

prepositour: a scholar appointed by the master to oversee the rest.

prerogative court: 1) an English probate court; 2) the name of the court which in many states handled probate matters. Only New Jersey retains the old title.

presbyter: 1) a priest; 2) a Presbyterian church elder; 3) an official of the early Christian church who taught, administered and acted as a priest.

prescription: the title to real property by using it uninterrupted for a long time. Time, in this case, was originally indefinite but now is limited by the statutes of limitations.

presentment: a grand jury's statement in a case which has been brought into court.

presents: when the phrase "by these presents" is found in a document it literally means "this document or instrument."

President: Pennsylvania and New Hampshire were first headed by an executive council of which one member was named president. New Hampshire, Delaware and South Carolina had single heads of state. These states, at a later date, all changed the title to governor.

Presidents of the United States

George Washington	1789-1797
John Adams	1797-1801
Thomas Jefferson	1801-1809
James Madison	1809-1817
James Monroe	1817-1825
John Quincy Adams	1825-1829
Andrew Jackson	1829-1837
Martin Van Buren	1837-1841
William Henry Harrison	March-Apr.1841
John Tyler	1841-1845
James K. Polk	1845-1849
Zachary Taylor	1849-1850
Millard Fillmore	1850-1853
Franklin Pierce	1853-1857
James Buchanan	1857-1861
Abraham Lincoln	1861-1865
Andrew Johnson	1865-1869
Ulysses S. Grant	1869-1877
Rutherford B. Hayes	1877-1881
James A. Garfield	1881
Chester A. Arthur	1881-1885
Grover Cleveland	1885-1889
Benjamin Harrison	1889-1893
Grover Cleveland	1893-1901
William McKinley	1897-1901
Theodore Roosevelt	1901-1909
William H. Taft	1909-1913
Woodrow Wilson	1913-1921
Warren G. Harding	1921-1923
Calvin Coolidge	1923-1929
Herbert C. Hoover	1929-1933
Franklin D. Roosevelt	1933-1945
Harry S. Truman	1945-1952
Dwight D. Eisenhower	1952-1960
John F. Kennedy	1960-1963
Lyndon B. Johnson	1963-1968
Richard M. Nixon	1968-1974
Gerald R. Ford	1974-1976
James E. Carter	1976-1980
Ronald W. Reagan	1980-1988
George W. Bush	1988-1992
William Clinton	1992-

presidios: Spanish military settlements in California and in the Southwestern states. Soldiers at these posts had their families with them and were farmers while pro-tecting Spanish interests.

press: a large cupboard where clothes were kept.

press gang: see impressment.

press money: see prest money.

prest: (Norman) pastor.

prestidigitator: a magician.

prest money: an obsolete phrase for money given in advance to induce men to enlist in one of the armed forces. Sometimes called press money.

presumptive settler: a squatter.

pretermit: 1) to leave something undone; 2) to suspend; 3) to interrupt; 4) to let pass unnoticed.

pretermitted child: a child born after the father's will has been executed and the child was not mentioned in the will. Usually such a child can inherit property under a state statute.

prevention: jurisdiction.

pricasour: a hunter.

pricer: a person whose duty it was to regulate the prices of a market.

pricker: 1) any sharp-pointed instrument; 2) a light horse man. There was at one time a cavalry regiment termed the "prickers."

pricking: a way of voting, usually for selectmen. Names of candidates were written on a piece of paper which was passed around and each man pricked a hole by the names of his choice. The person having the most holes was chosen first, the next highest second, etc.

pricking aches: convulsions.

pricking iron: a tool used by a saddler.

pricking knife: a carpenter's tool.

pricking note: a note concerned with the shipment of goods. The customs officer has inspected the goods as they were loaded onto a ship and the ship's captain has given a receipt for the goods.

pricking wheel: a tool used by a saddler.

prick louise: a nickname for a tailor.

prickly ash (xanthoxylum): the root of this plant was used to cure rheumatism.

priest: 1) a member of the gentry who lived on church land which an English lord donated to the village church. He received tithes and administered them for the church. Sometimes called a parson; 2) this term is occasionally found in reference to marriages outside of Friends' (Quaker) meetings, but it is not to be understood as referring necessarily to a member of the Catholic clergy. More frequently the "priest" referred to was an Anglican clergyman or a minister of a Protestant denomination.

priest ill: the ague.

prig-napper: a stealer of horses.

prima facie: "at first view." Something assumed to be correct in the absence of evidence to the contrary; a fact is true until it is proved otherwise.

primage: see hat money.

primary record: a record made by someone who knew at the time an event occurred. The record is usually the first and best record available.

primary sources: original documents.

primer fine: one-tenth of the value of produce grown in one year on land which had been the subject of a suit. This tax was paid by the plaintiff who brought the suit to regain possession of the land into court.

primogeniture: 1) the state of being a first-born child of the same parents as one's siblings; 2) the right of the eldest son to inherit the property or title of his intestate father. The personal property, both money and goods, was then equally divided among the deceased man's children.

princess: 1) a female member of the royal family; 2) a prince's wife; 3) a style of a dress; 4) a daughter of a king or queen; 5) a king's (or queen's) son's daughter.

principal meridian: a geographical term which refers to a reference line used in surveying and dividing land in certain parts of the United States. The meridian numbers progress from low to high as they were surveyed from east to west. The meridian lines on either side of the principal meridian are twenty-four miles apart.

pringle: a small silver Scotch coin equal to a British penny.

prisage: a king's right to take a portion of wine for his own use.

prius: before, prior to.

private: a soldier who does not hold rank of any type.

privateer: a privately owned, armed vessel commissioned by a government in wartime to prey upon the enemy's commercial activities. The Admiralty Court had to condemn the captured booty, which led to the creation of records useful to genealogists. This information is found in Admiralty Court records.

privateerism: disorderly conduct.

privateer papers: power of attorney, signed by a ship's officers and crewmen which allowed the prize money to be distributed to others.

private land claims: these were claims for acreage lying in what are now lands within the United States, but earlier were owned by other governments (England, France, etc.) and were allegedly sold or given to claimants by these other countries.

private letters: letters carried by individuals or groups other than government. For example, ships carried mail from one port to another on a more or less regular basis.

privigna: stepdaughter.

privignus: stepson.

privity: 1) a secret plan; 2) a person's private business; 3) an obsolete word for an intimate relationship; 4) a mutual interest between two people in something.

privy: 1) a secret among a few; 2) private knowledge of which few know; 3) an outside toilet.

privy coat: a light, defensive coat of mail which was concealed under an ordinary garment.

Privy Council: 1) a panel appointed to advise the ruler of a country: king, emperor, governor, etc.; 2) a group whose actions are known only to a few.

prize: enemy property which has been captured.

Prize Court: a special Admiralty Court convened to determine how the shares gained from a prize ship are to be distributed.

prize ships: when any enemy ship is captured during wartime it is referred to as a prize. See prize court.

prized: mechanically forced, e.g. tobacco into a barrel or a nail from a board.

PRO: Public Record Office.

Pro.: Province.

pro.: 1) probated; 2) proved; 3) provost.

pro: for.

pro anno: for the year.

proavia: great grandmother.

proavus: great grandfather.

prob.: 1) probably; 2) probated.

probable: provable.

probably: provable.

probal.: probable.

probang: a probe with a soft end to put into the throat, which has medication on it or is used to remove foreign matter.

probate: the legal process of settling an estate. Until the Revolution the Church of England was almost supreme in probate matters. Today, probate has become an inclusive term to describe all the matters which a probate court handles.

probate court: in some states, the name of the court in which estates are settled.

probate packet: loose papers which contain records of an estate settlement. These are usually filed in envelopes by probate case numbers.

probate records: papers generated by the settlement of an estate.

proceed: to take a degree, as at a university.

proceedings: 1) a record of transactions; 2) events, happenings; 3) a legal measure; 4) to carry on an action.

process: as in "due process of law." A series of actions taken in an orderly manner.

processioner: a type of a surveyor in England and the United States, especially Virginia and Kentucky. His job was to decide upon property boundaries to mark, and describe them in the processioner's book. Occasionally, the total acres and property boundaries determined by the processioner will be found in old minutes of a church in whose parish boundaries the land in question was located.

processioning, land: each four years, all landowners in a community would ride or walk along the boundaries of all their plantations. Surveyors who accompanied this procession would redraw any disputed lines. This custom came from England to Virginia as a means of avoiding disputes arising from poor surveys or loss of boundary markers such as trees.

prockesy: a proxy.

procl., procla., prol.: proclamation.

proclamation money: in 1704 a British royal proclamation was issued which fixed uniform coin values in the Colonies, including foreign coins whose value was based upon the bullion content of each coin. The purpose of this proclamation was to promote trade directly with England but it was not enforced and the Colonists completely ignored it.

Proclamation of 1763: a dividing line designed to separate the territory of American settlers and that of American Indians. It followed more or less the tops of the Appalachian Mountains.

proctor: one who collected alms for lepers or other persons who were unable to do it themselves.

Procurator Fiscal: a Scottish lawyer who practices in lower court.

procuratory: in Scotland this is the permission of one person to conduct business for another.

professional mourner: a person who

attends the funeral of a stranger for pay.

professional soldier: a soldier, officer or not, who serves in the regular army for pay.

progenitor(s): 1) those living before a person: father, grandfather, great-grandfather, etc. who are part of one's direct line; 2) a source, a beginning for development.

progeny: all descendants of a common ancestor.

progress: tours of the sovereign and court to various parts of the kingdom.

projection survey: see office survey.

projector: an inventor of ideas or projects, e.g. settling a town in a different area.

prom.: promoted.

promissory note: a document in which the author promises to pay at a certain time, or when demanded, a given sum of money. Sometimes called "note of hand."

promotor: an informer.

pronephew: a great-grandson.

proof: 1) documents or other evidence, which established the truth of a statement or claim; 2) land is said to be proof when it is of excellent quality.

prop.: property.

propinquity: kin, related.

propositus: in a genealogical chart, this is the ancestor from whom a line descends.

propounder: a person who offers something for consideration, discussion, etc.

propr.: proprietor.

proprietary colonies: to settle new colonies in the 1600s, England made large grants of land to small groups and individuals (proprietors) who could, if they wished, sell the land. Laws and court decisions of these colonies were subject to review by England but the colonists were allowed to appoint almost all government officials. Pennsylvania, Maryland, Maine, New York, New Jersey, Delaware, and Carolina were all proprietary colonies.

proprietor: 1) an owner; 2) a person who manages an establishment; 3) historically, an original purchaser or grantee of town land. In New England, they had the responsibility of locating house lots, setting aside a town common (market place or green), laying out of pastures and highways; 4) a term to denote all original purchasers or grantees of town land. They held closed meetings during which all matters which pertained to town land were acted upon.

Proprietor's Court: it was possible for appeals from the county court to be heard before this court, except for less important civil cases.

prosecute: to try in court, or to proceed legally against another.

prostatitis: inflammation of the prostate gland.

protection certificates: American seamen about 1797 had to carry these identification papers. If they did not have their papers with them, they could be forced into service on British vessels and were treated as prisoners of war.

pro tem: "pro tempore," temporarily.

prothonotary: 1) a county clerk; 2) in Great Britain and in some states of the United States this person is the chief clerk of a court or the person who registers wills, etc. into the court.

protocol: 1) an original record from which a certified copy may be issued; 2) a preliminary agreement used as a basis for a final agreement; 3) an official account of a proceeding; 4) a code of ceremonial behavior.

protokoll: (Norman) records.

proud: a swelling which is sore and inflamed is sometimes called proud flesh.

prov.: proved. A will has been proved when probate has been granted.

provand: provisions.

provant master: a person who provided wearing apparel for soldiers.

provenance: place of origin.

provender: corn, oats, hay, straw, or a mix of grain used as food for domestic animals, horses, cows, etc.

prover: see approver.

provesour: surveyor.

province: a division of a country which functions independently of, but is a member of, a confederation of counties.

provincial court: Based on English law, this high court heard appeals for all types of criminal law cases from lower courts.

provisioner: a person who sold supplies to settlers, etc.

provost marshall: a temporary military prison is called a provost. The person in charge of it is called a provost marshal. He is also in charge of military police.

provostry: the provost's office.

prowor: a priest.

proxenete: an agent, one who brings two people together, e.g. a go-between in a marriage, a spokesman, etc.

proxy: a person allowed by another to act in his behalf.

prunella: a stout, durable cloth which was made of silk but later of wool. It was used for clergymen's robes and later for the uppers of women's shoes.

Prussia: a state which occupied approximately the northern half of Germany.

prvd: proved.

pryowre: 1) the first; 2) the chief.

ps: pieces.

pseudonym: a fictitious name used to disguise the real name of an author.

psoas abcess: an abscess of the loin muscle, usually associated with tuberculosis.

p s d: p = pound, s = shilling, d = pence, which are denominations of English money.

Pt.: 1) point; 2) port; 3) petition.

pt.: a pint, which contains sixteen fluid ounces, or four gills.

ptf.: plaintiff.

pub., publ.: published, publication.

puberty: females who have attained the age of twelve and males who have become fourteen years old are said to have reached the age of puberty.

public: 1) an inn; 2) an alehouse.

publican: 1) in England this person owns or manages a tavern or pub; 2) a collector of taxes in early Rome; 3) any collector of a tax, toll, etc.

Public Domain: land which belonged to the United States in parts of the midwest, south, and west. If it was not reserved for a special purpose as parks or reservations, it could be disposed of by sale, the bounty land system, etc.

public house: 1) an inn, tavern, etc. In England this term usually refers to a place where alcoholic beverages may be used on the premises; 2) a community building for everyone's use; 3) a place for entertainment; 4) an obsolete phrase for a brothel.

public land: see Public Domain.

public vendue: an auction sale.

pucksy: a quagmire.

pudding pie: a piece of meat dipped in batter and baked in a deep dish. It had the properties of both a pudding and a pie.

puddings: intestines.

puder: a misspelling of pewter.

Pueblo Indians: a Southwestern tribe whom the Spanish named for the dwellings built in canyons on the sides of cliffs in which they lived. They now live in Arizona and New Mexico.

puella: girl.

puer: boy.

puerperal: related to childbirth.

puerperar exhaustion: died during childbirth (labor).

puerperium: childbirth.

puerpual fever: childbed fever. Blood poisoning following childbirth. If a woman died shortly after childbirth, it was most often due to this condition.

puffer: a person who attends an auction and by prearrangement bids in order to make the price of an object go higher. Also known as a shill.

puggard: a thief.

pugger: usually a child whose job it was to walk on clay until it was reduced to a smooth, even substance used to make bricks.

puking fever: milk sickness.

pull: to injure or damage a cause.

pullaile: poultry.

pulley pieces: armor for the knees.

pullover: a road along the seashore.

pulpit cuffer: a preacher of fiery sermons.

pulter: 1) the royal officer who was in charge of the poultry; 2) a miner who conveyed coal from hewers.

Pulver Wednesday: Ash Wednesday.

pulvering day: any day when a community assembled to lease rental farmland which belonged to the town.

pump drill: a tool used by a blacksmith.

punch: a tool used by a 1) stone mason; 2) saddler; 3) blacksmith to make holes, decorate the surface of work, remove a pin from a hole, etc.

punch clod: a clodhopper.

puncheon: 1) a cask which held wine or beer; 2) a tool used by a goldsmith, cutler or stone cutter. It was hit on one end by a hammer. The other end shaped the work; 3) a log split in half and placed so that the smooth side faced into a puncheon house. The rough, rounded side was so placed to form part of the exterior wall.

punch plier: a tool used by a bootmaker.

punky: 1) dirty; 2) a chimney sweeper.

punnet: a round fruit basket which was usually shallow.

pupil: in Scotland a girl up to twelve years of age or a boy up to fourteen.

pur.: purveyor.

pur autre vie: for another's lifetime.

purchase: land bought by a colony, person, or government from the American Indians. Used often in place names, but also used in identification of nearby land.

purchased court: a session not on a regular court schedule. The costs of this session were paid for by either the plaintiff or defendant, rather than the government.

pure finders: collectors of dog manure. The alkaline properties of this substance were used to cure leather.

purkey: a variety of wheat.

purn: a tool for holding a vicious horse by the nose while the blacksmith shod him.

purser: the officer on a ship who is in charge of financial matters.

purser's name: an assumed name. An impressed seaman expected to find an opportunity to leave the ship at the earliest possible moment. Therefore, he assumed an alias to avoid detection. He gave this alias to the purser to enter into the ship's books.

pursourver: (Norman) to survey.

pursuer: a plaintiff.

pusayle: 1) a guard; 2) an archer.

putative: reputed, supposed.

putative father: a term used to designate the alleged father of an illegitimate child.

put by: an early nineteenth century phrase which meant that food or some other article that was not needed at the moment had been preserved for use at a later time. Storing in root cellars, pickling, smoking, drying and, later, canning were some of the methods of preserving food.

putrid: decayed or foul.

putrid fever: diphtheria.

putter out: 1) a distribution; 2) one who, when going abroad, deposited money on the condition that he receive a high interest upon his return. It was proportional to the dangers of the journey and his chance of returning to claim it.

pvt.: private.

pymt.: payment.

pyd., pyed.: now this word is usually spelled "pied." It means spotted black and white.

Q: quarto, oversized book. The term is found in bibliographies or on catalogue cards in a library.

q.: 1) farthing; 2) qt. or qts.; 3) a query.

qaly: qualifying.

Q.C.: Queen's Council (which see).

Q.M.: 1) Quartermaster. The army officer in charge of provisions and supplies; 2) Quarterly Meeting (Quakers).

Q.M.D.: Quartermaster's department.

Qm. Sgt.: Quartermaster Sergeant.

qt.: quart.

qtr., qrtr.: quarter.

quacksalver: a cheat or quack.

Quadragesimal: something which lasts for a period of forty days, such as Lent.

Quadragesima Sunday: the first Sunday in Lent and the fortieth day before Good Friday.

quadrangle map: a map published by the United States Geological Survey which shows one particular area of land in detail. It can be ordered from a master map showing a large portion of a state.

quadrant: a device for taking the altitude of stars, moon, etc. above the horizon to determine the latitude and thus aid the navigation of a ship.

quadrel: a brick, tile, or stone used during the late seventeenth century which cut into a square.

quadrille: 1) a card game played by four people which was popular at the beginning of the eighteenth century; 2) a square dance for four couples or the music played for this dance; 3) graph paper.

quadriloge: a work compiled by four authors.

quadrimus: four years old.

quadripartite: participation by four parties.

quadroon: one-fourth black. A child of a mulatto and a white.

quaich, quaigh: a shallow cup which was quite common at one time in Scotland.

quaire: 1) a quire; 2) a pamphlet; 3) a book.

Quaker: a religious group also known as the Society of Friends or Friends.

Quaker calendar: Quakers did not write the name of a month until 1752, but chose to use numbers with March as the first month. January 9th would be written 9th 11th month.

Quaker gray: see hemp.

Quaker gun: an inoperable or dummy gun on a ship or fort. The name comes from Quaker opposition to war.

"Quaker meeting:" any meeting where there is a long period of silence.

Quaker records: Quaker churches kept detailed records of births, marriages, and deaths. Many of these have survived and are kept in church repositories. Some have been published.

quality make: gentry.

Quanhado: an Indian tribe which belonged to the Comanche family.

quar: a stone quarry.

quarier: a wax candle which is a lump of wax with a wick in the center. It is also called quarion and is frequently mentioned in very old inventories.

quarion: see quarier.

quarne: see querne.

quarrier: a worker at a quarry.

quarryman: a craftsman who splits and removes stone from the ground. He may also form it into rough or finished shapes.

quart: three pounds of butter.

quartage: 1) housing for military personnel or payment in lieu of such housing; 2) a tax, pension, salary, etc. paid four times per year; 3) an Irish land measure.

quarter: 1) literally means one-fourth of a ship, but more commonly means the portion behind the beam (the widest portion of the ship); 2) one quarter of anything; 3) a measure of grain.

quarter eagle: a gold coin which had an eagle on one side, as did the ten dollar gold eagle coin. The quarter eagle was worth a quarter of ten dollars or two and one-half dollars.

quarterer: a lodger.

Quarterly Court: a petty court on the county level which meets in some states every three months, e.g. Kentucky.

Quarterly Meeting: a Quaker high-ranking business meeting which occurs every two or three months and includes matters pertaining to several monthly meetings.

quartermaster: the officer in charge of issuing clothing, food, etc. He assigns housing and when the troops are in the field, he marks out a camp area.

quartern: a quarter of a standard weight: pound, ounce, etc.

quarters: house(s), apartment(s), or other living arrangements for military officers and men, single or married, on land or aboard ship.

quarter section: one-fourth of a section of land: 160 acres.

Quarter Sessions: an English court which served a county and met four times a year to consider minor criminal cases. See courts of pleas and quarter sessions.

quartle: one-quarter of something.

Quarto: a large book too tall for most library shelves. They will be found in a special section and will be so marked in the card catalogue.

quash: to annul, abate, or put an end to.

quaste: 1) quashed; 2) smashed.

quatrusze: (Norman) fourteen.

quattezime joar: (Norman) fourth day.

que: a cow.

Queens of England: See Kings and Queens of England.

Queen Anne's War: fought in 1701 and 1714, this was the American counterpart of the war of the Spanish Succession. The main war was fought simultaneously in Europe. It took place mostly in the West Indies, in New England, and on the Carolina coast. The New York border did not suffer attack because of an alliance with the French and Iroquois Indians. Peace negotiations began in 1711 in Europe, resulting in an armistice in America in October 1712. All those who fought were volunteers.

Queen's Attorney: see King's Attorney.

Queen's or King's Counsel: barristers can earn the title of Queen's Counsel which confers certain privileges and may lead to a judgeship.

queer customers: vagrants, tramps, recluses, fugitives, eccentrics, prostitutes, self-appointed street preachers, gamblers, con-men, etc., all of whom were itinerants.

querele: a complaint.

querestar: a chorister.

querne, quarne, quern: the simplest of hand mills. Made of stone about three inches thick, set in a wooden frame which turned against another stone set underneath it. The top stone was turned by hand with a stick put into a hole which had been chipped in the stone.

querrour: a quarry worker.

quest: an inquest.

questant: a candidate or a person who is seeking something.

quest house: a building, which usually adjoined a church, where inquiries into wrongdoings were held.

questman: those who were chosen annually according to the custom of a parish to assist the church wardens in an inquiry, and who also presented the offenders to the church court for punishment.

questmonger: a juryman.

quetoure: a swelling, a scab.

quick march: three and three-fourths miles per hour or one hundred and ten paces (275) feet per minute.

quick step: see quick march.

quickstocke: livestock.

quid pro quo: "what for what." Consideration, as in money paid for land.

quietus: a final settlement of an obligation, court order, or debt.

quilting party: sometimes called a quilting bee, this usually was an all-day gathering of ladies to tie a comforter, or quilt a bed cover. Luncheon was served, gossip exchanged, and work finished painlessly.

quilts: patchwork quilts were a necessity because they conserved small pieces of cloth and they were valuable enough to mention in wills. However, quilting originated in China, where even now quilted uniforms are worn by the Chinese.

quine: whence.

quinine: a bitter medicine used to treat malaria, fevers, etc. It was introduced to Europe from Peru in the seventeenth century.

Quinquagesima: the Sunday before Lent begins; also called Shrove Sunday.

quinsy: acute tonsillitis.

quint: a coin which was not accepted by Congress in 1783. It was to have been made of silver and would have been worth about thirty-five cents.

quire: 1) twenty-four sheets of paper which are the same size; 2) a section of leaves in a book; 3) an old word for a choir.

quire bird: one who has recently come out of prison and seeks a place to live, work, etc.

qui tam: "who as well." A case brought into court whereby an informer can sue another for the state at the same time he sues for himself. The penalty assessed is split between the informer and the state.

quit claim: free from claim.

quit claim deed: a document transferring the interest a seller had in a property. It does not guarantee that the seller was the sole owner.

quite: 1) free; 2) acquit; 3) pay off.

quiteclamaunce: (Norman) a release.

quite claym: free from claim.

quit rent: an early type of property tax which was assessed by the Crown. The governor of each colony was responsible for distribution the funds which were collected by the sheriff of each county. It could be paid either in cash or in tobacco. The use of quit rent was abolished during the Revolutionary War.

quo: 1) at or to what place; 2) how far? to what end?; 3) because; 4) whereby.

quod vide: which see; see reference.

quorum: the legal number of persons which is necessary to conduct the business of a group.

q.v.: see quod vide.

R

R: 1) Range, in a legal description of land; 2) Rabbi; 3) River; 4) Road; 5) on a Revolutionary War pension jacket, R means "rejected."

r.: removed.

R.A.: Rear Admiral.

rabbate: to abate.

racking torture: agonizing.

rackrent: an exorbitant rent.

racks: the sides of a wagon.

rack up: to supply horses with their food for the night.

rack yard: the farmyard where animals are kept. So called from the racks kept there.

radegunde: a sort of a boil.

radknight: in early England this man,in lieu of rent, paid his landlord by riding horseback while performing his duties.

raft: the first of large scale river craft. It could be large enough to load a Conestoga wagon which was about sixteen feet long and six to seven feet wide and also carry food, seed for planting at the destination, the animals from horses to chickens. Literally the whole equipment for a farm.

raglar: an officer in South Wales who collected fines, etc.

ragman: a person whose business is to collect old cloth or clothes for sale.

ragman's roll: 1) a Scottish collection of documents in which nobles state that they are loyal to Edward I, King of England; 2) an obsolete word for a long list, catalogue, etc.

rag picker: a person who makes money by picking up trash of many types from city streets for his livelihood.

raid: a quick and rapid movement by or against hostile troops primarily to obtain information by capturing prisoners.

rail fence: poles cut from straight trees, laid in a zig-zag pattern to form a barrier to keep cattle in or out. Sometimes called a Virginia fence.

rail splitter: a person who split logs into rails or smaller pieces with which fences could be built.

"rains:" a reckoning of time based on one rainy season each year. This term was used by Africans as "moons" was used by Indians.

raising: in pioneer days neighbors would gather together on a specified day to build, or raise, a barn. It might not be completely finished, but it would be capable of providing shelter for animals and their provisions. The women gathered together at the site and provided food for the workers. In a sense, it became a social gathering and party.

rake: 1) a large-tined tool used on a farm to gather grass, hay, etc. for storage; 2) gunfire along a row of troops, etc.; 3) an incline, either vertical or horizontal.

rake maker: a person who makes wooden rakes usually of ash which makes a very smooth handle. The tines are made of willow as a rule.

raker: a person who raked and removed filth from the streets, generally called "Jack Raker."

ram: a male sheep.

rambooze: an early drink made of wine, ale, sugar and eggs.

ramel: rubbish, especially bricklayer's rubbish or stony fragments.

rampart: an embankment which serves as a defense against attack.

randy beggar: a tinker.

Range: townships in a line or tier running from north to south. In a legal description a capital R is used as the abbreviation for Range.

rangers: 1) in Colonial America a special troop of men under the British was used to guard frontiers against Indian attacks. During the Revolution some of these men continued to work on the frontiers; others sided with the British; 2) an elite group of World War II soldiers skilled in raids and attacks on special targets, even those behind enemy lines; 2) state police in Texas; 3) in England this person is a park superintendent; 4) a general term in this country applied to park officers.

rangs: rangers.

rank: 1) any number of men side by side in a line; 2) a step or degree on a graduated scale of authority.

rank and file: all soldiers below the rank of sergeant.

rape: 1) an old term which means to capture and forcibly remove; 2) to plunder or abuse an area; 3) a plant which belonged to the mustard family which was used as animal feed; 4) pulp, seeds, peel, etc. after the juice was extracted. This residue was used as a filter when making vinegar.

raper: a ropemaker.

raser: a variation in spelling of raze; a person who tore down buildings.

raser house: a barber's shop.

rash: a smoothly woven cloth which when made of silk was called silk rash. If it were made of wool it was referred to as cloth rash.

rasp: a tool used by a 1) farrier; 2) carpenter.

rat.: rated.

ratables: 1) persons eligible to have their property assessed and to be taxed for this property, real or personal; 2) in the settling of an estate this has the sense of being proportionate, e.g. a ratable distribution of John Wood's estate.

rate: 1) an enlisted man's rank in the navy; 2) the class to which a ship belongs.

rate books: a collection of assessors' lists of property upon which an owner owed taxes.

rated commodities: goods whose value was set by law for exchange purposes in lieu of money.

rate list: this list usually contains a person's name, the amount and value of his property, plus time, e.g. 140 acres rated @ 2p 2s 10d. An actual assessment list, if it can be found, will give more detailed information.

ratepayer: taxpayer.

rates: taxes.

ratine: a fabric which is woven from a nubby yarn in a loose honeycomb weave popular during the Civil War. Sometimes called sponge cloth.

rating: see ratteen.

ratoner: a rat catcher.

rats bane: white arsenic, a rat poison.

ratten: to destroy or take away a workman's tools, or otherwise keep him from working, for not paying his natty to the fund, or for having offended the trade union in any matter.

ratteen: an obsolete spelling for ratine (which see).
rattle, rattles: a gurgling sound heard from the throat area.
ravener: a plunderer.
R.C.: Roman Catholic.
rcdr.: recorder.
rcpt.: receipt.
RD.: release of dower rights.
Rd.: Road.
re: a reference to something. Many times this term is used in listing an adoptions in county court minutes. Hunt for adoptions in the "I" section of an index, rather than in the "A" section as it may be listed "In re John Ancestor."
read out of meeting: when a Quaker performed an act in a manner disapproved by his church, he was disowned or read out of meeting.
real: 1) applies to land, buildings, etc. as opposed to personal property; 2) an old Spanish coin of silver used in the early United States. It took eight reals to make one dollar, hence the phrase "pieces of eight." Sometimes called a milled dollar.
real daughter (D.A.R.): a woman whose father gave service in some capacity during the Revolutionary War.
real estate: 1) land, with or without buildings; 2) real property; 3) in a few southern states slaves fell into this category rather than being classed as chattel.
real property: land, real estate. Real property may not be disposed of by will unless the person making the will is twenty-one or older. See also real estate.
realms: see dominion.
reals: see bits.
realty: relating to land and buildings. Sometimes called fast estate.
ream: a quantity of paper which originally was twenty quires (480 sheets). Today, it is five hundred sheets.
reamer: a tool to increase the size of a hole.
reap: 1) a bundle of corn; 2) to harvest.
reap hook: a farmer's tool used in harvesting grain; a sickle.
reappd.: reappointed.
rebel: 1) a person who supported the South during the Civil War; 2) a name given in the plural form to the Southern Confederacy.
rec.: 1) record; 2) receive or received; 3) recorded.
recd., reced.: received.
receipt: a written statement which acknowledges that property has been received by the writer.
received on certificate form: in the Quaker records when a certificate of membership has no state following the name of the monthly meeting who issued the certificate, it is presumed the state of both monthly meetings mentioned is the same.
received on letter from: in the Society of Friends (Quaker) church letters of membership from most Protestant churches were received by the church.
receiver: 1) a court appointed manager of a business which is bankrupt; 2) the person who has been appointed to collect money; 3) a person who is in charge of caring for the property of others.
receivership: the state of property being in the custody of a receiver (which see).
recess: 1) a public place where one can buy food and eat it on the premises; 2) a period of time during which normal activity ceases.
recidivist: an habitual criminal.
recital: a general term used most frequently in deeds to describe the reason that a contract is being drawn. Most of the time this is a straight business deal, however the "recital" may indicate a relationship between the parties involved or a relationship with a previous owner.
recognitors: a jury.
recognizance: 1) a promise made to a court official in which a person says he will do a particular thing; 2) the sum of money which a person will give to the court; 3) an old meaning is a token, badge or pledge.
reconnaissance: a movement by personnel in uniform to obtain information of military value in an area. Observation does not require movement.
reconstruction: 1) rebuilding; 2) reestablishment.
Reconstruction: the period of time at the end of the Civil War when the South

rebuilt.

reconveyance: a deed in which real estate which has been sold to another person is transferred to the original owner.

record: 1) recorded; 2) to witness; 3) testimony.

recorded: in Quaker records it was noted when a member appeared to have the gift of the ministry or to become a minister within that denomination.

recorder: 1) an official of county government whose duties are concerned with caring for land records; 2) a person in a mining camp who keeps a record of each person's rights to hunt for valuable ore in a specific area; 3) a wooden musical instrument.

record keeper: 1) notary public; 2) secretary; 3) recorder, sometimes registrar; 4) town clerk.

Recorder's Release: in county deed books where mortgages are recorded, releases (mortgage paid) are also recorded, usually following or with the mortgage. Sometimes, however, releases were not noted. At a much later date (more than twenty years) the mortgage was released by a notation called a "Recorder's Release."

recpts.: receipts.

recruit: to reinforce an army or military unit when men or supplies are suddenly needed. New men in the service are sometimes called "raw recruits."

rectangular survey system: a method of surveying in which territories were divided into numbered townships, each six miles square. Each township was further divided into thirty-six sections. Then land descriptions could be broken down into northwest 1/4 of Section 2, or further "the south 1/2 of the northwest 1/4 of Section 2" and, therefore, provide an accurate location. The land description in its entirety will read, for example: S1/2 NW1/4 S2 T8N R VIII east of the third Principal Meridian. When a person uses this description he should locate the land by reading the description from the end back to the beginning.

rector: 1) a minister; 2) a school headmaster.

recureless: irrecoverable.

recusant: 1) a person who refuses to conform; 2) a person of another faith who refuses to attend services in the Church of England.

redar: 1) a person who advises or explains; 2) a thatcher.

redback: a certificate printed on red paper and issued by Texas at the time that it was an independent republic (ca. 1834). Texas was unable to pay interest on these certificates and soon they were worthless.

redcoats: the slang term used during the Revolutionary War for British soldiers because they wore red uniforms.

redemption: 1) to be rescued from something; 2) to buy something again; 3) to regain an item which was offered as a pledge by paying in full for it; 4) to turn paper money into coins.

redemptioner: a person who, of his own free will, bound himself as a servant for an agreed number of years. For this servitude he received his passage to America.

red lattice: an ale house, so called from its red lattice work instead of windows.

redoubt: 1) a reinforcement wall built within a fort; 2) a wall built as protection.

redubbors: those who buy stolen cloth and disguise it by dyeing it a different color.

reduce: 1) annul; 2) set aside legally.

reed billy: a bundle of reed.

reedholder: a thatcher's bow fastened to the roof to hold the straw.

reef: an itch or eruptive disorder.

Rees: see Rickarees Indians.

reeve: 1) a person who was responsible for enforcing local laws in English and American towns, e.g. making certain that hogs were properly marked with their owner's brand and that they had rings in their noses to prevent their doing damage to the ground; 2) an officer of an English manor; 3) an agent of the king during the Anglo-Saxon era.

ref.: reference.

refectory: a restaurant.

referee: a court officer who takes testimony in a case, investigates it and reports this testimony to the court. He does not make a ruling in the case.

refers: reference.

refiner of pewter: the person who melted and mixed tin and lead to make the alloy called pewter.

reflectory: a restaurant.

reformado: a disbanded soldier; anyone whose company was closed down.

reft: a robbery.

refugee: 1) a person loyal to Britain during the Revolutionary War who sought protection in territory controlled by British forces; 2) a person from Canada or Nova Scotia who aided the Americans in the Revolutionary War; 3) a person who left one side to help or seek protection from the other side during the Civil War; 4) used to describe land set aside in the United States for the British who preferred to stay in this country after the Revolutionary War.

Refugee Tract —1798: this area consists of parts of now Franklin, Licking, Fairfield, and Perry Counties in Ohio, set aside for Canadians who had helped the United States during the Revolutionary War and who had been forced to leave their homes because of this aid. The acreage not claimed was later sold at not less than $2.00 per acre to the highest bidder at the Chillicothe Land Office.

reg.: register.

regd.: registered.

regent: 1) the person who has been appointed to the position of ruling a monarchy when the King or Queen is not present or is too young to assume his or her responsibilities; 2) a member of a board which governs an institution, e.g. a state.

regiment: this is the largest permanent group of soldiers which is commanded by officers who serve continually.

register: 1) the list of officers which includes their rank, date of commission, etc.; 2) a large, heavy book in which public records are officially entered by the officer in charge; 3) a duly authorized official who is charged with keeping official records, e.g. the register of deeds; 4) a book of church records.

register of mesne conveyance: in some states this is the office in the courthouse where land records are housed.

register of voters: this list of voters contains the name and address of each voter, plus the state or country where he was born. If he is a naturalized citizen the time and place of his naturalization is listed.

register of wills: some large cities have this office in which estates are settled.

registers of actions: see docket books.

registrar: an official record keeper of deeds, of college student records, etc.

registry: a place for depositing wills, deeds, etc.

regnal: this term refers to years of a sovereign's reign.

regt.: regiment.

regtl.: regimental.

regular preacher: a salaried minister who was present to conduct church business and church services on a regular basis, as opposed to a circuit rider minister who came only once every four to six weeks.

regulars: 1) professional soldiers who are permanently in the army as opposed to militia who are in volunteer groups. The United States regular army began in 1789; 2) men who did hauling on a regular basis as opposed to short-term, light load, part-time haulers.

regulator: 1) a surveyor who helped plat the town of Philadelphia; 2) a member of a volunteer organization which pretended to keep order, but in reality performed illegal or violent acts; 3) a group of average backwoods citizens who resented deeply the oppressive, tyrannical and mercenary representative of the Carolinas government. They formed an association to vote the corrupt officials out of office and to try to reform local government. This attempt failed, but it proved a decade before the Declaration of Independence that those unschooled frontiersmen were capable of armed resistance and this was proved again during the Revolution; 4) a secret organization of law-abiding citizens who banded together in the early nineteenth century to combat lawlessness. As time went on they, too, committed lawless acts until in Illinois they were made to realize that these acts would not be tolerated by the state government and both the Regulators and the Flathead organizations died out.

reinstated in membership: in Quaker records this phrase indicates that after a member was disowned he could be reinstated by condemning his misconduct.

reinstd: reinstated.

rejoinder: the statement in which a defendant makes a reply to the plaintiff's statement, and vice versa. In other words, one side of a type of conversation in a courtroom.

reinstd.: reinstated.

reister: a German horse soldier.

rel.: 1) relative; 2) released (found in Quaker church records); 3) religion.

relay station: a designated place on a stage coach or mail route where tired horses were changed for fresh ones, and mail was both picked up and left.

reld.: relieved (of duty).

release: 1) a relinquishment of some right or claim by one person in favor of another; 2) see also discharge.

release of dower: see dower release.

release of lien: when a debt which has had a lien placed on it is satisfied, the person who holds the lien then files a statement that the lien has been paid.

release of mortgage: see mortgage release.

relebe: a fine paid by a tenant at his admission to a copyhold.

relevainthes: the revenue obtained from fines, etc. paid by a tenant on the death of his ancestor.

relict: from the Latin relicta, left. 1) a widow; 2) see also consort.

relicta: widow.

relictus: widower.

relief: 1) a fine paid to a feudal lord for a tenant's entering upon the estate which was lapsed by the death of the tenant's ancestor; 2) change of watch duty; 3) fresh troops to replace tired troops.

relief book: a replacement book of deeds. This would occur if a courthouse burned, then landowners would bring their deeds to the authorities who would re-record the deeds.

relinquish dower: a woman could give up her rights to inherit a portion of her deceased husband's estate by joining her husband in a conveyance of his lands or by accepting a legacy in lieu of a dower, or by assenting to a provision by way of jointure.

relinquishment: to abandon, give something up, surrender a thing, waive a right, etc.

relocation: when a survey for a warrant is in conflict with an earlier survey, the warrant holder could ask that another survey be made.

rem: removed.

remainder man: the person who receives what is left of an estate after all debts and inheritances have been paid.

remand: to send back, e.g. to send back a case to the court from which it came to be acted upon there or to send back a prisoner to jail after a preliminary hearing until the trial starts or the hearing is resumed.

remitter: 1) this word is used to describe a case where a person has a valid title to an estate and also has a defective title to the same estate. He owns the estate under the first and good title; 2) to restore a previous claim or right; 3) to put a case into another court for further action.

remitting fever: malaria; a fever which keeps recurring.

removal: 1) to change a job, a residence, etc.; 2) to be dismissed or put out; 3) to kill.

removal order: an official document prepared by overseers of the poor to require a person or persons to go back to the settlement from which they had come.

removed: a person's or family's change of residence from one place to another. Used interchangeably with moved.

ren.: renunciation.

renegade: 1) in the military sense a turncoat, deserter or one who joins the enemy forces; 2) a person who does not obey the laws of his area or country.

renounce: 1) to give up or abandon, as in giving up citizenship in a former country and acquiring citizenship in another country; 2) a court document created when an executor named in a will did not wish to be responsible for the estate settlement and so stated. Sometimes a reason is given, e.g. "too far away," which is a clue to family migration. If a widow renounces administration she may name her successor and give the relationship, e.g. if this would be her father, a maiden name is revealed.

rent: 1) a payment to an owner for the use of a house, land, equipment, etc.; 2) an old word for income.

rent rolls: a list of persons in an area who rented land.

renunciation: a refusal to execute or administer an estate. Sometimes called a disclaimer.

repayre: a carrier of sea fish.

repeater: 1) a person who tries to vote more than one time in an election; 2) a gun which fires several shots without needing to be reloaded; 3) communications by using signals; 4) anything or anyone who repeats something.

repl.: replacement.

replevin: a legal action taken to regain possession of specific personal property alleged to have been unlawfully taken.

replication: an answer or response. See rejoinder.

rep: a ribbed or corded cloth sometimes used as an upholstery fabric.

rep.: 1) report; 2) representative; 3) reprint; 4) reprinted.

report or reported: in Quaker records when a member was reported to the monthly meeting or was complained of for acting in a manner contrary to church rules, a committee was appointed to confer with him. Later, the committee reported to the monthly meeting with a recommendation for retaining or dismissing the person. Sometimes the abbreviation inf (informed) was used instead of report.

reported records: statements that are found in printed genealogies, histories, etc., but have no sources cited.

Republican calendar: a French Republic change in the calendar which was in use for a period of about ten years. It was used not only in France, but in French-occupied countries.

requiescat in pace: "rest in peace."

requisition: the official request, or demand, for supplies, etc.

res: a thing, things.

res.: 1) residence; 2) resides.

resd.: resigned.

research: the process used to hunt an ancestor or solve a problem.

reservation: 1) land which has been set aside by the Federal government for the sole use of an American Indian tribe. Indians residing on this land are generally referred to as Reservation Indians; 2) land set aside for a special purpose such as bounty land or school land.

reset: to receive stolen property knowingly.

resians: inhabitants, residents.

residium: see residue.

residuary clause: a statement in a will which mentions "all the rest and residue" of my property.

residuary devisee: see residuary legatee.

residuary estate: all property which has not been bequeathed to others at the time a will has been written. This is called a "residuary clause." See also after-acquired property.

residuary legatee: a person who receives an inheritance of an estate's residue or remainder. The phrase often used in a will is: "the remainder I give to ..."

residue: 1) what is left after part has been removed or disposed of; 2) the part of an estate which is left after all debts, bequests, etc. have been paid.

residuum: see residue.

respondent: the person called upon to answer an appeal. For example, if a defendant appeals a decision of a lower court to a higher court, the original plaintiff (the person bringing the suit) becomes the respondent in the higher or appellate court.

rest a case: to stop, without a judge's order to do so, introduction of any more evidence.

restar: a person who arrests others.

restraining order: see injunction.

restraint on alienation: in feudal England land could not be sold; it was passed on by inheritance and this restriction was called "restraint on alienation," which restraint later became illegal.

resurvey: another survey made to redetermine land boundaries.

ret: found in Quaker records, this abbreviation means retained or returned.

ret., retd.: retired.

reten: 1) garrison; 2) followers.

reticule: a lady's net or string purse. At a later time it was made of fabric.

retour: the verdict of a jury.

retting hemp: hemp was left in the field where rain, dew and freezing weather caused the stems to ret (rot) and therefore soften. Then the hemp could be easily broken and made ready for shipment.

return(s): 1) a report of a unit which gives the officers' names and gives data about others who have been assigned to the unit; 2) a document sent to Congress listing officers and a tabulation only of enlisted personnel. These were carefully kept to ensure that the army did not grow too large and perhaps make an attempt to overthrow the government; 3) bring or send back. A court officer, such as a sheriff, brings back to a court an account of delivering or failing to deliver a notice or other paper; 4) in England this term means the election of a Member of Parliament.

Rev.: 1) Reverend; 2) revolution; 3) revised.

reve, reeve: a bailiff.

revenuer: a term used by producers of illegal whiskey to describe a federal officer charged with enforcing the laws against distilling untaxed liquor.

revenue stamp: a stamp affixed to a document which showed that a tax due was paid.

reverse index: the index which lists the names of persons other than the main names in a court's book of documents.

reversion: 1) to return an estate to the person that gave it (or his heirs) after a contract for use of the estate has elapsed; 2) an old word for what is left after a meal.

revestiary: a vestibule or room in a church where the priest put on the sacred garments. Hence the term vestry.

reville: a bugle call signalling all men to arise.

revival: a number of evangelistic meetings held on consecutive days for the purpose of creating religious enthusiasm. These were often treated as social events, with people coming from miles away. There were also rivalries as between the "forty-gallon" Baptists and the "sprinkle-wrinkle" Methodists. Both of these titles were derived from the method of baptism, with Baptists believing in immersion (streams were often used) and the Methodists believing in a sprinkling on of waters. See also camp meetings.

revocation: 1) to recall or withdraw; 2) to make void, e.g. draw up a new will which voids a previous will.

revolution: a change in the government of a country which is done quickly by force.

Rev. War: Revolutionary War.

Revolutionary War: fought from 1775 to 1783, this was the first time in Colonial history when all men, young and old, were called to serve in the armed forces. Beginning after the end of the French and Indian War in 1763, the opposition to Britain's Colonial policies grew until thirteen of the twenty-two British Colonies revolted and won independence. Until October 1777 the bulk of the fighting was in the North; after that most of it was in the South.

rewars: (Norman) governors.

Rex: king.

reys: (Norman) kings.

rhine: (Norman) queen.

Rhynland duim: a Dutch measure of 1.03 inches.

Rhynland morgen: a Dutch square measure of 2.103 acres.

Rhynland rode: when the word rod was used in Dutch records it was always the Rhynland rod, consisting of twelve Rhynland feet.

Rhynland voet: a Dutch measure which equalled 12.36 inches and was used for long measurements, such as land.

rial: an English gold coin.

rialle: 1) royalty; 2) good conduct.

ribbed road: see corduroy road.

ribbon cane syrup: a fine quality cane

syrup which contained sucrose and was made in Louisiana and Georgia sugar houses as their choicest product.

Rickarees Indians: also called Arickarees or Rees, these Indians were of Pawnee ancestry and lived near the upper Missouri River.

rick cloth: a large canvas sheet put over an unfinished stack.

rickets: 1) body deformities caused by malnutrition in childhood; 2) also a blight in corn.

riddle: a large, coarse sieve.

riddler: a dealer in wool.

ride: a saddle horse.

rideable: passable with horses.

ridge tile fork: a tool used by a brick maker.

riding: Yorkshire, England has three administrative districts: North, East, and West Riding. Riding can refer to any of these three or a comparable division elsewhere.

riding chair: a one-horse vehicle of light weight, similar to a gig.

riding the fair: the steward of a court baron attended by the tenants of the baron would ride through a town, proclaiming a fair was to be held on a certain date in a particular town.

reiz: (Norman) nets.

riflemen: light infantry men who were expert marksmen.

riflowr: 1) robber; 2) plunderer.

rigadoon: a lively dance which was popular during the seventeenth century. The music or rhythm for this dance was also named "rigadoon."

rigger: a person who installed, adjusted and dismantled ropes which braced or moved parts of a ship.

rigging: the ropes (or chains) which support the masts and arrange the sails of a sailing vessel.

right of dower: see dower.

right of election: see dissent.

right of presentation: a patronage right which belonged to those who either built or endowed parish churches.

right of survivorship: if two or more people own property jointly and one lives longer than the other(s), he receives the entire estate by being the surviving member of the joint ownership.

right stripe: underworld slang meaning one who is willing to commit a crime. A criminal comrade.

rigor: 1) a sudden cold chill accompanied by fever and muscle stiffness; 2) hardship; 3) stiffness.

rijksdaelder: a Dutch coin worth two and one-half guldens.

rill: see drill.

ring finger: so called because commonly a ring is worn upon it, especially the left hand. It is said that from the ring finger there is a sinew so small and tender that it reaches the heart, therefore it ought to wear a ring as a crown for its dignity. In old time marriage ceremonies, the wedding ring was placed first on the thumb, then removed and placed on each finger until the third finger was reached and this is where the ring stayed.

ringle: 1) a metal ring for a pig's nose to keep it from tearing up the soil; 2) a metal ring used in horses' harnesses; 3) a ring used to pull a door knocker.

ringleader: the person who opens a ball.

R.I.P.: requiescat in pace, rest in peace.

riparian right: when a person owns land on a river or lake bank (riparian property), the use of water for fishing, irrigation, etc. is his.

ripe men: reapers.

ripier: a robber.

ripper: a tool used by a slater.

rippier: a person who transports fish inland to market it.

riprap: a protection constructed of carefully placed loose rock to prevent soil erosion on the banks of a body of water.

rithe: a small stream which appears during a heavy rain.

rivermen: a general term used to refer to unlicensed employees on a boat.

river workers: as itinerants worked at many occupations they walked around the country, some took to rive travel, and all supported themselves by their trade: grist millers, blacksmiths, entertainers, traders, etc. This was true along the ocean shore also where there were hucksters or peddlers of the sea.

R.L.D.S.: Reorganized Church of Jesus

Christ of Latter-day Saints. See Mormon.

road agent: 1) a robber of stage coaches; 2) a New England term for a surveyor.

road commissioner: see commissioner of roads.

Road or Turnpike Lands—1827-28: three percent of land proceeds after 1802 was allotted to build roads to the east coast. This was the beginning of a highway system of which the National Road (Road 40) is a part.

road overseer: see overseer of the road.

roadster: 1) a wanderer, at times not entirely honest; 2) a buggy suitable for travel; 3) a horse fitted for the road.

robe: dressed animal skins which were sewed together and used as a blanket or a rug.

roberdsmen: a gang of lawless vagabonds in the fourteenth century.

rocf: see received on certificate form.

rock salt: halite. Rock-like lump of salt.

Rocky Mountain spotted fever: a serious disease accompanied by fever. It is contracted by humans from the bite of a tick and is non-contagious.

rod: a lineal measurement of land which equals sixteen and one-half feet or five and one-half yards. See also Rhynland rode.

rode: 1) a company of horsemen; 2) a harbor of ships.

rodman: 1) a surveyor's assistant; 2) see chockerman.

roede: a linear measure used in western Germany which equaled 12 voeten. The Dutch linear measure of the same name equaled 13 voeten. The plural of roede is roeden.

rogation: 1) an obsolete word for a formal request; 2) a begging for charity.

rogation days: the three days before Ascension Day (which see). The week in which Ascension Day falls is referred to as rogation week.

Rogation Sunday: the fifth Sunday after Easter or the Sunday before Ascension Day.

rogue money: a tax paid by a county. These funds are used to apprehend, prosecute, and maintain criminals in jail.

rolf: see received on letter from.

rollar: a tool used by a brick maker.

rolling road: a roadway, usually in the south, made by the rolling or pulling with oxen of casks filled with tobacco to a waterway for shipping.

roll paper: wallpaper.

rolls: a list or lists of people's names. The name probably came from documents which could be rolled to form a cylinder.

rollster: see roster.

Rom.: Roman.

romage: 1) to set a ship in order; 2) to clear the hold of goods; 3) to remove things in the ship from one place to another.

romal: a square of silk or cotton which sometimes had a pattern. Sometimes they were called handkerchiefs. There were three types: silk romals, cotton romals, and romals garrub.

Roman numerals: a number system used regularly in Roman times, and still used occasionally. Symbols may be written in either capital or lower case letters.

I= 1	V= 5	VIIII= 9
II= 2	VI= 6	IX= 9
III= 3	VII= 7	X= 10
IV= 4	VIII= 8	XI= 11
XII= 12	XIIII= 13	XXV= 25
XIII= 13	XIX= 19	XXVI= 26
XIV= 14	XX= 20	XXVII= 27
XV= 15	XXI= 21	XXVIII= 28
XVI= 16	XXII= 22	XXVIIII= 29
XVII= 17	XXIII= 23	XXIX= 29
XIII= 18	XXIV= 24	XXX= 30

XXXI = 31 (continue with the 30s as with the 20s). XL or XXXX = 40 (XL is more commonly used). Continue with the 40s as with the 20s.

L = 50 (for remainder, use symbol for larger number first, followed by I, II, III, IV, etc.).

LX = 60; LXX = 70; LXXX or XXC = 80; LXXXX or XC = 90 (LXXX and LXXXX are more commonly used).

C = 100; CI = 101 (continue as before). CXI = 111; CXXI = 121; CXXXI = 131 etc. CL = 150; CC = 200; CCC = 300; CD or CCCC = 400.

D = 500; DC = 600; DCC = 700; DCCC = 800; DCCCC or CM = 900.

M = 1000; MC = 1100; MDCCVI4 =

1706; MDCCCXC = 1890; MXM = 1990.

When a symbol or group of symbols for a smaller number precedes a symbol for a larger number, the smaller symbol(s) is subtracted from the larger. When a symbol for a larger number precedes a symbol for a smaller number, the numbers are added. Use the smallest number of symbols possible.

romney: a sheep bred in England which has long, coarse wool.

rood: 1) a measure of length, which varied from state to state, five and one-half to eight yards. This term is sometimes used to describe an area up to one-fourth of an acre; 2) a crucifix, a cross; 3) a measure for timber; 4) a measure for wine.

room: see in room of.

roomer: a person who lives in another's house but seldom, if ever, eats his meals there.

rooming house: 1) a place where persons may rent a room in which to sleep on a daily, weekly or monthly basis. They obtain their meals elsewhere. It is not a hotel but a private home operated by a person who lives there; cf. boarding house; 2) a heated building near a church in New England where a half-frozen congregation could warm up following a long morning service in an unheated church building. The churches were unheated because fuel was expensive, and because they sometimes they also served as a storage place for gunpowder which could be ignited by sparks. The instructional sermon could easily last as long as two hours. Also called a Sabbaday house.

root doctor: one who practiced medicine seriously and used parts of plants to cure his patients of any number of ailments.

rope bed (corded bed): a rope was tightly stretched back and forth through holes drilled in the bed frame, or around wooden knobs to substitute for springs.

roper: 1) a rope maker (sometimes spelled raper); 2) a crafty fellow; 3) a rogue.

roper: a maker of rope.

rope ripe: fit for hanging, a phrase applied to anyone very wicked.

ropery: the place where rope is made.

rope walk, rope yard: a factory building with a long passage along which a worker walks while making rope, laying strands in a prescribed pattern.

rope yarn Sunday: a navy term for the time allotted for the repair of clothing and other personal items.

roquelaure: a man's knee-length cloak.

rose cold: hay fever believed to be caused by pollen from roses.

rose noble: a gold coin stamped with a rose.

roseola: or rose rash, a mild childhood disease characterized by three days of fever, followed by an outbreak of rose-colored spots.

rose ryal: a gold coin.

rosin: the by-product or residue after turpentine has been made from a pine tree. Rosin was used in early days in combination with tar and yellow wax to form "poor man's plaster."

rosin end: a shoemaker's thread.

roster, rollster: the list of officers who are fit for duty in order of seniority.

rot: a body of six soldiers.

rother: 1) the rudder of a ship; 2) a sailor.

roudge: a rough, coarse cloth.

rough-hewn: 1) a person who is not refined; 2) an unfinished board.

rough rider: 1) in the British cavalry this man was a non-commissioned officer whose job was to train horses or to make an unruly horse behave; 2) the same term was used in this country as early as the Civil War; 3) the name given to Theodore Roosevelt's volunteer cavalry regiment raised from among cowboys and western law enforcement officers to fight in the Spanish-American War; 4) one who breaks in horses.

rough settler: a mason who only did rough coarse work, as well as walls, etc.

rounder: 1) a cowboy whose job is to drive cattle into a group so that they may travel or receive specialized care; 2) a boring tool; 3) a Methodist minister; 4) an English game similar to baseball; 5) a tower which is round in shape; 6) an officer who makes the round of posted sentinels.

Roundhead: a contemptuous term for member of the English Parliament during the seventeenth century, so called because they had their hair cut in a shorter style than their colleagues, the Cavaliers.

roundhouse: a round building where train engines are repaired or stored. Inside the building is a turntable which can bear a locomotive and can be turned to provide access to any one of many tracks radiating from the center of the building.

rounding knife: a tool used by a 1) tanner; 2) currier.

round nosed pliers: a tool used by a blacksmith.

round shave: a tool used by a 1) beasom maker; 2) cooper.

round tilth: sowing land continuously without allowing time for it to lie fallow.

rounge: a wheelbarrow.

roup: an auction.

rout: 1) a disorderly, overwhelming, disastrous defeat; 2) a grassy yard used to hold stray animals.

routed: if an animal strays and is impounded it remains, when unclaimed, three days and nights in the pound or penfold. Then it is taken to a rout until the owner can be found. It is not unusual to see ads in small English papers beginning: "routed at ______ two pigs, etc."

rover: 1) an archer; 2) an old word for a pirate ship.

rowell: anything circular.

Royal Highlanders: a fraternal organization begun in 1896 by a hardware dealer, W. E. Sharp of Aurora, Nebraska, to preserve Scottish history. Now the organization has been changed from a fraternal benefit society to an insurance company located in Lincoln, Nebraska. The emblem of this society, which might be found on a tombstone, featured hearts and the letters P.F.V., signifying prudence, fidelity, and valor.

Royalist: a supporter of England and her cause during the Revolutionary War.

royals: 1) taxes; 2) members of the royal family in England.

royster: an inventory.

rpt: see report or reported.

r.r: railroad.

R.R.: a type of land sale in early Illinois, railroad land sales.

rst: see reinstated in membership.

rubella: German measles.

rudder: a flat, vertical blade, hinged at the rear of a vessel by which the ship is guided through the water.

rudge wash: cloth made from unprocessed sheep's wool.

rudge wool: a kersey cloth made of wool as it comes from the sheep's back; not washed after shearing.

rue bargain: a bad bargain. When a man withdrew his banns of marriage, he considered it a rue bargain.

ruffle and flourish: a steady beat of the drums with a bugle fanfare used when showing honor to a high official at a reception.

ruff tree: the roof beam of a house.

rule: a tool used by a 1) stone mason; 2) carpenter.

rule nisi: see nisi.

rule of descent: a prescribed list of people to whom property is distributed when a person dies intestate. If a person dies leaving no will, no widow, and no kin, the estate reverts to the county of residence.

rumfustian: a popular drink among some sportsmen during the late nineteenth and early twentieth centuries.

run: 1) to survey, usually a boundary line; 2) a small creek.

runaway: 1) a fugitive; 2) a horse which has escaped from human control; 3) a receding chin.

rundlet: 1) a small keg; 2) a container which holds liquid equal to fifteen English gallons or eighteen United States gallons.

runiple: a large debt accumulated little by little.

runner: 1) a deserter; 2) a messenger; 3) a person hired as a collector of varying items; 4) a policeman; 5) a tout; 6) a fast sailboat; 7) a smuggler; 8) a blockade runner; 9) a small stream; 10) see millstones.

running the bottle: after a wedding, the father of the groom (or a representative) would wait at his gate with a bottle of whiskey for a group of visitors who gathered together for this occasion. At a given signal the race began, with the winner receiving the bottle, drinking a toast to the bride and groom, and then sharing the bottle with others in the party.

running with the land: a phrase used to describe a contract that goes with the land. This action is passed from owner to owner, therefore the new owner is obliged to abide by the action of a former owner. For example, a right-of-way for a utility.

rushlight: made from reeds dipped in tallow and placed inside a holder to provide light.

russel: a 16th century clothing fabric of wool which came in several colors including green and red.

rusticoat: a countrified person.

rustler: 1) a person who steals livestock; 2) an animal which rummages around for its food.

rutter: 1) a directory to show the proper course of a vessel; 2) a rider or trooper (from the German). The term was usually applied to a fine, dashing, boasting, gallant man who was so fashionable that he spoke much in foreign languages.

R.W.: 1) Revolutionary War; 2) Red War.

ryptage: a wine made in Portugal.

S: 1) South; 2) section (which see); 3) in a Revolutionary War pension jacket, this means survivor.

s: 1) shilling (a unit of English money); 2) son; 3) signed; 4) small; 5) in manuscripts "s" was often substituted for "z."

s and h: son and heir.

saalez du mun fel: (Norman) sealed with my seal.

sabbaday house: see rooming house.

sabbata recutita: the day of circumcision, the seventh from birth.

sabre, saber: the long, broad and heavy sword, either straight or curved, which was used by a cavalryman.

sacerdos: priest.

Sachem: a North American Indian chief, also called Sagamore.

Sac Indians: a member of the Algonquin tribe who lived in Michigan and later in Wisconsin, where they joined the Fox tribes and during the Revolutionary War supported the British.

sackcloth: a coarse cloth, usually black, worn when in mourning.

sacrament: an oath.

sacrarium: a vestry. The place where the priests' robes were kept.

sacro: sacred.

saddle: a seat for a rider, usually made of wood and leather, which is held in place on a horse's back by a strap passing under its stomach.

saddlebags: attached to a horse's saddle these containers made of leather, plain or decorated, carried the rider's possessions. If he were a peddler, his wares could be carried in these bags.

saddle cloth: the cloth put between the saddle blanket and the saddle. It is usually decorated in the rear corners with the insignia of the branch of service or the insignia of the regiment to which the rider belongs.

saddler: 1) the craftsman who once made and repaired only saddles for horses but now repairs all types of leather goods, except shoes and boots; 2) a saddle horse.

saddle-tree maker: the person who makes or repairs the framework of a saddle (saddletree).

sad iron: an iron made of solid metal which was heated on a stove and used to press clothes.
safe: a light, simple wooden cupboard in which food was stored. It was usually placed in a cool place.
safe conduct: written permission given by a military commander which allows one or more persons to pass through certain localities under military control, in order to move supplies, carry on trade, or other reasonable cause.
Sagamore: see Sachem.
sagatheco: see sagathy.
sagathy: a fabric of wool with silk mixed in at times.
sager: a lawyer.
sailing master: a navigator, especially aboard a sailing ship.
sailleires: (Norman) keepers of the seals.
sail loft: a "factory" consisting of a large room or loft where sails for ships were cut out and sewn.
sail looser: a person appointed to 1) loosen the sails when starting out from a dock, or to 2) loosen the sails to dry.
sail maker: 1) a person who makes and repairs sails; 2) an old navy rank given to a warrant officer.
Saint Anthony's fire: see erysipelas.
Saint Elmo's fire, Saint Elmo's light: so called for the patron saint of sailors, this is a fire-like glow caused by static electricity, which is seen at the tips of masts, tops of trees, etc.
Saint Hugh's bones: shoemakers' tools.
Saint Vitus dance: most often a child's disease. See also chorea.
salamander: 1) a red hot poker used to ignite gunpowder; 2) a hot dish which, when held over a dish of food, will brown the food.
sale bill: a record of property sold at a public auction: what the article was, who purchased it and how much was paid for the item.
salere: salt seller.
saleratus: an ingredient found in baking powder.
sale with right of redemption: a sale in which a vendor reserves the right to take back property by returning the money paid.
Salic Law: a French law which prohibited females from occupying the throne.
Salish Indians: a friendly tribe of Indians who lived in western Montana. Other nearby tribes, who fixed their hair in such a way as to appear pointed, referred to the Salish as flatheads, for their hair was fixed and appeared flat. Eventually the Salish, or flatheads, moved further north in Montana where they lived on a lake named Lake Flathead.
saloon: around the middle of the nineteenth century a saloon was a respectable place of business, e.g. an ice cream parlor and not necessarily a place to purchase alcoholic beverages.
saloon keeper: a bar and grill "proprietor."
saller: (Norman) a saddler.
salster: a dealer in salt.
saltbox (house): an early American house which had two stories in the front and one in the rear. It had a rear roof which sloped from the peak down to the level of the first floor ceiling. This type of house was designed so that the owner would not have to pay the higher tax which was imposed on a two story house.
salted paper photographs: these photographs were made by a chemical process which deposited particles of silver within, instead of on top of, the paper. As a rule, they were mounted on thick paper.
salter: 1) a supervisor of salt works; 2) a person who mines, evaporates, or sells salt; 3) a person who preserved fish or meat by putting it in a barrel of salt. Now some meat is salted by injecting it with salt; 4) an embalmer; 5) a seller of salt; 6) a dispenser for salt.
saltern: a building where salt is processed.
salt fund: contributions of money for the poor and veterans' families.
salt horse: meat, usually beef or pork, preserved by a salting process.
salt house: a building, usually located near the ocean, where salt is refined or stored. An obsolete name is salt coat or salt cote.

salt lick: a spot which is saturated with salt deposits (usually in crystalline form) and toward which animals naturally gravitate to lick the salt as a supplement to their diets.

salt marsh: a low lying area which periodically is flooded with salt water.

salt meadow: a grassy area which lies close enough to sea water to be flooded periodically by the salty water.

salt petre (peter): potassium nitrate, a vital ingredient in gunpowder, sometimes found as crystals in caves. Because petrus in Latin means rock, saltpeter is sometimes confused with rock salt (sodium chloride).

salt pit: a type of reservoir which is found along an ocean which holds sea water used to make salt.

Salt Reservations—1824: in pioneer days, salt was a luxury and salt springs located in Delaware, Muskingum, and Jackson Counties, Ohio were valuable. This land was held in reserve by the federal government to avoid a salt monopoly being formed. Later, the springs were sold when drilling salt wells produced better salt.

salt spring: similar to a salt lick but a mixture of salt and water. It, too, was a popular spot for deer, buffalo, etc. to obtain salt needed in their diet.

saltstone: an obsolete word for rock salt.

salt suck: a salt lick so wet that the animals frequenting it secured salt by sucking it rather than licking. Licks became sucks in wet weather and many sucks became licks in dry seasons.

salvage: property rescued from a disaster, e.g. from a shipwreck.

Salvation Army: a charitable and religious group organized by the Reverent William Booth in a military manner.

salver: a serving tray.

salvo: several guns shot at one time, e.g. as a salute to an important person.

salyne (un): (Norman) a salt pit.

Samaday: (Norman) Saturday.

Sambo: three-fourths black, a child of a mulatto and a black.

samite: a rich silk cloth, with silver or gold threads woven into it.

sammaron cloth: fabric finer than hemp cloth and coarser than cloth made of flax.

sampler: a piece of linen cloth which was used as an inexpensive embroidery pattern book and a beginning school book, but developed into a more elaborate form of the art of embroidery.

samson: a tool used by a wheelwright.

Sanborn insurance map: a detailed map developed in 1876 in New York City for the purpose of indicating dwellings and outbuildings and their proximity to fire-fighting equipment. These maps were produced for many other cities, which used them not only in fire-fighting but for city planning, assessments, etc.

sand: in pre-revolution days when most houses did not have carpets, sand was spread over the floors and swept in fancy designs. Later when wood floors were common in kitchens, fine sand was used as a scrub powder.

sandler: a person who transported sand or gravel from one location to another.

sandwichman: a person who had advertising signs hanging from his shoulders on both his front and back sides.

sanguinous crust: an old term for a scab.

sans issue: without children.

santee: a flannel cloth worn about the abdomen and loins as a sanitary bandage. Also called a gazondheid.

sanzack: the governor of a city.

saponarius: soap maker.

sappers and miners: soldiers who dug beneath enemy fortifications. They now belong to the Corps of Engineers.

S.A.R.: Sons of the American Revolution.

saracen: a fine, soft silk fabric of plain or twill weave used for clothing or curtains.

sarcenet: see saracen cloth.

sarpelere: a coarse canvas made of hemp.

sartor: a tailor.

s.a.s.e.: self addressed stamped envelope.

sasines: 1) possession of feudal property in Scotland; 2) the instrument under which land in feudal Scotland was rented; 3) the deed which transferred land in feudal Scotland; 4) the act of transferring of land by giving a symbol

such as earth, stones, etc.
sassafras: bark of a small tree with which a tea is made.
satchel: a bag small enough to be carried by hand or by a strap from the shoulder.
satinet: a silk or silk and cotton mixture which had a satin weave. It was used for ladies' summer clothing.
satinisco: a poor quality satin. Other similar fabrics were perpetuana and bombazine.
satisfaction: in Quaker literature this term indicates that a member who failed to live up to the rules of discipline was dealt with by the monthly or business meeting. The person might give satisfaction by signing a statement that he or she had come to a "sight" and "sense" of their offenses and had experienced a true repentance. That the individual might do this was in all cases the desire of the meeting.
satisfied: paid in full.
satty: a type of frigate.
Saturno: Saturday.
sauseflemed: red spots or scabs on the face.
sawing dogs: tools used by a chair bodger.
saw horse: a wood board parallel to and about two feet above the ground. It is supported by a pair of legs at each end, and is used for supporting boards which are to be sawed and as a base for planks on which to stand while painting a ceiling, etc.
saw mill: a machine which cuts logs into lumber. It is driven mechanically or by humans, horses, etc.
sawpit: a pit, dug or naturally hollow, over which a log is placed in order that it can be more easily sawed into lumber. A two-man saw was used with one of the sawyers pulling the saw down into the pit, while the other stood on the log and pulled the saw back up. See pitman and top sawyer.
sawyer: a person who cuts logs to make lumber.
Saxe-Coburg: the family name of English King Edward VII, son of Queen Victoria. His son, King George V renounced all ties to Hanover and the family name became Windsor. Hostilities between England and Germany at the time of World War I were involved.
Saxons: persons of German origin who conquered England and remained in power until the Normans conquered England.
say: a fabric with a fine serge-like texture, part silk in the beginning but later entirely of wool. It was used for linings, curtains, petticoats and when used by the Quakers for aprons it was dyed green.
sayer: a poet.
sayweaver: probably the person who wove a fabric called say. It was a thin fabric made of silk or wool with a weave similar to that of serge.6
S.C.: 1) Society of the Cincinnati; 2) a type of land sale in early Illinois, in which land was sold to support schools.
sc.: see scilicet.
scab or scabies: a skin disease which has scaly eruptions. Sometimes called sanguinous crust.
scabbing hammer: a tool used by a stone mason.
(the) scald: see achor.
scaldhead: a person afflicted with ringworm on the head.
scale dish: a milk skimmer.
scanteloun: a carpenter's measure.
scantling: 1) a measured size of stone, wood, ships, etc.; 2) to estimated the size of an article, animal, etc.; 3) an allotted amount; 4) a pattern; 5) of insignificant size; 6) an obsolete word which meant to build a small ship.
scarfed: decorated with flags.
scarlatina: scarlet fever.
scarleteer: 1) a soldier whose uniform was an intense red; 2) one who holds the degree of Doctor of Philosophy and wears the red gown of his university, e.g. Oxford.
scarlet rash: a reddened rash, especially that caused by German measles.
s.c.c.: sworn chain carrier.
schale: a ladder.
schedule: a census questionnaire which has been filled out by the enumerator (census taker).
schedule form: a census questionnaire

which is blank.

schelling: a Dutch silver coin.

schepel: a Dutch dry measure which equaled approximately three-fourths of a bushel of wheat or a little more than one bushel of salt.

schepen: in the Dutch areas of New York this person was a public officer whose duties were similar to those of an alderman.

scherche: church.

schilling: a Dutch coin worth six stuivers.

schinckel: an iron wagon of a peculiar design which was used in two or three provinces of the Netherlands.

schnitzel-bank: Pennsylvania Dutch name for a shaving horse.

school lands: part of each township was to be sold for the use of schools.

schoolmaster: a person who teaches in or operates a school.

school street: the university.

schrimpschonger: a person who carves bone, ivory or whale's teeth into beautiful and useful objects. This art form was usually done by men who spent long periods of time at sea. Sometimes corrupted to scrimshander.

Schwenckfelders: these were members of an unorganized religious group named for Casper von Schwenckfeld of Silesia, eastern Germany, a non-conformist of the early sixteenth century. After traveling first to England, the group sought religious freedom in this country settling in southeastern Pennsylvania where some of their descendants live today.

Sci Fa.: Scire Facias.

scil.: see scilicet.

scilicet: 1) a word used to clarify an unclear sentence; 2) an introductory clause; 3) a clause which specifies something: to wit ...

scinn: a skinner of hides.

scire facias: to renew a judgment after some time has elapsed.

scirrhus: 1) a hard tumor, cancerous in nature; 2) an organ which has become hard.

scold: a person who swore at or berated another person. This act was punishable by ducking the offender in a pond.

scolers: (Norman) scholars.

scoop wagon: see conestoga wagon.

scooter: a piece of iron pointed and bent, which was dragged along the ground to make a row to plant seed.

score: 1) twenty yards; 2) twenty pounds weight mark or notch.

scot: to assess, for tax purposes.

scot and lot: a parish tax for support of schools.

scotch cloth: an inexpensive, sleazy cloth made of nettle fiber used for bed linen and window curtains.

Scotch-Irish: people of northern Ireland descended from Scotch settlers of Ireland. Many have emigrated to the United States.

scout: 1) a person sent ahead of, or on the side of, an army unit or a group of pioneers headed west. He observed movements and strength of troops or Indians; 2) a college errand boy; 3) an underworld term for a watchman; 4) a small division of land; 5) a Dutch river boat with sails.

scovel: a baker's tool.

scraper: a tool used by a 1) wheelwright; 2) cabinet maker.

screffe: the sheriff.

screws: rheumatism.

screw shoulder vein: a tool used by a saddler.

scriba librarius: clerk.

scribe: 1) an official accountant; 2) a clerk or official transcriber of records into registers; 3) to mark wood or metal with a sharp instrument.

Scrie Facias: a legal document based upon a record which requires a person to give a good reason why the record should not be enforced, annulled, etc. or what ever has been asked. From the Latin "and it was ordered that."

scrimer: a fencer.

scrimshander: see schrimpschonger.

scrimshaw: useful and beautiful articles carved of bone, ivory or whale's teeth.

scrip: 1) one of several documents which states that the person who possesses it is entitled to exchange it for something, e.g. land or money; 2) paper certificates issued in a financial emergency to be used in lieu of money.

script: 1) a manuscript; 2) printer's type which resembles handwriting with connected letters; 3) handwriting.
scripta litera manet: the written word remains.
scrivener: 1) a writer of letters; 2) a transscriber; 3) a writing master; 4) a person who drew up legal documents; 5) a person who, at a client's request, loaned money without interest, for which duty he received a commission.
scrivener's palsy: writer's cramp.
scrutiser: see vadlet.
scrofula: tuberculosis of glands, joints and bones, etc.
scroll: a tool used by a blacksmith who made decorative wrought iron.
scroll wrenches: a tool used by a blacksmith in making decorative wrought iron.
scru.: scruple.
scrumpox: see impetigo.
scruple: an apothecary's measure which contains twenty grains.
scrutineer: a judge at an election.
scudder: a tool used by a 1) tanner; 2) currier.
scuffer: a type of plow.
scunning: disease of the heart.
scupper: 1) an opening which has been cut into the side of a ship or wall, of a building, for drainage purposes; 2) a pipe, trough or other device to aid in the draining process; 3) a British term for an ambush.
scurvy: rarely heard of today, one hundred and fifty years ago it was a deadly disease. The simple medicine was lemon or lime juice, which contains vitamin C, and sunshine. Sailors in the British navy who received lime juice to prevent scurvy were known as "limeys."
scutage: a tax paid instead of giving military service.
scutch: 1) a hammer used by a brick layer; 2) the process of separating woody fibers from flax during the production of linen.
scutelaire: (Norman) the officer in the king's household who was to take care of the dishes, etc.
scutter: to have diarrhea.
S.C.V.: Sons of Confederate Veterans.
S.C.W.: Society of Colonial Wars.
scythe: 1) a farmer's grass or grain cutting tool; 2) a weapon which had a long, curved blade.
sd.: said.
s'd.: a scribe's abbreviation for "said," found in legal documents.
S.D.A.: Seventh Day Adventist.
S.D.I.: Signer of the Declaration of Independence.
SE.: southeast.
sea: a large quantity of anything.
sea dog: naval slang for an older, more experienced seaman.
seafaringman: a person who sails a ship or who goes to sea as a business or to travel.
Sea Fencibles: a coast guard.
sea island cotton: a type of cotton which is grown on the southeastern coast of the United States and in the West Indies. It has a very long, silken fiber and is sometimes called "Egyptian cotton."
sea lawyer: a sailor who argues with those in authority and, while doing so, attempts to make the navy regulations appear to be on his side.
sealed: the union of a family "for time and all eternity." Persons born into a previously sealed Mormon family are sealed at birth. Others may be sealed in person, or by proxy (after death), in a ceremony which takes place in a temple (into which only Mormons in good standing may go).
sealed and delivered: see signed, sealed and delivered.
sealed records: documents not to be used by the public, e.g. adoption records.
sealer: 1) the person who attaches the seal to a document; 2) an inspector of weight and measurement; 3) a ship which hunts seals.
sealer of leather: a person, who with two other honest, experienced men, inspected all leather tanned in the town. Deficient leather was destroyed, good leather was "sealed" or stamped with their own distinctive mark. He also inspected finished shoes and boots, along with other leather goods to insure their quality.

sealer of measures: see weight viewer.
sealer of weights and measures: a person charged with the responsibility of seeing that all buying and selling was accurate and met set standards of commerce.
seaman: see navy rank.
seaman apprentice: this man has been through a basic training course and is learning the trade of seaman.
seaman recruit: this man usually receives the same pay as a seaman apprentice but has not gone through a basic training course.
seamen's protection certificates: these proofs of citizenship were authorized by an Act of Congress in 1796 to prevent seamen from imprisonment by Great Britain. An application was filed with the collector of customs, a fee of twenty-five cents was paid, and for this the seaman would receive a certificate to carry with him. The applications are now housed in the National Archives and are indexed.
seamer: usually a child who had the job of sewing the back seam of knitted stockings.
seam set: a shoemaker's instrument for smoothing the seams of boots and shoes.
seamstress: a woman who is skilled in sewing dresses, but does not make fancy embroidered pieces.
search: to look for information in a record, public or private.
searcher: a person who, during the Colonial period, was officially appointed as an inspector of meat, leather, fish, butter, etc.
searcher and sealer of leather: see sealer of leather.
searchers: persons appointed to examine corpses and report the cause of death.
sease: an obsolete form of cease, which was still used as late as 1860 in Massachusetts.
seasoned troops: 1) those who have become used to climate or local conditions and, therefore, are not likely to become victims of local diseases; 2) those who have fought numerous times, know how to protect themselves and are unlikely to panic.
seat: 1) to form a town; 2) to settle an area; 3) to assign church pews to persons in the order of their social importance in a New England community.
seat aze: a tool used by a chair maker.
seat house: the manor house on an estate.
seating: 1) to settle in a country; 2) to provide a house; 3) material used in upholstering chairs; 4) a support for something.
seat iron: a tool used by a saddler.
seau: a water pail.
sec.: 1) section; 2) security; 3) second.
secatour: an executor.
secessionist: a supporter of the South and its principles during the Civil War.
second: 1) an obsolete word for one half; 2) to relieve an officer temporarily from his regiment to perform a task in another unit.
secondary records: documents stating facts which were supplied by a person who was not present at the event which is being described. This record also could be made by a person who was present at the event, but who had allowed a considerable amount of time to elapse before recording the facts. Therefore, the account is likely to be less accurate.
secs.: securities.
secret diseases: an old way of mentioning venereal diseases.
section: 1) part of a battalion or company assigned to military movements; 2) a measurement of land which consists of one square mile or six hundred and forty acres.
secture: an executor.
security: money, or something of value, which is promised to make certain that an obligation or promise is fulfilled. Similar to a bond.
secuty: security.
sedan chair: a covered, enclosed, portable chair for one person. It was mounted on two poles in order that it could be carried by two or four men.
seedsman: 1) a person who sells seed; 2) a person who sows seed by hand or machine; 3) a florist; 4) (archaic) a foreman on a farm, whose duty it was to sow the corn.

sefynt: seventh.
sei (heir de): (Norman) heir of his body.
seieant: (Norman) sixty.
seigniorage fini: a fee no longer charged by a lord for the granting of a privilege.
seigniour: (Norman) lord, owner.
seine: a drift net for catching fish.
seised: see seized.
seisen, seizin: possession of property, either real or personal.
seit house: a dwelling house.
seized: in legal possession of.
sekilman: an invalid.
selectman: 1) a New England town officer chosen from among the town board members to carry out the directives of the board; 2) a New England town board member elected annually. This board reported persons who were not in church on Sunday and required anyone walking around town to go to church. These duties were in addition to regular town business.
select meeting: a Quaker meeting of ministers, elders, or counselors authorized by the monthly meeting.
self marriage: the offence of marrying without parental consent for which a court could levy a fine. Sometimes when a couple felt that their parents were unfairly withholding their consent, they could sue the parents, sometimes quite successfully.
sem: needlework.
seminary: 1) an English Roman Catholic priest educated abroad; 2) a school, often a girls only school; 3) a college for ministers.
Seminole Indians: a tribe who lived in Central Florida and who fought with the British during the Revolutionary War.
sempiternum: a 17th century cloth similar to perpetuana (which see).
semple: a medicinal herb.
sempster: a seamstress.
sempstress: a dressmaker.
senage: a monetary tribute paid to a high-ranking church official at Easter.
sending out: the custom of allowing children to be raised in another home, one perhaps closer to a school, to learn a trade, to put a child out of harm's way, to allow a closer position to a medical doctor, to let a friend care for a child after the death of a parent, etc.
Seneca Indians: residents of New York state. They were the largest and most warlike of the Six Nation group of Indians. Defeated tribes were taken into the Seneca tribe, thus enlarging their number. They were allies of the United States during the War of 1812.
Seneca rattlesnake root: a "cure" for pleurisy which was popular with traveling medicine men for years after it won an award of one hundred pounds from the Virginia Colony.
senee: (Norman) wife.
seneschal: 1) an official in an English city, province, or church; 2) the person who was in charge of administering domestic affairs in the king's or lord's households.
senex: senior, aged, old.
senility: the degenerative effects of old age upon a person's mind. Many times in a census an aged person will be listed as insane, when probably he was only senile.
Senior: 1) a father known by the same name as his son, e.g. John, Sr. and John Jr.; 2) sometimes used when the person is an uncle or cousin.
senior officer: the highest ranking line-officer at any time or place. If two officers have the same rank, the one who has held that rank the longest is the senior officer.
sennachie: a professional genealogist in Ireland and Scotland.
sennight: a common abbreviation for a period of one week or seven days and nights. A sennight day is the same day in the next week.
Senr.: Senior.
sentinel: a soldier of low rank who was posted at a certain point and was charged with allowing the passage of authorized persons and repelling all others.
sentry: see sentinel.
seoptisme: (Norman) seventh.
seor: (Norman) sister.
seor (la): (Norman) the elder.
separated: this word is used when a man and his wife have agreed to live apart,

although they are not divorced.

separate examination: the questioning of a married woman without her husband being present, in order to establish that she understands and is acting of her own free will and not as her husband forces her to do.

separatist: 1) a person who has left an established church; 2) a person who disagrees or does not wish to conform to established customs.

Sephardim: Jewish persons of Spanish or Portuguese ancestry.

sepoy: a cavalry soldier of India who served a foreign power, especially one who was in the British army.

sept: 1) a screen which divides two areas; 2) a division of a nation into parts; 3) an enclosure saved for a particular purpose; 4) a tribe; 5) a class.

septain (diz et): (Norman) seventeenth.

Septembrale: (Norman) September.

septicaemia: a blood infection.

Septuagesima Sunday: a period of time which lasts from the third Sunday before Lent for seventy days. It ends with the Saturday of Easter week.

sepulcra: cemetery.

sepulturae locus: burial ground.

sequela: aftermath of a disease.

sequester: 1) to separate; 2) to temporarily remove a person's property, e.b. to hold property until he has paid his debt.

sequestration: 1) isolation; 2) authorization to hold property of a person until he obeys a court order; 3) confiscation.

ser., serv.: 1) servant; 2) service.

serarius: locksmith.

sere month: August.

serf: in early England, a person who farmed approximately thirty acres. For this privilege, in lieu of rent, he worked a few days a week for the lord who owned the land. A villein.

serfe: (Norman) a female slave.

serge: see cabbis.

sergeant: see army rank. 1) a sheriff's officer; 2) a soldier; 3) a squire, an attendant on a person of rank; 4) a royal servant.

sergeant-major: an experienced, senior, non-commissioned officer who commands other sergeants and others of lesser rank.

sergeanty, serjeanty: 1) an obsolete word used when speaking of a number of squires; 2) any one of several providers of personal services to a feudal lord; a steward, a constable, etc.

sergt.: sergeant.

sermonary: a collected group of sermons written by one or more persons.

seron: a bale or package of goods enclosed in an animal's hide.

serpigo: a skin disease such as ringworm, etc.

sert.: servant.

serv.: service.

servant: low social status was not implied by this word during Colonial days. It meant only "one who serves," for example, as an apprentice served.

servery: a butler's pantry.

service: 1) time spent in the armed forces or as a servant; 2) allowance of food; 3) set of dishes.

serviens: see vadlet.

seskar: a small Scotch coin.

sester: a jar, pitcher for liquid, etc.

set, sett: 1) a lease; 2) a patterned cloth.

sete: a city.

set off the dower: a division of property. During the administration of an estate the widow is given her portion (one-third) by means of a document.

setors: (Norman) sailors.

set square: a tool used by a stone mason.

setter-out: 1) an editor; 2) an author.

sett hammer: a tool used by a blacksmith.

setting brake: a tool used by a rake maker.

settl.: settled, settlement.

settle: an uncomfortable bench with a high back and sides but which, when pulled up to a fireplace, created a warm place to sit with the drafts kept away. Some settles had drawers or chests underneath the seat portion.

settlement: the final itemized account of the expenses of an estate and a list of how the property was divided among the heirs. Often referred to as the final account.

settlement certificate: a document carried by working class persons to support their right to settle in a community.

settlement day: the day when accounts are paid.
settlets.: settlements.
settlor: a person who makes a settlement.
setyme (dis): (Norman) seventeenth.
sev.: several.
sevener: a criminal whose sentence is to be jailed for seven years.
seven night: a week.
Seven Ranges: in 1786 this was the first survey of land west of the Ohio River and was a part of the Congress Lands. It sold slowly, at $2.00 per acre in lots of not less than 640 acres (a section), as there were better buys in others parts of Ohio and Kentucky. It was located on the eastern border of Ohio in Jefferson, Monroe, Carroll, Harrison, Belmont and Washington Counties, Ohio. This was the first time that the rectangular system of surveying was used in this country and the only one made under the Continental Congress.
severalty: to own real property in one's own name.
sevt.: servant.
Seward's Folly or Seward's Icebox: Alaska, which was purchased from Russia in 1867 while Seward was Secretary of State. The wisdom of this acquisition was not widely appreciated at the time.
Seward's Icebox: see Seward's Folly.
sewerage: to use sewer waste as a fertilizer.
sewing awl: a tool used by a boot maker.
sewing clerk: 1) a person who deals in gloves; 2) the person who collects sewed articles from home workers.
sewster: a seamstress.
Sexagesima Sunday: the second Sunday before Lent.
sexennial: 1) a period of time which continues for six years; 2) an event that happens every six years.
sextant: see quadrant.
sextary: a pint and a half. It varied in measure in different countries.
sexton: the person paid to care for a church and/or cemetery, to toll the church bell, dig graves, etc.
seynmaker: a person who made fish nets.
seyowners: noblemen.
seze: (Norman) sixteen.
Sgt.: Sergeant.
Sgt. Maj.: Sergeant Major.
shadowgraph: a "picture" formed between a light and the surface of a wall by movement of a person's hands.
shag: 1) cloth used to line cloaks, church cushions, etc. When made of silk it would be called silk shag; 2) see also duffel.
shagbush: an obsolete term for a hang gun.
shakefork, shackfork: a two-tined pitchfork.
shakes: 1) a common name for malaria; 2) cracks which appear in pieces of wood, caused by exposure to sun and weather.
shaking: the ague.
shalloon: a tightly woven wool fabric used for linings. It must have been fairly expensive, for sometimes a glazed calico was substituted for shalloon in lining a coat.
shallop: a small, open fishing boat powered by men using oars, by wind, or a combination of both. It had storage for the catch and operated fairly close to shore.
shamble: 1) a footstool; 2) a table for displaying goods in a store; 3) a stall where meat or fish was sold; 4) a meat or fish market; 5) a slaughterhouse.
shamboats: usually boats on a river provided entertainment on the boat while tied to shore. They moved from place to place at night.
shandygaff: a mix of beer and ginger-beer.
shank's mare, to go by: a form of transportation, to walk.
shant: 1) a quart; 2) a pot of something to drink, e.g. beer, etc.
shanty boat: a lumberman's houseboat. A shanty man is a man who deals in lumber.
shaping knife: a shoemaker's paring knife.
shappers: 1) makers; 2) creators.
share, plow: see coulter.
sharecropper: a farmer who works another person's land in return for a portion of the harvest.
sharping corn: a customary gift of corn

which was given each year at Christmas to the smith who sharpened plowshares, etc. It was not to be more than half a bushel per farm.

sharps: an inferior flour.

sharpshooter: 1) an old army term denoting a rifleman; 2) the rank, in pistol or rifle shooting, below an expert.

sharpshooters, hauling: farmers who hauled freight during an extremely busy season and were so named for their shrewdness in hauling only at the time when rates were high.

shattuck: a grapefruit.

shave: 1) one of any number of tools used to scrape or remove the surface of wood, a hide, etc.; 2) extortion; 3) a barber; 4) to cut a ground growth, such as grass, off.

shaving horse: a tool used by a cooper.

shaw: 1) a woods; 2) underbrush on the border of a field.

shawm: a musical instrument of the oboe family.

Shawnee Indians: a tribe of American Indians who in 1648 lived in Wisconsin. Tecumseh was a noted chief of this tribe in Indiana in the late eighteenth and early nineteenth centuries.

sheared sheep: the wool (hair) was cut from the sheep in the spring season. This not only provided raw material to make clothes, but kept the animal cool in the summer.

shearing knife: a thatcher's tool.

shearling: 1) a year old sheep which has had its wool shorn once; 2) the short wool sheared from a shearling; 3) a hide from a lamb or sheep with the wool still on it, which is later tanned.

shearman: 1) a cloth worker; 2) the person who cuts the wool from a sheep.

sheaves: this method of harvesting was used in Biblical days and is now obsolete. Bundles of grain were cut near the ground and fastened together to dry. They were then transported to the thresing floor.

shed: 1) a structure with a nearly flat roof and only one side, where it is attached to the building; 2) a single room attached to a house; 3) a small independent building usually used for storage.

sheepbiter: 1) a petty thief; 2) a person who enjoys mutton meat; 3) a womanizer.

sheepcote: a shelter for sheep.

sheepfold: a pen for sheep.

sheepherder: a person who cares for and keeps sheep together, usually in unfenced areas.

sheepman: a person who owns and breeds a large number of sheep.

sheepmaster: the person who hired and supervised sheepherders and paid them from the town treasury. His main duty, however, was to establish the grazing areas and move the flock from area to area as necessary.

sheep's head: a simpleton, fool.

sheepskin: 1) a sheep's skin from which parchment is made; 2) a diploma; 3) sheared sheep skin used to make a jacket.

sheep yoke: a light device which fitted around the neck of a sheep to enable it to pull a load.

sheerings: hay made from the least desirable pasture land.

shekir: a chess game.

shell auger: a tool used by a wheelwright.

shellback: naval slang for a person who has gone through the traditional initiation when he crossed the equator for the first time.

shell fire: the phosphorescence sometimes seen in farmyards. It is caused by decaying straw, etc.

sheltroune: a regiment of soldiers.

shepster: 1) shearer of sheep; 2) a cloth cutter.

sher.: sheriff.

sheriff's deed: when a person fails to pay the taxes due upon his property it is sold, usually at public auction. The deed is issued by the county sheriff and is entered in the grantor index under the sheriff's name.

sheriff's posts: posts set up at the doors of the sheriff's office where royal proclamations were tacked. It was the custom to remove your hat while reading them.

sherry vallies: a heavy, outer pair of pants worn for horseback journeys.

shetar: an archer.
sheth: a part of a field.
shgs.: shillings.
shifter: 1) a superintendent; 2) a cozener or cheater.
shill: see puffer.
shilling: an English monetary unit.
shingles: a disorder of the nerves also referred to as herpes zoster. An old belief was that if the rash was in the middle of the body and went all the way around and met, the person would die.
shinguard: wooden guards worn by a farmer to protect his legs during the thrashing by flail process.
shinplasters: a derogatory name for fractional paper money issued during the Civil War in 3, 5, 10, 15, 28, and 30 cent amounts to stop hoarding of silver coins. Although it was necessary for trade, it quickly became torn and dirty. Although replacement cost was high, it was used until confidence in greenbacks was restored.
ship boy: an attendant for the captain of a ship.
ship carver: a person who carved the elaborate figurehead for a ship's prow.
ship chandler: a person who deals in equipment and supplies for ships.
shipe: a shovel for cutting turf.
ship lord: the owner of a ship.
shipman: 1) a mariner; 2) the master of a barge.
ship master: the owner or the captain of a merchant ship.
ship money tax: in England, from 1634-1649, a tax was levied mainly on landowners to "build ships for the Navy," but in reality it was to replenish the King's pockets. The records which survive serve as a census for the area.
ship's articles: an agreement signed by all the crew and the ship's master. This agreement shows the working conditions under which the men consented to sail.
ship's fever: typhus.
ship's husband: a person employed by the owners of a ship to oversee repairs, etc., while the ship is in the harbor. He may be a part owner of the ship.
ship's last: a Dutch dry measure which equalled about three and three-quarters cubic yards or two and one-half tons of cargo.
ship's log: the book kept by the captain of a ship which records the daily movements of and events aboard the vessel. It contains notations about weather, injuries to crew members, deaths and births on board, an account of the ship's course, etc.
shipsmith: a blacksmith who worked aboard a whaling ship. His job was to keep the harpooners' equipment in good repair.
ship's papers: various types of records, for example the ship's log. They are considered proof of the legality of a voyage.
ship spy: a telescope used on the coast.
shipwright: a person who built ships.
shire: 1) an English county; 2) a breed of work horses which were brown with white markings. They were named for the counties whose names end in shire, in west and central England.
shireman: any person who did not have the good fortune to be born in this county or a neighboring one. He was sort of a foreigner; his speech betrayed him.
shirereeve: a sheriff.
shirrene: a sheriff.
shoat: a young hog weighing about 100 to 180 pounds.
shoddy: goods of poor quality.
shod shovel: a wooden shovel tipped with iron.
shoe finder: a dealer in a shoemaker's tools.
shoe hammer: a tool used by a bootmaker.
shoeing smith: see farrier.
shoe pack: a leather moccasin-type shoe.
shoe wiper: the servant who cleans shoes each night.
shop knife: a tool used by a basket maker.
shopocrat: a member of a body of wealthy shopkeepers who aspire to some social importance.
shopwalker: a British floorwalker in a store.
shopworker: a factory employee, or skilled artisan, who usually works indoors.
shore patrol: the navy equivalent of the

army's military police.

shoresman: a person who stays on land but furnishes supplies, money, etc. for active fishermen.

short bit: see bits.

shorthorn: beef cattle, bred in England, which have shorter than usual horns.

Shoshone Indians: a tribe which inhabited the northwestern United States.

shot: 1) a foot soldier who carried fire-arms; 2) the term also applied to a shooter who was an extremely good marksman.

"shotgun:" an armed guard who rode with the driver of a stage coach.

shott: 1) a field; 2) a plot of land.

shot tower: a high (for example, a 170 foot) tower from which melted lead was dropped through a screen into water, forming lead shot for guns. It is said that this was inspired by a plumber's night-mare in which raindrops turned to lead as they fell. He then experimented with lead dropped from a church tower.

shot with a plane: accurately squared.

shoulder-clapper: a bailiff.

shout: 1) a hill; 2) a small, nearly flat-bottomed boat.

shr.: sheriff.

shrefe: sheriff.

shrieve: a sheriff.

Shropshire: a breed of English sheep which produce both white wool and good meat.

shroud: garments which are put on a corpse for burial. Many times special garments were made for this purpose, but now usually regular clothing is used. In ancient times a shroud was often a length of cloth wound around the corpse and was called a winding sheet.

Shrove Tuesday: the day before Ash Wednesday, the first day of the Lenten season.

Shrove Sunday: see Quinquagesima.

shrump shouldered: hump backed.

sh. sh.: sharpshooters.

shilling: an English silver coin.

shucker: 1) a person who removes the outer covering from ears of corn; 2) a machine which does the task of removing the outer covering from ears of corn; 3) a person who removes the oysters from their shells.

Shutten Saturday: the Saturday in passion week when Christ's body laid enclosed in the tomb.

shutting in: to harness a horse to a wagon.

shutting out: unharnessing a horse from a wagon.

shuttle: used to hold a bobbin filled with thread from the spinning wheel. It is passed from side to side between the warp threads on a loom to form cloth.

S.I.: Staten Island (New York).

siatica: an obsolete spelling of sciatica (which see).

sibberidge: the banns of matrimony.

siblings: brothers and/or sisters of the same parents.

sibman: a relative.

sibrede: relationship; kindred.

sic: a Latin word which means "thus" or "so." It is usually written enclosed in parentheses to denote a word, phrase, or passage which may appear incorrect. It indicates that the original has been quoted verbatim.

sichten with a mathoech: found in old Dutch records, this is a tool used when cutting buckwheat.

sick book: the bound volume in which the names of military personnel who need medical help are written.

sickle: a sharp, curved knife which was used to cut grain before it was bound into sheaves (which see). It also could be used for cutting weeds.

sickness: the plague was called "the sickness" for distinction's sake.

sic transit gloria mundi: thus passes away the glory of this world.

side arms: weapons which are worn on a belt at the side of the body when not in use.

side axe: a tool used by a chair bodger.

side board: 1) a table suitable for meals, placed on one side of room; 2) a cupboard placed on a dining room wall for storage and for serving dishes of food; 3) a removable board placed on the side of a wagon to provide extra seating space.

sidelong: to fetter by tying a foreleg and a hind leg together as a preventative for

straying.
side man: see sworn man.
sidemen: assistants to the church warden.
siege: a systematic attack upon a fortified area in a continued effort to obtain possession.
siegle: (Norman) age.
sietans: (Norman) sixty.
sight: the device which enables a person to aim a firearm.
signal corps: the branch of the service which is in charge of conveying orders. This was done with flags, banners, lights or rockets until the invention of the telegraph.
signed, sealed and delivered: a phrase which was usually found at the end of a deed, followed by the signatures of the witnesses. It meant that the document was authentic and the transaction was finished. Few states today use the seal.
signiory: 1) government; 2) dominion; 3) domain or lordship; 4) seniority.
sikernesse: security.
sil.: 1) son-in-law; 2) sometimes means stepson; 3) sister-in-law.
silence cloth: the forerunner of a table pad, so named because dishes and flatware would make less noise when placed on the table. It was used under the tablecloth.
silenced: ministers prohibited from preaching were said to be "silenced."
silent brigade: see night riders.
silhouette: this is the profile of a person, cut from black paper. It was the cheapest method of preserving a likeness prior to portraits.
silk rash: see rash.
silk throwster: a person who twists silk fibers to make thread.
sill: the wood beam that rests upon the foundation of a building.
sillery: a French wine which was popular in England, particularly for celebrations.
silleurs: (Norman) mowers.
silver gelatin photographs: as its name implies, this picture consists of silver in gelatin which produces a black and white image in a variety of tones. In use today, this process does not require a heavy backing such as was applied to earlier photos.
silverlings: silver coins.
silver rent: rent money, not service.
silver riband: a ribbon used as a decoration, woven with silver threads.
silversmith: a person who repairs and fashions objects from silver. See goldsmith.
sime: (Norman) sixth.
simitorie: (Norman) church yard.
simity: flat-nosed.
simplex et pura: simple and pure.
sinapism: a mustard plaster.
sindon: a thin, fine weave goods made of cotton or linen.
sine: without.
sine anno: without year.
sin eaters: it was an ancient custom at funerals to hire poor people, who were to take upon themselves the sins of the deceased.
sinede: assigned.
sine die: without date (in case of a court or other meeting, an indefinite adjournment).
sine loco: without place.
sine nomine: anonymous.
sine parole: without issue.
singel: the roof of a house.
singing men: choristers.
single crease: a tool used by a saddler.
sinking fund: a sum of money set aside for the purpose of paying off the principal of a debt at the time it becomes due.
sinking fund bond: a bond issued which has the provision that a certain sum or a percentage of the issuing company's income be deposited in a special sinking fund. This money would be reserved to pay the entire bond issue.
Sioux Indians: see Dakota Indians.
sir: 1) a gentleman; 2) a term of respect; 3) when applied to priests and curates it was more of a scholastic title; 4) a title given to a person who had taken his first degree in a university.
sire: 1) a breed or sort, e.g. a good sire of pigs, cabbages, etc.; 2) to father.
siress: 1) a mother; 2) a matron.
Sir John: a priest.
sis.: sister.
sister: 1) a daughter of the same parents. Sometimes this term referred to a step-

sister, a half-sister, or a sister-in-law; 2) a form of address by members of the same church, e.g. Sister Jane or Sister Johnson.

sister church: a church of the same denomination in another location.

sister german: a full sister.

sister-in-law: sister of a person's spouse. In Colonial days this term could refer to a step-sister.

sister law: sister-in-law.

sister sone: nephew.

site: (Norman) sixteenth.

sithcundman: the head or chief of a town or parish.

sitiophobia: a fear of food.

sitting: a space in the pew of a church sufficient for one person.

situate: 1) to locate (a house, land, etc.) in an area; 2) sited.

Six Nations: see Iroquois Indians.

sizer: a thin piece of brass with a round hole in it. It was used to see if a cast bullet was perfectly round.

sizer of pipe staves: an inspector of the boards which formed the sides of casks. If bundles of staves were to be exported from the town, the inspector had to place his town's seal on them.

S.J.: Society of Jesus.

skeddle: 1) to run quickly as if in a panic; 2) in a military sense to withdraw hastily or secretly from the enemy's presence.

skeet: a long-handled scoop which was used to tighten sails on a ship so they would hold the wind better.

skepe: 1) a wooden pan which separated the wheat from the chaff by throwing the grain in the air and catching it in the pan. The wind blew away the chaff. The process was a form of threshing called winnowing; 2) a fishing vessel.

skerrings: hay made from the bad part of pasture land.

skiff: a small bateau (boat) used as a tender to a larger craft.

skiff dish: a hatter's tool.

skimmer: a kitchen tool used to remove fat from broth, cream from milk, etc.

skin-dresser: see tanner.

skinflint: a miser, a person who is thrifty to extremes.

skinker: a tapster, a drawer of ale.

skinner: 1) a dealer in animal skins; 2) see also cowboy; 3) the person who drives horses which pull a heavy load; 4) a group of mounted men who claimed to be loyal to the British and to the Americans. They plundered and raided without regard for anyone.

skinners: a band of men who, during the Revolution, professed loyalty to the American cause but roamed "neutral territory" between the opposing armies, robbing those who refused to take the oath of allegiance. These men not only stole cattle to sell to the highest bidder but switched uniforms to rob and murder in Westchester Co., New York. No one was safe from either cowboys or skinners.

skip boy: a ship boy, a boy who is an attendant to the captain of a ship.

skip kennel: a footboy.

skipper: naval slang for the captain of a ship.

skipple: see schepel.

skirmish: a minor battle between two opposing armies.

skirret: a root vegetable comparable to a parsnip, but sweeter.

SL: a type of land sale in early Illinois, which was saline land along the Ohio River.

slab: 1) a bricklayer's assistant; 2) a puddle; 3) a flat, mass of anything solid. An old word for a concrete road.

slander: a malicious, untrue statement spoken to harm a person's reputation.

slasher: a tool used by a wattle hurdle maker.

slater: a craftsman who, with special knowledge of roof geometry, cuts and fastens slate or tile to a roof.

slates, roofing: roofing slates from Wales and Cornwall were produced in different sizes. The smallest were 15" x 8" and were called ladies. Other sizes were named countesses, dutchesses, doubles, slabs, and flags.

slave: a person owned as property of another person.

slave declaration book: a book kept at the request of state authorities. The contents include a collection of statements by emigrants to another area that the slaves brought with them are not for sale but are personal slaves.

slave schedule: the portion of censuses which refer to slave owners and their slaves until after the Civil War.

sleaker: a tool used by a 1) tanner; 2) currier.

sleazy: a linen that took its name as an abbreviation from silesia and not from its wearing ability, which was quite good. It is not to be confused with a sleazy or cheap piece of cloth.

sledge hammer: a very heavy hammer used by a blacksmith, farmer, builder, and laborer in general.

sleeper: a wooden beam used to support a floor.

sleeping partner: a term used in business, which meant a limited partner.

slekt: (Norman) family.

sley: a weaver's tool.

s.l.g.: sine legit. Without legitimate issue (children).

slide box wheel: a tool used by a boot-maker.

sling: a Colonial cold drink made most frequently of gin, water, sugar, and flavored with lemon or lime. When it was served hot it was flavored with mint or nutmeg.

slinger: 1) a person who steals cloth, yarn or the like from clothiers, with the idea of making it up and marketing it; 2) a person who used a sling.

slip down: old milk which is slightly curdled.

slitting mill: a tool which cuts metal into strips of various widths which can be used to make nails, brackets, hinges, etc.

sloes: milk sickness.

sloop: used in deeper water as a depository for catches of fish. The fish were caught and brought to the sloop from smaller flat-bottomed, steepsided rowboats which had pointed bows and sterns.

slop: 1) a loose, outer jacket; 2) baggy, loose pants which were worn by sailors; 3) cheap clothes; 4) waste liquid of any kind; 5) live underbrush; 6) to run over.

slop dealer: a person who owned a store where cheap, ready made garments were sold.

slop seller: one who sells cheap, ready made clothing in a store called a slop shop.

slote: 1) a crossbar; 2) an obsolete word for a dead bolt.

slough: 1) a narrow ditch designed to drain water from a swamp area; 2) a slow moving channel of water; 3) a pond; 4) sometimes used as a verb: to sink in swamp land.

slows: see milk sickness.

sluice: the last portion of the mill race which as it reached the millwheel carried the water under or up and over the wheel. It was also called a mill run, mill way, mill stream, or mill flume, depending upon the locality.

slumgullion: meat and vegetable stew, sometimes shortened to slum.

SM: a type of land sale in early Illinois, which was land sold to support higher education.

sma: small.

small arms: portable fire arms: rifles, carbines, pistols, muskets, etc.

small clothes: pants which end at the knee; breeches.

small coal: charcoal.

smallpox: a very contagious disease characterized by fever and eruptions on the skin. Not to be confused with chicken-pox, a milder disease.

smally: an obsolete word for a weak, thin liquid.

S.M.D.: Society of Mayflower Descendants.

smelter: a person who works in a smeltery where ore is melted to produce a pure metal.

smeth: a medicine or ointment to remove hair.

smethymene: smiths.

smiddy, smethy: a blacksmith's smithy or shop.

smith: a worker in metals.

smithy: the blacksmith's shop where he does his work.

smock mill: a type of windmill which was more popular than the post mill. It sat upon the ground and only the top part was turned to face the wind.

smoke house: a small windowless house

built over a pit where a low fire could be kept burning to cure meat. After this curing process the meat would be wrapped in flour sacks, then in news-papers. Then the package would be buried in a bin of wheat where, for a year or so, it would keep quite well.

smoke jack: the mechanism used to turn a meat roasting spit. It used the current of hot air in a chimney as a driving force.

"smoker-back" hollow knife: a tool used by a chair maker.

smout: to work at odd jobs when out of constant employment.

snakefence: an interlocking rail fence made from rails arranged in a zigzag pattern. Also called a worm fence, Virginia fence or a rail fence.

Snake Indians: see Shoshone Indians.

snakeroot: a plant which was used as a medicine for snake bites.

snakestone: see madstone.

snakeweek: see adderwart.

sned: 1) to prune trees, shrubs, etc.; 2) a tool for pruning.

sniper: an expert shot who fires at individuals among the enemy.

snippet: 1) a small portion of cloth, thread, yarn, literary passages, etc.; 2) a small person.

snob: 1) a journeyman shoemaker; 2) an obsolete word for a townsman; 3) a person of no rank; 4) a game of cricket.

snobber: a shoemaker.

snobscat: a shoemaker.

snow: 1) a method of telling time used by Indians. The winter season marked the passing of a year; 2) a small sailing ship.

snowball hammer: a tool used to remove snow and ice which would collect in the hollowed section of a horse's foot. If the snow and ice were allowed to build up, the horse lost his grip on slippery ground, as well as becoming painful to the horse.

"snow the bridges:" in northern states when a covered bridge was constructed, it not only kept out rain, but snow. Most towns had to allot money to pay men to put snow on the bridge floor in order that sleighs, and other equipment designed for use on snow, could get through.

snow warden: in states where snow fell, this person had the job of keeping the streets covered with an even layer of snow in order that the runners of sleighs could move easily.

s/o: son of.

soapboiler: a person who makes soap by boiling ingredients in a large container until the mixture is quite thick.

sobrine: (Norman) kinswoman.

soc., socs.: society, societies.

socage, soccage: an ancient tenure by which tenants were obliged to cultivate the lord's lands. It allowed a man to have the use of land by paying rent, but he was not obliged to serve in the military.

socer: father-in-law.

Society: 1) in New England this term referred to a church parish or portion of a town which had its own church; 2) a Protestant assemblage whose members attended the same church. For example, Baptist Society, Christian Society, etc.; 3) abbreviation for "Society of Friends" (Quakers).

Society of Friends: a Protestant church sometimes known as Quakers (which see).

Society of the Cincinnati: an organization formed in 1783 by men who had served as officers during the Revolutionary War. General George Washington was the first president of this patriotic brotherhood designed "to preserve the memory of the American Revolution." It is named after a Roman general, Lucius Quintius Cincinnatus, who left civilian life to fight in Rome. Certain descendants of these officers are eligible for membership in the society.

sock: 1) the drainage of farmland; 2) a heavy fall of rain; 3) a plowshare.

sock and scythe: plowing and mowing.

socrus: mother-in-law.

Soft-Shell: the opposite of Hard-Shell in religious, politics, personality, etc. Not rigidly conservative.

sogn, sokn: (Norman) parish.

sojurnaunt: 1) an entertainer; 2) the host.

soke: 1) a privilege, franchise. An exclusive right claimed by, e.g. millers. They ground all the corn used within the manor or township where their mill stood; 2) a right or franchise to govern a specified geographic area. It allowed the holder to collect rents and fees, and to hold court and levy fines and other punishments.

sokeman: the person who had land under a socage arrangement.

soken: 1) a toll; 2) a district held by tenure of socage.

soke-reeve: the person who was in charge of collecting a lord's rent.

sol., sold.: soldier.

sold up: when a man had become bankrupt or insolvent, he was said to be "sold up."

Sole: Sunday.

soler: a person who puts new soles on shoes.

soliciter: obsolete spelling of solicitor.

solicitor: an English lawyer. See also barrister.

solid: 1) a tool used by a saddler; 2) a Quaker term which means that a subject has been discussed and deliberated at length earnestly and prayerfully.

solyer: (Norman) a shoemaker.

somerland: ground that lies fallow all summer.

son and daughter: 1) members of the same tribe, group, clan, etc.; 2) followers of a leader; 3) male or female infant offspring of the same parents.

son-in-law: a daughter's husband. In Colonial days it sometimes referred to a step-son.

Sons of the American Revolution: a patriotic organization, membership is comprised of men who have a direct ancestor who fought in or provided some other service during the American Revolution.

Sons of Liberty: 1) patriots who fought against Britain in the Revolutionary War; 2) a secret society formed to aid the escape of Confederate soldiers from northern prisons.

sooner: a person who tried to obtain choice public land before the government declared the land open for settlement.

soosey: a striped cotton fabric imported from India. It usually was made of silk and cotton.

sop: meat juice or a combination of juices in which bread is dipped just before consuming.

soporose, soporous: similar to a coma.

sor: 1) a wooden tub used by a brewer, or by housewives to wash their glasses in; 2) sorrow.

sore throat distemper: quinsy.

sorghum molasses: the lowest grade of molasses made from cane grown most often from Kentucky south to the Gulf. It was made into a thick syrup early in the fall.

soror: sister.

sorter: 1) one who grades hides or produce by weight, color, etc.; 2) a filing clerk.

sortie: the movement into enemy-held territory which was of a tentative or temporary nature.

soster: (Norman) sister.

sotre: an auditor's office.

sought: illness. Later, this word was in use only in speaking of animal sickness.

soukinge fere: a foster brother.

soulez (femes): (Norman) single woman.

soul scot: 1) a fee paid by the family of a deceased person to the church where he was a member; 2) a mortuary.

soul silver: the whole or part of the wages of a retainer or servant, originally paid in food, but afterwards converted into a money payment.

soum: 1) the number of cattle or sheep put to pasture in a field; 2) a unit of measure for sheep: either five or ten sheep.

soundex: a system of indexing surnames that sound alike. Consonants have certain values, vowels are ignored. The first letter of the name and three digits are used, e.g. Evans = E152. This system is used to index the 1880, 1900 and 1910 censuses and some states use the soundex code on drivers' licenses.

sound mind: a person capable of making his own decisions.

soun piere: (Norman) his father.

soupless: no food.

sourdough bread: a pioneer basic bread, served with fried or cured meat and a hot beverage. The dough, made with home-grown yeast, was kneaded in the pan. See also starter.

souse: headcheese. A meat and gelatine product, usually made from the head of a cow or pig.

souter: a cobbler.

Southern army: the Confederate army in the Civil War.

Southwest Territory: the area known in 1790 as the "Territory of the United States south of the Ohio River," most of which we know today as Tennessee.

sovereign: 1) an English gold coin; 2) a person or group of persons who possess the power to rule, such as a king, queen, etc.; 3) an effective treatment; 4) an independent state; a sovereign state.

sovereyne: 1) a husband; 2) a provost; 3) a mayor.

sovran: an old, rare spelling of sovereign.

sow: a female hog.

sowdears: soldiers. Properly, hirelings or those who received pay.

sowding: soldering.

sowle grove: February.

sowster: a seamstress.

sp.: 1) spinster; 2) without issue; 3) abbreviation for dsp, which see.

spaeman: a fortune teller; prophet.

spaining: summer pasturage for cattle.

spallier: a laborer in a tin works.

spalling hammer: a tool used by a stone mason.

Spanish American War: this war lasted one year, 1898, and was fought only in Cuba. The origin was in the Cuban insurrection of February 1895. There were 5,000 casualties but only 400 of them were caused by battle; the rest were caused by disease. The two governments terminated hostilities on 12 August 1898. Some personnel also served during the Philippine Insurrection.

Spanish milled dollar: a Spanish silver coin.

Spanish real: a coin of silver worth one-eighth of a dollar which was used in some southern states. See also eleven penny bit.

spanshakell: a device for fastening chains or ropes.

spar: a term which means mast, boom, gaff, etc. but in the building of a ship it referred to the small fir trees on which men stood while making repairs.

sparables: shoemaker's nails.

spar hook: a tool used by a thatching spar maker.

spastic croup: see croup.

spats: a type of gaiters which stopped at the ankle. They were used by men who dressed in a fashionable manner.

S.P., Dom: State Papers, Domestic.

spear: 1) a public auction was sometimes referred to as "goods sold under the spear;" 2) a soldier who carried a spear.

spears: heavy armed cavalry.

specie: 1) metal coins; 2) repayment; 3) anything used in trading.

specie payment: some businessmen preferred to be paid in precious metal, e.g. gold or silver either made into coins or not, as they did not trust paper money.

specific performance: to follow a contract according to its stated terms, from beginning to end.

speculator: 1) a person who bought and sold blacks when slavery was prevalent; 2) also applied to a person who buys property cheap and who hopes to make a quick profit when it is sold.

spence: 1) a pantry; 2) a man's double-breasted overcoat; 3) a life preserver.

spendinage: money.

spensere: a dispenser of provisions.

spere: 1) to ask, to inquire; 2) a spy.

spermaceti: found in sperm whales and dolphins, this is a fatty mass which was used to make candles and some medicines or ointments.

sperviter: the person who cared for hunting hawks, just as a falconer cared for falcons, especially a keeper of sparrow hawks and musket hawks.

sperm whale: the oil in the very large head cavity of this whale was "lighter and purer" than the whale oil previously used, so it made a brighter flame for lamps, candles, and beacons.

spes: hope.

S.P.G.: Society for the Propagation of the Gospel.

sphragistic: a person who studies, collects and deals in seals or signet rings.

spicer: a grocer.

spider: an iron frying pan which had three long legs to raise it above the coals of a fire for use as kind of a dutch oven. Now the term, if used at all, refers to a cast iron frying pan.

spillway: after the water which powered the mill had done its task, the waterway to carry the water back to the stream was known by different terms depending upon the locality: mill tail, washway, mill wash, tail race.

spina bifida: drainage of the spinal fluid through a hole at the base of the spine (a congenital disorder).

spinde: a pantry.

spinner: a person who made yarn from sheep's wool which had been carded.

spinning house: a building in a compound used to spin wool into yarn.

spinning money: six pence.

spinning wheel: a tool used by a wool worker which makes thread by compressing and twisting the fibers.

spinster: 1) a spinner of yarn either in a factory or her home to earn money; 2) an unmarried woman.

spiral auger: a tool used by a wheelwright.

spirit level: a tool used by a 1) stonemason; 2) carpenter.

spirits: 1) men who practiced the trade of kidnapping people, selling them to the captains of ships bound for America, who would then, in turn, sell the victims as indentured servants; 2) a beverage with alcohol added; 3) an alcoholic liquor made by distilling or fermenting grain, fruit, etc.

spiritual court: church court.

spiser wife: a woman who sold spices and general groceries.

spital, spitall, spittal, spittle: 1) a hospital; 2) a roadside building which offered shelter for travellers.

spite fence: a fence, usually high, which a landowner erects in order to shut off light from his neighbor's buildings.

spittle: 1) a place where diseased and poor people were housed during the sixteenth and seventeenth centuries; 2) a little spade.

spit turner: a boy or dog employed to turn the spit for roasting meat.

splent: 1) lath; 2) inferior coal.

splits: thin strips split from white oak saplings of four to six inches in diameter and used to make chair seats and baskets.

spoils: property taken from the enemy.

spoke dog: a tool used by a wheelwright.

spoke lever: a tool used by a wheelwright.

spoke set gauge: a tool used by a wheelwright.

spokeshave: a tool used by a wheelwright, chair maker, wood carver, and carpenter.

spoke tongue gauge: a tool used by a wheelwright.

spoliation: 1) plundering; 2) robbery; 3) the act of altering or destroying a document so it is no longer presentable in court as evidence.

sponge cloth: see ratine.

sponsor: 1) a godparent; 2) a surety; 3) a person who strongly supports another.

spoon auger: a tool used by a wheelwright.

spoon carver: a person who makes wooden spoons, usually of sycamore wood.

sporadic cholera: see cholera.

sporyar: a spurrier or spur maker.

spotted fever: typhoid fever or a fever accompanied by tiny hemorrhages which appear on the skin.

spotter: a detective.

spouse: the person to whom another person is married. If you are married, you are a spouse.

Spr.: Sponsor.

sprig: a rail.

sprits: an alcoholic beverage.

spruce beer: a beverage made from twigs of spruce trees and sugar. Yeast may be added to start fermentation.

sprue: see thrush.

spurrier: a person who made spurs.

spurrings: marriage banns.

spur royal: a gold coin.

spy: 1) a person who, in disguise, under false pretenses, or secretly, goes behind the enemy's line to gain information; 2) the pilot of a vessel.

Sq.: Squadron.

sqr.: square.

square chain: see chain, square.

squad: 1) the infantry equal of a section; 2) a number of men who are drilled together; 3) the smallest unit in the United States Army.

squadron: 1) two or more divisions of a ship; 2) a group of cavalry men; 3) in Colonial New England, a division of land in a settlement; 4) an obsolete term for a school district.

squaine: 1) a herdsman; 2) a servant.

square: a tool used by a 1) stone mason; 2) carpenter; 3) slater.

square jawed tongs: see hollow tongs.

square pig awl: a tool used by a bootmaker.

squatter: a person who built a cabin, cleared a few acres and settled on unclaimed (usually public) land. As a rule, he had not formally applied for title to his site.

squerer: (Norman) a squire.

squire: 1) a landed gentleman, in the feudal system this person ranks next to a knight; 2) see also coistrell; 3) an attendant for a person of rank; 4) a lawyer; 5) a justice of the peace; 6) to convoy.

squire of the body: a knight's attendant.

Sr.: Senior.

ss.: scilicet (which see).

S.S.: see Supra Scriptum.

St.: 1) Saint (when used as a prefix); 2) Street.

ST: a type of land sale in early Illinois; land sold for internal improvements.

stabbing awl: a tool used by a bootmaker.

staddow: a combmaker's tool.

staff officer: officers who direct the army's actions beginning with the regimental level. The regimental officer is concerned with only his own unit while a staff officer deals with a larger section of the army.

stagecoach: the horse and passenger wagon which carried passengers and mail. It was designed more for speed than the cumbersome conestoga wagon and, consequently, traveled farther in a day. See Concord wagon for a physical description.

stage driver: a person who drove a team of horses which pulled a stagecoach behind them.

stail engine: a tool used by a rake maker.

stake: a tool used by a rope maker.

stake knife: a tool used by a 1) tanner; 2) currier.

stall: a doorless pew in a church.

stallage: 1) a tax upon a booth (stall) at a fair or market; 2) a stand upon which a cask can be placed.

stallman: 1) a person who helped with horses in the stable; 2) an underground section of a coal mine in which a miner and his partner or assistant worked.

stamine: linsey-woolsey cloth or a garment made from it.

stammel: usually dyed red, this cloth was really linsey-woolsey. The shade of red which the fabric was dyed became called "stammel color."

stamp: a tool used by a blacksmith.

Stamp Act: an English parliamentary law (1765) which required publications and documents produced in the United States to bear a tax stamp. This law was strongly objected to and was later repealed (1766).

stamp iron: a branding iron.

stamp man: a person who crushes ore with a heavy instrument powered by water or steam.

stanchion: the first stanchions were posts at intervals along a trough. Later, it was a device of vertical and horizontal boards. One vertical board was moveable in order to allow the cow's head to be slipped in when fastened. The cow had space to move and eat but could not get her horns out. This forced the cow to stand fairly still while she was being milked.

standard: 1) the flag under which men and women unite in a common cause; 2) a banner or flag.

standard interrogatories: questions answered in court by the crew and officers of a prize vessel. The questions usually asked concern birth place, citizenship, wife and family, fellow crewmen and the officers, details of the voyage itself, etc.

standard keeper: see weight viewer.

stands: forerunners of today's motels or tourist courts.

stangey: a tailor.

starboard: the right hand side of a ship as you face the front.
starching brush: a weaver's tool.
starchmaker: the person who makes a stiffener for cloth after laundering or during the manufacturing process.
starter (sour dough starter): before the days when yeast could be purchased in a store, a housewife would make a started by putting flour, salt, and water into a crock kept near a fire to stay warm and to bubble and ferment. Then it would be put aside to become sour dough to make bread, pancakes, etc. A cup of the starter was always kept in the crock, more flour and water added and the crock placed in a warm place for the contents to sour for the next meal. When pioneer men would go out to hunt or tend animals, scout or bring back supplies, they carried a half gallon crock of starter.
state: 1) to deed land to a person or several persons; 2) to survey and build a road between two points.
state census: a census taken by a state in between federal censuses, e.g. 1845, 1855, 1865. As a rule, these do not contain names, other than the head of a household but can, with careful study, reveal the composition of a family.
state church: a church recognized by law as a country's official church. This church is supported by the government and frequently its records are more complete and better than those of a denominational church.
state-land states: states which kept title and control of land owned by the state were, in addition to the 13 original states: Kentucky, Maine, Tennessee, Texas, Vermont and West Virginia, after the split-off from Virginia.
State of Franklin: created in 1784, this temporary state, unlike Transylvania and Westsylvania, was a true state with its own laws, courts, etc. Settlers set up this state when North Carolina ceded the Watauga region to Congress. It was not recognized by either North Carolina or Congress and became known as the Lost State of Franklin or Frankland.
statery: merchandise.
statesman: 1) a person who occupies his own estate; 2) a small landholder.
stathe: 1) a wharf; 2) a dock for merchandise.
station: 1) a farm owned by a pioneer would carry his surname, e.g. Smith's Station. Many times it would be large and well-fortified enough to be used as a place of refuge for other pioneer families against Indian attacks; 2) in other in-stances this term with a family surname meant a group of families settling to-gether as protection against Indians; 3) one Methodist-Episcopal congregation, usually the one where the minister lived; 4) a stagecoach stop which usually carried a person's surname as a prefix; 5) an underground railway temporary stop during the Civil War when slaves were aided in reaching the north; 6) often used instead of fort.
stationer: 1) a seller of paper, pens, ink, etc.; 2) a seller of books; 3) a publisher.
station staff: an early device used in measuring land. It was a straight pole, divided and marked into feet and inches.
status plat: a map on which has been noted enough information to determine ownership of federal land, its use, and its availability.
status quo: as matters stand now.
statute of limitations: a limitation of time during which an action may be brought into court.
statute mile: 5,280 feet, as defined by law.
statutes: 1) written laws passed by governments, from Federal to local representatives of the people; 2) gatherings of farm servants, possibly held by statute, in the early part of May at various places in the country. Prospective employers attended to hire servants for the coming year. At these gatherings, the servants were distinguished by symbols of their talent, e.g. a groom would have a couple of straws in his hat, a carter or wagoner would attach a piece of whip cord to his hat or a shepherd a lock of wool, etc.
statutes of limitations: a varying amount of time determined by state or federal

governments during which a suit may be started and after which a person may never start the suit.

statutory: demanded by the laws of a state or country.

statutory law: a type of common law in which determinations are based upon statutes passed by Congress, state legislatures, county and cities, etc.

stave: a narrow piece of wood joined edge to edge with other pieces to form a barrel or to form the sides, lining, etc. of a ship.

stay law: a statute which specified certain conditions under which mortgages and judgments against individuals would not have to be paid immediately. It delayed a threat of foreclosure, but it was considered unconstitutional in some states. Also called stop law or relief law.

steading, stedding: a building lot which has been set aside for that purpose.

steam packet: a steam-powered ship which ran regularly between at least two places and which carried cargo and passengers.

steaver: 1) a collier who superintended the coal pit; 2) a banker.

stee: 1) a ladder; 2) a stile.

steelyards: a portable scale suspended horizontally from a hook or held in a person's hand. Also called a lever scale.

steeping rain: a soaking rain.

steeple house: a church.

steer: 1) a male bovine (bull) which has been desexed at an early age; 2) an ox of less than four years old; 3) the hide of a steer; 4) a rudder; 5) a helmsman, one who steered a boat; 6) a handle for a plow; 7) a pile of wood; 8) strong; 9) to govern.

steerage: undesirable cabins in the lowest portion of a passenger ship available for a low fare.

steersman: a pilot. See helmsman.

stemma: a genealogical chart or tree.

stent: the right to use pasture land.

steonn: (Norman) stepson.

step: 1) used in front of mother, father, brother, etc. to denote a relationship by a remarriage, e.g. a step-child is the child of a person's spouse by a former marriage; 2) the distance between the heels of a man walking or running. Half and back step equals fifteen inches. Right and left step equals ten inches. Quick step equals thirty inches. Double time step equals thirty-six inches.

step-father: father to wife's child by another marriage.

stepony: a popular early English wine.

stereographs: a popular object for parlor tables from the 1850s to the 1920s. This special viewer allowed a three-dimensional picture to be seen by placing two identical pictures side by side on a card that was viewed through lenses.

stern: see aft.

stet: a proof-reader's mark indicating that words or letters which were crossed out earlier should, instead, be retained. "Stet" is written in the margin, and a series of dots (...) is used to show which characters are to be retained.

steve.: stevedore.

stevedore: a person who has the job of loading or unloading the cargo of a merchant ship in harbor.

stevedore troops: persons in the military who are employed as unskilled laborers.

stewd.: steward.

steward: a sailor whose duty is to serve meals.

St. Hugh's bones: shoemaker's tools.

stibille: a carpenter's tool.

stifadre: step-father.

stiff: a blacksmith's anvil.

stile: wooden steps leading up and over a fence.

stillborn: dead at birth.

still house: a distillery.

still room: 1) the housekeeper's room; 2) an area in a house where cordials and perfumes were distilled; 3) a pantry where preserves and various supplies were kept; 4) the area where tea and coffee were prepared for the table.

stirp: 1) a race; 2) a family; 3) a line of descendants. Plural, stirpes.

stirpe: 1) a race; 2) a family.

stirpes: the ancestor from whom a family is descended. See also per stirpes.

stirrups: the portion of a saddle which supported the rider's feet. These were made of iron or wood and varied in shape according to the part of the country in which they were made.

stitcher: a person who sews clothing or other articles together and, at times, decorates garments with top-stitching.

stitcher knife: a tool used by a bootmaker.

stitch pricker: a tool used by a bootmaker.

stithy: an anvil.

stive: flour dust which filled the air while grain was ground into flour.

stiver, stuiver: a Dutch coin made of nickel which had a small value, hence the phrase "not worth a stiver."

stockade: 1) an area enclosed by a high picket fence made of trees, ten to twelve inches in diameter, cut twelve to fourteen feet in length and used as the principal defense against Indians; 2) a jail.

stocking apple: an apple suitable for cider.

stockinger: a person who knits or weaves stockings.

stock-in-trade: an accumulation of anything necessary to conduct a business, e.g. articles for sale by a storekeeper.

stock mark: a brand (which see).

stocks: punishment in which the criminal was made to sit in a public place with his feet confined in holes between boards. See also pillory and vanes.

stoker: see fireman.

stomacher: 1) a man's vest; 2) a cloth with medication on it which was put on a person's chest to cure a cold, etc.; 3) a jeweled and highly ornamented piece of women's clothing; 4) a person filled with resentment.

stomatitis: see thrush.

stone: 1) a measure of weight; 2) a grave marker either of field stones or a slab with or without an inscription.

stone ax: a stone worker's axe.

stone cutter: 1) a person who cuts inscriptions on tombstones; 2) a person who shapes stones for building.

stoned: 1) fortified with stones; 2) something made of stoneware; 3) a male animal which has not been castrated.

Stonehenge: a famous circle of stones located in England. Sometimes cold, unappetizing potatoes are likened to the stones in this circle.

stone horse: a stallion.

stoneman: a highly skilled mason who was capable of shaping stone for building.

stoner: a mason.

stone rake: a sturdy hook-toothed rake used by a farmer to collect and fill boxes with stones to be placed on the road bed, thus making the road more suitable for all-weather travel. Each box of stones was worth a fixed amount toward payment of taxes.

stonewarden: a supervisor of road repair.

stoop: an old term for a porch without a roof. Usually the term was qualified as front stoop or back stoop.

store boat: a floating store which sold legal or illegal merchandise and sometimes would carry a passenger or two. Many times it would be a family moving westward who sold goods along the way to support themselves.

store bought: see boughten.

stores: supplies for use in the military service.

stoup: 1) a little cask; 2) a bucket; 3) a container used for liquid, holy water, etc.

stout: an extra-strength ale.

stove: broken in or crushed; as the side of a ship.

stover: 1) fodder for cattle; 2) provisions.

St. Peter's canvas: a strong cotton cloth used upon which women could embroider designs.

straddle: 1) a young sapling; 2) the bottom portion of a haystack; 3) a base which supports a stack of lumber, etc.

strain: 1) lineage; 2) descent.

strait: a passage which connects two parts of a sea.

strake: a metal tire for wagon wheels.

strand twister: a tool used by a rope maker.

stranger's court: in Colonial days this court could meet rather quickly and hear the case of a traveller, thus not delaying his journey until the next scheduled session of court.

stranger's fever: an illness which people felt particularly attacked newcomers to an area. At one time it was a name for yellow fever.

strangery: a rupture or stricture; painful urination.

straw joiner: a thatcher.

straw men: see men of straw.

strawstack: after the grain has been threshed from the wheat stem, the stems were piled high and used during the winter months as barn bedding and as roughage and shelter for animals.

strays: see estray books.

street cleaner: a street sweeper who did not wear a white uniform. Also called a mudlark.

strength: 1) a castle; 2) a fortress; 3) number of laborers hired by a farmer.

stretchers: the horizontal pieces of wood which steady the legs of a piece of furniture; rungs.

stricker's hammer: a tool used by a slater.

strictland: an isthmus.

strike: 1) an iron spear; 2) a bushel.

string: 1) a fence row; 2) an old term for a horse whip.

stringer: a person who made strings for bows.

strocal: a glassmaker's tool.

stronghold: a place of security, e.g. a fortress.

stroud: a coarse woolen cloth, blanket or garment used by the British when they bartered goods with North American Indians. It was probably named for Stroud, a textile manufacturing town in Gloucestershire, England.

struma: goiter or scrofula.

Stuart: as Queen Elizabeth I died unmarried, James I of the Stuart family (the sixth King of Scotland) ascended to the throne. The Stuart family continued to rule England through Queen Anne's reign.

"stub book:" a large book used in issuing land warrants. Blank certificates were bound in a book with a perforated line separating the stub from the warrant. A short abstract describing the warrant (date, name, number of acres, etc.) was written on the certificate and repeated on the stub. Sometimes a cross would be drawn across both pieces of paper before separation to discourage forgery attempts.

stuccoworker: 1) a person who decorates with or makes designs in stucco, a mixture of Portland cement, sand and lime which may be applied to outside walls of a building; 2) a person who works with fine plaster inside buildings.

studdles: weaver's tools.

stuff: a woven wool fabric used in England.

stuff gown: a junior barrister and the robes he wore.

stuiver: a Dutch coin worth about two cents.

stuiver gold: an arrangement made at all public sales in early New York City of both real and personal property. It was stipulated that the buyer should pay for his purchase at the rate of twenty-one stuivers to a guilder. The odd stuiver was the auctioneer's fee, about two and one-half cents.

sub.: subsistence.

subaltern: every officer is subaltern to the ranks above him, but generally this term refers to a commissioned officer of a rank lower than a captain. This term was used first by the British and later by Colonial America.

sub-foreman: see driver.

suborn: 1) to bribe someone to give testimony, etc.; 2) to commit perjury; 3) to obtain evidence unlawfully; 4) to give support to another.

subp.: subpoena.

subpoena: an order from a court to appear before it as a witness under penalty for non-appearance.

subpoena duces tecum: an order from a court which is personally served, ordering a person to bring into court a tangible item which he has in his possession and which is needed as evidence at a trial.

subscribe: 1) to sign a document; 2) to give a statement; 3) to give allegiance; 4) to admit a wrong; 5) to vouch for a person; 6) to contribute money to an organization.

subscribing witness: a person who signs a document as a witness.

subscription book: 1) a book sold in advance of publication by a salesman going from house to house; 2) a book which has a list of subscribers printed in it; 3) see county history books.

subsidy book: tax lists.

subsidy tax: the reputed value of an estate was taxed at twenty-five percent on land and twelve percent on the approximate value of goods.

Subsistence Department: the section of the United States army which dealt with buying and issuing supplies of all kinds to other sections of the army personnel. Now these duties are assumed by the Quartermaster Corps.

subsister: a prisoner who had no money.

substitute broker: a person whose business was to procure the services of a poor person, etc. to perform the duties in the military of a wealthy man who did not care to go to war and who could pay for this substitution.

substitute soldier: a person who served in the armed forces for another. He was paid by the one who should have served.

subtack: sublet.

successions: a term used in some probate courts to indicate the line of descendants who are involved in an inheritance case.

sucken: 1) a fee paid at a grinding mill with ground grain. Also called thire or multure; 2) the duty of a feudal tenant to take grain only to the manorial mill to be ground.

sudor anglicus: see sweating sickness.

sufferage:1) an obsolete word for permission; 2) the right to vote, as in women's sufferage.

sufferers: Connecticut citizens whose homes had been burned by the British and were given certificates for land in the Western Reserve. Many times these certificates were given or sold to younger men.

sufferer's lands: land in northern Ohio given to citizens of several Connecticut towns whose property was burned by the enemy, with the assistance of Benedict Arnold, during the Revolutionary War. See firelands.

Suffolk: 1) an English-bred sheep which had a black face and legs; 2) a short legged, sturdy work horse; 3) a little black hog bred in England.

suffragan: an assistant bishop.

sugarhouse: a better name would be sugarshed, for it was many times constructed of a pole frame with rough lumber nailed to three sides. It contained the large fire pit over which at least fifty gallons of sap would be reduced to a gallon of maple syrup.

Sugar House prison: a sugar house converted into use as an infamous prison in New York City during the Revolutionary War.

sugaring off: to take sap from maple trees and boil it down to make sugar.

sugar on snow: partially boiled down maple sugar which is poured over ice or snow to make an edible confection.

sugarplum: a small ball of candy.

suit broker: a person who made a trade of obtaining the suits of petitioners at court. He was sometimes termed a suit jogger.

suitor: 1) a follower; 2) a petitioner.

suling: plowland.

sull: a plow.

sullerye: (Norman) tillable land.

sullow: a plow.

sulphur and molasses: a spring tonic widely used at one time. It was believed to have a great medicinal value each spring.

sulung: a measurement of land (120 acres) used in Kent, England. See also carucate and hide.

summary: 1) a shortened report which mentions only main points; 2) court proceedings or courts-martial which have been shortened considerably by omitting formalities; 3) an obsolete word for supreme.

summary court: a special court created in Southern states for slaves.

summary court martial: a special court martial which cannot confine a man to more than 30 days in jail or fine him more than two-thirds of one month's pay.

summer beam: see sumpter beam.

summer complaint: acute gastroenteritis.

summerland: ground which lies fallow for a year.

summons: 1) a court order or writ to appear before a court; 2) an order or writ of the reigning sovereign of England to appear at the national council or in Parliament. This summons went to each bishop, earl and baron and a general summons was issued to a sheriff for all the knights and freeholders; 3) a notice to a defendant in a case that he is to appear in court. If he chose not to appear he could have a judgment issued against him.

sump hole: a cesspool.

sumpter: 1) a saddlebag; 2) an animal which carries bags of merchandise or camping gear, etc. on its back; 3) the strongest work animal on a farm, which was usually a horse or ox; 4) the person who drives a packhorse.

sumpter beam: the main beam that held up most of a house. It was named for the sumpter work animal and was sometimes corrupted to "summer beam."

sumptuary laws: these restrain excess in dress, furniture, eating, etc.

Sunday clothes: best wearing apparel kept for use only on Sundays and holidays.

Sunday Saint: a person who never missed going to church twice on Sunday, nor an opportunity of reviling or cheating his neighbors during the rest of the week.

Sunday's fellow: Monday.

sundries: when found in an inventory, this term means various small articles which are too numerous to mention individually.

sun fiuz: (Norman) his son.

sup.: supply.

super cargo: 1) a title which indicates the officer of a merchant ship who is in charge of the cargo. He is also in charge of any commercial affairs connected with the voyage; 2) an agent for a merchant in charge of foreign business.

superintendent: see overseer.

superior circuit court: the name in some states for a probate court.

superior court: 1) the highest court in a state; 2) a court which is between a supreme court and a lower court.

superior officer: one who has a higher rank or who ranks higher by seniority within the same bracket.

supervisor: the overseer of a will, now an executor.

supr.: superintendent.

supra: 1) before; 2) earlier or above in this document.

supra scriptum: Latin "as written above." A legal phrase used to avoid repetition in long documents.

supreme court: 1) in the Colonial era this was the highest court in a colony and had jurisdiction over a wide area. It often performed the duties of an appellate court. Not all states or colonies had this court; 2) some states now still have this court but it is lower than the appellate court; 3) the Cherokee Indians had this court as their highest court; 4) it is the highest court in the United States today with the entire title of Supreme Court of the United States.

supreme court record: documentation of appeals made to the supreme court from a lesser court.

surbatre: a bruise.

surety: a person who of his own free will makes himself liable for another's debts and obligations if that person defaults.

surg.: surgeon.

surgeon: a physician. In the Revolution, he served in a civilian capacity.

surgian, suringer, surjoner: surgeon.

sur. mate: surgeon's mate.

surname: a person's last or family name.

surrender: to give up, by mutual consent, a lease before the expiration date.

surrogate: 1) a person who was substituted or appointed for another; 2) in a few states, an officer of the court who has control over probate or guardianship matters.

surrogate wife: a mistress.

sursanure: a wound which has healed outwardly but not inwardly.

survey: 1) the procedure of accurately locating land by description any place on the earth's surface; 2) a species of auction in which farms are disposed of for three generations.

surveyor: 1) a general term for a town officer, the person who was the overseer of several departments or works; 2) the officer in a royal household who supervised the preparation of food and drink; 3) a head magistrate of an area; 4) an architect.

surveyor general: the federal officer appointed to survey public land in a designated area.

surveyor of the highway: the person who supervised highway workers in Colonial days. Each adult male was required to give six day's labor on public roads per year.

surveyor's droughts: see droughts.

surveyor's measure: a unit of measurement used by a surveyor of land. The length is sixty-six feet (a gunter's chain).

survey plat: usually a single township map which contains the locations of surveyed land.

surviowre: an overseer.

survivorship: see right of survivorship.

susceptor: 1) a godfather; 2) a supporter.

susceptous: godparent.

suspensive: a suspended judgment; a temporary stop, e.g. the defendant moved for a suspensive.

suspensive appeal: a case which has or is being brought to a higher court and has been temporarily stopped.

suster doughtere: a niece.

sustre: a sister.

sutler: a person who follows an army from camp to camp selling food, drink and small supplies to the troops.

sutler's cabin: a soldier's tent.

sutor: shoemaker, cobbler.

sutter: 1) (obsolete) sutler; 2) (archaic) a cobbler or shoemaker.

Sutton Law: Dr. William Sutton was the first president of the Kentucky State Medical Association. This bill, requiring collection of vital statistics for Kentucky, was passed on the ninth of January 1852. All clergymen, doctors and midwives were to report these events. This practice continued until the 29th of August 1862 when the General Assembly repealed the law. Not until 1910 was the law repassed. Filmed copies of these records are available for most Kentucky counties. They are especially valuable for early birth and death records.

S.U.V.: Sons of Union Veterans.

S.W.: 1) Southwest; 2) a type of land sale in early Illinois: swamp lands.

swabber: a person on a ship whose duty was to keep the decks clean.

swage: a finishing tool used by a blacksmith.

swage block: a tool used by a blacksmith.

swager: a brother-in-law.

swain: 1) a young male attendant for a knight; 2) a male servant; 3) a laborer on a farm; 4) a bread for the meals of servants.

swaine: 1) a herdsman; 2) a servant; 3) a youth not quite old enough to be an esquire; 4) anyone not a knight in the fourteenth and fifteenth centuries.

swaler: a dealer in corn, or rather one who bought corn and converted it into meal before he sold it again.

swamper: 1) a person engaged in clearing a road to haul lumber; 2) a person who lives in a swampy area; 3) a maintenance worker in a saloon.

swamp lands: located mainly in Ottawa, Wood, and Sandusky Counties, Ohio this land was given by the federal government to Ohio on the condition that the land be drained and made useable. This type of land existed in other states also.

swamp sickness: milk sickness.

swanikins: see swanskin.

swanskin: a fine, thick, soft flannel which gained its name from the extraordinary whiteness of the cloth.

sward: an area of land, usually sodded.

swart rutter: a German horseman.

sway: a thatcher's tool.

sweating sickness: a main symptom, rather than an illness, characterized by profuse perspiration. See also day fever.

swedge block: a blacksmith's tool which was used in forming various shapes. A swage.

swelled neck: a goiter.

sweep, mill: the pole attached at one end to the mill and at the other end to the source of power used to run the mill: horse, mule, cow, etc. As the animal walked in a circle, it pulled the sweep around, which turned the mill.

sweep net: a large fish net.

sweeps: see bateau.

sweetmeats: 1) sweet, small cakes made usually of maple sugar by bakers, resembling fancy candy. These led to candy and candy bars as we know them; 2) a linseed oil and varnish mix used in the manufacture of patent leather.

swele: 1) a swelling; 2) a tumor.

Swem's index: an alphabetical compilation of names found in eight genealogical or historical quarterlies for the state of Virginia.

swepe: 1) a whip; 2) a crop of hay; 3) a baker's malkin.

Swethens: Swedes.

swill: 1) a partially liquid feed for hogs; 2) something which reminds one of garbage.

swinacie: quinsy.

swine: a collective term for pigs, hogs, and sows.

swine cote: a pig sty.

swine flu: a very contagious influenza first found in swine.

swineherd: 1) a man employed to care for hogs, pigs, etc.; 2) the boar (male hog) who is the "head" of the herd.

swine same: lard.

swinyard: a keeper of swine.

swiss muslin: this somewhat stiff, sheer fabric is made of cotton. It is a plain weave cloth which is covered with raised dots in a regular pattern.

switchel: a beverage made of molasses, honey, water, rum, ginger and vinegar, etc.

swizzle: a mixture of ale and beer.

swizzle-stick: made from the top of a small tree, it was used to beat eggs.

swod: a basket for measuring fish.

swon: sworn.

sword: a general term for a metal hand weapon carried at the side and consisting of a fairly long blade fixed in a handle. As it is a very personal weapon, its surrender to the winning side has always been considered a token of submission and the breaking of a sword, a ceremony of humiliation.

sword-cane: a cane, or walking stick, which conceals a sword or dagger.

sword cutler: a person who makes swords.

sword player: a juggler with swords.

sword sliper: a sword maker.

sworn brothers: brothers in arms bound by the ancient laws of chivalry.

sworn man: a church officer in a sixteenth century church who assists a church warden. A later name for this person was a side man.

syer: sire or father.

syles: the "principal" load-bearing rafters of a building.

Symmes purchase: located in southwest Ohio along the Ohio River between the Miami rivers, this land was sold in 1794 by the U.S. government for sixty-seven cents an acre to John Cleve Symmes in appreciation for his support of the Continental Army. This land was a part of Hamilton, Butler and Warren Counties, Ohio.

syncope: fainting.

synod: 1) a council of clergymen of one denomination who are gathered together to discuss church affairs; 2) a convention or assembly.

syphillis: one of the venereal diseases (least common but most serious).

syphilitica: see syphillis.

syre: (Norman) father.

T 1) township in a legal description of land (which see); 2) tablespoon of which one equals about one-half of a fluid ounce.

t.: teaspoon, a liquid measure, which contains one fluid drachm, or about sixty drops.

tabby: a general term for silk taffeta. Originally applied to a striped taffeta, but later it included silks of an even color, either waved or watered. The name came from the area of Baghdad where it was first made.

tabellarius: record keeper.

tabes: progressive wasting from a chronic disease.

tabine: a silk fabric, sometimes with gold or silver woven in it.

table: 1) to board, to live at the table of another; 2) to take Holy Communion.

tablemen: men employed at table games, e.g. dice players.

tabler: 1) a person who keeps boarders; 2) a person who is a boarder.

tabling: a linen material from which table clothes were made.

tabularium: an archives or office where records are kept.

tack: 1) to hire pasturage for cattle; 2) a horse's harness and other equipment; 3) a lease.

tacker: 1) a person who finishes cloth; 2) a shoemaker's waxed thread.

tack hammer: a tool used by an upholsterer.

tacking end: a waxed thread with a stiff end which was used by a shoemaker.

tack lifter: a tool used by a bootmaker.

tacksman: a leaseholder.

tack to hire: 1) pasturage for cattle; 2) a shelf suspended from the ceiling to hold supplies such as bacon so animals cannot reach the supplies; 3) a path or cause-way.

taedium vitae: weariness of life.

taffeta, taffety: one of several different fabrics made of silk, linen, wool and silk, challis, thin wool, or cotton in many colors from pastels to jewel tones.

taffety: a thin silk cloth.

tail, taille: 1) a tax in France upon poor people; 2) a limitation of inheriting land to heirs of his/her body; 3) the bodice or upper part of a dress.

tail corn: see tail ends.

tail ends: hardly marketable, inferior corn which was usually consumed at home. Also called tail corn.

tail, estate: see estate tail.

taillage: a tax.

taillager: a collector of taxes.

tailleur: another spelling of tailor.

taillurs de amans: (Norman) cutters of diamonds.

tail male: at one time, there was a system of indivisible land grants in Georgia. If a person died without sons, the title to his land went back to the trustees of Georgia. There also were restrictions on the maximum size of a person's holdings and leases were forbidden.

tailor's chair: a legless chair with a back used by a tailor when he sat on the floor.

tailorship: the work of a person skilled in the art of sewing, especially men's suits.

tail race: see spillway.

taken work: a piece of maintenance (husbandry) work, not day work.

taker: a purveyor.

talbotype: a stable image produced with a special paper by a photographic process invented by W. H. Fox Talbot. Also called calotype.

talesman: one who is summoned to serve as a juror to complete the jury when all others have been excused for any one of several reasons.

talesmen: people chosen from an audience to sit on a jury when the supply of called jurors has been exhausted.

taliage: a tax.

tall: tax.

tallager: a person who collected a toll (tax).

tall clock: the name used for what we now call a grandfather clock.

tallow: animal fat which, when combined with other ingredients, will make soap, candles, etc.

tally: 1) an account; 2) upon the tally, upon credit; 3) to live together without marriage; 4) five dozen (of produce, e.g. cabbages, melons); 5) a luggage tag; 6) to label goods; 7) to be the banker at games.

tally clark: the person who checks the cargo of a ship against the bill of lading.

tally ho: a fast day-coach which ran between London and Birmingham, England.

tallyman: 1) a clerk; 2) an accountant; 3) a person who sells articles on an installment plan.

tamarine: a type of wool cloth.

tamer: a team of horses.

tamlin: a miner's tool.

Tammany: the central Democratic party housed in Tammany Hall in New York City.

tammy: a fine wool cloth of very nice quality which many times had a glazed finish.

tandem: a linen cloth which was made in Silesia.

tanist: under Irish tribal law this person was the lord second in rank to the chief of the tanistry system. See tanistry.

tanister: see tanistry.

tanistry: in Ireland before 1604 this was the equal division of lands after the death of the owner among his sons, whether or not they were legitimate. If one of the sons died, his son did not inherit but a new division was made by the tanist or chief.

tankard: a tall, drinking mug usually made of pewter or silver, with a lid and one handle.

tankard bearer: a person who brought water from a centralized supply for the use of the citizens of London.

tanner: a craftsman who cures animal skin to produce leather.

tannikin: a Dutch woman.

tansy: 1) an herb used in cooking; 2) a festival held on Shrove Tuesday.

tansy oil: a tonic made from a plant.

tantara: the sound of a bugle, trumpet or horn.

tap: a tool used by a metal worker to produce internal threads.

tapeman: see chockerman.

taper auger: a tool used by a 1) cooper; 2) chair maker.

taper bit: a joiner's tool.

tapester: a tapestry maker.

tap house: an inn or tavern where liquor is stored in casks and is served from these casks.

tapisser: a maker of tapestry.

taplash: a weak or stale beer.

tapper: an innkeeper.

taps: the last prescribed bugle call, or signal, at night which signifies that lights must be put out and noise cease. This call is also played at military funerals or at gatherings honoring military dead.

tapster: a bartender.

tapstere: the woman who had the care of the tap in a public house or inn.

tarbarelle: a combustible missile used in ancient warfare.

tar box: a box used by shepherds for carrying the tar used to mark sheep or anoint their sores, etc.

targe: a light shield worn by an archer or a member of the infantry.

tarlatan: an open, thin, plain weave cloth made of cotton which has been glazed or stiffened.

tartar, tartarin, tartarine: a rich, elegant fabric of the fifteenth and sixteenth centuries, probably a Chinese export.

tartarin: silk cloth.

tar-water: a tar and water mix which was used for medicinal purposes.

task: 1) a feudal tax of a fixed amount which was payable to a king or lord; 2) a fixed amount of work for a person to perform; 3) to tax.

tasker: 1) a person who worked and was paid for each individual piece or task; 2) a thresher, in some areas called a reaper.

taskmaster: an overseer.

task work: 1) work taken by the piece instead of an hourly wage; 2) forced labor.

tattoo: the night bugle call preceding taps. It tells the troops to go to their sleeping quarters. See also evening gun.

taulpinier: (Norman) a mole catcher.

tavern: 1) a business where alcoholic liquor is either sold to take elsewhere or drink on the premises; 2) a house where travelers were provided a room and meals for varying lengths of time; 3) a cellar.

taverner: the person who kept a tavern.

tavern keeper: the person who ran a tavern.

tavern token: a coin issued by a tavern keeper. A slang expression for "tipsy" was " to swallow a tavern token."

tawer: a leather dresser, a tanner.

taws: a piece of tanned leather.

taxables: a Southern term for males sixteen years of age and older who were obliged to pay a poll tax. Church of England clergymen, paupers and disabled persons were exempted. Many persons over 53 with no sons or any other person performing military duty paid a double tax for real and personal property.

taxage: taxation.

tax deed: a document transferring real property which has been sold for the owner's failure to pay the taxes.

taxers: two English officers chosen on an annual basis to determine if all weights and measures were correct.

tax exempt: see exempt from tax.

tax list: a list of persons in an area who own certain kinds of property which can be taxed: cattle, horses, carriages, billiard tables, as well as real estate. By comparing lists of consecutive years one can determine when the head of a household dies. The description of land or personal property is the same but the Christian name is that of a female, likely his widow. If a young son becomes an adult and the father has one less cow and horse, it may be assumed that he helped his son get started. The information varies with what information was needed by the taxing unit. By following tax lists year after year they can be considered an annual "census."

taye: 1) (Norman) grandmother; 2) to spread manure as fertilizer on land.

tayelable: (Norman) taxable.

tayon: (Norman) grandfather.

tealie: a tailor

team: a litter of pigs.

teamer: a team of five horses.

teamerman: a wagoner, carter or driver of a teamer.

teamster: a driver of two or more horses pulling a vehicle.

teasing (willying): the first of two steps in preparing fiber, by loosening and disentangling it, for spinning into thread. This is the point where the colors of wool are mixed if so desired. See carding.

teathe: dung of cattle.

ted: 1) to spread hay; 2) to turn flax which has been spread to dry.

teeled: buried.

teenage: longer wood used to make, or mend, hedges.

teepee: see tipi.

teeter cum tawter: a seesaw.

teg: a two-year-old sheep.

teguler: (Norman) tiler.

teind: a tithe.

teinten: to die.

telegrapher: a person who sends messages by using a series of dots and dashes.

telling beads: prayer beads.

temoin: French. A witness.

tempis fugit: time flies.

temple mold: a mold or pattern used by masons.

temporal court: civil court (in contrast to a church court).

tempore: in time of.

tempus fugit: time flies.

tems bread: made of sifted or fine flour.

temsing chamber: the sifting room where flour is put through a temse (sieve) to refine it.

temulence: drunk, intoxicated.

tenancy: a temporary occupation of lands or buildings which belong to another person to whom rent is paid.

tenancy at will: rental for as long as both parties desire to continue. It can be ended upon written notice of either party.

tenancy by the entirety: this type of ownership is not recognized in most states today unless it is written into a document with specific details. It is believe that this type of estate originated with the old common law belief that a man and his wife were one person and that person was the man. It is a joint ownership of land by both husband and wife with right of survivorship.

tenancy in common: this is ownership by separate titles of property held concurrently. There are no rights of survivorship and any one of the parties may terminate the cotenancy.

tenant: 1) a person who pays rent to live in a house, on a farm, etc.; 2) a person who owns land by any kind of a document. A tenant farmer can either pay cash rent or share in the profit from crops. The owner usually pays for fertilizer and anything that benefits the land and the tenant farmer provides labor and machinery. The ownership of livestock, seed, etc. are shared.

tenant farmer: this person farmed for and paid rent on an English lord's land. See also tenant.

tenants in common: see tenancy in common.

tenants, joint: see joint tenancy.

tende: 1) tenth; 2) tithe.

tender: 1) a waiter at an inn; 2) a formal offer made by one person to another; 3) a small ship acting under orders of a larger ship; 4) money; sometimes called legal tender.

tenderfoot: a person new at a job.

tenement: 1) holding by tenure; 2) a room or several rooms used by one family in a large building which houses several families.

teniente: a lieutenant.

tennandry: 1) tenants who help with harvesting; 2) manual labor on the roads ordered by the feudal lord.

tennies: a slaughterhouse. Also called a fennies.

tenor: 1) a Colonial term which described the value of silver. In used there was old tenor, middle tenor or new tenor which described fluctuating rates. By 1750 it ceased to be lawful money; 2) a general intent of the substance of a document; 3) an exact copy; 4) the value of a bill as printed on it, e.g. 10, ten.

ten sight: ten times.

tentage: 1) a camp; 2) a tent.

tenter: 1) a person who took care of cows; 2) a watchman; 3) a hired collector of tolls; 4) a tool used by a cloth dyer.

tenth and fifteenth: a taxpayer was obliged to pay a tenth or fifteenth of the value of moveable property in tax, thus the name tenth and fifteenth.

tenthedel: tenth part.

tenure: 1) the right to hold property such as real estate; 2) the right to hold a job indefinitely unless one is proved to be incompetent.

terce: life rent allotted to a widow as part of her husband's estate. There is one provision attached—they must have been married for a year and a day or have had a child.

tercian: eighty-four gallons of liquor.

termers: persons who visited the city at term time (when court was in session), the fashionable season. This word was generally applied to those who came for intrigue or tricks.

termined: judged.

terminer: a person who makes a decision.

Terr.: 1) Territorial; 2) Territory.

terre: land.

terrenus: tenant.

terre tenant: a person who holds land. Sometimes spelled ter tenant.

terrier: 1) a register or record of a survey of land in England; 2) an auger.

Territorial Papers of the United States: a series of books containing various documents generated by the states when they were territories. They contain: petitions of inhabitants, land titles, official correspondence.

Territory of the United States South of the Ohio River: this was the full name of the southwest territory. Sometimes on old deeds it is called Territory South of the Ohio River.

territory, Territory: 1) land which is not in a state, but is owned by the state or by the federal government; 2) when used with a capital T, this was an area which had a government of some type and also had not been admitted to the United States.

ter tenant: see terre tenant.

tertia: 1) the third part; 2) the ancient term for dower.

tertius: the third. One of three names added when there are three people who have the same surname in the same place, e.g. Smith minor, Smith major,

Smith tertius.

test, teste: see attest.

testable: legally able to dispose of property by a will or witness a document.

testament: see will and testament.

testamentary: 1) referring to a will; 2) given by a will; 3) appointed by a will.

testamentary bond: a bond given to a probate court by the executor of an estate to ensure that he will settle the estate in the manner desired by the testator. Some wills name Joe Blow to serve without bond, in which case no bond is posted.

testamentary guardian: a child's guardian who has been named by the father in his will or in a deed.

testament dative: an administrator appointed by the court for an intestate estate.

testament testamentor: this phrase is used to indicate that an executor was named by the deceased in his will.

testate: when a person dies and leaves a will, he dies testate.

testator: the person making a will. See devisor.

testatrix: a female who makes a will.

teste: 1) witness; 2) one who validates a document by acknowledging that a signature is correct.

tester: 1) a six pence; 2) armor for either a man's or a horse's head.

testimonium: this phrase is usually found at the end of a document and means "in witness whereof."

testimony against: a Quaker report concerning persons in violation of church rules who were not repentant. The report approved at the next business meeting would be read at the close of First Day Meeting.

testy: a witness.

tetter: a general word used to describe any skin eruption.

tew: 1) to beat hemp; 2) to tow; 3) rope used to tow a boat; 4) to work hard.

tewter: a tool used to break flax.

Texas Panhandle: a narrow strip of Texas in the extreme northern part of the state between New Mexico and Oklahoma.

textor: weaver.

thacker: a person who puts thatch on a roof, a thatcher.

thane: 1) a person who could hold land given him by his feudal superior; 2) a person who was a free servant of a feudal lord; 3) a person who held land awarded by a king of Scotland; 4) the head of a clan in Scotland; 5) a Scottish nobleman.

tharborough: a constable; every third borough had a constable.

tharfe: a number or company.

thaser: 1) a thatcher; 2) a builder.

thatch: 1) stems of plants carefully laid a foot or more deep to make a roof. Wheat straw was common, but not very durable; 2) a roof made of stems of plants, reeds, palms, straw, etc.

thatcher: a person who thatches.

thatching spale: a tool used by a thatcher.

thatching spar maker: a person who practices a trade similar to and often conducted along with wattle hurdle making. He cuts and prepares the material used in a thatched roof.

thayn: a nobleman.

theak: thatch.

thede: 1) a brewer's instrument; 2) country, land, kingdom.

theines: servants.

The Late Hostilities: the Civil War.

The Lost Cause: the Civil War.

theme: the right which a person has when he is caught with stolen goods. He can then name the person who gave him the goods.

theow: a slave.

The Recent Unpleasantness: the Civil War.

therfbreed: unleavened bread.

these presents: see presents.

The Southern Uprising: the Civil War.

thewe: 1) a slave; 2) a bondsman.

they appeared: a Quaker term found in records. It means that appointed representatives are present at a meeting.

thick set: a stout cotton cloth with a twill weave and a very short nap.

thief: a tool used by a cooper.

thirdborough: an early English policeman or constable.

third father: a great-grandfather.

thirl: 1) to restrict (England); 2) an opening; 3) to pierce something. See also sucken.

thither: to go from this toward another place.

thoft fellow: a fellow oarsman.

thole: an owner's right to charge a fee for goods transported through his property.

thornback: a female who did not marry by the time she was thirty years old.

thorowstone: a flat gravestone.

thorp, thorpe: a village or hamlet.

thorps men: villagers.

thrall: 1) a slave; 2) a captive.

thramp with: a loose noose used to tie cows to their stalls.

threap ground: disputed land.

three-cent piece: a silver, later a silver and nickel, coin in existence from 1851 until it was discontinued by Congress in 1873.

three-cocked hat: a triangular-shaped hat formerly worn by naval officers.

thresher: a furniture duster.

thridde half: two and one half.

thride: thread.

thrift box: a kind of a penny bank, this was a pottery container so constructed that coins cannot be removed without breaking it.

throw out land: acreage depleted and made worthless because the same crop was grown on it year after year.

throwster: a person who throws or winds silk thread.

thrummed: knitted.

thrush: a fungus infection of the mouth and throat characterized by tiny white spots and many times coupled with fever and inflammation of the digestive tract. This most often is found in babies and young children.

thundering preacher: the itinerant parson who harangued, raised his voice loudly, acted and used the very dramatic hell-fire and damnation oratory which became common among the rural residents of pioneer America.

thurshouse: a hollow cave in a rock or hill which served as a dwelling house for a poor family.

thurt saw: a cross-cut saw.

thwart saw: see cross-saw.

thyzle: a cooper's adze.

T.I.B.: Temple Index Bureau. A catalog for finding ancestors in a Mormon temple. No longer in use.

ticket: a tradesman's bill written on a card or ticket.

ticketings: weekly sales of ore.

ticklenburg: a coarse, uneven linen cloth named for a town in Westphalia. It was about twice as strong as osnaburg, which was popular in England. About 1800 its name was always stamped on the cloth.

tide mill: a mill powered by the coming and going of the tide. The mill had to be caulked and kept as water-tight as a ship.

tidewaiter: a customs inspector. His name came from this act of standing by the water's edge waiting for the tide to change so an incoming ship could dock.

tidewater: an area which includes bays, rivers, etc. where a tide rises and falls. It is not necessarily salt water.

tide waiter: 1) the customs officer who oversees loading of a ship's cargo; 2) an English laborer whose job is to tow ships in or out of the harbor at high tide.

tied cottage: a small house owned by an employer for the use of his worker.

tiffany: a thin, transparent fabric of silk or cotton.

tike: 1) an old horse or man; 2) corn; 3) a common sort of a dog.

tilder: a machine kept in a cellar which tilts a cask to the proper angle.

tile kill: a kiln for firing tiles.

tile punch: a tool used by a brick maker.

tile stone: a tile.

tiliere: husbandman.

tiliers: husbandmen.

tillage: 1) the process of improving land in order to grow crops; 2) crops growing on tilled ground are sometimes referred to as "sixty acres in tillage."

tiller: a farmer.

tille thakkers: tilers.

tillman: a farm laborer.

timber: 1) to build something from wood; 2) to supply with timber; 3) to sort timber into beams, planks, etc. for use in building.

timber leaves: wooden shutters.

timberline: the higher areas of a mountainous region where it begins to be too cold for trees to grow. Above the timberline there are few or no trees.

timberman: the person who measures, installs, and maintains timbers used in a mine.

timber master: the person who examines lumber and pronounces it fit for use.

timber mill: the mill which cuts timbers for building purposes.

timber right: to own the trees but not the land upon which they grow.

timber vessel: a wooden bowl.

timwhisky: a light one-horse carriage. Also called a gig, a whisky.

tinctor: dyer.

tincture: liquid medicine with an alcoholic base.

tine former: a tool used by a rake maker.

tinker: tinsmither; a person who makes inexpensive articles from sheet metal.

tinner: a sheet metal worker.

tinsin: satin cloth.

tinter: a person who dyes cloth, yarn, etc.

tinters: (Norman) tinkers.

tintype: a positive photograph on a very thin iron plate, which had been coated with a thin layer of tin to retard rust. Sometimes called a ferrotype.

tip cart: see tumbrel.

tipi: or teepee. An American Indian's house made of animal skins. Sometimes when a white man needed shelter he would trade with an Indian for an old tipi.

tippling: haymaking.

tippling house: a tavern.

tipstaff: a constable or bailiff.

tire: 1) to arm (a soldier); 2) to plaster a building; 3) to dress.

tireman: a dealer in dresses and all kinds of ornamental clothing.

tirewoman: a milliner.

tiring boy: one who stirs the color about in printing cloth, etc.

tiring room: a dressing room.

tiseours de drapes: (Norman) weavers of cloth.

tissue: a light-weight, delicate fabric which had a gauzy texture and sometimes had a gold or silver thread running through it.

tissue ballot: small ballots (2 1/4" by 1 1/2") printed on thin sheets of paper which were hard to separate, thus making "skillful" ballot counting easier when necessary. These ballots were sometimes called "kiss-verse" tickets from the small, sentimental verses contained in candy wrappers and printed on similar paper.

tithable: a person sixteen to sixty who was obliged to pay taxes.

tithe: 1) a tenth of something; 2) a portion of income paid to a church or government, usually a tenth.

tithing: 1) an administrative unit in England, including ten families or an area consisting of a tenth of a hundred; 2) to pay a percentage of income to help support a church.

tithingman: 1) a person who gave one-tenth of his income to the church; 2) a person whose official job was to wake those worshipers who nodded, keep order and make certain that persons attended church in Colonial New England. He also made certain there were no loafers in taverns who should have attended church; 3) men appointed by a jury of the court to represent their towns, to appear in court two times each year to report those who had violated a by-law of the court, e.g. a boundary post in poor condition. One term was as long as a man would care to serve.

tixteresces: (Norman) weavers.

tn.: 1) town; 2) township.

To: to wit.

toad bit: a disease in cattle.

tobacco: used in early Virginia as money when metal for minting coins was scarce.

tobacconist: 1) a person who sells products made of tobacco; 2) an obsolete word for a person who has a habit of using tobacco.

tobacco roller: a man who rolled hogsheads of tobacco with a team of horses from the farm to the shipping point.

tobine: a stout, twilled variation of the fabric called tabby.

tocher: a dowry.

toddy: a Colonial hot drink made from an alcoholic liquor, water, sugar and spiced with cinnamon, cloves, or nutmeg and

garnished with a piece of fruit.
tofet: half a bushel.
toft: 1) a knoll on which one could build a house; 2) the land on which a house and outbuildings are built.
toillier: (Norman) a weaver.
tokin: alarm bell.
toll: money paid for a privilege, such as the use of a road.
tommy: provisions.
toller: 1) a bell ringer; 2) a toll gatherer.
toloun: (Norman) toll.
tomahawk: a light war hatchet used by North American Indians.
tomahawk grant: a term for early land claims. A squatter cut a blaze or mark on each tree that surrounded his choice of land. After doing that he went to the land office to ask that his ground be surveyed and a title granted to him.
tommy: provisions.
tondour de drap: (Norman) the person who cut the cloth.
tongs: long-handled pliers used to hold hot metal while it is being worked by a 1) wheelwright; 2) blacksmith.
tonic: a strengthening medicine, which is either a patent or homemade medicine. A tonic frequently used in springtime was sassafras tea.
tonnage: 1) the cubic contents of a ship calculated in tons by the builder; 2) a tax upon casks of imported wine; 3) a fee charged to rent a ship; 4) a fee payable at a port on tons of cargo which are transported.
ton, navy vessel: one hundred cubic feet.
tonsor: barber.
tontine: an annuity toward which a group of people contribute money with the one who survives the longest reaping all the benefits.
toothing: bricks left protruding from a common wall, ready for a house to be built next to it.
Top.: topographical.
top: a tool used by a rope maker.
topens: a two penny coin.
topsman: a merchant vessel. See also top sawyer.
topographical map: a map which shows the surface features of land, such as rivers, streams, mountains, etc.
topography: a detailed exact description of an area.
topping plane: a tool used by a cooper.
topping pot: an allowance of beer given at harvest time when the hay mow was filled to the top.
topple over: a phrase used to describe livestock when they sell for double their cost.
top sawyer: the man who worked above the sawpit, also called a topman.
topsman: 1) a foreman; 2) a bailiff.
torale: (Norman) a kiln.
tornator: turner.
torrens system: named for the man who developed this plan of title registration whereby government guarantees a title. This simplifies transfers of title and renders title insurance unnecessary.
torril: 1) a worthless woman; 2) a horse.
tort: any non-criminal wrongdoing that does not involve the breaking of a contract, such as libel or slander.
Tory: 1) a person loyal to the British government during the Revolutionary War period. Also called a loyalist; 2) a person who is disloyal to a cause, for example, a Southerner who sympathized with the Union; 3) a traitor.
tory irish: a robber.
tosier: basket maker.
to smile: to take a drink of whiskey.
tote-road, pack-road, horseways: a trail used by horses laden with two hundred pound loads going single file, tied together, led by a man and followed by another man to keep the horses moving. This method grew from several families going together and hiring drivers and helpers to freight "trains" whose owners opposed the building of dirt roads because such roads would allow wagons to put them out of business.
touch box: a receptacle for lighted tinder which was carried by soldiers as sort of a matchbook.
touffa: a small shed near a farm house used to store garden tools and agricultural implements.
tougher: 1) a portion; 2) a dowry.
tounders de herbis: (Norman) sheep shearers.
tounischmen: townsmen.

tourney: see turning mill.

towboats: these boats push barges loaded with freight.

tow cloth: a very coarse, heavy, serviceable linen which during the eighteenth century would be purchased by plantation owners for their slaves to use in making their clothing. Bags or very coarse clothing were made of tow cloth and tow was also used to make ropes. Sometimes called tow linen.

to wit: that is to say; namely.

town: 1) a name for a township. It provided certain governmental duties performed elsewhere by a county; 2) village; 3) farm yard.

town clerk: the records in his keeping were minutes of town meetings, land transfers, brand marks of cattle and horses, etc. He kept what records there were of births, marriages, and deaths that were directly connected to other town business.

town crier: a person who roamed the streets of a town calling out "ads" for lost articles, animals which had strayed, the time of day, etc. Also called a herald or bellman.

town hall: a building housing the seat of local government.

town husband: an officer of the parish who collected money from the parents of illegitimate children for the maintenance of the children.

town meeting: a gathering of town citizens to conduct an open hearing on town business. Every man was eligible to attend these New England meetings, usually held annually. Officers were elected and laws were passed for the community. Special meetings could be called on a need-to-have basis.

town place: a farmyard.

Township: 1) thirty-six square miles of land; 2) a governmental unit responsible for an area of approximately thirty-six square miles; 3) thirty-six sections each one mile square; 4) a local governmental unit.

Township, numbered survey: usually found in the public domain states and bounded by geographic references which are used in describing or surveying real estate.

Township planting: laying off of land by survey into townships and selling it by complete townships to one or more persons.

townsman: see selectman.

town ward: an official title used in the late 1700s for the person who had the job of controlling fires in a town.

tow row: money paid by porters to anyone who undertook to find them work.

t.p.: see title page.

Tp.: Township.

t.p.m.: title page mutilated.

tr.: 1) troop; 2) transferred; 3) see treated.

trace: a path made first by animals, then by men, which gradually widened with use into a road; 2) a trail. See also buffalo trace.

trachelos: the neck.

tract: 1) a piece of land of any size; 2) a short book on a specific subject; 3) a booklet whose subject is usually religious and which is given free to the public.

tract book: a geographic record of sections of land. One copy was kept in the local district land office and another copy was sent to the federal government.

tract books: earliest land records of individual counties arranged by Range, Township and Section or by the metes and bounds surveying system.

tract society: a group of people organized for the purpose of giving out Bibles and literature about religion.

trader: a person who maintains a place of business and sells his goods from it.

trading cloth: see duffel.

trading vessel: a ship in any branch of commerce which is regularly used to transport goods for trade or barter. Sometimes called a trader.

trail: see trace.

traile bastons: a company of persons who bound themselves together by oath to assist one another against anyone who displeased a number of the body. They arose during the reign of Edward the First and judges were appointed expressly for the purpose of trying them. Their name was supposed to de-rive from the long staffs which they carried.

trailing beer: beer given to mowers as a fine by persons who walked over the grass before it was cut, thus mashing it down.

traillez: (Norman) taxed.

Train Band Days: in Colonial days local militia paraded on training or regimental muster days. This event would be attended by peddlers, booths might be set up, relatives would be present to watch the training process and a fair-like atmosphere would prevail.

"training band:" see militia.

trait (gens de): (Norman) cross-bowmen.

traitor: a person who betrays his country to an enemy.

trammel: a metal device attached to a horse's legs, used to make him walk slowly.

tramper: a traveling mechanic.

trampler: a lawyer.

trans.: transcribed. Sometimes used to indicate a book of deeds which have been copied from the deed books of the parent county. The land now lies in the new county, so the presence of the Trans. book can lead to earlier records.

transcribed: a record compiled or copied from an original record or from a record which has been compiled previously.

transl.: translation.

translator: a cobbler.

transporter: a person whose passage to this country was paid by another person. Therefore, he was "transported."

tranter: a carrier.

trapper's cabin: a one-room cabin, usually quite small with a roof made of sod.

traps, fish: made by basket weavers, or net workers, in varying shapes and designs depending upon the type of fish to be caught in the trap.

traunter: a peddler.

traveler: 1) a name given to very different tools used by a wheelwright and a rope maker; 2) a measuring device used to determine the circumference of a wheel, of which one revolution equalled one foot. It was used by wheelwrights and blacksmiths to measure without using a rule; 3) see also traveling missionary.

traveling missionary: a circuit rider or itinerant preacher of any one of a number of sects. The rigors of this calling kept many men from marrying, and those who did marry found it necessary to pursue an additional trade. Some became tailors, carpenters, teachers and more than one, believing that healing mens' bodies was as necessary as healing mens' souls, practiced medicine as a sideline.

traverse: 1) the area adjacent to a blacksmith's shop where horses are shod; 2) a dispute; 3) a formal denial.

traverse jury: see petit jury.

traverseles (lines): (Norman) cross lines, collateral lines.

travisher: a tool used by a chair maker.

trawe: where a farrier shoes horses.

tread road: a road made of two strips of pavement upon which the wheels of vehicles ride.

treason: the act of aiding an enemy of the country of which one is a citizen. Sometimes called leze majesty.

treasurer: this officer not only kept financial accounts, but if a bill were paid in produce he was obliged to find storage for the produce.

treasury note: a certificate which called for interest to be paid to the owner or a note payable upon request of the purchaser. These were issued by the treasury of a colony. The Republic of Texas and the Confederate Union also issued documents of this type.

treated: in the Quaker church when a member had a complaint made against him by another number, a committee was appointed to treat or deal with the offense. They were to try to get him to acknowledge his error.

treaty: a formal agreement between two or more nations specifying the actions each will take under a given set of circumstances. This may relate to trade, navigation, war, Indians, etc.

Treaty of Greenville—1796: after General Anthony Wayne defeated the Indians, a treaty was signed at Fort Greenville which ended Indian attacks on settlers in the midwest. Most of the land in Ohio was given to the United States under this treaty and enabled migration to the northwest to start.

treeksin: three weeks from now.

treen: 1) see trencher; 2) also the old plural form of tree.

treet: a kind of bran.

tregar: a linen fabric.

treltres: (Norman) traitors.

trembles: see milk sickness.

trencheours: (Norman) carvers.

trenchepaine: the person who cut bread at the royal table.

trencher: a twelve inch square block of wood with a hollow in the middle for food. These sometimes were shared by man and wife or by children. A person who could eat the entire contents by himself was called a "good trencherman."

trencher coat: a cloak worn by servants and apprentices.

trencher man: a good eater.

trenket: a shoemaker's knife.

trepeget: a military engine for projecting stones, arrows, etc.

tresail: a great-grandfather.

trespass: to cross land, enter a house, etc. of another person without permission.

tresze: (Norman) thirteen.

treys: (Norman) three.

treytour: (Norman) a traitor.

trial jury: see petit jury.

tricker: an old spelling for the trigger of a gun.

trickling: small intestines.

trifallow: to till ground for the third time.

trimmer: 1) a person who finishes an article; 2) a person who cuts excess from an article during manufacture; 3) a person who distributes the weight of cargo on a ship in order that the ship will handle properly.

trimming bill: a tool used by a wattle hurdle maker.

trine immersion: to immerse a person three times during baptism in the name of the Father, the Son and the Holy Ghost (the Trinity).

Trinity Sunday: the Sunday after Pentecost when a festival is held to honor the Trinity (Father, Son, and Holy Ghost).

trip: 1) a small flock of sheep, herd of goats, or flock of birds; 2) race or family.

tripartite: participation by three parties.

trippet: one-quarter pound.

tritor: thrasher.

troacher: a dealer in smuggled goods.

trodden paths: another name for a trace. See buffalo trace.

trolly: a low, heavy cart.

trolubber: 1) a ditcher; 2) a hedger.

trompour: a trumpeter.

tronage: a toll based on the price charged to weigh wool in the market.

tronour des laines: (Norman) weighers of wool.

trover: a court case intended to recover the worth of personal property which another person has illegally acquired and kept.

trover and conversion: an action to obtain damages against a person who has, without any right, used personal property which belongs to another person as his own.

trowe, troye: (Norman) a sow.

trowel: a tool used by a 1) stone mason; 2) plasterer.

trow mother: reputed, but not proven, mother.

truchman: an interpreter.

truck shop: in some manufacturing areas this was the place where workmen received food, clothing, etc. in lieu of money for their wages.

truck system: payment of wages in goods instead of in cash. Even more disadvantageous to workers than the company store.

true bill: when a grand jury has heard the evidence in a case and they are satisfied that there is sufficient evidence to bring the accused into court, they issue a bill of indictment—a true bill.

true form: verbatim.

trug: 1) a milk pan made of wood; 2) a shallow garden basket used for gathering flowers; 3) a measure of grain, two-thirds of a bushel.

trug framing table: a tool used by a garden basket maker.

trugger: a closely-woven basket resembling a tub or boat. It is oblong and shallow with a tall handle.

trunk-peddler: a traveling seller of small items that could be carried in one or two small tin trunks strapped to his back.

trunnel: 1) a small wooden peg with many sides which was used to fasten down shingles; 2) a wooden pin used in framing a house and its trussed roof.

trussing bed: a portable bed.

trust: property held or used to benefit the owner.

trust deed: see deed of trust.

trustee: 1) a person to whom is entrusted the care of property of another person; 2) a selectman or councilman of a city whose power was general in nature; 3) a superior court officer; 4) an official designated to guide policy and protect property of a school, township, etc.; 5) a church official; 6) a person who is appointed to protect the interests of another person by legally keeping a debtor from selling property and not paying his debts; 7) in the Quaker church, this is the person appointed by the meeting and confirmed by the court to hold title to property.

ts: tombstone.

tte: fatt (which see).

tubber: a cooper.

tubman: see postman.

tuckaway: a table which could be made smaller in some manner and put in a corner to allow more room for other activities in a pioneer cabin.

tucker: 1) see walker; 2) a fuller.

tucker in: a chambermaid.

Tudors: the royal family from which came the Kings and Queens of England from Henry VII to Elizabeth I.

tuffold: a small outbuilding.

tuft: a grove or plantation.

tuition: guardianship over orphaned minors.

tulke: 1) a man; 2) a knight.

tum: to card wool for the first time.

tumbestere: a dancer.

tumble care: a cart drawn by a single horse.

tumbrel: a cart tipped backward in such a way that the contents can be emptied from the cart.

tun: 1) a large cask which held 252 wine gallons; 2) a tub; 3) a chest; 4) a measure for wine.

Tunker: see Dunker.

tunnel: 1) in some areas this term is used to mean a funnel; 2) an obsolete term for a chimney flue.

tup: a ram.

tupman: a breeder of rams.

turbary: where there is a soil suitable for growing peat or turf which may be dug to use as fuel. May be in a commons area or on another person's land.

turbe: squadron, troop.

turfegraver: a plowman.

turf graft: see turbary.

turnbench: a watchmaker's tool.

turncoat: 1) a person who refuses to associate any longer with his former political party or other group and usually joins one having opposite principles; 2) a deserter from the army who joins the enemy.

turner: a person who shapes objects: pottery on a potter's wheel, wooden articles on a lathe, etc.

turney: a lawyer.

turning chisel: a tool used by a 1) wheelwright; 2) turner.

turning mill: this mill usually specialized in woodworking and used the water power to run a lathe on which the miler fashioned many wooden objects for home and work. This combination of lathe and power was called a tournery.

turnpike: these were toll roads with toll gates built by private companies in the late 1700s. They were dirt roads and were not passable in rainy weather for obvious reasons. A durable hard surfaced (broken stone) road was made by an Englishman who had seen this type of road in his own country and, from that time on, the roads in America improved steadily. Toll (on a round trip basis) was not charged to persons attending church services, going to vote, going to the mill or blacksmith, and the doctors or a midwife also passed through with no charge.

turnpike lands: see road or turnpike lands.

turns: a watchmaker's tool which preceded the lathe. It was used for making cylindrical objects.

turnspit dogs: dogs trained to run in a cylindrical device to keep the spit turning to cook the meat on the spit over the open fire.

tuscarora rice: a "sure cure" for "consumption" made of Indian corn and sold in the early 1700s.

Tuscaroras Indians: an Iroquois tribal member, these Indians lived in North Carolina until the early 1700s, when a savage war was waged. The Tuscaroras Indians, who were left, moved north with the Five Nations.

tutor: guardian.

tutor-at-law: a person who has been lawfully appointed for a task.

tutor dative: a guardian appointed by the court.

tutor nominate: a guardian appointed in a will.

tutorship: a guardianship in Louisiana.

Twelve-Mile Square Reservation —1805: located in Lucas County, Ohio, this reservation was the site of the old British Fort Miami. Settlers had settled near this fort for protection before the United States obtained the fort. Therefore, Congress gave the settlers their improved land before a general subdivision was made.

twesdie: (Norman) Tuesday.

twibill, twilbil: 1) a double-headed ax used to kill people in battle during the Middle Ages; 2) a hook for cutting beans.

twindles: twins.

twinlinges: twin children.

twitchel: 1) a narrow passage; 2) an alley.

twivete: a carpenter's tool.

Two-Mile Square Reservation—1805: located in Wood and Sandusky Counties, Ohio, this land was deeded by Indians to the United States under the Greenville Treaty.

Twp.: Township.

Ty.: Territory (which see).

tycoon: 1) a powerful leader of men; 2) an astute businessman.

tympanitis: see air swellings.

typewriter: 1) a machine which produces letters (1827 to present); 2) the person who uses such machines (late 1800s).

typhlitis: an inflammation in the intestine.

typhus fever: prevalent among sailors and passengers at sea and in military establishments. It is transmitted to humans by fleas and lice. Sometimes mistakenly called typhoid fever.

tyre dogs: a tool used by a wheelwright.

tythable: see tithable.

tythe: see tithe.

tythingman: see tithingman.

Uuc: in Quaker records this means "under care of."

U.C.: upper Canada.

u.d.: see ultimo die.

U.D.C.: Daughters of the Confederacy, United.

uekte: (Norman) illegitimate.

ufflers: bargemen not in constant employ who assist occasionally in towing.

U.G.S.: Utah Genealogical Society.

U.K.: United Kingdom.

ulster: northern Ireland.

ult.: abbreviation for the Latin word "ultimo," which means "last." This word is used frequently to indicate the preceeding month, for example, "8 October—Joe Ancestor died on the 17th ult." Therefore, the person died 17 September, the month before October.

ultimo die: final day.

ultimus: end, the last.

unassd.: unassigned.

under dealings: Quaker church members who have disobeyed a discipline rule to such an extent that the business meeting wants an investigation conducted into the cause of the offense and are appointing a committee to accomplish this.

underground railroad: a cooperative effort by various citizens who opposed slavery to aid slaves who were trying to escape from the south to get to the north. Much of the traveling was done at night and households would shelter the slaves in secret hiding places during daylight hours.

underground stations: safe houses where, at great risk to themselves, people sheltered fugitive slaves on their way to northern states or to Canada.

under sail: the movement of a sailing vessel as a result of wind blowing against its sails.

undertaker: 1) this occupation appeared in this country during the first half of the nineteenth century. A woodworker made coffins as a sideline. A sexton, in addition to tolling the bell and digging the grave, came more and more to making funeral arrangements. The livery stable rented carriages and thus came to furnish a hearse as part of his services. The laying out of the body progressed from friends and neighbors performing this service to a nurse who would "lay out" her patient. Finally, the coffin makers added a furniture store and then undertaking became a profession now referred to as a funeral director; 2) see also enterpriser.

ungdom: (Norman) youth.

ungkarl: (Norman) bachelor.

unhairing knife: a tool used by a tanner.

Union case: see photo cases.

"Union List:" a bibliography compiled from several sources.

unite: a gold coin.

United Confederate Veterans: an entirely male organization which no longer exists, it comprised of veterans of the Southern armies of the Civil War.

United States Military Academy: this school was formed in 1802 at West Point, New York to train young men as officers in the army. It was the first engineering college in the United States.

United States military lands: in 1796 two and a half million acres of land east of the Scioto River in central Ohio were given to pay officers and soldiers of the Continental Army for their services in the Continental army.

units: groups such as divisions, brigades, regiments, etc. in the army and corresponding groups in other branches of service.

unk.: an abbreviation for "unknown" used frequently in early census records in answer to the question "born where?."

unlaw: 1) to pay a penalty; 2) to annul a law; 3) illegally; 4) a bad habit.

unlocated balance warrant: in some states when a survey was returned to the land office for a lesser number of acres allotted in the original warrant the land office officer could issue this certificate for the remaining acres of the grants.

unm.: unmarried.

unofficious will: a will which ignores the fact that the testator has natural heirs.

unorg.: unorganized.

unprobated will: a will which was never entered into probate. Sometimes these wills will be handed down to descendants because they have never become a court record.

unrecuring: incurable.

unseated: 1) a tax list category of persons being taxed who owned land but did not live on that particular parcel; 2) removal from a position of high rank.

unseated lands: unoccupied or unsettled areas.

unsolemn will: a will with no executor named.

uphand sledge: an iron hammer large enough to require lifting with both hands.

upholder: 1) an upholsterer; 2) a person who keeps something from sinking, upright; 3) the person who maintains a building, engine, etc. in good working order.

upholster: 1) to cover furniture with cushions, fabric, springs, etc.; 2) to furnish the interior of a house with draperies, rugs, etc.

upl: in Quaker records this means "using profane language."

upland: 1) high land; 2) land in the interior of a country.

upon: when found in old court records and used as a prefix, this term indicates that something has been done, e.g. upon petition, the petition has already been presented.

upon commissioner's report: found in old court records, this term means that a report has already been received from those appointed to study the situation.

upper cutter knife: a tool used by a bootmaker.

upse Dutch: a heavy Dutch beer very popular at one time in England.

upright: a tool used by a basket maker.

upright-man: the leader of a group of beggars.

upse Dutch: a popular heavy Dutch beer in early England.

urchin: 1) a hedgehog; 2) a friend; 3) a hunchback; 4) a pitiful child.

urinch milk: whey.

U.S.A.: United States Army.

U.S.C. Art.: United States Colored Artillery.

U.S.C. Cav.: United States Colored Cavalry.

U.S.C.G.: United States Coast Guard.

U.S.C. Inf.: United States Colored Infantry.

usher: 1) an obsolete term for an assistant teacher in a private school; 2) obsolete term for a male escort for a lady.

U.S.M.C.: United States Marine Corps.

U.S.N.: United States Navy.

usufruct: to use and have the profit from land or other property which belongs to a group and which may be used only as long as the person is a member of the group.

usurer: a person who lends money at a high rate of interest.

usury: the old term for all interest paid on money. Now the term is used for interest at a higher rate than is legal.

U.S.V.: United States Volunteers.

ut: how, in what way.

Utah Indians: see Ute Indians.

Ute Indians: a warlike member of the Shoshone who lived in parts of Colorado, New Mexico, Nevada and Utah. Sometimes they were referred to as Utah Indians.

uterine brother and sister: siblings who have the same mother and different fathers.

ut infra: as below.

utroque: both sides, both directions, etc.

ut supra: as above.

ux, uxor, uxoris: wife.

uxorium: an unmarried man subject to a fine or tax upon his marital state.

uyrgaens: a Dutch measure: as far as one can walk in an hour's time.

uzzard: the letter z.

V: a letter which was partially replaced by the letter "U," beginning in the eighteenth century. It is sometimes used instead of a U in old English documents and in carved marble or other stone. It is sometimes printed for "W," or vice versa.

v.: 1) volume; 2) versus.

vacant land: government land or land to which no one holds a title. The land could be occupied but if the title has not been passed to the person on the land or if the land has reverted back to the government, it is vacant land.

vacation: the interval between the end of a court session and the start of the next.

vaccary: a cow pasture.

vachery: a dairy.

vadlet, valet: this word had various meanings. Sometimes it signified the heir of a nobleman or knight. At other times it means a young man retained in the king's or some great man's family and who was a candidate for honor. Often a young gentleman who served in the army was known by this word, as was at times a yeoman.

vails: gifts to servants.

vair: squirrel fur used as a trim or lining.

valet des chivalx: (Norman) a groom.

valid: legally binding; sufficient to be upheld by the court.

validate: to verify or confirm formally a theory, fact, document, etc.

valise: an old term for a suitcase.

vallation: 1) a wall used by the military in a defensive action; 2) to construct a wall for military defense of an area.

vallow: a press for cheese.

van: 1) an abbreviation for vanguard; 2) a machine which separates, using air, the husk from the grain.

Van Buren elm: Martin Van Buren vetoed an appropriation for maintenance of the National Road. In Plainfield, Indiana, people dug out one of the many potholes and filled it with water. The driver for Van Buren's campaign coach was part of the plot. He drove through the "pot hole," which dumped the President in the water near a tree which became known as the Van Buren elm. Van Buren signed the next road appropriation.

vandue: vendue; a public auction.

vane man: a surveyor's assistant.

vanes: the latticed, arm-like extensions on a windmill. The sails were attached to the vanes to use the wind to turn the grinding machinery.

vanesection: an old term for bleeding.

vanguard: the front line of defense on land or sea.

vanity book: another name for a county history book whose pages describe all the subscribers (for they were charged to have their biographical sketch published) as fine, upstanding, devout persons, whether they were or not.

vant currier: advanced guard.

var.: variant, variation, various.

vara: 1) a Spanish and Portuguese linear land measurement: 1 vara = 31 to 34 inches, 36 varas = approximately 100 feet, 1900.8 varas = approximately 1 mile; 2) a Texas unit equal to 33.33 inches; 3) a Spanish badge of office known by a cane used by the office holder.

varioloid: 1) a disease which resembles smallpox; 2) a mild form of smallpox which can occur in a person who was vaccinated against smallpox.

varles: (Norman) servants.

varlet: (Norman) 1) a yeoman; 2) a servant; 3) a young man who acted as a page for a knight; 4) a scoundrel.

varleton: (Norman) a groom.

vassal: 1) under the feudal system this person was obliged to serve and be loyal to an English lord for which, in return, he received the protection of the lord; 2) a slave, servant, one dependent on another for his livelihood.

vat: see wheel hoop.

vault: 1) a burial chamber situated beneath a church, partially underground, or in a tiny building on a cemetery lot; 2) an outside toilet.

vavasour, vavassor: 1) an inferior gentryman; 2) a tenant in the feudal system who ranked below a baron or a peer.

V chisel: a tool used by a chair bodger.

V.D.M.: see voluns Deus.

veelez viscountz: (Norman) old sheriffs.

veers: young pigs.
vefue, vefues: (Norman) widow, widows.
veifuage: (Norman) widowhood.
veiltee: (Norman) old age.
veloutine: a woolen fabric.
velyarde: an old man.
venator: a hunter.
vendage: harvest.
vendee: used in some courthouses instead of "grantee."
vendor: used in some courthouses instead of "grantor."
vends: a limited sale of coal.
vendue: an auction sale.
vendue master: an auctioneer.
veneours: (Norman) hunters.
venerdy, venardy, venredi: (Norman) Friday.
venesection: bleeding.
venetians: a cloth suitable for suits or dresses which had a fine, closely woven surface.
venire: a group of people who have been served a notice to appear in court as possible jurors.
venire facias: an order from a court to a sheriff requiring him to obtain a specified number of qualified people to serve on a jury.
venire facias de novo: an order to call a jury for a new trial.
venue: the county where a certain court case should be tried because it is the area where the crime took place.
veors: (Norman) 1) viewers; 2) surveyors.
verbatim: literally.
Verbi Dei minister: minister of the word of God.
verd: verdict.
verdugo: hangman.
verge: 1) a wand carried by a church official as a badge indicating his rank; 2) a wand held by a person while he swore his loyalty to his feudal lord; 3) a boundary; 4) the area surrounding the royal palace in England.
verger: 1) a church official who acted as an usher, caretaker, etc.; 2) the official who carried the verge before a dignitary.
vermifuge: a medicine, no longer used, which rid the intestines of worms or other parasites. When a child ground his teeth together while asleep, his mother could consider this a symptom and he would be given a dose of this vile-tasting medicine.
vermis: a worm.
vern: a partner in a mine.
vernage: a white, sweet Italian wine which had a higher than common alcohol content. It was sometimes used in cooking.
verser: a poet.
versus: in court records this means one against another.
very fee: full wages.
vesle: (Norman) small.
vessel: one-eighth of a sheet of paper.
vest, vestre: (Norman) west, western.
vested remainder: estate to be enjoyed later.
vestry: 1) a closet or small room in which is hung the outer garments worn by church officials during a service; 2) a layman who acts as a trustee of parish or church property.
vetera: old.
veteran donation: this land grant was given by Texas to all veterans who had ninety or more days of service in the Texas Revolution and were poor. If the veteran's widow did not remarry, she was allowed the donation.
vetula: little old woman.
vetulus: little old man.
vewter: a keeper of hounds.
veyle (le): (Norman) the elder.
veylles: (Norman) towns.
V.F.W.: Veterans of Foreign Wars.
vessel: the general term for all ships, boats, etc. used on rivers, canals, lakes, or oceans.
vicar: 1) a clerical assistant to an archbishop in ecclesiastical matters; 2) a person that takes another's place and acts for him; 3) in England, a priest who receives a salary instead of tithes; 4) in the Episcopal church, a minister who cares for another minister's church; 5) an officer of a church who represents a supervising clergyman.
vicarage: 1) the house where a vicar lives; 2) the duties performed by a vicar; 3) the salary paid to a vicar for his work.
Vice-Admiral: see navy rank.

vicereine: the wife of a viceroy.
viceroy: a person deputized to govern a colony, country, etc. in the place of its ruler.
victualler, vicualer: 1) a tavern keeper; 2) a person who supplies food to army or navy units; 3) a ship which carries provisions to army or navy units.
vide infra: see below.
videlicet (viz, vizt): namely, to wit, easy to see (used to note an explanation).
vide supra: see above.
vidi: see.
vidner: (Norman) witnesses.
vidua: widow, relict.
viduus: widow, widower.
viel: (Norman) senior, elder.
vielse, vigsel: (Norman) wedding.
viewer and culler: a person who examined and certified the size and quality of pipe staves. This was required in all New England seaport towns which exported staves. See packer and sizer of pipe staves.
view (the road): lay it out; decide the best way for the road to run from point A to point B.
viewer: an inspector of a number of things.
vigilantes: 1) a secret group of citizens who banded together presumably to preserve law and order; 2) person in the north who aided escaping slaves; 3) southern citizens who tried to control and intimidate slaves and restrain Union sympathizers.
villa: a country house.
village: a group of houses smaller in number than a town, but larger than a hamlet.
village/borough: in some states a town is referred to as a village or borough.
villein: 1) see serf; 2) an old spelling of villain, which at that time meant a worker on a farm; 3) serfs in feudal England. They were freemen except for their obligations to the feudal lord, to whom they were still considered slaves and as such must obey him.
villeinage, villenage: the conditions under which a serf had the right to live on or own his land.
villeez: (Norman) townships.
vine dresser: a person who prunes and cultivates grapevines in a vineyard.
vintager: grower of grapes.
vinter: a wine dealer.
vintner: a maker or seller of wine.
viper's dance: St. Vitus' dance.
vir.: generally means "husband."
virgate: one of several measures of land used in England which equals approximately one-fourth of an acre.
Virginia Companies: two grants, each of ten thousand square miles, were obtained by two English land promotion companies. One, located in Plymouth, colonized Northern Virginia and the other, in London, colonized Southern Virginia. These companies are usually called the London Company and the Plymouth Company.
Virginia fence: a rail fence. See snake fence.
Virginia Military District of Ohio—1784: this land was retained by Virginia to satisfy the claims of her soldiers for service in the Revolutionary War. These four million plus acres lie between the Scioto and Little Miami Rivers north of the Ohio River and are bounded on the north by Auglaize, Hardin, and Marion Counties, Ohio.
Virginia panhandle: the counties that now lie in northeastern West Virginia in the "handle" of the pan formed by West Virginia.
virgin swarm: a division of a swarm of bees.
virgo: virgin, maiden.
vir viduus: widower.
Vis.: Viscount, Viscountess.
Viscount: 1) the name of an earl's deputy; 2) an old term for a sheriff; 3) a member of English nobility, ranking just below an Earl and Count and above a Baron.
visitation: 1) an official visit; 2) a church feast held on July 2 which commemorates the visit of the Virgin Mary to Elizabeth; 3) the trip to obtain information on land owners to form the Domesday Book (which see).
visitation pedigree: see herald.
visitations: in England heralds went out into the country and collected pedigrees

to give honors to individuals.
visney: a cherry brandy imported in England from Turkey.
vita brevis: life is short.
vital records: see vital statistics.
vital statistics: public records of births, deaths, marriages, etc.
viticulture: the knowledge and skill of growing grapes.
vitious intromission: to unlawfully take, borrow, etc. with the personal property of a deceased person.
vitler: a tavern keeper.
vitrage: a thin cloth which, when used as window curtains, still lets sunlight in.
vitriarius: glazier.
vitricus: stepfather.
vitry: a light durable canvas.
vittery: see vitry.
vix.: namely.
vix or vx: wife.
viz, vize, vizt: see videlicet.
voet: a western Germany linear measure of 12.36 inches. The plural of voet is voeten.
void: no longer legal and binding.
vol.: 1) volume in a series of books; 2) volunteer.
vols: volunteers.
voltigeurs: 1) light infantry; 2) sharpshooters.
voluns Deus: minister, one who serves God.
volunteer: 1) a person who serves the federal government of his own free will and is not a member of the permanent armed forces. However, during a national emergency anyone serving at anytime, regardless of the circumstances under which he entered the service, may be considered a volunteer; 2) a person who gives a service for which he receives nothing in return; 3) a person who concerns himself with affairs which do not legally nor morally concern him.
volvulus: an obstruction of the bowel caused by twisting itself.
von: (German) of; in a name it usually indicates nobility.
voucher: a receipt or some other document which proves a transaction was made.
vounze: (Norman) eleven.
v.r.: vital records.
v.s.: vital statistics.
vs.: see versus.
vulcan: a blacksmith.
vyre: an arrow for a cross-bow.

W: 1) west; 2) will; 3) when found in a Revolutionary War pension jacket it means widow; 4) with; 5) sometimes printed as VV or substituted for "V."

w.: wife.

w/1, w/2: first wife, second wife, etc.

Wabash and Erie Canal: this canal was to be constructed from Toledo, Ohio (located on Lake Erie) to Evansville, Indiana and was to be the longest canal in the United States, 452 miles of waterways. After bankrupting Indiana, the project was abandoned.

wad: line or rank. In land surveying, when surveyors were setting out their stakes, they were said to wad in a line. Therefore, it was taken to signify a line and it was said of a person, they were all in the same wad when connected together in any way with business, etc.

wadler wife: the keeper of a register office for servants.

wadmal: a coarse, heavy wool fabric used in England and the Scandinavian countries to make sturdy outer wear.

wadset: land given as security for a mortgage which may be recovered upon payment of the debt.

waferer: a person who sold wafers, a type of cake.

wafrestere: the maker of wafers used for consecration at the sacrament.

wafter: 1) a boat which carries passengers, or 2) its master.

Wag.: wagoner.

wagonage: 1) the fee paid for hauling in a wagon; 2) a collection of various types of wagons is called a wagonage.

wagoner: 1) a hauler of food and manufactured products, successor to a pack-horse man. The wagoner carried supplies for troops in the Revolutionary War which was considered grounds to receive a pension. Also called a teamster.

wagon-master: the person in charge of several wagons which either transported freight or were occupied by pioneer families traveling westward.

wag-on-the-wall: clock works designed for a tall or hall clock but, instead of housing the clock and pendulum in a fine cabinet, the clock works were placed in a box with a hole in the bottom through which the pendulum extended. This was hung on a wall.

wagon train: a group of wagons traveling in a convoy to move freight, army supplies, or pioneers westward.

waif: 1) unclaimed goods; 2) a child alone, with no home or family.

wain: 1) a cart or wagon; 2) a home or dwelling.

wainbote: the amount of wood which a tenant could cut from a lord's woods to repair his wains or carriages.

wain men: wagoners.

wainscot: to attach wood panels to a wall. It usually covered only the bottom half of a wall and absorbed many dents which would have destroyed wallpaper.

wainwright: a maker and repairer of carts and wagons.

waist-coat: vest.

waist iron: a tool used by a bootmaker.

waiter: 1) a watchman; 2) a lord or lady-in-waiting; 3) official of the London stock exchange who wears a uniform; 4) the tray used to carry a tea service or light meal; 5) a customs official.

waits: musicians.

waive: to relinquish or abandon a right.

wakemen: watchmen.

wakemete: provisions for wakes.

walker: a person who, after the weaving process, literally walked upon the cloth in a trough. Also called a tucker, fuller, dresser.

walking inspection: see processionary lands.

walking purchase: an area around which a person can walk in a day and a half. It is a method of land measurement.

walk mill: a fulling mill.

wallage: a loose bundle of anything.

wall coping mould: a tool used by a brick maker.

waller's hammer: a tool used by a stone mason.

walloon: a person from southern Belgium and the adjoining portion of France.

wamlokes: unwashed wool.

wampum: beads fashioned from shells and used by native American Indians as money.

wang tooth: a grinder.
wanters: unmarried persons; those who want mates.
wapentake: a subdivision of an English shire which corresponded to a hundred. It had its own court system, officers, etc.
War between the North and South: the U.S. Civil War.
ward: 1) a minor child who has a guardian; 2) an administrative division of a large city; 3) see watch and ward.
ward and watch: see watch and ward.
warden: 1) a keeper; 2) a cooking pear which was available in the late fall and early winter; 3) an English high official in government; 4) a port superintendent; 5) a trustee of an institution; 6) an Oxford College headmaster; 7) a watchman.
ward room: the dining cabin for officers. Usually on the main deck.
warehouse: 1) a work house for masons, etc.; 2) a British wholesale or large retail store in England.
War for Abolition: the U.S. Civil War.
War for Emancipation: the U.S. Civil War.
War for Southern Freedom: the U.S. Civil War.
War for the Preservation of the Union: the U.S. Civil War.
warlock: a traitor.
"**warned:**" see warning out.
warning out: a stranger to an area, or sometimes a widow and her children, who were without proper security and were likely to become public charges were "warned out." Later records show that they sometimes remained in the community despite the warning.
War of 1812: the war lasted from 1812 to 1814. It was a conflict between the United States and Great Britain, arising from the attempt of the United States to maintain the freedom of the seas against British and French interference, and an attempt of the West and South to seize an opportunity to take Canada from Spain. It was during this war that the burning of Washington occurred. The peace treaty was signed 24 December, 1814. In 1850 and 1855 Congress passed an act for bounty land. These warrants were totally negotiable. The veteran could sell his warrant for money, give it away, trade it, etc. Some warrants were sold before the service was rendered.
War of 1861-65: the U.S. Civil War.
War of Northern Aggression: the U.S. Civil War.
War of Secession: the U.S. Civil War.
War of Southern Independence: the U.S. Civil War.
War of Southern Rights: the U.S. Civil War.
War of the Blue and Gray: the U.S. Civil War.
War of the Confederacy: the U.S. Civil War.
War of the Rebellion: the U.S. Civil War.
War of the Sixties: the U.S. Civil War.
War of the Southern Planters: the U.S. Civil War.
War of the Southrons: the U.S. Civil War.
War over Slavery: the U.S. Civil War.
War over States Rights: the U.S. Civil War.
warming stone: a stone put by a baker into his oven. When the stone had turned white the oven was hot.
warp: the thread which runs the length of a piece of cloth.
warper: the person who threaded a loom with long warp threads.
warping bat: a tool used by a wool worker.
warps:distinct pieces of plowed land separated by furrows.
warrant: 1) a court order. In some states this is necessary before each step of the probate process is taken; 2) a court order for the arrest of a person by a policeman; 3) a document which gives a person the right to receive specified property or services; 4) a document which gives a person the right to act in a way which would ordinarily be prohibited. This term was used interchangeably with "certificate;" 5) a receipt for goods which have been stored in an English warehouse; 6) a certificate given to a military man when

he is appointed to the grade of warrant officer.

warrant duplicate: see duplicate warrant.

warrant officer: the highest grade of non-commissioned officer. Ranked below a commissioned officer.

warranty deed: a deed which says that the seller has a clear title to the property he is selling and will defend that title.

warren: 1) the privilege, given by the king, of hunting wild game; 2) a place set aside by the king in which to keep game, e.g. rabbits, pheasants.

warriner: keeper of a warren.

warrior's path: see great Indian warpath.

wary breed: worms in cattle.

washman: a beggar who solicited charity with sham sores or fractures.

wash water: a ford.

washway: see spillway.

wasting: consumption.

watch and ward: 1) by the old common distinction "watch" was used for guard by night and "ward" for guard by day; 2) an unbroken watch of a guard against Indians, fire, etc.; 3) the service of a watchman required by a feudal lord; 4) sometimes a duty of a constable.

watching candle: the candle which provided light for the person who sat all night with a corpse.

watchman: a person who looked for criminals, unfriendly Indians, etc. and during the night would "call" out the time, weather and if all was quiet would finish with "all's well." However, if something went wrong, he would shout a warning to the citizens.

water closet (w.c.): a polite term for a toilet.

watercourse: a stream often used in metes and bounds descriptions of land.

water leder: a water carrier.

waterman: 1) a person skilled at working with boats; 2) one who earned his living by fishing; 3) the person who gave horses water while they waited at a cabstand.

water paragoon: see paragon.

water workers: makers of meadow drains and wet ditches.

wattle hurdle: a woven fence used by sheep raisers replaced now by wire and electric fences. Wattle is still used for screening in yards and gardens in town.

waugh mill: a fulling mill.

waver: a common pond serving the whole village.

wax chandler: probably the person who made candles from beeswax.

wax end: a waxed thread used by a shoemaker.

way goose: a party given by an apprentice to his fellow workmen.

way wardens: keepers of private roads.

w.b., w.bk.: will book.

w.c.: 1) with costs; 2) see water closet.

w/c: in Quaker records this means "with consent of."

W.D.: 1) War Department; 2) Warranty Deed.

wd.: ward.

wds: wounds.

weak in body: a phrase used in early wills; it meant that the testator's health was not good. Usually followed by a claim that his mind was clear.

weard/writere: 1) testator; 2) word writer.

weaver: a person who weaves rugs, cloth, etc. for his living.

web: a weaver.

webber: a person who wove cloth.

webster: a weaver of cloth.

weddle-fere: husband; wife.

weddiger: a guest at a wedding.

wedge: a tool used by a chair bodger.

wedlake: marriage.

wedlock: a wife.

wedman: a husband.

wedwede: widowhood.

Weekly Meeting: the Sunday service of the Society of Friends.

weepers: persons, sometimes professionals, who attended funerals to swell the crowd and make the deceased appear to be more important.

wedge and feathers: a tool used by a stone mason.

weight viewer: the person who inspected scales so that a retailer would not give a short weight. Today this person would be concerned with weights and measures. Sometimes called a standard keeper.

weir: a 1) dam; 2) fence; 3) fish trap.

well-hook: see grapnel.

wells: underparts of a wagon.

Wells Fargo Colt: so called because the gun issued by the express company to its guards was a small five-shot, 31 caliber, percussion-cap revolver issued by the Colt Gun Company in 1848.

well-sweep: a device consisting of a bucket fastened to the end of a pivoted and counterweighted pole used to raise water from a well. It was cheaper than a pump and would not crack or freeze in winter, therefore it was used for many years.

Welsh uncle: first cousin of a parent.

welt plough: a tool used by a bootmaker.

wem: 1) a spot or blemish; 2) the womb; 3) a belly.

wenche: a black female slave. The term is often used on tax lists.

werke: work.

werke day: work day.

Western Reserve: sometimes referred to as New Connecticut, this was land in the northeast corner of Ohio which was owned by Connecticut.

West Point: see United States Military Academy.

Westsylvania: the Westsylvania Land Company was formed in 1776. It covered a large part of the Appalachian Mountains and included some of southwestern Pennsylvania, all of present day West Virginia and northeastern Kentucky.

wever: a river.

wey: a measure of weight. A wey of coal was approximately three tons.

weyne: a wagon.

weysluyp: a Dutch tool similar to a harrow which was passed over ground in the spring to level molehills.

wh: with, which.

whacker: a driver of a team of horses, oxen, etc.

whaleman: a person who worked on a whaling ship.

whaler: a person who catches whales or the ship engaged in the business of catching whales.

whang: rawhide strips used for shoestrings, etc.

whangley: a very hard cheese made from old or skim milk.

wharfboat: this boat houses company offices from a mooring on the shore.

wharfinger: 1) the person or company in charge of berthing ships to be loaded or unloaded; 2) one who represents a ship owner at a wharf to ascertain the amount or condition of cargo.

whart: one quart.

wharter: a quarter.

what way: a guidepost.

wheat cradle: a farmer's tool. Basically, a scythe with an attached wooden frame which collected the cut wheat and allowed it to be placed on the ground for easier harvesting.

wheat shocker: the person who bound cut wheat into a bundle and stacked several bundles together to dry.

wheel hoop: millstones were enclosed in a custom-made circular wooden box which was also called a vat, hoop, husk, curb.

wheelspun: a strong, coarse yarn.

wheelwright: a person who made wagon and carriage wheels and installed metal tires on the wheel rims.

whereas: a word which prefaces a recitation of facts.

whetlebones: vertebrae of the back.

whetstone: an abrasive stick used to sharpen hard steel.

whig: buttermilk.

Whig: 1) a person who sided with the Colonial side against the British during the Revolutionary War; 2) a person who was against Andrew Jackson's ideas and principles; 3) a member of one of various British or United States political parties, most of which were conservative.

whim: see wim.

whip: there were several kinds and designs of whips but they all had lashes and were used to make an animal obey or go faster. Also used to punish people.

whiparse: a schoolmaster.

whip jack: a vagabond who pretended to be a distressed seaman when he begged for alms.

whir-to-woo: buttermilk.

Whiskey Insurrection: an outbreak in western Pennsylvania in 1794 caused by the imposition of taxes on domestic distilled goods. The people of western Pennsylvania, where large quantities of whiskey were made, resisted the collection of the revenue by excise officers forcibly. The insurrection became gen-eral in several counties, buildings were burned, mail tampered with, govern-ment officers insulted and abused. George Washington, as President, finally called out the U.S. military and put down the insurgentcy. Leniency was shown to the offenders and the excitement died away.

Whiskey Rebellion: fought in 1793-94, when Pennsylvania rebelled against a tax imposed upon whiskey by the United States government.

whisky: see timwhisky.

white: silver money.

white acre, witacre, whitaker: a name given to one particular piece of land, as opposed to another particular piece of land referred to as a black acre.

white ale: an ale pale in color.

white back: white poplar tree.

white house: a dairy house.

white money: silver.

white powder: a gunpowder which exploded with little noise and smoke.

white rent: rent to be paid in silver (money). See black rent.

whitesmith: 1) a tin worker; 2) a person who finishes metal; 3) any worker in metal who is not a blacksmith.

whitester: a bleacher of linen.

white swelling: phlegmasia. Thrombosis of large veins in the leg accompanied by swelling, hardness, and much pain. It occurred quite frequently after child birth and is also called milk-leg.

whitewing: a street sweeper who wore a white uniform while performing his tasks.

whitlow: a felon; a painful inflammation of tissue deep in a toe or finger near the nail.

whitney: see witney.

Whitsunday: see Pentecost.

Whitsuntide: a festival to commemorate the descent of the Holy Ghost upon the Apostles. It is said that newly baptized persons wore white garments on Whit-Sunday. This feast is moveable, always being exactly seven weeks after Easter.

whitster: a whitesmith.

whitsun farthings: customary dues from parochial churches to their cathedral.

whittawer, whitetawer: 1) a collar maker; 2) one who tanned white leather; 3) a maker of harnesses and saddles.

whooping cough: an infectious disease, now almost extinct, characterized by a convulsive cough and an intake of breath that had a crowing or whooping sound.

whyster: one who bleaches cloth.

wic: a week.

wicken tree: a mountain ash tree.

wid.: widow.

wide coat: a heavy outer coat.

widow: a woman whose husband is deceased.

widow bewitched: a woman who is separated from her husband.

widower: a male whose wife is deceased.

widow's bench: a share of a husband's estate which some widows enjoy besides their jointures.

widow's mite: 1) the portion of a man's estate which was given to his widow; 2) a small amount of money given to a cause willingly. So-called for the two mites a widow gave to the temple (Mark 12:42).

widow's walk: a platform with a rail which went around the highest part of a house situated on a seacoast. Here a wife could watch for her husband to come home after a sea voyage.

widr.: widower.

wife modir: a mother-in-law.

wifler: a huckster.

wifles: unmarried.

wifly: unmarried.

wifman: a female.

wigger: a wig maker.

wiggin: mountain ash tree.

wigster: a wig maker.

wike: 1) a home; 2) a dwelling.

wildcat bank: an unreliable bank, oil well, etc. that is outside the bounds of a legitimate business practice.

wild nettle: a weed from which clothing for Virginia pioneers was made. It was cut when still green and then treated as flax to make a linen-like thread which was woven with buffalo hair to make a durable cloth.

wilf: a willow tree.

wilghe: a willow tree.

will and testament: the word "will" means a document in which the testator distributes his or her real estate. "Testament" is the document in which the testator distributes his or her personal property.

will contest: any type of controversy which concerns whether or not a will is eligible to be probated.

willow bench: a share of a husband's estate enjoyed by his widow, besides that which was held jointly.

willying: see teasing.

wim: an engine or machine worked by horses, used for drawing ore.

winder: a woman who had charge of a corpse between time of death and the burial.

winding sheet: see shroud.

windmill: a mill with large vanes or arms (usually four) and sails which made use of wind to power a mill. A windmill ground corn, sawed wood, ground bark for a tanner, pumped sea water for salt making, ground flour, chocolate, snuff, etc.

window peeper: the district tax assessor.

window tax: an early English tax charged for each window or opening to let light into a building.

windrow: 1) sheaves of corn set up in a row, one against another. They are stacked this way so that the wind may blow between them to dry the corn; 2) a row of grass in haymaking.

Windsor: the family name of the rulers of England since World War I. See Saxe-Coburg.

wine gallon: a measure of wine, based on the English gallon of 231 cubic inches, 160 fluid ounces English, and 128 fluid ounces U.S., which has become the standard for a gallon in the United States.

Winnebago Indians: a tribe who lived around the lake of the same name in Wisconsin and took part in several wars. They moved further west in the middle nineteenth century.

winnowing: see skepe.

winter cricket: a tailor.

winter fever: probably pneumonia.

winteridge: winter food for cattle.

winter weeds: chickweed; a hearty weed which flourishes in winter.

wintle end: the stiff end of a shoemaker's thread.

wipes: a fence made of brushwood.

wire drawer: the person who pulls metal through a series of progressively smaller holes to form wire of varying thicknesses.

wisewoman: 1) a midwife; 2) a female fortune teller; 3) a woman who dispenses charms.

wissere: 1) teacher; 2) director.

wit.: witness.

Witan: a council in early England whose function was to select a king from among suitable candidates of royal birth.

witchwood: a mountain ash tree.

Witembre: (Norman) October.

witewood: a covenant.

withe: a small flexible branch used in place of a rope.

withes: thin strips of wood or bark, hung between rafters for drying fruits, vegetables, etc.

witness: 1) a person who saw an event occur, a document signed, etc. and who can swear that his description of what he saw is the truth. In Virginia for many years three persons were required to witness a document when most states required only two signatures. When a document with three witness signatures is found a researcher might think about searching Virginia records.; 2) a godmother.

witness corner, witness tree: a surveyor's mark. A tree or rock on which is carved a reference, plus the initials w.c., to the corner of a tract of land.

witness tree: see witness corner.

witney: a loosely woven, heavy cloth suitable for blankets which was made at Whitney, England. At one time a cloth suitable for coats was made at Whitney.

W.O.: 1) Warrant Officer; 2) presumed to mean white oak when found in old records.

w/o: wife of.

wobster, wobstar: a weaver.
wod: an ox.
Wodenis: Wednesday.
wodewe: a widow.
wolf: 1) a wooden fence which, when placed across a ditch in the corner of a field, will prevent cattle from straying via the ditch; 2) a fishing net; 3) a disease of the legs; 4) a bit for a restless horse.
wommel: an auger.
woning: a dwelling.
wooden ditch: see mill race.
wooden pipe: see mill race.
wooden ruff: the pillory.
woodhacker: a woodman.
woodman: a carpenter.
wood monger: 1) a dealer in wood used as fuel; 2) a dealer in timber used to build houses.
woods colt: a child born out of wedlock.
woodsman: 1) a cutter of trees; 2) a person who removes logs from a forest; 3) a person who lives in a woods or goes there quite frequently. As a rule, he is skilled in survival and hunting.
woodward: an English officer who had charge of patrolling a wooded area.
woolcomber: 1) a person who removes tangles from wool fibers and discards those which are too short; 2) the person who runs a machine which accomplishes the above task.
woolen worker: a weaver's aide.
worke: a week.
workfarm: a farm where those who have a short-term sentence are obliged to do whatever farm work needs to be done.
workhouse: 1) a jail where those who committed petty crimes are obliged to work while they are confined; 2) an English poorhouse; 3) a workshop where something is manufactured.
worm fence: see snake fence.
worm fever: fever accompanying intestinal worms.
wormfit: see also vermifuge.
worms: parasites which look like earthworms and which live in the human body.
worsted: a long fibrous wool which is twisted tightly into a thread or yarn. When woven into cloth, it has a hard, smooth finish which wears well. The yarn, used for knitting, has the same qualities and both thread and yarn have acquired the name of worsted.
wort: beer in the making.
w.p.: white poll.
W.P.A. (historical records): Works Progress Administration, a Federal make-work program introduced during the middle 1930s. Many old records were copied, inventories of courthouse records were made, local histories were written, etc. by persons who otherwise would have been unemployed.
wrapper: a housecoat, robe, etc.
W.R.H.S.: Western Reserve Historical Society.
wright: a person who did the designing, making and erecting of machinery, for example, a millwright, a wheelwright.
wringhouse: a building for cider making.
writ: 1) a written order of a court addressed to a sheriff or similar officer who must carry out the instructions of the court. After receiving the order he must return a report to the court officer who issued the document; 2) a scroll of writing.
writend: 1) a writer; 2) a legatee.
writer: a solicitor.
writ of attachment: see attachment.
writ of capias: a formal arrest document.
writ of certiorari: see certiorari.
writ of fieri facias: see fi fa.
writ of inquiry: an order to the sheriff which directs him to determine, with the help of a jury, damages which cannot have a dollar and cents value placed on them.
writ of restitution: a process by which a person who has won an appellate case can retrieve property which had been unjustly taken away from him in a prior judgment.
writ of summons: see summons.
writ of venditioni exponas: an order to a sheriff to sell goods of a person who owes the court money.
writ of venire facias: see venire facias.
wroken: a Dutch woman.
Wyandot Indians: see Huron Indians.

X: 1) Christ; 2) Christian; 3) when the person who was to authenticate a document could not write his name, someone else would write his given name and surname. Then, the signer would mark an "X," usually between the two names, and the second person would write "his mark" or "her mark." Usually, one of these words was above and the other below the "X."

xch.: exchange.

Xn.: Christian.

xped: Christened.

Xr.: Christian.

Y

y: see i.

y.: year.

yaits: oats.

yale: a small quantity.

yankee: name given to North Americans in general, but to New Englanders in particular. It is not a complimentary term in the southern United States.

Yankee Invasion: the Civil War.

yankee peddler: see chapman.

yard: a garden.

yard land: 1) a quantity of land which varies from fifteen to forty acres. In some places a quarter of an acre was called a yard of land; 2) a barn or pen for animals; 3) a farmyard.

yard man: 1) the laborer who had charge of the farmyard; 2) a person who worked in a lumberyard, shipyard, etc. or cared for the yard of a public building.

yard master: a superintendent of a railroad yard.

yat: 1) a gate; 2) a heifer.

yaud: a horse or mare.

yaw: a fast turn from directly ahead to the right or left, caused by poor steering.

yawney box: a donkey.

yd.: graveyard.

ye: 1) the; 2) you (plural); 3) you (singular), particularly when referring to a noble; 4) the use of ye for "the" is a carryover from the old Anglo-Saxon letter "thorn.".

year day: 1) an anniversary; 2) a day on which prayers were said for the dead.

yearling: an animal, person, or anything, especially a horse, more than a year old.

Yearly Meeting: an annual quarterly business meeting at which activities of all the monthly meetings under its control are reported. Annual reports are published by this group and are distributed to the members. The churches of the Orthodox branch of Friends are united under the Five Years Meeting.

year's provisions: a widow was entitled to supplies for a year from her husband's estate. Some men listed these supplies in their wills or charged a son with his mother's support. By reading these supply lists, one can discover much about an ancestor's way of life. Also called year's support.

yele house: a brewery.

yeman: 1) a servant of a rank next to a squire; 2) a person of middling rank.

yeme: 1) uncle; 2) to protect; 3) to care for; 4) to rule.

yende: India.

yeoman: 1) an experienced man capable of keeping account of supplies and costs; 2) a farmer who tills his own small acreage; 3) a person who can be counted on to work diligently and effectively; 4) a clerk or writer in the navy.

yeoman fewterer: a dog keeper.

yeoman's bread: bread for everyday use.

yere: 1) an heir; 2) ear; 3) year.

yermen: men hired by the year.

yets: oats.

yett: a gate.

yewre: a water bearer.

yewys: Jews.

yh: used in some old manuscripts for y, e.g. yheme = yeme (uncle), yhe = ye.

yherde: 1) yard; 2) rod.

yhere: a year.

yith: an ecclesiastical district in England. 1630: I give unto the poor of the Parish of St. Nicholas Atwode (Thanet, England) 20 pounds to be paid among the poorest sort of people of the said YITH within one year of my disease."

Y.M.: a Quaker yearly meeting.

ym: them or him.

ympnys: hymns.

yngynore: a maker of engines.

ynnys: lodgings.

yo: you.

yoke: 1) a pair of oxen; 2) part of a working day; 3) a hiccough; 4) a grease found in wool.

yoky: wool as it comes from a sheep's back.

yoo, ewe: a female sheep.

yore: this word usually refers to an old time, long ago. However, in an inventory it appears to be used in the sense of antique.

Yorkist: 1) a member of the Plantagenet (which see) families from which fourteen of England's kings descended; 2) a supporter of the Plantagenets.

york pence: a copper coin used during Henry VI's reign.

york shilling: a coin used in early New York.

Yorkshire hunters: the name of a regiment formed by men from Yorkshire.

yort: 1) a yard; 2) a field.

younger children: all of a man's children except the eldest sons. They had fewer rights than the eldest son. Daughters who were older than the eldest son were included among the "younger children."

your obedient servant: written above a signature in a letter, this is equivalent to today's "yours truly."

yr: year.

yraut: (Norman) a herald.

yr., yrs.: year, years.

yrfe: 1) an inheritance; 2) a sword.

yt: it or that.

Z: often used in Scottish books to represent "Y."

zak: a Dutch measure consisting of three schepels.

Zane's Tracts: from 1796 to 1802 three one-mile-square pieces of land were given to Ebenezer Zane, for which he agreed to open a road from Wheeling, West Virginia to Maysville, Kentucky. They were located at Zanesville, Lancaster, and on the east bank of the Scioto River across from Chillicothe, Ohio.

zax: a tool used by a slater.

zed: English English for the letter "z."

zephyr: one of any number of lightweight items made from a high quality wool.

zin: 1) the sun; 2) a son.

zinnila: a son-in-law.

Zivershsack: a bag, closed at both ends, with an opening in the middle. When carried across a man's shoulder the weight is evenly distributed between the front and back. An Aesop's fable calls it a Zivershsack wallet; a man put his neighbors' faults in the front section and his own faults in the back section. Therefore, he could not see his own faults but he could always see those of his neighbors.

zonarius: girdlemaker.

Zouaves: a body of French light infantry whose uniform was unusual and brightly colored. The name was assumed by a number of volunteer regiments in the Union army during the Civil War. They wore a uniform similar to that of the Zouaves.

& c, & ca: et cetera.

$: 1) United States dollar; 2) Spanish milled dollar.

Appendix A

Dutch Given Names

Many historical trails lead back to New Amsterdam (now New York) and back to the Netherlands. The names encountered along these trails seem strange to speakers of English. Naturally, these names tended to be Anglicized after English power prevailed in North America. Two lists are presented here: the Dutch-English list may be more useful for those tracing from early days to the present, while the English-Dutch list may be better for those who are looking backward in time.

The Pennsylvania Dutch, needless to say, are not Dutch at all, but Deutsche (German). Dutch names ending in "je" e.g. Dirkje, Klaasje) and "ken" are diminutives and apply either to little boys or females, as we say Billy, Nelly, etc.

Dutch-English First Names

Dutch	English
Aaghie, Aaghje, Aaght, Aagje	Agatha
Aaitje, Aaltje	Adeline
Aarend, Aart	Arthur
Abegail	Abigail
Absulon	Absulom
Adda	Adeline
Adela	Adelaide
Adriaantje	Adrianna
Aefje, Aefjee	Eva
Aeltie, Aeltje	Adelina
Aengenietje, Aengenietye, Agnietie, Agnietje	Agnes
Alana	Helen
Albertus, Alburtus	Albert
Aletta	Adela, Letitia
Alicia	Alice, Lettice
Alida	Adeline, Adela
Anate	Ann, Anne
Andries	Andrew
Anecke	Ann, Anne
Angenetye	Agnes
Angie	Anna, Nancy
Anginette	Agnes
Anita	Ann, Anne
Annaatje, Annatie, Annatje, Annatjie	Ann, Anna, Anne
Anneckie, Anneke	Anna, Nancy

Anneken, Annetje .... Anna, Nancy
Antie .... Ann, Anne
Antonetta .... Antoinette
Antye, Ariantye .... Adriana
Arie, Arien .... Aaron, Adrian
Arlond, Arnout .... Arnold
Asel .... Asael
Assepoester .... Cinderella
Augustijn .... Augustine
Baachie .... BerBalt, Balthaser
Baltas .... Balthaser
Baltie, Baltje .... Elizabeth
Baltus .... Balthaser
Barber .... Barbara
Barent .... Bernard
Bartel, Bartholomeus ... Bartholomew
Bartje .... Bertha
Bastiaan .... Sebastian
Bata, Batje .... Bertha
Baudewyn .... Baldwin
Becki .... Rebecca
Beletje .... Isabella
Belettie, Belitje, Bell . Isabella, Arabella
Bella. Belletjie ..... Isabella, Arabella
Bengemen .... Benjamin
Betje .... Betty
Betsy .... Elizabeth
Boduwyn, Boudewyn .... Baldwin
Brechje, Bregetje, Bregetta .... Bridget
Bregette, Bregezie .... Bridget
Breghje, Bregie .... Bridget
Calvijn .... Calvin
Carel .... Charles
Carly, Carlyn, Caroly .... Caroline
Carroline, Carye .... Caroline
Casparis .... Jasper
Catalina, Catalyntie, Catalyntje, Catalyntjen, Catarina, Catelina, Catelyntye, Cathalyna, Cathalyntie, Catharin, Cathelina, Cathleen, Cathlintie, Cathlyntje, Cathryntje, Catlynte, Catlyntie, Catlyntye, Catreina, Catriena, Catrientje, Catrina, Catryna, Catryntjie, Cattalyntjen, Cattelyntie, Cetje .... Catherine
Charlina .... Caroline
Chattie, Chatty ..... Catherine (Kitty)
Christiaan .... Christian
Christinje .... Christina
Christoffel .... Christopher
Christyntje .... Christiana
Citty .... Catherine
Claasje .... Claudie
Cladious .... Claude
Claes .... Nicholas
Claessie .... Nicole
Cloudy .... Claude
Coen, Coenraad .... Conrad
Cornelis .... Cornelius
Crumeline .... Crommelin
Cryenus .... Quirinus
Cytie .... Sophia
Daam .... Adam
Daatje .... Adelina
Dammas .... Thomas
Deetje .... Adelina
Denys .... Dionysius
Derick, Derrick, Diederick ... Theodore
Diewertje .... Deborah
Dirck .... Theodore
Dirckie .... Theodora
Dirick, Dirk .... Theodore
Dirkje .... Dorothy
Doortje .... Dorothea
Doris .... Theodore
Dorotea .... Dorothea
Douwe .... Dow, Dowie
Dries .... Andrew
Dunis .... Anthony
Dyne .... Dinah
Echie .... Agatha
Effie .... Eva
Elena .... Helen
Elesebath, Elizabet .... Elizabeth
Elsje, Elzie .... Alice, Lettice
Emalyne, Emmetje .... Emma
Engelite .... Angeline
Engeltie, Engeltje .... Angelica
Enretta .... Harriett
Epje, Epke .... Egbert
Ernst .... Ernest
Ethelbert .... Albert
Ethelyn .... Ethel
Eva .... Eve
Evert .... Everard
Evertie .... Everarda
Eytie .... Ida
Feitjin .... Sophia
Felipe .... Philip
Femmetie, Femmetien, Femmetye .... Sophronia
Filip, Filips .... Philip
Floortje .... Flora
Floris .... Florence
Francina .... Francisca, Frances
Frans .... Francis, Frank
Franscyntje ...... Francisca, Frances

Fransytie . . . . Francisca, Frances
Frenky . . . . Frances
Frientye . . . . Catherine
Frinckye . . . . Frances
Fytie . . . . Sophia
Geerje . . . . Gertrude
Geert . . . . Godfrey, Gerard
Geertje, Geertruy, Geertruyd . . Gertrude
Geertye . . . . Gerardina
Geesie, Geesje, Geesye . Grace, Charity
Gellis . . . . Giles
Gerardus . . . . Gerard
Geresolveert, Geresolvert . . . . Resolved
Gerretie . . . . Gerardina
Gerrit . . . . Gerard, Garret
Gerritie, Gerritje, Gertchen, Gertje
. . . . Gerardina
Gertruit . . . . Gertrude
Getty . . . . Catherine (Kitty)
Geurtje . . . . Gerardina
Giel . . . . Michael
Giertje . . . . Gertrude
Gillis . . . . Giles
Gitty . . . . Catherine (Kitty)
Goris . . . . George
Govert . . . . Godfrey, Gerard
Gretchen, Grietie, Grietje . . . . Margaret
Grietzie . . . . . Margaret, Madge, Peggy
Griselda, Grissel . . . . Grishild
Guysbert, Gysbert, Gyslbert . . . . Gilbert
Hannes . . . . John
Hans . . . . Jack
Hansje . . . . Johanna
Harman, Harmanus, Harmen, Harmon
. . . . Herman
Hendrick . . . . Henry
Hendrickje . . . . Henrietta, Harriett
Hendrickus . . . . Henry
Hendrickye . . . . . . Henrietta, Harriett
Hendrik, Hendrikje, Henricus . . . Henry
Hervey . . . . Harvey
Hesje, Hetty . . . . Esther
Hevlyn . . . . Evelyn
Heyltje . . . . Huldah, Hail
Hieronimus, Hieronymus
. . . . Hierom, Jerome
Hilah, Hillegonda, Hilletje . . . . . Huldah
Huygen . . . . Hugh
Hyer . . . . Hierom, Jerome
Hyltje . . . . Huldah
Jaap . . . . Jacob
Jaapje . . . . Jemima
Jacobus . . . . James
Jacomina, Jacomintie, Jacomyntje,
Jakomina . . . . Jemima
Jan . . . . John
Janche, Janije, Janneke . . . . Jane
Janneken . . . . Joan
Jannetie, Jannetje, Jannitje . . . . Jane
Japic . . . . Jacob
Jaquemyntie . . . . Jemima
Jas . . . . James
Jeannetie . . . . Jane
Jeletie . . . . Julia
Jennecke, Jenneke, Jennica . . . . Jane
Jeremias . . . . Jeremiah
Jeronimus . . . . Hierom, Jerome
Jesyntje . . . . Justina
Jillis . . . . Giles
Joana, Joanna . . . . Jane
Jochem . . . . Joachim
Johan . . . . John
Johanna . . . . Joan
Johanneke . . . . Jane
Johannes . . . . John
Jonitia . . . . Jane
Jooris, Joost . . . . Justus, Jocelyn
Joris . . . . George
Josina . . . . Juarina
Josine . . . . Juarine
Josyntje . . . . Juarina
Jurge, Jurgen, Jurian, Jurjen . . . . George
Kaarl . . . . Charles
Kaatje . . . . Catherine
Karel . . . . Charles
Kasper . . . . Jasper
Katheryn, Kathy, Katrientjie, Katryne.
Katryntje, Kattelyntie, Kattelyte,
Katy . . . . Catherine
Kees . . . . Cornelius
Kerstan . . . . Christian
Keziah . . . . Cassia, Kezia
Kittie . . . . Catherine
Klaartje, Klaartye . . . . Clara, Clare
Klaas, Klaasje . . . . Nicholas
Klassve, Klasyne, Klazina, Kobus Nicole
Koris, Korn, Krelis . . . . Cornelius
Kristiaan . . . . Christian
Kryn . . . . Quirine
Laenette, Lana . . . . Helen, Magdalene
Laurens, Laurentz, Laurenz . . Lawrence
Lea, Leah . . . . Helen, Magdalene
Leendert . . . . Leonard
Leentje . . . . Helen, Magdalene
Leisabeth . . . . Elizabeth
Lena, Leni . . . . Helen, Magdalene

Lenoor, Leonora	Eleanor
Letje	Letitia
Leynje	Helen, Magdalene
Liene	Helen, Magdalene, Caroline
Lientje	Caroline
Lieve	Leo
Lieven	Elizabeth
Lodewyk	Ludovicus
Lotje	Charlotte
Lourens, Loures, Lowerens	Lawrence
Ludovicus	Louis, Lewis
Lukas, Luytje	Luke
Lybetie, Lysbet, Lysje	Elizabeth
Maaicke, Maartje	Mary
Maas	Bartholomew
Maayke	Mary
Machtel, Machtelde	Matilda
Macia, Maike, Mally	Mary
Manus	Herman
Mareus	Marius
Margarita, Margaritta, Margrietje, Margrietze, Margritje	Margaret
Maria, Mariah, Marica, Maricka	Mary
Marietje	Maria
Marietta, Mariken, Maritjen, Marretye, Marrietta, Marritje	Mary
Mart	Martin
Marta	Martha
Marte, Martyen	Martin
Martyntie, Martyntje	Martina
Marya, Maryette	Mary
Maryntyntie	Martina
Marytje	Mary
Matewis, Matheas, Matheus	Matthew
Matie, Matje	Martha
Matthys	Matthias
Meewes	Bartholomew
Metje, Mettje	Martha
Mewis	Bartholomew
Meysie	Mazie
Mietje	Mary
Morinus	Marinus
Mouris	Maurice
Myrette, Myrtie, Myrtle	Mary
Naatje	Anna
Neeltje, Neeltjen	Cornelia
Neil	Cornelius
Nelje, Nella, Nelletje	Cornelia
Nicolaas	Nicholas
Nicolaes	Nicholas
Nicolaus	Nicholas
Nieltjin	Cornelia
Niesje	Agnes
Noach	Noah
Obadja	Obadiah
Orsinius	Ursinus
Osseltei	Ursull
Ota	Ortho
Otho	Otto
Pakke	Margaret
Pauel, Paulus	Paul
Paulyntje	Paulina
Pauwel	Paul
Peggie	Margaret
Petrus	Peter
Phlip	Philip
Piet	Peter
Pieterje, Pietertje, Powles	Paul
Rasana	Rosina
Roelof	Ralph
Roosje	Rose
Rosena	Rosina
Rudelft	Rudolph
Rutgert	Roger
Ryck, Rykaard	Richard
Saal, Saartie	Solomon
Saartje	Sarah
Sander	Alexander
Sanneke, Santje	Susanna
Sarahette, Seertie	Sarah
Sherrard	Gerard
Sophya	Sophia
Staats	Eustice
Stoffel	Christopher
Styntje	Christiana
Tannecke, Tanneke, Tanneken	Ann
Teewis	Matthew
Teunis	Anthony
Teunitje	Antonia
Teuntje	Eunice
Theodorus	Theodore
Theunis	Anthony
Thryntie	Catherine
Thys	Matthias
Tiebout	Theobold
Tietje, Tietye	Letitia
Tina, Tinie, Tiny	Catherine
Titje, Tittye	Letitia
Tones, Toontye	Anthony
Treintje, Trientie, Trientje	Catherine
Truytje	Gertrude
Tryntie, Tryntje	Catherine
Tuenis, Tunis	Anthony
Tymen	Timothy
Tys	Matthias
Ursel	Ursula

Vinnie . . . . Lavinia
Vroutie, Vroutjer, Vroutie, Vroutjer,
Vrouwete . . . . Sophronia
Weart . . . . Wiert
Wientie, Wientje . . . . Lavinia
Wilhelmyntie . . . . Wilhemina
Willem . . . . William
Willemfye, Willempie, Willempje,
Williememe . . . . Wilhemina
Wouter . . . . Walter
Wynca, Wyntei, Wyntie, Wyntje.
Wyntye . . . . Lavinia
Yacobes . . . . James
Yaennje. Yaennye, Yanaca, Yannetie
. . . . Jane
Ydje . . . . Ida
Yellis . . . . Giles
Zacariah . . . . Zachary
Zanneke . . . . Susanna
Zara . . . . Sarah
Zephronia . . . . Sophronia
Zilpha . . . . Zilla

English-Dutch First Names

English . . . . Dutch

Aaron . . . . Arie, Arien
Abigail . . . . Abegail
Absulom . . . . Absulon
Adam . . . . Daam
Adela . . . . Aletta, Alida
Adelaide . . . . Adela
Adeline . . . . Aaitje, Aaltje, Adda, Aeltie
. . . . Aeltje, Alida, Daatje, Deetje
Adrian . . . . Arie, Arien
Adriana . . . . Ariantye, Adriaantje
Agatha . . . . Aaghie, Aaghje, Aaght
. . . . , Aagje, Echie
Agnes . . . . . . Aengenietje, Aengenietye
. . . . Agnietie, Agnietje, Angenetye
. . . . Anginette, Niesje
Albert . . . . Albertus, Alburtus, Ethelbert
Alexander . . . . Sander
Alice . . . . Alicia, Elsje, Elzie
Amilia . . . . Emalyne, Emeline
Andrew . . . . Andries, Dries
Angelica . . . . Engeltie
Angeline . . . . Engelite, Engeltje
Ann . . . . . Antye Anate, Anecke, Anita,
. . . . Antye, Annatjie, Antie, Anytie
. . . . Tannecke, Tanneke, Tanneken
Anna . . . . . . Angie, Annaatje, Annatie
. . . . Annatje, Anneckie, Anneke
. . . . Annetje, Naatje, Anate, Anecke
. . . Anita, Annatjie, Antie, Antye, Anytie
Anthony . . . . . Dunis, Teunis, Theunis
. . . . Tones, Toontye, Tuenis, Tunis
Antoinette . . . . Antonetta
Antonia . . . . Teunitje
Arabella . . Belettie, Belitje, Bell, Bella
Arnold . . . . Arlond, Arnout
Arthur . . . . Aarend, Aart
Asael . . . . Asel
Augustine . . . . Augustijn
Baldwin . . . . Baudewyn, Boduwyn
. . . . Boudewyn
Balthaser . . . . Balt, Baltas, Baltus
Barbara . . . . Barber
Bartholomew . . . . Bartel, Bartholomeus
. . . . Maas, Meewes, Mewis
Benjamin . . . . Bengemen
Bernard . . . . Barent
Bertha . . . . Baachie, Bartje, Bata, Batje
Betty . . . . Betje
Bridget . . . . Brechje, Bregetje, Bregetta

. . . . Bregette, Bregezie, Breghje, Bregie
Calvin . . . . Calvijn
Caroline . . . . Carly, Carlyn, Caroly
. . . . Carroline, Carye, Charlina
. . . . Leynje, Liene, Lientje
Cassia . . . . Keziah
Catherine . . . . Catalina, Catalyntie,
. . . . . . Catalyntje, Catalyntjen, Catarina
. . . . Catelina, Catelyntye, Cathalyna
. . . . Cathalyntie, Catharin, Cathelina
. . . . Cathleen, Cathlintie, Cathlyntje
. . . . Cathryntje, Catlynte, Catlyntie
. . . . Catlyntye, Catreina, Catriena
. . Catrientje, Catrina, Catryna, Catryntjie
. . . . Cattalyntjen , Cattelyntie, Cetje
. . . . Chattie, Chatty, Citty, Frientye
. . . . Getty, Gitty, Kaatje, Katheryn
. . . Kathy, Katrientjie, Katryne, Katryntje
. . . . . Kattelyntie, Kattelyte, Katy, Kittie
. . . Thryntie, Tina, Tinie, Tiny, Treintje
. . . . . Trientie, Trientje, Tryntie, Tryntje
Charity . . . . Geesie, Geesje, Geesye
Charles . . . . Carel, Kaarl, Karel
Charlotte . . . . Lotje
Christian . Christiaan, Kerstan, Kristiaan
Christiana . . . . Christyntje, Styntje
Christina . . . . Christinje
Christopher . . . . Christoffel, Stoffel
Cinderella . . . . Assepoester
Clara . . . . Klaartje, Klaartye
Clare . . . . Klaartje, Klaartye
Claude . . . . Cladious, Cloudy
Claudie . . . . Claasje
Conrad . . . . Coen, Coenraad
Cornelia . . . . . Neeltje, Neeltjen, Nelje
. . . . Nella, Nelletje, Nieltjin
Cornelius . . . . . . Cornelis, Kees, Koris
. . . . Korn, Krelis, Neil
Crommelin . . . . Crumeline
Deborah . . . . Diewertje
Dinah . . . . Dyne
Dionysius . . . . Denys
Dorothea . . . . Doortje, Dorotea
Dorothy . . . . Dirkje
Dow, Dowie . . . . Douwe
Egbert . . . . Epje, Epke
Eleanor . . . . Lenoor, Leonora
Elizabeth . . . . Baltie, Baltje, Betsy
. . . . Elesebath, Elizabet, Leisabeth
. . . . Lieven, Lybetie, Lysbet, Lysje
Emilia . . . . Emalyne, Emeline
Emma . . . . Emmetje
Ernest . . . . Ernst
Esther . . . . Hesje, Hetty
Ethel . . . . Ethelyn
Eunice . . . . Teuntje
Eustice . . . . Staats
Eva . . . . Aefjee, Effie
Eve . . . . Aefje, Eva
Evelyn . . . . Hevlyn
Everard . . . . Evert
Everarda . . . . Evertie
Flora . . . . Floortje
Florence . . . . Floris
Frances . . . . Francina, Franscyntje
. . . . Fransytie, Frenky, Frinckye
Francis . . . . Frans
Francisca . . . . Francina
. . . . Franscyntje, Fransytie
Frank . . . . Frans
Garret . . . . Gerrit
George . . . . Goris, Joris, Jurge
. . . . Jurgen, Jurian, Jurjen
Gerard . . . . Geert, Gerardus
. . . . Gerrit, Govert, Sherrard
Gerardina . . . Geertye, Gerretie, Gerritie
. . . . . Gerritje, Gertchen, Gertje, Geurtje
Gertrude . . . . Geerje, Geertje, Geertruy
. . . . Geertruyd, Gertruit, Giertje, Truytje
Gilbert . . . Guysbert, Gysbert, Gyslbert
Giles . . . . . Gellis, Gillis, Jillis, Yellis
Godfrey . . . . Geert, Govert
Grace . . . . Geesie, Geesje, Geesye
Grishild . . . . Griselda, Grissel
Hail . . . . Heyltje
Harriett . . . . . . Hendrickje, Hendrickye
Harvey . . . . Hervey
Helen . . . . Alana, Elena, Laenette
. . . . Lana, Lea, Leah, Leentje
. . . . Lena, Leni, Leynje, Liene
Henriet . . . . Hendrickye
Henrietta . . . . Hendrickje
Henry . . . . Hendrick, Hendrickus
. . . . Hendrik, Hendrikje, Henricus
Herman . . . . Harman, Harmanus
. . . . Harmen, Harmon, Manus
Hierom . . . . . Hieronimus, Hieronymus
. . . . Hyer, Jeronimus
Hugh . . . . Huygen
Huldah . . . . Heyltje, Hilah
. . . . Hillegonda, Hilletje, Hyltje
Ida . . . . Eytie, Ydje
Isabella . . . . . . Beletje, Belettie, Belitje
. . . . Bell, Bella, Belletjie, Belletjie
Jack . . . . Hans
Jacob . . . . Jaap, Japic

James . . . . Jacobus, Jas, Yacobes
Jane . . . . Janche, Janije, Janneke
. . . Jannetie, Jannetje, Jannitje, Jeannetie
Jane . . . . . . Jennecke, Jenneke, Jennica
. . . . . . Joana, Joanna, Johanneke, Jonitia
. . . Yaennje, Yaennye, Yanaca, Yannetie
Jasper . . . . Casparis, Kasper
Jemima . . . . Jaapje, Jacomina
. . . . Jacomintie, Jacomyntje
. . . . Jakomina, Jaquemyntie
Jeremiah . . . . Jeremias
Jerome . . . . Hieronimus
. . . . Hieronymus, Hyer, Jeronimus
Joachim . . . . Jochem
Joan . . . . Janneken, Johanna
Jocelin . . . . Jooris
Jocelyn . . . . Joost
Johanna . . . . Hansje
John . . . . Hannes, Jan, Johan, Johannes
Juarina . . . . Josina, Josyntje
Juarine . . . . Josine
Juarua . . . . Jooris
Julia . . . . Jeletie
Justina . . . . Jesyntje
Justus . . . . Joost
Kezia . . . . Keziah
Kitty . . . . Chattie, Chatty, Getty, Gitty
Lavinia . . . . . Vinnie, Wientie, Wientje
. . . . Wynca, Wyntei, Wyntie
. . . . Wyntje, Wyntye
Lawrence . . . . Laurens, Laurentz
. . . Laurenz, Lourens, Loures, Lowerens
Leo . . . . Lieve
Leonard . . . . Leendert
Letitia . . . . Aletta, Letje, Tietje
. . . . Tietye, Titje, Tittye
Lettice . . . . Alicia, Elsje, Elzie
Lewis . . . . Ludovicus
Louis . . . . Ludovicus
Ludwig . . . . Lodewyk
Luke . . . . Lukas, Luytje
Madge . . . . Grietzie
Magdalene . . . Laenette, Lana, Lea, Leah
. . . . Leentje, Lena, Leni, Leynje, Leynje
Margaret . . . . Gretchen, Grietie, Grietje
. . . . Grietzie, Margarita, Margaritta
. . . . . . Margrietje, Margrietze, Margritje
. . . . Pakke, Peggie
Maria . . . . Marietje
Marinus . . . . Morinus
Marius . . . . Mareus
Martha . . . . Marta, Matie, Matje
. . . . Metje, Mettje
Martin . . . . Mart, Marte, Martyen
Martina . . . . Martyntie, Martyntje
. . . . Maryntyntie
Mary . . . . . Maaicke, Maartje, Maayke
. . . . Macia, Maike, Mally, Maria
. . . . . Mariah, Marica, Maricka. Marietta
.. Mariken, Maritjen, Marretye, Marrietta
. . . . Marritje, Marya, Maryette, Marytje
. . . . Mietje, Myrette, Myrtie, Myrtle
Matilda . . . . Machtel, Machtelde
Matthew . . . . Matewis, Matheas
. . . . Matheus, Teewis
Matthias . Matthias, Matthys, Thys, Tys
Maurice . . . . Mouris
Mazie . . . . Meysie
Michael . . . . Giel
Nancy . . . . . . Angie, Annaatje, Annatie
. . . . Annatje, Anneckie, Anneke
. . . . Anneken, Annetje
Nicholas . . . . Claes, Klaas, Klaasje
. . . . Nicolaas, Nicolaes, Nicolaus
Nicole . . . . . Claessie, Klassve, Klasyne
. . . . Klazina, Kobus
Noah . . . . Noach
Obadiah . . . . Obadja
Ortho . . . . Ota
Otto . . . . Otho
Paul . . . . Pauel, Paulus, Pauwel, Powles
Paulina . . . . Paulyntje
Peggy . . . . Grietzie
Pernel . . . . . Pieterje, Pietertje, Pietertzie
Peter . . . . Petrus, Piet
Petronella . . Pieterje, Pietertje, Pietertzie
Philip . . . . . . Felipe, Filip, Filips, Phlip
Quirine . . . . Kryn
Quirinus . . . . Cryenus
Ralph . . . . Roelof
Rebecca . . . . Becki
Resolved . . . . Geresolveert, Geresolvert
Richard . . . . Ryck, Rykaard
Roger . . . . Rutgert
Rose . . . . Roosje
Rosina . . . . Rasana, Rosena
Rudolph . . . . Rudelft
Sarah . . Saartje, Sarahette, Seertie, Zara
Sebastian . . . . Bastiaan
Solomon . . . . Saal, Saartie
Sophia . . . Cytie, Feitjin, Fytie, Sophya
Sophronia . . . . . Femmetie, Femmetien
. . . . Femmetye, Vroutie, Vroutjer
. . . . Vrouwete, Zephronia
Susanna . . . . Sanneke, Santje, Zanneke
Theobold . . . . Tiebout

Theodora . . . . Dirckie
Theodore . . . Derick, Derrick, Diederick
. . Dirck, Dirick, Dirk, Doris, Theodorus
Thomas . . . . Dammas
Timothy . . . . Tymen
Ursinus . . . . Orsinius
Ursula . . . . Ursel
Ursull . . . . Osseltei
Walter . . . . Wouter
Wiert . . . . Weart
Wilhemina . . . Wilhelmyntie, Willemfye
. . . . Willempie, Willempje, Williememe
William . . . . Willem
Zachary . . . . Zacariah
Zilla . . . . Zilpha

Appendix B

Nicknames

A nickname is a name in addition to, or substituted for, the name given a child by its parents. This bestowing of other names is not a new custom. Whenever there has been more than one James Jones in a town they have been distinguished, not only by Senior, Junior or a numerical designation, but by a physically descriptive name. A red-headed James Jones naturally became known as Red James, Red Jones or plain Red. A short man became known as Shorty while his slim friend was Slim. Or, contrary to the obvious, a heavy man could be called Slim as a satirical nickname. Perhaps a person who always wore a red stocking cap came to be known as Redcap and a compulsive talker earned the nickname of Gabby, unless that name had been given to an unusually quiet man. Other characteristics, both physical and mental, led to Dizzy (usually used with Dame), Sleepy, Happy, Holy Joe, Peeping Tom and many more.

Pet names bestowed by loving parents may stick, although fortunately in most cases, not for long: Precious, Honey, Baby, Lambie Pie. Husbands add to confusion with Sweetie Pie, Pet, Sugar.

Most public figures are happy to have nicknames, especially those which are flattering, and gradually their real names become lost except to their immediate families. The late Bing Crosby, Bogey (Humphrey Bogart), Jack Benny, and Teddy Roosevelt are so familiar to us that most would not remember their real names. States have their nicknames also—Hoosier (Indiana), Sooner (Oklahoma) and even the United States as Uncle Sam. The Republicans were called the Grand Old Party which quickly was shortened to G.O.P. Lawless men have had nicknames that stuck with them until death: Scarface Al Capone, Baby Face Nelson, Pretty Boy Floyd.

Initials can constitute a nickname; B.J. or J.F.K. My father, whose name was William, used to recite a verse which illustrates how one person may possess more than one nickname, each used by different people. "Father calls me William, Sister calls me Will, Mother calls me Willie, but the fellers call me Bill!" However, do not forget that some persons really were named Billy, not William. What appears to be a nickname offers a false clue and can lead to a fruitless search for a non-existent name. The name Elizabeth illustrates that many names have been derived from one name. Many of these are now used and accepted as given names, e.g. Elisa, Elise, Eliza, Elsie.

A familiar form of a name if achieved by adding "ie" or "y" to a name—Jean becomes Jeanie or Jeany. Surnames lend themselves to becoming changed to form a nickname: Mac for all the surnames beginning with Mc or Mac. Jonesey (Jones), Smitty (Smith), and Mitch (Mitchell) are examples of nicknames derived from surnames.

There are nicknames that leave us more than one clue, in fact too many clues, e.g. Al or Bert. Don't forget the names derived from rocking a baby and half-singing to the child: Mary, Mally, Molly, Polly; Maureen, Maurie, Dorie. These may leave us far removed from the child's real name.

Nickname	**Given Name**
Ab, Abbie	Abner, Absolum
Ab, Abbie, Abbey, Abby	Abigail
Abe, Abie, Aby	Abraham, Abel
Abram	Abraham
Addy, Add	Ada, Adela, Adeline
Ade	Adam
Ag, Aggie, Addy	Agatha, Agnes
Al	Adeline, Alan, Albert, Alberta, Alfreda, Alice, Alvin
Alay	Algernon
Alce	Alice
Alec, Alex, Alick, Al	Alexander
Alf, Alfie, Alfy	Alfred, Albert
Algy	Algernon
Alla	Alexandria
Allie, Ally	Adeline, Alberta, Alfreda, Alice, Aileen, Alicia, Allison
Ana	Anastasia
Andy	Andrea, Andrew, Angela, Angelica, Anita, Annienn, Anna, Ann
Annie	Anna
Anty	Anastasia
Ara	Arabella
Arch, Archie, Archy	Archibald
Arnie	Arnold
Art, Artie, Arty	Arthur, Arthurine
Aus	Austin
Ava	Avis
Bab, Babie, Babby, Babs, Bar, Barb, Barbary, Barbie	Barbara
Baldy	Baldwin
Barney, Barnie	Barnabas
Bart, Barth, Bartie, Bat	Bartholomew, Bartley, Barton, Bartram
Bartle	Bartlemy
Bass, Bast, Bastin, Basty	Sebastian
Bea, Bee	Beata, Beatrice
Becca, Beck, Becky	Rebecca
Bel, Bell, Belle, Bella	Arabella, Belinda, Elizabeth, Isabel, Isabella, Mirabel
Belle	Mabel, Sybil
Ben, Bennie, Benny	Benedict, Benejah, Benton, Reuben
Ben, Benjie, Benjy, Bennet	Benedict
Bennie, Benny	Benjamin
Bern, Berni, Berny	Bernard
Berni, Berny	Bernice
Bert, Bertie	Albert, Alberta, Bertha, Bertram, Bertrand, Egbert, Gilbert, Herbert, Norbert, Osbert
Berta, Bertie, Berty	Bertha
Bess, Bessie, Bessy, Bet, Bette, Bettie, Betty, Beth, Betsey, Betsy	Elizabeth
Bev, Bevvy	Beverly
Bias	Tobias
Biddy, Brig	Bridget, Brigid
Bill, Billie, Billy	William
Bith	Tabitha
Bob, Bobby	Robert
Bobbe, Bobbi, Bobbie	Roberta
Boots	Bertha
Bram	Abraham
Bren	Brenda
Bridey	Bridget
Brie	Bridget
Burt	Burton
Cage, Cager	Micajah
Cal	Caleb, Calvin
Cam, Camm, Cammie, Cammy	Camelia, Camerson
Cana, Caner, Caney	Elkanah
Candie, Candy	Candace
Carrie, Carry	Caroline, Charlotte

Carey, Cary . . . . . Charles, Charlotte
Carey, Carrie, Cary . . . Carol, Carola
Cass, Cassie, Cassy . . . . . . Cassandra, Catherine
Cath, Cathie, Cathy . . . . . Catherine, Cathleen
Celia . . . . Cecilia
Cephus . . . . Josephus
Cerna . . . . Lucerna
Ces . . . . Cecil, Cecilia
Chad, Charley, Charlie, Chas, Chaz . . Charles
Chatty . . . . Charlotte
Ches, Chet . . . . Chester
Chick . . . . Charles
Chris . . . . Christabel, Christian, Christopher
Chris, Chrissie, Chrissy, Christie, Christy Christine, Christopher
Chuck . . . . Charles
Cilla . . . . Priscilla
Cindy . . . . Lucinda
Cis, Cissy . . . . Cecilia, Cicily
Clar, Clarri . . . . . eClarence, Clarice, ... Clarinda
Clay . . . . Clayton
Clem, Clemmie . . . . Clement, ... Clementine
Cleo . . . . Cleopatra
Cliff . . . . Clifford
Clo . . . . Chloe
Col, Cole . . . . Coleman, Colin
Con, Connie, Conny . . . . . Constance, Consuela
Con, Connie, Cur . . . . tConrad
Corbie, Corby . . . . Corbert
Cornie, Corny . . . Cornelia, Cornelius
Corrie, Corry Cora, Cordelia, Cormick
Curt . . . . Curtis
Cy . . . . Cyrus
Cindy, Cyn, Cynth . . . . Cynthia
Cindy . . . . Lucinda
Daff, Daffy . . . . Daphine
Daisy . . . . Margaret
Dal . . . . Dallas
Dan, Dannel, Dannie, Danny . . Daniel
Dandy . . . . Andrew
Daph, Daphie . . . . Daphne
Dave, Davie, Davy . . . . David
Deb, Debbie . . . . Deorah, Debra
Dee . . . . Audrey, Deloris, Dolories, Dorothy
Dee, Deedee . . . . Deidre
Del, Dell . . . . Della
Delia . . . . Cordel
Den, Dena, Dee, Dina . . . . Magdalena
Dennie, Denny, Deny Denis, Marsden
Detta . . . . Henrietta
Di . . . . Diana, Diane,Dinah
Dick, Dickie, Dicky . . . . Richard
Dixey, Dixie . . . . Benedict
Dodie . . . . Doris
Dol, Doll, Dollie, Dolly . . . Dorothea, Dorothy
Dolly . . . . Mary
Dolph . . . . Adolph, Randolph
Don, Donn, Donnie, Donny . . Donald
Dora . . . . Eudora, Dorothea
Dora, Dori, Dory . . . . Dorothea, Isadora, Theodora
Dore . . . . Dorothy
Dori, Dorrie, Dorry, Dory . . . . Delores, Dorene, Dorothea, Dorothy
Dorie . . . . Pandora
Doro . . . . Dorothy
Dosia . . . . Theodosia
Dot, Dottie, Dotty . . . . Dorothy
Doug, Dougie, Duggie . . . . Douglas
Drew . . . . Andrew
Dru, Drus, Dursie . . . . Drucilla
Dud . . . . Dudley
Dug . . . . Douglas
Duke . . . . Marmaduke
Dulce, Dulcia, Dulcie . . . Dulcibella, Dulcinea
Dunc . . . . Duncan
Eb, Ebbie, Eben . . . . Ebenezer
Ed, Eddie, Eddy . . . . Edgar, Edmund, Edsel, Edward, Edwin
Eadie, Eda, Ede, Edie . . . . Edith
Edny . . . . Edna
Efrem, Eph . . . . Ephram
Effie . . . . Euphemia, Evelyn
El . . . . Eldon
Eli . . . . . . Elias, Elihu, Elijah, Elisha
Elisa, Eliza, Elsie . . . . Elizabeth
Ella . . . . Ellen, Helen
Ellie, Elly . . . . . Eleanor, Ellen, Helen
Elvie . . . . Elvira
Ely . . . . Elias
Elzy . . . . Elizabeth
Em . . . . Emmett
Em, Emmie, Emmy . . Emeline, Emilia, Emily, Emma, Emrnelina, Enie, Ena
Ep, Eph . . . . Ephraim
Eppie . . . . Euphemia

Ern, Ernie . . . . Ernest
Erna . . . . Ernestine
Essie . . . . Esther
Etta, Etty, Ellie . . . . Esther, Henrietta
Evie, Evy . . . . Eva, Eve, Evelyn
Ez . . . . Ezra
Fan, Fannie, Fanny . . . . Frances
Fee . . . . Felicia
Ferd, Ferdie . . . . Ferdinand
Fifi, Fifine . . . . Josephine
Flip . . . . Philip
Flo, Florrie, Flory, Flossie, Flossy . . . Florence, Flora
Fran, Frank, Frankie . . . . Francis
Fran, Francie, Frannie, Franny Frances
Fran, Frankie . . . . Frank
Fred, Freddie, Freddy . . . . . . Alfred, Ferdinand, Freda, Frederick, Fredricka, Wilfred
Free . . . . Frieda
Fritz . . . . Frederick
Gab, Gab, Gabby . . . . Gabriel
Gabi, Gabie, Gabby . . . . . . Gabrielle
Gael, Gail, Gale, Gay . . . . . lAbigail
Garrie, Garry . . . . Garret, Garth
Gar, Gary . . . . Garvin
Gatty . . . . Gertrude
Gen, Genny . . . . Guinevere
Gena, Gene, Gene, Gina . . . . Eugenia, Regina
Gene . . . . Eugene
Geof, Geoff . . . . Geoffrey
George, Georgia, Georgie . . . . Georgiana, Georgina
Geri, Gerri, Gerry . Gerald, Geraldine
Gerry . . . . Garett, Gerald
Gert, Gertie, Gerty . . . . Gertrude
Gib, Gil, Gillie . . . . Gilbert
Gibbie . . . . Gabriel
Gill . . . . Gillian
Ginger, Ginny . . . . Virginia
Gib, Gip, Gipper, Gyb . . . . . . Gilbert
Glad . . . . Gladys
Glory . . . . Gloria
Gracie . . . . Grace
Greg, Gregg . . . . Gregory
Greta . . . . Margaret
Griff . . . . Griffin
Gritty . . . . Margaret
Gus, Gussie . . . . . Augustus, Gustave
Gussie, Gussy, Gusta . . . . . . Augusta
Gwen, Gwenn . Guinevere, Gwendolen
Hal . . . . Harold, Henry
Ham . . . . Graham
Hank . . . . Henry
Har, Harl . . . . Harley
Harry . . . . Harold, Henry
Hart . . . . Hartley, Hartwell
Harv, Harve, Herv, Herve . . . . Harvey, Hervey
Hat, Hatti, Hattie, Hatty . . . . Harriet, Henrietta
Hec . . . . Hector
Hedy, Heddy . . . . Hedda
Hen . . . . Henry
Henni, Henni . . . . Henrietta
Hepsy . . . . Hepzibah
Herb, Herbie, Herby . . . . Herbert
Hetti, Hetty . . . . Esther, Harriet, Henrietta, Hester
Hi, Hy . . . . Hiram, Hyman
Hildie, Hildy . . . . . . Hilda, Hidegard
Hitty . . . . Mehitable
Honey . . . . Honora
Horrie, Horry . . . . Horace
Howie . . . . Howard
Hubie . . . . Hubert
Hugh . . . . Elihu
Hughie . . . . Hugh
Ik, Ike, Ikey . . . . Isaac
Irv . . . . Irvin
Issy, Iz, Izzy . . . . Isadora, Isidore
Jack, Jackie, Jacky . . Jacob, Jamesina John, Jonathan, Julius
Jackie . . . . Jacqueline
Jaime, Jamie . . . . James
Jake . . . . Jacob
Jan . . . . John
Jan . . . . Janice
Jan, Janie, Janey . . . . Jane
Jary . . . . Garett, Garry
Jeanie . . . . Jean
Jed, Jeddy . . . . Jedediah
Jeff . . . . Godfry, Jeffrey
Jem, Jemmie, Jemmy . . . . James
Jen, Jenni, Jennie, Jenny . . Guinevere, Jennifer
Jenkin . . . . John
Jerrie, Jerry . . . . Geraldine
Je, Jerry . . . Gerald, Jeremiah, Jerome
Jess, Jessy . . . . Jasmine, Jessamine, Jesse, Jessi, Jessica
Jeth . . . . Jethro
Jill . . . . Julia
Jim, Jimmie, Jimmy . . . . James
Jobey, Joby . . . . Joseph

Jo, Jodie, Jody, Judy . . . . Josephine, Josephus, Judith
Jock . . . . John
Joe . . . . . Josepha, Josephine, Jotham
Joe, Joey, Jos . . . . Joel, Joseph
John . . . . Jonathan
Johnnie, Johnny, Jonnie, Jonny . . . John
Jon . . . . Jonathan
Jone, Jonie . . . . Joan
Jose . . . . Joseph
Josh . . . . Joshua
Josie, Jozy . . . . . . Josepha, Josephine
Joy . . . . Honor, Hope, Joyce, Joscelin, Mercy
Ju, Judie, Judy . . . . Judith, Judy
Jule . . . . Julia, Julian, Julius
Julie . . . . Julia, Juliana
Kara, Kata, Kate, Katie, Kath, Kathie, Kathy, Katty, Kay . . . . Katherine, Kathryn, Kathleen
Ken, Kenny . . . . . Kendall, Kendrick, Kenelm, Kenneth, Kenyo
Kim . . . . Kimball, Kimberly
Kit, Kittie, Kitty . . . . Catherine, Katherine, Kathryn
Kit . . . . Christopher
Kon . . . . Konrad
Kri, Kriss . . . . Christopher
Kurt . . . . Konrad
Ky . . . . Hezekiah
Lali . . . . Eulalah
Lani . . . . Elaine
Lari . . . . Laura
Larry, Laurie, Lawrie . . . . Laura, Laurence, Lawrence
Leafy . . . . Relief
Lecty . . . . Electa
Lee . . . . Dudley, Leander, Leila, Leslie, Stanley
Lee, Lennie, Lenny . . . . Leona
Lela, Lelah, Lelia . . . . Lillian
Lem, Lemmie . . . . Lemuel
Len, Lennie, Lenny . . . . Leonard
Lena . . . . Eleanor, Helena, Leonora, Selena
Lennie, Lenny . . . . Helen
Leo, Lepp . . . . Leopold
Les . . . . Leslie, Lester
Leta, Lettie, Letty . . . . Letitia, Lettice, Loutitia
Letty . . . . Charlotte
Lew, Lou . . . Lewis, Llewellyn, Louis
Li . . . . Elihu
Lib, Libbie, Libby . . . . Elizabeth
Liddie, Liddy, Lide . . . . Lydia
Lige . . . . Elijah
Lil, Lili, Lilla, Lillie, Lilly, Lily . . . . Lillian
Lila, Lilah . . . . Delilah, Lillian
Lilla . . . . Elizabeth
Lin . . . . Lionel
Lina . . . . Adeline, Caroline, Charlotte
Linc . . . . Lincoln
Linda, Lindie, Lindy, Linnie, Linny Belinda, Malinda, Melinda
Lisa, Lise . . . . Elizabeth, Louise
Lisbeth, Lisette . . . . Elizabeth
Lish . . . . Elisha
Lissa . . . . Melissa
Liv, Livi, Livia, Livvi . . . . Olivia
Liz, Liza, Lizzie, Lizzy Eliza, Elizabeth
Lodi . . . . Melody
Lois . . . . Louise
Lola . . . . Delores
Lolly . . . . Laura
Lonny . . . . Zebulon
Lori, Lorie, Lorrie . . . . Laura
Lorrie, Lorry . . . . Laurence, Lawrence
Lotta, Lotte, Lottie, Lotty . . Charlotta, Charlotte
Lou, Louie . . . . Louis, Louisa, Louise
Lu, Lucie . . . . . Lucas, Lucille, Lucy
Luc . . . . Lucas
Luce . . . . Lucius
Lucie, Lucy . . . . Lucia, Lucille, Lucinda, Lucretia
Luke . . . . Lucas, Lucian, Lucius
Lula . . . . Louisa
Lura . . . . Lurana
Lyn, Lynn . . . . Jocelyn
Mab . . . . Mabel
Mabel . . . . Mehitable
Mad, Mada, Maddie, Maddy . . . . Madeline, Matthew
Madge . . . . Margaret
Mae, May . . . . Mabel, Mary
Mag, Maggie, Maggy . . . . Margaret, ... Magdalene
Magda . . . . Madeline, Magdalene
Maidie, Maidy . . . . . Maida, Margaret
Mame, Mamie . . . . . Margaret, Mary
Manda, Mandy . . . . Amanda
Manny . . Emanuel, Immanuel, Manuel
Mara, Mari, Maria . . . . Maria, Mary
Marcy . . . . Marcia
Marge, Margie . . . Margaret, Marjorie

Marget, Margot . Margaret, Marguerite
Marsh . . . . Marshall
Marth, Marti, Marty . . . . Martha
Marv, Merv . . . . . Marvin, Mervin
Mat, Matt, Mattie, Matty . . . Martha, Mathilda, Matilda, Matthew, Mattia
Maud, Maude, Maudie . . . Magdalene, Matilda
Maury . . . . Maurice
May . . . . Margaret
Max, Maxie, Maxey . . . . Maximilian, ... Maxine, Maxwell
Meg, Megan, Meggie, Meggy . . . . . Margaret
Mel . . . . . . Melody, Melville, Melvin
Melia, Melie . . . . Aelia, Emily
Mell, Mellie, Melly Amelia, Melanie, ... Melinda
Mena . . . . Philomena
Merci, Mercy . . . . Mercedes
Mert, Myrt . . . . Myrtle
Meta . . . . Margaret
Mick, Mickie, Micky . . . . . . Michael
Midge . . . . Margaret
Mig, Miggy, Migsy . . . . Margaret
Mike . . . . Michael
Mil, Milli, MillieAmelia, Camilla, Emily, Mildred, Millicent
Milt . . . . Milton
Mimi . . . . Mary, Wilhelmina
Min, Mini, Minnie, Minny . . Minerva, Minna, Wilhelmina, Mary (in Ireland)
Mina, Minna . . . . Wilhelmina
Mira, Mirey . . . . . . Almira, Mirabel
Mitch . . . . Mitchell
Moe, Mose, Moss . . . . Moses
Moll, Mollie, Molly . . . Mary, Martha
Mona . . . . Ramona
Monty . . . . Montague
Mort, Mortie, Morty Mortimer, Morton
Mur . . . . Muriel
Myra . . . . Almira
Nab . . . . Abel
Naby, Nabby . . . . Abigail
Nada, Nadia . . . . Nadine
Nan, Nana, Nance, Nannie, Nanny . . . Ann, Nancy, Hannah
Nanty . . . . Anthony
Nap . . . . Napoleon
Nat, Nate, Natie . . . Nathan, Nathaniel
Nat, Nattie . . . . Natalie
Neal, Neil . . . . . Cornelius, Edward
Ned, Neddy Edmund, Edward, Norton
Nelia, Nell, Nellie . . . . Cornelia, Eleanor, Helen
Nelie . . . . Cordelia, Cornelia
Nell, Nellie, Nelly . . . Eleanor, Ellen, Helen
Nemire . . . . Nehemiah
Neo . . . . Neville
Nessa, Nessie . . . . Agnes
Net, Nettie, Netty . . . Agneta, Antonia, Henrietta, Natalie
Neza . . . . Agnes
Nib . . . . Isabella
Nic, Nick, Nicky . . Dominic, Nicholas . . . . Nicodemus
Niki, Nikki . . . . Nicole
Nina, Ninette . . . . Ann
Nita . . . . Anita, Juanita
Nob . . . . Robert
Noe, Node . . . . Noah
Noll, Nollie, Nolly . . . . Oliver
Nonie . . . . Nona
Nora . . . . . Eleanora, Elnora, Leonora
Norine, Norrie . . . . Honora
Norm, Normy . . . . Norman
Normi, Normie . . . . Norma
Norrie . . . . Eleanor, Nora, Norah
Nullie . . . . Ursula
Obe, Obed, Obie . . . . Obediah
Odo . . . . Odell
Ollie, Olly . . . . Olive, Oliver, Olivia
Omy . . . . Neoma
Ora . . . . Aurelia
Os, Ossie, Oz, Ozzie . . Orson, Osbert, Oscar, Osmond, Oswald, Oswell
Ote, Otie . . . . Otis
Paddy . . . . Patrick
Pam . . . . Pamela
Pat, Patsy, Patti, Pattie, Patty . . . . . . Martha, Matilda, Patricia
Pat, Pate, Patie, Patsy, Paty, Patty . . . Patrick
Peddy . . . . Experience
Peg, Peggie, Peggy . . . . Margaret
Pen, Pene, Pennie, Penny . . . Penelope
Perce, Percy . . . . Percival
Perr . . . . Perry
Perry . . . . Peregrine
Pete, Petey . . . . Peter
Phelia . . . . Orphelia
Pheney . . . . Josephine
Phil, Phip . . . . Philip, Philippa
Pol, Poll . . . . Polly
Poll, Pollie, Polly . . . . . . Mary, Paula

Pop . . . . Robert
Pris, Prissel, Prissy . . . . Priscilla
Pru, Prud, Prue, Prudie, Prudy . . . . . . Prudence
Quill . . . . Quillon
Rab . . . . Robert
Rae, Ray . . . . Rachel
Rafe, Raff . . . . Ralph, Raphael
Ran, Rand, Randy . . . . Forand, Randall, Randolph
Randie, Randy . . . . Miranda
Ray . . . . Raymond
Reba . . . . Rebecca
Reg, Reggie . . . . Reginald
Rena, Rene, Reni, Rennie, Renny . . . . Irene, Serena
Reta, Rita . . . . Clarita, Margaret, Margarita, Norita
Rho, Rhody . . . . Rhoda
Rich, Richie, Rick, Ricky, Ritch . . . . Richard
Rick, Ricky . . . . Eric, Garrick, Patrick
Riddy, Rilda . . . . Serilda
Ro, Roly, Rolly . . . . Roland
Rob, Robbie, Robby . Robert, Roberta
Rod, Roddy, Rory . Roderick, Rodney
Rodi, Rodie . . . . Rhoda
Rodge . . . . Roger
Roe . . . . Monroe
Rome . . . . Jerome
Ron, Ronnie, Ronny . . . . . Reginald, Ronald, Veronica
Ros, Roz . . . . Roscoe, Roswell
Rosa . . . . Rosina
Rosie . . . . Rosa, Rosalind, Rose, Rosamond, Rosemary, Rosetta, Rosina, Rosita
Ross . . . . Roscoe
Rox, Roxie, Roxy . . . . Roxanne
Roy . . . . Leroy
Rube . . . . Reuben
Rudy, Ruddy . . . . Rudolph
Rufe . . . . Rufus
Rus . . . . Cyrus
Russ . . . . Russell
Sade, Sadie . . . . Sarah
Sal . . . . Salome, Salvador
Sal, Sallie, Sally . . . . Sara, Sarah
Sam, Sammie, Sammy Sampson, Samuel
Sandy . . . . Alexander, Sandra
Shel, Shell, Shelly . . Sheldon, Shelley
Shep, Shepp . . . . Shepard
Sherry . . . . Sheridan
Sherm . . . . Sherman
Shir . . . . Shirley
Si, Sy . . . . . . Silas, Simon, Sylvester
Sid . . . . Sidney
SigS . . . . iegfried, Sigismund
Sil . . . . Priscilla, Silvester
Silla . . . . Drusilla, Priscilla
Silvie . . . . Sylvia
Sim . . . . Simeon, Simon
Sinty . . . . Hyacinth
Sis, Sissy . . . . Cecely, Cecilia
Sisely . . . . Cecilia
Sol, Solly . . . . Solomon
Sonny . . . . Tyson
Sohie, Sophie, Sophy . . . . Sophia
Stacey, Stacie, Stacy Anastasia, Eustace
Stan . . . . . Standish,Stanislas, Stanley
Stell, Stella . . . . Estelle, Esther
Steph . . . . Stephanie
Steve, Stevie . . . . Stephen
Stevie . . . . Stephanie
Stew . . . . Stewart
Stu . . . . Stuart
Sue, Susi, Susie, Susy, Suzie, Suzy . . . Susan, Susanna, Suzanne
Suke, Suky, Sukey . . . . Susanna
Syl, Sylvie . . . . Sylvia
Tab, Tabbie, Tabby . . . . Tabitha
Tad . . . . Thaddeus
Taffy . . . . David
Tallie . . . . Natalie
Tam, Tammie . . . . . Tamsin, Tamzine
Tavi, Tavia . . . . Octavia
Ted, Teddy . . . . . . Edward, Theodore
Teddi, Teddie . . . . Theodora
Terry . . . . Theresa, Torence
Tess, Tessa, Tessie . . . . Theresa
Thad, Thady . . . . Thaddeus
Than . . . . Nathan
Thea, Theda, Thia . . Althea, Anthea, ... Theodora
Theiss . . . . Matthias
Theo . . . . Theobald, Theodora, Theodore, Theodosia
Tibbie, Tibby . . . . Isabel
Tice . . . . Matthias
Tilda, Tillie, Tilly . . . . Matilda
Tim, Timmie, Timmy . . . . . Timothy
Tina, Teena, Teeny . . . . . . Albertina, Augustina, Christina, Ernestine, Justina, Justin
Tine . . . . Catherine
Tish, Tishi, Titia . . . . Letitia, Loutitia

Tobe, Toby . . . . Tobias
Tom, Tommie, Tommy, Thom . Thomas
Tonia, Tony . . . . Antonia
Tony . . . . Anthony
Tracy . . . . Theresa
Trella . . . . Esther
Trev . . . . Trevor
Trina . . . . Catharina, Cathleen
Triss, Trissie Trissy, Trix, Trixie, Trixy Beatrice
Truda, Trude, Trudy . . . . . . Gertrude
Ty . . . . Tyler, Tyron, Tyson
Ursie, Ursy . . . . Ursula
Val, Vallie Valarie, Valentina, Valentine
Van, Vannie . . . . . . Vanessa, Vanora
Vern, Verne . Laverne, Verna, Vernon
Vet . . . . Sylvester
Vi . . . . Viola, Violet
Vi, Viv, Vivi, Vivia, Vivie . . . Vivian
Vic, Vick, Vicky . . . Victor, Victoria
Vin, Vince . . . . Vincent
Vin, Vinny . . . . Galvin, Vincent
Vina . . . . Alvina
Vina, Vinia, Vinnie, Vinny . . . Lavinia
Virg, Virgie . . . . Virginia
Virg, Virgy . . . . Virgil
Von, Vonnie . . . . Yvonne
Wal, Wallie, Wally, Walt . . . . Wallace, Walter
Wat, Wattie, Watty . . . . Walter
Web, Webb . . . . Webster
Wendy . . . . Gwendolen
Wes . . . . Wesley
Wilf, Wilfie, Wilfy, Wil . . . . . Wilfred
Will, Willie, Willy . . . . William
Willa, Willie . . . . Wilhelmina
Win, Wyn . . . . Winslow, Winston
Win, Wina, Winnie, Winny . . . . Edwina, Winifred
Winn, Wynn . . . . Edwin
Woody . . . . Woodrow
Xina . . . . Christina
Zach, Zack, Zacky . . . . . . Zachariah
Zeb . . . . Zebulon
Zed . . . . Zedekiah
Zeke . . . . Ezekiel